THE
LONDON
COMPOSITOR

Documents relating to
Wages, Working Conditions
and Customs of the
London Printing Trade
1785–1900

EDITED BY

ELLIC HOWE

Published for
THE BIBLIOGRAPHICAL SOCIETY
by GEOFFREY CUMBERLEGE
OXFORD UNIVERSITY PRESS
LONDON
1947

Printed in Great Britain by William Clowes and Sons, Limited,
London and Beccles

CONTENTS

PREFACE

In the autumn of 1937 Mr. Stanley Morison handed me a pile of photostats and documents, and suggested that I should apply myself to their study. The originals from which the photostats were made are in the possession of the Cambridge University Press, and were, in the main, formerly the property of the late Charles T. Jacobi, of the Chiswick Press. They consist mainly of documents issued by the London compositors' trade union at the beginning of the nineteenth century, and were originally sent by the committee to the first Charles Whittingham, founder of the Chiswick Press. Mr. Morison had long intended to publish this material, and had gone so far as to have the Jacobi collection set up in type. Mr. Michael Clapham, now of the Kynoch Press, but formerly on the staff of the University Press, also compiled a check list, of which a few copies were printed.

Just prior to the outbreak of war in 1939 I had completed the arrangement, not only of the Cambridge documents, but of the even greater number found in other collections. Throughout the summer of 1939 our anti-aircraft defences had been maintained in a state of semi-mobilization, and my departure for a month's service appeared a tedious but nevertheless necessary interlude before finally preparing the book for the press. Three weeks later the Germans invaded Poland.

My wife packed the manuscript in a hat-box, and delivered it to Mr. Morison at the offices of the Monotype Corporation in Fetter Lane. There it remained until late in 1940. Many bombs fell near, but the Corporation's premises were not hit. By that time I had forsaken the sand-dunes at the mouth of the Humber for the northern suburbs of London. The hat-box was fetched from Fetter Lane, and in the evenings, often to the sound of the anti-aircraft barrage and the drone of German aeroplanes overhead, I attempted to work. When not required, the manuscript was stored, always in its hat-box, in an Anderson air-raid shelter. During the last great raid of the 1940–41 series the Fetter Lane offices of the Monotype Corporation were destroyed and in the same night Mr. Morison lost his home and most of his books.

Towards the end of 1941 I left the Army on being transferred to a department of the Foreign Office. For two busy years the hat-box lay unregarded, but the possibility of the manuscript being destroyed by an unlucky bomb could not be disregarded. My wife suggested the precaution of having the book set up in type, and two or three sets of galley proofs sent to friends in different districts. Thus, in December 1943, the first of one hundred and seventy-five galleys was composed. The work was still in progress in the following February when the Germans launched a series of short but sharp air attacks on London. The type was being set by a firm of printers which had leased the building on the site of Strahan's original King's Printing Office. The nearest bomb fell about a hundred yards away.

At about that time the proofs were shown to my friend Mr. F. C. Francis, Honorary Secretary of the Bibliographical Society, and in due course I was informed that the Council of the Society had done me the honour of accepting this book for publication when ready.

In June 1944, a few days after the Armies of Liberation had landed in Normandy, the Germans began to launch pilotless aircraft on London, causing great damage and destruction. It is true that there existed several copies of the book in galley proof, but I was now also the worried owner of about five hundred pounds' worth of typesetting, which had been paid for. The flying bombs fell all round my printing office, but it was never hit. Finally, I was able to borrow a lorry, had the galleys loaded on to it, and early one morning set forth for Messrs. Clowes's printing works at Beccles. It was the first time in the long and distinguished history of the firm that an author had arrived with two tons of his own type metal ! As I write these words, in February 1945, explosive rockets occasionally fall within earshot, but the Russian armies are massing on the Oder, and the end of both the war and the making of this book seems near.

Although it is not usual to include war memories in the preface to a book of this sort, I ask the reader's indulgence. It is, however, largely a product of the war years, and although the completion of this book often appeared to be as distant an event as the conclusion of hostilities, I was loth to abandon the task, despite frequent uncertainty as to what the next day would bring.

My thanks are due to many who have helped with advice or the loan of material. I am particularly indebted to the Governors of the St. Bride Foundation, and to Mr. W. Turner Berry, their Principal Librarian, for the loan of a great deal of material, and for his constant and ever-willing help during many years. The

London Society of Compositors have also generously allowed me unrestricted access to its archives, and to borrow whatever I required. I am grateful to Mr. A. M. Wall, until lately Secretary of the L.S.C., for these facilities. Mr. F. A. Davies, Assistant Secretary, a veteran member of the trade, has given me the benefit of his long experience, and Mr. F. J. Mayer, the News Secretary, has similarly helped. Another Society member, Mr. Harold E. Waite, has not only read the book in proof, but made many useful suggestions, and to him I am particularly obliged.

Mr. Walter Lewis, Printer to the University of Cambridge, has kindly allowed me to examine the collection of documents at the University Press, and was so good as to photograph such of them as were required. The Master, Wardens and Court of the Stationers' Company, of which the writer is a Liveryman, have allowed me to use a duplicate set of Apprentice Registers for the Eighteenth Century, and several other documents which it had not been found necessary to evacuate during the war. I am ever mindful of their sympathetic interest and kindness.

I am indebted to Mr. R. E. Jones, Deputy Keeper of Records of the Corporation of London, for answering my questions on the subject of City customs and regulations; also to Mr. John Drage, of the Fanfare Press, who was of great assistance in preparing the copy for the printer. The index has been prepared by Mr. F. Garfield Howe, to whom I am also obliged for his helpful criticisms.

Lastly, I must thank the three friends who have followed the fortunes of this book with benevolence and unstinted help. Many are in debt to Mr. Graham Pollard, and none more than myself. Mr. F. C. Francis has given me much support and encouragement. Finally, I express my gratitude to Mr. Stanley Morison for directing my prentice hand to the undertaking of this work. Mr. Morison has guided my studies for almost as long as I have been a member of the printing trade, and it is to him that I dedicate this book with affectionate regard.

ELLIC HOWE

LONDON
February 1945

INTRODUCTION

(i) *The Emergence of the Permanent Journeyman*

Research into the social and economic history of the printing, bookbinding, bookselling and allied trades has in the past been somewhat neglected. The connection between such studies and other bibliographical investigations is important, since the physical appearance of any printed document depends largely upon the technical methods used in its manufacture, and these in turn are closely related to economic factors. From the time of the Industrial Revolution onwards, the key to the understanding of the economic and social history of any trade is to be found, where they survive, in the archives of the appropriate Trade Union, or "continuous association of wage earners for the purpose of maintaining or improving the conditions of their working lives". The purpose of this book, therefore, is to print and elucidate the principal documents relating to arrangements between masters and men: wages, working conditions and customs of the London printing trade from 1785 until the end of the nineteenth century. This covers the period during which the trade was transformed from a manual craft, using a technique almost identical with that already developed by 1500, into a fully mechanized industry.

The year 1785 represents a convenient point of departure, since in that year was negotiated the first known agreement between the principal master printers and a compositors' *trade union*. It is important to note that the employers, who made certain written concessions in respect of piece-work prices, probably had no official mandate from the masters at large, while those who accepted the new terms on behalf of the compositors represented a bustling and energetic minority. Some forty master printers signed the document setting forth the revised prices. There were at that date at least one hundred and twenty-four London printing offices. In 1793, when further agreements were made, some seven hundred compositors put their signatures to resolutions or petitions, but Union discipline had not yet become strong and there were plenty who were apathetic or who were compelled to accept worse terms from the smaller masters.

The novel character of the 1785 agreement can be better appreciated if we consider an earlier state of affairs. In the sixteenth and seventeenth centuries labour policy was under the control of the Stationers' Company. As was the case with many of the other old craft guilds, the Company's influence was much diminished in the eighteenth century. Old traditions, however, die hard, and it was not until the closing years of the century that we find both employers and employed entering into bi-lateral agreements without reference to the old machinery of negotiation provided by the Company. The 1785 Scale of Prices, then, was a convention between a group of entrepreneurs, acting independently of the Company (upon whose Livery all the leading personalities among the employers were represented), and the workmen.

Some brief review of the Company's traditional attitude towards labour problems is necessary to our understanding of later events, but for any discussion of the economic and social history of the London printing trade between 1557, when the Company received its first Charter, and the end of the eighteenth century, we are handicapped for lack of essential documents. The Company's Court Minutes from 1603 onwards have yet to be published in calendar or transcript form, while much other material in the Company's archives still remains to be examined.

The essence of mature trade union practice is free negotiation between employers and employed. The discipline of the old guilds did not admit such a course. In the case of the Stationers' Company, its governing body, the Court, was chosen from among the senior and most influential Liverymen, who were all masters. The workmen, too, were members of the Company, but their status as Freemen or Yeomen was lower, and they were bound to accept the decisions of the ruling oligarchy. In the sixteenth and seventeenth centuries the Company's supervision of all aspects of the trades it represented was at once authoritarian and paternal. Thus the independence of the journeyman was closely controlled, and the liberty of action of the individual master printer, in his capacity as an entrepreneur, was equally circumscribed. These factors are well illustrated in the documents reprinted in the next section.

While the master was unable to engage in free and unrestricted competition, it was made equally difficult for the capable and ambitious journeyman to rise into the ranks of the employers. The former could not depend upon a free supply of labour, because entry into the trade was closely controlled, and he might only employ trained journeymen who had served an apprenticeship. Men who had served their time, and were free of the

Stationers' Company by servitude, were first of all hindered in their efforts to better themselves by the great expense involved in becoming a successful master printer, and secondly by the limitation in the number of printing offices allowed to function. Hence a situation from which the trade unions later developed: the existence of a class of permanent journeymen of which the majority had no hope of becoming masters.

Caxton set up his press at Westminster in 1476. It is probable that most of his workmen were aliens. During the first years of the sixteenth century all the master printers in England were foreigners. By 1557, although the number of foreigners had increased, they were no longer the employers but their servants, with little hope of altering their status for the better. Throughout the preceding quarter of a century the tendency had been for all economic legislation to protect native merchants and craftsmen against competition from the foreigner in their midst.[1]

The Charter further confirmed the policy, by restricting the right of any individual to set up a printing press at will. Its twelfth paragraph limited the privilege to members of the Company, who were required to have served an apprenticeship and be admitted Freemen of the City of London. The latter course was extremely difficult for aliens, and a body of printing craftsmen unable to rise from the ranks was immediately created.[2]

The position of the native-born craftsman was almost as unsatisfactory. In the Middle Ages it had been possible for an apprentice to set up as a master after he had completed his period of indentures, although he might serve for a few years as a journeyman to save capital for starting on his own account. But the system which grew up in the latter half of the sixteenth century, whereby the copyrights of all the most profitable books fell into the hands of printers able to pay the best prices for them,

[1] A good account of the background of the sixteenth-century printing trade in England may be found in the introduction to Duff, E. G., *A Century of the English Book Trade* (London, 1905). See also Worman, E. J., *Alien Members of the Book Trade during the Tudor Period* (London, 1906).

[2] The Freedom of the City was a closely guarded honour. There were three ways of obtaining it. Men whose fathers were Freemen at the time of their birth could claim Freedom by patrimony. Secondly, anyone who had served an apprenticeship to a Freeman was entitled to be made free of the City. Lastly, there was redemption, or purchase, the only method left open to foreigners whom earlier legislation had prevented from being apprenticed. The right of redemption depended upon the favourable attitude of the guild authorities of the applicant's craft. Freedom of the City was thus essential to aliens who wished to become masters.

militated severely against a young man anxious to enter an expanding and highly competitive market.[1] By 1580 the price of copyrights, the cost of which had long been rising, had put them beyond his reach. For instance, the Queen's Printer's Patent, and the outlay on printing the Bible, cost Christopher Barker over £3,000. Reference to his *A Note of the State of the Company of Printers . . . with a valuation of all the letters patent concerning printing*, which was written in 1582, will show that the majority of books in common demand, such as Bibles, law and school books, were protected by patents.[2]

The *Newe Decrees of the Starre Chamber for Orders in Printinge* of 1586, promoted by the Court of the Stationers' Company to facilitate the enforcement of copyright, finally thwarted the ambitions of the average young journeyman, for they ordained that no more printing offices were to be opened without license of the Court of High Commission, until the present "excessive number was abated". (Barker had reported in 1582 that there were "22 printing howses in London. . . .") The number of boys permitted to be apprenticed to each master was also laid down, but this maximum was greatly in excess of the twenty or so who could become master printers, and it is clear from the new regulations that a permanent class of journeymen was envisaged.[3]

The decrees of 1586 were not explicit as to the number of firms allowed. The total was at the discretion of the Court of High Commission. It is evident that the problem was not finally settled, for in 1615 the Court of the Stationers' Company made an order to the effect that only twenty-two printers were to be allowed to exercise their craft in London, which suggests that interlopers had appeared. The famous Star Chamber Decrees of 1637 were designed to supplement and reinforce those of 1586. The fifteenth paragraph is of particular importance, since it specifically limited the number of master printers to twenty. The number of printing presses these men might own was also clearly defined. The Master and Upper and Lower Wardens of the Stationers' Company were allowed three apiece, while the remainder of their colleagues were

---

[1] Copyright was secured either by Royal Patent or by entry in the Register of the Stationers' Company. Neither method had been used exclusively before 1557.

[2] B. M. Lansdowne MS. No. 48, reprinted in Arber, *Transcript of the Registers of the Company of Stationers of London*, 1554–1640 (London, 1875–94), Vol. I, p. 114 *et seq.*

[3] The Master and Upper Warden of the Stationers' Company were allowed three boys; the Under Warden and Livery two, and the Yeomanry or Freemen one each.

to possess no more than two. The maximum number of apprentices was the same as in 1586.

The Courts of Star Chamber and High Commission were abolished in 1641, and there was consequently no legal sanction to enforce the 1637 decrees after that year. By 1660 the number of master printers had risen to sixty.[1] The Licensing Act of 1662 was the last piece of legislation framed to confine the trade within well-controlled bounds. Its provisions had great similarity with the Star Chamber Decrees of 1586 and 1637. Once again there was the limitation of the number of master printers to twenty, and the same regulations concerning the maximum number of presses to be kept and apprentices indentured. The Act of 1662 was periodically re-enacted until 1695, when it was allowed to lapse. After the latter date, therefore, the principal obstacles preventing the free expansion of the London and provincial printing trades were removed. The ambitious journeyman, hitherto prevented from becoming an employer, was now theoretically able to rise into the ranks of the masters.

(ii) *Some Regulations and Customs of the London Printing Trade, 1587–1734*

As a prelude to the documents of the late eighteenth and nineteenth centuries, a number of earlier pieces and extracts from contemporary literature are reprinted in this section. Documents relating to the government's control of the printing and bookselling trades during the sixteenth and seventeenth centuries have been omitted, since they are contained in Arber's *Transcript*.

This control, on political and religious grounds, had the effect of limiting the size and output of the London printing trade. It is apposite to note that, while the Parisian and French printers generally were subject to equally close control, the quality and volume of work executed there was greatly superior to the products of the craft in London. Whereas in London the number of presses a man might own was limited, in Paris there was a statutory minimum. The overseers of the Parisian trade also insisted upon a certain standard of quality being maintained, although this deteriorated in the seventeenth century. Its revival during the eighteenth century was due, in no small measure, to the example set by the Royal Printing Office. In France, and in the Low Countries as well, the master printers still counted in their ranks

---

[1] See *Harleian Miscellany* (London, 1774–6), Vol. III, p. 277.

men of substance and learning. Their London colleagues were, in comparison, neither erudite nor influential.

The documents in this section illustrate several important factors. The regulations of 1587 and 1635 were clearly for the protection of the new class of permanent journeyman, unable to rise into the ranks of the masters and still, withal, strongly conscious of its rights as Freemen. They were mainly designed for the prevention of unemployment. I have included the description of "Ancient Customs used in a Printing House" taken from Moxon's *Mechanick Exercises* (1683). Although this passage has often been reprinted, its importance justifies its inclusion in a book of this nature. The Chapel system, described by Moxon, survives to this day. This was the earliest form of Trade Union in the printing trade, and when individual Chapels began to send delegates to collective meetings, the nucleus of a Trade Union organisation, as we now understand it, was established. This does not appear to have taken place regularly until after 1785.

(a) THE REGULATIONS OF 1587

On 11 December, 1587, *"certen orders concerning printing"* were put into force by the Stationers' Company, designed to alleviate the discontent of the journeymen. Whether any of the regulations were in force at a previous date is not known. The orders of 1587 are, indeed, of the greatest historical importance, since they record the right of the compositors to any advantage accruing from the existence of standing formes. It was set forth that such formes, from which an impression had already been taken, and which had not been broken up or distributed, should not be used again without some compensation to the journeymen, since their regular use materially lessened the amount of work available for the workmen. Two centuries later and more, the compositors' right to standing formes, or "fat," was often a matter for dispute.

The regulation limiting the number of impressions that could be taken from a forme was also for the protection of the journeymen. The necessity for the frequent resetting of books in great demand provided work for hands which would otherwise have been idle. Exceptions were made in the case of certain devotional and school books, of which larger impressions might be taken, although a maximum was clearly defined. But the latter books were in such constant demand that their execution always provided a measure of work for the men. The regulation, then, provided work at the expense of the more profitable patents and copyrights.

A Copie of Certen Orders Concerning Printing

1. ffyrst that no fórmes of letters be kept standinge to the preiudice of Woorkemen at any tyme.

2. Secondly that no booke to be printed excede the number of 1250 or 1500 at one ympression except any book whatsoeuer of the non pareille letter [*i.e. size of type*] and the brevier letter,[1] and also except iiij ympressions yerely of the *grammer* and lykwise iiij ympressions yerely of the *Accidence* seuerall[y] in 4to or 8uo and also all *prymers* and *Catechisms*. and that euery of th[e] impressions of *grammers Accidences prymers* and *Catechismes* and of all bookes of the none pareill letter and brevier letter be not aboue 2500 or 3000 at the most and except also *the statutes* and *proclamacons* with all other bookes belonging to ye office of her maiesties printer which by reason of her maiesties affayres are to be limited to no numbers.[2] And except all *Calenders* printed Red and black[3] and also except all *Almanackes* and *prognostications*.

3. Thirdly that no Apprentice nowe beinge be employed either in composing or woorkinge at the presse while any woorkman prynter hable to discharge suche work and reasonably requiring the same (and beinge of honest and good behaviour) shall want woork. Nor that hereafter (the yeres of theise beinge expired) any more Apprentises be into any printinge house taken other then according to ye meaninge of ye Decree made in the Starrchamber bearinge date the 23 Day of June [1586] in ye xxviijth yere of the reign of the Quenes maiestye that nowe is. And that if any woorkman shall over hardly behaue him self either in his woork or in Demaunding of wages That then the controuersie to be decided by ye Master, wardens, and assistentes of the Company of Staconers of London or any other by their appointment.

4. Neuertheles yf any Master Printer supplyinge the place of A

---

[1] The exception was probably made for the following reason: brevier and nonpareil are both small sizes of type, 8 pt. and 6 pt. in modern measurement. For instance, a book containing 160 pp. set in either of these sizes would provide much more work than one set in pica, or 12 pt., the measure and the depth of setting being equal, and the types set solid. Therefore, because of the extra labour involved and wages paid, additional impressions were allowed.

[2] Proclamations were printed by the King's Printer under Patent, and were generally required by the Government in a hurry. In his memorandum of 1582, Christopher Barker remarked that "*Proclamations* come on the suddayne, and must be returned printed in hast: wherefore by breaking of greater worke I loose oftentymes more by one Proclamacon, then I gayne by sixe, before my servantes can comme in trayne of their worke agayne, and in many yeres there hapeneth not a proclamation of any benefit at all."

[3] Printing in two colours involved no extra setting, but necessitated passing the sheet twice through the press. This extra cost in pressman's wages may have been the reason for the concession. There are some sixteenth century frisket sheets, with the black forme blanked out for printing the second colour, in the Victoria and Albert Museum, London. I do not think that a separate forme for each colour was used at that period.

Journeman shall at any tyme hereafter haue occasion of busynes or any other ympedyment That then yt shalbe Lawfull for the prentyce of suche Master Prynter to Woork in his maysters place duringe suche tyme as his master shall not in his own person ymploy him self and his own personal woork in printing.

5. And lastly that yf it shall happen at any tyme hereafter the copy [*i.e., a publication enjoying what was then roughly equivalent to our existing copyright protection*] of any man to be out of prynt and that after warninge shalbe gyven him and registred in the hall book at a Court of Assistentes for the reprynting thereof, the owner of the same doo not within Sixe monethes (after suche warning and regestring in the said book) reprynt or begyn to reprynt the same and procede orderly with the ympression to ye finishyng thereof / as he conveniently may so that the Aucthor of any suche copy be no hinderance therevnto That then it shalbe Laufull for the Journemen of the said Company to cause and gett any suche book or copy to be printed to ye vse of ye Company during ye Impression then to be printed of ye same copy. Savinge and alowinge to the owner of the copie a ratable parte with them in ye same Impression in proffitt and charge as yt shall fall out to euery seuerall partener in euery suche Impression According to the order and discretion of the Master, and Wardens of the Company for the tyme beynge.

6. Provided alwaies that yf the Journemen to whose benefit the Contentes of these present Articles and orders doo tend or any of yem [*them*] by ye Consent of the moore parte of the said Journemen shall not hold them selues content therewith but shall move or begyn any newe sute peticon or complaint to or against the Mayster Wardens and Gouernours or any other of the Society contrary vnto or further or otherwyse then shalbe Consonant and Agreable to the Contents and trewe meaninge of these present Articles and orders That then and from thensforth these said artycles and orders and euery thinge in them Conteined shalbe as vtterly void and frustrate in all intentes and purposes as thoughe the same had neuer ben had nor made Any thinge Whatsoeuer to the contrary thereof in any wise notwithstanding.

(b) THE REGULATIONS OF 1635

Half a century separates the last document from the one that follows, which Arber described as an "Arbitration Case." The regulations here reproduced, dated 16 November, 1635, were drafted by the Stationers' Company in answer to a petition from the journeymen. Five of the nineteen paragraphs concerned the control of the large number of apprentices who were irregularly bound, and who had no right to work in the trade. The remaining clauses clearly defined certain rules of the trade. The text in square brackets is by Arber.[1]

Whereas a Peticion and Declaracion annexed of the Jorneymen Printers exhibited to the Master Wardeines and Assistantes of this Company

---

[1] State Papers Dom. Charles I., No. 301, Art. 105. Reprinted by Arber.

Concerning divers abuses which they desire reformacion of was referred vnto vs whose names are hervnto written. Wee haue taken into our consideracion the Complaintes of the said Jorneymen against the excessive numbers of persons brought vpp to the Art of Printing, some of which learne the trade and are not bound at all by Indenture to any, others bound to men free of this Company and other Companies and turned over to Printers to serve out their tyme[,] others are disorderly bound at the Scriveners, other Printers by profession take Partners vnto them and their partners get Apprentices bound to them, and others are bound at the [Stationers'] Hall aboue the number that each one is to haue. As also of extraordinary numbers of some Bookes printed at one Impression And like wise of the abuse of standing formes, with other matters of great preiudice to them. And allso wee haue considered the Complaint of divers Master Printers concerning the wrong and losse that they suffer by the negligence and misdemeanour of some Jorneymen printers. ffor reformacion whereof, and for prevention of future Complaints, wee have composed theise Articles following. Notwithstanding wee submit the same to the better Judgement of your Worships:

1 That those servantes which are not bound at all, and are kept and brought vpp to worke at the Trade of printing shalbe presently [*i.e., at once*] put away, and the Master or Masters ffyned for keeping them contrary to the allowed ordinance of this Company.

2 That those that are at this tyme bound to ffreemen of this Company not being Printers, or any other Company and afterward (to evade the Decree [*of the Star Chamber of the* 23rd *June,* 1586]) haue beene put to or turned over to Printers, whereby to learne the Art of printing. That they shalbe forthwith reformed or removed. And that yf anie shall hereafter be soe bound or turned over as aforesaid, he or they shalbe presently put away, and the Master soe keeping him or them shalbe ffyned at the discretion of the Master Wardeins and Assistantes, or the more part of them.

3 That those which are not presented at the [Stationers'] Hall, and allowed there to be the Apprentice of him or them that presents him, and bound by the Clarke of this Company, The Master or Masters of such shalbe warned to the Hall, and there ffyned as shalbe thought fitt. And likewise such further order taken as shalbe considered for redresse.

4 That those which haue beene bound according to Order, and before their tyme expired haue come away or otherwaise hauve beene putt away, and soe the Master or Masters of such, haue others bound in their stead That the presentment of such soe gone away shall be [e]razed out of the Hall Booke, and the Indentures delivered vpp, yf they can be come by. And for the more certeinty of such not to be made free in tyme to come, The Clarke of the Company shall from tyme to tyme keepe Register of the names of all such soe gone, when others are presented in their Roomes.

5 That those, that are become partner or partners in anie printing house, shall not be suffered to take any Apprentice. Nor shall there be allowed by reason of anie Copartnershipp anie more Apprentices, then the Master or Owner of such Printing house shalbe capable to haue by his Ranke and degree in this Company And for those that are

already taken, such speedy redresse to be had as shall be thought fitt by the Master Wardeins and Assistants or the more part of them.

6 That no Printing formes be kept standing, but the *Psalter, Gramar, Accidence, Almanacke Prognostication, Primer* or *Absee* [*i.e., ABC*]. And [the type of] those [works] to be distributed once a yeare, and the Letter [*type*] to be new cast, which vppon viewe shalbe found defective. And that noe Bookes printed of the Nonpariell Letter exceed aboue the number of 5000. And of the Brevier 3000. Except the Priveledge granted to the Company and the *Testament*, belonging to the Kinges Printers Commonly called [Sir J.] Cheekes *Testament*, and of that 6000. at the most. And of all other Bookes 1500. or 2000. at the most. But yf occasion shall require to haue a greater number than the said 2000. That then vppon good reasons shewed to the Master and Wardeins, the said Master and Wardeins may permit to be printed 3000. but noe greater number in any wise.[1]

7 That noe Master Printer shall lay on anie greater quantity of Paper then will fynish the Impression agreed for, according to the porporcion aforesaid, except Two quires vpon a heape to perfect the said Impression.[2]

8 That where a Jorneyman and Apprentice worke togeather, they shall both take their worke as it falles out and not otherwise, the one the ffirst part, and the other the Last, as at ffirst they agree.[3]

9 That yf anie standing forme shall on necessary occasion be vsed (yf anie compositor in that house want worke at that tyme) he shal be paid for that fforme, as yf he had composed it, excepting such fformes as before excepted.[4]

10 That every Jorneyman Printer shalbe allowed for the Hollydaies as

---

[1] The sixth paragraph, in Arber's opinion "bears witness in the increased number of copies allowed to an impression to the general growth of the English book trade. For unless the Compositors had been kept fully employed with new books, they would not have suffered such large editions of the more popular old ones."

The King's Printer purchased the copyright of Sir John Cheke's version of the New Testament in 1606. See Pollard, A. W., *Records of the English Bible* (Oxford, 1911), p. 335. The maximum impression of 6,000 may be contrasted with the King's Printers' previous right, as allowed in his original Patent, to print as many copies as he wished. On the subject of limitation of impression reference should also be made to Greg and Boswell, *Records of the Court of the Stationers' Company*, 1576–1602 (London, 1930), *passim*.

[2] Two quires would be the equivalent to an extra fifty sheets, "to make *Proves, Revises, Register-Sheets, Tympan Sheets,* and to supply other accidents that may happen at the *Press,* either by naughty Sheets, or Faults committed in *Beating, Pulling, Bad Register, &c.*" Moxon, J., *Mechanick Exercises* (London, 1683). Reprint of New York Typothetæ, 1896, p. 354.

[3] If the journeyman was on piece-work, this rule would be of great importance. It would prevent the Master from giving all the "fat," such as short pages, blanks, half-titles, etc., to the apprentice, who received no wages. "Fat" work, being quickly and easily set, would be profitable to a man on piece-work. If the journeyman were paid a fixed weekly wage, the relative ease or difficulty of the copy provided would be of little account to him. Owing to lack of evidence, it is impossible to deny or affirm that piece-work existed at that period.

[4] *Cf.* regulations of 1587 (p. 16): "I. ffyrst that no formes of letters be kept standinge to the preiudice of the Workemen at any tyme."

heretofore, but yf it shall happen anie Jorneyman to loose his worke, then the said Jorneyman shall not onely pay for the losse of his owne worke, but for his fellowes allso, that loose their worke through his default.[1]

11 That every Jorneyman Printer shall forever hereafter, haue of the Master Printer with whome he worketh, in lieu of an Auncyent Custome which they the said Jorneymen Printers haue had, for to have a Copie of every Booke they worke vppon, Three Pence a weeke. But yf it shalbe proved any Jorneyman Printer to take or convay away out of the Printing-house where he worketh, or receive from any other Printinghouse any printed Copie or booke, or any Sheet or Sheetes of paper printed belonging to anie Booke. Or shall lay on anie Sheet or Sheetes of his owne paper, or other mens, thereby to gett Copies. That then every Jorneyman soe offending herein, shalbe forever hereafter vncapable of anie benefitt by theis Orders now agreed vppon. As also forever to be vncapable of the benefit of Hollidaies, or anie other benefit or advantage in this Company.

12 That noe workeman that doth vndertake a place to performe worke, shall put anie other man to doe the same worke for him, except he be a sufficient workeman, without consent of the Master, nor for a longer tyme, then the Master shall thinke fitt.

13 That noe workman shall rayse his wages aboue the now vsuall Rates. Nor noe Master Printers abate the prices they now give. But in case of difference, the Master and Wardeins to decide it.[2]

14 That the Custome of the Kinges Printinghouse, for wages, Holly-daies, Copies, and other benefittes to workemen, to contynue, as now, and heretofore it hath beene.

15 That noe workman lend Letter without consent first obteyned of the Master, on paine to loose the benefit of Hollydais and Copies.[3]

---

[1] The "Hollydaies" were those of the Church, such as Christmas Day and Good Friday. The second half of the rule discouraged the intemperate from celebrating "St. Monday" by not returning to work. This particular saint was, I think, recognized by both the English and French printing trades. *Cf.* Franklin, B., *Memoirs of the Life and Writings of Benjamin Franklin* (London, 1818). Second Edition. Vol. I., p. 71.

[2] What the "now vsuall Rates" were is not known. There does not appear to be any contemporary evidence to show what the workmen earned in 1635.

[3] This rule did not legislate so much against type being lent to a rival firm, as to a secret or unlawfully conducted press. Apparently the practice was an old one. Fifty years before, in his evidence to Star Chamber as a defendant in an action brought against him by John Day, Roger Wolfe declared "that one Adam a seruant of Master purfo(o)ttes dyd lende him some letters wherewith he imprynted the said boke." (Arber ii. 761). It may well be asked how an employer had so little control over the use and disposal of his property. Arber suggests that "The composition then was not necessarily done in the master-printer's house where he kept his press. Of course, such portion of it as was executed by himself and his apprentices was done there; but that which was committed to the journeymen compositors, who were for the most part householders, was pro-bably done in their houses and paid for by piece work; a custom which was facilitated by most of the books then printed, being almost always in some one size of type." (ii. 22.)

There is, however, no evidence that such was the case, or that payment by the

16 That the Compositors keepe their Cases cleane / and dispose of all Woodden Letters, and Two Lyne letters And keepe their Letter whole while worke is doing, and after bind it vpp in good order. But yf they faile herein, Then the Master to cause the same to be done, and abate for it, out of his wages Provided he [*the Compositor*] receive it in like manner as aforesaid.

17 That what worke shalbe spoiled by workemen, they having where-with sufficiently [*i.e., proper tools and materials*] to discharge their worke, They shall allow for Paper, printing, and other Charges to reprint the same, that soe workmanshipp may be the better heeded.

18 That noe Master Printer shall hereafter permit or suffer, by them-selves, or their Jorneymen any Girls, Boyes, or others, to take off anie Sheetes from the Tinpin [*tympan*] of the Presse, but that hee that pulleth at the Presse shall take off every Sheet himself.[1]

19 That yf anie Compositor or Presseman, or anie other shall hereafter erect or set vpp, or cause to be erected or set vpp, or consent, or be privy vnto the setting of anie printing Presse or presses in any Corner or secret place vnlawfully, or shall worke or cause to worke at such Presse or Presses, or compose or sett, or cause to be composed and sett anie Letter or Letters in or for any such printing house, contrary to the Decree in the Starrechamber, made in the 28th. of Queen Elizabeth. As also the allowed Ordinances of this Company. That then every such partie or parties, soe offending, besides all such punishmentes, as is allready prouided in that behalf, shalbe forever vncapable of anie benefitt ef theis Orders, now agree vppon, of Hollidayes, Coppie money, pencion in the Hall, or anie other benefitt whatsoever in this Company.

piece was made in the printing trade. From the practical point of view the existence of home work is improbable. There would be loss of time owing to shortage of sorts, common enough in a printing office, but far worse when the compositor has to make a journey to fetch them. Also there is the trouble of con-veying the completed galleys to the printing office, and the risk of their being dropped in crowded streets, with disastrous results. Arber evidently did not appreciate the ease with which a galley can be "pied."

Again, there is no evidence that the practice of home work prevailed on the Con-tinent. The iconography of the sixteenth- and seventeenth-century printing office demonstrates time and again, that, unlike in the present day, the composing and press rooms were combined in one. (Although Moxon did write that in England in his day "it is not very customary.") Therefore, if types were lent by the journeymen, it must be assumed that they were lent direct from the printing office.

[1] This clause prevented the employment of unindentured, unskilled labour for the performance of trivial tasks, since there was the possibility that such hands might later be set to more productive work. "The *Press-man* sometimes has a Week-Boy to *Take Sheets*, as they are Printed off the *Tympan:* These Boys do in a Printing-House, commonly black and Dawb themselves; whence the Workmen do Jocosely call them *Devils;* and sometimes *Spirits* and sometimes *Flies*." (Moxon, J., *op. cit.*, p. 373.) The term Fly-boy persisted to the middle of the nineteenth century. The introduction of the automatic flyer, invented by Hoe, in 1846, which placed the printed sheets in a heap after they were received from the cylinder, caused the eventual disappearance of this class of labour in the printing trade.

(c) THE CHAPEL

The Chapel, or organization of journeymen in a printing office, enforced the recognized customs of the trade, was a mutual benefit society, and in cases of dispute negotiated with the employer. It is unlikely, however, that there was any organized union of the principal chapels in the London trade much before 1800. The earliest information about the Chapel system is to be found in Joseph Moxon's *Mechanick Exercises.*

The origin of the term is obscure. Moxon suggested that "the style was originally conferred upon it by the courtesie of some great churchman, or men (doubtless when chapels were in more veneration than of late years they have been here in England), who, for the books of divinity that proceeded from a printing-house, gave it the reverend title of Chapel." A more usual, although probably equally inaccurate suggestion, was the one proposed by Savage and many other writers: "The term is supposed to have had its origin from the first introduction of printing into England by Caxton, who executed his works in a chapel adjoining Westminster Abbey."[1] The fact that the expression was also used in France would suggest that it did not originate with the situation of Caxton's Press. Radiguer conjectured that printers' Chapels existed in France before the middle of the sixteenth century.[2] The word *Chapelian* to designate a member of a Chapel was certainly in use in Paris in the eighteenth century.[3]

The Chapel rules, as given by Moxon, show that it was both a disciplinary and benevolent institution, run on severely practical financial lines. There were the fines inflicted upon the untidy and unruly, entrance fees for new members and levies on certain occasions. The clause stating the remuneration for holidays other than Sundays provides some argument for the existence of piece-work at that date, since the sums to be allowed, ranging from 2s. 6d. to 4s., were "to be paid proportionably for what they undertake to Earn every Working day. . . ." Moxon concluded with an account of the feast held by the printers, masters and men, "on or about May day" every year in Stationers' Hall.[4]

---

[1] Savage, William, *Dictionary of the Art of Printing* (London, 1841).

[2] Radiguer, I., *Maîtres Imprimeurs et Ouvriers Typographes* (Paris, 1903), p. 96.

[3] *Cf. Reglement pour le Bon de la St. Martin, fait entre les ouvriers de M. Herissant, et de son consentement, en vertu d'un Memoire a lui adressé et signé de tous les ouvriers.* November 10, 1760. (Bib. Nat. MS. Franç., 22064.) This document is quoted in Morin, L., *Essai sur la Police des Compagnons Imprimeurs* which appeared serially in *L'Intermediaire des Imprimeurs,* May 1897-June 1898.

[4] Omitted in the present work. It is interesting to note that the great banquet

Ancient Customs Used in a Printing House

Every *Printing-house* is by the Custom of Time out of mind, called a *Chappel;* and all the Workmen that belong to it are *Members of the Chappel;* and the Oldest Freeman is *Father of the Chappel*. I suppose the stile was originally conferred upon it by the courtesie of some great Churchman, or men (doubtless when Chappels were in more veneration than of late years they have been here in *England*) who for the Books of Divinity that proceeded from a *Printing-house*, gave it the Reverend Title of *Chappel*.

There have been formerly Customs and By-Laws made and intended for the well and good Government of the *Chappel*, and for the more Civil and orderly deportment of all its Members while in the *Chappel*; and the Penalty for the breach of any of these Laws and Customs is in Printers Language called a *Solace*.

And the Judges of these *Solaces*, and other Controversies relating to the *Chappel*, or any of its Members, was plurality of Votes in the *Chappel*. It being asserted as a Maxim, *That the Chappel cannot Err*. But when any Controversie is thus decided, it always ends in the good of the *Chappel*.

1. Swearing in the *Chappel*, a *Solace*.
2. Fighting in the *Chappel*, a *Solace*.
3. Abusive Language, or giving the Ly[e] in the *Chappel*, a *Solace*.
4. To be Drunk in the *Chappel*, a *Solace*.
5. For any of the Workmen to leave his Candle burning at Night, a *Solace*.[1]
6. If the *Compositor* let fall his *Composing-stick*, and another take it up, a *Solace*.
7. Three *Letters* and a *Space* to lye vnder the *Compositers Case*, a *Solace*.
8. If a *Press-man* let fall his *Ball* or *Balls*, and another take it up, a *Solace*.
9. If a *Press-man* leave his *Blankets* in the *Tympan* at Noon or Night, a *Solace*.

These *Solaces* were to be bought off, for the good of the *Chapel:* Nor were the price of these *Solaces* alike: For some were 12d, 6d. 4d. 2d. 1d. *ob*. according to the nature and quality of the *Solace*.

But if the Delinquent prov'd Obstinate or Refractory, and would not pay his *Solace* at the Price of the *Chappel;* they *Solac'd* him.

The manner of *Solacing*, thus.

The Workmen take him by force, and lay him on his Belly athwart the *Correcting-stone*, and held him there while another of the Workmen, with a Paper-board, gave him 10 l. *and a Purse*, viz. Eleven blows on his

of the Parisian printing trade, in celebration of the Feast of St. Jean de Latran, was held at much the same date, namely, on 6 May. For details see Lottin, A. M., *La Messe du Martyre de S. Jean, Apôtre et Evangéliste, devant la Porte Latine à Rome, patron de la Communaute des Libraires* (Paris, 1789.) The only known copy of this work is at the Bib. Carnavalet, Paris. It is quoted by Thoinan, E., *Les Relieurs Français* (Paris, 1893).

[1] Savage stated that this fine was never remitted. The amounts in his day were sixpence for a workman, double for the overseer, and half-a-crown for the master.

Buttocks; which he laid on according to his own mercy. For Tradition tells us, that about 50 years ago one was *Solaced* with so much violence, that he presently Pissed Blood, and shortly after dyed of it.

These nine *Solaces* were all the *Solaces* usually and generally accepted: yet in some particular *Chappels* the *Work-men* did by consent make other *Solaces*, viz.

That it should be a *Solace* for any of the Work-men to mention Joyning their Penny or more apiece to send for Drink.

To mention spending *Chappel-money* till *Saturday* Night, or any other before agreed time.

To play at *Quadrats*, or excite any of the *Chappel* to Play at *Quadrats;* either for Money or Drink.[1] This *Solace* is generally Purchas'd by the Master-Printer; as well because it hinders the Workmens work, as because it Batters and spoils the *Quadrats:* for the manner how they Play with them is Thus:

They take five or seven more m *Quadrats* (generally of the *English Body*) and holding their Hand below the Surface of the *Correcting Stone*, shake them in their Hand, and toss them up upon the *Stone*, and then count how many *Nicks* upwards each man throws in three times, or any other number of times agreed on: And he that throws most Wins the Bett of all the rest, and stands out free, till the rest haue try'd who throws fewest *Nicks* upwards in so many throws; for all the rest are free: and he pays the Bett.

For any to *Take up a Sheet*, if he receiv'd *Copy-money;* Or if he receiv'd no *Copy-money*, and did *Take up a Sheet*, and carryed that Sheet or Sheets off the Printing-House till the whole Book was Printed off and Publisht.[2]

Any of the Workmen may purchase a *Solace* for any trivial matter, if the rest of the *Chappel* consent to it. As if any of the Workmen Sing in the *Chappel;* he that is offended at it may, with the *Chappels* Consent purchase a penny or two penny *Solace* for any Workmans singing after the *Solace* is made; Or if a Workman or a Stranger salute a Woman in the *Chappel*, after the making of the *Solace*, it is a *Solace* of such a Value as is agreed on.

The price of all *Solaces* to be purchased is wholly Arbitrary in the *Chappel*. And a Penny *Solace* may perhaps cost the Purchaser six Pence, Twelve Pence, or more for the *Good of the Chappel*.

Yet sometimes *Solaces* may cost double the Purchase or more. As if some *Compositor* haue (to affront a *Press-man*) put a Wisp of Hay in the *Press-mans* Ball-Racks;[3] If the *Press-man* cannot well brook this affront, he will lay six Pence down on the *Correcting-Stone* to purchase a *Solace* of twelve Pence upon him that did it; and the *Chappel* cannot in Justice

---

[1] A custom known in the nineteenth century as "Jeffing." Savage, W., *op. cit.*, shows the earliest use of the word that I have seen. The typefounders played the same game, but called it "Bogleing." There is an account of the niceties of the practice in Southward, J., *A Dictionary of Typography* (London, 1870-71), art. Jeffing.

[2] *Cf.* paragraph 11 of the Arbitration Case dated 1635, here reprinted at p. 20.

[3] The pressmen were then nicknamed "horses."

refuse to grant it: because it tends to the *Good of the Chappel*: And being granted, it becomes every Members duty to make what discouery he can : because it tends to the farther *Good of the Chappel*: And by this means it seldom happens but the Agressor is found out.

Nor did *Solaces* reach only the *Members of the Chappel*, but also Strangers that came into the *Chappel*, and offered affronts or indignities to the *Chappel*, or any of its Members; the *Chappel* would determine it a *Solace*. Example,

It was a *Solace* for any to come to the *Kings Printing-house* and ask for a Ballad.[1]

For any to come and enquire of a *Compositor*, whether he had News of such a Galley at Sea.

For any to bring a Wisp of Hay, directed to any of the *Press-men*.

And such Strangers were commonly sent by some who knew the *Customs of the Chappel*, and had a mind to put a Trick upon the Stranger.

Other Customs were used in the *Chappel*, which were not *Solaces*, viz. Every new Workman to pay half a Crown; which is called his *Benvenue:*[2] This *Benvenue* being so constant as Custome is still lookt upon by all Workmen as the undoubted Right of the *Chappel*, and therefore never disputed; yet he who has not paid his *Benvenue* is no Member of the *Chappel*, nor enjoys any benefit of *Chappel-Money*.

If a Journey-man Wrought formerly upon the same Printing House, and comes again to Work on it, [he] pays but half a *Benvenue*.

If a Journeyman *Smout* more or less on another Printing House, and any of the *Chappel* can prove it, he pays half a *Benvenue*.[3]

I told you before that abusive Language or giving the Lye was a *Solace*: But if in discourse, when any of the Workmen affirm anything that is not believed, the *Compositor* knocks with the back corner of his *Composing-stick* against the lower Ledge of his *Lower Case*, and the *Pressman* knocks the Handles of his *Ball-stocks* together: Thereby signifying the discredit they give to his Story.

It is now customary that Journey-men are paid for all Church Holy days that fall not on a *Sunday*, Whether they Work or no: and they are by Contract with the Master Printer paid proportionally for what they undertake to Earn every Working day, be it half a Crown, two shillings, three shillings, four shillings, &c.

[1] The terms "cock-robin shop" and "hedge-printer" are still used in a derogatory sense to describe a small, badly equipped office or its owner. It would appear that the expression "Ballad House" was the seventeenth or eighteenth-century equivalent. See Gent, Thomas, *Life of Thomas Gent* (London, 1832), p. 73. It would, then, be out of place to demand the text of the latest song from the King's Printer.

[2] An additional argument supporting the French origin of the Chapel. Very similar regulations are quoted in Momoro, A. F., *Traité Elémentaire de l'Imprimerie* (Paris, 1793), p. 73. See also Arber, E., *op. cit.*, Vol. I, pp. 36-37.

[3] "Workmen when they are out of constant Work, do sometimes accept of a Day or twos Work, or a Weeks Work at another Printing-house: this By-work they call Smouting." Moxon, J., *op. cit.*, p. 390. This practice is now called Casual Work or "grassing." Today's meaning of *Smouting* is when a man has a full engagement at one office and works also at other offices in his spare time, *e.g.*, evenings or in five-day week houses on Saturdays.

It is also customary for all the Journey-men to make every Year new Paper Windows, whether the old will serve again or no; Because that day they make them, the Master Printer gives them a *Way-goose*[1]; that is, he makes them a good Feast, and not only entertains them at his own House, but besides, gives them Money to spend at the Alehouse or Tavern at Night; And to this Feast, they invite the *Correcter, Founder, Smith, Joyner,* and *Inck-maker,* who all of them severally (except the *Correcter* is his own Civility) open their Purse-strings and add their Benevolence (which Workmen account their duty, because they generally chuse these Workmen) to the Master Printers:[2] But from the *Correcter* they expect nothing, because the Master Printer chusing him, the Workman can do him no kindness.

These *Way-gooses,* are always kept about *Bartholomew-tide.* And till the Master-Printer have giuen this *Way-goose,* the Journey-men do not use to Work by Candle Light.

If a Journey-man marry, he pays half a Crown to the *Chappel.*

When his Wife comes to the *Chappel,* she pays six Pence: and then all the Journey-men joyn their two Pence apiece to Welcome her.

If a Journey-man haue a Son born, he pays one Shilling.

If a Daughter born, six Pence.

The *Father* of the *Chappel* drinks first of the *Chappel Drink,* except some other Journey-man have a *Token*; viz. Some agreed piece of Coin or Mettle markt by consent of the *Chappel:* for then producing that *Token,* he *Drinks* first. This Token is always given to him who in the Round should have Drank, had the last *Chappel-drink* held out. Therefore when *Chappel-drink comes in,* they generally say, *Who has the Token?*

Though these Customs are no *Solaces*; yet the Chappel Excommunicates the delinquent; and he shall have no benefit of *Chappel-money* till he haue paid.

It is also Customary in some Printing-houses that if the *Compositor* or *Press-man* make either the other stand still through the neglect of their contracted Task, that then he who neglected, shall pay him that stands still as much as if he had Wrought.

The *Compositers* are Jocosely call'd *Galley Slaves*: Because allusively they are as it were bound to their *Gallies.*

And the *Press-men* are Jocosely call'd *Horses*: Because of the hard Labour they go through all day long.

An Apprentice when he is Bound pays half a Crown to the *Chappel,* and when he is made Free, another half Crown to the *Chappel;* but is yet no Member of the *Chappel*: And if he continue to Work Journeywork in the same House, he pays another half a Crown, and is then a Member of the *Chappel.*

A *Founding-House* [*i.e.,* a type foundry] is also call'd a *Chappel:* But I

---

[1] The origin of the term is obscure. The explanation to be found in most works of reference, that a wayz or stubble goose was the chief dish at the feast, is not accepted by the compilers of the O.E.D. After the introduction of railways, the wayzegoose generally took the form of a day's outing to the sea or some beauty spot. The custom seems almost to have died out.

[2] In the Parisian trade the men solicited contributions from the individuals who supplied their office with types, ink, etc. Morin, L., *op. cit.*

suppose the Title was originally assum'd by *Founders*, to make a Competition with *Printers*. The Customes used in a *Founding-House* are made as near as may be to those of a *Printing-House:* but because the Matter they Work on, and the manner of their working is different, therefore such different Customes are in Use, as are suitable to their Trade, As

First, To call *Mettle* Lead, a Forfeiture.

Secondly, A Workman to let fall his *Mold*, a Forfeiture.

Thirdly, A Workman to leave his ladle in the *Mettle* Noon or Night, a Forfeiture.

(*d*) EXPERIENCES OF THOMAS GENT

The autobiography of Thomas Gent, well known as a master printer in York in the eighteenth century, contains an account of his initiation as a member of the chapel of a London printing office about the year 1712.[1]

Being as inconsiderate youth is, too soon, over fond of novelty, being invited to another place, under Mr. Mears, in Blackfriars, I very indiscreetly parted with my mistress, which entirely lost me the favour of that knowing gentlewoman. On my entrance amongst a number of men, besides paying what is called Benmoney, I found, soon after, I was, as it were, to be dubbed as great a cuz as the famous Don Quixote seemed to be when he thought himself a knight, and that the innkeeper was lord of the castle, in the yard of which he judged that the honour was conferred: though the insipid folly thereof, agreeably to their strange harangues in praise of the protecting charms of cuzship, which, like the power of Don Waltho Claterbank's infallible medicines, would heal all evils, whether curable or not, was not very agreeable to my hearing; yet, when the master himself insisted it must be done, I was obliged to submit to that immemorial custom, the origin of which they could not then explain to me. It commenced by walking round the chapel (printing rooms being called such, because first begun to be practised in one at Westminster Abbey;) singing an alphabetical anthem, tuned literally to the vowels; striking me, kneeling, with a broadsword; and pouring ale upon my head: my titles were exhibited much to this effect, "Thomas Gent, baron of College Green, earl of Fingall, with power to the limits of Dublin bar, captain general of the Teagues, near the Lake of Allen, and lord high admiral over all the bogs in Ireland." To confirm which, and that I might not pay over again for the same ceremony, through forgetfulness, they allowed me godfathers, the first I ever had before, because the Presbyterian minister, at my christening, allowed none at his office; and these, my new pious fathers, were the un-reverend Mr. Holt and Mr. Palmer. Nay, there were witnesses also, such as Mr. Fleming, Mr. Gibbings, and Mr. Cocket, staunch journeymen printers. But after all this work, I began to see the vanity of human grandeur; for, as I was not yet a freeman, I was discharged as a foreigner in about a fortnight or three weeks' time.

---

[1] *The Life of Mr. Thomas Gent, printer, of York, written by himself* (London, 1832), p. 16. The manuscript of this book, dated 1746, was apparently completed in its author's fifty-third year.

(e) EXPERIENCES OF BENJAMIN FRANKLIN

Benjamin Franklin, who worked in London both as pressman and compositor in 1725, also recalled his experiences of the customs of the London printing trade in his Memoirs.[1]

Watts, after some weeks, desiring to have me in the composing-room, I left the pressmen; a new *bien venu* for drink was demanded of me by the compositors. I thought it an imposition, as I had paid one to the pressmen; the master thought so, too, and forbad my paying it. I stood out two or three weeks, was accordingly considered as an ex-communicate, and had so many little pieces of private malice practised on me, by mixing my sorts, transposing and breaking my matter, &c., if I ever stept out of the room; and all ascribed to the *chapel ghost*,[2] which they said ever haunted those not regularly admitted; that not-withstanding the master's protection, I found myself obliged to comply and pay the money; convinced of the folly of being on ill terms with those one is to live with continually.

(f) THE INITIATION CEREMONY

There is a good account of Chapel customs and the prescribed ceremonies for admission in *The Country Journal: or, The Crafts-man*, for 24 May, 1740.

When a printer first sets up, if it was an House that was never used for *Printing* before, the Part design'd for that Purpose is consecrated by the *senior Freeman* the *Master* employs, who is the *Father or Dean of the Chapel;* and the chief Ceremony is drinking Success to the *Master*, sprinkling the Walls with strong Beer, and singing the *Cuz's* Anthem, of which more hereafter; at the Conclusion of which there is a Supper given by the *Master*.

All the Workmen are Call'd *Chapellonians*, who are obliged to submit to *certain Laws*, all of which are calculated for the Good of the whole Body, and for the well-carrying on of the *Master's* Business. To the Breach of *these Laws* is annex'd a Penalty, which an obstinate Member sometimes refuses to pay; upon which it is left to the Majority of the *Chapel*, in Convocation assembled, whether He shall be continued any longer a *Chapellonian;* and if his Sentence is to be discontinued, He is then declared a Brimstone; That is an *excommunicated Person*, and deprived of all Share of the Money given by Gentlemen, Authors, Booksellers and Others, to make Them drink, especially that great annual Solemnity, commonly call'd the *Way-Goose Feast*.

While He continues in this State, he can have no Redress for any Mischief that is done Him; so that, in a short Time, He is glad to pay the *Penalty*, which He had incurr'd, and a *discretionary Fine* besides, to reconcile Himself to the *Chapel*.

---

[1] *Memoirs of the Life and Writings of Benjamin Franklin* (London, 1818), Vol. I, p. 69.

[2] This elemental was also known as "Ralph." See p. 121.

When a Boy is to be bound Apprentice, before he is admitted a *Chapellonian*, it is necessary for Him to be made a *Cuz*,[1] or *Deacon;* in the performance of which there are a great many Ceremonies. The *Chapellonians* walk three Times round the Room, their right Arms being put through the Lappets of their Coats; the Boy who is to be made a *Cuz*, carrying a wooden Sword before Them. Then the Boy kneels, and the *Father of the Chapel*, after exhorting Him to be observant of his Business, and not to betray the Secrets of the *Workmen*, squeezes a Spunge of strong Beer over his Head, and gives him a *Title*, which is generally That of *Duke* of some Place of the least Reputation near which He lives, or did live before; such as Those of *Rag Fair*, *Thieving-Lane*, *Puddle Dock*, *P-ssing Alley*, and the like. This being done, the *Father of the Chapel* gives the Boy an Account of the Safety He will enjoy by being made a *Cuz*, which is that whatever Accident may happen to Him, no ill consequence will attend it, such as *Falling from an House*, or into the *Thames*, etc.

Whilst the Boy is upon his Knees, all the *Chapellonians*, with their right Arms put through the Lappets of their Coats, as before, walk round Him, singing the *Cuz's* Anthem, which is done by adding all the *Vowels* to the *Consonants* in the following Manner.

Ba-ba; Be-be; Bi-bi; Ba-be-bi; Bo-bo; Ba-be-bi-bo; Bu-bu; Ba-be-bi-bo-bu—And so through the rest of the Consonants.

It should be noted, however, that the ceremonies and customs described above were primitive compared with those practised in the German-speaking countries at the time. While in England the affair of the initiation was an agreeable piece of tomfoolery, an excuse for a tipple, the German counterpart involved a complicated ritual. For an account of the German formulary, see Blades, W., *An Account of the German Morality Play entitled "Depositio Cornuti Typographici"* (London, 1885).

(*g*) CHAPEL RULES OF 1734

The following document, dated 1734, and originally printed as a broadside, is by far the most complete and interesting compilation of its sort at present known. The wording of these Chapel Rules makes me suspect that they were as much for the protection of compositors engaged on piece-work as in the interests of their employers. The emphasis on the necessity for the orderly disposal of types and other material will be noted. Piece-work is unprofitable unless all the necessary equipment is immediately available and in its correct place.

The seventh paragraph of the rules applying to both compositors and pressmen is of interest. Men who were "not free, but having a

---

[1] The expression was exclusive to the printing trade (O.E.D.).

right" were those who had served a normal apprenticeship, but had not bothered to take their Freedom. They paid more for their *Bienvenue*. Throughout the eighteenth century, about one in three of the boys apprenticed to London printers became Freemen of the Stationers' Company. The Freedom was indispensable for those who wished to become master printers. It also qualified journeymen to partake of the Company's charity in old age or sickness.

RULES AND ORDERS TO BE OBSERVED BY THE MEMBERS OF THIS CHAPEL[1]

BY THE COMPOSITORS

I. Title Pages to be clear'd by the Person who compos'd them, within a Week after laid up, Notice being given, on the Forfeiture of 2*d*.

II. For every Page or Piece of Letter ty'd up with Braces, Whitelines, or more than four Fractions, or with one whole Word of *Greek* of more than three Letters, or with Letter of a different Body, to forfeit 2*d*.

III. The Stones, Nest of Drawers, &c. to be clear'd by those who last us'd them, within half an Hour after Notice, on Forfeiture of 2*d*.

IV. For every Capital or other Thing pick'd out of Matter, without putting in something of like Size, the Person so doing to forfeit 1*d*.

V. The Sweepings of every one's Place to be clear'd within a Day, on Pain of forfeiting for every Day 2*d*.

VI. No Sorts to be put by in Papers, or otherwise, but to be put into the Bump-Case; or if the Bump-Case will not hold them, or there be no Bump-Case, into a Coffin in the Basket or Cupboard belonging to the Fount, on Pain of forfeiting for every Paper or Sort so put by 2*d*.

VII. Pye belonging to any Person, to be clear'd within two Days after Notice, on Pain of forfeiting 2*d*.

VIII. Cases to be put into the Frame or Rack within two Hours after done with (if Room) on Pain of forfeiting for each Case 1*d*.

IX. Braces, Fac-totums, Head-pieces, Tail-pieces, Slips, two-lin'd Letters, to be put into their proper Places in two Hours after done with, on Forfeiture of 1*d*.

X. *Greek* to be distributed within four Hours after the rest of the Letter in which it is used, on Pain of forfeiting for every Offence, in every Form 2*d*.

XI. Proof or Revise to be begun to be corrected within a Quarter of an Hour after requir'd, by the Master, or by the Fellow-Workman,

---

[1] British Museum. MSS. Add. 27799, f. 88. (Place Papers). See also MSS. Harl. 5915 *Orders to be observed in this Printing-House.* (n.d.) and a broadside in the St. Bride Collection, *Rules and Regulations to be observed by the Compositors and Pressmen employed by Mr. Jones at the Conference Printing Office,* 14, *City Road, London* (1808).

unless it appear to the oldest Freeman Compositor, that the Stone cannot be come at, on Forfeiture of 1*d.* '

XII. He that lays up an Act or Job for his own Conveniency, to tie up the Pages and Indorsement immediately, if not done with. If done with, he that compos'd the Job, or fill'd up the Blanks, to tie them up in Pieces convenient for Papering, in two Days after Notice given of their being laid up, on Forfeiture for every Day's Neglect for every Page or Indorsement, of 2*d.*

XIII. Every Form for Distribution, or Papering up, to be wash'd in the Sink, on Pain of forfeiting for each Form 2*d.*

XIV. If a Form, after laid up and wash'd by the Compositor, remains in the Sink an Hour, after Notice to take it away, the Compositor to forfeit 1*d.* and for every Hour after 1*d.*

XV. The Person appointed for papering up Letter, &c., to paper up the same within Eight Days after Notice given of its being tied up for that Purpose, on Forfeiture (for every Eight Pages, Pieces proper for papering up) of 2*d.* for the first Eight Days; and for every Day after 1*d.*

XVI. No Mixtures of Founts, especially Lower-Case Letters to be permitted; nor of Capitals, without the Consent of the Master, on Forfeiture, for every Mixture of Lower-Case Sorts, of 6*d.* per Sort; and for every Mixture of Capitals, *per* Sort, of 2*d.*

BY THE PRESS-MEN

I. Proofs to be made in a Quarter of an Hour after defin'd except in Cases of extraordinary Hurry, and no Press empty, of which the two eldest Freemen to be Judges, on Pain of Forfeiture of 2*d.*

II. All work to be taken in Turn, as brought to the Press, except in such Work as may require Dispatch, or the Compositor will want the Letter, on Forfeiture for every Form so transgress'd upon, of 2*d.* each Person, or 4*d. per* Press.

III. If a Form be imposing, and there be a Necessity for the Proof or Revise to be made, the Proof-maker for the Time being to forfeit, if he cap his Balls, and neglect the Proof, having Notice of it, 2*d.*

IV. For every Form not wash'd in a Quarter of an Hour after off, the Person offending, to forfeit 2*d.*

V. For leaving the Ink-Tub uncover'd; for Ball-Nails not put in the Shoe; for every Frisket standing on the Ground one Hour; for dipping Balls in the Lye-trough; for every Offence to forfeit 1*d.*

VI. For every Form left half an Hour in the Sink, after rincing, the Press-man offending, to forfeit 1*d.*

VII. Every Form to be rubb'd over immediately after making a Proof or Revise, on Forfeiture of 2*d.*

VIII. The Press-men are desir'd to put in the Drawer, one of a Sort of every Job, with their Names, the No. wrought, and Day of the Month.

RULES RELATING TO BOTH

I. Every Person fighting or striking in the Chapel, if taken in Earnest on the Spot, to forfeit 1s.

II. For every Time the Hammer or Sheeps-foot is used to lock up or unlock a Form, at the Press, or the Stone, instead of the Mallet and Shooting-stick, the Person to forfeit 2d.

III. For leaving a Candle lighted in the Chapel, without giving Charge of it, if the Person go out of the Limits of the Chapel, to forfeit 4d.

N.B. The Limits to be understood every Place within each of the two Houses in *Salisbury-Court.*

IV. Breaking a Window in the Chapel to mend it in two Hours at their own Expence; or the Master to deduct the Charge out of the Person's Wages: Or if a Window be broke by the Casement being left open, the Person who left it open to incur the same Penalty.

V. To pay the Chapel for a Job on one's own Account 6d.

VI. Gaming of all Sorts, either for Money, Beer, or any other Liquor, prohibited, on the Penalty of every Person who offends, for every Game or Chance, paying 6d.

VII. Every Freeman's Bienvenue, if the first Time of his working in the House, 18d. Every one not free, but having a Right, 2s. 6d. Every one having no Right, 5s. An Apprentice, 5s. The eldest Freeman to pay 1s.

VIII. No Smoaking to be permitted in the Chapel, except a Dispensation from the Master be obtain'd for the Sake of the Person's Health, on the Penalty of forfeiting each Time 2d.

IX. Any Difference arising, to be determin'd by the two eldest Freemen; and if they cannot agree, a third to be chosen by Consent of both, as an Umpire, whose Determination shall be decisive.

X. All Money arising to the Chapel, to be divided, and not spent; and to pass by Seal.

XI. If a Person be refractory, and refuse Payment for any of the Penalties above mentioned, the Master, on due and satisfactory Proof, is impower'd to stop the same out of the Wages of the Person offending.

N.B. A Stick or Quoin to be put between each Form, and no Pot, Plate, Earthen Ware, or any thing that may probably damage the Face of the Letter, to be put thereon.

No Person to be brought into the Printing-house, except it be some Stranger to the Trade, who (out of Curiosity) desires to see *Printing.*

As nothing is proposed by these Orders, but good Rule, and what shall be equally for the Advantage of every one, all Cavilling, Stratagems, or Snares to promote Forfeitures, otherwise called Polling, is agreed to be avoided.

And we the under-written engaged to comply with all and singular the above Articles.

[Then follow 20 signatures.]

August 30, 1734.

(iii) *The London Printing Trade in the Eighteenth Century*

Prior to the passing of the Licensing Act in 1662, there were seventy printing offices in London.[1] The Act stipulated that further masters were not to be admitted until their number was reduced by death or retirement to twenty. A year later there were ten less,[2] and by 1668 the total was as low as thirty-five.[3] Sir Roger L'Estrange, in his capacity of Surveyor of the Press, had not been inactive. Some thirty years after the repeal of the Licensing Acts, when Samuel Negus compiled his list of master printers in 1724, there were seventy-five firms in London and twenty-eight in the provinces.[4] There was, therefore, no great expansion of the trade compared with its state seventy years previously. In 1785, when John Pendred published his list of printers, he recorded one hundred and twenty-four.[5] In 1808, Caleb Stower printed two hundred and sixteen names and addresses in his *Compositor's and Pressman's Guide to the Art of Printing*. Thus, during the space of eighty-four years, the number of employers increased threefold.

Although there was no limitation of the number of printing offices, the prospective master printer was still subject to the trading regulations of the City of London. The right to trade was restricted to Freemen of the City. The Freedom could nominally only be obtained by men who were already free of a Livery Company. In both cases Freedom by servitude or patrimony cost less than Freedom by redemption or purchase. It was made a fairly expensive matter for an outsider, a provincial or a foreigner to buy the right to set up in business. At the end of the eighteenth century the old regulations were still in force, but it was only by the most strenuous efforts that the City restricted trading to its Freemen. The Wardmote Inquests continued to present non-

[1] *The Case of the Free Workmen Printers* (London, n.d.) gives this number. Kitchin, G., *Sir Roger L'Estrange* (London, 1913), p. 178, suggests 1665 as the date of publication. But the Licensing Act, 14 Car. II, c. 33, par. xi, provided that no fresh master printers were to be admitted until their number was reduced to twenty. This pamphlet must therefore have been published before 19 May, 1662, the last day of the Session in which the Act was passed.

[2] L'Estrange, R., *Considerations and Proposals* (London, 1663), reprinted in Timperley, C. H., *Encyclopædia of Literary and Typographical Anecdote* (London, 1842), p. 532 *et seq.*

[3] *A List of the Several Printing Houses taken* 12 *July*, 1668. S. P. Dom. Car. ii, 243 (126).

[4] Printed in Nichols, John, *Literary Anecdotes*, Vol. I, p. 288 *et seq.*

[5] *The London and County Printers, Booksellers and Stationers Vade Mecum* (London, 1785). [Bodleian Library].

citizens for engaging in wholesale trade, and the City Chamberlain to prosecute them for so doing; the penalties were recovered in the Lord Mayor's Court. In theory it was also still necessary for a Master to secure a licence before he could employ a non-Freeman in his business. However, throughout the century this regulation was never strictly observed in the printing and allied trades.

In the nineteenth century the City authorities found it increasingly difficult to maintain the situation; they could not keep pace with the non-Freemen, who set up shops or engaged in retail trade in an unostentatious manner. The story of the next half-century is one of unavailing effort to maintain the old exclusive trading rights, and at the same time to meet reasonable grievances.

In 1835 it was resolved that persons should be admitted to the Freedom without having to join a Company and the fee for purchase by redemption was reduced from £25 to £5. Even this concession was not sufficient inducement for many retailers to take up the Freedom. In 1846 a very large number of actions was pending against non-citizens and one was taken as a test case. The defendant, a wholesale dealer, won his case, and henceforth no attempt was made to restrain wholesale dealers. In 1848 the fee for freedom by redemption was further reduced to 46s. 8d. In 1854, faced with taking proceedings against some two thousand small traders, the Common Council repealed their Acts of 1606 and 1712, which prohibited the employment of non-Freemen as journeymen or hired servants. Finally, on 18 December, 1856, an Act of Common Council was passed to abolish all laws and customs which prohibited any other persons than Freemen from carrying on business by retail or exercising any handicraft or other lawful trade or calling within the City.

The original Stationers' Charter of 1557 stated in its twelfth paragraph that no "person shall practise or exercise the Art or Mystery of Printing . . . unless the same person is or shall be one of the Society of the foresaid Mystery or Art of a Stationer . . ." This regulation was not strictly enforced. An examination of the Company's apprentice registers for the eighteenth century shows that boys bound to Freemen of the Company were occasionally turned over to Freemen of other Companies, who exercised trades under the nominal control of the Stationers. The formula for recording the turn-over usually ran in this fashion: "John Smith, apprentice of Joseph Wood, Printer Citizen and Stationer, turned over to Henry Jones, Printer Citizen and

Leatherseller." How many Freemen of other Companies were active in the printing and allied trades is not known, but I do not think that there were a considerable number before 1800.

Negus's list details the master printers practising a generation after the repeal of the Licensing Act, and contains seventy-five names. Our knowledge of them is insufficient. We know little of their background, or how many of them succeeded to the business of their fathers or other relatives, and for how long they had wrought as journeymen, after serving their time, before launching out into trade for themselves. The answers lie buried in the archives of the Stationers' Company, now stored in a place of safety owing to the danger of enemy action. Meanwhile some valuable information is contained in a *Calender of Masters and Apprentices*, 1684–1718, and in a duplicate set of Apprentice Registers, 1730–1815, which still remain at the Hall. The former lists the employers in alphabetical order, but with no details as to their trade, together with the names and dates of indenture of their apprentices during the period. The Apprentice Registers contain evidence from which the number of boys taken by individual printers can be estimated, as well as the number of years during which an employer was active.

A typical entry reads: "John Poplett, son of John of Jewin Street, Fellowship Porter, apprenticed to John Abraham of St. Swithin's Lane, in consideration of £30. Seven years." We are thus able to assess the boy's social and economic background in the light of his father's calling, and the amount, if any, of premium paid. These two sources, the Calender and the Registers, make possible the annotation of both the Negus and Pendred lists. While there is a gap of twelve years between 1718 and 1730 for which no details are available, there is sufficient material to indicate the scale on which apprentices were recruited during the century. The number of boys apprenticed to an individual firm over a certain period also enables us to judge whether the business was of any size or importance. Unfortunately there is little or no information telling us the actual number of journeymen employees working in individual offices.

An examination of Negus's list demonstrates how limited was the intake of boys in his generation and, in turn, the small size of the average firm. William Burton, for instance, indentured but three apprentices between 1718–33, or one every five years. John Humphreys took five in fifteen years; John Watts, a printer of some importance, three in eight years. The largest employers appeared to be Henry I Woodfall, seventeen in twenty-two years; James Bettenham, seventeen in thirty years; William I and II Bowyer, twenty-four in thirty-eight years; and Samuel Richardson eighteen in thirty years. But these men were practising the craft well into the middle of the century. The printers whose working life was drawing to an end in 1724 operated on a far smaller scale.

For the period 1730–1815 about one in three apprentices had premiums paid on their behalf. If we take the principal employers on Negus's list we find that Henry I Woodfall received premiums in six out of seventeen instances, averaging £25; Bettenham twelve out of seventeen, averaging £25; William I Bowyer seven out of twenty-four, £20; and Samuel Richardson thirteen out of eighteen, £37. At least five future master printers served their time with him. The premiums paid throughout the whole of the century range from £5 (often paid by the Treasurer of Christ's Hospital) to a maximum of £100. The average was probably about £20.

Negus's list is now reprinted. I have added the first name of most of the men he recorded, together with the date of their decease, if known. I have also attempted, where possible, to set forth the number of apprentices indentured by their predecessors and successors, generally members of the same family, thus indicating a firm's intake of boys over as long a period as possible. It must be emphasized, however, that this list will give us no more than a cross-section of the trade in the eighteenth century. It is nevertheless useful in one important respect, for it indicates that many of the offices which ceased to exist shortly after 1724 were probably small indeed, while some of the masters at the beginning of their career conducted businesses in the middle years of the century which were considerably greater in size.

KNOWN TO BE WELL AFFECTED TO KING GEORGE

ARIS (*Samuel I*), d. 1739 c. Creed Lane. 1725–30, 4 apprentices. 1 premium, £5. Thomas Aris, later of Birmingham, was either son or brother. 1731–41 he indentured 8 apps. 3 premiums, average £10. In 1742 a boy was turned over to Robert Penny, Printer, Citizen and *Leatherseller*. Aris wrote from Birmingham that the boy did not wish to leave London.

BASKET (*John*), d. 1742. Black-friars. 1692–1718, 10 apps. 1724–41, 14 apps. Succeeded by son Thomas, d. 1761. 1738–53, 5 apps.

BOTHAM (*William I*), d. 1748. Jewin St. 1702–18, 6 apps. 1724–32, 1 app. 1 prem., £10. Son William free 1732. 1734–48, 4 apps. 4 prem., average £35.

BRIDGE (*Samuel*) and/or (*Daniel*), Little Moorfields. 1696–1703. S. B. indentured 3 apps. D. B., 1705–15, 2 apps. 1724–44, 2 apps.

BUCKLEY (*Samuel*), d. 1741 Amen Corner.

BURTON (? *William*), d. 1736. St. John's Lane. 1718–33, 3 apps.

DARBY (*John II*), d. 1733. Bartholomew Close. 1699–1718, 8 apps. 1724–28, 2 apps. 1 prem., £25.

DOWNING (*Joseph*), Bartholomew Close. 1704–18, 4 apps. 1724–26, 1 app. 1 prem., £25.

DOWNING (*William*), St. John's Lane. 1697–1718, 5 apps. 1724–38, 2 apps. 2 prem. of £25.

HUMPHERIES, *i.e.* HUMPHREYS (*John*), d. 1740 *c.* Bartholomew Lane. 1698–1712, 5 apps. 1727–29, 2 apps. 1 prem., £21.

HUNTER (*William*), d. 1725 *c.* Jewin St. 1717–18, 2 apps.

HOLT (*Sarah*), St. John's Lane. 1704–12, 3 apps.

JANEWAY (*Richard II*), White-friars. 1698–1710, 3 apps. 1731–32. 3 apps.

JENOUR (*Matthew*), Giltspur St. 1701–17, 5 apps.

LARKIN (*George II*), Bishopsgate St. 1696–1706, 2 apps. 1730–40, 3 apps.

LEACH (*Dryden I*), Old Bailey. 1705–17, 6 apps. 1724–28, 2 apps. 1 prem., £10. His son Dryden II free 1745. 1745–66, 7 apps. 2 prem. £15, £30.

MOUNT (*William*), late of Tower Hill. 1718, 1 app.

NEGUS (*Samuel*), Silver St., near Wood St. 1715, 1 app. 1725, 1 app.

NORTON (*Roger*), Little Britain.

PALMER (*Samuel*), d. 1732. Bartholomew Close. 1717–18, 2 apps. 1725, 3 apps.

PARKER (*Andrew*), Goswell St. 1709–18, 3 apps.

PARKER (*Edward*), Salisbury St. 1705–13, 3 apps.

PEARSON or PEIRSON (*William*), d. 1737 *c.* 1698–1714, 7 apps. 1725–34, 6 apps. 2 prem. £52, £10. Alice Pearson (widow?), 1737–38, 2 apps. 2 prem., average £10.

PICKARD (——).

RAYLTON (——), George Yard, Lombard St. 1726, 1 app.

READ (*James*), d. 1745 *c.* 1704–17, 6 apps. 1728–38, 9 apps. 2 prem., average £10. His son Thomas free by patrimony 1725. 1730–45, 7 apps. 5 prem., average £20. Mary Read, widow of James, 1747–49, 4 apps. Daughter Elizabeth, later Mrs. Nunneley, free by patrimony 1752. 2 apps. in that year.

ROBERTS (*James*), d. 1754. Warwick Lane. 1703–18, 5 apps. 1726–41, 6 apps. 4 prem., average £20.

STAPLES (*Robert*), St. John's Lane. 1714, 1 app. 1728, 1 app., being his son Alexander, subsequently a printer in York.

TOOKEY (*Robert*), d. 1725 *c.* behind the Royal Exchange. 1709, 1 app.

WATTS (*John*), d. 1763 and TONSON (*Jacob*), d. 1735. Covent Garden. 1709–17, 3 apps. 1725–49, 15 apps. 3 prem., average £10.

WILKINS (*William*), d. 1751 *c.* Little Britain. 1706–18, 4 apps.

WILMOT,*i.e.*WILMER(*Thomas*), Fenchurch St. 1704–18, 6 apps. 1726–27, 3 apps. 1 prem., £10.

WOOD (*Thomas*), Little Britain. 1718, 1 app.

WOODFALL, the family of:[1]

NON-JURORS

BETTENHAM (*James*), d. 1774. St. John's Lane. 1725–55, 17 apps. 12 prem., average £25.

BOWYER (*William I*), d. 1737, and (*William II*), d. 1777. 1699–1714, 5 apps. 1727–65, 24 apps. 7 prem., average £20.

DALTON (———), St. John's Lane.

SAID TO BE HIGH-FLYERS

APPLEBEY, *i.e.*, APPLEBEE (*John*), d. 1750 *c*. Fleet Ditch. He was a member of the Leathersellers' Company. Apprentices were turned over to him by Stationers in 1738 and 1748.

BADHAM (———), Fleet St.

BARBER (*John*), d. 1741. Lord Mayor of London 1732–33 1718. 1 app.

BRUGES (*Henry*), Jewin St. 1704–18, 4 apps.

CLARK (? *Henry*), Thames St.

CLUER (*John*), d. 1728. Bow Church Yard. 1726, 1 app. Succeeded by Thomas Cobb. 1728, 1 app.

COLLINS (———), Old Bailey.

EDLIN (*John*), near the Savoy.

GENT (*Thomas*), d. 1778. Pye Corner.

GRANTHAM (*John*), Paternoster Row. 1702–18, 4 apps.

HEATHCOTE (*J.*), Baldwin's Gardens.

HIND (*Luke*), Old Bailey. 1733–63 at George Yard, Lombard St. 5 apps.

HUMPHERIES (*J.*), Silver St.

ILIVE (*Thomas*), Aldersgate St. 1698–1708, 4 apps. Father of Jacob (free 1726) and Abraham (free 1737). 1732–50, 17 apps. 2 prem. £14, £26.

JAMES (*George*), d. 1735. Little Britain. 1727–35, 3 apps. 2 prem. £10, £20.

LEE (———), St. John's Lane.

LIGHTBOY (———), Old Bailey.

MEERE (*Hugh*), d. 1724. Old Bailey.

MIDWINTER (*Edward*), Pye Corner. 1702–17, 4 apps.

MIST (*Nathaniel*), Great Carter St.

MOORE (*John*), Southwark.

---

[1] Henry I. d. 1747. St. Clements Danes 1725–1747. 17 apps. 6 prem., av. £25.

Henry II. d. 1769 *c*. free 1735.
    1735–47. Little Britain, 9 app. 4 prem., av. £23.
    1749–66. Paternoster Row, 14 app. 4 prem., av. £28.

George. d. 1771 *c*.
free 1741.
1742–63 Charing X.
10 app. 2 prem.
15 gns., £105.

Henry Sampson I. d. 1805. free 1760.
    1764–86. P.N.R. 12 apps. 4 prem., av. £20.

William. d. 1803. free 1769.
1769–90 Salisbury St.
14 apps. 3 prem.,
av. £15.

George. d. 1844. free 1788.
    1796–1813. P.N.R. 21 apps. *Henry Sampson II.* d. 1833. free 1789.
    1814+. Angel Ct.   1790 Salisbury Sq., 1 app. *Thomas.*
                                                      free 1795.

Henry Dick. d. 1869.

MOTTE (*Benjamin*), d. 1738. Aldersgate St. 1697–1715, 9 apps.

NORRIS (——), Little Britain.

NUTT (*Elizabeth*), In the Savoy. Widow of John Nutt, d. 1716 *c.* 1704–13, 5 apps. Eliz. Nutt, 1716, 1 app.

POWELL (——), Aldersgate.

REDMAYNE (*William*), Jewin St. 1699–1710, 5 apps.

RICHARDSON (*Samuel*), d. 1761. Salisbury Court. 1729–59, 18 apps. 13 prem., average £37. Succeeded by nephew William Richardson, 1762–82, 8 apps. 2 prem. £5, £42.

SAYS, *i.e.*, SAYES (*William*), Aldersgate St. 1703–18, 5 apps. 1728–33, 3 apps. 1 prem., £5.

SAYS, *i.e.*, SAY (*Edward*), d. 1769. Bishopsgate St. until 1732.

Warwick Lane until 1744. Ave Maria Lane until death. 1725–66, 21 apps. 13 prem., average £32.

SHARP (*Thomas*), Ivy Lane. 1718, 1 app.

TODD (——), Fleet St.

TOOK (——), Old Bailey.

WILDE (*Allingham*), d. 1770. Aldersgate St. 1727–68. 19 apps. 2 prem., average £10.

ROMAN CATHOLICS

BERRINGTON (*E.*), Silver St., Bloomsbury.

CLIFTON (*Francis*), Old Bailey.

GARDINER (——), Lincoln's Inn Fields.

HOWLETT (——), Lincoln's Inn Fields.

The following figures, based on an examination of the apprentice registers, show the number of boys indentured to masters in the principal crafts represented in the Stationers' Company during the period 1730–1815.

Printers	3,318
Stationers	1,007
Bookbinders	946
Booksellers	593
Copperplate printers, engravers, mathematical instrument makers, printsellers, typefounders, etc.	832
Miscellaneous trades: drapers, builders, bakers, tailors, watermen, etc.	754
	7,450

Of this total premiums were paid by	2,778
Turned over from one master to another ..	994
Eventually became freemen	3,426
Came to London from places more than 12 miles distant	1,400

The graph printed on p. 512 shows the fluctuations in the intake of apprentices during the period. The plots are calculated on the basis of the total number of boys indentured to each trade in periods of five years. It will be noticed how the rise and fall for individual trades closely follows the graph for the total; furthermore, that the intake by binders, stationers and booksellers was fairly static compared to that of the printers. The number of the latter increased gradually from 1730–70. For the next fifteen years there was a decline. Indeed, the Compositors' Scale of Prices of 1785, the first trade union agreement, was signed at a time when the recruitment was at its lowest since 1760. It is possible that this fall was partly due to the after-effects of the American War of Independence (1775) which seriously diminished the export of books, for which America had previously been a valuable customer. Hence fresh labour was in less demand. From 1785–95 the intake increased considerably, and reached the highest level yet attained. During the next five years, perhaps as a result of the outbreak of the Napoleonic Wars, there was once again a steep decline. The first ten years of the new century, however, saw a phenomenal increase; close on nine hundred indentures were registered at Stationers' Hall. For the five years ending 1815 the total fell, but the 1815 figure of 360 was still higher than the 1795 total of 310 registrations.

In 1785 there were about 124 London printing offices, while in 1808 there were at least 216. Between 1800 and 1810 a large number of men went into business for the first time. This much is demonstrated by the new names in the apprentice registers.

After the year 1815 it is doubtful whether the Stationers' Company apprentice registers provide a trustworthy guide, from a statistical point of view, to the London printing trade. I surmise that there were many small master printers who were neither Freemen nor Liverymen of the Company, and did not therefore register their boys at the Hall. It is clear that the traditional apprenticeship system, in its strictest and most formal sense, has broken down. The proprietors of the larger firms could not possibly have lodged, fed and clothed the influx of boys taken since 1785. John McArthur, who was Andrew Strahan's manager, indentured 82 boys between 1800–15. Eight of them paid premiums, the average sum being £15. Luke Hansard and his two younger sons, who were partners in his business, took 60 apprentices in the period 1801–10, of whom two paid premiums. His eldest son, Thomas Curson Hansard, who conducted his own independent business, registered 48 boys, for six of whom premiums were paid. The average fee was £42.

It is clear that after the turn of the century fewer premiums were paid than in the past. This was because the old "indoor" apprenticeship system, whereby a boy lived as a member of the master's family, had come to an end.[1] In the old days, I think, premiums were paid for two reasons. Firstly, as an inducement for a master to take a boy. Such premiums were not necessarily very high. In scores of instances £5 or so was paid by Christ's Hospital, other Charity Schools, or the Churchwardens of a parish, on behalf of boys who obviously never subsequently rose above the status of a journeyman. Secondly, where a higher fee was expended, a parent often expected his son to be taught all the intricacies of the business, in order that the lad might be well equipped to enter the ranks of the employers in due course. In the nineteenth century premiums were paid mainly for the minority of "indoor" apprentices, since the employer was put to some expense for their sustenance during the period when they were essentially non-productive members of his staff.[2]

One hundred and twenty-four names of London master printers were listed by John Pendred in 1785. Andrew Strahan's business was set down twice, since it was divided into two parts: the office known as the King's Printing House, which he conducted in partnership with Eyre, his co-patentee, and his own private business, founded by his father *c.* 1739.

Of these hundred and twenty-three master printers, I have been able to identify ninety-five. That is to say, something is known of their background, the name of the master to whom they were apprenticed, the date of their Freedom, the span of their working life, the number of boys apprenticed to them and so on. Where possible, Pendred's list, now reprinted, has been annotated in so far as the available information and space permit.

Fifteen of the individuals exercising the trade of master printer in 1785 were the sons, daughters or near relatives of master printers. In thirty out of ninety-five instances, a premium was paid on their behalf when they were apprenticed as youths. The highest sum was £40 and the lowest £5. The average was £23.

[1] "Of the 600 [printing trade] apprentices now in London not more than 90 are *in-door* apprentices—that is, apprentices living with their masters' houses, all the rest are *out-door* apprentices." Francis Place in *The Gorgon* (London, 28 Nov., 1818), p. 222.

[2] For an account of the decline of the indoor apprentice system, see Dunlop, O. J., *English Apprenticeship and Child Labour* (London, 1912), Chapter XIV.

In forty-five out of ninety-five cases, therefore, a master was possessed of some initial advantage.

It has been stated that fifteen of our master printers succeeded to their respective concerns by inheritance. We also know something of the social background of some of the remaining eighty. Of these, eight sons of "gentlemen" formed the largest group. Booksellers and apothecaries came next, with four and three each. The writer has counted twenty-eight other trades. It would be tedious to detail them all. Suffice to say that there were butchers, bakers, candlestick-makers, a maltster, distiller, and innholder, a musician, a coffin maker, a fan maker and a parish clerk. Of clerks in holy orders there was but one. Earlier in the century many sons of clergymen were apprenticed to printers, booksellers and stationers. Their premiums were often paid by the Steward of the Corporation of the Sons of the Clergy. It is significant of changing fashions that there were no sons of peruke makers, a trade which had provided many apprentices earlier in the century.

While it would be an exaggeration to say that there have been as many Scots printers exercising the trade in England as Scots engineers on the high seas, or Scots gardeners on English flower beds, yet they have long been a notable feature of the craft in this country. Both William Strahan and Archibald Hamilton senior served their time north of the Tweed, and purchased their Freedom by redemption in 1738 and 1749 respectively. Their businesses were undoubtedly the largest yet known in the London trade. Buchanan McMillan, son of Findley McMillan of Inverness-shire, Gentleman, who was listed by Pendred, was a prominent newspaper printer throughout the era of the Napoleonic Wars. We must also mention William Faden, recorded by neither Negus nor Pendred, but nevertheless a substantial master printer from about 1744–76. He was apprenticed to Richard Harbin of Esher in Surrey in 1726, being registered at the Hall as "William Mack-faden, son of William of Wapping, Mariner. £10 premium." He was turned over to Samuel Palmer in 1730 and was made free in 1733. Between 1744–46 he indentured four boys in the name of Macfaden, but henceforth abandoned the prefix and was known as Faden.

If we examine the list of forty-one signatories to the Scale of 1785, printed on p. 74, we find that all save one are to be found in Pendred's directory. The exception is John Plummer, who was not a master printer in his own right, but the manager of William

Lane's printing office, which was attached to his publishing business. The first three names on the list are those of Strahan, the King's Printer; Hughs, the Printer to the House of Commons; and Nichols, Printer of the House of Commons Votes. It is significant that the leading printers to the legislative body should take pride of place, for governmental printing was rapidly increasing in both amount and importance. Strahan and Hughs conducted two of the largest firms in the trade, of a size and importance far exceeding any concern existing in Negus's day. The fourth name, that of Archibald Hamilton, represented one of the most influential periodical printing and publishing houses of the day. While many of the other printers active in 1785 were at the head of firms far greater than those existing two generations back, there were still a great many small concerns, employing but a few journeymen. However, the existence of even a minority of large-scale offices was now sufficient to create favourable conditions for the emergence of the compositors' trade union. For in those offices the concentration of many workmen under one roof engendered that sense of solidarity, security, and resistance necessary to secure recognition and respect from employers who were inclined to regard the journeymen's organizations with suspicion and hostility rather than approval. Pendred's list, now reprinted and annotated, will indicate the growth of the London printing trade since 1724.

LONDON MASTER PRINTERS, 1785

ABRAHAM (*John*), St. Swithin's Lane. s. of Guy A., of Berkhampstead, Schoolmaster, app. Mary Say 1776, free 1783, livery 1790. d. 1808. 1786–1807, 13 apps. 5 premiums, average £26. 1811 described as "Price Current Office." Family carried on business until 1859.

ADLARD (*William*), Salisbury Sq. s. of Charles A., of St. Ives, Tailor, app. Thos. James of Cambridge 1751, free 1759, livery 1776. d. 1820. 1767–89, 27 apps. 10 prem., average £12. His son James free 1789. 1800–15, 13 apps. 5 prem., average

£20. Book and periodical printers. Firm exists to-day.

ALEXANDER (*Alexander*), Black Lion Yd., Whitechapel Rd. Printer of Hebrew Liturgical Books. Firm existed until 1828 c.

ALLEN, 3 Maiden Lane, Cheapside.

ALMON (*John*), 183 Fleet St. d. 1805. 1788 founded *Sunday Chronicle*.

ANDREWS, 10 Little Eastcheap.

ANDREWS, 14 Beach Lane, Whitecross St.

AXTELL & CO., 17 Little New St. (i) Samuel Axtell, s. of William A., of Hempsted, Herts.,

Butcher, app. Samuel Richardson 1759, free 1766. 1769–81,
10 apps. 1 prem. £50. (ii) son
John app. Charles Rivington
1763. free 1770. 1773–97, 8
apps.

AYRE (*Ralph*), 14 Brydges St.,
Covent Garden. s. of Ralph A.,
of Oxford, Musician, app. William Faden 1753. £21. 1776–
90, 11 apps. 1 prem. £20. Newspaper proprietor and printer.

BAILEY, 7 Featherstone St., Bun-
hill Row.

BAILEY (*Thomas*), 22 Petticoat
Lane. Was at same address in
1763.

BAILEY (*Thomas II*), 5 Star
Alley, Mark Lane. s. of (i) Thomas I Bailey, s. of Thomas B.,
of Wapping, Yeoman, app. William Osborne 1733, free 1741.
1745–70, 9 apps. (ii) Thomas II
Bailey, app. his father 1760,
free 1767. 1793–95, 3 apps. 3
prem., average £7. (iii) *c.* 1817
firm became Burton & Co.
(iv) 1821 Burton, Clay & Co.
(v) 1827 Clay. The firm is still
in existence as Richard Clay
& Co., Ltd.

BAILEY (*William*), The Little a,
42 Bishopsgate Within. s. of
Thomas I Bailey, app. his
father 1758, free 1767. 1768–93,
14 apps. 5 prem., average £7.

BALDWIN (*Henry*), 108 Fleet St.
s. of Robert B., of Farringdon,
Berks., Apothecary, app. Edward Say 1749, free and livery
1756. d. 1813. 1759–94, 30
apps. 9 prem., average £25. His
son Charles free 1796. 1796–
1815, 25 apps. 2 prem. £2, £30.
Newspaper printers and proprietors. Firm existed until
after 1850.

BARKER (*James*), Russell Court,
Drury Lane. s. of Jeremiah B.,
of N. Minns, Labourer, app.

William Griffin 1766, livery
1801. 1776–1802, 10 apps. 1
prem. £4.

BARKER (*John*), 1 Shoemaker
Row, Blackfriars. s. of Ralph B.,
Citizen and Vintner, app. to
William Lear 1764, free and
livery 1771. d. 1831. 1777–95,
7 apps. 1 prem. £50.

BARR (*James*), 18 Catherine St.,
Strand. s. of James B., of
Coleman St., Trunk maker, app.
Robert Lloyd 1769. £30 prem.
1784–95, 4 apps., 4 prem.,
average £21.

BASSAM (*Robert*), 53 St. John's
St. s. of Robert B., of Whitecross St., Coffin maker, app.
Thomas Hamilton 1768, free
1775, livery 1782. 1787–1805,
8 apps. 2 prem., average £10.

BATE, 16 Goodge Street.

BELL, 33 Fulwoods Rents, Holborn.

BENSLEY (*Thomas II*), 2 Swan
Yard, Strand. s. of (i) Thomas I
Bensley, 1753–80, 6 apps. 1
prem. £20. (ii) Thomas II
Bensley, app. his father 1774,
free and livery 1781. d. 1835.
Subsequently moved to Bolt
Court. 1782–1813, 30 apps.
6 prem., average £50. A leading
book printer. His two sons
carried on the business until
c. 1826.

BLYTH (*Francis*), 2 Queen's Head
Alley, Paternoster Row. s. of
John B., of St. Giles, Apothecary, app. Charles Green Say
1752, free 1760, livery 1781. d.
1788. 1766–84, 11 apps. 2 prem.,
average £5. Newspaper printer.

BOND (*Daniel*), 9 Union Buildings, Leather Lane.

BRADLEY, Suffolk St., near the
Mint, Southwark.

BREWMAN (*Draper*), 18 Little
New St. Newspaper printer.

BROOKE, 11 Little Eastcheap.

BROOKE (*Samuel I*), Hanging Sword Alley. s. of Rev. Samuel B., of Gamston, Notts., app. Thomas Harrison 1761, free 1768, livery 1769. 1771–95, 11 app. 1 prem. £20. Succeeded by his son Samuel II, free 1795. 1797–1815. 14 apps. 3 prem. 1 £5, 2 at £40. Specialized in government printing. At 35 Paternoster Row until 1836.

BROWN (*Matthew*), 3 Windmill Court, Pye Corner. s. of (i) Robert Brown of W. Smithfield. 1739–74, 17 apps. 5 prem., average £16. (ii) Matthew Brown, free 1767. d. 1817 c. 1778–1787, 5 apps. 3 prem., average £8.

BROWN (*William*), 22 Poppin's Court. 1785–86, 3 apps.

BROWN, Fair St., Horsleydown, Southwark.

BUCKTON, 8 Great Pulteney St.

BUTTERS (*Robert*), 10 Poppin's Court. s. of William B., of Glasgow, Carpenter, app. Archibald II Hamilton 1765, free 1772. 1778–1807, 18 apps. 1 prem. £10.

CARPENTER (*William*), 14 Fetter Lane.

CAUSTON (*Richard*), 21 Finch Lane.

CLARKE & CO. (*i.e., Charles CLARKE*), 6 Northumberland Court, Strand. s. of Charles C., of Clerkenwell, Sawyer, app. Thomas Parker 1766, £25, livery 1780. 1774–1801, 20 apps. Business was then purchased by William Clowes.

COGHLAN (*James Peter*), Duke St., Grosvenor Sq. s. of James C., of the Parish of St. George, Hanover Sq., Stonecutter, £15. app. Samuel Cope 1746, free 1754. Printer to the Society of English Catholics.

COLLINS (*Thomas*), 3 Nevills Court, Fetter Lane. 1796–1809, 6 apps. 2 prem. £5, £20.

CONSTABLE (*Daniel*), 6 Old Bailey. s. of Joshua C., of Clerkenwell, Butcher, app. Thomas Harrison 1770. £21, free and livery 1777. 1782–85 3 apps. 1 prem. £15. Shortly afterwards emigrated to N. America.

COOPER (*Joseph*), 134 Drury Lane. s. of John C., of Cornhill, Bricklayer, app. Chas. Rivington 1753. £21, free 1761, livery 1771. d. 1808. 1763–1798, 25 apps. 6 prem., average £25.

COUCHMAN (*Stephen*) and FRY. Queen St., Upper Moorfields. S. C. free by redemption 1774. 1789–1812. 11 apps. 1 prem. £63. Firm still exists.

COX (*Edward*), 73 Little Queen St. His son John Lewis Cox app. George Bigg 1791, free and livery 1798. 1799–1812, 10 apps. Firm later became Cox and Wyman and still exists under the latter name.

COX (*Henry*), 3 Lovells Court, Paternoster Row. 1775–79, 2 apps. 1 prem. £40. His son Charles app. his father 1779, free and livery 1786. Conducted the business until 1797, when he died.

DAVIS (*Jonas*), 61 Chancery Lane. s. of William D., of Southwark, Gentleman, app. Thomas Bailey 1770, free 1777. 1783–1798, 25 apps. 3 prem. of £50. 1 prem. £5.

DIXWELL (*James*), 148 St. Martin's Lane. s. of Alexander D., of Loughborough, Gentleman, app. John Moore 1744, £20., free 1752. d. 1788. 1760–88, 19 apps. 3 prem., average £10.

EVERINGHAM (*John*), 1 Dean St., Fetter Lane. Free 1751.

1753–78, 10 apps. 4 prem., average £10.

FAWCET, Shoemaker Row, Blackfriars.

FENWICK (*Henry*), 63 Snow Hill. s. of Henry F., of White-chapel, Distiller, app. J. Oliver 1754, £20, free and livery 1761. d. 1822. 1763–1811, 33 apps. 7 prem., average £5. Firm existed until 1822.

FORD (*Samuel*), 14 Cross Key Court, Little Britain. s. of John F., of Pangbourne, Maltster. app. Thomas Harrison 1768, free 1775, livery 1777. d. 1812. 1783–1811, 4 apps. 3 prem., average £17. Took Tew as a partner in 1804. The latter was still conducting the business in 1842.

GALABIN (*John William*) and BAKER (*William*), 1 Ingram Court. (i) J. W. G., s. of John G., of Greenwich, Watchmaker, app. Joseph Kippax 1753. Livery 1776. d. 1824. 1767–1795, 19 apps. 5 prem., average £25. (ii) W. B., s. of William B., of Reading, Schoolmaster, app. Joseph Kippax 1758, £20, free 1766, livery 1776. d. 1785. 1767–83, 8 apps. 4 prem., 3 at £20. 1 prem. £100. (iii) Gala-bin's three sons conducted the business 1793–1805, 10 apps. prems. £20, £50. (iv) *c.* 1805. William Marchant became a partner, later sole proprietor. Firm still exists as Marchant, Singer and Co., and is controlled by Messrs. Witherby.

GEOGHEGAN (*Thomas*), 3 Kent St., Borough. s. of Constantine G., of the Borough, Farrier, app. William Robins 1767, free 1775, livery 1790. 1775–1801, 11 apps. 5 prem., average £20.

GILBERT (*William II*), Cree Church Lane. Grandson of (i) Stephen Gilbert, 1728–49, 4 apps. Son of (ii) William I, 1747–59, 3 apps., and (iii) Ann, his widow, 1767–68, 2 apps. (iv) William II, free by patri-mony 1767. 1773–78, 3 apps. 3 prem., average £15.

GOLDNEY (*Henry*), 15 Pater-noster Row. s. of Edward G., of London, Gentleman, app. Wil-liam Richardson, 1759, £21, free and livery 1767. 1778–90, 5 apps.

HAMILTON (*Archibald I*), 4 Falcon Court, Fleet St. Free by redemption 1749. d. 1793. 1749–89, 24 apps. 7 prem., average £20. His son Archibald II app. his father 1755, free and livery 1762. d. 1792. 1762–93, 28 apps. 5 prem., average £20. His grandsons (i) Archibald III 1795–99, 4 apps. 1 prem. £30, and (ii) Samuel, 1800–1812, 19 apps. The latter had his office at Weybridge.

HARRISON, 20 Warwick Lane.

HARRISON (*Thomas*), 18 Pater-noster Row. s. of Thomas H., of Reading, Basket-maker, app. Edward Owen 1738, free 1750, livery 1751. 1751–81, 11 apps. 4 prem., average £20. It is probable that H. had retired by 1785, but the business was car-ried on by his partner Samuel I Brooke, *q.v.*, until James II, s. of James I (see Harrison and Co.) came of age. The Harrison family still carry on the business in St. Martin's Lane.

HARRISON AND CO., 2 Red Lion Court, Fleet St. (i) James I Harrison, younger brother of Thomas, app. Edward Say 1743, free and livery 1754. d. 1769. 1755–66, 8 apps. 3 prem., average £20. (ii) his widow Mary, 1771–82, 7 apps. 3 prem., average £12. (iii) William

Thorne, app. M. H. 1771, free 1778. 1783–98, 6 apps. 1 prem. £20.

HARRISON, 57 Newgate Street.

HART (*Harris*), s. of (i) John H., of the Parish of St. Bride, Printer. 1732–59, 13 apps. 2 prem., average £20. (ii) Harris, H., app. his father 1742, free 1749, livery 1753. 1765–73, 5 apps. 1 prem. £31.

HAWES (*Robert*), 40 Dorset St., Spitalfields. He also exercised the trade of typefounder.

HESSE, 1 Leman St., Goodfields Fields.

HETT (*Richard II*), Wild Court, Wild St. s. of Richard H., of the Poultry, Bookseller, app. Saml. Richardson 1744, £40. 1755–74. 9 apps. 1 prem. £30.

HEYDINGER (*John*), 7 Queen's Court, Great Queen St. d. 1814. He was also a valuer and auctioneer of printing material.

HINDMARSH (*Robert*), 32 Clerkenwell Close. Free and livery 1794, d. 1835. 1795–7 2 apps.

HODGSON, 18 George Court, St. John's Lane. He was also a "letterpress brass engraver and cutter in wood."

HOLLIS (*James II*), 21 Shoemaker Row. s. of James H., of Lambeth Hill, Printer, app. his father 1761. 1794–1811, 4 apps.

HOOD (*Catherine*), 24 Warwick Lane,? widow of (i) Edward H., s. of John H., of the Parish of St Martin's, Ludgate, Leatherseller, app. Saml. Nevill 1736, free 1743. 1763–68, 2 apps. 2 prem., £2, £21. (ii) Catherine H., 1770–77. 3 apps.

HUGHS (*Henry*), near Gt. Turnstile. s. of (i) John H. 1732–67, 17 apps. 8 prem., average £20. (ii) Henry H., free and livery 1769. d. 1811. 1769–97, 27 apps. 1 prem. £40. The business passed c. 1800 to Luke Hansard, father of T. C. Hansard, first printer of the *Parliamentary Debates*.

JARVIS, 283 Strand.

JENOUR, opposite St. Dunstan's Church.

JOHNSON (*Edward*), Ludgate Place. d. 1789 c.

JONES (*Stephen*), 138 Fetter Lane, s. of Giles J., of Villiers St., Gentleman, app. John Everingham 1778, £10. 1791–96, 3 apps.

JUSTINS (*William*), 6 Albion Buildings, Bartholomew Close. s. of Saml. J., of Sherborn, Cordwainer, app. Robert Goadby 1769. 1786–95, 6 apps. His son Edward free 1800. 1800–13, 5 apps. 2 prem. £30, £52.

LAIDLER, 13 Princes St., Soho.

LEDGER (*Henry*), Maze Pond, Southwark. s. of Robert L., of Southwark, Dyer, app. Henry Baldwin 1773. In 1789 he was trading as a buckram stiffener, glazer and callender.

LEWIS, 5 Sherborne Lane.

MACKINTOSH (*William*), Peter St., Borough.

McMILLAN (*Buchanan*), 35 Henrietta St. s. of Findley McM. of Inverness-shire, Gentleman. app. Thomas Wright 1773. 1784–1813, 15 apps. 1 prem. £20. Newspaper and book printer.

MARCH (*John II*), George Yard, Tower Hill. s. of (i) John I. 1727–50 c. 10 apps. 2 prem., average £5. (ii) John II, app. his father 1747, free and livery 1754. d. 1798. 1765–98, 8 apps. (iii) John III, s. of John II. d. 1803. The business passed to Henry Teape.

MARSHALL (*John*), 4 Aldermary Churchyard. s. of (i) Richard

M., of the same address, Printer, Citizen and Wheelwright. 1771–72, 2 apps. (ii) John M., app. Edward Gilbert 1771, turned over to his father 1772. 1786. 1 app.

MILLER, 74 Rosemary Lane, Tower Hill.

MILLIDGE (*Josiah*), 37 Maiden Lane. s. of Josiah M., of Wiltshire, Maltster, app. Mary Read 1749. d. 1786 c. 1770–81, 7 apps.

MOORE, Drury Lane (Great A). Pendred also lists him as a typefounder. 1809, Joseph Kenton Moore took an app. prem. £20. Firm existed in 1822 as Moore and Son.

MOORE (*Elizabeth*), 11 Grocers Alley. Widow or daughter of (i) John M., s. of John of St. Martin's Lane, Bookbinder, app. Henry I Woodfall, 1733. 1740–66, 20 apps. 4 prem., average £30. (ii) Elizabeth M., 1770–85, 5 apps. d. 1787 c., succeeded by (iii) John Bryan, s. of Thomas of Seething Lane, Staymaker, app. to Elizabeth M., 1781, free 1790. 1790–1814, 9 apps. 2 prem., average £10. His sons carried on the business until c. 1840.

NEWCOME, 9 Wych St.

NICHOLS (*John*), Red Lion Passage. s. of Edward N., of Islington, Baker, app. William II Bowyer 1759, £20, free and livery 1766. d. 1826. He was Bowyer's partner and successor. 1766–99, 20 apps. 6 prem., average £35. His son John Bowyer Nichols succeeded to the business. 1801–1813, 14 apps. 2 prem., average £12. The firm was conducted by the Nichols family until 1940. Printers of the House of Commons Votes.

NORTH (*Thomas*), 4 Little Tower Street. s. of Joshua of the Parish of St. Botolph, Aldgate, Fanmaker, app. Charles Say 1770, livery 1790. 1785–1807. 7 apps. 4 prem., average £30.

PACE, 56 High St., Borough.

PARAMORE, Windmill Hill, near St. Luke's Hospital.

PARKER (*Thomas II*), 4 Bull Head Court, Jewin St. Grandson of (i) Henry I P., 1725–28, 4 apps. (ii) His widow Ann, 1733–37, 4 apps. (iii) Son Thomas I, free 1740. 1740–70, 23 apps. 12 prem., average £20. (iv) Grandson Thomas II, free 1765. 1770–93, 8 apps. 1 prem. £20.

PHILLIPS, 2 George Yard, Lombard St. Probably successor of Luke Hind. The firm existed until c. 1826.

PRATT (*W.*), 25 New Round Court, Strand. Firm existed in 1794.

REDMAYNE (*Graham*), 8 Creed Lane. s. of Samuel of Jewin St., Printer, app. Thos. I Parker 1741.

REYNELL (*Henry*), 21 Piccadilly. s. of Richard R., of Air St., Apothecary, app. John Money 1760, free 1767, livery 1789. d. 1811 c. 1774–1810, 13 apps. 3 prem., average £35. Succeeded by son Henry Carew R., app. his father 1791. d. 1859.

RICHARDSON, 47 Duck Lane, Westminster.

RIVINGTON (*John*), 5 Badger Yard, St. John's Square. s. of John Rivington of Paternoster Row, Bookseller, app. Chas. Rivington 1770, £50, free and livery 1777. d. 1785. 1777-83, 9 app. 2 prem. £25, £80. Succeeded by his widow Anna. 1787, 1 app. The firm was well known throughout the nineteenth century as Gilbert and

Rivington, book and oriental printers, and in 1907 was purchased by Clowes.

RIVINGTON (*Charles*), 5 Noble Street, Foster Lane. s. of Charles R., of St. Paul's churchyard, Bookseller, app. Samuel Richardson 1746, free 1753. 1753–89, 29 apps. 9 prem., average £30. 1 prem. £100.

ROZEA (*Jessington*), 91 Wardour St. s. of Jessington R., of Marylebone, Gentleman, app. Thomas Jones, Bookseller, 1766, free and livery 1782. d. 1790 c. 1782–89, 6 apps. 2 prem., average £25. After his death the firm was taken over by Sampson Low. 1794–95, 2 apps. 1 prem. £20. Firm existed in 1800.

SABINE (*Thomas*), 81 Shoe Lane. s. of Cornelius S., of Steeple Ashton, Wiltshire, Schoolmaster, app. Thomas Bailey 1758, free 1765, livery 1780. 1775–95, 15 apps. His sons carried on the business until 1824.

SAY (*Mary*), Ave Maria Lane. Daughter-in-Law of Edward Say (see Negus's list) and widow of his son (i) Charles Green Say, app. James Bettenham 1735, free and livery 1743. d. 1775. 1749–72, 20 apps. 5 prem., average £15. (ii) Mary Say, 1775–85, 5 apps. In 1794 the firm was conducted by one Vint, who may have been her second husband.

SHAW (*Richard*), Silver St., Whitefriars. He was a member of the Clothworkers' Company. d. 1801. The firm still exists, having been in Fetter Lane since 1810 c.

SKIRVEN (*John*), Corner of Old Gravel Lane. s. of Alexander S., of St. Martin's Lane, Cabinet Maker, app. William Bailey

1769, free 1776, livery 1787. d. 1817 c. 1778–1809, 12 apps. 4 prem., average £15. His son John app. his father 1809. The firm existed until 1824 c.

SMITH (*William I*), Castle St., Oxford Market. 1787–99, 5 apps. 3 prem., average £10. Father of William II, free 1795, and Joseph, free 1799, who conducted separate businesses in King St., Seven Dials 1800–1810.

SPIERS, 1 Chapel Alley, Long Acre.

SPILSBURY (*Thomas*), 57 Snow Hill. Free by redemption 1776. d. 1795. 1776–95, 21 apps. 5 prem., average £20. Succeeded by his sons William, free and livery 1789, and Charles, free 1796, livery 1799. 1798–1810, 13 apps. 6 prem., average £20.

STAFFORD (*George*), 6 Fleet Market. Free by redemption 1787, livery 1788. 1788–95, 17 apps. 2 prem., average £21.

STEEL (*Henry Draper*), 51 Lothbury. s. of Henry S., of Tower Hill, Bookbinder, app. his father 1768, free 1775, livery 1776. d. 1818. 1781–89, 6 apps 3 prem., average £16.

STOCKEN, 58 Haymarket.

STRAHAN (*Andrew*), 10 Little New St., and 8 East Harding St. (The King's Printing Office). s. of (i) William I Strahan, free by redemption 1738, livery 1742. d. 1785. 1739–83, 48 apps. 23 prem., average £32. (ii) His son William II, app. his father 1754, free and livery 1761. 1762–85, 15 apps. 5 prem., average £20. (iii) His son Andrew, app. William II 1763, free and livery 1770. d. 1831. 1778–1806, 45 apps. 7 prem., average £20. (iv) Andrew Strahan's Manager, John McArthur, 1800–15, 82 apps. 8 prem., average

4

£15. A. S.'s nephews, Andrew and Robert Spottiswoode, succeeded to the business, which was divided into two in the middle of the century. The private business is now known as Spottiswoode Ballantyne, and the King's Office as Eyre and Spottiswoode.

STUART, Blake Court, Catherine St.

STUART and STEVENSON, 2 Martlett Court, Bow St.

TRAPP (*Henry*), 1 Paternoster Row. s. of Michael T., of Margate, Parish Clerk, app. Mary Lewis 1759, free 1768. 1774–88, 8 apps. 2 prem., average £10.

VIGEVENA (*Joseph*), 9 Huggin Lane. s. of Joseph V, of Blackfriars, Perfumer, app. Samuel Chandler 1771, free 1779, livery 1792. 1803, 1 app. £5 prem.

WADE (*John*), 163 Fleet St. 1778–80, 2 apps. 2 prem., average £18.

WALKER, 6 Bolt Court.

WALTER (*John I*), Printing House Square. 1800–12, 11 apps. Founder, proprietor and printer of *The Times*.

WATTS, Queen St., Grosvenor Square. 1804–10 *c.* the firm was known as Watts and Bridgewater, thenceforth as Bridgewater until after 1872.

WHITWORTH (*James*), Playhouse Yard. s. of John W., of Blackfriars, Tailor, app. Thos. Bailey 1757. 1778, 1 app.

WILKINS (*Thomas*), 45 Cow Lane, W. Smithfield. s. of Thomas W., of Northampton, Gentleman, app. William Oliver 1772, £21. 1782–97, 12 apps. 2 prem., average £20.

WILKINSON, Clare Street. (Law House).

WOODFALL (*Henry Sampson I*), corner of Ivy Lane, Paternoster Row. See Negus's list.

WOODFALL (*William*), corner of Dorset St. See Negus's list.

WORRALL (*Thomas*), Montague Court, Spital Square.

WRIGHT (*Thomas*), 4 Peterborough Court. s. of Thomas W., of Wolverhampton, Bucklemaker, app. Archibald Hamilton 1758, free and livery 1766. d. 1796. 1767–93, 23 apps. 6 prem., average £25.

(iv) *The Compositors' Documents*

It would have been more satisfactory if this book could have as its title *The London Compositor, 1476–1900*, thus covering the first four centuries of printing in England. Documents of a date prior to 1785 are unhappily so few in number, that such a description would hardly be justified. Such of them as are appropriate are printed in section (ii) of this Introduction. There exists, it is true, a considerable body of material covering regulation of the trade by the Government and the Stationers' Company, but these documents primarily concern the intimately related aspects of politics and State censorship. Few concern the relations between masters and men, and thus working conditions and customs. This lack of material may perhaps be explained by the fact that there is no evidence to prove the existence of a printer's trade union before 1785. The Webbs defined a trade union as a "continuous association of wage-earners for the purpose of maintaining or improving the conditions of their working lives." Until such an association was in being, there was neither opportunity nor necessity for the continuous codification of relationships between employers and employed.

Our material for the period 1785–1900 consists of four main classes of documents.

1. Memorials addressed to the employers. These concern such matters as piece-work or weekly wage rates, the limitation of apprentices and the non-observance of time-honoured customs. They were, in fact, requests for concessions of one kind or another, and formed the basis of subsequent negotiations.

2. The printed reports of Meetings, on matters arising out of the Memorials, held by the compositors at large or their delegates.

3. The Quarterly and Annual Reports of the London Union of Compositors (1834–45) and the London Society of Compositors (1845 onwards).

4. The Reports of Committees appointed by the trade union to investigate a specific problem.

In addition, there are the printed papers issued by the Association of Master Printers at various dates.

I have also extensively quoted from the professional literature of the printing trade published in the eighteenth and nineteenth centuries: the manuals of Luckombe, Stower, Hansard, Johnson, Savage, Gould, Southward and others. In addition, much valuable material has been discovered in trade periodicals and the reports of Parliamentary Select Committees.

The Compositors' Documents are gathered in three main collections. The St. Bride Foundation, in the City of London, possesses an extensive collection, including many printed before 1800. These are housed in the Technical Reference Library of Works on Printing, the most considerable of its sort in this country. The Cambridge University Press also possesses a fair number, including some unique items. Lastly, there are the archives of the London Society of Compositors. The L.S.C. does not own many early items, but has preserved full records of its transactions from 1848 onwards.

No attempt has been made to reprint every known document, since their number is far too numerous. It has been my endeavour, however, to select such documents as will throw light on some of the principal factors in the economic history of the London printing trade during the period. This book, therefore, does not attempt to provide a consecutive record of events. It is neither a history of the London trade, 1785–1900, nor a formal record, year by year, of the Compositors' Union and its relations with the employers, although the documents now reprinted are undoubtedly essential material for either project. They are equally valuable for any detailed study of the *products* of the trade during the century and a quarter they cover. These products range from billheads to Bibles, from advertising circulars to daily newspapers; hence their importance to bibliographers. Our material throws immediate light on the following aspects of the nineteenth-century London printing trade.

1. The continued increase in the size of individual offices and of the trade as a whole—the industrialization of the craft.

2. The tendency towards specialization: the existence of offices undertaking specific kinds of work, such as book, jobbing, newspaper, periodical and parliamentary printing, as distinct from the eighteenth-century firms which undertook all classes of work with equal facility.

3. The influence of the London Scale of Prices for Compositors' Work, upon whatever aspect of the trade is under examination.

4. The effects of mechanization, particularly in the composing room.

This book, then, deals almost wholly with the affairs of the compositors, since they alone have provided any substantial body of records. This is due to the continuous existence, from 1785 onwards, of their Union. Such was not the case with the Master Printers' Associations, nor with the trade organizations of the pressmen, printing machine minders or other workmen employed in and around printing offices. But even had such material been plentiful, the compositors' documents would still hold pride of place. The compositor was traditionally the representative craftsman of the printing trade. He still is, in spite of the claims of the printing machine managers, lithographers and photogravure process workers. The composing room is the nerve centre of the printing office, since therein is performed the "art and mystery" of printing, the assembly of the printing surface. The subsequent production of copies, whether on a handpress or a high-speed newspaper rotary machine, although requiring a measure of skill, is at best a mechanical business. Compositors, as a class, are familiar with the manipulation of other men's words, with the task of translating manuscript text into the disciplined state the multiplication of copies demands. The compositor well trained in his profession thus understands something of the use of words, of orthography, correct printing and so on. During the period covered by the documents in this book compositors were more skilled in these matters than now. Therefore, when occasion arose, they had no difficulty, intellectual or technical, in printing their own observations on matters affecting their trade. Hence, I think, the number of documents issued by them.

The material in this book, therefore, comes within the field of the economist, of the social historian, and of the specialist in the history of trade unionism and labour relations. My approach is that of a student of the history of printing, and as such I have selected and interpreted my material.

(v) *Expansion of the London Printing Trade*, 1785–1896

Pendred listed 124 firms. In 1808, according to the list printed by Stower in his *Compositor's Guide*, published in that year, there were 216 offices. Johnson's *Typographia* (1824) and the *Rules of the London Trade Society of Compositors* (1826) recorded 306 and 323 firms respectively. This number does not appear to have been greatly exceeded during the following quarter of a century. By 1870 there were nearly 600 firms and in 1900 at least 700 offices. In 1818 Francis Place's anonymous correspondent stated that there were "233 master printers now in London; ten years ago there were not more than 130." [1] This estimate is puzzling, since Stower listed 216 names in 1808, and Rhynd 210 in 1804. It is possible that Place's informant ignored one-man shops or very small concerns.

Statistics as to the number of compositors and pressmen are uncertain. While there is a quantity of documents with long lists of compositors' names appended, there is no means of knowing how many men abstained from participation in trade union affairs. The following totals show the number of signatories at various dates between 1793–1816 :

1793. 539 compositors (presumably excluding newsmen).
1793. 145 newspaper compositors.
1801. 492 book compositors.
1807. 242 pressmen.

[1] See p. 132.

1807. 464 book compositors.
1809. 722   „   „
1809. 198 newspaper compositors.
1816. 717 book compositors.

Writing in 1818 Place's correspondent stated that there were then 1,882 compositors in London, and 600 apprentices. Since only 717 men supported the petition to the employers in 1816 we can perhaps assume that at that time only about half the compositors were members of the union. Place's friend estimated the number of pressmen at 500, with 200 apprentices.

The *Report of the Proceedings of the Delegated Meeting of Compositors*, 12 December, 1833, stated that 185 delegates represented 1,200 journeymen in book-offices, while the Annual Report of the London Union of Compositors for 1834 recorded that there were upwards of 1,700 names on the books of the Union. The Annual Report for 1839 recorded 1,343 men and 534 boys working in ninety-five of the three hundred firms then in existence. In 1850 Edward Edwards, Secretary of the L.S.C., estimated that there were 3,000 journeymen compositors and 1,500 boys, as well as 850 men and 450 boys working at the press. In his evidence to the Select Committee on Stationery Contracts in 1896, Charles Bowerman, then Secretary of the L.S.C., stated that 10,000 men were members of the Society, while about 3,000 more were outside it. There were, at that date, about 700 printing offices in London.

As to the number of men employed in individual firms, statistics for the earlier part of the century are rare. Place's informant provided figures for twelve firms only. The average number of compositors, pressmen and boys employed in them was 20 and 9 respectively. The average given by the 1839 Report was 14 men and 5 boys to each office, but these latter figures apply to compositors only. If we include the pressmen, machine-room staff, warehouse and clerical departments, it is probable that by 1839 the medium to large-sized firms employed anything from thirty to a hundred men. In any case, the statistics for 1839 exclude the house of Spottiswoode and Company, Her Majesty's Printers (successors to the Strahan family). Spottiswoode's was, in the eyes of the Union, an "unfair" house, and closed to its members. At that time the firm employed 121 compositors and 55 apprentices in the composing department. It was the most considerable business in the country.

By the end of the century there were at least half a dozen firms employing over five hundred men, and many with payrolls of a hundred.

The fact that the three principal master printers specializing in work for the legislature headed the list of signatories of the Scale of 1785 has already been noted. The lengthy Report of the Finance Committee of 1796–97 and the mass of returns relative to the Slave Trade, published in the following year, were indicative of the scale upon which State printing was required. Both these items were printed in the office of Henry Hughs, under the supervision of Luke Hansard, who was to succeed to the business within a year or two. There was, at the same time, a steady increase in the number and size of newspapers, books, pamphlets and advertising circulars. The growth in the number of newspapers was a direct result of the interest and participation of the new and increasingly influential mercantile middle class in current affairs. The French Revolution and the Continental Wars created an appetite for news and comment. Burke's *Reflections on the French Revolution* sold 32,000 copies within a year of publication. The development of trade and industry was an equally important factor, since the promotion and transaction of business required an ever greater amount of printed matter.

Although there was more and more printing required, the trade's customers wished it to be delivered with expedition. In default of mechanical aids to speedier production, the number of operatives was increased. Since the compositor is a skilled craftsman, additional labour could only be supplied by the indenture and employment of extra apprentices. Boy labour had the additional merit, in the master printers' eyes, of being cheap. It was not until comparatively late in the nineteenth century that the Unions were able to prevent excessive recruitment into the trade. But since the public's expenditure on printing grew throughout the whole century, the craft was able to absorb additional manpower without much difficulty. By 1800, however, the old apprenticeship regulations, with their insistence on formal indenture and abode in the employer's house, all to the strictest letter of the law, had begun to break down. The documents printed in Chapter IV illustrate this development very clearly.

Not only were more hands employed in the trade as a whole, but their methods of work were organized for quicker production. This was achieved by the institution of the "Companionship" system, which worked in favour of both masters and men. The employers obtained faster production on certain types of work, and the men were enabled to increase their piece-work earnings. The compositors were assembled into "companionships" of half a dozen or so men, headed by a "clicker." There could be any number of 'ships, according to the size of the office. In his *Compositors' Handbook* (London, 1854), Thomas Ford remarked that "a judicious distribution of employment in every business is the only means of expediting it. This is forcibly illustrated in the printing business, where, in order to meet the wishes or requirements of publishers and the public, pamphlets and even volumes of no ordinary size must often be commenced and completed within an incredibly short space of time. To effect this object properly, it is required to possess an almost unlimited supply of materials, and to divide the labour to be performed, in proportion to its extent, amongst a certain number of compositors. These are called a Companionship." He went on to say that "companionships are of two kinds; one, in which each person takes copy from the overseer—composing and completing it—the other called a Clickership, where the work or copy is given out, made up, completed, charged and received for in gross, under the management and control of a person styled a Clicker, *i.e.*, a working overseer."

Ford did not make it clear that the Clicker was not an overseer appointed by the management, but by the men. Since there could be a number of 'ships in an office, so would each have its clicker. The fundamental feature of the system was that small groups of men organized themselves for speedy production on the basis of piece-work payment. The function of the clicker was to keep his team supplied with copy, to attend to those phases of production which could not be paid for at piece rates, such as make-up and imposition, and to act as clerk to his group. As piece-work involved the making out of bills for the precise amount of work accomplished, the concentration of clerical work in the hands of one man saved much time and argument. The clicker was not paid by the firm, but by his companionship. His earnings were always equal to or slightly above those of the best piece-worker in the group.

There is no doubt that the companionship system generally resulted in higher wages as well as in an accelerated rate of production, since the members of the 'ship were able to concentrate solely upon the task of composition. In 1809, however, the compositors were already complaining that their earnings were diminishing owing to "the great number of hands that are put into companionships." [1] Twenty-five years later the first decade of the century was regarded as a golden age of plenty. "Those who can remember the state of the Trade for a few years previous and subsequent to 1810, and can call to mind the fact of each compositor having three or four stock works in hand, and the booksellers' and authors' loud complaints at the tardy progress of their works, may well be struck with surprise, when we behold the state to which our Trade is reduced. All employment has become uncertain—no situation is permanent—and, instead of having three or four volumes in stock, a dozen and sometimes a score of compositors are huddled on to a work which in former times would have been an employment only for one." [2]

The companionship system in book and general offices persisted until the end of the century. The introduction of composing machinery, which took place at that time, revolutionized composing-room methods. One machine could achieve the output of at least four hand compositors, and thus the case-hands were only required for corrections, make-up and imposition, which were paid for on a time basis.

(vi) *Specialization*

The development of offices specializing in distinct varieties of printing began towards the end of the eighteenth century. Probably the newspaper printers were the first to organize themselves for a specific type of production. According to the Newspaper Compositors' Report of 1820, referring to the practices in force before 1793: "Most of the papers were small folios; and they were nearly all connected with, or done in Book-houses; the eldest apprentice upon a press of matter, was usually called upon to assist. Upon the subdivision of the labour into galleys, and the size of the paper extending, a man was employed if any deficiency arose in the quantity required." [3] By 1793 the newspaper compositors had become separated from the book hands, and from that time onwards they negotiated agreements with their employers independently from their colleagues in the book and jobbing trade. Newspaper offices dropped out of the general trade, or kept separate companionships for that class of work.

By the middle of the nineteenth century there were firms

---

[1] See Document XLIII, p. 144.
[2] See Document LXV, p. 228.
[3] See Document CIII, p. 378.

specializing in Stationery Office contract work (Clowes); periodicals and books (S. and R. Bentley; Clay, Son and Taylor, and other firms in the Paternoster Row district); gift books and colour printing from wood engravings (Vizetelly and Edmund Evans); law printing (firms in the vicinity of the Temple and Lincoln's Inn); foreign and exotic languages (Watts and later Gilbert and Rivington); theatrical printing (Fairbrother, Johnson); printing in gold (Howlett and Son); security printing (Whiting and Branston). The development of the railway system after 1850 was the foundation of the fortunes of the houses of McCorquodale and Waterlow, which were the first specialists in poster, time-table and ticket printing.

(vii) *The London Scale of Prices for Compositors' Work*

Next to nothing is known of compositors' wage rates or methods of charging for piece-work before 1785. From that date, however, our information is plentiful. Throughout the nineteenth century the London compositors worked in accordance with their Scale of Prices, which grew out of the initial agreement made between the employers and themselves in 1785. By 1805 the early agreements had become consolidated in a Scale containing twenty-seven articles. In 1810, after a lengthy series of negotiations, the Scale was revised. Its twenty-two paragraphs were to remain in force until 1891. This was the Book Scale.

The object of the Scale was to regulate rates of payment for the manifold varieties of work undertaken by the men in the general trade: books, settings in foreign and exotic languages, dictionaries, schoolbooks, periodicals, pamphlets, complicated settings for accounts and tabular matter, music, mathematics and jobbing. It also stipulated the charges for corrections, nightwork, overtime and other emergencies. As specialization or new inventions developed, there were formulated the News Scale (1820), the Parliamentary Scale (1836), the Composing Machine Scale (1894). As occasion arose, certain Addenda were grafted on to the Scale of 1810 and, generally in agreement with the employers, explanatory paragraphs appended to elucidate obscure or disputed points. It must be emphasized, however, that the Scale itself was never tampered with. For the majority of compositors it had the force of law. Members of individual offices were quick to resist infringement of the Scale by one of their number or by their employer, while the compositors' Union watched over the interests and actions of the trade as a whole. The master printers mostly recognized the Scale. There were occasionally disputes over the interpretation of a clause, but there were few, if any, attempts to repudiate the agreement as a whole.

The greater part of the articles of the Scale stipulated the price to be paid for composing various types of work, *e.g.*, ordinary book composition as opposed to dictionaries. The basic rate of payment was per 1,000 ens. For instance, bookwork composition —"common" or straightforward matter—was charged $5\frac{3}{4}d$. per 1,000 if leaded and $6d$. if solid. The equivalent rates for dictionaries were $6\frac{1}{4}d$. and $6\frac{1}{2}d$.

Corrections were paid $6d$. per hour. It would thus appear that about 1,000 letters per hour was the normal speed of setting for hand composition. This was not, in fact, the case. The composition rate also included the cost of distribution. Therefore a compositor had to be capable of setting at least 1,500 ens per hour if he were to earn the normal rates. Varieties of composition for which more was charged than for common matter were those *"attended with any extra trouble* beyond usual descriptive matter . . . and therefore such gazetteers or dictionaries as contain many references, italics, contractions, etc., take the advanced price as dictionary matter." [1]

It must be remembered that the normal type cases would not include all special sorts, accents, bold-faced letters, etc. The compositor would therefore have the trouble of working from several pairs of cases and, equally important, distributing his used matter back into the correct receptacles. All this would tend to diminish his speed of composition. Hence the higher charges for intricate work.

The compositors succeeded in obtaining a rise of $\frac{1}{2}d$. per 1,000 ens in 1866, together with a reduction of the hours of labour from 63 to 60 per week. This was the first advance since 1810. In 1872, when negotiations broke down, the men were able to impose an advance of a further $\frac{1}{2}d$. per 1,000, and the reduction of hours to 54 per week. In 1891 came the third and last increase in prices during the period covered by this book. In that year a number of concessions were obtained.

It may well be asked why more than half a century was to elapse

---

[1] Scale of 1810, Art. 4, note. See p. 175.

before the composition prices agreed in 1810 were increased, and why the Scale as a whole persisted unchanged and unchallenged until 1891, for such was the case. This was due to several causes. Firstly, there were no violent upward changes in the cost of living. Secondly, there was the steady increase in the amount of work available and fairly full employment for all hands. Thirdly, although the price per thousand appears to be pitifully small, the compositors did not reckon to subsist entirely upon the return for straight composition, but reaped the benefit of work for which higher rates were paid. Of the latter there were many varieties, as reference to the Scale will show.

Piece-work, then, was the rule in the London printing trade during the last century. The establishment hands were often elderly journeymen, no longer able to hold their place in the bustle of a companionship, but who were content to attend to the more leisurely tasks of odd jobbing and clearing away used matter. They were paid the establishment wage of 33s.–36s. The piece-hand would reckon to earn more, by the exercise of both energy and skill.

In 1891 the Scale of 1810 was fundamentally revised and redrafted. This was done at the instigation of the London Society of Compositors, but in co-operation with the employers. There was also an advance in prices. Within a few years of the new agreement, however, less and less work was done on the piece, and the majority of hands in the general trade were "on the establishment" and uniformly paid the 'stab rate of 38s. per week.

The new advances in prices killed the traditional piece-work system. The employers found the terms of the new Scale too much in favour of the men, especially the extras for table-work and other complicated settings. Their reaction was to give their piece-workers a fortnight's notice and to offer them employment on the establishment. The men had no alternative but to accept. Thus, in the general trade, the London Scale of Prices for piece-work fell into disuse. The newspaper men, however, remained piece-hands, whether they were hand or machine compositors. Such is their status at the present day. In 1924 piece-work was revived for composing machine operators engaged on weekly periodicals.

(viii) *The News Scale*

From 1793 onwards the News Compositors separated from the book-hands. That is to say, they negotiated their own agreements with the daily newspaper proprietors as to wages and methods of

working. In view of the nature of daily newspaper composition
and make-up, no very elaborate Scale of Prices, such as was
evolved in the general trade, was necessary. For the newsmen the
principal factors were: the price per galley of 5,000 ens of long
primer or minion, the time allowed for the composition of stated
quantities of lines, since speed was important in newspaper
printing, and the sums to be paid for overtime.

The early history of the news compositors appears to be more
concerned with the apprentice question than with piece-work
rates or hours of labour. Before 1810 the employment of boys on
daily newspapers was hotly resisted by the journeymen, and by
that date they had succeeded in excluding them.

The first News Scale was formulated in 1820, being the result of
the labours of a Committee, which also issued a comprehensive
Report detailing all agreements reached between the news compositors and their employers during the previous half-century.
This Report is printed in full.[1] A few months after the publication of the Report and Scale, the formation of the News Society
took place, the membership of which was restricted to men
employed on daily and weekly newspapers. In 1833 this Society
refused amalgamation with the newly founded London Union of
Compositors, which already contained the London Trade Society and
London General Trade Society of Compositors. The London Union
thereupon founded a rival News Society. This latter organization
published two valuable reports on the methods of work and payment in various London newspaper offices. *The Times* printing
department, exceeding those of its rivals in size and importance,
was made the subject of a searching inquiry, since the compositors
at Printing House Square were not members of either of the news
compositors' trade societies. *The Times* office had been considered
"unfair" since 1816, and remained so until 1914, when the
property was purchased by Lord Northcliffe.

The rival News Societies amalgamated in 1853. The News
Scale had not been altered since its compilation in 1820, but in
1868 the original document was completely redrafted. Although
an increase in the price per 1,000 was requested from the newspaper proprietors in 1874, no advance was given and it was not
until 1891, when the News Scale was once again extensively
revised, that the newsmen obtained any concessions. Upon this
occasion the price per galley was not altered, but a number of
important extras were interpolated in the Scale; it was the payment

[1] See Chapter XV, p. 372.

for these more complicated types of composition which earned the newsman his additional wages. It is probable that the average skilled hand could earn something over £3 per week. At no time were establishment hands in book and general houses paid more than 38s.

No sooner was the News Scale of 1891 in operation than it was once again the subject of review. This was due to the increase, at that time, of displayed advertising. Until this time the conventional newspaper advertisement was set in the body types normally used for the text of the paper. We now find the innovation of the whole-page insertion, composed in a variety of display faces, and in a number of different measures which were not those of the standard column width. Furthermore, there was the new practice whereby the purchasers of space provided stereotype blocks of their advertisement, since any number of plates could be cast from a mould, and an identical design supplied to a number of publications. This practice was due, no doubt, to their dissatisfaction with the quality of display setting accomplished by the newspaper compositors, who were more accustomed to handling solid matter, and to the fact that the public were better able to recognize an advertisement which had the dual merits of distinctiveness and ubiquity. As time went on, an increasing number of displayed advertisements were set by specialist typesetting houses with access to stereotyping plants. The News Compositors, however, established their right to set the whole of the paper, and the space filled by all such matter set outside is charged by them, on its first appearance, as common matter.

While the prices paid for extras had been much increased since 1868, the rate per thousand ens and per galley still remained the same as in 1820. The proprietors refused an advance of ½d. per 1,000 in 1874, and again in 1893. On the latter occasion they insisted that, before any discussions could be held, a Scale of Prices for machine composition must be arranged. The introduction of composing machinery was a new factor, and one which was to revolutionize printing technique in all sections of the trade.

(ix) *The Introduction of Composing Machinery*

The difference between the type-setting machines and the Linotype matrice composing and slug casting apparatus, first used in this country in 1889, must be explained. The type-setting machine consisted of magazines loaded with normal printing types. The operation of a keyboard released the types from their containers, whence they fell by gravity and were moved to the "stick". At this point they were justified by hand, either by the keyboard operator or by an assistant sitting beside him. The galleys would be corrected by hand, and the pages made-up, imposed and printed off in the usual manner. Distribution was effected by hand or a separate machine. Where the latter was employed, specially nicked types were required. These type-setting machines were capable of at least 6,000 ens per hour, when operated by a moderately skilled man. This was three times the output of a really fast hand-compositor. It was found, however, that although the use of the machines both increased and speeded up production, their employment was uneconomic unless the distribution could wholly be attended to by cheap labour, either youths or females. Such a course was never tolerated by the London Society of Compositors, and type-setting machines were therefore rarely used in London. Outside London, where trade union restrictions were not so firmly enforced, a different state of affairs prevailed, and a number of provincial newspapers used the machines between 1870–1900.

The introduction of the Linotype, first used for a New York daily sheet in 1886, produced far-reaching results. Movable types stored in magazines were replaced by matrices. Manipulation of the keyboard released the matrices, which were directed to a point at which they were justified to the correct measure by wedge-shaped spaces. The line of matrices was then mechanically trans-ferred to a position in front of a mould, into which molten type metal was automatically pumped. A line-o'-type, or solid slug, was then ejected, completely ready for make-up, unless corrections were required, which were made by resetting the line completely. The matrices were then automatically lifted from the mould and returned to their respective magazines. Used type matter was melted down. The time was later to come when the equipment of a composing room could be judged, not by the amount and variety of types held in cases, but by the variety and excellence of design of the matrice repertory. The success of the invention, both in the provinces and in London, was immediate. The problem of dis-tribution disappeared, and the slugs were easier to handle in a busy newspaper composing room than loose type. The endless expense of replenishing the type cases was also at an end, since a freshly cast printing surface was used for every issue, thus afford-ing better quality stereotype plates.

The effects of the introduction of the Linotype on the hand-compositors' calling were several. At first the men feared for their employment, and in fact for a few years a number of men were displaced. It was not long, however, before the constantly expanding turnover of the printing trade called them back and, indeed, many more in addition. In the meantime, except on newspapers, the breakdown of the piece-work system was beginning and the tendency was for men to be engaged at establishment rates of pay. As I have pointed out, the increased prices for tabular work and other extras were militating against piece-work in the general trade, where employers preferred to pay the minimum 'stab rate of 38s. at the risk of obtaining a smaller output for their money. The increasing use of composing machinery still further influenced the tendency, since the earning capacities of skilled operators were very much higher than those paid to even the best hand-compositors. The Scale, therefore, became practically a dead letter, and by the end of the nineteenth century there was little piece-work in the general trade. It continues to be employed by compositors on London daily and weekly newspapers, and in certain weekly periodical houses, since in such cases fast production is essential. Since the large revenue derived from the sale of advertising space is often out of all proportion to the cost of production or the income from copies sold, the proprietors can afford, and are obliged to pay, high piece-work rates to ensure quick and uninterrupted production.

(x) *Aspects of the London Printing Trade in the Nineteenth Century*

On the whole relations between employers and employed were friendly throughout the century. Even during the period 1800–10, when the rises in the cost of living consequent upon the Napoleonic Wars brought about the long struggle on the part of the journeymen which resulted in the Scale of 1810, complete deadlocks were shortlived, and a compromise solution always obtained. This was due, perhaps, to the fact that the barriers between masters and men were not firmly fixed. There were many small employers who had but recently left the ranks of the journeymen. And when, after the conclusion of the wars, the country settled down to a lengthy period of industrial expansion, the vested interests in the printing trade acquired neither the power nor the aloofness from the employees such as was manifest in heavier trades and industries. The compositors' trade union was both recognized and respected by the employers and arbitration of disputed points was the accepted method of settlement. The existence of the Scale, and its strict observance by all parties, contributed to this factor. It also served to prevent unfair competition on both sides. In times of slackness it was made difficult for a workman to undercut his fellow journeymen by offering his services below the standard rates. Uniformity in wage rates blunted the edge of economic rivalry between one master and another.

We do not hear much about intense competition among the masters, but then the turnover of the London trade was constantly increasing. The chief threat was from the country printers, who could afford to work at cheaper rates than those prevailing in London. This aspect will be mentioned again.

The disputes in the 1830's over the prices to be paid for composing the wrappers or paper covers of periodical publications indicate the expansion in that section of the business. The Union Committee's *Report of the Proceedings respecting Periodical Publications*, published in 1832, stated that there were at that time fifty weekly periodicals and that they afforded employment for nearly two hundred persons. "Although these periodicals are now so numerous, they may all be said to have taken their rise from the establishment of the *Poor Man's Guardian*, which led the way to its more celebrated successor *The Penny Magazine*. The great success of which latter publication produced the number of rivals and imitators already stated." [1]

New technical developments such as stereotyping, mechanical type-setting and printing machinery are all mentioned in the documents, with observations as to their effect on the compositor's trade. In 1834 the men complained ".... where are the heavy standard works, which used to afford constant employment to some of the largest houses in the trade? They have been stereotyped, and all are gone from the compositor's hand, while the capital which was employed by the Masters in the production and reproduction of these works, is laid out by them in the purchase of machinery and the fabrication of stereotype plates. . . ." [2]

The first composing machine, or mechanical type-setting apparatus, the Young-Delcambre invention, was working in London between 1841 and possibly 1846. The men were hostile to what they considered a threat to their employment. It was not,

[1] See Document LVII, p. 192.
[2] See Document LX, p. 209.

however, until fifty years later that the problem became acute, since in the intervening period composing machinery was never used in London other than experimentally, and then only in a few instances. The exception was at *The Times*, where the Kastenbein machine was operated from 1872 onwards; but since that office did not employ union labour, and was a law unto itself, no complaint was or could be made.

The size of the sheet upon which books or periodicals were printed affected the price to be paid for make-up and imposition. The effect of the growth in the use in printing machinery, which was considerable after 1840, was that larger sheets could be printed than were possible with the handpress. This development is clearly shown by the compositors' desire, in 1845, to specify a maximum sheet size for charging purposes.[1]

Social and economic influences outside the printing trade are also shown in the documents. They were ultimately reflected in the Scale or its Addenda. For example, the reduction of the Newspaper Stamp Tax from 3*d.* to 1*d.*, which took place in 1836, was noted in the Annual Report of the London Union of Compositors for that year. Apparently the immediate effect was to stimulate work in the provinces rather than in London, although the metropolitan trade was soon to reap the benefit.

The repeal of the Advertisement Tax in 1853 "extended advertising both greatly in quantity, and from octavo pages of bourgeois and brevier to quarto pages of nonpareil and pearl, at the same time greatly increasing the quantity of Standing Advertisements."[2] The above extract relates to the dispute in 1856 on the subject of charges for standing advertisements on periodical wrappers, and demonstrates the influence of outside events on the Scale.

Improvements in communications also had their effects on the compositor's calling. The introduction of the Penny Post in 1839 brought increased prosperity to the trade, since direct mail advertising by printed circular or catalogue now became an economic proposition. In addition, proofs could be despatched with greater facility and less expense than before. It is possible that the innovation also worked, to some extent, to the detriment of the London trade, since contact with country printers, whose charges were less, was henceforward made easier. But this factor did not become of much consequence until the development of the railway system.

[1] See p. 257.
[2] See Document LXXVIIIA, p. 266.

The documents relating to the compositors' negotiations with the employers in 1866, proposing an advance in prices and shortening of the hours of work, provide useful evidence. The men pleaded that for rent "the working man is now called upon to pay from 15 to 20 per cent. more than he did a few years back; nor is this all, as he is compelled, by the large displacement of population arising from the requirements of our railroad system and other improvements, to seek lodgings far away from his work, thus increasing considerably the cost of family living. . . ."[1] The masters argued in reply that they had "the strongest possible evidence that large and increasing quantities of work are going into the provinces, to Scotland and to the Continent, owing entirely to the question of price." Economic carriage rates on a widespread railway system undoubtedly did much to assist provincial printers to gain a footing in the rich London market.

The deterioration in the standards of printing, so evident during the century, were due to piece-work in the composing room, to the increasing employment, from 1840 onwards, of the steam-driven printing machine in the press-room, and to the use of cheap machine-made papers. A high standard of type-setting cannot be achieved if the niceties of spacing must be sacrificed to speed, and celerity was required if a compositor was to earn an adequate wage. The printing machine, with an average production capacity of about 1,250 impressions per hour as opposed to the 250 obtained by the traditional handpress, was first used by *The Times* newspaper in 1814, but it was not until some thirty years later that the machines were extensively employed in the general trade. Their product could never compare with the best standards of handpress work, and until late in the century fine printing continued to be executed at the press. By 1890, however, American two-revolution machines were capable of good-quality work, and machine presswork of the highest order has been possible since that date. Machine-made paper, manufactured in the reel, was first produced in this country in the early 1800's, and the progressive substitution of material other than rags for paper making was manifested in the progressive deterioration of quality in book papers and newsprint. Inferior papers, coupled with careless and unplanned type-setting, account for much of the mediocrity of nineteenth-century printing. The use of narrow, condensed types was another disagreeable feature of British printing between 1830–60. These were known to the compositors as "thin" founts.

[1] See Document LXXIX., p. 269.

The more extreme versions were much disliked by them, not on æsthetic grounds, but because they were uneconomic to compose on piece-work rates. Thus, if the normal pica em was taken as a standard, a measure of 12 ems (24 ens) would contain more letters if set in a condensed face than if set in the conventional width types to which we are now accustomed. Why were these monstrous designs so widely accepted? Their appeal was utilitarian rather than æsthetic. It is probable that they were particularly designed for periodical printing, which flourished from 1830 onwards. There was the necessity of providing as much reading matter as possible within the limits of the one or two sheets which, folded into quarto or octavo, comprised the average periodical. Book faces were not so condensed, since a far greater number of sheets were employed, and the new convention of the three-volume novel encouraged rather than hindered the use of wide-set types and an open style of composition.

The introduction of mechanical composition did nothing to improve the appearance of book typography at the time, and it was not until the manufacturers of the Monotype composing machine produced a remarkable repertory of matrices, comprising designs based on the classic typefaces of the preceding centuries, that the product of the composing machine began to equal, if not outrival, the work of the great typefounders of the past. But this typographical renaissance did not take place until immediately after the last European War. The work of William Morris did not have any effect on the trade during his lifetime, and while there are many traces of his influence after his death, their discussion does not come within the scope of this book.

The influence of newspaper printing technique on that of the general trade must also be noted. Both the steam-driven printing machine and mechanical composition were originally developed and used for newspaper production. Such was also the case with wet-flong stereotyping. *The Times* was responsible for each of these innovations, being followed in due course by other journals. Competition necessitated the employment of the most efficient apparatus, even at the cost of great capital expenditure. These technical advances were only taken up by the general trade when they had been perfected by the newspaper printers.

The study of the London printing trade and its products in the nineteenth century is in its infancy. It is hoped that the collection of documents reprinted in this book will provide both clues and material for the more detailed inquiries which will follow in due course.

CHAPTER I

THE FOUNDATION OF THE LONDON SCALE OF PRICES
1785–1805

We now come to the main purpose of this book, a detailed examination of the London Scale of Prices for compositors' work from the year 1785, when the first known agreement was signed between masters and men, until the end of the nineteenth century, by which time the economic and technical organization of the trade presented the features which are recognizable to-day.

The agreement of 1785 specifically referred to the prices to be paid for certain kinds of piece-work, and it may well be asked why, in view of the antiquity of the London trade, no similar document can be found of an earlier date. Indeed, the extracts printed in the Introduction refer to almost everything except what a man might receive as the price of his labour.

At this point it may be as well to summarize our sources of information concerning wages or piece rates prior to 1785. Arber's *Transcript of the Registers of the Company of Stationers of London* (1554-1640) provides no help, and while a few figures are to be found in Greg and Boswell, *Records of the Court of the Stationers' Company*, it is impossible to prove that the rates there mentioned apply to journeymen compositors or pressmen. They might equally well appertain to bookbinders, claspmakers, or warehouse or shop assistants. Moxon noted the custom of paying the men "for all Church Holy days that fall not on a Sunday . . . proportionately for what they undertake to Earn every Working day, be it half a crown, two shillings, three shillings, four shillings, &c." [1] The use of the words "undertake to earn" suggests a piece-work system, the men undertaking to produce according to their known capabilities. On the other hand, there may have been a sliding scale for weekly establishment rates, again governed by a man's acknowledged skill. But neither the one nor the other supposition can be proved.

[1] See p. 25.

There are, however, a few indications in contemporary literature for the rates paid in the eighteenth century up to 1785:

Thomas Gent, *The Life of Mr. Thomas Gent, printer, of York, written by himself* (London, 1832), p. 90. Gent was paid 20s. per week in London in 1719.

James Watson, *The History of the Art of Printing* (Edinburgh, 1713), p. 21 : "For my Part, I'd rather give a Crown a Day to a good Press-Man, who brings Reputation to my Work and preserves my Letter, than Eighteen Pence to one who must certainly destroy it by careless and base Working."

The author of the *General Description of all Trades* (London, 1747), *art. Printer*, stated that "A Compositor may earn a Guinea a Week, if he is Expert in his Business and gives close Application, and a Pressman may get as much: But many of them play great Part of their Time."

Horace Walpole, *Journal of the Printing-Office at Strawberry Hill* (London, 1923), p. 80. Walpole agreed to pay his pressmen one guinea per week in 1759.

Lawrence Wroth, *The Colonial Printer* (Portland, Maine, U.S.A., second edition, 1938), provides valuable evidence concerning eighteenth-century American wage payments. He reprints a document in the possession of the American Antiquarian Society, written in the hand of Benjamin Franklin and endorsed by Isaiah Thomas. It consists of *Prices of Printing Work in Phila*[a] 1754, and includes retail prices for book and jobbing work and, more important, a short scale of prices for compositors' and pressmen's piece-work. It may safely be presumed that the American colonial printing trade inherited its methods of working and trade customs from London, upon which it was always to some degree dependent for men, equipment and ideas. I do not know whether the Philadelphia scale of 1754 was actually based on contemporary London practices.[1]

A century, more or less, passed before Moxon's book was followed by further trade manuals, and the two published in the latter half of the eighteenth century provided no information

---

[1] See also Stewart, E., *A Documentary History of the Early Organisation of Printers*. (*Bulletin of the* [*U.S.*] *Bureau of Labour*, No. 61. Nov., 1905, pp. 857-1033). This gives details of the first constitution of the Philadelphia Typographical Society and its scale of 1802, besides much other useful information concerning the American printing trade during the early part of the nineteenth century. Loft, Jacob, *The Printing Trades* (New York, 1944), is useful for the study of the American trade from the end of the last century to 1939.

about the prevailing methods of remunerating compositors or pressmen for their work.[1] The first mention of any Scale of Prices in a technical work addressed to the English printing trade is in Caleb Stower's *Printer's Grammar* (1808). On p. 418 he gave "An Account of the different Advances in Journeymen's Wages, from the Year 1785 to 1805, with the present Regulations and Scale of Prices." In an introductory paragraph he noted that "In the early stages of the printing business, the mode of paying the workmen employed in it must have been similar to those of every other business or manufactory in its infancy; viz., on established weekly wages. The idea of laying down fixed charges for different kinds of work was not suggested for nearly two centuries after the discovery of our art; nor indeed till the year 1785 had there been any regular scale of prices printed."[2] John Johnson and T. C. Hansard, who published books with the same title, *Typographia*, in 1824 and 1825 respectively, reproduced or paraphrased Stower's remarks without any alteration. Hansard added the following note :

Moxon, my oldest authority in printing, is silent upon the subject. As far back (previous to 1785) as I have been able to trace any fixed price, it appears that composition was paid in some degree according to the size of type used; upon the very rational principle, that a compositor had much less interruption in the actual operation of composing, or picking up, his thousands, when working upon small type, than he would have when upon large, by the more frequent making-up, imposing, correcting, etc. Thus, English type was at one period paid at fourpence, Long Primer three-pence half-penny, Brevier three-pence farthing. In Edinburgh, about fifty years ago, Brevier was two-pence halfpenny, while English was four-pence per thousand.[3]

In 1836 the London Union of Compositors issued a handbook known as *The London Scale of Prices for Compositors' Work: agreed upon, April 16, 1810, with explanatory notes*. The first twenty-six pages of this work contained a "History of the London Compositors' Scale of Prices." Although the introductory remarks merely consisted of meagre expansions from Stower, Johnson

---

[1] Smith, John, *The Printer's Grammar* (London, 1755). Luckombe, Philip, *A Concise History of the Origin and Progress of Printing* (London, 1770).

[2] [Knight, Charles.] *The Guide to Trade. The Printer* (London, 1838), p. 36, suggested that in 1774 the compositors received 20s. per week, and "About this period a system of paying per 1,000 letters was first established." As far as the latter statement is concerned, there is no adequate proof that Knight was correct.

[3] Hansard, T. C., *Typographia* (London, 1825) p. 778. *Cf. A copie of certen orders concerning printing*, para. 2, p. 16, *supra*, where it is made clear that the small sizes of type were probably more profitable to compositors than large ones.

and Hansard, there was much useful information in this section of the book. Concerning the earliest scale the following remarks were made :

> . . . we do not find any records by which we can conclude that paying by the piece or per thousand was the *general* practice of the trade at an earlier period than the year 1785. It is highly probable that some masters paid by the piece, in the same way that compositors are now paid in Germany—that is, by an agreement between the employer and the employed, for the price to be paid per sheet, regulated by the time occupied by the compositor in setting up the first sheet—but that there was an acknowledged scale to regulate the price of the various works, is extremely doubtful. In all cases, however, where the works were cast up, the price does not appear to have exceeded fourpence per thousand for the largest size type, while a somewhat less price was paid for the smaller.

The first regular and acknowledged compositors' scale for the payment of piece-work is by one writer stated to have been agreed to at a general meeting of masters, who assembled in the month of November 1785, to consider eight propositions submitted to them in a circular form from the whole body of compositors, with a view to advance the price of labour. That part of the trade, however, who were the most materially interested in the adjustment of the price of labour, namely, the compositors, do not appear to have been present when these propositions were discussed, or to have been permitted to offer any arguments in their favour; but the masters assumed the right to set a price upon the labour of others, although a short time afterwards they repelled with indignation an attempt of the booksellers to interfere with their practices and profits.

It is not essential, at this period, to know whether the scale was agreed to by a general meeting of masters, or by a committee, but the merit of forming the basis of the scale for regulating the price of the compositor's labour, certainly belongs to the journeymen, who, on the 6th of April, 1785, submitted to the masters eight propositions for this purpose, five of which were agreed to, and three rejected by them, after they had been laid before them upwards of seven months.

No copy of the original memorial submitted by the compositors survives, but its terms are set forth in the account of the general meeting held by the Masters.

[DOCUMENT I]

At a General Meeting of the Master Printers, at the Globe Tavern, in Fleet-street, on Friday, the 25th of November, 1785, to consider of the Propositions of the Compositors.

Resolved unanimously, That the answers following be given :

Prop. I. That the price of work, paid for by letters, be advanced from fourpence to fourpence halfpenny per thousand.

Answer. Granted; including English and Brevier, and, in leaded matter, the ems and ens at the beginnings and ends of the lines not to be reckoned in the width.[1]

Prop. II. That heads or folios, and direction lines, be included in the casting-up of all work.

Answer. Rejected; half a crown in the pound having been given in the first article.

Prop. III. Provided nevertheless, That the above mode of calculating prices shall not operate against the compositors in those works that are not customarily paid for by letters, such as smaller sized folios, quartos, octavos, etc. or works done in Great Primer, or any larger sized type, not heretofore paid by letters; but that such works bear an advance upon their accustomed price, proportionate to what is now proposed as the additional rate of other works.

Answer. Inadmissible in any degree as to any rise upon these articles.

Prop. IV. That the compositors employed on daily newspapers, now paid at the rate of one pound seven shillings per week each, be in future paid one pound eleven shillings and sixpence per week, and over hours as at present.[2]

Answer. This cannot be a matter of general regulation, as the trouble of every paper differs from that of another.

Prop. V. That pamphlets of five sheets, and under, be paid one shilling per sheet above what they come to by letters.

Answer. Allowed.

Prop. VI. That all works printed in any foreign language, though common type,[3] be paid fivepence per thousand.

Answer. Allowed, when wholly in a foreign language.

Prop. VII. That all dictionaries, done in Brevier, in the manner of a lexicon, be paid fivepence halfpenny per thousand; but not to extend beyond fivepence to dictionaries of science, or such as from their nature can be considered as only common matter.

Answer. Agreed to pay fivepence per thousand for all dictionaries of two languages, in Brevier or larger type; but not for English dictionaries, unless attended with peculiar trouble.

---

[1] "It appears to have been the practice, in all leaded matter, to indent an em or en at the beginning and end of the line, to prevent commas or other thin types from slipping." Gould, J., *The Letter-Press Printer* (London, 1876), p. 159 *n.* Mr. Waite tells me that the custom is still occasionally followed.

[2] The separation of the newspaper and book compositors did not take place until a few years later. Many of the masters who signed the above agreement were proprietors or printers of newspapers.

[3] *i.e.* in roman as opposed to *Fraktur*, Greek types or exotic characters.

Prop. VIII. That the price of Greek be advanced in the same proportion as that of common work.
Answer. Allowed.

Resolved unanimously, That the preceding advance in prices shall commence from the first of January, 1786; but not to extend to any works at that time unfinished.

Resolved, That a committee be appointed to enforce the above resolutions.

A. Strahan	J. Cooper	Henry Draper Steel
H. Hughes	H. Goldney	D. Bond
J. Nichols	E. Cox	Thomas Wilkins
A. Hamilton	D. Constable	Tho. Parker
Fr. Blyth	Thos. Spilsbury	John Plummer
M. Say	Matthew Brown	Ja. Andrews
T. Wright	Buch. Millan	Henry Trapp
H. Baldwin	J. Davis	G. Redmayne
J. Almon	Richard Causton	Wm. Adlard
Cha. Clarke	Harrison and Brooke	R. Ayre
W. Woodfall	John Wm. Galabin	J. Dixwell
Harrison and Thorne	Robert Butters	Jessington Rozea
Robert Hindmarsh	Thomas Bensley	W. Justins
H. S. Woodfall	John March	

Early in 1793, when the Scale of 1785 had been in existence some seven years, the compositors sought for certain concessions. Whereas in 1785 no discussion was held between the employers and employed, upon this occasion the men were given the opportunity to send representatives to confer with the masters.

[DOCUMENT 11]

The Address of the Compositors of London to the Master Printers.

London, Feb. 14, 1793.

Sir,

Seven years have now elapsed since we addressed the master printers on the subject of an advance of prices; with gratitude we call to our remembrance that they then deemed our application worthy their attention, and that they thought fit to redress, in part, the grievances we complained of. As we disclaim all proceedings militating against justice, or that are subversive of decent and respectful behaviour, we presume that any communication, which the present situation of the business renders necessary to be opened with our employers, will be received in a manner suitable to its importance, and with candour coinciding with its equity. Impressed with this idea, we respectfully submit the two following propositions for your sanction :

I.　That all works be cast up with the heads and directions inclusive.
II.　That em or en quadrats, or whatever is used at the beginnings and ends of lines, be considered each as a letter, and be included as in the above article.

The reason we beg to offer that heads and directions should be included in the future estimation of works, is, that they are to all intents and purposes a part of the page; and that the former are often attended with peculiar trouble, especially when composed in a type different from that employed on the body of the work, sometimes consisting of capital and small capital letters united, and frequently of italic capitals, which require the utmost skill of the compositor to space with neatness and propriety; insomuch, that the time employed in this part of the business would be fully sufficient (in many instances) for the composition of four lines of the ordinary matter : this trouble, when it is extended to the supplying running titles for two or three sheets of letter, occasions a considerable drawback from the earnings of the compositor, and is a hardship which we hope our employers can have no objection to remove.

With respect to em or en quadrats, in works printed with distances, it is to be observed, that in general the advantage supposed to be derived to the compositor from the use of leads, etc., is lost by the cutting of milled leads,[1] as well as by the introduction of two or three cast leads in a line; which, with the extra trouble occasioned in collecting em or en quadrats, in correcting and over-running matter so composed, and especially in clearing-away, form a substantial plea for their being allowed in the calculation of the price of the work.

Your acquiescence to the above propositions is all that the compositors ask or expect; and we trust, that when the more than proportionate increased price of every article of life, since the last rise in 1786, is considered, our requisition will meet with the hoped-for compliance.

The communication of your sentiments to the compositors in your office, or in any manner agreeable to the masters in general, to the committee of compositors at the Hole-in-the-Wall, Fleet-street, on or before the first of March, will be respectfully received by

Your humble servants,

[*Then follow 539 signatures*]

---

[1] "The great expense of this article [*i.e.* cast leads] in a printing office made it necessary, as far back in time as the oldest printers can remember, to have recourse sometimes to sheet or milled lead, particularly where leads were required for any unusual measure; or upon occasions where the office was not provided with that particular variety wanted, and time would not allow of the slow process of casting, even when the letter founder was in reach. The sheet-lead, in such cases, having been procured from the flatting-mill, was cut by the compositors, by hand, with shears." Hansard, T. C., *op. cit.*, p. 448. Hansard stated that cast leads cost him 2s. 4d. per lb., while the milled lead cost no more than 5½d. per lb.

[DOCUMENT III]

*At an Adjourned Meeting of the Committee of Master-Printers,[1] on Monday
the 11th Day of March 1793, in consequence of a Circular Letter from the
Compositors, dated the 14th of February last, requesting,*

 I. That all works be cast up with the heads and directions inclusive;
 II. That em and en quadrats, or whatever is used at the ends of
lines, be included as in the above article;

The committee, having held a conference with a deputation from the
compositors at large, agree to recommend to the master printers to
comply with the first request; understanding that the head-line (whether
larger or smaller) is to be reckoned like the text; and that, where the
length of the page is not exact even ems, if it does not exceed an en, it
is not to be considered as a line. Directions and signatures to be reckoned
in the gauge.[2]

The above increase of price to commence on Lady Day next, but not
to extend to any works at that time unfinished.—In periodical works, to
commence with the next new volume after Lady Day.

The compositors, who attended for their brethren, declared themselves
satisfied with the above advance, and have acceded to the reasons given
by the committee why the second request cannot be complied with.

On 18 December, 1795, the master printers of London sat in
conference to consider a letter from the compositors, dated
23 November, 1795. No copy of this letter has survived, but the
printed report of the employers' General Meeting reproduced
the demands for an advance in prices contained in it.

 1. That from and after the 1st of January, 1796, all works, hitherto
paid for by letters at the rate of fourpence halfpenny per thousand, be
advanced to five pence, and that all other works bear a proportionate rise.

 2. That all jobs, not exceeding one sheet, be paid at the rate of six
pence per thousand.[3]

 3. That all works, printed on a type of a larger size than English, be
cast up as English.

---

[1] There is a note on the copy of the document at St. Bride to the effect that
the Committee consisted of Messrs. Barnard, Brook(e), Gosnell, Davison and
Baldwin.

[2] "The injustice of this latter stipulation seems to have been so evident,
as to cause its tacit abandonment by the masters; and the custom has accordingly
been to pay extra for the headline, when it is set up in a *smaller* type than the
text." *The London Scale of Prices*, 1836, p. 9.

[3] "JOB. Any thing which printed does not exceed a sheet, is termed a Job,
and is paid for extra to the compositor, because there is no return of furniture
or of letter : he has generally to put up fresh cases, and has some additional
trouble in getting the right letter, and in making up the furniture." Savage, W.,
op. cit.

The threat of competition from country printers, working at prices substantially lower than those in force in London, was also mentioned by the employers. This problem was not to become acute until after the introduction of Penny Postage in 1840.

[DOCUMENT IV]

At a General Meeting of the Master Printers, convened by the Committee to consider of certain Propositions submitted to them by the Compositors for an advance upon the price of their work.

Globe Tavern, Dec. 18, 1795.

Mr. Davis having been voted into the Chair,

The letter from the compositors [dated 23 Nov. 1795] was read; when, after a deliberate discussion; it having been declared by some gentlemen present that offers had been repeatedly made by country printers to serve the booksellers £20 per cent. under the present London prices, and the recent advance having been duly considered; the first, second, and third propositions, were separately declared to be inadmissible : but, to prevent misunderstanding in future, respecting the third it was

Resolved, That, from the 1st of January, 1796, all works printed in a larger type than English shall be cast up, and paid for, as half English and half Great Primer.

Resolved, In answer to the propositions concerning apprentices, That all regulations of that sort must necessarily belong to the masters.

Resolved, That a copy of these resolutions be printed, and sent round to the trade.

J. DAVIS, *Chairman.*

[Then follow 36 signatures]

In the autumn of 1800 the compositors decided to present a further petition to the masters. A "Plan of Prices," containing five propositions was annexed to the compositors' preparatory letter, circulated among themselves. Four more paragraphs were added before a communication was sent to the masters. No copy of the original memorial in its revised form exists, but the nine propositions were printed in the *London Scale of Prices* from which they are here extracted.

[DOCUMENT V]

[From the Compositors' Committee to the Compositors.]

Hole-in-the-Wall, Oct. 24, 1800.

Sir,

You are hereby requested to call together the compositors of your office, and lay before them the annexed plan of prices, which the persons who have undertaken to conduct the business, think the most proper that can be adopted in the present embarrassed and divided situation of our affairs. But as it is not their intention to dictate, but to offer a plan, by which the opinion of each individual can be ascertained without the confusion of a general meeting, they recommend to the gentlemen to write on the blank leaf of this letter any alterations which they may think necessary in the following propositions; and that when the said plan is approved of, or altered according to their judgment, that they deliver it to a delegate appointed by them to attend at a meeting of the compositors, to be held at the Hole-in-the-Wall, on Monday, the 27th day of October, at seven o'clock precisely; for the purpose of finally agreeing to a plan of prices, which shall take place the 10th day of November 1800. As the master-printers, by refusing to answer our humble petition and letters, have shewn that they have no intention to pay the least respect to our just claims (which the distresses of the times sufficiently warrant), and leave us no resource but what must arise from our own firmness and determination.　　　　　　　　　　　　　　　　　　　　　　　　　　　　A. Z.

P.S. Please to remember, that in order to prevent confusion, none but delegates can be admitted on the meeting night, and the return of this letter shall be their ticket of admission.

[*Then was printed a "Plan of Prices" containing five clauses*]

"PLAN OF PRICES" AS FINALLY PRESENTED TO THE EMPLOYERS[1]

1. That all works done from a manuscript copy, common matter, be paid for at the rate of $5\frac{1}{2}$d. per 1000; and all works done from a printed copy, common matter, be paid for at the rate of 5d. per thousand.—Note. Works done from a printed copy, with interlineations, or that do not preserve their original form, to be considered as manuscript copy.

2. That minion, nonpareil, and pearl, be subject to a proportionate increase, according to the first article.

3. That not less than 6d. per hour be paid for corrections.

4. That all works done in two columns in a page (folios and quartos excepted), be paid one shilling per sheet extra, and when exceeding two columns to be paid for as tabular.—Note. This article does not extend to figure or rule-work.

5. That jobs of a sheet and under be paid for at the rate of $6\frac{1}{2}$d. per thousand.

6. That all works in a larger sized type than English be cast up as English.

7. That ems or ens, or any indentation, be included in the width of the page.

8. That all works paid heretofore double, be considered as liable to a proportionate increase; also works, or such parts of works, as are partly figures and partly plain matter, to be paid one and one-half, such as arithmetical works, and works where calculations are made.

9. That the above resolutions commence on all works put in hand on or after the 10th day of November 1800, and on all periodical publications at the commencement of each volume.

[1] Reprinted from *The London Scale of Prices*, 1836, p. 10.

The author of the historical introduction to *The London Scale of Prices* stated that "The masters, however, declined acceding to these articles, but, to meet the demands of the journeymen half-way, offered them an additional halfpenny per thousand. The journeymen did not deem this advance sufficient; and, indeed, the offer of the masters must excite surprise, when the difference in the price of provisions between the two periods is considered; for the price of bread, from 1785 to 1800, had advanced from 7¾d. to 1s. 7½d. a quartern, meat from 3½d. to 7½d. per lb., and every other necessary of life in equal proportion." [1]

[DOCUMENT VI]

At a Meeting of the Master Printers of London and Westminster, held for the purpose of taking into further consideration the state of the trade, both in respect to their workmen and their employers.

December 24, 1800.

It was stated, That a general dissatisfaction still remained among the compositors, concerning the advances granted them at a former meeting, (Nov. 29*); they expecting to have had an additional allowance of one halfpenny per thousand on works printed from MS. copy.

* "On that day the masters agreed to advance one halfpenny, or ten per cent. but it was even then so confined, that it did not operate on many works. The idea of compositors adhering to an additional halfpenny on manuscript copy was never permanent; it was, indeed, not an unfair proposition, considering the bad state in which some copy is placed into the compositors' hands; but it was well-known that the usual mode of master's undertaking work could not be set aside; and it was thought it would justify the claim of fifteen per cent. advance; and might be the cause of having the copy something better."

The same was taken into consideration; and, upon deliberate discussion, it was found impracticable to comply with their expectation; the meeting being convinced, that to make any distinction between manuscript and reprint would be an unjustifiable departure from the established and long approved principles by which works have been appreciated :—But, considering the extreme and increasing pressure of the times (the article of bread alone having arisen to the unusual price of 1s. 7½d. the quartern loaf) it was

Resolved, That, upon the first article of the compositors' scale, one farthing more per thousand be allowed in general, without making any distinction between manuscript and reprint; to take place on all works begun on or after the 1st of January, 1801.

[Then were printed two paragraphs concerning an advance granted to the Pressmen. See p. 96.]

[1] *Op. cit.*, p. 11.

COMPOSITION SCALE AS NOW AMENDED

I. That the scale of 1785 (whereby an advance of 2s. 6d. in the pound was given)—as amended in 1793 (when the further advance of including head-lines and directions was acceded to,) and is subsequently amended in 1796 (respecting works done in larger type than English)—is a fair and applicable scale to judge and appreciate works by.

II. That the following further advances and regulations be made on the above scale :

First—That the price of works paid for by letters be advanced from 4½ to 5¼d. per 1000, including English and Brevier.

Second—That all works printed in any foreign language, though common type, be advanced to 5¾d. per 1000, including English and Long Primer—In Bourgeois or Brevier to 6d. per 1000.

Third—That all dictionaries of two or more languages, in Brevier or larger type, in quarto and octavo, be advanced to 5½d. per 1000. If in duodecimo or eighteens, to 6d. per 1000.

Fourth—That corrections be advanced to 5d. per hour.[1]

III. That jobs, and other works not specified in the above prices, or in the annexed schedule, bear a proportionate advance.

J . N I C H O L S , *Chairman.*

JOB MASTERS' RESOLUTIONS

First—That every article under one sheet, be considered a job, and be paid 6½d. per 1000.—3d. to be considered as 6d.—under 3d. to be lost.

Second—One sheet and under five, to be cast up as usual, with 1s. a sheet for the imposing.

Third—Corrections on all jobs to be paid 6d. per hour.

Fourth—All jobs, not hitherto paid by letters, to be allowed 6d. in every 3s.[2]

Fifth—All jobs in foreign languages to be paid 7½d. per 1000.

Sixth—The imprint not to be included in the square of the page.

Seventh—Jobs having two or three head rules, and four columns to be considered tabular, all above to be reckoned table-work. The first to be paid one-half. The second double price.

"It appears that the booksellers were offended at the advance which the masters proposed to grant to the compositors; for we

---

[1] "The price previously paid for corrections per hour is presumed to have been fourpence halfpenny, upon the principle that the composition of one thousand letters per hour is the average result of labour. This estimate, however, is very erroneous; and in the above scale of 1800 it will be seen that the compositor on book work when correcting was to have fivepence per hour, but when correcting jobs, he was to have sixpence per hour; the reason for this difference is not stated." *The London Scale of Prices*, 1836, p. 14, *n.*

[2] "By this stipulation it was intended that broadsides, bills in parliament, and other such work as had a definite charge, were to be increased in price one sixth." *Ibid.*, p. 14. *n.*

find that, previous to the rise just noticed, a circular from the booksellers was addressed to the master printers, expressing their uneasiness at the contemplated increase of the wages of the journeymen." [1]

When the employers met to discuss the points arising out of the revised Scale, the booksellers' interference was answered by four resolutions.

[DOCUMENT VII]

At a further Meeting of the Master Printers, finally to adjust and settle the business above-mentioned.

January 7, 1801.

Mr. J. Nichols in the Chair;

The meeting was informed, That much uneasiness prevailed amongst the booksellers respecting the above advances; and a circular letter from them to the master printers of London and Westminster, dated January 2, 1801, signed W. Davies, Chairman, was read :—and those gentlemen who had, by request, attended two meetings of the booksellers, having reported what transpired thereat. The above resolutions, after full and deliberate discussion, were unanimously confirmed.   And it was further

Resolved, *nem. con.* 1. That the said resolutions be signed by the company present, and left with the secretary for the signatures of those who could not attend this meeting.

2. That the said resolutions, together with this day's proceedings, be printed and circulated to the master printers of London and Westminster.

3. That the above advances, both to compositors and pressmen, being grounded on known practical scales hitherto acted upon with ease and advantage to the workmen, and with justice to our employers, are recommended to be generally adopted.

4. That we will not take into our employment any workman, without previously inquiring whether he has left his last place fairly; and that encouragement and protection be given to the sober and industrious. [2]

[*Then follow 33 signatures*]

The compositors were in a conciliatory mood, and expressed their solidarity with the master printers against the interference of the booksellers.

---

[1] *The London Scale of Prices*, 1836, p. 15. No copy of the booksellers' letter is known.

[2] A workman left a situation unfairly if he departed without giving proper notice, or in debt or "horse" to his late employer. "If any journeyman set down in his bill on Saturday night more work than he has done, that surplusage is called *Horseflesh*; and he abates it in his next bill." Moxon, *op. cit.*; Savage, *op. cit.* uses the term *horse*; Ringwalt, J. L., *American Encyclopaedia of Printing* (Philadelphia, 1871) has "*Dead-horse.* Matter charged before it is set." [Pasko, W. W.], *American Dictionary of Printing* (New York, 1894). "*Horsing-it.* To read proof without a copy holder."

[DOCUMENT VIII]

At a numerous Meeting of Delegates, on Tuesday, Jan. 20, 1801, at the Harlequin, Drury-Lane, representing the great body of compositors, to take into consideration the above resolutions of the Master-Printers in granting a further Advance on labour of 15 per cent.

Resolved, That the resolutions of the masters of book-houses in the printing business, though not directly agreeable to our propositions, are adequate to our wishes; and that we are not ungrateful in the receipt of our requests, nor negligent of their attention.

Resolved, That the jobbing masters' resolutions, though not the same as stated in Article III of the book-master's resolutions, is nearly adequate to our propositions, and that we shall from gratitude as well as inclination accede to the 1st, 2nd, 3rd, 4th, 5th, and 6th.

To the seventh, jobs having three columns to be considered tabular, with or without rules; all above to be reckoned table-work. The first to be paid one half, the second double price.

At the above meeting the resolutions of the booksellers having been laid before the compositors, it was unanimously

Resolved, That the interference of booksellers between the master printers and journeymen, is unhandsome, and their resolutions insulting; and that we shall adhere firmly to those masters, notwithstanding any future threats or temptations.

[Then follow 492 signatures]

[DOCUMENT IX]

At two several General Meetings of the Master Printers of London and Westminster, held on the 5th and 17th inst. John Nichols, Esq., in the Chair; to take into consideration the great inconveniences which have arisen to the Masters, and dissatisfaction to the Men, from the different Prices paid for the Imposition of Works done in Eighteens, and the various modes of paying for the Alteration of Margins.

York Hotel, 17th Jan., 1803.

Resolved unanimously,

1. That these meetings have nothing more distant from their intention than advancing upon, or abridging, the present established prices.

2. That as it appears that various customs have long prevailed in the payment to compositors for works done in eighteens, there be hereafter paid one shilling per sheet for imposing Long Primer eighteens, and one shilling and sixpence per sheet for imposing Small Pica, Pica, and English eighteens; not, however, extending this regulation to those eighteens done in a larger body than cast up to, or in a smaller type than Long Primer.

3. That this meeting, having received a letter from the compositors (signed Joseph Freeman, Philemon Chalk, G. Adams, William Goff, Nichs. Middleton, P. Egan,[1] Charles Fagan) submitting the question

---

[1] Pierce Egan (1772–1849), author of *Life in London*, 1821, and other sporting works.

respecting the alteration of margins to the decision of the committee of master printers, do resolve, That when a similar application shall be received from the pressmen, the committee of master printers be requested forthwith to give a meeting to a select number of compositors and pressmen, and report the result of such meeting to the trade at large, in order to enable them to come to a determination on the subject.[1]

4. That the committee of master printers do meet at the above place on Wednesday, the 2nd of February ensuing.

T . B E N S L E Y , *Secretary.*

[1] "ALTERATION OF MARGIN. In works that are published in different sizes, this is the changing of the margin from the small paper to the large paper edition, when at press." Savage, W., *op. cit.* 1841.

CHAPTER II

THE SCALE OF 1805

According to the compiler of *The London Scale of Prices* (1836), p. 17, in 1801 the journeymen "established a Society with the design of correcting irregularities, and endeavouring to promote harmony between the employers and the employed, by bringing the modes of charge from custom and precedent into one point of view, in order to their being better understood by all concerned."[1]

Early in 1805 the compositors' Society approached the employers with the suggestion that a complete Scale of Prices be drafted by common consent. In negotiating its compilation with the employers the compositors were not seeking an advance in the current prices, but rather a clarification of established customs and methods of charging. The compositors' committee drafted a "Prepared Scale of Prices," dated 20 January, 1805, which was circulated among the journeymen, together with a letter soliciting their approval. A few days after the proposed Scale received the general support of the trade, it was submitted to the masters, accompanied by the following letter.

[DOCUMENT X]

To Master Printers

February 9, 1805.

Gentlemen,

The many disagreeable differences that occur on the introduction of almost every new work, from the want of a regular scale of prices, have long been the cause of serious inconvenience to the printing business;— the inexperienced part of the profession have often been misled in their charges from the want of such guide, and in too many instances the employer has taken advantage of their situation, by disputing or denying

---

[1] There is reason to believe, however, that the Union Society, founded in 1801, was descended from an earlier institution. The London Society of Compositors possesses an incomplete copy of the *Rules and Orders to be observed by the Members of the Phœnix: or Society of Compositors. Instituted March* 12, 1792, *at the Hole-in-the-Wall, Fleet Street, London, printed for the Society*, 1792. The "Phœnix" was a friendly society. The subscriptions were "2s. 3d. monthly: 2s. to the box, 3d. to be spent, increased to 2s. 6d. each quarterly night: 3d. to the Secretary, 3d. to be spent." It will be noticed that the headquarters of the "Phœnix" were later taken over by the Union Society.

custom, and by refusing to acknowledge precedents, which have been hitherto the only reference.

Sensible that nothing can tend more to the advantage of the journey-man than a perfect good understanding with his employer, we submit, with every mark of respect, the following fair (and correct as far as can be ascertained) scale for your approval; feeling confident your candour will do justice to the purity of our intentions, when you find we have not attempted a rise on established usage, farther than a proportionate advance on articles always allowed extra, but not included in the scale of 1801, thereby leaving an uncertainty in the charge;—rather relying on your liberality for any addition you may please to make, than wishing to urge the necessity of the times as a claim, the peculiar distresses of which you are, gentlemen, well acquainted with.

We have found the task of forming the present scale a very difficult one, from the intricate nature of our trade, which will not allow of its being perfect; many works, from their peculiar nature, must depend on amicable agreement; yet, to such as can be regulated, we have devoted our attention, keeping strict justice in view, and considering our employers interest on an equality with our own : for, surely, if ninety-nine grievances existed, and eighty of them could be remedied, it is not an argument, because the whole cannot be accomplished, that the greater part should not be settled. We have, therefore, endeavoured to form such a scale as may guide future charges, and prevent the trouble and inconvenience which have hitherto been experienced from the want of a knowledge of the fair and customary prices.

The ground-work of altercation is founded on the many different customs prevalent in our trade : to reduce those differences into one acknowledged system is our object, and we look for your concurrence with a strong degree of satisfaction :—the accomplishment of our wishes will then be our reward, and we shall no longer behold those disputes which at present reflect but little credit on a profession that gives light to every other.

As, gentlemen, we disclaim every thing that might be construed into disrespectful behaviour, so we trust we shall meet with that candour from our employers the nature of our communication entitles us to; being ready to receive your sentiments in whatever manner you may think proper to disclose them, but must urge your earliest consideration of our proposal.

[*Then was printed the Scale of Prices proposed by the Compositors*[1].]

The candour of our employers will easily appreciate our motives for introducing the above articles in a scale, when it is recollected that such charges above the per thousand were mostly known half a century back, when every article of life was more upon an equality with the then price of labour. Even at the present time the majority of houses in town acknow-ledge their propriety, by paying to the amount of this scale; though others, more particular, refuse their justice, because we cannot produce them in print; and it certainly will be to the benefit of the employer and the employed, that one general scale should alone be known and abided by.

---

[1] Limitations of space make it desirable to omit all draft Scales.

On the article of dictionaries, you will, gentlemen, assuredly acknowledge the fairness of our charge; the last rise only allowing ten per cent. on such, though they were always considered as twenty per cent. under other works; and, even with the proportionate advance, will at no time be reckoned as desirable work by the journeyman. It is scarcely necessary to observe, that English, or English and foreign dictionaries, vary but little in the loss of time to a compositor, upon an examination of Boyer,[1] the English, Spanish, Portuguese, Entick,[2] and the pronouncing dictionaries, and other works of like description of the present day. With respect to gazetteers and geographical dictionaries being paid the same as those of language, without referring to the ancient custom of paying such works extra, Cruden will determine why they are now mentioned, where the multiplicity of capitals, small capitals, figures, points, and a continual run upon sorts, render them very disadvantageous, and place them on a footing with the most difficult dictionaries—vide Walker's, Brooke's, &c. &c.

With respect to ems and ens at the beginning and ends of lines, we beg to urge the extreme hardship they have long been to the journeyman, and especially at the present period, when their necessity is done away by the cheapness of cast-leads; and the argument no longer standing good, that the journeyman derived equal benefit with the employers as, with the exception of a few houses, milled-leads are nearly out of use, and it is only to the advantage of the employer they are used, in order to accommodate his assortment of cast-leads.[3]

There are many other inconveniences materially infringing on the time of the compositor, reducing the last rise of fivepence farthing per thousand, and which, without introducing into this scale, we would rather leave to your adoption, contenting ourselves with the liberty of suggesting the propriety of drawing a line whereby such may be remedied for the future.

Bad copy has always been considered by the liberal part of our employers, as entitled to an extra charge, from the consideration of the time it takes a journeyman to discover the meaning of a slovenly author—to arrange in many cases his copy—to point his intricate sentences; and then, to be subject to the caprice of the corrector, who generally proves his superior judgment at the expence of the compositor—Scarcely any two persons agree in their modes of punctuation,—and most houses in town have their peculiar method, not only in this, but in spelling, dividing, &c. &c. all which becomes a heavy burden on those who have to support it; we therefore presume, that where a loss is experienced, the most proper person to bear such would be the author, who derives the benefit, and through whose carelessness it is we have the principal reason to complain of the evil.

We likewise beg to call your attention to the alarming increase of apprentices, not only to the injury of the journeyman, but time will prove to the great detriment of the employer.—It is a known fact, that

[1] Abel Boyer (1667–1729) published a French–English dictionary.

[2] Entick, John, *The New Spelling-dictionary teaching to write and pronounce the English Tongue with Ease and Propriety* (London, 1784).

[3] See footnote to p. 75.

some gentlemen of the profession, (even in the city) have taken apprentices for the term of four, five, or six years, according to the extent of the premium—against established usage, and to the injury of the lads themselves, who will not be allowed their privilege to the trade without serving the full term of seven years.—As it is a mutual detriment, we leave to your better judgment to make the proportion of apprentices to the number of journeymen in each house—Again expressing our hopes that these suggestions will not be slighted, but meet with fair, cool, and rational consideration.

We have thus, gentlemen, submitted to you the result of our most mature deliberation. We have carefully endeavoured to avoid the introduction of any article that might be construed into the idea of exaction, and there is not one in the scale, but what we can justify from custom, precedent, and sound argument. Your answer to our proposals is requested by Saturday, the 16th instant, that their speedy settlement may for ever put to rest those disputes which it is the earnest wish of the trade to see effected.

We are,

Gentlemen,

[Then follow 533 signatures]

The master printers took immediate notice of the letter printed above, and appointed a committee of eight to meet an equal number of representatives to be sent by the men. The employers' committee was also empowered to treat with the pressmen who sought a "Scale of new Prices." No copy of the pressmen's application has been found.[1]

[DOCUMENT XI]

At a General Meeting of the Master Printers, held here this Day, to take into Consideration

    I. A Scale of new Prices offered by the Pressmen : And
    II. A Letter of Regulations received from the Compositors :

    Present
        John Nichols, Esq. in the Chair,

Mess.		Mess.		Mess.		Mess.	
Abrahams		Bye		Hansard		Smith	
Adlard		Couchman		Harvey		Stratford	
Auld		Davison		Hempsted		Swann	
Baldwin		Dewick		Keating		Taylor	
Barfield		Fisher		Lane		Teape	
Baylis		Flint		Law		Thompson	
Bensley		Galabin		M'Dowall		Thorne	
Blackader		Galton		Plummer		Whiting	
Brettell		Gillet		Ruffy		Wilks	
Brooke		Glendinning		Savage		Wilson	
Bryer		Gosnell		Shaw		Woodfall	
Burton		Hales		Skirven		Wright	

---

[1] Documents relating to the pressmen are printed in chapter III. See p. 95.

After the most deliberate Discussion, it was Resolved Unanimously,

That the following Eight Gentlemen, viz. Mess. *Nichols*, *Hansard*, *Bensley*, *Woodfall*, *Baldwin*, *Gillet*, *Shury*, and *Ruffy*, be appointed a Committee, to meet an equal Number from the Body of Pressmen on Monday the 18th Inst. at the York Hotel; and an equal Number from the Body of Compositors on Tuesday the 19th Inst. at the same Place, at Eleven o'Clock each Day, to confer on their respective Propositions, and report their Proceedings to the next Meeting.

Resolved,

That this Meeting do now adjourn to Stationers' Hall on Thursday the 21st Inst. at Eleven o'Clock in the Morning.

(Signed) J. N I C H O L S, *Chairman.*

York Hotel, Bridge Street,
Feb. 13, 1805.

Every Gentleman is requested to make this known by delivering the enclosed Copies to the Men in his own House.

The masters' committee reported progress at a General Meeting held at Stationers' Hall on 23 February, 1805. The bulk of their printed summary of the proceedings concerned their unsatisfactory relations with the pressmen (see p. 99). Negotiations with the compositors proceeded more smoothly, since it was realised that they required a clarification of existing customs and charges rather than an advance in prices. The relevant paragraphs are here reprinted.

In a few days after publishing this Notice from the Masters to the Pressmen, the Compositors circulated an Address to Master Printers, dated February 9, 1805; in which, after assigning their reasons, they respectfully offer a fair Scale for the Masters' approval, rather relying on their liberality for any addition, than wishing to urge the necessity of the times as a claim;—and conclude their Address, by urging the earliest consideration of their Proposal; and requesting an answer by Saturday the 16th Instant.—This Proposal was entitled "Compositors' Scale of Prices,"—and consisted of 30 Articles and seven subsequent Paragraphs; concluding with printed signatures of 533 Compositors.

In consequence of this Address from the Compositors, and the Pressmen still persisting in their demands, a second General Meeting of the Trade was held on the 13th of February, to take into consideration both these circumstances.

This Meeting appointed a Special Committee of Eight to confer, on Monday the 18th, with an equal number of Pressmen, and on the next day with an equal number of Compositors; which Special Committee held nine distinct Meetings : the result of which is contained in the following.

In this state of things your Committee adjourned their sitting till the evening, when they proceeded to investigate the Compositors' proposed Regulations. On first examining this Business, it was thought a labyrinth and sea intricate and unfathomable : but, in the free conference which followed with the Deputation from the Compositors, after three successive meetings and laborious discussions, your Committee are pleased in having it in their power to state, that much was done to compose the differences and variations alleged in their Address. The Compositors' Scale of Prices extended to several minute articles which, in some houses, but little doubt is entertained, bore hard upon the individual Compositor. To assimilate the great variations in the multiplicity of the business of the Capital, and the customs of different houses, it was soon found that an explanation was nearly the sum and substance of the Compositors' wishes. With this idea before them, your Committee entered cheerfully into an investigation of the Articles one by one; classing and combining the different regulations proposed, and thereby endeavouring to make, as near as local circumstances would permit, one universal system for the Composing branch of the Business.

After the several amendments had been mutually agreed to, some observations dropped from the Compositors respecting the unequal multiplication of Apprentices in several houses; but, as your Committee did not feel themselves at liberty to enter into that business, and it being only a remark by the Compositors, your Committee conceive nothing more to be necessary on this head than merely to notice the circumstance.

In the same spirit and inclination, that nothing should be lost sight of which even in idea might bear hard on the Compositors, your Committee cannot omit the opportunity of mentioning the real difficulty creeping by degrees into the Trade, to the expense of the employer, the retarding of business, and the sources of complaint from the Workmen, by the hasty manner in which Copies for the Press are too frequently prepared.

Upon the whole, your Committee came to the unanimous Opinion, That the Compositors' Scale of Prices, as amended by your Committee, be recommended for the adoption of the Trade at large.

At an Adjourned Meeting of the Master Printers, held two days later, the following supplementary resolution was passed.

[DOCUMENT XII]

Stationers' Hall, 25 Feb. 1805.

The Adjourned Meeting resumed and concluded their Deliberations on the Compositors' amended Scale; and confirmed the Resolutions of Saturday.

Resolved. That the Special Committee do inform the Booksellers of their Proceedings, and immediately furnish them with a copy of these Resolutions.

Adjourned,

J. N[ichols],

The compositors assembled on 6 March, 1805, and the Booksellers' resolutions of 28 February were discussed. (These are reprinted on p. 102.) It was regretted that the Booksellers had drawn no distinction between their affairs and those of the pressmen.

[DOCUMENT XIII]

At a Meeting of Compositors held at the Hole-in-the-Wall, Fleet-street, convened by General Summons, on Wednesday, March 6th, 1805, the following Resolutions were unanimously agreed to:

Samuel Charles Fawcett, in the Chair,
Mr Davenport being indisposed :

Resolved, That it is with regret we have read a resolution entered into at Stationers Hall, on Thursday, February 28th, 1805, by the booksellers, and an advertisement in most of the newspapers, signed by the master printers and booksellers, wherein the line of distinction is not drawn between the two branches of the profession, but implicating us in measures which we neither avow nor support; and that we feel it a duty to ourselves, to request our employers, in their future reports to the public, to let them know the compositors are a distinct branch from the pressmen.

An anonymous letter having been sent to the committee of master printers, it was

Resolved, That the propriety of the conduct of the compositors is a complete refutation of the calumnies contained in such letter; and that we do consider the writer as actuated by the worst of motives—possessing a mind stained with the black dye of an incendiary—envious of the high situation we hold in the opinion of our employers—and wishing to thwart that good understanding, which it is the interest of every well-thinking man to maintain.

The meeting taking into consideration the present state of the business, and the distress that must eventually occur to men with families, should the present contest between their employers and the pressmen long continue, do

Resolve unanimously, That we lament the hostility which at present exists between the pressmen and their employers, of which we are likely to be the first sacrifices; and though we think every compositor ought, as far as possible, to refrain from working at press, or any other measure which may be, or even appear to be, hostile to either party, if necessity drives the compositor to press, we cannot think he ought to be held culpable by his fellow-workmen.

Resolved, That if the committee can devise any means to reconcile, or tending to reconcile, the differences between the pressmen and their employers, they will be entitled to the gratitude of the business at large.

Resolved unanimously, That the thanks of this meeting be given to the committee of master printers who met the deputation of compositors at the York Hotel, for their polite and gentlemanlike attention in arranging their adopted scale of regulated prices.

From reflections thrown out by an individual in the meeting on the conduct of the committee, and the committee having expressed their determination to retire on the next monthly night, it was

Resolved, That the present committee have uniformly acted for the welfare of the business, and have the confidence of its members; but their resignation at the present time, on account of the *calumnies* of an individual or individuals, would be inconsistent with their general good conduct.

In consequence of a dispute relative to the proceedings of the general meeting of Friday evening last, and the conduct of the chairman on that evening being called in question, it was

Resolved, That the thanks of this meeting be given to Mr Davenport, for his upright conduct on Friday evening last in the chair.

S. C. FAWCETT, *Chairman.*

The Scale of 1805 is an important document, since it was the basis of the Scale of 1810 which, with the amendments introduced in 1816, 1847, 1866 and 1872, remained in force until 1891. If we compare the Scale of 1805 with that of 1801, it will be seen that while no advance per thousand was given from english to brevier, specific charges were now agreed for minion, nonpareil and pearl, and the rates for various extras laid down and recognized by the employers.

[DOCUMENT XIV]

Regulations and Scale of Prices for Compositors' Work, as adjusted and agreed to in February 1805.

Article 1. All works in the English language, common matter, including English and Brevier, to be cast up, as settled in December 1800, at fivepence farthing per thousand; if in Minion (being a type not very prevalent), to be cast up at fivepence halfpenny; in Nonpareil, sixpence farthing; and Pearl, eightpence; heads and directions, or signature lines, included. A thick space to be considered an en in the width, and an en to be reckoned an em in the length of the page : and, where the number of letters amounts to five hundred, a thousand to be charged; if under five hundred, not to be reckoned : and if the calculation at per thousand shall not amount to an odd threepence, the odd pence to be suppressed in the price of the work; but where it amounts to or exceeds threepence, there shall be sixpence charged.

2. Works printed in Great Primer to be cast up as English; and all works in larger type than Great Primer as half English and half Great Primer.

3. All works in a foreign language, though common type, to be cast up at fivepence three farthings per thousand, including English and Long Primer; if in Bourgeois or Brevier, sixpence per thousand; Minion, sixpence farthing; Nonpareil, sevenpence; and Pearl, eightpence three farthings.

4. English dictionaries of every size to be paid fivepence three farthings per thousand. (In this article are not included gazetteers, geographical dictionaries, dictionaries of arts and sciences, and works of a similar description, except those attended with extra trouble beyond usual descriptive matter.) Dictionaries of two or more languages of every size to be paid sixpence per thousand. If smaller type than Brevier, to take the proportionate advance specified in article 1.

5. English grammars, spelling books, and works of those descriptions, in Brevier or larger type, to be cast up at fivepence halfpenny per thousand; if in two languages, or foreign language, to be cast up at fivepence three farthings per thousand.

6. Small sized folios, quartos, octavos, and works done in Great Primer or larger type (English language) which do not come to six shillings when cast up at the usual rate, to be paid as follows : English and larger type, not less than six shillings; Pica, seven shillings and sixpence : English twelves to be paid not less than nine shillings and sixpence; and Pica not less than ten shillings and sixpence per sheet.

7. Reviews, magazines, and works of a similar description consisting of various sized letter, if cast up to the different bodies, to be paid two shillings per sheet extra.

8. Pamphlets of five sheets and under, and parts of works done in different houses, amounting to not more than five sheets, to be paid one shilling per sheet extra; but, as it frequently occurs that works exceeding a Pamphlet are often nearly made up without a return of letter, all such works shall be considered as Pamphlets, and paid for as such.

9. Works done in sixteens, eighteens, twenty-fours, or thirty-twos, on Small Pica and upwards, to be paid one shilling and sixpence extra per sheet. If on Long Primer, or smaller type, one shilling per sheet extra. Forty-eights to be paid two shillings per sheet extra, and sixty-fours two shillings and sixpence per sheet extra.

10. Works requiring an alteration or alterations of margin, to be paid for each alteration one shilling to the pressmen if altered by them, and sixpence to the compositor as a compensation for making up the furniture; if altered by the compositor, then he is to be paid one shilling for the alteration, and the pressmen sixpence for the delay. *This article to be determined on solely at the option of the employer.*

11. Bottom notes consisting of twenty lines (or two notes, though not amounting to twenty lines), and not exceeding four pages, *in every ten sheets*, in quarto or octavo :—one page (or two notes, though not amounting to one page) and not exceeding six pages, in twelves :—two pages (or two notes, though not amounting to two pages) and not exceeding eight, in eighteens or above; to be paid one shilling per sheet :—but under the above proportion no charge to be made. Bottom notes consisting of ten lines (or two notes, though not amounting to ten lines) in a pamphlet of five sheets or under, and not exceeding two pages, to be paid one shilling per sheet extra. Quotations, mottos, contents to chapters, &c. in smaller type than the body, to be considered as notes. [Where the notes shall be in Nonpareil or Pearl, in twelves, the number of pages to be restricted to four; in eighteens, to five pages : and, if the number

of sheets or notes in a volume shall exceed what is stipulated, to take the proportionate advance.]

12. Side notes to folios and quartos not exceeding a broad quotation, if only chap. or date, and not exceeding three explanatory lines on an average in each page, to be paid one shilling per sheet; in octavo, if only chap. or date, and not exceeding three explanatory lines on an average in each page, one shilling and sixpence per sheet. Cut-in notes in smaller type than the body to be paid for in a similar manner.

Side and bottom notes to many, particularly historical and law works, if attended with more than ordinary trouble, to be settled between the employer and journeyman.

13. Greek, Hebrew, Saxon, &c. or any of the dead characters, if one word and not exceeding three lines in any one sheet, to be paid for that sheet one shilling extra : all above to be paid *ad valorem*.

14. Greek without accents to be paid eightpence per thousand; if with separate accents, ninepence half-penny per thousand : the asper not to be considered an accent.

15. Hebrew, Arabic, Syriac, &c. to be paid double :—Hebrew with points to be cast up as half body and half points doubled.

16. Music to be paid double the body of the sonnet type.

17. Index matter, though but one measure, to be paid one shilling per sheet extra.

18. Booksellers' catalogues to be cast up at sixpence per thousand, not including the numbering.

19. Em and en quadrats, or whatever is used at the beginning or end of lines, to be reckoned as an em in the width.

20. Night work to commence and be paid for, from eleven o'clock till one, one shilling; till two, one shilling and sixpence; and threepence per hour extra till six.—Morning work, commencing at four o'clock, to be paid one shilling extra.—Sunday work to be paid twopence per hour, provided it amount to not less than one shilling.

21. Jobs of one sheet or under (except auctioneers' catalogues and particulars) to be cast up at sixpence halfpenny per thousand; if done in smaller type than Brevier, to take the proportionate advance specified in article 1.

22. Jobs in foreign language of one sheet or under (except auctioneers' catalogues) to be cast up at sevenpence halfpenny per thousand; if done in smaller type than Brevier, to take the proportionate advance specified in article 1.

23. Where two pages only are imposed, either opposite to or at the back of each other, they shall be paid for as two pages; but if with an indorse, or any other kind of matter constituting a third, then to be paid as a sheet, if in folio; a half-sheet if in quarto, and so on.

24. Broadsides, such as leases, deeds, and charter parties, above the dimensions of crown, to be paid the double of common matter; on crown and under, to be paid one and one-half common matter.—The indorse to be paid one-fourth of the inside page.

25. All corrections to be paid sixpence per hour.

26. The imprint to be considered as two lines in the square of the page.

27. Different volumes of the same work to be paid for distinctly, *ad valorem*.

This scale to commence on Monday, the fourth day of March 1805.

Any disputes that may arise in future, we agree to refer to the decision of the committee of masters.

On behalf of the Masters.	*On behalf of the Compositors.*
(Signed) John Nichols	(Signed) Edward Davenport
Luke Hansard	James Atkinson
Thomas Bensley	Charles Fagan
George Woodfall	S. Charles Fawcett
Charles Baldwin	William Magrath
Thomas Gillet	Philemon Chalk
Dav. Nathan Shury	Charles Higly
William Ruffy	Henry Dench

CHAPTER III

PRESSMEN'S SCALES
1794–1816

The date of the first agreement between the masters and the pressmen is indicated in the *Report of the Special Committee of Masters Printers*, dated 23 February, 1805. This is printed on p. 99. The employers "first took into consideration the Pressmen's Scale of Prices, and proceeded to investigate and compare the different rises and regulations which have taken place from the year 1787, when the first scale was formed; and in order to have a comparative view of the whole, they caused to be drawn out, for their own information, on one sheet, the two Scales as proposed and acceded to in 1787 and 1794, and as advanced upon, at the Pressmen's own request, in December 1800, and then acceded to by the Masters on account of the unusually high price of bread and every necessary article of life : to which they also added the Scale of Prices now demanded by the Pressmen."

No copies of the presswork Scales of 1787 and 1794 have been found. A document relating to the advance of 1794 reads as follows:

[DOCUMENT XV]

The Committee of Master Printers, having taken into Consideration the Article of Broadsides (as referred to them by the last General Meeting of the Trade),

Resolved,

That it is their Opinion, that 8*d. per* 100 should be paid for any Number not exceeding 500; but, should the Number be more than 500, then the Whole to be paid for at the Rate of 1*s.* 4*d. per* Token, unless the Form should require three Pulls—in that Case, One-third more to be allowed. No Form to be deemed a Broadside that comes in at one Pull.

By order of the Committee,

T. BENSLEY, *Sec.*

York Hotel, October 20, 1794.

It will be noted that prices for presswork varied according to the number of impressions required. With two men at the press, one to ink and the other to pull the forme, a production of 250 sheets per hour, printed on one side, was expected.

"It is the general custom to print of every work what is termed an *even* number, either 250, 500, 750, 1,000, &c. These quantities are set out for the wetter in *tokens* : viz., for 250 [sheets] one token, containing 10 quires 18 sheets; for 500, two tokens, one 11 quires, and the other 10 quires and a half. . . ." [1]

Whereas in Moxon's time a *quire* was made up of twenty-four sheets, with ten quires to a token, at the beginning of the nineteenth century the token was equivalent to ten quires [and] eighteen sheets, or 258 sheets.[2] Thus, on 250 sheets "the [eight] overplus sheets are allowed for tympan sheets, register sheets, and other incidents, such as bad sheets, faults committed in beating [inking], pulling, bad register, &c. . . ."[3]

When the employers met on 24 December, 1800, "for the purpose of taking into further consideration the state of the trade, both in respect to their workmen and their employers,[4] a communication received from the pressmen was deliberated.

It was further stated, That the pressmen had solicited the masters to reconsider their former petition :—The same being done; and the like consideration influencing the meeting as had induced their giving a further advance to the compositors; it was

Resolved, That instead of the former regulations of the press-work scale, an advance of one halfpenny per hour, each column, be allowed upon all volumes begun after 1st of January 1801.

[DOCUMENT XVI]

SCHEDULE OF PRESSWORK PRICES, 1801

FOLIOS *On Medium or Demy*	1000 and up d.	750 and 500 d.	250 d.
Not exceeding 52 Pica ems, upon Small Pica and upwards	4½	5	5½
If on Long Primer, Bourgeois, or Brevier .	5	5½	6½
All above 52 Pica ems, upon Small Pica and upwards	5	5½	6½
If on Long Primer, Bourgeois, or Brevier .	5½	6	6½
Long Primer and upwards, on Copy or Crown .	4½	5	5½

[1] Stower, C., *The Printer's Grammar* (London, 1808), p. 403.
[2] According to Savage, *op. cit.*, the newspaper quire was reckoned at twenty-five sheets, for the convenience of the Stamp Office.
[3] Stower, *ibid*, p. 404. Further useful information is given in the evidence of George Woodfall before the Select Committee on Copyright Acts (London, 1818), p. 66.
[4] See p. 79.

	1000 and up	750 and 500	250
	d.	d.	d.

QUARTOS
On Medium or Demy

Not exceeding 40 Pica ems, upon Long Primer and upwards	$4\frac{1}{2}$	5	$5\frac{1}{2}$
If on Bourgeois or Brevier	5	5	$5\frac{1}{2}$
All above 40 Pica ems, and less than Long Primer	5	5	$6\frac{1}{2}$
If on Bourgeois or Brevier	$5\frac{1}{2}$	$5\frac{1}{2}$	$6\frac{1}{2}$
Brevier and upwards, on Copy or Crown . .	$4\frac{1}{2}$	5	$5\frac{1}{2}$

OCTAVOS
On Medium or Demy

Not exceeding 24 Pica ems, upon Small Pica and upwards	$4\frac{1}{2}$	5	$5\frac{1}{2}$
If on Long Primer, Bourgeois, or Brevier	$4\frac{1}{2}$	5	$6\frac{1}{2}$
All above 24 Pica ems, on Brevier or upwards .	5	$5\frac{1}{2}$	$6\frac{1}{2}$
If less than Brevier	$5\frac{1}{2}$	6	$7\frac{1}{2}$
Brevier and upwards, on Copy or Crown . .	$4\frac{1}{2}$	5	$5\frac{1}{2}$

TWELVES
On Medium or Demy

Not exceeding 21 Pica ems, upon Long Primer and upwards	$4\frac{1}{2}$	5	$6\frac{1}{2}$
If on Bourgeois or Brevier	5	$5\frac{1}{2}$	$6\frac{1}{2}$
All above 21 Pica ems, upon Long Primer and upwards	5	$6\frac{1}{2}$	$7\frac{1}{2}$
If on Bourgeois or Brevier	$5\frac{1}{2}$	$6\frac{1}{2}$	$7\frac{1}{2}$
Long Primer, Bourgeois, or Brevier, on Copy or Crown	$4\frac{1}{2}$	5	$6\frac{1}{2}$

EIGHTEENS

If not less than Small Pica	$4\frac{1}{2}$	5	$6\frac{1}{2}$
If on Long Primer, Bourgeois, or Brevier . .	5	$5\frac{1}{2}$	$6\frac{1}{2}$
If less than Brevier	$5\frac{1}{2}$	$6\frac{1}{2}$	$7\frac{1}{2}$

TWENTY-FOURS AND THIRTY-TWOS

If not less than Small Pica	5	$5\frac{1}{2}$	$6\frac{1}{2}$
If on Long Primer, Bourgeois, or Brevier . .	$5\frac{1}{2}$	$6\frac{1}{2}$	$7\frac{1}{2}$
If less than Brevier	6	$7\frac{1}{2}$	$8\frac{1}{2}$

POCKET BOOKS
Octavo

Post. or Crown, 21 Pica ems wide, 35 long . .	$4\frac{1}{2}$	$5\frac{1}{2}$	$6\frac{1}{2}$

7

	1000 and up *d.*	750 and 500 *d.*	250 *d.*
Twelves			
Pot, such as ladies and christian ladies table part, 6 mo. 35 Pica ems wide, 26 long . . .	4½	5½	6½
Pot, such as ladies and christian ladies miscellany part, 16 ditto wide, 26 long	4½	5½	6½
Copy, christian gentleman's, 20 wide, 35 long .	4½	5½	6½

SCHOOL BOOKS

Twelves

Copy or Crown, not exceeding 17 Pica ems wide, and 31 long, nor less than Brevier. . .	4½	5½	6½

Octavo

Copy or Crown, not exceeding 21 Pica ems wide, nor less than Long Primer . . .	4¼	5	5½

N.B. School books on Copy or Crown are defined to be Palairet's French Grammar, Chambaud, Salisbury Spelling Book, Fox's Lessons, Ward's Latin Grammar, and all of a similar description.

BILLS IN PARLIAMENT

	d.
From No. 4 inclusive to any No. under 100 . . .	4
If 100, and under 200 . .	4½
If 200 or 250	5
Above 250, and under 400 .	4
If 400 or 500	4½
Above 500, and under 700 .	4
If 700 or 750	4½
All above 750	4

ALMANACKS

	d.
Royal Broadsides . . .	6½
Demy ditto, size Wing or Cambridge	5
Goldsmith, Calendar form .	5
Do. Prog.	4½
Twelves Demy, 19 ems w. 34 long Calendar sheet .	5
Do. Prog.	4½
Do. Crown, size Rider . .	4½
Octavo foolscap, 20 ems w. 34 l. Calendar and Prog. .	4½

N.B. Side notes to be reckoned in the width, bottom notes not to be regarded.

Works on Royal paper to be paid one halfpenny per hour more than the above prices.

Ditto on Foolscap or Pot, not less number than 1000, and worked at one pull, 4*d.*

Ditto in square pages (like Entick's Dictionary), and works for the Public Offices to be paid one halfpenny per hour more than allowed by the scale of 1794.

Fine paper of the same size, if included within the token, not to be charged extra; but if of a larger size, then to be paid according to the scale.

Three or more proofs pulled at one time to be charged 3½*d.* per form; and if made ready to be charged as a token.

Cards, large or small, to be paid 6*d.* per 100.

₊ That jobs and other works not specified in the above scale shall bear an advance of one halfpenny per hour more than was paid previous to the above date.

When the compositors submitted their draft Scale to the employers in February 1805, the pressmen also made certain proposals to the masters. No copy of this document survives. The masters issued a circular with the heading *Printing Business. London: January, February and March* 1805, in which a summary was printed of all negotiations with compositors and pressmen. This is now reprinted, with the exception of those paragraphs concerning the compositors, which will be found on p. 88.

[DOCUMENT XVII]

PRINTING BUSINESS.

LONDON:

JANUARY, FEBRUARY, *and* MARCH 1805.

In the month of January, a Letter, accompanying a new and extensive Scale of Presswork Prices, was delivered generally to the Masters in the Printing Business, signed by their respective Workmen. This Scale was entitled "The Pressmen's Scale of Prices," and peremptorily fixed, by them, to take "place on Monday the 4th of February following."

In consequence of this request of the Pressmen, a Meeting of the Trade was held, at the York Hotel, on February the second; when a general answer was published, "that the Scale of 1800 was the only Scale which could be adhered to; but that any reasonable observations on particular parts of that Scale, would be taken into consideration."

The pressmen persisted in their demands, and a Special Committee of the employers held a number of meetings. Extracts from their final report follow :

REPORT

February 23, 1805.

The Special Committee of Master Printers, appointed by the General Meeting of the Trade, held at the York Hotel on Wednesday the 13th, entered with diffidence, on Friday the 15th instant, upon the arduous task assigned them, and continued their deliberations from day to day until this morning; and do now report as follows :—

They first took into consideration the Pressmen's Scale of Prices, and proceeded to investigate and compare the different rises and regulations which have taken place from the year 1787, when the first scale was formed; and, in order to have a comparative view of the whole, they caused to be drawn out, for their own information, on one sheet, the two Scales as proposed and acceded to in 1787 and 1794, and as advanced upon, at the Pressmen's own request, in December 1800, and then acceded to by the Masters on account of the unusually high price of bread and every necessary article of life : to which they also added the Scale of Prices as now demanded by the Pressmen.

On investigating this comprehensive view, they were struck with amazement at the enormous and disproportionate advance upon the current works; in which a submission to the Pressmen's demands would have involved every principle of justice and equity, and probably tended to the ultimate ruin of every branch of the literary concerns of the United Kingdom.

Their astonishment was most seriously increased by observing that, while the Pressmen's Scale speciously held out no advance on some works, yet, by narrowing the dimensions, they virtually enhanced every work, till finally the Elementary Books and more useful tracts of literature would take an advance of from thirty to forty per cent.

Notwithstanding these apparent obstacles, any reasonable hopes of accommodation with the Pressmen seemed to your Committee to be insurmountable; yet they were encouraged to enter upon the unpleasant and difficult task of endeavouring so to arrange the prices of those works which by imaginary construction might admit of some advance, hoping that the Pressmen would, from that principle of conciliation so generally manifested by their Masters, join with and afford your Committee the desirable opportunity of bringing matters to an amicable adjustment, by offering an amended Scale for your approbation. These hopes, however flattering, and these labours, great and difficult as they were, have proved of no avail;—for the Pressmen did not think proper to give the proposed Meeting.

[*Then was printed an account of the negotiations with the Compositors.*]

The attention of this Meeting must now be imperiously called to the state in which many Houses will shortly be placed through the violent and combined proceedings of the Pressmen, who (in consequence of the necessary and justifiable refusal on the part of the Masters to comply with their arbitrary, unjust, and unexplained demands), gave warning, at their respective houses, on Saturday the 9th of February; which warning will terminate this evening.[1]

To such a mischievous length has this Combination proceeded, that not only those Men who are paid by piece-work are quitting their situations, but they have driven those also who are upon established and stated weekly salaries, through intimidation, unwillingly to follow the same pernicious example of giving warning.

Such outrageous and unlawful combinations can only tend to a complete stop to all public and private business, to the probable ruin of some concerns, and to the utter impossibility of conducting the Printing

---

[1] There is no evidence to show why the pressmen were so very much more intransigent than the compositors.

Business upon any certain and equitable principles; to this may be added the ruin of many industrious families, and an additional charge on the Poor's Rates of several Parishes.

To compensate the Labourer for his extra labour, is a maxim ever to be held in remembrance; and that the measure of that compensation should be adequate to the times we live in, and suitable to the profession in view as it stood at any recent or given period, is also a maxim of which your Committee have never lost sight. But the Pressmen, not content with altering their own accepted Scale of Prices in 1800; not content with reverting back to an abandoned Scale of 1787 (the first ever introduced for Press-work in the Printing Business); not content with narrowing the dimensions of their work; not content with advancing per ems in such a ratio as to set at defiance all comparison and all fair rate of labour;—on the first refusal of compliance on the part of individual Masters to their exorbitant demands, in a body, and in one night, went to the length, in many instances, of deserting their employers.

Feeling, as your Committee could not but feel, for the situation of those houses thus involved, and for the innocent and industrious workman thus drawn into the vortex of this most alarming combination, they found great difficulty in applying or recommending any remedy to repel such an unjust aggression, without involving the innocent with the guilty.

As the deliberations were necessarily to be reported to the Trade at large, some easement was felt to the measures about to be proposed, from a confidence that they will meet that serious discussion their importance requires; and that, whatever may be the ultimate determination of this Meeting, it will be strictly adhered to.

Your Committee's proposal is therefore short, and simple in its application; but they do hope it will eventually convince the Pressmen of the error into which they have fallen, and prevent the necessity of adopting those lawful measures, which the Masters, in justice to the Public and themselves, might otherwise reluctantly be driven to pursue.

Their Proposal is :

That we solemnly and seriously pledge ourselves not to take into our employment, on any pretence or under any circumstances whatever, any Pressman who may apply at our respective offices for that purpose, till all those, who are now under the warning they themselves have given, do quietly and peaceably return to their respective situations to work upon the terms of the Scale as settled and mutually agreed upon in December 1800 : And that no Master will, on any pretence whatever, engage any one or more Pressmen upon any Stipendiary or Weekly Agreement, or otherwise, with a view to evade this necessary and justifiable Proposal, or do any act which may in anywise tend to violate or infringe upon the true intent and meaning thereof. And that no one will receive any work taken from any other Gentleman of the Trade pending the present dispute.

The Master Printers, at a Meeting held at Stationers' Hall on 25 February, 1805, resolved "That the Special Committee do inform the Booksellers of their Proceedings, and immediately furnish them with a copy of these Resolutions."

The booksellers met at Stationers' Hall a few days later, and passed the following resolutions :

[DOCUMENT XVIII]

At a General Meeting of the Booksellers of London and Westminster, held at Stationers' Hall, on Thursday, Feb. 28, 1805;

Mr. Davies in the Chair;

Resolved unanimously,

That the recent Conduct of the Master Printers, in firmly and unanimously resisting the exorbitant and unjustifiable Demands of their Journeymen, has entitled them to the Approbation and Gratitude of every Branch of the Community, and demands, in a particular Manner, the Support of this Meeting pledged to them most unequivocally.

That, as the most effectual Means of co-operating with the Master Printers on this Occasion, the Parties now present, following the Example set them by the various Departments of Public Business, the great Corporate Bodies, &c. do collectively and individually engage to suspend the Printing, both in Town and Country, of all Works, periodical or of any other description, belonging to any of them, till the Journeymen Printers see the Impropriety of their Conduct, and are satisfied to work according to the Scale of Prices mutually agreed upon between their Masters and themselves in December 1800, when the Price of Bread and other Necessaries of Life was much higher than at present, or till additional Apprentices, or other Persons, are rendered capable of executing the Business.

That these Resolutions, together with all the Signatures, be printed and distributed as extensively as possible amongst the Booksellers and Printers of the United Kingdom.

WILLIAM DAVIES, *Chairman.*

Resolved,

That the Thanks of this Meeting be given to the Chairman for his able and impartial Conduct in the Chair.

[Then follow 90 signatures]

Agreement had been reached with the compositors, but the pressmen still remained on strike. The master printers met on 9 March, 1805, and decided to retaliate by taking additional apprentices at press. The periodical publishers and booksellers supported the employers by agreeing to withhold sales and distribution of new works until such time as labour had been found.

[DOCUMENT XIX]

PRINTING BUSINESS

At a General Meeting of Master Printers, held at Stationers' Hall on Saturday the 9th of March, 1805, to take into Consideration the present Critical State of the Printing Business;

It appearing that upwards of 250 Pressmen had within the last fortnight voluntarily quitted their respective Houses of Employment, thereby leaving, on their part, all public and private Business nearly at a stand, and utterly preventing the possibility of completing in due time many important Papers actually wanted by Government, as well as the various Periodical Publications for the ensuing Month, to the great detriment of the Revenue as well as to the Proprietors of the said Works;—

Agreed Unanimously,

That an adequate Number of Apprentices be immediately taken, at the rate of not less than One to each Press throughout the Metropolis.

It also appearing, That from the arbitrary and unprincipled Influence of the Pressmen over many of the Apprentices, in different Houses, they are, through fear and intimidation, deterred from working in such a manner as their respective Masters may judge proper for the furthering of Business;

Agreed also Unanimously,

That Application be immediately made to Parliament, for leave to bring in a Bill to regulate the Printing Business, and for the better settling of Disputes between Masters and their Journeymen.

And it also appearing, That, under the cover of Friendly or Benefit Societies, Journeymen Printers, as well as various Bodies of Mechanics, and other Workmen, separately associate in their respective callings, not so much for granting Assistance to each other in case of Sickness, as for the too obvious purpose of compelling their Employers to raise their Wages;

Agreed Unanimously,

That the Special Committee do notice this matter to the Right Honourable Gentleman[1] by whom they have already been favoured with an interview on that Business.

It also further appearing, That it will be of the highest importance that the Resolution entered into by the Booksellers on the 28th of February, should be strictly adhered to;

Agreed Unanimously,

That a Deputation from the Special Committee do wait on the Booksellers, expressing the firm Determination of the Master Printers to avail themselves of the liberal Support pledged to them by the Booksellers most unequivocally.

(Signed) J. N I C H O L S, *Chairman.*

---

[1] Presumably a member of the Government.

[DOCUMENT XX]

MONTHLY PUBLICATIONS

Two Meetings having recently taken place; the first, of the Proprietors and Publishers of Reviews, Magazines, and other Periodical Publications; the other, of the Booksellers of London and Westminster; the Resolutions adopted at those Meetings are respectfully submitted to the Public.

Chapter Coffee-House, 18th March, 1805.

At a numerous Meeting of the Proprietors and Publishers of Reviews, Magazines, and other periodical Publications,

It being stated that the whole of the usual Works cannot be got ready for Publication by the First of next Month, on account of the Journeymen Pressmen refusing to Work at the regular Prices—

Resolved unanimously,

To postpone the Publication of every Work as above described, intended for next Month, till the Master Printers can conveniently complete all the usual Periodical Undertakings; and that no advantage shall be taken by publishing any Works that may happen to be finished, until a day of publication, to be determined at a future meeting.

J. NICHOLS, *Chairman.*

Stationers' Hall, 20th March, 1805.

At a very numerous Meeting of the Booksellers of London and Westminster—

In consequence of the Resolution of the Proprietors and Publishers of Reviews, Magazines, &c. and as the Parties now present are more strongly than ever impressed with the propriety of supporting the Master Printers in their resistance to the unreasonable demands of the Pressmen,

Resolved unanimously,

That, in due attention to the general Interests of the several Proprietors above mentioned, we whose Names are hereunto subscribed will defer the circulation of all Periodical Publications whatsoever, in conformity with the above Resolution; trusting that the Readers and Patrons of those Works will liberally and cheerfully submit to a delay, which has for its object the prevention of a very considerable increase in the Price of Books.

Resolved, That this Resolution (signed by the Chairman) be advertised, with that of the Proprietors and Publishers of the Periodical Publications, in the London Newspapers.

W. DAVIES, *Chairman.*

The pressmen did not receive the concessions they had demanded in 1805 and eventually returned to work. In December 1806, and again in April 1807, further petitions were addressed to the employers.

[DOCUMENT XXI]

Sir,

Early in December last, Copies of the inclosed, without the signatures, were delivered to Master Printers, individually, and a few to Mr. Bensley, as Secretary of the Society, requesting him to lay them before the Masters at their next meeting, to which we never received any kind of answer, nor could we account for the seeming neglect, until informed by a friend, that the Masters could not notice any anonymous address. This objection, we hope will now be considered as done away, and flatter ourselves we shall be made acquainted with your opinion at an early period.

You will please to observe the inclosed is the request of the BOOK-WORK PRESSMEN Only, and that there are not the names of any Pressmen employed upon Daily Newspapers, annexed to it.

Your's, with all due respect,

April 6, 1807.   The Pressmen, as signed in the inclosed.

The Journeymen Printers (Book-Work Pressmen) to their Employers

Gentlemen,

We humbly presume to submit this address to your candid and serious consideration, and sincerely hope it will meet with that kind of treatment which is the surest method of preserving that cordiality so essentially necessary between employers and their journeymen : we only request, that if any thing is advanced which may be deemed unreasonable, or if any of the circumstances noticed are not justifiable, that such, or any other error that may occur, may be candidly pointed out, as we do not profess to be equal to so arduous a task; we trust you will look upon them, not as being designed, but merely through inadequacy, as we hope our conduct will prove.

On comparing the scale published by the employers in 1787 with the one published by and with the sanction of the employers and journeymen in 1794, it will be found in the Folios that one halfpenny is granted for 750s and 500s, above 52 pica ems, on Longprimer, &c. and not any thing upon the other articles—In the Quartos of the same scales it will be found, there is one halfpenny granted upon the 750s and 500s for an additional 6 ems in width ! and not any thing upon the 250s ! and for Bourgeois &c. the scales are exactly the same, excepting the additional 6 ems ! ! Octavos will be found to correspond in proportion, gaining one halfpenny for 3 ems, upon Smallpica, &c. and giving 3 ems upon Longprimer, &c.—Twelves will be found to answer in like manner. Eighteens, Twenty-fours and Thirty-twos, no alteration whatever.— Now, Gentlemen, by a fair investigation of the above, we presume you will find that the scale of 1794, is not equal to the one of 1787.—We beg leave, likewise, to draw your attention to the vast increase of labor occasioned by the additional ems, as it thereby becomes necessary to lengthen the pages in proportion, for the sake of uniformity; and this proves still more severe upon pressmen as they become aged, and all works so enlarged as to render it very difficult for them to do it that justice expected. From what has been above premised, it will appear, that previous to 1787, there was not any kind of scale, that, in that year one was published by the employers, but it did not answer the intended purpose of preventing disputes, as several of them paid previously, and continued to pay various prices for the same sized works; in this state it remained until 1794, when the pressmen urged the necessity of a scale regulated and sanctioned by both parties, and a request made by the pressmen of an advance upon the 750s, 500s and 250s—A new scale was made and signed by employers and journeymen : but we humbly presume, the former part of this will shew how far the journeymen succeeded in obtaining any advance on the above numbers. Thus it will appear, we believe, that there is not any difference in the scales of 1787 and 1794, except what is by far overbalanced by the great increase of labor.

In 1800, the employers were solicited to advance one halfpenny upon all works (to take place January 1, 1801), and was granted, which, upon a fair calculation of twelve hours per day, may be estimated at three shillings per week : this we presume, must be allowed to be the only advance for nineteen years, which the scales will prove; how much longer we are not prepared to say exactly, but can answer for two years, making twenty one !

When the very great advance that has been made upon every necessary article of life, (which we deem useless to enumerate), is taken into consideration, and when you reflect how the disadvantages to the pressmen by paper being so much thinner than formerly, which consequently renders it more difficult to work; likewise, if a man has the misfortune to spoil any work, the very great advance upon paper requires a remuneration to cover the additional risk. You allow that a man ought to be able to earn thirty three shillings per week, to do so upon the scale, he must do twelve token per day, of work at five pence halfpenny per token : it is unnecessary to state the great difficulty of doing it, when it is considered how often there is occasion to wait for forms, revises &c. When we allude to the quantity of work, we mean to take the business generally, for it must be allowed there are times when work is very scarce, which we are happy to think is not the case at present.

When the above remarks are impartially considered, we flatter ourselves that you will be indulgent enough to look upon the following alterations as moderate, and the above statement as candid and just, and that you will consider them worthy your kind attention.

ALTERATIONS, &c.

That Folios, Quartos, Octavos and Twelves be advanced one halfpenny per hour, and one penny per hour upon all Forms containing more than twelve pages.—Jobs, &c. not mentioned in this, to be advanced according as they rank in the scale.

P.S. Your sentiments communicated, by Letter, addressed to the Pressmen, at the Rainbow, Fleet Street, will be duly attended to, and esteemed a particular favor,

By your very Humble Servants,
The Undersigned Pressmen.

[*Then follow 242 signatures*]

The General Meeting of the Master Printers of London and Westminster held at Stationers' Hall on 1 May, 1807, was mainly concerned with Apprentice questions, and the report of the proceedings will be found on p. 126. It was, however, resolved that the pressmen's demands should not be granted.

After the business had proceeded thus far—A Letter from the Pressmen, requesting an advance of Prices, was laid before the Meeting, which being read, and various observations made thereon, it was

Resolved unanimously,

That it appears to this Meeting that any alteration in the Scale for Presswork as amended in 1794, and further advanced upon in 1800, is wholly unnecessary.

Resolved unanimously,

That the foregoing Resolutions be printed and circulated through the Trade, together with the Signatures of every Gentleman present.

G. WOODFALL, *Chairman.*

The compositors memorialized their employers for a revision of the Scale of 1805 in April 1809, and in November negotiations were still proceeding. At this stage the pressmen also petitioned for an advance in prices. When the employers met on 15 January, 1810, to consider the compositors' demands, they resolved to consider the pressmen's application.

[DOCUMENT XXII]

Sir,

We, the Journeymen Pressmen, most respectfully solicit your Interest in our Behalf, in Consequence of the enormous Price of every necessary Article of Life, and the great Encrease upon House Rent.— We feel Ourselves under the disagreeable Necessity of soliciting you for an Advance on the present Scale of Prices, they being inadequate to the Support of our Families : We therefore trust you will make such Augmentation as you may think proper. We flatter ourselves you will not reject our Solicitation as your own Knowledge of the above Statement must convince you it is not erroneous.

We are,

SIR,

With due Respect,

Nov. 30, 1809. THE PRESSMEN.

The Master Printers met again on 8 February, 1810, and the pressmen were granted an advance of one halfpenny per token on all quantities and classes of work.

[DOCUMENT XXIII]

At a Special General Meeting of Master Printers, held this day, to take into consideration a Letter received from the Pressmen, requesting an Advance of Wages, and on other important business.[1]

Stationers' Hall, Feb. 8, 1810.

J. Nichols, Esq. in the Chair

Messrs.	Messrs.	Messrs.
Bensley	Gosnell	Law and Gilbert
Whittingham	Vogel and Schultz[e]	Hazard
Davison	Thompson	Swan and Son
Nichols and Son	Ryder and Weed[2]	Barfield
Woodfall	Mercier and Chewet	Corrall
Baldwin	Valpy	Stower
Taylor	Squire and Warwick	Bennett
Shury	Harding and Wright	Tyler
Bryer	Heseltine	J. & E. Hodgson[3]
M'Creery	Ellerton and Byworth	Downes
Brettell	Davidson	Diggens
Clowes	Darton and Harvey	Flint
Barnard	Delahoy, Jun.	Dean
Page	T. C. Hansard	Hamilton
Brooke	Harper and Co.	Sidney
Galabin and Marchant		

It was unanimously resolved,

I. That some advance be granted to the pressmen, on the scale of December 1800.

Resolved,

II. That the scale of 1787, which classed the different works, and formed columns of 1000 and upwards—750 and 500—and 250—whereby the prices to be paid were more easily and satisfactorily amended, and which was subsequently amended and advanced upon in 1794, and again advanced upon in December 1800—is a fair and equitable scale to act upon.

Resolved,

III. That an advance be made on the scale of December 1800 of one halfpenny per hour on each column throughout, upon all new works commencing after the 28th day of February, 1810.

Resolved unanimously,

IV. That it be distinctly understood that the advance shall not take place on any works but those which are paid by the scale.

---

[1] The " other important business " concerned the Compositors, and the latter half of Document XXIII is reprinted on p. 167.

[2] *i.e.* Rider and Weed.

[3] *i.e.* J. and E. Hodson.

When the employers met in January 1816, "for the purpose of taking into consideration the state of the Trade in general, in consequence of the alteration of the Times" they were successful in imposing reductions on both the compositors (see p. 189) and the pressmen. "In the Pressmen's Scale every token above the first four Tokens to be paid one half-penny per hour less than the Scale of 1810." There was no resistance from the men. With the conclusion of the Napoleonic War, the year before, the cost of living had fallen, and the employees were not disposed to dispute what was, in effect, an arbitrary decision on the part of the masters.

CHAPTER IV

THE APPRENTICESHIP QUESTION
1586–1818

The *Newe Decrees of the Starre Chamber for Orders in Printinge*
of 1586 appears to be the earliest document regulating the employment and indenture of apprentices in the printing trade. The
eighth paragraph stipulated

§8. *Item* that for the avoydinge of the excessyve number of Prynters
within this Realme, yt shall not be lawfull for any person beinge free of
the Cumpany of Staconers, or usinge the trade or mistery of pryntinge,
booksellinge, or bookebyndinge, to haue take and keepe hereafter at one
tyme any greater number of Apprentices than shalbe hereafter expressed,
that is to sayes Everye person that hath been or shalbe master or upper
warden of the Cumpanye whereof he is free to keepe three apprentices
at one tyme, and not aboue. And everye person that is or shalbe under
warden or of the Lyvery of the Cumpanye whereof he is free, to keepe
twoo Apprentices, and not aboue.

And euery person that is or shal be of the yomanry of the Cumpanye
whereof he is or shalbe free, to keepe one apprentice (yf he himself be
not a Journeyman) and not aboue.

Provyded alwayes that this ordinaunce shall not extend to the Quenes
Maiesties prynter for the tyme beinge for the service of her maiestie and
the Realmes. But that he be at liberty to keepe and haue apprentices to
the number of Sixe at one tyme.

The Regulations of 1587 and 1635, both reprinted in the Introduction, also contained clauses on the same subject. The Star
Chamber Decree of 1637 and the Licensing Act of 1662 permitted
Members of the Stationers' Company to take apprentices according to the scale set forth in paragraph 8 of the 1586 Decree
printed above. These two enactments limited the number of
master printers to twenty, but there was constant evasion of the
rule, and the prescribed maximum number was probably seldom
adhered to. Thus the quantity of apprentices indentured was also
excessive. According to *The Case of the Free Journeymen Printers*,[1]
published before 19 May, 1662, there were 150 apprentices in the
London printing offices, while Roger L'Estrange recorded the
same figure in his *Considerations and Proposals* (London, 1663).

[1] See footnotes on p. 33.

That the uncontrolled entry of juvenile labour into the trade was a matter of concern to the journeymen is shown in their petition of 23 October, 1666. This does not give the number of masters, but states that there were one hundred and forty workmen "who have served seven years to the art of printing, under lawful masters." Their Memorial was issued about six weeks after the Great Fire of London, at a time when the trade must have been in a great state of disorganization. Without doubt, much equipment had been destroyed, work was at a standstill, and unemployment growing. Hence their desire to eliminate irregular or boy labour. The Memorial follows:

[DOCUMENT XXIV]

*The Case and Proposals of the Free-Journeymen-Printers,
in and about London, humbly submitted to Consideration.*[1]

Whereas, there are at this present, in and about the city of London, to the number of a hundred and forty workmen printers, or thereabouts; who have served seven years to the art of printing, under lawful master printers, and are reduced to great necessity and temptations for want of lawful imployment, occasioned partly by the encroachment of forreigners, and partly by supernumerary apprentices and turn-overs,[2] which have increased the number almost to twice as many in the whole, as would be sufficient to discharge all the publick and lawful work of the kingdom. The work-men printers above mentioned, have unanimously agreed upon, and presumed humbly to offer these proposals following; always submitting themselves to what other course or provision soever authority shall judge more expedient for their redress.

1. That no forreigners (that is to say) such an one as hath not served seven years to the art of printing, under a lawful master printer, as an apprentice, may be entertained or imployed by any master printer for the time to come.

2. That a provision may be made to hinder the increase of apprentices, and a limitation appointed as to the number; the said restraint and limitation to take effect and commence from the present session of Parliament.

3. That no turn-overs be received by any master printer, but from a master printer; and that no master printer turning over any apprentice to another master printer, may be permitted to take any other apprentice in his place, till the full time of the said apprentice so turned over be expired : For otherwise, the restraint and limitation of apprentices will

[1] A broadside of this petition is in the British Museum, 816 m.12 (50). It is reprinted in L. Brentano's introduction to Smith, J. T., *English Guilds* (London, 1870), p. clxi *n*.

[2] TURN-OVER. An apprentice whose indentures are transferred to another master on the death, retirement or failure of his original one; also the action or process of turning over an apprentice (O.E.D.). The use of the word in the document printed above is the earliest example given.

be evaded, and the number supplyed by turn-overs; under which name is understood, such persons as being bound apprentices to one master, are turned over to serve the residue of the time with another.

Licensed October 23, 1666. Roger L'Estrange.

After the abolition of the Licensing Act in 1695, entry into the trade was unrestricted, provided that the apprenticeship regulations, as laid down by the Statute of Apprentices (5 Eliz. c. 4), and applying to all trades, were duly enforced.

"The customary enforcement of the apprenticeship prescribed by the Elizabethan statutes, and the high premiums often exacted from parents not belonging to the trade, long maintained a virtual monopoly of the better-paid handicrafts in the hands of an almost hereditary caste of 'tradesmen' in whose ranks the employers had for the most part served their apprenticeship."[1] Thus the old legislation, with its insistence on the full term of seven years' servitude and the strict formality of indentureship, tended to keep the supply of juvenile (and therefore cheap) labour within bounds.

But by the end of the eighteenth century the old apprenticeship regulations were becoming a dead letter and the Statute of Apprentices enforced with increasing laxity.

The expansion, both in the size and number of offices, of the London printing trade seemed, from the employers' point of view, to demand the sweeping away of all restrictions on the supply and employment of labour. The journeymen's reply to this diluting tendency was to attempt to insist on the enforcement of the apprenticeship laws. Only thus, in their opinion, would their trade be protected from the results of unrestricted competition among their employers.

The documents which follow show that the journeymen were not successful in their attempts at apprentice limitation and that the problem of a floating population of cheap juvenile labour was a vexing one. Reference should be made to the graph printed on p. 512.

In 1789, John Walter, founder, printer and proprietor of *The Times* newspaper, wrote:[2]—

. . . in May 1786, I perceived that the minds of the men employed in my Printing House had been poisoned by some of the enemies to the

---

[1] Webb, S. and B., *History of Trade Unionism* (1920 Edition), p. 45.

[2] The following extracts are taken from Walter, J., *An Address to the Public* (London, 1789), reprint of 1883, p. 34. See also *The History of "The Times"* (London, 1935), Vol. I, chap. I, and Appendix II, p. 468 *et seq.*

Logographic method of business, and that they threw every obstacle that they could in my way. I had originally taken several apprentices in order to counteract the general plan, against my undertaking; and on this additional proof of that necessity, I added one more, or what was tantamount, took a boy on what is termed in the trade, on *liking*.

The consequence of this was, a threatening letter from the Typographic delegates in the following words :

To Mr. Walter [from The Compositors]

Sir,

At a general Meeting of the Trade, the following Resolution was agreed to.

Resolved, That any Master not having a legal Right to the Printing business,[1] cannot be allowed apprentices, as it was the general opinion that no Journeymen, in such cases, can in future work with them.

By order of the Meeting,

W. LARMAN, *Sec.*

Friday Night, *At Hughes's.*
12th May.

The following was sent by the same party to the Pressmen. May 23, 1786.

Gentlemen,

At a general Meeting of the delegates, it was the opinion that, "If Mr. *Walter* does not give a positive answer respecting the lad being bound, the Pressmen shall only work the paper that is wet, and then leave the House, and give notice to the Secretary of the answer, in order to acquaint the Trade."

Walter threatened to prosecute if his pressmen combined against him, and opposition from them died down. Walter thereupon advertised for boys in the columns of his own paper, *The Times*. In his own words :

This advertisement I sent afterwards to the *Daily Advertiser*, but even they, impartial as the Proprietors hold themselves to be, returned my money, and refused to insert the article.

The cause of this, as I am informed, was owing to a resolution of the Journeymen Printers not to work in any house with those who had served an Apprenticeship to me; and, to further their plan, they subscribed a sum of money to take Counsel's opinion on the question. "Whether my patent could, according to law, allow as it did, a right to take any number of apprentices;" and for the further purpose of prosecuting me, if I took another Apprentice.

---

[1] Walter had never been apprenticed as a printer. He was a Freeman of the Mason's Company.

The compositors were summoned to hear Counsel's report, of which no details are available, at the Hole-in-the-Wall public house in Fleet Street on 1 October, 1787. It is interesting to note that the men were already meeting at this house at this date. The address appears as their headquarters on *The Rules and Orders to be observed by Members of the Phœnix*, dated 1792.[1]

It is possible that the document printed below may have some connection with the first John Walter's dispute with his journeymen, details of which follow. It was published and circulated by the journeymen.

[DOCUMENT XXV]

[RESOLUTION]

General Meeting held June 4, 1787

I. That no apprentice bound to learn the art and mystery of printing, after the 21st day of August, 1787, whose indenture, contract of servitude, or real apprenticeship, shall appear to have been for a less term than seven years, be from such servitude entitled to follow, or exercise the said profession.

II. That any person now employed, and working as a journeyman, who shall be discovered not to have fulfilled the term of his indenture, &c. and provided the term of such indenture be not expired when the discovery is made, shall be compelled to quit his employment, and notice thereof sent to the different printing offices, in order that the compositors may not be injured in their employment by such lawless intruders.

[The first of these resolutions is founded on the Act of 5 Eliz. cap. 5; the second on that of 6 Geo. III. cap. 25—Lenity having, however, for a long time defeated the salutary intent of these statutes, and accumulated much injury to the profession, the printers of London are determined to give every efficacy in their power to the law, and enforce the penalties on its violators : the better to facilitate which, and guard against the possibility of every future infringement, the following resolution was also unanimously passed.]

III. That the compositors in every printing office, where they have any doubt, or ground of suspicion, examine the indenture or other right of persons on their first coming to work; strictly, however, governing their conduct by the spirit of the foregoing resolutions, in order that no individual, who does not come within their obvious meaning and import, may be idly abused, or wantonly thrown out of employment; but nevertheless, any person so suspected, obstinately refusing to give the required information, shall be considered as without claim to the rights and privileges of a journeyman.

Further adopted May 2, 1796.

In 1793 the newspaper proprietors had been obliged, under the threat of a general strike, to grant a considerable advance in prices

See p. 84*n*.

to the compositors employed by them. "The Employers conceiving that they had been *forced* to accede to the rise in the month of April preceding, appeared determined to take advantage of the men, by paying themselves for their defeat by the difference of prices between apprentices and journeymen." The proprietors' attempt to displace men by boy labour was immediately resisted by the news compositors. A printed protest, dated 1 October, 1793, with five propositions subjoined, was circulated among both the book and news compositors, who were invited to express their agreement. Extracts from the circular and the text of the propositions will be found in the *Report of a Committee appointed to draw up a statement of the regular mode of working on Newspapers* (1820) which is reprinted in this work.[1]

As a result of the compositors' representations, the principle that apprentices should not be employed on daily newspapers appears to have been accepted by the majority of employers.

The system [of employing apprentices], however, commenced in the month of October [1793], upon one Journal, which lasted about five years —and upon another which continued nearly eleven years; but in the end you were successful; and men were again engaged upon these Journals on a fair principle. The fate of some who had worked with the boys should have served as a warning—they were neglected, despised, and ultimately driven from the profession.[2]

The above passage makes it possible to fix the date of publication of three undated documents in the St. Bride collection.

1. A handbill entitled *Typographical Black List No. 1*, arraigning one "Michael Alder . . . who has, in a manner which must ever reflect disgrace on his name, accepted a situation on the *Morning Chronicle*, a newspaper once remarkable for the respectability of its Compositors . . ."

2. A foolscap folio broadside listing the "Beings who are now acting as compositors on the *Morning Chronicle*."

3. A circular from the late companionship of the *Morning Chronicle*, stating that the Printer had insisted upon the introduction of an apprentice, and now reprinted.

[DOCUMENT XXVI]

[1793]

Gentlemen,

An Advertisement having this Day appeared in the *Morning Chronicle*, for Compositors on that Paper.—It is deemed necessary to state the Reasons

---

[1] p. 372 *et seq.*   [2] Ibid.

why such Advertisement has appeared; and the present Companionship quit their Situation.

An attempt to force an Apprentice on the Paper, who cannot be an equal Companion, contrary to every principle of Justice, and to the injury of the Business, and a refusal from the Companionship to admit him, has induced the Printer of the Paper above-mentioned, to give a general *Warning* (collectively) to the Companionship, under the futile Idea of their not having begun Business at a proper Hour; though he has since declared, they fully accomplished the Quantity of Matter required within the proper Time, and has since expressed a Wish to retract that *Warning:* yet he still, to use his own Words "persists in his design of taking an Apprentice, and if they refuse to teach him, he must either do it himself, or endeavour to find a set of Men that will." He has farther demanded as a *matter of Right*, (not request) that should the Paper not go to Press before Six o'Clock in the Morning, the Companionship shall commence Business at the usual Time, contrary to a previous public Agreement.

This concise Statement is laid before you for Consideration, and to guard you against any Misrepresentation that may take place; and to evince to you that that Companionship have acted with the general Opinion of the Trade, not doubting but it will meet with your hearty support.

A few weeks later the following was circulated by the compositors' committee to men employed in the general trade:—

[DOCUMENT XXVII]

To Compositors

Hole-in-the-Wall, Fleet Street, Nov. 24, 1794.

Gentlemen,

As no redress could be obtained by the petition to the Company of Stationers,[1] to stop the increase of apprentices, it was unanimously resolved, at a general delegated meeting, held the 3d of November, "That in future any youth being introduced into a printing office as an apprentice, the delegate of such office, or any other gentleman working therein, shall immediately procure from the boy a knowledge of his parents or friends that put him out, that they may, either personally or by letter, present them with the address to parents, and guardians, (which may be had any Monday evening of the committee at the Hole-in-the-Wall) and inform them of the present ruinous state of the trade, in consequence of being overstocked with apprentices."

Several gentlemen being very backward in their subscriptions to the fund, are earnestly intreated to make good their deficiencies, by any sum per week they may please to give, in order to prevent farther contributions from the trade in general.

----

[1] The Company's archives are not at present available for inspection and the Petition, if it survives, cannot therefore be reproduced.

Although the Union Society was successful in negotiating the terms of the Scale of 1805, the limitation of apprentices remained beyond its powers. Reference to the graph printed on p. 512 shows how great was the increase in boy labour in the years 1800–1810. A circular headed *To Parents and Guardians* was circulated by the journeymen in 1805. Its object was to dissuade the entry of further boys into an already overcrowded trade.

[DOCUMENT XXVIII]

TO
PARENTS and GUARDIANS.

That it is the duty of every Parent and Guardian to carefully consider the provision he hopes to make for those tender objects, whom Nature or Law has put under their care, we deem it absolutely necessary to inform them of the motives, which actuate the Master Printers in their present Proceedings; that they may not be seduced by *delusive professions* to destroy the *future welfare* of those who are under their *protection* by introducing them into a Business, which is threatened with a redundancy of Journeymen; and which will inevitably involve in poverty all those who augment their number! We beg leave to inform the candid Public, that there are at this time about *Two Hundred Pressmen* out of work, owing to a trifling advance which they solicited (on account of the pressure of the times) and which has been denied them.[1] A Bill has since been presented to the Legislature, and we are content to wait the result of that august Assembly. We, therefore, returned to our different Employers, preferred our services, which was refused, unless we would sign a paper, the purport of which we considered as signing away all rights to a Business which we have gained by a servitude of seven years, and premiums to different amounts. Judge what our feelings must be; it is not only a sacrifice of seven years of hard labour, but a sacrifice for life, provided the Master Printers persevere in their unjust, not only unjust, but we will say, cruel proceedings.

We beg leave to inform the Public one of the Resolutions entered into by the Masters is, that they will put one Apprentice to every Journeyman; by that means one half of the business will be completely thrown out of work, their Trade entirely lost, and themselves, together with the unhappy youths, reduced to beggary ! ! !

The Journeymen Printers having thus impartially stated their case for Public consideration, leave it to be reflected upon with that candour and liberality for which the present æra is so justly celebrated.

The circulars written under the pseudonyms "Miles's Boy," "A Compositor," and "A Terrier," published in 1806 and the

[1] See p. 103.

following year, provide some information on the changing conditions of apprenticeship. In the printing trade, the time-honoured system had broken down. The apprentice, bound for seven years, living in his master's house, and receiving no wages, was replaced by the out-door apprentice, who was paid, to a greater or lesser degree, for his labour, and not subject to strict discipline.

The letters of "Miles's Boy" to his friend Chms [Chims?], although containing much scurrility and nonsense, provide an interesting account of the labour problems of the time. The "Miles's Boy" letters and those from "A Compositor" were printed in three columns on broadsides ranging from crown folio to royal quarto in size. A single manifesto signed "A Terrier" was arranged in single column on a foolscap folio sheet. These formats were simple enough to produce and convenient for distribution. It is evident that these compositions were sold for the benefit of their authors, as well as for the entertainment or edification of the trade. "Miles's Boy" mentions that his sheet could be purchased for twopence.

Nine different examples of these ephemera survive.[1] The first three letters of "Miles's Boy" are dated from Monument Yard, 4, 18 August, 15 September, 1806. They drew replies, sober and well-reasoned, from "A Compositor" on 18 October and 17 November. "Miles's Boy" replied to his critic on 21 December. The last of the series, from the pen of "A Terrier" was published on 9 March, 1807. There is also an undated communication from "Miles's Boy," who had changed his address from Monument Yard to Liberty Hall. Finally there is a sixteen-page 12mo pamphlet, undated, with the title *No. 1 of a Black List, or Typographical Characteristics: with a Variety of Anecdotes. . . . by Myles's Boy. Printed for, and may be had of Ralpho.*

The following extracts are from the first three letters of "Miles's Boy" and the first of the two communications signed "A Compositor":—

[DOCUMENT XXIX]

(4 August.) Your note of last August gave me great satisfaction, wherein you informed me that the *Chronicle* was cleared of the obstacles that had clogged your entrance for some years. There I was out-generalled, about the year 1793, and have never lost sight of the disgrace which overwhelmed me—Oh! what a falling off, in a few years, is there in the spirit of men! When that paper was shut from every *good man*, none but the veriest wretches from book-house rat-holes were found to fill up the vacancies.[2]

---

[1] St. Bride collection.   [2] See p. 385.

It was to rouse the *sleeping slave* that I have been so often induced to come forward. A.B. once sent me to Strahan's, which I then found a shocking receptacle of *blacks*[1] and *boys*, and as it *was*, so it *is*, and ever will *continue*. I mean to take a peep into some of these *slaughter houses*, such as Flint's, Dewick's, Savage's, Sidney's, Cox and Baylis's,* Hansard's, &c. &c. of which I shall give you an account in my next, together with some anecdotes of those concerned in the bringing up, viz. *Jack Heath*, *Jack Poplet*, Miserable *Phillips*, *Dick Reeves*, Gloucester *Leonard*, Bill Haydon, Purser *Morris*, (worth about 12s., receives 33s. per week) and *William BAYES*, from Cambridge, well known in a Certain List, now before me, and a *Handbill*, which was issued, a few years ago, from the appartments he then occupied, which stated Mr. B. as *a tall, thin, black man*, &c. &c. who had thinned *his lodgings*.

* Printers to the Hon. East India Company !—*Thirty-two Apprentices!!*—Surely they recruit for the Company; or how can Mr. B. justify himself, as a freeman of London, for having, in violation of his oath, taken so many boys by *foreign indentures?* It would be a good hint to the *Society for the Suppression of Vice*, that they might, instead of hunting lollypop sellers on a Sunday morning, do their country a service, by preventing any master from having *Out-Door Apprentices*, who, finding no check, are hurried into every vice, and end their lives, 'e'en in their teens,' on the gallows. *Oh, Billy Vizetelly, Oh !!!* Mr. B. is one of the York Council ![2]—*what a farce!*

.   .   .   .

(18 August). I promised you, in my last, that I would take a view of those places which have become notorious receptacles for boys, and that I would also give you an account of some gentlemen whose names I intended should grace a *list*, which, when printed in *black letter*, always reflects a degree of *credit* on those so *honoured*.

.   .   .   .

You know that a great number of boys, friend Chms, were taken to *case* soon after the York Treaty[3] was signed, and that though your Society was thereby acknowledged, (how, indeed could it be otherwise, after they had called upon you to do them hommage, and promising you justice in all their proceedings?) yet, in some places, your members were threatened with their discharge the first opportunity. (I am not positive that it was by Mr. *Baylis*). Did they deem you as heretics, with whom it was dangerous to keep their faith?—It is contrary to the spirit of Englishmen to consider a man guilty till he has been tried; yet these *merciful judges* have written horse[4] upon punishment, for fear that you, by any subsequent act, should require its administration.

Trusting to the honour alone of this tribunal, did you demand an *equality* of power with it in giving judgment?—Have you since the signing of the treaty, given the least cause of complaint by any act of rebellion? —Have you not lately again acknowledged its supremacy by a second

---

[1] The reference is probably to "black-tailed *rats*." "RAT. A compositor or pressman, who executes work at less than the regular prices. . . ." Savage, *op. cit.*

[2] The Master Printers met at the York Hotel.

[3] The Scale of 1805, negotiated at the York Hotel.

[4] See on p. 81*n*.

choice of representatives?—You have; and after having done so, I say it is vexatious on the part of the masters (some only, I mean, though the rest should not sanction it) to introduce so many boys into their houses. One who was chosen on their committee, directly after an exchange of signatures had taken place, has *Thirty-two ! ! !* Another has a round dozen, and this man was formerly on the journeyman's committee, when they remonstrated with their employers on the injury the business sustained by a disproportionate increase of apprentices—Mr. *Sidney* must recollect employing me as a messenger *"To Parents and Guardians."*[1] Mr. *Wright* also has ten or a dozen. Mr. *Flint* has sixteen or seventeen very nice *chickens*; another, Mr. *Mac-something*, whose olfactory nerves were so offended by *Hawley's* breach of decency, has above his share. *Dewick* has too many. At *Strahan's* it must be expected; apprentices are taken there, as *current cash*, or, according to *masonic rule*, to bring things upon the *square*.[2] The elder Mr. *Hansard*[3] has his share of lambs, as they are called, (I suppose of Colonel Kirk's kind) of which a specimen may be seen, every Monday, at the *Robin*. Mr. *Luke* has seven or eight, which, added to the old gentleman's[4] *flock*, have become too formidable for their keepers. They perfectly understand each other, in *lane* or *fields*,[5] and have already, at one year's keeping, played such tricks that any one may be convinced of the consequences. Mr. *Thomas* is commencing on a grand scale, (having seven or eight) with the able assistance of Mr. *Bayes:* but I'll not *overlook* him.

You know very well, friend Chms, the effects that may be expected to result from this system of crowding a number of low-bred boys together, making them their own masters before reason has taken its seat, and given them opportunities, not having them under their own roof, of running down the stream of vice at a pretty rate indeed ! ! Many of these, besides their being kept out of their master's house, receiving wages, contrary to law, are also, unlawfully, bound for a less term than seven years. (I shall furnish you with their names). How much credit is not due to the parties concerned in this *kidnapping* business ?

Recollect, friend Chms, how Kennington Common and the Old Bailey were adorned, during a former rage for boys, with them for several sessions. What assistance did not the system afford (about fifteen years since) to the East-Indian army and to his Majesty's Colony of New South Wales ?—How great a number ran or were sent to sea ?—It were needless to tell *you*, that in the short space of two years, *Thirty Out-door Apprentices to Printers* received their sentences for crimes committed in London and Surry ! ! !—I could give you their names, but that would hurt the feelings of their relatives. You may expect, however you may lament it, that, in the way in which they are now taken, as many more, in the same space of time, will be registered in the judge's calendar. They begin just as their pre-

---

[1] This circular is printed on p. 117.

[2] William Preston, Strahan's partner, was a prominent Freemason.

[3] T. C. Hansard, eldest son of Luke Hansard (1752-1828).

[4] The "old gentleman" was Luke Hansard. Mr. Luke was Luke Graves Hansard, younger brother of T. C. Hansard.

[5] The family had two offices. One was in Parker's Lane, off Drury Lane, and another at Great Turnstile, Lincoln's Inn Fields. T. C. Hansard had his own business, at that time at Peterborough Court.

decessors did—*Oroonoko tobacco, girls,* and *cutters*—and the general conversation, at present, of these journey-boys is of nothing but Hansard's *lambs* and their two cutters, one for each house, which neither the floggings of *Governor Wall,* nor the preachings of St. Luke,[1] will be able to do away; indeed they feel their own consequence so much, that one party tossed the O. in a blanket,[2] and the other promised them assistance in any way, by the mouth of their coxswain, who can boast a bringing up by the notorious *Neddy Ashford.*

(September 15). *Ralph,*[3] who you know very well, is a good fellow; he does every thing in his power to please me, and though he is very old must not be despised. He has been constantly employed for the last month either in collecting anecdotes about the town, or answering messages at my door, for I assure you that I have been tormented by visitors in Monument Yard since you received my first letter, but I am determined to be seen by no one for the future.

By skilful management, Ralph has found his way into most of the *Ratteries* about town, and has hitherto escaped very well, notwithstanding the threatenings held out of *capping,*[4] &c.; he takes a peep at Mr. Bayes in the morning, visits Mr. Heath in the forenoon, and just before dinner calls at Mr. Flint's.

I told you in my second letter the consequences to be expected from such numbers of lads being crowded together, of the truth of which we have almost daily proofs. Wouldst believe, friend Chms, that on August 26, the young gentlemen of *St. Luke's* were pulled up (their own expression) to a police office, to answer a complaint for an assault on the pot-girl. . . . All this they did, and *only* paid 11s. each for their *lark,* and had an admonition from the magistrate to amend their conduct for the future. This had as much effect as would singing psalms to a dead horse, for the same gentlemen, on Sept. 1, attempted to smother a poor journeyman *pig*[5] in the dust-hole, and they certainly would have taken his life

---

[1] St. Luke, *i.e.* Luke Hansard senr. He was apt to combine piety with priggishness, hence the nickname.   [2] O., *i.e.* Overseer.

[3] "Every chapel is haunted by a spirit, called Ralph. When any man resists the decision of the chapel, and it is determined to enforce it, Ralph, or the spirit, is said to walk; and whatever mischief is done to the resisting party to enforce submission, which is always performed secretly, is invariably imputed to Ralph, or the spirit." Savage, W., *op. cit.* See also p. 28, *Experiences of Benjamin Franklin.*

[4] "C A P P I N G   A   M A N. Wrapping one of the blankets with which the pelt balls are capped about a man's head, and tying it round his neck. This most filthy and disgusting punishment is very rarely inflicted in a press room; yet I have read an account of a trial at the Old Bailey for an assault, in which this act was the ground of offence." Savage, W., *op. cit..* When the ink balls were wrapped up at night, after the day's work, they were said to be "capped."

[5] "P I G. Pressmen are called pigs by compositors, sometimes by way of sport, and sometimes by way of imitation; in the same way the press room is called a pigstye. When the compositors wish to teaze them, they will grunt when a pressman goes into the composing room. In Moxon's time they were called Horses." Savage, W., *op. cit.*

had not the compositors interfered, which occasioned a battle-royal— *boys* and *men*—and the combatants were only separated by sending an express for the elder Mr. Hansard, who, upon his arrival, read the Riot Act, and put the aggressors to flight.

The two replies of "A Compositor" to "Miles's Boy" were more serious in tone and content. His observations add little to our knowledge of events, but the following paragraph is of some interest :

What a gloomy prospect has a compositor before him by finding those introduced around him who, from their numbers, will, in three years, deprive him of half his loaf, and running the risk of losing the other half by stereotype printing, which will certainly engross our larger and popular works, (vide Andrew Wilson's advertisement) and leave us nothing but the floating pamphlets of the day.[1]

The worst fears of "A Compositor" were not immediately to be realised. Indeed, many years were to pass before the majority of standard works were stereotyped. That the London compositors were hostile to the new process can easily be understood, since by its use reprints would not necessitate resetting in type. It must be added that, before 1816, when a reduction was imposed by the masters, reprint copy was considered "fat" by the compositors.

The agenda for discussion for a compositors' meeting to be held on 4 February, 1807, shows that the limitation of apprentices was still a pressing problem to which no solution had been found.

[DOCUMENT XXX]

Union Society

Agreeably to Art. 4, of Code of Laws,[2] you are requested to attend a General Meeting, which will be held on Wednesday next, Feb. 4, 1807, at the Hole-in-the-Wall, Fleet-Street.

Signed by Order,

E. DAVENPORT, *Sec.*

---

[1] A process of stereotyping from plaster-of-paris moulds had lately been perfected by Andrew Wilson, "a printer of respectability in London," in conjunction with Lord Stanhope. The latter had already been instructed in the practical side of the business by Tilloch and Foulis of Glasgow, who had rediscovered the long-forgotten technique of William Ged. For an account of Ged's life and works, see Nichols, John, *Biographical Memoirs of William Ged* (London, 1781). Later developments, historical and technical, are fully described in Hansard, T. C., *op. cit.* Wilson's claims are here subjected to severe criticism.

[2] No copy of this Code of Laws is known.

Chair to be taken at half past eight precisely.

The following resolutions were submitted by a member to the consideration of the society on the last meeting night (Jan. 19) and, on motion, were ordered to be printed and circulated for the consideration of the General Meeting.

So important a subject it is hoped will urge every man to do his duty, and come prepared for the discussion.

Resolved,

I. That no person pretending to have a right to follow the printing business, from having been employed seven years unmolested, shall have the right thereby acquired admitted, unless he produce satisfactory proof of such occupation.

II. That no person whose indenture is ante-dated, or collusively executed, through interest or connexion, previous to the commencement of actual servitude, shall, at the expiration of such covert indenture or covenant, be admitted to possess a right to follow the printing business.

III. That no person purchasing his time, or making other considerations for the same, unless he continue in the service of the master he originally contracted with for the term of such indenture, shall be considered as having a legal right to follow the business.

IV. That no overseer, journeyman, or reader, be allowed to take an apprentice either from his employer, or any person unconnected with the business, except in the case of a father taking his own son; but no man to have more than one son as an apprentice at the same time.

V. That no journeyman be allowed to bring up a son-in-law, as his apprentice, on any account whatever.

VI. That every journeyman employed in any house where a poundage, or other apprentice, is taken as a turn-over, do consider it his duty to enforce the necessity of such an apprentice entering on his second contract within one month after his introduction; as the particular means not only of preventing illegal apprenticeships, but of any encouragement being given to run-away apprentices.

VII. That no journeyman shall take a boy (not even his own son) to work or assist, nor shall any journeyman work or assist with an apprentice, in any manner whatever, on any of the morning or evening papers.

VIII. That no apprentice from the country shall be admitted to work in town, unless he be fairly acquitted by his country master, and regularly turned over to one in London.

IX. Having ascertained that the practice of binding boys to the printing business for a less term than seven years has become common in the country parts of the kingdom, contrary to, and in defiance of, the laws, to the great detriment of both masters and journeymen in the metropolis, and to the injury of the lads so taken, it is absolutely necessary that every well-wisher to the profession should oppose, at all hazards, such an innovation; that it therefore becomes the bounden duty of every man, or set of men, to demand the production of the indenture, or other document, of any person engaged to work with him or them, in order to a strict investigation of its fairness, as well as his right to occupy the station of a journeyman; and if such indenture, or document, should not prove satisfactory to such man, or set of men, he or they shall immediately refer the said indenture, or document, with a statement of attendant circumstances, to the committee, who are authorised to give such advice, and take such measures as the case may require. Should the disputed party not be able to prove the legality of his claim, by a seven years' servitude, he must be regulated, if he stops in London, by resolutions 6 and 8.

X. That it is the duty of every man to oppose the introduction of persons into the profession who are not intended to fulfil the legal term of apprenticeship, but who are brought in only with the view of procuring such an insight as may enable them to earn their subsistence, thereby depriving the fair journeyman of his chance of employ in a business to which he has devoted seven years of his youth.

XI. That owing to the alarming increase of apprentices, the following be adopted as a fair proportion of boys to men employed, viz. From one man to five men, one boy—from five to nine men, two boys—from nine to fourteen men, three boys—from fourteen to twenty men, four boys, and upwards in the same proportion; and that, in consequence of the injury the business has received from the great increase of apprentices, any journeyman, from this date, who shall undertake to bring up a boy where the above proportion is overcharged, shall be considered inimical to the profession, and an enemy to its interests.

The eleventh resolution on the agenda of the compositors' meeting called for the limitation of apprentices according to the number of · men employed in any office. The employers met at Millington's Hotel on 9 March, and put forward propositions which would immediately defeat any such measure.

[DOCUMENT XXXI]

It appearing to this meeting that there is a scarcity of compositors in the Trade, arising from the great increase of business, from periodical publications, book work, and newspapers. And it appearing to this meeting that there are nearly three hundred compositors engaged on newspapers alone, not one of them being an apprentice,

Resolved unanimously,

That taking into consideration the present state of the Trade, we do individually agree to take as speedily as possible, such number of apprentices at case as may be deemed advisable, in the present exigency, to remedy the evil, and suitable to our individual situations.

Resolved unanimously,

That every Gentleman present do give to the Committee a list of the apprentices at case he now has, and that at the expiration of two months he do give in another list, containing the number of apprentices at case then in his office, by which means the Committee may ascertain what increase has taken place in the Trade, since the present ninth of March.

Resolved unanimously,

That we will not engage any compositor without enquiry of his last employer, personally if in Town, or by Letter if from the country.

Resolved,

That a deputation from this meeting be appointed to wait on the most respectable Master Printers not present at this meeting, to obtain, if possible, their sanction to the foregoing resolutions.

The booksellers met at Stationers' Hall on 28 April, 1807, and signified their approval of the measures taken by the master printers. It is probable that copies of the resolutions passed at the master printers' meeting of 9 March, had been circulated among them. The master printers met again on 1 May. The report of booksellers' proceedings follows :

[DOCUMENT XXXII]

At a General Meeting of the Booksellers of London and Westminster, held at Stationers' Hall, on Tuesday, April 28, 1807; Mr. Davies in the Chair.

Resolved unanimously.

That the Thanks of this Meeting be expressed in the strongest manner to the Master Printers, for the Communication from their Committee, which has this day been read from the Chair; the whole tenor whereof clearly evinces that that very respectable body, whilst disdaining the influence of a narrow and shortsighted policy, which would prefer present and individual advantage to permanent and general good, and scorning to compromise their lasting respectability and independence for the indulgence of temporary ease and quiet, are also firm friends to the best interests of Literature.

That no apprehension of the possibility of temporary inconvenience shall prevent this Meeting from cheerfully and steadily co-operating with the Master Printers at the present juncture.

That this Meeting is convinced, by the substantial reasons given in the written Statement of the Master Printers, of the extreme inadequacy of the present number of Journeymen Printers to the Work to be executed; and therefore, in order to encourage a further increase of Apprentices throughout the Printing Business, so that there may always be a sufficient number of capable persons educated thereto, this Meeting pledges itself collectively and individually, to give every preference in their power, and every means of facilitating the Education of Apprentices, to those Master Printers who are most attentive to so salutary a measure.

That, in order to carry into effect the foregoing Resolution, this Meeting do request the Master Printers to circulate, monthly or quarterly, as long as the same may appear advantageous, and amongst such Booksellers as they may think proper, an authenticated account of the number of Apprentices in each of the Printing Offices in London and Westminster.

That this Meeting will heartily co-operate with the Master Printers in an Application to Parliament, or in any other legal way, to put a stop to the present unwarrantable combinations amongst the Journeymen.

That these Resolutions, together with all the Signatures, be printed, and distributed amongst the Master Printers of London and Westminster.

WILLIAM DAVIES, *Chairman.*

Resolved,

That the Thanks of the Meeting be given to the Chairman, for his conduct in the Chair, and attention to the business of the Meeting.

[*Then follow* 68 *signatures*]

[DOCUMENT XXXIII]

At a General Meeting of the Master Printers of London and Westminster, held at Stationers' Hall, on Friday, May 1, 1807; to take into consideration the present state of the trade :

Mr. Woodfall in the Chair ;

A Report of the Committee on the comparative situation of the Printing Business since 1770,[1] and the Address to the Booksellers, with their Resolutions in consequence, being read,

Resolved unanimously,

That the Printing Business has, for the last thirty years and upwards, been progressively increasing; and that there is not an adequate number of hands either in, or training up to, the business, to do the work required.

Resolved unanimously,

That it appears, from the unlawful and dictatorial combinations of the Compositors, that not only the Bookselling Trade, and Authors and Literature in general, but the Master Printers in particular, have suffered great inconvenience, and considerable loss and detriment; and that the prosperity of the Printing Business is thereby in imminent danger.

Resolved unanimously,

That it also appears that the Compositors have within the last four months in part, and in some instances entirely, left their Masters, at a time when there has been abundance of work and an evident scarcity of hands; thereby leaving such Masters with scanty, or without any, means of carrying on their business, except by the introduction of APPRENTICES; and then, having created the necessity of taking more Apprentices, made *that* the reason for such desertion : thus conspiring to strike a deadly blow at the prosperity both of the Masters and the Journeymen; and even aiming, and in some instances avowedly so, to consummate a Master's ruin.

Resolved unanimously,

That this danger arises from the aforesaid artful, pertinacious, and unlawful combinations of the Compositors; who by attempting to limit the number of Apprentices, would, if not frustrated, have completely the means within their power of enhancing the price of labour, and would render the Trade unable to enter into a competition with other markets

No copy is known.

where such causes do not operate; and by thus obstructing the increase of workmen, the employment and extent of our capital would be materially cramped, and the spirit of enterprise and the liberty of trade, so congenial to British Literature, would be in danger of being extinguished.

Resolved unanimously,

That it is therefore necessary, in order effectually to prevent such evils, for every Gentleman of the Profession immediately to take some Apprentices, and to continue so doing from time to time; convinced that no other measure can preserve the flourishing condition of the Printing Business, secure our rights from the greatest restraint, and insure to Literature that freedom and encouragement in which the public, as well as ourselves, are so deeply interested.

Resolved unanimously,

That when any Journeyman leaves, or gives warning to leave, our employ from motives with which we are not satisfied, his name, and reason for quitting, if assigned, be forthwith sent in circulation; and that we will not, on any pretence whatever, engage such Journeyman unless his last place has been left fairly, and clearly exempt from any question.

Resolved unanimously,

That this meeting do instruct the Committee to make a report, from time to time, to the Booksellers, of such Master Printers, who, neglecting their own obvious interest, and that of the Trade at large, shall employ or give encouragement to any Journeyman who may leave his Master on account of his taking Apprentices.

Resolved unanimously,

That the Committee be instructed with the fourth Resolution of the Booksellers, respecting the return of the number of Apprentices in the Printing Offices of London and Westminster.

Resolved unanimously,

That the Thanks of this Meeting be given to the Booksellers of London and Westminster, for their so speedily calling a Meeting of that respectable body, for their spirited Resolutions entered into at that Meeting, and for their ready and timely co-operation with the Committee of Master Printers in stemming the present combination among the Compositors.

Resolved unanimously,

That a Deputation from this Meeting do wait on the Booksellers with the Thanks of the Trade, and with the proceedings of this Day.

Resolved unanimously,

That the thanks of this Meeting be given to the Chairman for his attention to the business of the day.[1]

The above resolutions drew forth an answer from the compositors, of whom four hundred and sixty-four signed a letter of protest and explanation to the booksellers. This document is of considerable length and tedium. Only its most pertinent paragraphs are reprinted.

[1] The concluding paragraphs, concerning the pressmen, are reprinted on p. 107.

[DOCUMENT XXXIV]

TO THE BOOKSELLERS OF LONDON AND WESTMINSTER[1]

. . . The compositors then assert, that they have not attempted to *limit* or *restrain* their employers in their endeavours to introduce and educate apprentices, so as to produce a *sufficient number of capable* persons to answer the demands of literature. They have only declared their objection to the introduction of an enormous number of apprentices, in such a mode that it is almost impossible that *capable* workmen should be produced.

The Compositors have not objected to apprentices generally, but only to one species of apprentices; namely, OUT-DOOR APPRENTICES.

Out-door apprentices are those who do not board and reside in the houses of their masters, but only resort to their offices for the purposes of business. They receive a regular weekly stipend, or a certain proportion of their earnings, to board themselves.

This mode of apprenticeship has long had the reprobation of every person who has had an opportunity of observing its effects. It is peculiarly dangerous in an extensive city like this, teeming with incentives to vice and profligacy. Numerous have been its victims to the violated laws of the country; and by it vice and dissipation have been diffused to a lamentable extent.

Every person must likewise be struck with the illegality of it, for it is a direct violation of the indenture. There, it is said, that the youth is to serve from the day of the date of his indenture "after the manner of an apprentice"; but this novel practice has nothing of the manner of an apprentice in it. It might as well be said, after the manner of a journeyman. The indenture afterwards recounts many of the errors, and vices which the apprentice is required to abstain from. Surely, it is not expected, that persons of their age can be restrained by empty, dry, formal precepts, inserted in their indentures; it must therefore be intended as a charge to the master to use his endeavours to preserve them from those faults by salutary restraint. And how can they be thus restrained unless they are under their master's roof? When an apprentice for instance is apprehended at any unseasonable hour in any criminal or disorderly action, and carried before a magistrate, on his situation in life being learnt, his master is sent for, and interrogated as to the cause of his apprentice being out at so improper a time, and on it being discovered that he does not board in the house of his master, what is the conduct of the magistrate? Why, he requires that he should be immediately taken into his master's house, or turned over to another. And this is necessarily accompanied with a reprimand to the master. The passage in the indenture adverted to above, "after the manner of an apprentice," is thus explained in a subsequent passage, towards the conclusion, "finding unto his said apprentice meat, drink, apparel, lodging, and all other necessaries, according to the custom of the city of London." By this practice the youth are neither found in meat, drink, apparel, lodging,

[1] British Museum. MSS. Additional. 27799. f.97., n.d.

or any other necessaries; but converted into a kind of indentured journey-man. Every idea of apprenticeship is violated. You are most of you citizens of London, gentlemen, yourselves ; and when you are made acquainted with these flagrant breaches of your own salutary laws and customs, will surely not countenance the practice, nor impute blame to others for *resisting it*.

But, notwithstanding those great and manifold evils, and this evident illegality, many master-printers have recently increased it to an un-paralleled extent. The compositors have naturally been alarmed, as it threatens to deprive them of the just and honourable means of sub-sistence, which have been acquired by the care and purchase of their parents and friends, and by a legal servitude of seven years; and they conceive, that so far from being calculated to attain the object which the booksellers, and every other person interested in literature, have in view, it militates directly against it.

[*Then follow 464 signatures*]

The employers circulated a black list of compositors who had left their employment on the introduction of fresh apprentices.[1] This is now re-set in much the same style as the original. The latter, however, was printed on a foolscap folio sheet.

[DOCUMENT XXXV]

COMPOSITORS

Extract from a printed Paper circulated by the Compositors in February, 1807 :—"Resolved, That when we have given our Employers fair Notice (which shall be done in the month of March), we will RESIST their taking Out-Door Apprentices."

JANUARY—MAY, 1807

Messrs. Hansard & Sons' Office.[2]

J. Sandford	Thomas	J. Clarke	— Bibby
J. Clap ¶	Rogerson	E. Yeates	J. Jones ¶
T. Moffat	S. Reeves	J. Elliot	S. Kathrens
W. Brown	Wm. Cooper ¶	W. Jackson	J. Davenport
W. Whitelaw ¶	John Redford ¶	T. Baker,	W. Mackintosh. ¶
D. Robertson	J. Thomson ¶	*discharged.*	
J. B. Spence ¶	Joseph Sutton ¶		
D. Walsh, jun.	J. A. Trevor ¶		
J. Coppin ¶	Charles Sloman ¶		
J. Germain	J. White		

These Compositors gave warning subsequent to the first of January; and, with the exception of those marked thus (¶), completed the usual fortnight.

[1] The employers used the same measures in 1810, when the compositors were fighting for an advance in prices. *Cf.* Report of meeting of master printers on 15 Jan., 1810, p. 160, and resolutions passed by compositors on 18 Jan., 1810, p. 162.

[2] "Among the combinations of workmen in the year 1805, the Printing

9

Thomas   John Jenkins   †
     Woolley † W. Bethell,
William   *discharged.*
     Thomas †

† Expressly because Apprentices
were taken.

Mr. Bulmer's Office.

J. B. Parker   C. Wright
I Chapman   D. Lewis
H. Lyon   G. Chisolm
J. Cox   J. Orchard
J. Freeman   George Robbins.
John Chapman

Gave warning, and have left, expressly because Apprentices were
taken.

Mr. Gosnell's Office.

G. Gall and Son — Newman
R. Burton and   T. Verrall
     Son   E. Justins.
R. Halsted

These have recently given warning,
and left, expressly on the introduction
of one Apprentice.

Mr. Whittingham's Office.

Richard Ireland Wm. Taylor
James Heyes   Samuel Metcalf
Wm. Watkins   J. Thompson
John Griggs   T. Corne.

Gave warning expressly on the introduction of one Apprentice.

Mr. Bryer's Office.

— Goodwin   — Guthrie.

Mr. Adlard's Office.

— Davenport   — Shaw.

Mr. Brooke's Office.

Israel Pottinger James Beck
Christopher   James Hollis.
     Pottinger   Samuel Adams.

Left on account of Apprentices.

Trade did not escape, and the Standing Order for the delivery of printed
Bills before their first reading was deemed by the workmen a good opportunity
to try an experiment of forcing a rise of wages in Mr. Hansard's Printing Office.
The Pressmen were put in front of the battle; twenty-four of them simultaneously left their work. Their master lost no time in seeking and finding
unemployed men in the streets and stableyards, and he was seen by more
Members of Parliament than one in a working jacket, and, with his sons,
instructing these men by precept and example. In the year 1807, his compositors,
a more instructed sort of workmen, to the number of thirty, insisted upon
restraining the introduction of new hands by apprenticeship, and upon their
right (as it was too usually acquiesced in) to print as they pleased, according to
the manuscript furnished to them; that is, in a diffuse manner. In House of
Commons Table work (Accounts and Column) this last alleged privilege would
have been peculiarly expensive to the Public, and Mr. Hansard withstood it
accordingly. His door was never again opened to the mutineers, and no degree
of personal inconvenience was regarded until they were replaced from the
country and other adventitious circumstances." *Report from the Select Committee on Printing done for the House,* 1828. Evidence of J. Rickman.

Mr. Marchant's Office.	Left on account of Apprentices.
Joseph Simpson Benjamin Rogers	————————
Epenetus Smith S. Kathrens	To be continued.
John Pierce Harney	
Richardson Robert Toplis.	

————————

During the five years ending 1810, a total of 585 boys were indentured to freemen of the Stationers' Company alone. How many were taken by men free of other Companies, but practising as Master Printers, is not known. During a similar period ending 1815, the total indentured was 360, indicating a considerable reduction.

[DOCUMENT XXXVI]

[1813]

An Address from the Journeymen Printers (Pressmen), to the Master Printers of London.

Gentlemen,

Impressed with the most lively sense of gratitude for your very handsome behaviour towards us upon a former occasion, when you were pleased to acquiesce in our solicitation for an Advance of Prices for our Work,[1] and entertaining a sanguine hope that our present request will not be thought unreasonable, we are emboldened once more to address you, and trust that our very calamitous situation will be deemed a sufficient apology for so doing, and not thought unworthy of your serious consideration.

It is with the utmost concern we witness the present very depressed state of the Printing Business, and of Trade in general; and we cannot help expressing our apprehensions, that the period is far distant ere any change for the better is likely to be effected : and it is with heartfelt sorrow we have to say, that, from these circumstances, and owing to the multiplicity of Hands now in the Profession (which in a short time will be still further increased, there being a great number of Apprentices in the different Charitable Institutions who are upon the eve of becoming Journeymen), there are, at this moment, *numbers of us totally out of employ, and have been for some time past,* many of whom have served you a faithful Apprenticeship. And it is no less lamentable than true, that there are several amongst us who have numerous families to support, but from the above-mentioned causes, are rendered wholly incapable of providing for them.

Under these truly distressing circumstances, we have most humbly to entreat, that you will be pleased to *discontinue for a certain period augmenting your number of Apprentices;* which, Gentlemen, you will

[1] 1810. See p. 108.

perceive, would not only in some measure tend to ameliorate *our* present condition, but prove equally beneficial to the rising generation.—We have not presumed to name any period, but leave that for your better judgments to determine.

Trusting that our unfortunate situation will appear to you of sufficient interest to excite your attention, and that this our present application will not prove unavailing, we remain, with sentiments of the most profound respect,

Your obedient and very humble Servants,

Jan. 1, 1813.   THE PRESSMEN OF LONDON.

*** For the better understanding between Employers and Journeymen, we beg leave to inform you, that should any Pressman, leave his situation either in debt or with *horse*, by directing a line "To the Pressmen of London, at Mr. DOWLE's, the *George, East Harding-street, Shoe-lane*", the said person will be sought after, and information given to the Employer he may have so unhandsomely left, where he may be found.

The following information was contained in a letter addressed to Francis Place (1771-1854), the famous radical politician and resolute fighter for the repeal of the Combination Acts.[1] His informant, whose signature is not appended, provides most valuable information as to the strength of the London trade in 1818. The statistics demonstrate the almost complete breakdown of the old apprenticeship regulations, and show that the journeymen's fears for their livelihood, expressed in all the preceding documents, were not unfounded.

[DOCUMENT XXXVII]

Sir

After the most careful enquiries, the following are the answers I have to make to your questions :—

1. There are 233 master printers *now* in London;—ten years ago there were not more than 130.

2. There are 1882 compositors (apprentices and journeymen).

3. There are about 700 pressmen (apprentices and journeymen).

4. Out of the above one may reckon near 600 composing apprentices and 200 press apprentices.

5. Out of these apprentices not more than 60 compositors and 30 press apprentices are *in-door* apprentices.

6. Of Masters in the country, there are at least one in every market town throughout England and Wales, taking as an average *one* apprentice

---

[1] Brit. Mus. MSS. Add. 27799, f. 99. Place used the material for an article on "Journeymen Printers" published in *The Gorgon—A Weekly Political Publication* (No. 28), 28 November, 1818. See also p. 41, footnote.

each, which the moment he is out of his time, they send a-drift, and take on another, for which they usually receive a good premium. So that the country sends to town every *seven* years as many men as there are Masters in the country.

7. Out of the above men and apprentices—50 newspapers *in London* employ 200 men and 50 boys, compositors, and about the same number of pressmen.

8. *No rise* since 1813—but on the contrary *a fall* in 1815, of 1s. 6d. in the £. to the compositors, and 8d. in the £. to the pressmen.[1]

List of twelve respectable master printers, and the men and apprentices they employ, now, in 1818.

	PRESS		COMPOSITORS	
	Men	Boys	Men	Boys
1 . . .	5	1	20	5
2 . . .	4	4	8	2
3 . . .	4	2	16	3
4 . . .	32	5	40	12
5 . . .	4	6	8	17
6 . . .	12	2	8	2
7 . . .	8	3	10	3
8 . . .	7	6	9	6
9 . . .	12	2	7	5
10 . . .	4	2	7	5
11 . . .	4	4	7	5
12 . . .	4	2	2	7
	100	39	142	72

[*An average of 20 journeymen and 9 boys in each office.*]

Of late the apprentices taken are much fewer than formerly :—the trade also is more precarious than 6 or 7 years ago. Masters are more shy of taking apprentices now, because they may not have always work for them. The two largest houses in London had, at one time, no less than 220 apprentices between them.

---

[1] These dates are incorrect. The last advance in prices was given in 1810, and the reduction made in 1816.

CHAPTER V

THE NEGOTIATIONS FOR THE SCALE OF 1810

The compositors were satisfied with the Scale of 1805 for some years. It was not until early in 1809 that they again approached the employers. "On the 13th April, 1809, an address was presented by the journeymen to their employers, soliciting a considerable advance . . . with a stipulation that 2s. 6d. per sheet should be paid for all periodical publications, whether cast up to the different bodies or not."[1] No copy of this address has been found, nor the answer, if any, sent by the masters. Nevertheless, the compositors pressed their claims for an increase in wages, for two weeks later they sent in another letter, emphasizing the rise in the cost of living and included a "Proposed Amended Compositors' Scale of Prices." In 1800 the price for the composition of common matter, in all sizes from English to Brevier, had been fixed at 5¼d. per 1,000. The journeymen now required 6½d., an increase of approximately twenty per cent. The other clauses in the Scale of 1805 were also to be subject to various advances, ranging from twenty to fifty per cent.

[DOCUMENT XXXVIII]

TO MASTER PRINTERS

Hole-in-the-Wall, Fleet Street, April 29th, 1809.

Gentlemen,

We request your candid perusal of the following statements and representations. And we solicit your assistance to preserve us from the abyss of indigence into which they show we are rapidly sinking, owing to the accumulated enhancement in the price of every article of life; and to restore us, in some degree, to the condition of being able to acquire, by our industry, such a portion of the necessaries and comforts of existence as we have heretofore enjoyed.

As we are desirous to give substantial proof of the justice and reasonableness of our request, we present to your view the following statements :

---

[1] *The London Scale of Prices*, 1836, p. 22.

COMPARATIVE PRICES OF THE NECESSARIES OF LIFE

IN 1801				IN 1809			
Meat, per pound ..	£0	0	7½	Meat, per pound ..	£0	0	10
Butter, ditto	.. 0	1	0	Butter, ditto	.. 0	1	4
Cheese, ditto	.. 0	0	9	Cheese, ditto	.. 0	1	0
Tea, ditto	.. 0	6	0	Tea, ditto ..	.. 0	8	0
Sugar, ditto	.. 0	0	9	Sugar, ditto	.. 0	1	0
Soap, ditto..	.. 0	0	8½	Soap, ditto	.. 0	1	0½
Candles, ditto	.. 0	0	9	Candles, ditto	.. 0	1	1
Salt, ditto ..	.. 0	0	3½	Salt, ditto ..	.. 0	0	4½
Strong Beer, per pot	0	0	4	Strong Beer, per pot	0	0	5
Coals, per bushel ..	0	1	3	Coals, per bushel ..	0	1	10
Rent, per week	0	4	0	Rent, per week	.. 0	6	0
	£0	16	5½		£1	2	11

It is observable that in the foregoing statements, one material article, indeed the most material according to the usual mode of appreciating the necessaries of life, is omitted; namely, Bread. Our reason for the omission is, that its excessive high price, at the period of our last advance, being regarded as temporary, and its present great price having all the appearance of a degree of permanence, comparison is necessarily precluded. Moreover, it being particularly mentioned in the documents we possess relative to our last rise, the peculiar circumstances of the case in this point appeared to us to demand particular notice.—In the first place let it be observed, that, at the period of our last rise, Bread was at double its former average price; it could not therefore be the foundation of what was granted us, as we received only a rise of a sixth.— In the next place permit us to suggest, that, as the excessive price of Bread in the years 1800 and 1801, was universally attributed to temporary causes, so far as Bread was considered, it is reasonable to suppose, the Journeyman were prompted to ask, and their Employers induced to comply, according to what was judged likely to become its average price. Now, on this view of the subject, that is, regarding its average, which we trust is the right way of considering it, we submit to you, Gentlemen, whether what we now ask might not be justly complied with: for, taking the average in 1785 at 7d. the quartern loaf; the expected average in 1800 and 1801 at between 9d. and 10d. which justifies what we then received; surely, according to all present appearances, its future average is likely to be far enough advanced beyond its average at all former times fully to support our present request, even if it depended on so narrow a basis as the mere article of Bread.

We have not given a catalogue of the innumerable little articles which a family require, as it would be tedious to read, though they have equally increased in price, and many in a much greater proportion than those we have mentioned; neither have we said anything of wearing apparel, though holding an essential rank among even the necessaries of life. It would be wrong entirely to pass over another source of very weighty expences attendant on a family; we mean the ailments or more serious diseases, which perpetually occur; often produced, and certainly much aggravated, by the contractedness of the apartments which our straitened circumstances compel us to occupy.

You will perceive, Gentlemen, that we propose considerably less than the comparative statement of even our absolutely necessary expenses require. The pressing nature of our necessities dictates this line of conduct, in order to obtain a prompt and ready compliance. We trust to your liberality for this moderation having its desired effect, by urging you to afford us relief as speedily as possible.

We have endeavoured to form as correct statements as possible, in order to enable you to judge of the reasonableness of what we request. If there be any error in our statements, we conceive it is on the side unfavourable to ourselves; but, even were it otherwise, no trifling error would operate to the disadvantage of what we propose, our propositions being so clearly within the limits of the advance of prices which justice sanctions and which our necessities require.

The altered Scale and Regulations we present with deference for your approbation. Whatever calumny or wild rumour may say, we assure you, we entertain no intentions hostile to your interest, or tending to the interruption of business. We seek by peaceable means to obtain what is barely necessary, with rigid economy, to "provide for the day which is passing over us." It has been our endeavour to give an ingenuous and faithful view of our case, and we rest in full assurance that your bene- volence and consciences will dispose you to comply with our request, conformably with the golden and universally approved rule—"Do unto others as you would have them in like circumstances do unto you."

[*Then follows the proposed Scale of Prices, together with* 795 *signatures*]

The master printers met to consider the proposed scale, but were evidently not prepared to discuss it with the men.

[DOCUMENT XXXIX]

At a General Meeting of the Master Printers of London and Westminster, held this Day, to take into consideration a "Proposed amended Compositors' Scale of Prices."

Stationers' Hall, May 25, 1809.

Mr. Woodfall in the Chair

The Regulations for Compositors' Work, as adjusted and agreed to in the Year 1805 (which bore a material advance on the Scale of 1800); and the injurious consequences of any further advance at the present juncture, having been maturely considered, it was

Resolved, That it appears to this Meeting that any advance on the Scale of Compositors' Work, as adjusted in 1805, is at present inexpedient and impolitic.

Resolved, That the above Resolution be printed, and circulated generally to the Trade.

G. WOODFALL, *Chairman.*

Resolved, That the Thanks of this Meeting be given to Mr. Woodfall for his conduct in the Chair, as also for his indefatigable attention to the general Interests of the Trade.

The masters had asserted that the 1805 Scale "bore a material advance on the Scale of 1800." The compositors drafted another memorial to the employers, in which they claimed that the above statement could not be true, since, when their representatives met with the masters in 1805, they had specifically disclaimed any intention of soliciting a rise.

[DOCUMENT XL]

To the Committee of Master Printers. Copy of an Address generally circulated to Master Printers.

Hole-in-the-Wall, June 23, 1809.

Gentlemen,

When you consider the powerful motives by which we were impelled to request an advance of prices, the strong grounds on which the propriety of that request was founded, and the painful corroboration of its reasonableness by daily experience, you must be convinced that, to afford us consolation for the delaying of compliance, some very cogent reasons are necessary. Instead of which we have only the general assertion "that any advance is at present inexpedient and impolitic." The reasons which lead to this conclusion are entirely concealed from us, for we cannot regard what is said respecting the Scale of 1805 as constituting any part of the grounds on which it is founded; as, if what is advanced on that subject were consistent with fact, it would apply to the justice or necessity, rather than the policy or expediency of compliance with our request.

We mean not to offend, but our consciences dictate to us, as a duty to our profession, to protest against the assertion that the Scale of 1805 bore a "material advance on the Scale of 1800." It is true that in two of the articles which compose the Scale of 1800 there is something additional allowed us, but those are not material articles. And even if there were a material advance on the *Scale* of 1800, it would not follow that we obtained an advance of prices in 1805; for when the extent of the *Scale* of 1805 is considered, and how small a part of it can have reference to the very few articles of that of 1800, it must be acknowledged that no general inference can be drawn from the comparison.

The object of the Scale of 1805 was to embody in a printed document those rules of charging which before rested entirely on remembered custom; and, consequently, from obvious causes, were liable to produce a diversity of practice unfavourable to a right understanding between Journeymen and their Employers. In forming that Scale, a governing principle was, for mutual concessions to be made by both parties on some articles, so that on the whole the just interests of each might be preserved. If it so happened that the concessions by the Master Printers were on those articles which had previously appeared in print, we assure ourselves that our Employers would not act so unfairly as to wish to avail themselves to our disadvantage of such an accidental circumstance.

It is a question among the Journeymen whether they were losers or gainers by the Scale of 1805, but this is merely matter of opinion, not easy to determine. The advantages they contemplated from it were the termination of vexatious disputes with their Employers, and a more clear and permanent basis to their interests. The ready co-operation of the Master Printers to attain those desirable ends they are at all times willing gratefully to acknowledge. Many Journeymen have complained that their interests suffered, while others have expressed gratitude for what they considered a degree of liberality honourable to their Employers. But no one ever regarded it as an advance.

However, there is much stronger proof that we had no advance in 1805 than mere opinion on the Scale. When the Committee of Master Printers and the Deputation from the Compositors met to confer on the subject they commenced their conference by the Deputation of Compositors disclaiming on the suggestion of the Committee of Master Printers, all intention of soliciting a rise; and in the course of the discussion, on the articles, this declaration was referred to more than once as governing the proceedings. There is no instance on record of the Master Printers giving the Journeymen a rise unsolicited; and it can hardly be that the Journeymen had a rise given them immediately after they had disclaimed all intention of asking one, on being required so to do by their Employers. When we recollect too the manner in which the transaction of forming the Scale was concluded, we shall find it equally difficult to think that the Journeymen obtained an advance. The peremptory manner in which the *ultimatum* of our Employers was presented to us was utterly inconsistent with any idea we can conceive of the manner of persons conferring a gift.

Since the adoption of the Scale of 1805, the Master Printers, most likely to have correct ideas on the subject, we mean the Gentlemen composing the Committee, have repeatedly declared it was not a rise. This they have had the occasion of doing from the following circumstance. Some reprints, the last editions of which had been printed prior to 1800, and then underpaid, being put to press again subsequently to the adoption of the Scale of 1805, disputes arose between the Journeymen and their Employers. The differences were submitted to the Committee of Master Printers, who awarded an addition of a sixth, but the deficiency of the price proceeding from the works having been underpaid prior to 1800, the addition of the sixth did not satisfy the Compositors, who therefore requested the Committee of Master Printers to reconsider them, when the Gentlemen of the Committee took occasion to remind the Compositors, that the Scale of 1805 was not an advance. Here we have proof, both by word and *deed*, for the Committee would not have been so unjust as to give an addition of only a sixth if a further advance had taken place subsequently to 1800, the advance at that period entitling the Compositor to the addition of a sixth.

We have dwelt longer on the above subject than perhaps some will think necessary; but it was impossible to pass it over lightly, being so great a misconception, and in its tendency so adverse to our just interests, and the interests of those whose lot in life it may be to succeed us. And it had the greater effect on our minds as possessing all the force of novelty.

There is a circumstance also which, we hope, it will not be deemed improper in us to advert to, and make a few observations concerning, we mean the paragraph that appeared in the Newspapers, which first conveyed to us the painful intelligence that we should not receive that immediate relief we had hoped for. The words "highly improper," which were used in this paragraph, seemed calculated to give the public an unfavourable impression of our conduct, for it is a natural inference that what it is highly improper to give it is also highly improper to ask, and, we confess, on first reading, it caused us some uneasiness; but a little enquiry and reflection led us to views which in a great degree banished our disquietude. From its appearing immediately after the General Meeting of Master Printers, we concluded that it came directly from them, and that it could not injure us in the opinion of the public, who, knowing that every article of life had been risen upon us, instead of sentiments of disapprobation at our requesting an advance of wages, must pity our situation, and wish that our request should be complied with. To excite these sentiments, in order to obtain countenance for relieving our necessities as speedily as possible, we conceived to be the object of our Employers giving so much publicity to the transaction. From the well known justice, generosity, and humanity, of the British public, we entertain a confident hope that our Employers, by the conversation thus excited on the subject, will soon perceive the propriety of granting what we solicited.

We are aware that compliance may be attended with some difficulties at first, and even temporary loss, which, however, would in the end be amply reimbursed. On all similar occasions objections have been started, but the impediments have as often been surmounted. Were we acquainted with the nature of the circumstances which render compliance with our request "at present impolitic and inexpedient," we might even ourselves possibly contribute to remove the difficulties or avert the dangers. The public must ultimately bear the burden; and, as a part of the public, we must bear our due share. You, Gentlemen, stand between us and the public; we conceive our countrymen are too just, too generous, too humane, and even too wise, to be unwilling that we should be justly remunerated for our labour; and we have that reliance on you which assures us, that, far from obstructing the operation of those laudable principles for our benefit, you will facilitate them by your endeavours.

Suffer us to call your attention to another view of the subject. We not only took care to found our request on justice, but we also exerted our endeavours to make that justice apparent. The principles of justice are clear, certain, and perfect, while views of policy are frequently obscure, generally uncertain and deficient. The maxim that *sound* policy must have justice for its basis is a truth recognized and inculcated by the good and wise in all ages and countries; it is also acknowledged by all ranks of society, and seen equally by the peasant and the philosopher. How often do we hear it expressed in the trite, homely, but *sound* maxim "honesty is the best policy."

The reasons we have adduced we hope will be received as a valid excuse for not yielding implicit assent to the assertion that an advance of our prices is "at present inexpedient and impolitic."

Nothing is so efficacious in enabling men to endure evils as hope; nor can strength to support temporary burdens be so effectually inspired by any other means as a conviction that they are necessary, and a prospect of their being lightened. Actuated by these views and sentiments, the principal object of this address is to request, that you will explain to us the *reasons, why* compliance with our requests is "at present inexpedient and impolitic."

We are, Gentlemen,

[Then follow 795 signatures]

The last statement of the compositors' grievances apparently met with a sympathetic reception in some quarters. Finally, the masters' committee agreed to call a general meeting "to reconsider their request for an advance of wages." The following communication was circulated by the committee to their colleagues:—

[DOCUMENT XLI]

Sir,

The Committee of Master Printers think it proper to submit to the Trade a Letter received by Mr. Bensley, and the result of a Meeting held in consequence.

To Mr. Bensley, Bolt Court, Fleet Street.

Sir,

The Committee of Compositors beg the favour that you will lay the following before the Committee of Master Printers.

Gentlemen,

From the Answers which the Master Printers have generally given to the Compositors respectively employed by them, we entertain hopes that they are not unwilling to reconsider our Case, and therefore take the liberty to request (though we are sorry to be under the necessity of intruding so much on the Time of our Employers) that you will have the goodness to convene another General Meeting for that purpose.

Hole in the Wall,

Friday, July 28, 1809.

The Committee, in submitting this Letter to the Trade, are anxious to draw their attention more particularly to the important subject to which it refers; for though they had considered the Business to be finally settled by the Resolution of the Trade in May last, yet they deem a compliance with the wishes of the Compositors, in convening another General Meeting due to them, and therefore request you will make a point of attending at Stationers' Hall, on Thursday morning, the 7th of September next, at ten o'clock precisely, to reconsider their request for an advance of Wages.

The Committee have fixed the Meeting at a day so distant, in order to enable every Gentleman duly to weigh in his own mind the great importance of the Question to be discussed.

G. WOODFALL, *Chairman.*

York Hotel, August 16, 1809.

The masters' general meeting had been fixed for 7 September, 1809. Two days before, on 5 September, the compositors sent yet another circular letter to their employers. They quoted the five principal circumstances which, according to Adam Smith, "make up for a small pecuniary gain in some employments, and counter-balance a great one in others." The compositors sought "only to be restored, in some degree, to the station that they enjoyed during the latter half of the last century, and at the commencement of the present, for what they now ask will hardly raise them to a level with what they attained to by their last advance, in 1801, much less restore them the advantages they enjoyed even less than half a century back."

[DOCUMENT XLII]

To Master Printers

Hole-in-the-Wall, Fleet Street, London, Sept. 5, 1809.

Sir,

The Committee of Compositors, entertaining hopes that the Master Printers will reconsider the request for an advance of wages, which the necessities of the times lately compelled them to make, on behalf of their Fellow-workmen, solicit the favour of your attendance at any General Meeting which may be holden for that purpose.—At the same time they take the liberty of offering to your notice the following considerations in regard to the wages they are entitled to.

They have adopted as criteria, the five principal circumstances, which, according to Adam Smith, in his "Inquiry into the Nature and Causes of the Wealth of Nations," "make up for a small pecuniary gain in some employments, and counter-balance a great 'one in others.' "

I. *The agreeableness or disagreeableness of the employments themselves.*

The laying-up of forms, and handling of wet matter, particularly in winter; the leaning over the stone to correct; and dirtiness; we conceive, entitle the business to consideration under this head.

II. *The easiness and cheapness, or the difficulty and expenses of learning a business.*

Though perhaps no great degree of invention or ingenuity be necessary to form a Compositor, yet a quality as rare, and difficult of attainment, particularly by youth—*the power and habit of patient application*—is peculiarly necessary to form an efficient Compositor.

And we have the most respectable authority (Mr. Bowyer) for our support, when we affirm, that a greater degree of school-learning is necessary than in any other business. It is the difference in this respect, generally, that determined the branch of the printing business to which a youth is assigned; for when a boy is offered for an apprentice enquiry is constantly made respecting his education. And as the Compositor has generally to point what he composes, and often to correct the orthography, etc., it cannot well be denied, that a portion of literature, by no means contemptible, is requisite to qualify a youth for a Compositor.

III. *The constancy or inconstancy of employment.*

When the great exertion which is required during the winter months, and the season of parliament, and the great number of persons consequently employed, are considered, the probability of an insufficiency of employment for them in the summer months, and during the parliamentary vacation, is manifest.

IV. *The small or great trust which must be reposed in the workmen.*

Under this head the above-mentioned author observes, "The wages of goldsmiths and jewellers are everywhere superior to those of many other workmen, not only of equal, but of much superior ingenuity; on account of the precious materials with which they are entrusted." The workmen in the above businesses we find receive high wages on account of the trust reposed in them, although a breach of that trust, besides the loss of character, would expose them to the penalties of the law. Has not the Compositor an equal or superior trust frequently reposed in him ? Reputation and wealth are in most cases inseparably connected; and reputation is by many estimated as superior to wealth; and yet both might often be considerably affected by the treachery of the Compositor, and that with the sacrifice of character only, and without having anything to apprehend from the law. Nay, even imprudence in a Compositor might prove deeply injurious to his Employer. The premature publicity of information might often prove fatal or injurious to literary designs; and secrecy, if not essential, is highly desirable in innumerable instances. If, therefore, persons employed in the composing branch of the printing business have a trust reposed in them equal if not superior to those who are intrusted with precious materials, ought they not to be recompensed accordingly ? After mentioning the physician and lawyer as having the health, and sometimes life and reputation of their patients and clients in trust, the same author observes, "Such confidence could not safely be reposed in people of very mean or low condition. Their reward must be such, therefore, as may give them that rank in society which so important a trust requires." On the same ground it may be asked, ought such workmen as have the interests and reputation of their Employers sometimes in trust to be suffered to subside into a very mean and low condition ? Ought not a regard to character to be encouraged among them ? and ought they not to be afforded the means of supporting a condition in life sufficiently raised above that abject and necessitous state which precludes all attention to character ?

V. *The probability or improbability of success in an employment.*

If the mere acquisition of the capacity to drudge-out a livelihood by dint of unremitting application, early and late, were the point, it must be allowed that most succeed, at least during the continuance of youth and manhood; but a business should not be estimated merely by its immediate and ordinary advantage, its prospects should be taken into consideration; and viewing the business of a Compositor with a due regard to the prospects it affords, it labours under peculiar disadvantages. The capital required to set up as a master is so great, that no man, whatever may be his capacity as a journeyman, can rationally entertain expectations of ever acquiring a sufficiency by mere journey-work; while most working businesses afford almost a moral certainty to those employed in them, that, by industry, economy, and prudence, they may sooner or later emerge from the condition of journeymen. It is true, that the tools of some few businesses are more expensive to the journeymen than the implements of a Compositor, but when it is recollected, that they must have these tools to work at all; that they are usually furnished with a stock early in life, by their friends; and that little more is necessary to commence masters; it will very little weaken our comparative appeal under this head. Besides, the businesses in which expensive tools are necessary are very few; but numerous are those in which the men may, with facility, raise themselves to the rank of masters, enjoy every comfort and convenience, be respected, associate with our employers, and look down upon the journeyman compositor, drudging on to the end of life, his prospects blackening as years advance, and his powers and faculties decay.

We have said nothing on the score of bodily labour or injury to health (which the above quoted Author thinks might be classed with *Disagreeableness of Employments*); but when the intense attention necessary to dispatch business with expedition and propriety; the effects of that great attention on health, in the production of diseases incident to sedentary employments; and also, when it is recollected that considerable bodily exertion is necessary in some parts of our occupation, which becomes particularly oppressive on arriving at old age; we trust no one will deny that it ought to be taken into the account.

While other businesses are liberally paid on account of their claims on one or part of the principles above referred to as criteria, we can appeal more or less to *all*, and with very superior pretensions to one or two of the most important.

In comparing the wages of Compositors with the wages of other businesses, we should not omit to remark, that many of them, in which the regular wages are less, have the deficiency amply supplied by latent advantages, and perquisites, of a nature quite unknown to Compositors.

We have endeavoured to show the just pretensions of the composing branch of the printing business in respect to pecuniary recompense; and we trust that few will deny that it has superior claims. We have adopted the principles of the most respectable authority, which he applies generally, extending them to the liberal professions. The extensive utility of printing and the proximity of the art of composing to the higher professions, and liberal arts and science, would seem to entitle it to rank above mechanical and manufacturing employments; and consequently entitle it to a more liberal remuneration, as it is well known that rank in society can only be maintained by pecuniary means. The

Compositors, however, seek only to be restored, in some degree, to the station they enjoyed during the latter part of the last century, and at the commencement of the present; for what they now ask will hardly raise them to a level with what they attained to by their last advance, in 1801, much less restore them to the advantages they enjoyed even less than half a century back; as every person may satisfactorily convince himself by a careful examination, and comparison, of the prices of the necessaries of life now and at former periods, and the wages Compositors formerly received and what they now ask.

The General Meeting of masters took place on 7 September, 1809, and resulted in an emphatic refusal to acknowledge the claims of the compositors. A delegated meeting of the journey-men met on 13 September, 1809, and the report and resolutions of the employers' gathering were examined. It was not until 4 December, 1809, that the compositors issued a complete account of the transactions of both sides. They reprinted a document issued by the masters, containing the resolutions passed by them on 7 September, the three resolutions passed at the compositors' meeting of 13 September, together with a long and critical analysis of the terms of the masters' report. Finally, the men's committee requested the votes of their constituents on two propositions: that they should persist in their demands or, alternatively, that they should no longer "persevere in endeavouring to obtain an advance."

[DOCUMENT XLIII]

To Compositors

Hole-in-the-Wall, Dec. 4, 1809.

Gentlemen,

Your committee earnestly solicit your most serious consideration of the following resolutions of the master printers, and request your candid perusal of the subsequent remarks :

At a General Meeting of the Master Printers of London and Westminster, held this day to consider the application of the Compositors for an Advance of Wages.

Stationers' Hall, Sept. 7, 1809.

J. Nichols, Esq. in the Chair,

The chairman having stated the object for which they were convened, the several letters from the compositors, of April 29, June 23, Sept. 5, and their letter to the committee of July 28, were then read: and, after a deliberate discussion thereon, the following report of the committee was also read :

The compositors having earnestly solicited another General Meeting of the trade, to reconsider their request of the 29th of April last, for an increase of wages, your committee did not feel themselves at liberty to refuse their solicitation. In the mean time, your committee, having taken into mature deliberation the several papers circulated by the compositors, do make the following report:

That it appears to them,

1. That the statement of the compositors, as to the "comparative prices of the necessaries of life, in the years 1801 and 1809," is extremely incorrect.

2. That the inferences drawn by the compositors from their own statement are not only erroneous, but, in a great measure, irrelevant to their subsequent "proposed amended scale of prices."

3. That their "proposed amended scale of prices," contained in thirty-one paragraphs, is filled with perplexities, tending to a very considerable advance, even beyond their avowed request of £25 per cent. And your committee cannot help calling your attention to the last paragraph, which is in itself a sweeping clause, being a provision for every ideal circumstance, and which would ultimately tend to keep the trade in a state of perpetual litigation and turbulence.

Upon the whole, your committee feel themselves warranted in coming to the following determination :

1. That no advance whatever is necessary.

2. That the scale of 1801 is founded upon a fair and just estimation of the various descriptions of work; giving to the compositors, upon the ground of the then extreme and increasing pressure of the times, very great advantages; and, considering that the regulations adopted in the year 1805 have proved extremely beneficial to the compositors, your committee are decidedly of opinion that nothing has since arisen to justify, in the smallest degree, the admission of any further advance.

After a mature and ample discussion of the subject, it was

Resolved, (with one dissentient voice)

I. That, being unwilling to attribute to the whole body of compositors the offensive style of their late renewed application for an advance of prices, the master printers have again taken the subject under their consideration; and, after having attentively compared the expences of living, and the earnings of compositors, at various periods, are convinced that their condition has been of late years considerably improved.

Resolved unanimously,

II. That the master printers deem it right to express the great mortification they have felt from observing that the several advances, to which they have from time to time acceded, have been followed by diminished industry on the part of many of the compositors, and have increased, rather than allayed, their discontents.

Resolved, (with two dissentient voices)

III. That, for these and various other reasons, the resolutions of the General Meeting held on the 25th of May last, asserting the inexpediency and impolicy of any advance in the scale of compositors' work, as adjusted in 1805, be confirmed.

Resolved unanimously,

IV. That the report of the committee, and the resolutions annexed, be printed, and circulated to the trade.

J. NICHOLS, *Chairman.*

Resolved unanimously,

V. That the thanks of this meeting be given to the chairman for his attention to the business of the day, and to the general interests of the trade.

T. BENSLEY, *Secretary.*

We have presented you with the master printers' resolutions without any preface, and unaccompanied with comments, that you might form a clear unbiassed judgment of the document itself. We next lay before you the resolutions of the delegated meeting which was convened to consider it.

Hole-in-the-Wall, Sept. 13, 1809.

Resolved, That it is the opinion of this meeting, that the resolutions of the master printers are neither consistent with truth nor founded on justice.

Resolved, That it is the opinion of this meeting, that the business will act consistently with wisdom and justice by persevering in all justifiable means to obtain an advance.

Resolved, That the committee circulate the master printers' resolutions, with such remarks and explanations as they may think proper, and endeavour to obtain the sense of the trade at large.

We will now, in obedience to the last resolution, proceed to offer such explanations and remarks as appear to us to claim attention.

1. That the statement of the compositors, as to the "comparative prices of the necessaries of life, in the years 1801 and 1809, is extremely incorrect."

This assertion amounts to nothing; for, as they do not point out in what respects our statement is incorrect, that which they judge to be so may be to our own disadvantage. And there is good reason to think that, if they have discovered any errors, they are to our own disadvantage; for, had we represented things erroneously in our own favour, we have a right to conclude, from the general spirit and temper of their resolutions, that they would not have contented themselves with merely asserting it to be incorrect.—However, we must suppose, from their conclusions, that they mean to insinuate, we have stated the comparative prices of the necessaries of life between the years 1801 and 1809, greatly to our own advantage; and on this supposition we ground our observations.

Taking this assertion in the most candid point of view, we must account for it by conjecturing, that the master printers have compared the wholesale prices of some of the articles between the two periods, without making allowance for the increasing profits and demands of those who intervene between the wholesale dealers and the consumers. But, as taxes, and the prices of all the necessaries, comforts, and luxuries of life, have been constantly increasing since 1801, there can be no doubt that all who derive a profit, including the retailer (who has no one to consult between himself and the public), have increased their profits, and consequently contributed to enhance, extremely, the prices of the necessaries of life to us, since 1801. If the master printers have proceeded in this manner, they have not taken the right method of appreciating our statements, which refer to the retail prices of things, nor the right means of ascertaining the difference of price to us; which difference, from the causes we have before pointed out, must constantly grow greater from the merchants and wholesale-dealers to the retailers. The master printers may not have considered too that we do not enjoy advantages of which probably many of our employers avail themselves—the means of purchasing in large quantities, by which they save the increased charge of profit to the petty dealer, and may often anticipate any advance foreseen in the price.

We fear that you are too well convinced on the subject we are now considering by *experience*; but, as this point is fundamentally important to manifest the justice of what we have been asking, we hope you will be far from thinking time or trouble lost which is employed in endeavouring to make it as clear and evident as possible. With this view, we avail ourselves of a counter-statement inserted in the report of a committee of newspaper proprietors, in consequence of an application from the compositors on newspapers for an advance of wages. As the articles contained in the report from the newspaper proprietors are not quite the same as our's we can only make use of it so far as the same articles are contained in both.

Newspaper Proprietors' Statement of the Comparative Prices of the Necessaries of Life for 1800 and 1809

	1800 s. d.	1809 s. d.
Bread, per quartern	1 5	1 2¾
Meat, per pound	0 8½	0 10
Butter, ditto	1 0	1 4
Cheese, ditto	0 9	1 0
Soap, ditto	0 9½	1 0½
Candles, ditto	0 11	1 1
Small Beer, per gallon	0 6	0 8
Milk, ditto	1 2	1 4
Coals, per bushel	1 6½	1 10

Such of the articles contained in the newspaper proprietors' statements as are also contained in our's, incorporated with our's, at the prices stated by them.

	1800 s. d.	1809 s. d.
Meat, per pound	0 8½	0 10
Butter, ditto	1 0	1 4
Cheese, ditto	0 9	1 0
Tea, ditto	6 0	7 0
Sugar, ditto	0 9	1 0
Soap, ditto	0 9½	1 0½
Candles, ditto	0 11	1 1
Salt, ditto	0 3½	0 4
Strong Beer, per pot	0 4	0 5
Coals, per bushel	1 6½	1 10
Rent, per week	4 0	6 0
	17 1	£1 1 10½
		17 1
Fourth of 17s. 1d.	4 3¼	
Difference between 1800 and 1809 . . .		4 9½
Fourth of the amount of 1800 . . .		4 3¼
Surplus advance beyond the fourth . .		6¼

In the above incorporated statement, we have also reduced tea, under the year 1809, from 8*s.* to 7*s.*

It is also probable that the means by which the newspaper proprietors have collected their statements are liable to the same remarks that we have made on the probable means pursued by the committee of master printers. This conjecture is strengthened by the newspaper proprietors affirming, that the comparative statement of the compositors is made without authority, as it is not practicable to obtain authority for the retail prices, though it is for the wholesale.

As we have noticed the newspaper proprietors' statements, it may be proper to mention a remark they have made, "that meat is invariably cheaper in winter than at this season of the year," (it is dated June 30). On this remark it is necessary to observe, that meat is cheaper only during the Christmas quarter. We may also observe, that the newspaper proprietors seem to have forgotten how much dearer coals are in the winter than in the month of June.

We trust the above view of our statements possesses more weight than the unsupported assertion of the master printers' committee.

2. That the inferences drawn by the compositors from their own statement are not only erroneous, but, in a great measure, irrelevant to their subsequent "proposed amended scale of prices."

Your committee, in order to discover what was erroneous in this respect, naturally began by reading that part of our address which follows the statement, and could not discover any thing that could be called an inference : the first paragraph contains our reasons for not including bread in the preceding statement, and shows what we might reasonably request on account of the increase in the permanent price of that article;—the second paragraph points out to our employers some necessary articles which are not mentioned in the preceding statement;—the third endeavours to guard against any objection to our request, by remarking that the advance we ask is much less than the exigencies of the times require; and assigns as the reason for this moderation the pressing nature of our necessities;—the fourth also endeavours to guard against objections, by noticing, that in our statement we have inclined to the side unfavourable to ourselves, and that in our propositions we have kept clearly within the limits which justice sanctions and our necessities require;—the last paragraph expresses, first, the deference with which we propose the amended scale to our employers, then proceeds to profess the peaceableness of our intentions, and concludes with an appeal to the hearts and consciences of our employers. However, as we had not read the introductory paragraph, we at last perused that. Its first sentence requests what if we had been fortunate enough to obtain we might probably have been more successful in our following application —the candour of our employers. The subsequent part of the paragraph contains the only inference from our statement throughout the address : in it we infer, from the increased prices of the necessaries of life, that we are rapidly sinking into indigence. We apprehend there is little need of logic to convince those compositors who have families to support of the correctness of this inference.

We are next told that our inferences are in a great measure irrelevant to the "subsequent proposed amended scale of prices." The only inference which we find appears perfectly relevant : we infer from our statement of the comparative prices of the necessaries of life in 1801 and 1809 that we are rapidly sinking into indigence; and, having shown by the statement that the advance upon us since 1801 is upwards of one-fourth in the prices of the necessaries of life, request them to agree to the adoption of an amended scale, the basis of which is an advance of one-fourth per thousand in the estimation of common matter.

It is much to be regretted that the committee of master printers did not either give their own statements, inferences, and applications to the scale; or their arguments and objections to ours. The most cautious policy could not require suppression and concealment on this subject. What they might have objected to us on this point, if they could have had any well-founded objection, would have been of radical effect, and would have evinced a desire to dissuade; which is certainly more consistent with that social benevolence which ought to actuate every man, than a mere disposition to repulse a request.

3. That their "proposed amended scale of prices," contained in thirty-one paragraphs, is filled with perplexities, tending to a very considerable advance, even beyond their avowed request of 25*l.* per cent. And your committee cannot help calling your attention to the last paragraph, which is in itself a sweeping clause, being a provision for every ideal circumstance, and which would ultimately tend to keep the trade in a state of perpetual litigation and turbulence.

They begin this article by noticing the number of paragraphs contained in the proposed amended scale (31 articles, the present scale consists of 27). When it is considered that the "Regulations" of 1805 was the first attempt to comprise our rules of charging in a general printed scale, it cannot surely be surprising that experience should have discovered some defects; nor can it seem extravagant that, after the lapse of four years, four additional articles should have been found necessary. These four articles are :

"Folios or quartos, with three columns in a page, to be paid one shilling per sheet extra. Octavos, with two columns in a page, to be paid one shilling and sixpence per sheet extra, and upwards, in proportion.— Tabular and table matter, to be paid according to the custom of the trade."

"That on all works where, for the purpose of expedition, a number of hands shall be employed (exceeding four), and where the proportion shall not be equal to six sheets each, one shilling and sixpence per sheet be allowed; or the composition to be paid for by time."

"That parliamentary works, those issuing from the departments of state, and those hitherto paid sixpence per thousand, take the proportionate advance."

"Whatever is not specified in the above scale to be determined by the custom of the business, previous to the formation of the scale in 1805, with a proportionate advance; and those cases for which there is neither provision in the scale, nor any rule of previous practice, to be determined according to a fair estimate of labour or ingenuity."

We trust no reasoning is necessary to convince any compositor, of the least experience or reflection, of the propriety, and even necessity, of an addition to the scale of the nature of the above-mentioned articles.

They then complain of "perplexities tending to a considerable advance." This is itself not very clear. We cannot conceive how perplexities tend to an advance : the perplexities must be removed that the advance may be seen. We have endeavoured in the proposed scale to define the pecuniary charge of some parts which are now expressed by the words "proportionate advance," and we apprehend that these are the passages which perplexed the master printers' committee. But they are necessary, both for the sake of justice to the compositors, and harmony between them and their employers; for, when instances occur of works to be appreciated by articles containing the expression "proportionate advance," master printers frequently insist on an explanation disadvantageous to the compositor, and inconsistent with the right interpretation, and thence originate disputes, which cause vexation and loss of time to both parties, and generally terminate to the detriment of the interests of the one. Were the actual pecuniary sum stated these evils would be prevented.

With respect to its tending to an advance beyond 25*l*. per cent. which we avow as our request, we have to observe, that we did not present the scale peremptorily; but, as we say in the introductory address, with "deference." The scale presented by the compositors in 1805, underwent much alteration before it was adopted; we are not less willing to attend to rational objections now than the compositors were then. And, we may say, there is not an instance on record of propositions submitted by the compositors to their employers being entirely complied with— but the master printers formerly were candid and liberal enough to reason.

The committee then call the attention of their assembly to what they term "a sweeping clause" which they assert to be "a provision for every ideal circumstance," tending "to keep the trade in a state of perpetual litigation and turbulence." It is known to every man of experience and observation, that the greater part of the litigation and misunderstanding which has taken place in the business since 1805 has proceeded from the want of such an article. The address which introduced the scale of 1805 to the master printers contained this passage :—"Surely, if 99 grievances existed, and 80 of them could be remedied, it is not an argument, because the whole cannot be accomplished, that the greater part should not be settled." Accordingly, when the scale proposed by the compositors came to be discussed by them and their employers, it was found that they could not reconcile their ideas on some points, particularly the article relating to column matter. It was therefore understood between the parties, that those things which could not be reduced to a rule were to remain as they were previous to that period—to be remunerated according to the trouble and custom of the business; but since the adoption of the "Scale" many master printers have objected to paying whatever was not mentioned in it, however reasonable, however just, or however clearly ascertained by custom. This has been the cause of most of the recent disputes between journeymen and their employers; to guard against which was the object of this sweeping clause as they term it.

They have just been speaking of sweeping clauses—behold their next resolution !

1. That no advance whatever is necessary.

We think the entire want of truth in this sweeping sentence is so flagrant that no further remark upon it is necessary.

2. That the scale of 1801 is founded upon a fair and just estimation of the various descriptions of work; giving to the compositors, upon the ground of the then extreme and increasing pressure of the times, very great advantages :— And, considering that the regulations adopted in the year 1805 have proved extremely beneficial to the compositors, your committee are decidedly of opinion that nothing has since arisen to justify, in the smallest degree, the admission of any further advance.

Here they say "*is* founded upon a fair and just estimation of work upon the ground of the *then* extreme and increasing pressure of the times." There is an inconsistency between the *is* in the first sentence, and the *then* in the last too striking to be passed without notice. If the *is* in the first sentence were altered to *was* there would be consistency and propriety in that part of the article; which would then run "the scale of 1801 *was* founded upon a fair and just estimation of the various descriptions of work; giving to the compositors, upon the ground of the then extreme and increasing pressure of the times," which has nothing to do with the *now* increased, extreme, and increasing pressure of the times, in 1809.

With regard to the regulations of 1805, having "proved extremely beneficial to the compositors" if they mean that our prices were increased by it, we need only refer you to the refutation contained in the "Address to the master printers requesting their reasons why an advance was impolitic and inexpedient." (Dated June 23.)

We come now to the resolutions of the meeting of master printers :—

I. That, being unwilling to attribute to the whole body of compositors the offensive style of their late renewed application for an advance of prices, the master printers have again taken the subject under their consideration; and, after having attentively compared the expenses of living and the earnings of compositors, at various periods are convinced that their condition has been of late years considerably improved.

The first remarkable passage in this resolution which expresses their unwillingness to attribute to the whole body of compositors the offensive style of their late renewed application. We are at a loss to know letters or addresses they allude to, we took great pains to avoid saying anything in the least degree offensive, or which could even be made a handle of by those who might wish to be offended; and we feel confident that no expression in any thing that we have presented to the master printers, if taken in its genuine sense, and read with the context, can give offence to any one, however he may think himself elevated above us. But, as some may possibly think that this passage refers to some communication with which the trade at large are unacquainted, we here present you with the only communications which have not been printed and generally circulated.

To Mr. Bensley

June 26.

Sir,

Having learnt that the representatives of the compositors are not acknowledged by the committee of master printers (though entirely unacquainted with the cause), the committee acting for the journeymen take the liberty of requesting that you will present the enclosed to the committee of master printers.

It may be necessary to explain that the above application was complied with; but, as the committee of master printers did not think themselves justified in convening a meeting of their body, the following letter was addressed to the committee of master-printers :

To Mr. Bensley

Sir,

The committee of compositors beg the favour that you will lay the following before the committee of master printers.

Gentlemen,

From the answers which the master printers have generally given to the compositors respectively employed by them we entertain hopes that they are not unwilling to reconsider our case, and therefore take the liberty (though we are sorry to be under the necessity of intruding so much on the time of our employers) that you will have the goodness to convene another general meeting for that purpose.

Hole-in-the-Wall, Friday, July 29.

Since we saw this complaint, having perused our addresses and letters, we find that the supplicatory style of the first was rather departed from in those which followed; but this difference of style proceeded naturally from the different circumstances under which they were written : in the first, we endeavoured to make the master printers sensible of our sufferings, and dispose them to afford us that assistance which justice and humanity should prompt them to give; but those which followed, being in consequence of their refusal to comply with what we had requested in our first, had somewhat of an expostulatory air, but certainly contained nothing offensive.

We have also perused some communications which were addressed to the master printers by the compositors in former times, when they had occasion to make an application for an advance of prices, and we find them written in a bolder style than any the master printers have received from us during the present application. In those documents, the words right, claim, &c. occur not unfrequently. This language we have avoided. —In making this remark it is necessary to guard against misapprehension. We are far from wishing to inculcate that what we have been asking is not a right : we are fully convinced, that it is a claim not only supported, but even dictated, by justice.—But, in order to take the most likely course to conduct you with safety into the port of justice, we deemed it allowable, that we might steer clear of the shoals of pride, to use the language of request.

This may not be an improper place to advert to another point, on which our addresses may seem to countenance erroneous ideas. Though we have asked for the means of mere subsistence for the passing day we would not countenance an opinion, that we have not a right to participate in the enjoyments of improved society, or to the possession of the means of providing for the future. Our labour is as instrumental to the advancement of society as that of any profession; and those who are placed between us and the public enjoy their full share of the advantages. If you go into the houses of the master printers and booksellers you see them in possession of every accommodation which art and science has brought into general use. We have not less right to enjoyments than they, though we conceive that, under the present circumstances, we have not acted unwisely in limiting our endeavours to the obtaining of what is indispensable to mere decent subsistance.

We cannot leave this article, without observing, on the assertion that our "condition has of late years been considerably improved," that, even if the prices of the necessaries of life had remained stationary, our earnings must have been much diminished of late years by the great number of hands that are put into companionships. Formerly expedition-money was common; and work that required particular dispatch was better paid, as is recorded in the *Life* of Dr. Franklin. But we cannot be surprised, that those who, after attentively comparing the expences of living and the earnings of compositors at various periods, could think their condition considerably improved, should pass over this circumstance.

II. That the master printers deem it right to express the great mortification they have felt from observing that the several advances, to which they have from time to time acceded, have been followed by diminished industry on the part of many of the compositors, and have increased, rather than allayed their discontents.

As far as we can learn the imputation of "diminished industry" contained in this article is founded on the frivolous complaints of some master printers that their compositors do not go to business so early in the day as they ought : formerly the complaint was, that the compositors did not go to business so early in the week as they ought. We have more cause to be mortified, at finding that the increased sobriety and industry of the journeymen has rather increased than allayed the discontents of their employers. Formerly they were discontented with some reason, because their men, instead of going to their work on the Monday, absented themselves from their offices till the Wednesday, Thursday, or even Friday; now their discontent arises from some of their men not going to their business till eight or nine o'clock in the morning instead of five or six. So far as we can judge, instead of our advances having been followed by diminished industry, we are satisfied, on the best information that the case admits of, that for a series of years past, including all our advances within memory, the sobriety and industry of the compositors have increased, and are increasing; but we fear, by the discouragements of our employers, in endeavouring to prevent our receiving the due reward of our labour, is in danger of being diminished.

It is worthy of remark how soon our employers forget a just principle : in the resolution immediately preceding they would not attribute to the whole body of compositors the offence given by a part; here they assign, as one reason for refusing the request of the whole body of compositors, the idleness of a part of them. This last principle has too much characterised the conduct of the master printers of late years. They have even assigned, as a reason for destroying the harmony and connexion between the journeymen and their employers, an offence given by an individual, or an anonymous letter; for such is the alledged cause of refusal to acknowledge our representative in their committee. And they have never made any communication to your committee pending the present business.

The conclusion of this article seems to us to imply much that is well worthy of your notice, and very necessary to be clearly seen and fully understood : they seem to regret that our prices have been advanced in the course of the last 23 years (for the word several may be fairly construed to include the three advances we have had during that period), although the prices of the necessaries of life have been more than doubled during that time. They say these advances have rather increased than allayed our discontents, implying, that the successive advances we have had during that period were compliances from them, extorted by our complaints, instead of what they really were, an admission of claims which the change of circumstances rendered absolutely necessary on the principles of common justice.

This resolution directly conveys insult, and implies the grossest injustice. It shows how low they would have us reduced, and how they would treat us when so humiliated. We forbear to dwell longer on it, but earnestly entreat you fully to reflect on its tendency. Unless the light in which we view it be extremely erroneous, you cannot fail to be perfectly convinced by it, of the necessity of entire unanimity among ourselves, if we cherish any hopes of preserving our place in society.

III. That, for these and various other reasons, the resolution of the General Meeting held on the 25th of May last, asserting the inexpediency and impolicy of any advance in the scale of compositors' work, as adjusted in 1805, be confirmed.

However shy the master printers may be in producing reasons, we cannot be too well convinced of the reasonableness of the advance we have been soliciting; and therefore may take this occasion, as they will not afford us the opportunity of meeting their objections, of confirming our former reasons by additional reasons, as they confirm their former assertions and resolutions by additional assertions and resolutions. We have shewn that the advance we desire is just and moderate, by statements of the difference between the prices of the necessaries of life at the time of our last rise and at the present time; but, as there may be some, though we trust they are not numerous, who think we have asked too much, and as our unanimity cannot be too perfect, we will add a few reasons in support of the propriety of our propositions to the master printers. Having shown that we have asked less than the exigencies of the times require (for though we have used the newspaper proprietors' statements, we do not give up our own), the principle on which such persons rest their opinions seems to be, that we ought to ask much less than the exigencies of the times require. This, then, we will make the question—Ought we to ask much less than the exigencies of the times require ? Now, let any one put it to his own judgment and conscience, whether, when the prices of the necessaries of life have risen (if we were to estimate them duly), perhaps a third, can we, without gross folly, and a criminal sacrifice of the interests of our profession, endeavour to obtain less than a fourth ? If it be objected that printing will not bear it, that it will prevent reading, let it be recollected with what facility tradesmen (not omitting booksellers), increase the price of the articles they vend to the public, and how readily their increased demands are complied with, whether on articles of necessity, convenience, or pleasure; and that books are as necessary and useful in the present state of society as most things beyond the absolute supports of life; and let it be considered that the gratification of reading would be as unwillingly relinquished as any other pleasure to which mankind are attached—certainly not for the trifling augmentation of expence which the addition of our increase of prices would occasion. As we pay what is demanded of us, it is but fair that we should be paid in return; which the master printers who have agreed to these resolutions endeavour to prevent, and to choak the stream which would flow from the justice and reasonableness of the public. If we proceed on the principle of asking, every time we are necessitated to seek an advance, much less than the circumstances of the times require, to what deplorable state of poverty must we sink at last. As far back as any of us can remember, things have progressively increased in price, and latterly with accelerated rapidity. Since we had 4*d.* per thousand the value of articles of use or consumption, taken in the aggregate, has been doubled, which would justify our receiving 8*d.* per thousand (not including heads and directions) instead of 6½*d.*; and we can only judge of the future by the past.—We have thrown out these hints, as, if they are improved upon by a little calculation and reflection, so as to see the whole effect and ultimate tendency, of asking every time less than we have a right to, we trust no one will find any difficulty in resolving the question above proposed in the negative.

After the above suggestions, it can hardly be improper, and may even be necessary, to offer to your consideration, that the question at issue between us and our employers is—whether we are to have any advance at all? and to request you duly to consider, that, though it may be unwise for a mere majority to persevere in endeavouring to obtain an advance; yet, when the opinion of the business is ascertained to approach nearly to unanimity on that point, there is no other means of preserving that valuable and essential unanimity, than by every individual entirely acquiescing in, and firmly and zealously supporting, the resolutions of the majority, as to the nature and extent of the advance.—If this principle is departed from no common interest can ever be maintained.

We have endeavoured to execute the task assigned to us in the manner most likely to be advantageous to the interest of our profession. The document on which we have been commenting affords ample materials to inflame the passions and impel to rash measures. Perhaps that is the object of it. We have endeavoured to suppress our own feelings lest we should excite yours; and are inclined rather to cherish the idea that it emanates from individuals unfriendly to the journeymen (perhaps themselves enflamed and irritated by some casual unfortunate occurrences), than that it contains the deliberate uniform sentiments of the master printers at large. It may even proceed from individual design to create a breach between us and our employers, with a view to individual advantage; and, as it has never been officially communicated to us, nor to the compositors generally, in any regular and formal manner, we might even perhaps regard it as spurious. We should be glad, both for our own

satisfaction and for the sake of the character of the master printers to find
that it is so; but this we rather desire than expect. But if in the course
of our comments we have unconsciously [? departed] in any degree
from that calm and cool temper which we have endeavoured to preserve
we entreat you to guard your minds from the influence of our feelings
and to deliberate on your future proceedings with perfect calmness
Your situation is more arduous and difficult than it ever was at any
former period; you have more formidable obstacles to contend with
and consequently require more prudence. We say prudence, that is—care
and attention in your deliberations—and wisdom in your resolves—no
fear—"fear admitted into public councils betrays like treason."

You require also unanimity. As you have more to contend with than
ever you had, if you decide to persevere you will require more strength
than ever; and that strength can only exist with unanimity. In proportion
to our unanimity we have reason to expect attention and respect from
our employers. Let not any, therefore, refuse their aid (however specious
the pretences they may devise for their desertion of duty), in the hope
that others will acquire what they will gladly participate; for they must
not flatter themselves that they shall enjoy the fruit without contributing
to its production, as we must either recede altogether or advance as on
entire body. So at least it appears to us, and we feel a strong assurance
that such will be the general opinion.

It is now the time to deliberate. In order to afford the means of
ascertaining the real sense of the trade each man should conscientiously
and independently give his own opinion, regardless of what others do
Let him well consider the probable consequences of receding, and the
probable consequences of persevering, and decide accordingly; but
whether we retire or advance, it is our duty to know distinctly the—why

We will conclude with stating our conviction, that your preservation
or success, can only be hoped for on the condition, that, in deliberating
resolving, or acting, "Every man will do his duty."

Your committee have now to request the signature of each compositor
and, that the sentiments of the trade may be fully ascertained, it is hoped
that no man, however specious the motives that may prompt him to it
will be so unmanly, or indifferent to the interests of his profession, as to
decline to subscribe his name under one of the following heads :

Those who think we ought to persevere in endeavouring to obtain an
advance will please to sign their names here.

Those who think we ought *not* to persevere in endeavouring to obtain
an advance will please to sign their names here.

N.B. Attendance will be given at the Hole-in-the-Wall, to receive
these papers, with the signatures, on the following evenings : Saturday
Dec. 9, Monday, Dec. 11, Tuesday, Dec. 12, and Wednesday, Dec. 13.-
And also at Mr. Justs's, the Swan, Swan-Yard, Strand, on the following
evenings : Saturday, Dec. 9, Monday, Dec. 11, and Tuesday, Dec. 12
After the above dates their delivery will be useless.

The compositors did not abandon the struggle. A compromise was sought. A fresh draft of the Scale was made, and a differentiation between manuscript or printed copy and reprint copy was made. Some months earlier they had desired that common matter, in all sizes between english and brevier, should be paid for at $6\frac{1}{2}$d. per thousand instead of $5\frac{1}{4}$d. While the former price was still to hold good for manuscript copy, they were prepared to set reprint matter for 6d. per thousand. This would benefit the masters to a small extent, since they would only be required to pay $\frac{3}{4}$d. per thousand extra for this class of work, instead of $1\frac{1}{4}$d. In the revised draft scale the other half-dozen main clauses were altered accordingly, the difference between the two classes of copy being made. In principle, however, the subsidiary clauses were hardly different from those put forward in the previous April, although a few slight concessions to the masters were suggested.

[DOCUMENT XLIV]

To Master Printers

Hole-in-the-Wall, Fleet-street, Dec. 22, 1809.

Sir,

At no former period were the claims of the compositors to the liberality of their employers more justifiable, or more deserving serious attention, than at the present moment. Amidst accumulating hardships and difficulties, they have long waited, with anxious solicitude, for such a happy change of events and circumstances, as would have precluded the necessity of again intruding themselves to your notice. Disappointed, however, of their flattering expectations, and no ray of hope left to cheer them even with a remote prospect, when those evils of which they justly complain, and which press so heavily on our individual exertions, shall have a happy termination, they are once more forcibly impelled to the painful necessity of soliciting an additional advance to the present price of labour, without which it will be morally impossible for them to sustain the extreme pressure which the unexampled exigencies of the times are almost daily imposing on them.

The ready acquiescence evinced by their employers on similar applications, induces the compositors to trust, with some degree of confidence, that their present claims to an enlargement on the price of labour is so evidently justified by existing circumstances as not only to require your immediate attention, but also a speedy determination in their favour, by granting an advance in some degree proportionate to the enormous enhancement of every necessary of life.

Urged by the hardships and difficulties inseparable from a state of dependent and ineffectual exertion, the compositors beg leave to submit to your attentive consideration, the following [*proposed Scale of Prices, which is not reprinted*].

The above regulations, they conceive, would not be deemed exceeding the bounds of moderation, nor as bearing too heavily on the trade; and, though far inadequate to the necessities of the times, they will gratefully receive it as a desire on your part to alleviate their present embarrassments.

From a scrupulous desire not to depart from any thing that was agreed on between the compositors and their employers in 1805, we have preserved that scale as far as is consistent with the object of our request.— We present the above scale with deference : we have formed it, according to our views, to the best of our judgment; but shall gratefully receive the suggestions of our employers, with which we shall comply, so far as is consistent with our object, and willingly take upon ourselves whatever labour may be necessary to render it as correct as possible.

The compositors hope there will be no objection to works put in hand, on and after the first of January, 1810; and also volumes of periodical publications, being paid agreeably to the above scale.

[*Then follow* 612 *signatures*]

Following the publication of the new proposed Scale, the compositors' delegates were summoned to another meeting, arranged for 18 January, 1810. The journeymen were exhorted to persist in their demands, and it was stated that even the advance which they were endeavouring to obtain was inadequate in view of the heavy cost of living.

[DOCUMENT XLV]

To Compositors

Hole-in-the-Wall, Jan. 11, 1810.

Gentlemen,

You are requested to send delegates to a meeting at the Hole-in-the-Wall, next Thursday, Jan. 18, in the usual proportion (one from each office in which the number of persons employed do not exceed six, above that number, one for every six).

You are also requested to invest your delegates with full powers.

Chair taken at half-past eight.

A greater degree of unanimity never pervaded the printing business on any similar occasion than on the present; nor did the compositors ever make a proposal to their employers more just and reasonable; but, as our unanimity cannot be too extensive, nor our conviction of the justice of our claim too strong, we solicit your serious consideration of the following hints, which we embrace the present opportunity of suggesting.

The most general causes which do, or ought to determine the wages of journeymen, generally, are the following :—1. The demand for their services :—2. The usefulness, and the prices, of the articles produced by their labour :—3. The income which is necessary for their support.—

The first of these causes, though this is a time when there is the greatest demand for our services, we do not wish to press, because it has more the appearance of force than reason or justice. But it certainly requires us to remark the moderation of the compositors. They claim less now than they asked at a time far, very far, less favourable in this respect than the present. This circumstance should not only have a favourable influence on their employers, but also give satisfaction, and increase the ardour, of the few who happened to be in the minority at the commencement of this business, whom the majority have, with singular candour and moderation met as it were half-way.—With respect to the utility and price of books, though, no doubt, in justice and reason, it ought to have great weight, and probably would have with the public, we forbear, for obvious reasons, to canvass the subject in that view unnecessarily. We have taken the lowest, but the strongest ground, as it appeals to humanity as well as justice. To that ground we wish to adhere. But it is a kind of reason the full force of which is perhaps not easy to be seen, even by some among ourselves, however sensibly it may be felt by others. —There are some compositors who do not depend solely on the business for their subsistence; others have the advantage of a superior degree of swiftness in the execution of their work; a few have the good fortune (however precarious it must necessarily be) of situations peculiarly lucrative; while many do not know by experience, (the only true knowledge), the difficulties of supporting a family. We hope none of the above description of persons will be unmindful of the arduous situation of their fellow-workmen, who, with moderate abilities, and common average work, have the honourable misfortune of a family to support, with no other means than the produce of their labour as compositors.—To afford all some idea of the extreme inadequacy of the present average income of compositors to the maintenance of a family, we beg your attention to the following, we conceive, economical weekly expence of a man, his wife, and two children. It even proves the inadequacy of the advance we are endeavouring to obtain.

	s.	d.
Rent, per week	6	0
Bread and Flour, five quarterns	6	9¼
Meat 14 lb. at 9d. per lb.	10	6
Butter 2 lb. at 1s. 4d. per lb.	2	8
Cheese (average price 11d. per lb.) 1 lb.	0	11
Porter, ten quarts and a pint	4	4½
Candles, 1½ lb.	1	7½
Coals (one bushel and a half, average price 1s. 9d.)	2	7
Soap, Starch, and Blue	1	6
Tea, a quarter of a pound, at 7s. per lb.	1	9
Sugar 2 lb. at 9d. per lb.	1	6
Vegetables	1	6
Milk	0	7
Pepper, Salt, Vinegar, &c.	0	9
Cloathing, Shoes, and Mending	4	0

Total   £2   7   0¾

The masters met to discuss the compositors' communication of 22 December, 1809, which contained the revised Scale. A number of compositors had given notice, since payment on the basis of the new scale had been refused them. Severe measures were proposed against any journeymen who took the law into their own hands. Note was also taken of an application made by the pressmen. (See p. 107.)

[DOCUMENT XLVI]

York Hotel, Jan. 15, 1810.

At a Meeting of the Committee of Master Printers, held this Day—Present, J. Nichols, Esq., in the Chair: Messrs. Bensley, Woodfall, Baldwin, Whittingham, Davison, Taylor, and Shury:—and at which Messrs. Baylis, Clowes, Barnard, Stower, M'Creery, Valpy, Bryer, Law, Brettell, and Brooke, attended:—For the purpose of considering the Address of the Compositors, dated December 22, 1809:—

The gentlemen present, on referring to the proceedings of the general meeting of the trade, held at Stationers' Hall, September 7, 1809, were of opinion that no new circumstances had arisen since that period to justify any advance on compositors' work.

Resolved unanimously,—That, even had this meeting been of a different opinion, the conduct of several compositors, who have already given their employers warning, in consequence of a refusal to acquiesce in their demands of an advance, before the masters had time to deliberate thereon, renders nugatory any further consideration upon the subject.

Resolved unanimously,—That it be recommended to every gentleman immediately to circulate the names of those men who shall leave his employment in consequence of a refusal to accede to the advance demanded in the compositors' address; and that for every man so leaving his employ, he do immediately take an apprentice.

Resolved,—That the above resolutions be printed and circulated to the trade at large.

———————

In consequence of an application, communicated to this meeting by Mr. Bensley, from the Committee of Pressmen, soliciting an advance on the present Scale of Press-Work Prices,

Resolved,—That a General Meeting of the Trade be convened early in the next month, of which due notice will be given.

J. NICHOLS, *Chairman.*

The compositors' meeting arranged for 18 January, 1810, duly took place. Delegates from forty-seven offices attended.

[DOCUMENT XLVII]

Hole-in-the-Wall, Jan. 18, 1810.

At a Meeting of Compositors, held this Evening, at which were present Delegates from the following Offices, viz.

Messrs.

Adlard's	Gould's[2]	Savage's
Baillies'[1]	Hansard's Old-house	Squires'
Baldwin's	Hansard's New-house	Stower's
Barnard's	Harding & Wright's	Strahan's, King's H.
Bensley's	Harper's	Strahan's, Old House
Blackador's	Heeney's	Strahan & Preston's
Brettel's	Heseltine's	Stratford's
Causton's	Law and Gilbert's	Taylor and Co.'s.
Clowes'	Marchant & Gallabin's	Teape's
Coe's	M'Creery's	Townsend & Powell
Cundee's	Mercier & Chewet's	Vogel and Schulze
Davison's	Millan's[3]	Whiting's
Dennett's	Nichols and Son's	Wilkes'
Evans and Ruffy's	Phillips'	Wilson's
Gillett's	Plummer's	Woodfall's
Gosnell's	Pople's	

The following declaratory resolutions were unanimously agreed to :—
Resolved,

I. Previous to Sept. 15, 1809, the compositors stated substantial facts, and adequate reasons, for an advance of prices; to which the master printers answered by mere assertions, in the form of resolutions, unsupported either by fact or argument : and, though no new circumstances have arisen since the above period, the want of that relief which they had long needed has been more severely felt, from the circumstances universally accompanying the season of winter.

II. Although the original request of the compositors (in the year 1809), was for an advance of wages far more limited than the exigencies of the times required, such is their moderation, that their present claim is still more limited, notwithstanding the pressure of business would seem to favour them in increasing, instead of diminishing, their claims; and they might reasonably hope that this circumstance would not only obtain the attention, but also the acquiescence of their employers in their wishes.

III. The compositors have afforded their employers more time for deliberation than was thought necessary in 1800; and have fully evinced, by the patience they have shewn during many months of privation, that had their employers desired, in an amicable spirit, any reasonable time for deliberation, the compositors would cheerfully have consented to it.

---

[1] Probably a misprint. There was Bailey at 116 Chancery Lane and Bayley at Devonshire St., Bishopsgate. Mason, W., *The Printers' Assistant*, 1810.
[2] Gold of 103 Shoe Lane ? *Ibid.*   [3] *i.e.*, McMillan.

IV. The recommendation of a few master printers to their body to exclude the journeymen from their means of livelihood, by taking apprentices, rather than comply with the compositors' reasonable requests, is part of a wicked and cruel system of oppression, in the execution of which the poor deluded youths are first made the instruments, but will ultimately be the victims; as it must in its consequences, doom those who are already in the business, and those who may be apprenticed with this view, when the terms of their apprenticeships are expired, to a condition of slavery, want, and misery—in short, of absolute indigence and dependence.

Yet another memorial was sent to the masters. This defended the conduct of those journeymen who had left their work on the masters refusing to pay a higher scale, repeated their evidence that their earnings were not sufficient to obtain for them the ordinary necessities of life, and showed that the proposed advance would not increase the cost of the normal octavo volume to any large extent. It was also noted that some compositors were "assisting as extra hands on newspapers, to supply the deficiency of their utmost endeavours to obtain a livelihood on book work."

[DOCUMENT XLVIII]

Copy of an Address presented to the Master Printers

Hole-in-the-Wall, Feb. 5, 1810.

Gentlemen,

Several compositors having lately quitted their situations, seemingly on account of the refusal of their employers to pay the prices they had made on new works, founded on a new scale, more adequate to existing exigencies than the prices they had been paid for the nine years immediately preceding 1810, their conduct has by some been termed hostility. But why should it be so called ? The cause of their claim of increased remuneration for their labour is the increased demands on them for the necessary articles of subsistence and convenience. The compositors do not call this increased demand on themselves hostility : when the landlord raises his rent, the butcher, the baker, or any other tradesman, inform their customers that their articles must be paid an increased price for, though the increased demand be not complied with, the parties do not conceive malevolent sentiments towards each other. Nor do the compositors entertain sentiments of enmity to their employers, they only seek the means of honest maintenance for themselves and their families; and, they conceive that they are neither candidly, humanely, nor justly treated, by manifestations of hostility on the part of their employers. That their necessities are real, and that the means they have requested to enable them to supply those necessities, are not more than adequate, they trust the following facts will fully prove.

The compositors, from the best information they can collect, are of the opinion, that their average earnings do not exceed £1. 10s. 0d. per week; but, as their object is to convince their employers, having understood that the master printers have estimated the average at £1. 13s. 0d. per week, they prefer and adopt that sum. Calculating with a sufficient degree of accuracy for the purpose, it appears, that the advance will be as follows :—

Earnings per week

	On Reprints			On Manuscripts		
Average earnings per week previous to the advance	£1	13	0	£1	13	0
Advance	0	4	7½	0	7	9
Amount of earnings with the advance of prices	1	17	7½	2	0	9

It appears, from the above calculation, that a journeyman, if enjoying average work, and possessed of average abilities and industry, might expect, if employed on reprint works, to earn £1. 17s. 7½d. per week; if employed on manuscript works £2. 0s. 9d. per week; and as he might reckon being employed sometimes on reprint, and sometimes on manuscript works, the medium, as his average earnings, would be £1. 19s. 2½d.

Now, supposing him to have but the small family of a wife and two children to maintain, what would his weekly expences probably be—

	s.	d.
Rent, per week	6	0
Bread and Flour, five quarterns. . . .	6	9¼
Meat, 14 lb. at 9d. per lb.	10	6
Butter, 2 lb. at 1s. 4d. per lb.	2	8
Cheese (average price 11d. per lb.) 1 lb. . . .	0	11
Porter, three pints per day	4	4½
Candles, 1½ lb.	1	7½
Coals (average price) one bushel	1	9
Soap, Starch, and Blue	0	9
Tea, a quarter of a pound, at 7s. per lb. . . .	1	9
Sugar, 2 lb. at 9d. per lb.	1	6
Vegetables	1	6
Milk	0	7
Pepper, Salt, Vinegar, &c.	0	6
Cloathing, Shoes, and Mending	4	0
Schooling, Books, &c.	1	6
Benefit Society	0	10
Total £2	7	6¼
Average earnings	1 19	2½
Deficiency of the moderate means of subsistence for a small family	0 8	4

It must be evident to every considerate person that there are many other expences incidental to a family which cannot be foreseen; and, consequently, cannot be included in the above statement.

Some gentlemen seem to have no other objection to compliance with the request of the compositor than the reproach of other master printers, or the injury they may suffer in competition. But, with respect to the first objection, why should they fear reproach for their justice and liberality ? We are instructed by the highest authority, that "the labourer is worthy of his hire." And, with respect to the disadvantage in point of competition, those master printers who best remunerate their workmen will unquestionably obtain the best hands, and also be most efficaciously and cheerfully served by them, as "the nerve of industry, the hope of comfort, and pride of independence, constitute the great master-spring of human action."—Colquhoun's *Treatise on Indigence*, p. 233.

The compositors do not wish that their interests should occasion either trouble or difficulty to their employers, or to the booksellers. And they feel so assured of the justice and moderation of their object, and rely with such entire confidence on the justice, liberality, and humanity of their countrymen, that they are willing to state their own case to the public, and thereby facilitate the obtaining of a general compliance to whatever enhancement of the price of books their advance of wages may render necessary.

That the consequent increase on the price of books will not be very considerable, it will be easy for them to shew; as the following calculation fully proves.

We have taken the instance of a volume of 30 sheets octavo, at 13s. per sheet, from which a judgment may easily be formed by applying the proportion to other works. In addition to the reprint advance to 6d. per 1000 and the manuscript advance to 6½d. per 1000, we have taken an advance to 6¼ per 1000 as a medium, or average advance.

	at 6d. per thousand	at 6¼d. per thousand	at 6½d. per thousand
Advanced price on 30 sheets . .	£3 0 0	3 15 0	5 5 0
1000 copies at 1½ per copy advance	6 5 0	6 5 0	6 5 0
Surplus	3 5 0	2 10 0	1 0 0

If 2000 number were printed, three farthings on each volume would leave the above surplus; and as the number is increased, the advance on each volume will diminish, leaving the same surplus.

Some master printers who do not contradict the statements of the compositors as to the prices of articles of subsistence and use, nor deny the inadequacy of their earnings to their decent and comfortable maintenance, urge the supplying of the deficiency by an increase of exertion.*

---

* Masters should be informed, that the absence of some of their men is often owing to their having fatigued themselves, and exhausted their powers, by assisting as extra hands on newspapers, to supply the deficiency of their utmost endeavours to obtain a livelihood on book work.

The statements which we have here inserted, we trust, prove, that even were we in the acknowledged and tranquil enjoyment of the advance solicited, great exertion would still be necessary to supply the deficiency between the average earnings and the expences of even a small family. The following quotation from Adam Smith's *Wealth of Nations*, we hope also, they will not decline giving a due degree of consideration :

Excessive application during four days of the week is frequently the real cause of the idleness of the other three, so much and so loudly complained of. Great labour, either of mind or body, continued several days together is, in most men, naturally followed by a great desire of relaxation, which, if not restrained by force, or by some strong necessity, is almost irresistible. It is the call of nature, which requires to be relieved by some indulgence, sometimes of ease only, but sometimes too of hilarity and diversion. If it is not complied with, the consequences are often dangerous, and sometimes fatal, and such as almost always, sooner or later, bring on the peculiar infirmity of the trade. If masters would always listen to the dictates of reason and humanity, they have frequently occasion rather to moderate than to animate the application of many of their workmen. It will be found, I believe, in every trade, that the man who works so moderately, as to be able to work constantly, not only preserves his health the longest, but, in the course of the year, executes the greatest quantity of work.—Adam Smith, vol. i. book i. chap. viii.

We cannot reflect, without being convinced, that it is our indispenisble duty to endeavour to render our profession a source of effectual support to ourselves and families; nor can we, when fulfilling this duty, if possessed of common feelings, supinely rest under ungenerous threats, and unmerited reproach. At the same time we are fully sensible of the value of harmony and a good understanding between our employers and ourselves; and we lament that the law of the land precludes that facility of communication by which it might be most efficaciously promoted. But no considerations of a personal and private nature would operate as an obstruction to our exertions for the peace and prosperity of our business. If sentiments of benevolence, and a regard for our common interests should prompt you, Gentlemen, to any measures designed to restore universal harmony and good-will, whatever you may condescend to propose with that view, will be gratefully received, and met with correspondent dispositions and endeavours, as far as our duty will allow, by

Your humble servants,

THE COMPOSITORS.

N.B. Any communication addressed to A. Z. at the Hole-in-the-Wall, Fleet Street, will be received, and communicated to the compositors.

An account of the latest stages in the struggle was also sent by the London journeymen to their provincial brethren. No copy of the previous circular letter to the provinces, dated 4 August, 1809, can be found.

[DOCUMENT XLIX]

To the Compositors of the United Kingdom

(*not resident in the metropolis*)

Hole-in-the-Wall, Fleet Street, Feb. 6, 1810.

Gentlemen,

The circular letter which we addressed to you, dated Aug. 4, 1809, concluded with the following passage : "A cause founded so strongly in justice must produce perseverance, we hope, therefore, no delay of our object will induce you to think that it is abandoned. We trust that you will carefully abstain from whatever may counteract our views, but rather lend your endeavours to forward them." Accordingly, supported by justice, and urged by the most powerful of motives—necessity— which has become more imperious by the increased expences of house-keeping attending the season of winter, the compositors have renewed their endeavours to obtain an advance of price, and the request which concludes the passage above quoted they hope you will continue to comply with.

In our last address we informed you, that the advance of prices, which we had solicited, our employers had refused, alleging, that it was "highly impolitic and inexpedient at the present time." We then informed you, that we had presented a second address to them, requesting to know "the reasons why it was impolitic and inexpedient to comply with our request."

We were waiting in expectation of an answer to this last address, when we communicated with you. Not receiving any answer from the body of master printers, and encouraged by the favourable answers of the individual masters to their respective journeymen, we solicited their committee to convene a general meeting of master printers, to reconsider our case. This was complied with : the general meeting took place; but, inconsistently with their individual professions, they unanimously resolved, that their former resolution, asserting the "inexpediency and impolicy of any advance in the scale of compositors' work, be confirmed." It was now evident that we could expect nothing from further solicitation, at least for the present; we therefore abstained from any further application to the master printers (at the same time continuing our subscriptions and preserving our organization), till towards the end of December, when we presented a scale of advanced prices to the master printers to take place with the new year. In the address which accompanied it we expressed our willingness to consent to any modification of the scale, consistent with our interests, which they might suggest as necessary.

Instead of considering the difficulties which the journeymen have to struggle with; and the privations they are suffering, the committee of master printers, and a few who were not of the committee, met, and agreed to the following resolutions :

[*Then were printed the resolutions passed by the employers on* 15 *January,* 1810. *See p.* 160. *The resolutions voted on at the compositors' meeting on* 18 *January, were also given. See p.* 161.]

The conduct of the master printers has corresponded with their declarations; and many men are in consequence out of employment.

You will perceive by what has been related that we are engaged in an arduous struggle. The master printers, aided and instigated by the booksellers, have for some years past been preparing the means of preventing necessary advances in the price of our labour, according to the increase in the prices of provisions, etc. This they have done by taking a multitude of apprentices, in order to overstock the business. However, this part of the year being the most busy, we are not without hopes that we shall ultimately succeed.

We conceive that we have as much right to estimate our own labour as tradesmen have to put a price on the artices they deal in. Everything in the metropolis is sold at so great a price, and rents are so extravagantly high, that it is almost impossible to maintain even a small family. Our business, from having been one of the best, has become one of the worst. We state these things in order to put you in possession of information necessary to enable you to give advice to those parents and guardians who may be disposed to put their children to our business, with a view to their getting employment in London; whither, ere much time has elapsed, they may come only to starve, having exhausted their means in coming to town, and consequently being unable to return.

Your interests and ours are one, for the adversity or prosperity of the metropolis must naturally diffuse itself over the kingdom. At present we have the prospect of requiring every kind of aid and support to our cause which all who are connected with us by interest, or are desirous of promoting our success, have it in their power to afford us.

THE COMMITTEE OF COMPOSITORS

OF LONDON AND WESTMINSTER

The Master Printers remained adamant in their refusal to consider the compositors' demands. The following is the latter half of Document XXIII.

A manuscript letter having been read by the secretary, dated Hole-in-the-Wall, February 6, 1810,[1] signed "The Compositors," requesting that their former solicitations for an advance might not be overlooked by this meeting, a long conversation ensued thereon; when, in consequence of an inflammatory printed paper (purporting to be resolutions at a meeting of compositors, at which were present delegates from the offices of forty-seven master printers, dated Hole-in-the-Wall, Jan. 18, 1810) having been produced and read to this meeting, and from the offensive conduct of many of the compositors in circulating that paper, as well as in refusing to take works, except on the terms they had themselves presumed to dictate, it was

Resolved unanimously, That this meeting will not enter into any reconsideration of their demands.

[1] This was probably the *Address presented to the Master Printers*, dated 5 February. See p. 162.

Resolved unanimously, That the thanks of this meeting be given to Mr. Woodfall for his exertions in procuring the indemnity bill, and that he be requested to make further application on the subject.

Resolved, That the above resolutions be printed and circulated throughout the trade at large.

(Signed) J. NICHOLS, *Chairman.*

Resolved unanimously, That the thanks of this meeting be given to Mr. Nichols for his general attention to the interests of the trade, and for his conduct in the chair this day.

Adjourned.

The employers' complaints of the "inflammatory printed paper," and of "the offensive conduct of many of the compositors in circulating that paper," drew forth an answer from the men. They expressed regret for "the use which some individuals made of the paper." Once again the weekly budget of the normal family was presented, together with a request that another meeting of employers be called to reconsider their case.[1]

[DOCUMENT L]

To Master Printers

Hole-in-the-Wall, Feb. 17, 1810.

Gentlemen,

That we have manifested a degree of warmth, even in a single instance, we sincerely regret, and much more do we regret the use which some individuals made of the paper which contained the offensive passages; but we trust the candour and benevolence of our Employers will not suffer their minds to dwell on the unfortunate circumstances alluded to. When you consider, Gentlemen, the length of time (unparalleled on any former similar occasion) since we first solicited an advance of prices, during which we have patiently sustained the accumulated burden of the times, unequalled at any former period, we hope and trust, that, viewing the *whole* of our conduct, you will rather consider us as entitled to your favour and consideration than reproach and resentment. Actuated by these ideas we venture to request another meeting to consider our case.

Should we be happy enough to succeed in obtaining that relief of which we stand in such urgent need, assure yourselves, Gentlemen, that we shall prove that we are not deficient in those feelings which are deemed commendable, but that our gratitude will be evinced by our exertions to forward your business, and redeem the time which unfortunately has been lost. You cannot be unacquainted with the

[1] Since the weekly budget presented was the same as that of 5 February, it is not reprinted. See p. 163.

importance of a settled state of mind to efficient exertion in our employment; nor need anything be said to produce conviction, that mental tranquillity is incompatible with the present unsettled state of our business; which consideration we hope will induce you to an early compliance with our request.

Your humble Servants,

THE COMPOSITORS.

The compositors' first request for an advance on the Scale of 1805 had been made on 13 April, 1809. The masters had resisted every entreaty for nearly a year. Finally the employers showed some disposition to come to terms with their men.

[DOCUMENT LI]

March 12, 1810.

At a General Meeting of Master Printers, held this Day at Stationers' Hall, to consider the propriety of granting an advance to the Compositors—Present,

J. Nichols, Esq. in the Chair :

Messrs.	Messrs.	Messrs.
Woodfall	Brooke	Gosnell
Bensley	Page	Sidney
Whittingham	Coe	Allen
Baldwin	Moyes	Couchman
Taylor	Ryder and Weed	Burton
Shury	Stratford	Flint
Davison	Delahoy	M'Creery
Hansard, T. C.	Davidson	Dean, Hart Street
Barnard	Dean, Wardour Street	Valpy
Dennett	Vogel and Schultz	M'Pherson
Teape	Harding and Wright	Swan and Son
Law and Gilbert	Bryer	Ellerton
Darton and Harvey	Clowes	

A letter having been read from the Compositors, stating that *"all opposition to business was completely withdrawn on their part, and that they would rely upon the liberality of their Employers to grant them an advance on their labour adequate to existing circumstances"*—it was

Resolved,

I. That it appears to this Meeting that a moderate advance to the Compositors should be granted.

II. That a Special Committee be appointed to consider what that advance should be; in what manner it shall be made; and to regulate the present Scale of Prices for Compositors' Work accordingly.

III. That the Special Committee do consist of the following Gentlemen, in addition to those already on the present Committee :—*viz.*

Messrs. Hansard, Gosnell, Brooke, Stower, T. C. Hansard, Sidney, M'Creery, Brettell, Bryer, and Clowes.

IV. That these Resolutions be printed.

(Signed) J. NICHOLS, *Chairman.*

Resolved unanimously,

That the Thanks of this Meeting be given to the Chairman, for his impartial conduct, and attention to the business of the Day.

The new Scale of Prices was "Agreed upon at a General Meeting of Master Printers, at Stationers' Hall, London, April 16, 1810." For the first time a distinction was made between leaded and unleaded matter, more being paid for solid composition. There was an advance of one halfpenny upon leaded matter and three farthings upon solid. While the compositors had not obtained all the concessions demanded in their draft Scale of April, 1809, in the main they received increases ranging from 2s. to 3s. in the pound. The average increase may be taken as $12\frac{1}{2}$ per cent.

The compositors expressed their gratitude to the masters in the following terms :

[DOCUMENT LII]

To Master Printers

Hole-in-the-Wall, Fleet Street, London, May 17, 1810.

Gentlemen,

We request your acceptance of our thanks for your amelioration of our circumstances. The granting us an advance adequate to existing circumstances is a proof to us, that you would willingly advance our prices to an equality with our exigencies. Though we are sensible of the laudable motives by which you were induced to make a distinction between leaded and unleaded matter, we hope you will excuse our expressing apprehensions that it will not be productive of the salutary effects which are intended. To resume the object of this address, we present our thanks for the disposition you have evinced and the service you have done us, in the rise of prices which has been granted.

We are, Gentlemen,

Your faithful servants,

THE COMPOSITORS.

With the exception of the reduction of 1816 and the advances of 1866 and 1872, the clauses of London Scale of Prices of 1810 remained unchanged until 1891, when the whole Scale was fundamentally redrafted. The compositors had won a signal victory.

	previous to 1785	20th, 1785 Advance to	1793 Gave Heads and Directions.	1795 Works in larger type than English to be paid as English.	Dec. 24th, 1800	1805	April, 1809	1810
Including, English and Brevier	4d.	4½d.	—	—	Asked 5½d. for MS, copy and 5d. for reprint, i.e. advanced from 4½d. to 5½d.	The Scale of twenty-six Articles formed. 5½d.	6½d.	{ 5½d. leaded, 6d. solid.
Foreign languages	—	5d.	—	—	{ 5½d. 6d. Bourgeois or Brevier.	{ 5¾d. 6d. Bourgeois or Brevier.	{ 7½d. 7½d Bourgeois or Brevier.	{ 6½d. leaded, 6½d. solid. English-Brevier.
Dictionaries in two languages or foreign	—	5d.	—	—	5½d. Brevier upwards: 4to or 8vo—if 12mo or 16mo, 6d.	6d.	7½d. Brevier, upwards.	{ 6½d. leaded, 6½d. unleaded.
Corrections: Per hour	—	(4½d. ?)	—	—	5d.	6d.	7½d.	6d.
Grammars or spelling books	—	—	—	—	—	5½d. Brevier or or larger.	—	{ 6d. leaded, 6½d. unleaded.
Reviews or magazines with various size letters	—	—	—	—	—	2/- per sheet extra.	—	2/6 per sheet extra.
Index matter: one measure	—	—	—	—	—	1/- per sheet extra.	—	2/- per sheet extra.
Booksellers' catalogues	—	—	—	—	—	6d.	—	7d.
Night-work	—	—	—	—	—	11 p.m.-1 a.m. 1/-, until 2 a.m. 1/6, until 6 a.m. 3d. per hour extra.	—	10 p.m.-12 midnight 1/-, until 6 a.m. 3d. per hour extra.
Broadsides, leases, deeds, charter parties, etc...	—	—	—	—	—	Above Crown: double common matter; less than Crown, 1¼ common matter.	—	As in 1805.
Approximate increase, per cent.	—	12½%	10%	—	16½%	—	—	Average increase 12½%

CHAPTER VI

AN ANALYSIS
OF THE SCALE OF 1810

The Scale of 1810, largely based on that agreed to in 1805, was to remain the charter of the London compositors for eighty years. During that time many of its clauses were amended and a number of paragraphs added, but no changes were made in the original text, which was always reprinted in its integral form.

In 1836, when the compositors' reference book *The London Scale of Prices* was published, it contained explanatory paragraphs for each item of the Scale. And when masters and men met in 1847 to discuss certain addenda and revisions (although not of the main prices), the compositors' report of the proceedings contained similar details.

The Scale of 1810 is now reprinted together with the appropriate *glosses* of 1836 and 1847. The original text together with the addenda of 1816, 1847, 1866, and 1872, is printed parallel with the revised version of 1891 on pp. 328 *et seq.* of this book.

[DOCUMENT LIII]

Scale of Prices for Compositors' Work, agreed upon at a General Meeting of Master Printers, at Stationers' Hall, London, April 16, 1810: commencing on all Volumes or Periodical Numbers begun after the 30th instant.

Art. 1. All works in the English language, common matter, with space lines, including English and Brevier, to be cast up at 5¾d. per 1000;—if in Minion 6d. per 1000;—in Nonpareil 6¾d.—Without space lines, including English and Brevier, 6d. per 1000;—in Minion 6¼d.—in Nonpareil 7d.;—in Pearl, with or without space lines, 8d.;—heads and directions, or signature lines, included. A thick space to be considered an en in the width, and an en to be reckoned an em in the length of the page: and, where the number of letters amount to 500—1000 to be charged;—if under 500 not to be reckoned: and, if the calculation at per 1000 shall not amount to an odd threepence, the odd pence to be suppressed in the price of the work; but where it amounts to or exceeds threepence, there shall be sixpence charged. Em and en quadrats, or whatever is used at the beginning or end of lines, to be reckoned as an em in the width.

(1836). In casting up a work, although it be printed in half sheets,[1] it is cast up in sheets; in jobs less than a sheet, however, the casting-up is confined to the job,

---

[1] "HALF SHEET. When a forme is imposed in such a manner as to perfect itself, making two copies on a sheet, it is called a half sheet." Ringwalt, J. L., *American Encyclopaedia of Printing* (Philadelphia, 1871).

and the compositor loses or gains the five hundred letters, or the threepence (as stated in Art. 1.) as the case may chance to be.

By the term *common matter* is understood the usual description of bookwork, and not such matter as appeal cases, bills in parliament, etc., for which peculiar and distinct charges are made.[1]

Space Lines.—The reason of pearl being always paid the same price (whether leaded with a lead equal to its own body in thickness, or without a lead) has often excited surprise; but this surprise will cease when it is known that in the year 1810, when an advance of one halfpenny on leaded, and three-farthings on solid took place, *no advance whatever* was made on the price of pearl, which consequently when solid, which it most frequently is, does not have the advance which was granted in 1810; and the compositor in casting it up at 8d. receives only the price which was paid thirty years back. In 1805, the difference between the price of nonpareil and pearl was seven farthings; in 1810, the difference was one penny.

Head and White Lines.—The head or folio line and the white or direction line[2] are invariably reckoned in the square of the page. Head lines, when set up in a smaller type than the body of the work, are charged one shilling per sheet; and if any justification of figures, etc., occur, an allowance is made for extra trouble; but if the head be in larger type than the text, no extra charge can be made.

Reprints.—Annual reports of societies, with lists of subscribers, etc., are not reprints. If the copy for a book be print-copy, but derived from various sources, such book is an original work, and paid for as manuscript. Works with MS. insertions are paid extra per sheet—not less than 1s.,—but if materially altered or much interlined, or consisting of half manuscript and half reprint, are considered as original works, and paid for as if they were all manuscript. Reprinted pamphlets (when more than one sheet) are subject to the reduction above specified. No reduction is made for printed copy introduced into magazines, reviews, etc.

Diamond.[3]—It is the custom of the trade to pay tenpence per thousand for diamond, whether leaded or unleaded.

Ruby.[4]—This description of letter is not common, but it is paid an intermediate price allowed for those bodies between which it is cast; thus, a ruby (which is less than nonpareil and larger than a pearl) is cast up at $7\frac{1}{2}$d. leaded or unleaded.

(1847). This Article does not determine the price per 1000 of founts smaller than nonpareil. In future, ruby will be $7\frac{1}{2}$d. solid, $7\frac{1}{4}$d. leaded, being one-halfpenny increase upon the price of nonpareil. Diamond will be 10d. solid, $9\frac{3}{4}$d. leaded, which is a rise of 3d. per 1000 upon nonpareil. Upon all descriptions of work the extra price per 1000 for founts below brevier will be paid. The Article speaks of space lines or leads, and fixes no limit as to their thinness. In most offices 8 to pica leads are deducted for; and, in some, even 10 to pica, no matter the type they are used in. For years this has been a subject of considerable

---

[1] For details of Parliamentary Scale see chap. XIV, p. 365.

[2] "DIRECTION LINE, CATCH LINE, CATCH WORD. The first word of the following page set at the right hand end of the line of quadrats at the foot of each page . . . Catch words are now seldom used, except in reprints, to preserve uniformity in the different editions of each work." Savage, W., *op. cit.*

[3] "DIAMOND. The name of a type one size smaller than Pearl, and the smallest that is cast in the British foundries. It originated in casting a type with a pearl face upon a smaller body, for the purpose of getting in, in printing small Bibles; the founders subsequently cut it with a smaller face, and made it completely a distinct size." Savage, W., *op. cit.* (Diamond, $4\frac{1}{2}$ pts.; Pearl, 5 pts.)

[4] "RUBY. The name of a type, the next in size larger than Pearl and smaller than Nonpareil." *ibid.* ($5\frac{1}{2}$ pts.)

uneasiness, since injustice was upon the face of it; for a compositor had to deduct on a pica work just as much as he would if setting nonpareil, 8 to pica leads being used in both. This grievance is remedied, and the sizes of the type will now regulate the reduction for leads 8 and above to the pica, the basis being generally that of one-sixth of the body. Thus no deduction will be made for leads thinner than 6 to pica on founts larger than long primer, nor for leads thinner than 8 to pica on founts larger than brevier, nor for leads thinner than 10 to pica on founts larger than nonpareil, nor for leads thinner than 12 to pica when used with nonpareil or smaller type.

Stereotyped matter, when plaster of Paris is used, will be paid, with high spaces, $\frac{1}{4}$d. per 1000 extra; if with low spaces, $\frac{1}{2}$d. per 1000, as usual; but where the compositor has not the inconvenience of plaster of Paris, the extra will not be charged. This latter remark, however, supposes the compositor to impose his matter in the ordinary way; but if he has to impose it in small chases, he will then charge 1s. per sheet extra for the trouble occasioned by such imposition.

Bastard founts[1] of one remove will be cast up to the depth and width of the two founts to which they belong, as is the custom at present; and works printed in half-sheets will be cast up in sheets, with their proper extras.

The foregoing has been added to Article 1, which now declares the price per 1000 for founts down to diamond, decides what leads shall and shall not be deducted for, and settles the extra for stereotype matter, with the latest improvements therein. The granting by the masters so clear a definition in respect to leads, of which the Scale is silent, and compositors held liable to deduct for every kind of lead used, induced us to admit that pearl should not be excepted from the rule.

2. Works printed in Great Primer to be cast up as English, and all works in larger type than Great Primer as half English and half Great Primer.

(1836). This mode of casting up works, which was agreed to in 1796, applies also to jobs, but not to large-letter display broadsides, the charge for which will be found in the Appendix.[2]

3. All works in foreign languages, though common type, with space lines, including English and Brevier, to be set up at $6\frac{1}{4}$d. per 1000;—if in Minion $6\frac{3}{4}$d.;—Nonpareil $7\frac{1}{2}$d.—Without space lines, including English and Brevier, $6\frac{1}{2}$d.;—Minion 7d.;—Nonpareil $7\frac{3}{4}$d.;—and Pearl, with or without space lines, $8\frac{3}{4}$d.

(1836). In the scale of 1805, foreign works in bourgeois and brevier were paid one farthing per thousand extra; but in 1810 one price was established for type from english to brevier inclusive.

Works in the German language and common type are paid the same as other foreign works; but if the German character be employed, it is paid as Greek without accents. The same price is also paid for the Irish character.

(1847). This Article means, that "all works in foreign languages" shall be paid $\frac{1}{2}$d. per 1000 extra down to brevier, and $\frac{3}{4}$d. per 1000 extra for founts smaller than brevier; but an objection was raised to include, in this word "all," works in the Saxon language set up in ordinary roman type, its peculiarity warranting a higher charge. The extra labour caused was admitted, and Saxon works, with plain roman type, will be paid $\frac{1}{2}$d. per 1000 extra beyond the price of foreign.

---

[1] BASTARD FOUNT. Type with a face larger or smaller than its appropriate body.

[2] "Display broadsides, foolscap or crown size, are paid 5s.; demy, 7s.; royal, 8s. 6d.; and double crown, 10s."

When Saxon or German works are set up in the Saxon or German characters, then one penny extra per 1000 will be charged. So that a Saxon or German work, in its own character, will be cast up, if in English or brevier, solid, 7½d. per 1000, in minion 8d., in nonpareil 8¾d.

4. English dictionaries of every size, with space lines, including English and Brevier, to be paid 6¼d.:—without space lines 6½d. (In this Article are not included gazetteers, geographical dictionaries, dictionaries of arts and sciences, and works of a similar description, except those attended with extra trouble beyond usual descriptive matter.) Dictionaries of two or more languages of every size, with space lines, including English and Brevier, to be paid 6½d.: without space lines 6¾d.—If smaller type than Brevier, to take the proportionate advance specified in Article 1.

(1836). The words "of every size" allude to the dimensions of the page; because formerly (that is, by the scale of 1801) duodecimo and eighteenmo dictionaries were paid one halfpenny per 1000 more than those set up in 8vo. or 4to.

In framing the above article, it was intended that such gazetteers or dictionaries of the arts and sciences as were attended with *any extra trouble* beyond usual descriptive matter should be paid the above dictionary price; and therefore, such gazetteers or dictionaries as contain many references, italics, contractions, etc., take the advanced price as dictionary matter. For "Pharmacopoeias," see Appendix B.[1]

If the above works are in two columns an extra charge of not less than one shilling per sheet is made for column matter.

(1847). Although this Article says "dictionaries of two or more languages" shall be paid ¼d. per 1000 extra, we were successful in getting a just interpretation of these words, rendering Articles 3 and 4 consistent with each other. Thus, say a German-French dictionary. This dictionary is in foreign languages, and therefore entitled to be cast up according to Article 3, which says, "all works in foreign languages;" and Article 4 gives us the right to add to such cast-up ¼d. per 1000 for dictionary matter. The employers assented to the reasons mentioned, so that dictionaries wholly in foreign languages will now be paid ¼d. per 1000 more than the latter part of the Article, at first sight, seems to allow.

5. English grammars, spelling books, and works of those descriptions, in Brevier or larger type, with space lines to be paid 6d. per 1000;— without space lines 6¼d.;—if in two languages, or foreign language, with space lines 6¼d.;—without space lines 6½d.

(1836). There is a strange anomaly in this article. It was intended to allow the compositor one farthing per thousand extra for the trouble occasioned by the admixture of italic, the frequent occurrence of single letters and monosyllables in grammars, spelling books, etc.; but if a compositor be employed on a *grammar* wholly in a foreign language, it is paid no more for than if it were a foreign *work*. (see Article 3.) It should, however, to be consistent, be allowed the halfpenny for foreign, and the farthing for grammar, and be cast up at 6½d. with space lines, and 6¾d. without space lines.

The extra farthing per thousand for this kind of work is not to pay for column matter; but two column matter, in grammars, spelling-books, etc., is charged not

---

[1] *"Pharmacopoeias.*—These works, when differing in any material degree from common matter, are charged as dictionaries; and, when interspersed with Latin words, are charged as half foreign and half English. Medical signs are also charged extra, when they are numerous." (Appendix B, 1836.)

less than one shilling per sheet; three and not exceeding four columns are charged one and one-half; and above four columns are charged double.

School arithmetics, as well as the works above specified, are cast up at the above prices.

If the works specified above be in smaller type than brevier, they take the advance granted for such type in Article 1.

(1847). A like anomaly to that just mentioned has also been removed in this Article. The Scale gives no more for a French-German grammar than for an English-French or English-German grammar. The employers at once assented to the alteration proposed, and foreign grammars will now be paid ¼d. per 1000 extra beyond the price of foreign works, as settled by Article 3.

6. Small sized folios, quartos, octavos, and works done in Great Primer or larger type, (English language) which do not come to seven shillings when cast up at the usual rate, to be paid as follows:—English and larger type, not less than 7s.;—Pica 8s. 6d.;—English 12mo. to be paid not less than 10s. 6d.;—and Pica not less than 11s. 6d. per sheet.

(1836). By the words "cast up at the usual rate," is meant works cast up without their extras; and though this Article specifies small sized works in the English language, the principle is applied to foreign works also; and if foreign works amount only to the sums specified, they are entitled to an advance according to the number of thousands they contain, as regulated by Art. 3 of the scale. For example, if a foreign folio or 8vo. work, in english type, without space lines, contain 13,000 letters, it would come to 7s. 0½d. Now, as the same work in the English language would come to 6s. 6d. and would consequently obtain by this Article an advance of 6d., so the foreign work is entitled to the like advance, and is paid 7s. 6d.; if it were not so, the compositor would not receive anything for the work being in a foreign language.

(1847). Much unpleasantness has been occasioned in consequence of the different meanings given to the words "when cast up at the usual rate," as to whether the extras of the work were to be included, or otherwise. We did not deem it advisable to offer much opposition to the opinion expressed by the employers, as the price stated for Bills in Parliament corroborates their reading; and it was agreed that the words "when cast up at the usual rate" should be interpreted as "including every item of charge."

7. Reviews, magazines, and works of a similar description, consisting of various sized letter, if cast up to the different bodies, to be paid 2s. 6d. per sheet, extra.

(1836). The mere circumstance of a work being a periodical publication does not entitle it to the charge of 2s. 6d. per sheet. To justify this charge, the text must consist of two bodies, and be cast up to their respective founts. Publications, however, of more than one sized letter must not be cast up as all one body, to avoid the payment of the 2s. 6d. per sheet, but must be charged according to the proportion of type they contain, with the 2s. 6d. allowed by this article for the bodies.

Reprints of this description of work (if more than a sheet) are cast up at three farthings per thousand less than the current number, but the 2s. 6d. per sheet is charged. No deduction, however, is made for printed copy introduced into the current numbers of these works.

In reviews, magazines, etc., where leads are only occasionally used, or when used only in a small portion of the publication, no deduction is made.

Reviews, magazines, etc., are entitled to the charge for notes, although such notes are set up in one of the bodies used for the text.

All matter pulled in slips or galleys is made up at the expense of the employer.[1]

(1847). Where printed copy is partially introduced, or leads are occasionally used in reviews, magazines, publications, etc., no deduction will have to be made for such print copy or leads, unless with sizes of type leaded throughout according to the plan of the work. Under this Article, publications having two bodies of type in them are to be reckoned. The words "works of a similar description" determine this to be the meaning; so much so, that it was not considered necessary to define what constituted a publication.

8. **Pamphlets of five sheets and under, and parts of works done in different houses, amounting to not more than five sheets to be paid 1s. per sheet extra; but, as it frequently occurs that works exceeding a pamphlet are often nearly made up without a return of letter, all such works shall be considered as pamphlets, and paid for as such.**

(1836). Parts of works done in different houses, when unequal in their nature, are cast up according to the respective merits of the different parts; and if a sheet, or less than a sheet, it is considered a job, and cast up at the price specified in Art. 20 of the scale.

The expression *"nearly made up"* is indefinite; but in works where two-thirds of the matter are made up, one shilling per sheet is charged upon the whole.

In works of two or more volumes, when the letter of the first volume is all made up, and used for the second, no charge can be made for making up letter.

(1847). The words "nearly made up" will be considered to mean two-thirds. Consequently for works for which two-thirds of the letter have been made up without a return, either of its own or a similar work, 1s. extra per sheet throughout will be charged. But supposing the work be published in separate volumes, and the letter of the first volume be used for the second, or the second for the third, in such cases the charge for making up letter will not be made beyond the first volume. In all instances, however, it must be distinctly understood, that the letter and leads must be the same kind of letter, the same-sized leads; if not, the charge for making up letter will still stand good. Parts of work done at different houses will now be cast up according to their respective merits.

If they consist of a sheet, or less, they will be cast up as jobs; if over a sheet, and not more than five sheets, as pamphlets.

9. **Works done in sixteens, eighteens, twenty-fours, or thirty-twos, on Small Pica and upwards, to be paid 1s. 6d. per sheet extra. If on Long Primer or smaller type, 1s. per sheet extra.—Forty-eights, to be paid 2s. per sheet extra, and sixty-fours 2s. 6d. per sheet extra.**

(1836). This article does not apply to half sheets or sheets of double foolscap, double demy, etc., imposed as sixteens, as these are cast up and take the extras as octavo. Sixty-fours and forty-eights, in whatever type, are paid 2s. 6d. the former, and 2s. the latter, per sheet, extra.

(1847). The oft-repeated question, "What constitutes the boundary of a sheet of paper?"[2] has at length been answered. During the last few years, pages which

---

[1] "SLIPS. In printing encyclopaedias, dictionaries of arts or sciences, and similar works, which frequently undergo great alterations in the proofs, they are occasionally pulled on slips of paper, of the length and half the breadth of a demy leaf of paper. This is done on account of the facility of adding new subject matter, or taking some away, without having to over-run and to re-make up the sheet, after it has been imposed in pages." Savage, W., *op. cit.*

[2] See Pollard, Graham, *Notes on the Size of the Sheet* in *The Library* (Transactions of the Bibliographical Society), Fourth Series, Vol. XXII., No. 2, 3, 1941, and Document LXXVI, p. 256.

were wont to be called folio have been designated 4to, and quarto 8vo, etc., which is no other than increasing the size and number of the pages in the sheet at the expense of the compositors' extras. A limit is now made as to the size of what shall be termed a sheet. This will be arrived at by ascertaining the number of inches, width and breadth, the forme when in chase measures, including borders, rules, and inner margins. Thus, take an 8vo outer forme. Measure from the left corner of the first page to the right corner of the fourth page, just as imposed, and then measure from the foot of the first page to the foot of the eighth page, inclusive of the white lines, multiplying the dimensions by each other, and should the product be 520, or less, then the sheet shall be considered single; if exceeding 520, as two single sheets of half the number of pages of which the whole sheet consists, charging a quarto as two sheets of folio, 8vo as two sheets of 4to, etc., as the case may be, the standard being taken from a sheet charged as such during the last twenty years. By this simple method the trade will be protected against the ill-effects of large formes, and also readily ascertain whether the work being performed is imposed in single or double sheets.

10. Works requiring an alteration or alterations of margin,[1] to be paid, for each alteration, 1s. per sheet to the pressmen, if altered by them, and 6d. to the compositor, as a compensation for making up the furniture; if altered by the compositor then he is to be paid 1s. for the alteration, and the pressmen 6d. for the delay.—This article to be determined on solely at the option of the employer.

(1836). This article allows the employer to give the alteration either to the pressman or the compositor; but it more properly belongs to the compositor, and the general practice of the trade is for the compositor on the work to make the alteration. This Article does not apply to cases where a re-imposition or transposition of pages is required; in all such cases the compositor is entitled to charge his time.

(1847). No explanation respecting this Article was thought to be necessary.

11. Bottom-notes, consisting of twenty lines (or two notes, though not amounting to twenty lines) and not exceeding four pages, in every ten sheets, in quarto or octavo; one page (or two notes, though not amounting to one page) and not exceeding six pages, in twelves; two pages (or two notes, though not amounting to two pages) and not exceeding eight in eighteens or above, to be paid 1s. per sheet; but under the above proportion, no charge to be made. Bottom-notes, consisting of ten lines (or two notes, though not amounting to ten lines) in a pamphlet of five sheets or under, and not exceeding two pages, to be paid 1s. per sheet extra. Quotations, mottos, contents to chapters, etc., in smaller type than the body, to be considered as notes. [Where the notes shall be in Nonpareil or Pearl, in twelves, the number of pages to be restricted to four; in eighteens, to five pages.]—This article is intended only to fix what constitutes the charge of 1s. per sheet for bottom notes: all works requiring a higher charge than 1s. for bottom notes are to be paid for according to their value.

(1836). This article is by general acceptation understood to mean that, in a quarto or octavo volume, there must be one note of twenty lines, or two shorter ones, to constitute *any* charge, and that there must be on an average more than four pages in every ten sheets to carry a *higher* charge than one shilling a sheet; that is, in a work of forty 8vo. sheets, more than sixteen pages; for a fresh calculation is not made for every ten sheets. If, therefore, two notes, or one note of

---

[1] See p. 83, footnote.

twenty lines, occur in an octavo or quarto volume—and two pages or two notes in eighteens or smaller-sized works, one shilling per sheet is paid for such works throughout.

Where the notes exceed the quantity stipulated in the above article, an additional sixpence per sheet is charged, until the quantity of note entitles the compositor to a further advance, when, in order to ascertain what that advance should be, the whole of the notes are measured off, and cast up as a distinct body, and one shilling per sheet is charged for placing.

[*Then was given an example of a typical instance.*]

The usual rule for the type for notes is two sizes less than the text; i.e., English text has Small Pica notes; Small Pica text, Bourgeois notes; Long Primer text, Brevier notes; but when under this size a proportionately less quantity of note is required to constitute the above charges. Thus—If in a work set in Small Pica, the notes should be set in Brevier, which is three sizes less than the text; the same number of thousands should be composed for 1s. per sheet, as would be the equivalent to the number of thousands contained in the four pages of Bourgeois, i.e., if the four pages of Bourgeois contain 10,000 letters, no more than that number of Brevier should be composed without an increased charge.

To compensate the compositor for time employed in making up, altering references, etc., the notes, although in the same size as any type used in the text, take the charge of 1s. per sheet.

Notes upon notes, when set up in a smaller type than the note, are charged according to the rule laid down for notes.

(1847). We now come to one of the most important alterations made in the newly-arranged Scale, affecting, more or less, every office in the trade, newspapers excepted. It concerns bottom-notes—charging one shilling per sheet throughout a work if two notes occur therein. This and all the other Articles formed the basis of our arguments; the practice of the trade being valueless to us if opposed to the wording of the Article itself. In March, 1840, the Masters' Association issued a circular interpreting the Article to mean two notes for every ten sheets. This led to a Special Delegate Meeting of the trade in the same month, when the trade council caused to be read a report explanatory of the journeymen's reading. This report says:—"The first point to be considered is, whether the right claimed by the trade is authorized by the Scale?" Or, in other words, "Does the Scale sanction the present custom of the trade in the charge for bottom-notes?" This is answered by the trade being "entreated to bear in mind that if the members contend against the masters' interpretation, they will be contending for custom against a positive law;" and the report adds,—"In the opinion of the council, the Scale will not help us to claim 1s. per sheet for two notes in a volume. This is stated candidly and explicitly to you at the outset, that the trade council may be released from any odium hereafter of leading you into a contest for a charge which the Scale, taken by itself, cannot sanction." Enough has been shown to convince all present that the law and practice are at variance with each other. Be it borne in mind, then, that neither ourselves nor the masters could alter that law. As we found it, so we were necessarily obliged to consider it. At once, then, we confess that the words found in the Article "under the above proportion no charge to be made," were unanswerable; for to say otherwise, would be to persist in making a charge in the face of the sentence declaring that "no charge" shall be made. In addition to this testimony, the Secretary of the Masters' Association read from a minute-book a decision given in July, 1805, but a short time after the Scale was made. This decision was signed by five masters whose names are appended to the 1805 Scale. It established the masters' interpretation, and showed beyond doubt that the practice which has prevailed is directly opposed to the decision given. It was a work of twenty-nine sheets, and had five notes. No man would think he was doing wrong, following up the custom of years, if he charged for these five notes one shilling per sheet, or twenty-nine shillings. "But," said five of the eight gentlemen who framed the Article itself in 1805, "neither number nor lines justify the charge;" that is, there should be six, not five notes, or sixty lines of notes, to warrant a charge throughout. We found it impossible to gainsay the meaning of this decision, or to prove that the practice of the trade was in accordance with the Article. But knowing how vastly important the trade deemed this bottom-note question, some inquiry was made into the effect of the alteration. From a promiscuous library 192 volumes were examined. The result showed that the cases are extremely rare in which the compositor will be a loser, for 186 had sufficient notes to constitute the charge; three were without notes; one had a single note; and the other two might be called doubtful, the small type in them being explanations to wood-cuts. And if any man will look into a number of books, he will see that they are few indeed which, having notes, do not show two for each ten sheets they severally make. Cases of extraordinary sums paid were quoted; and were called iniquitous charges, paid to prevent disorder. One was a work of eighty-eight sheets; £4 8s. were paid for one note exceeding twenty lines, the difference in value of the note-matter over the text being about one shilling only. As it was in vain to follow up the subject, we determined upon obtaining a more liberal meaning to the actual wording than the resolution put before us gave. This we succeeded in, and we have no hesitation in stating that we believe a correct reading has now been arrived at.

The arrangement made does not cause separate castings-up; a great error has been committed in supposing the principle ever implied such a trouble; for suppose the work makes thirty sheets, if the compositor cannot show six single notes (half lines or even words will do), or three notes, in themselves amounting to sixty lines, such as 18 in one, 30 in the second, and 12 in the third, no charge will be made for notes; but showing the number of notes, or notes having the requisite number of lines, the charge of one shilling per sheet will be made throughout. To simplify the present rule, the compositor must show two notes in every ten sheets, or one note averaging in every ten sheets twenty lines. This latter amendment upon the original intention will be found, in many instances, to be a saving clause for the trade; for though there may be works making twenty sheets which fall short of having four notes, yet, in such works, there may be two notes which added together make forty lines. In such a case, the compositor will still charge 20s. for placing notes, the value of which may be said to be just trifling. Where notes exceed the maximum quantities stated in the Article, such as more than four pages in every ten sheets in 4to or 8vo, the compositor will then charge 1s. 6d. per sheet, although the exact value of the notes may not be more than 1s. 2d.; and where 1s. 6d. will not pay, then the whole of the notes must be measured off, their value charged, and 1s. per sheet extra added to the cast-up for placing. A plan has been laid down for measuring off notes, quotations, or small type inserted in the text of a work, making more than one line, by adding to each note, quotation, etc., an extra line for the space which separates the small type from the text type. Every reference is to be considered a note, if only a word; and if a work be in pica and the notes in bourgeois, or three removes from the text, the compositor will only be called upon to compose the same number of thousands as though the notes were set in long primer, or two removes, which is decided to be the proper distinction for notes to all works. In cases where there are notes upon notes, quotations, etc., set up in smaller type than the notes, 1s. per sheet extra will be paid on every sheet where such small type is found. Extracts, etc., set up in a type between that used for the text and that for the notes, will also be paid 1s. per sheet extra where they occur; but if it can be shown that the intermediate type course in three-fourths of the work, that is, in fifteen sheets of a work making twenty sheets, then the compositor will charge 1s. per sheet for placing throughout. With regard to this charge for mixture of type, it was stated by the employers to be a charge unknown in years gone by; and was but another mode of adding to the price per 1000 for making up, which was included in Article I.; that it had occasioned many of them great uneasiness in seeing a charge insisted upon of modern introduction, and though they had paid it, they had done so not as mixture of type, but looked upon works having it as occasioning additional trouble.

12. Side-notes[1] to folios and quartos, not exceeding a broad quotation, if only chap. or date, and not exceeding three explanatory lines on an average in each page, to be paid 1s. per sheet; in octavo, if only chap. or date, and not exceeding three explanatory lines on an average in each page, 1s. 6d. per sheet.—Cut-in notes, in smaller type than the body to be paid for in a similar manner.—Side and bottom notes to many, particularly historical and law works, if attended with more than ordinary trouble, to be settled between the employer and journeyman.

(1836). In casting up a work with side-notes, the side-notes are not reckoned in the width of the page.

Side-notes are cast up as double—that is, the length and breadth of the side-notes are taken, multiplied, and the product doubled. When the space between the note do not exceed a broad quotation it is reckoned in measuring off the notes. The side-note width of the guard line and head lines are reckoned in measuring the depth of the notes. The reglets[2] or leads between the text and side-note are reckoned in the width of the text, when the side-notes are cast up. One shilling per sheet for side-notes, in addition to their being cast up as double, is allowed for placing.

Under-runners from side-notes are reckoned in the side-note, and paid 3d. each, in addition.

When the bottom notes to law works, &c. are attended with extra trouble, in consequence of numerous contractions, an extra is paid.

(1847). Here was another equally difficult rule to determine, for the Article decides only a minimum charge, and this but for sizes down to 8vo. Side-notes to 12mo and smaller-sized works, or when side-notes exceeded the average mentioned, how they were to be reckoned and charged is not stated, neither is a principle laid down which shall govern a charge for side-notes throughout. The employers have never recognised the system adopted by the trade of casting off side-notes, but have given a fixed sum per sheet instead. The Article will now be found complete. The minimum charge for side-notes to 12mo will be 2s.; 16mo, 18mo, and smaller sizes, 2s. 6d. per sheet. Upon all sizes for side-notes set in nonpareil, 6d. per sheet additional will be paid; if in pearl, 1s. per sheet. For casting off side-notes a simple rule has been devised. The compositor will ascertain the exact number of appearing lines, and multiply the number by 3; that is, twice for composition, and once for making-up or placing; and he will find that heavily side-noted works, by this system, will amply pay; while those less noted will give a charge, in most cases, equal to the present custom. Side-notes and cut-in notes will be paid throughout if occurring in one-fourth of the work, and not in distinct portions. Thus, in a work of twelve sheets, if side or cut-in notes are found in three out of the twelve sheets, the charge for such side or cut-in notes will be upon the whole twelve sheets; if occurring in less than one-fourth, they will then be paid on those sheets in

---

[1] "SIDE NOTES or MARGINAL NOTES, are notes at the fore edge of the page, running from top to bottom, or placed opposite the matter to which they refer, when they are short." Savage, W., *op. cit.*

[2] "REGLET. A thin sort of furniture, of an equal thickness all its length. It is quadrat high, of several thicknesses." Hansard, T. C., *op. cit.*, p. 928.

which they appear. Double side-notes, or notes upon each side of the page, will be paid double the price specified for notes on one side of the page. As the trouble varies in respect to under-runners, or figures down the side of the page, it was deemed best that these should be left for settlement between the master and the journeymen.

13. Greek, Hebrew, Saxon, etc., or any of the dead characters, if one word and not exceeding three lines in any one sheet, to be paid for that sheet is. extra; all above to be paid according to their value.

(1836). The Saxon language is mentioned only in regard to the charge of one shilling per sheet, while the works wholly done in that language seem to have been unintentionally omitted in the scale; they are, however, paid the same as Greek without accents, according to Article 14.

The term "dead characters" is extremely indefinite; and the charge allowed by this article is not limited to the languages of such nations as are extinct, but includes all languages for which roman or italic types is not employed, such as Sanskrit and other oriental characters; also German, Irish, &c. &c.

This article defines only what charge is to be made for Greek, Hebrew, Saxon, &c. when introduced in small quantities in various parts of a sheet,— such as single words, half lines, or lines. If there be one word, and not more than three lines, the charge is one shilling for each character, in every sheet in which those characters occur; all above three lines is paid according to their value, preserving the is. per sheet for the first three lines. When the quantity of Greek, Hebrew, Saxon, &c. amounts to two-thirds, interspersed throughout the sheet, it is paid all as Greek, &c. or an equivalent price allowed for the admixture.

As it occasionally occurs that words in Greek, &c. are obliged to be set up in a different sized fount to the body of the work, when such is the case, extra is paid for justification.

For the convenience of employers, and that each sheet of a work may be paid the same price, it is sometimes the practice to ascertain the quantity contained in the work, and put an average price on each sheet. This was not formerly the general custom, nor is it, indeed, commendable, since by this mode it often happens that the task of setting up that part of a work containing the greatest quantity of Greek, &c. falls into the hands of those who have had no share of the lighter parts of the work, and thus endless and bitter disputes are caused by one man being called upon to perform that labour for which another has received the reward. The article limits the charge to "that sheet" and therefore a work in which small portions of Greek, &c. are introduced, should be charged according to the particular quantity in each sheet.

(1847). Greek, &c., exceeding three lines in any one sheet, will be paid is. additional to its value as cast up; the first three lines, entitling the charge of is., being deducted.

14. Greek, with space lines, and without accents, to be paid 8½d. per 1000; if with separate accents, 10d.; without space lines, and without accents, 8¾d.; with accents 10¼d. The asper not to be considered an accent. [If dictionary matter, to take one half-penny advance.]

(1836). By "separate accents" is meant the use of distinct accents with kerned letters.[1]

---

[1] " KERN OF A LETTER. That part which hangs over the body or shank." Hansard, T. C., *op. cit.*, p. 927.

The composition of grammars being attended with extra trouble, ¼*d.* per 1,000 is allowed for them. Therefore, Grammars in Greek, Hebrew, &c. take the advance specified in Article 5. Thus a Greek grammar without space lines and accents is paid 9*d.* per 1,000.

Jobs in Greek, &c. of one sheet or under are also paid 1*d.* per thousand more than the prices above stated.

It has been contended that works in Greek, Hebrew, &c. not being common matter, were not intended to be subject to the reduction upon reprints; but as the same advantage accrues to the compositor upon reprint Greek as upon reprint English, it is just that the reduction should be made; and therefore Greek, &c. set up from printed copy, is subject to the modification of the Scale proposed by the masters in 1816.

(1847). No addition has been made to this Article, it needing none. Alteration was not in the power of the Conference, otherwise no doubt it would have been attempted; the employers observing, that "the price of Greek without accents was extravagant, as the compositor could set plain Greek in almost the same time he could foreign matter."

15. Hebrew, Arabic, Syriac, etc., to be paid double: Hebrew with points to be cast up as half body and half points doubled.

(1836). The phrase "paid double" signifies double the price of common matter. Although Hebrew with points is alone stated to be cast up as half body points doubled; yet Syriac, or any other language or character with points, is cast up in the same manner.

Of the mode of casting up a work with points, the following is an example :— Supposing the work to be set up in small pica Hebrew with nonpareil points, it is cast up as half small pica and half nonpareil, that is each page is charged as if it were a page of small pica and a page of nonpareil.

Grammars, Dictionaries, &c. in these languages are cast up at double the price specified in Article 5.

This article applies only to works, or where several pages appear together. Small quantities of Arabic, Syriac, &c. are paid according to Article 13.

(1847). Upon the subject of Hebrew much discussion took place; it being contended that the Article could not be adhered to by London masters. It was said, too, that Greek and Hebrew works would be done in Germany, where wages were very low. The employers wished us to admit of a mutual settlement with respect to this kind of work, so that they might give to a compositor a certain price per sheet. This we objected to, as it allowed one man to have an advantage over his fellow-man, he being willing to take a less price than his neighbour. The employers said they could always have it done on the establishment; this we admitted, but added that that was a recognised system of working; whereas the other mode would be setting men in competition with each other. The rule was passed without addition.

16. Music to be paid double the body of the sonnet type.

(1836). That is, if the sonnet type be long primer, the square of the page is taken as long primer, and the amount which the sheet or job would be paid as long primer is doubled.

The rule is, however, little applicable to the present style of letter-press music printing, the composition of which is now usually paid an *ad valorem* price, as double the price of sonnet type would not pay. Indeed, in music wholly *instrumental*, Art. 16 would be useless as a guide, as there would be no *sonnet* type employed.

(1847). Here we had an imperfect rule, and but indefinite means to alter it. The Article is silent upon music which has no sonnet type, such as instrumental music. It was therefore inapplicable as a rule. The modern founts of music are very different to those formerly in use, and vary in thickness as well as mode of casting. No price could be settled upon to meet the whole of these founts, so it was agreed that music should be paid by agreement between the employer and employed; that is, the latter, if on an entire work, should get as much per week as their services are worth; and if setting up a few pages only, make such charge as will pay them for their labour and be just to the employer.

17. Index matter, though but one measure, to be paid 2s. per sheet extra.

(1836). The charge of 2s. per sheet for index matter does not include the charge for columns or tabular; and indexes cast up as tabular or table are charged 2s. in addition to what they come to by letters.

(1847). This Article has not been added to; the 2s. given for index matter per sheet being said to be good evidence of its being entitled to be cast up as distinct from the work. It was agreed, however, that column-matter, in indexes, should be charged the usual extra for.

18. Booksellers' catalogues (in whatever language) to be cast up at 7d. per 1000, not including the numbering.

(1836). The expression "not including the numbering" does not mean that the numbers are not to be reckoned in the square of the page, but that when the bookseller sends in his copy without numbers at the beginning of the article, or with incorrect numbers, and the compositor is required to alter them, or put in the numbers, he is entitled to make an extra charge for such numbering; in other words, 7d. per thousand does not include the charge for the trouble occasioned to the compositor by altering or marking in the numbers prefixed to the books.

If a bookseller's catalogue only makes a sheet, or less than a sheet, it is cast up at no more than 7d. per thousand.

Booksellers' lists or advertisements are charged as a job at 7d. per thousand when only making a sheet or under; but if done in smaller type than brevier, they take the proportionate advance specified in Article 1.

When notes or remarks in smaller type are inserted in a bookseller's catalogue, they are paid the same as bottom notes.

Catalogues in two columns are paid one shilling per sheet for columns.

The words "in whatever language" mean that the foreign languages, where roman type is used, viz. Latin, Italian, French, &c. take no extra charge; but Greek, Hebrew, Syriac, &c. are paid according to Article 13.

(1847). This Article applies to booksellers' catalogues only. "Not including the numbering" means, that when the compositor has to supply or correct the numbers used in a bookseller's catalogue, an extra charge shall be made equivalent to the lost time occasioned. The words "in whatever language" mean those in which common type is used.

19. Night work to commence, and be paid for, from ten o'clock till twelve 1s., all after to be paid 3d. per hour extra till six.—Morning work, commencing at four o'clock, to be paid 1s. extra—Sunday work, if not exceeding 6 hours, to be paid for 1s. if for a longer time, 2d. an hour.

(1836). The compositor's day's work is reckoned twelve hours; if, therefore, business require it, the compositor *on the piece* works from 8 till 10 in the evening, and from 6 to 8 in the morning, without any extra charge; but if required to come before 6, or called to work after 10, he immediately claims 1s., because he has already worked two hours beyond the ordinary time, without any extra charge. Sunday work, for any portion of time *less* than six hours, is paid 1s.

Compositors on the establishment, when required to work beyond the recognised hours, are entitled to charge extra.—See *Appendix*.

(1847). A long and animated discussion followed the reading of this Article, the employers wishing to be consulted in all chapel regulations respecting hours of work, commencing and ending; and mentioned the various interruptions their businesses were subjected to by chapels, &c. What they wanted was, that before any regulation was made, their consent should be obtained ere it was adopted. A resolution framed in accordance thereto was proposed. This we resisted, and said that chapels were a protection rather than an injury to employers. Some restriction was absolutely necessary, as many men would work in their meal-times and at extraordinary hours, if permitted, occasioning distrust and jealousy. Men were always anxious to fulfil, to the letter, the instructions of the overseer both as to coming early or working late; and chapels, after all, did but keep in order the refractory, when, but for them, disputes amongst the members would often be endless. Such a resolution, we stated, if allowed to be printed, would be discreditable to those we served. The employers ultimately consented to withdraw it. The Article remains as before.

20. Jobs of one sheet or under (except Auctioneers' catalogues and particulars) to be cast up at 7d. per 1000; if done in smaller type than Brevier to take the proportionate advance specified in article 1; if in foreign language, of one sheet or under, (except Auctioneers' catalogues,) to be cast up at 8d. per 1000; if done in smaller type than Brevier, to take the proportionate advance specified in article 1.

(1836). Auctioneers' Catalogues and Particulars, of whatever extent, or whether leaded or unleaded, are cast up at 6d. per 1,000; if any smaller type or other extras occur in a catalogue, they are paid in the same way as extras upon book-work. The conditions in smaller type, when standing, are paid as an ordinary page of the catalogue; but if set up, are charged according to the type in which they are set.

Jobs are not cast up as sheets or half-sheets, but according to the number of pages they may contain. They are also subject to the regulations in Art. 1.—*"A thick space,"* &c. see Art. 1 to end of that Article.

(1847). This Article excepts auctioneers' work, leaving it to be inferred that auctioneers' catalogues and particulars should be charged according to Article 1. We spoke of the labour this work often occasioned, and it was decided that it should be paid an uniform price of 6d. per 1000, leaded or solid. Under this Article came a description of work called one-sheet tracts, always in dispute, and generally composed by boys. The employers, it was said, could not pay them as jobs—they were never intended so to be considered. The letter, leads, white-lines, and furniture, were always the same; and to jump from 5d. to 7d. per 1000 for a reprint leaded tract, was too great to be allowed. These tracts seemed to us much to resemble one-sheet publications; and being sensible of the difference which this work presented from ordinary jobs, as also that journeymen seldom obtained them, but boys were kept constantly going, even to an unnecessary, and on the part of the employers, not desired, increase of their numbers, we consented to view these sheet-tracts as though they were publications; that is, allowing them to be cast up according to Article 1., adding to cast-up 2s. 6d., which is equivalent to $\frac{3}{4}$d., and sometimes 1d. extra per 1000; the only real difference being to the compositor, that he will deduct for reprint and leads; but a manuscript tract set in small pica will be found, by adding the 2s. 6d., to be close upon 7d. per thousand, and a reprint one equal to the ordinary price of manuscript. By this addition we settled a long-disputed description of work, we believe to the benefit of journeymen generally. Jobs partaking of the character of book-work will be cast up in sheets, and take the usual extras for notes, column-work, &c., as stated in the Scale.

21. Where two pages only are imposed, either opposite to, or at the back of each other, they shall be paid for as two pages; but if with an indorse, or any other kind of matter constituting a third, then to be paid as a sheet, if in folio; a half sheet, if in quarto; and so on.

(1836). This article has occasionally been misconstrued; and it has been supposed that if any matter be on the third page, the compositors ought to charge the job as four pages; this, however, is not the case—for, *in jobs*, it requires matter on three pages, in order that they may be charged as four. Thus, a circular of two pages, printed on the first and third page, is only charged as two pages; but if there be matter on the first, second, *and* third, it is charged as four; or if there be matter on the first and second, and an indorse on the fourth, it is charged as four. This definition will appear correct when it is observed that the indefinite article is used in the scale, which does not say, constituting *the* third, but constituting *a* third.

(1847). The following words were allowed to be added to this Article, because, by resorting to a different scheme of imposition, the same result could be obtained; and as we all along wished to procure for the piece-hands works which have hitherto been done by boys or on the establishment, but little harm could be done by agreeing that "works printed on alternate pages only, the blank at the back of each page not to be charged."

22. Broadsides, such as leases, deeds, and charter-parties, above the dimensions of crown, whether table or common matter, to be paid the double or common matter; on crown and under, to be paid one and one-half common matter.—The indorse to be paid one-fourth of the inside page, as common matter.

(1836). This article means that "common matter" or undisplayed broadsides, when set up in type "such as" is used for leases, deeds, &c. are to be charged, if larger than crown, the double of common matter, but if on crown or under, to be paid one and one-half common matter, as if as table, to be paid for as double. That this is the true interpretation of this article is evident from the introduction of the words "whether table or common matter," which were not in the Scale of 1805, and which were inserted to prevent more than double being charged for broadside tables above the dimensions of crown. In Ireland, table broadsides above medium are paid treble; but by the above article, however few or numerous the columns may be, the charge is to be that of double common matter.

(1847). Leases, deeds, and charter parties, here called broadsides, evidently mean undisplayed matter set up at a great width, occasioning infinite trouble in the composition. The Article means, then, broadsides set in one measure, in which case it pays, above the dimensions of crown, double price. When, however, undisplayed broadsides are set up in two, three, or four columns, one-fourth the price of common matter extra will be paid; if in five columns, one half; if in six columns, or more, double the price of common matter.

The Scale makes no provision for displayed broadsides. A price has, however, been put upon these, for which see Scale, p. 13.

23. All corrections to be paid 6d. per hour.

(1836). When blank pages at the end of a work are filled up on its return from the author with fresh matter, or booksellers' lists, or advertisements, the compositor charges the value of the matter, deducting the price of the blank, excepting the time for making up the blank. Matter driven out by the insertion of leads is charged by the compositor, but his time in doing so is not chargeable.

The compositors on the work are entitled to correct the author's proofs.

(1847). Arts. 33, 34, and 35, finishing the 1805-10 Scale, remain without addition.

24. The imprint to be considered as two lines in the square of the page.

(1836). In jobs, it is sometimes necessary to put the imprint nearly at the extremity of the paper, leaving a large blank between the last line and the printer's name. In all such cases, the blank is not cast up, but the job is considered to be two lines longer than the last line of matter. Previous to 1805, the imprint was not cast up when it had a large blank before it; but as the compositor frequently had to set up the imprint, it was agreed that he should charge two lines for it.

25. Different volumes of the same work to be paid for distinctly, according to their value.

No reference has yet been made to the wages of compositors "on the establishment," *i.e.*, working for a fixed weekly sum as opposed to payment by piecework. According to *The London Scale of Prices*, "it therefore becomes necessary to state that in 1744 persons so situated received 20s., in 1785 from 21s. to 27s., in 1793, 30s., in 1805, 33s., and in 1810, 36s. When the reduction in reprints took place, some of the employers reduced the wages of the compositors on the establishment to 33s., but this reduction was not general, and the most respectable houses still pay 36s. per week."[1] Thus, even a quarter of a century after the Scale of 1810 was accepted by the trade generally, the establishment wages had not increased. The compiler of the historical introduction to *The London Scale of Prices* was writing *circa* 1835.

[1] *Op. cit.*, p. 25. The reduction in reprints took place in 1816. See p. 189.

CHAPTER VII

EVENTS LEADING TO THE FOUNDATION OF THE LONDON UNION OF COMPOSITORS
1834

For six years the Book Scale arranged in 1810 remained without alteration, but on 16 January, 1816, the employers decided that reprinted works should be paid $\frac{3}{4}$d. per 1000 less than the basic rates settled in 1810, when no differentiation was made between manuscript and reprint copy. The pressmen were also confronted with a reduction in prices. "The reduction in the rate for reprints was agreed to in 1816 as a measure of self-defence against the competition of country offices."[1]

"This reduction is remarkable for two things:—1. That sixteen years prior, the employers absolutely refused to accede to a proposition put before them by the men, asking for an increase upon manuscript, and at the same time a distinction to be made between manuscript and reprint in the price per 1000. 2. That the document which enforced this alteration of what was called in 1800 'an unjustifiable departure from the established and long-approved principles by which works have been appreciated,'[2] was signed by twenty masters only, the men not being consulted, nor their remonstrances heeded when they sought for a definition of the ambiguous term reprint."[3]

A similar proposition had been made by T. C. Hansard, in the course of the employers' meetings in 1810. "He had long felt convinced that a graduated scale, to meet the various classes or qualities of work, and to equalize the rate of payment according to the various abilities of the workmen—to make a distinction between those works which might, from the ease of their execution, be given to apprentices and inexperienced hands, and those which, from their more difficult nature, could alone be sent away to distant

---

[1] Master Printers' Report, 12 March, 1866. See p. 279.

[2] See report of the *Meeting of the Master Printers of London and Westminster*, 24 December, 1800. p. 79.

[3] *Report of the Journeymen Members of the Arbitration Committee*, 1847. Extracts from this document are printed on p. 262 *et seq.*

country printing offices, that we might have something left for the employ of our young or aged, lame or indifferent hands—that, to effect all these purposes, a distinction ought to be made between *original, or manuscript works—print copy, but not exactly reprint works*—and, *precise reprints, line for line* and page for page."[1] The masters' committee, by a small majority, decided against him, and he seceded from the trade meetings altogether, forming a Scale of his own.

Following the publication of the document printed below, a signed protest from 717 compositors "employed in the largest houses in the metropolis" was sent to the employers and rejected by them.[2] "A strike followed this reduction; but, for want of unanimity, a society or leading power, and the sinews of war—funds, the trade was signally and completely vanquished."[3]

[DOCUMENT LIV]

Globe Tavern, January 16, 1816.

At a Meeting of Master Printers held this day, pursuant to notice, for the purpose of taking into consideration the state of the Trade in general, in consequence of the alteration in the Times;

It was the opinion of this Meeting, that it would be highly expedient that, after the 19th of February, the following modifications of the Compositors' Scale of Prices of 1810, as far as regards Reprints, and of the Pressmen's Scale of Prices, as far as regards all Numbers exceeding the first 1,000, should take place.

IN THE COMPOSITORS' SCALE

All Reprinted Works to be paid Three Farthings per 1,000 less than the Scale of 1810. All Manuscript or Original Works shall continue to be paid for as at present.

IN THE PRESSMEN'S SCALE

Every Token above the first Four Tokens to be paid One Halfpenny per hour less than the Scale of 1810.

Resolved, That the Master Printers be requested to communicate the above to their respective Journeymen.

G. Woodfall	Richd. and Arthr.	W. Bulmer
Andrew Spottiswoode	Taylor	Cox and Baylis
Charles Baldwin	Hy. Bryer	R. and R. Gilbert
Nichols, Son, and Bentley	A. J. Valpy	J. Adlard
Luke Hansard and Sons	Thos. Davison	J. and T. Clarke
J. McCreery	W. Clowes	Samuel Hamilton
Bensley and Son	James Moyes	Buchn. McMillan

[1] Hansard, T. C., *op. cit.*, p. 785.

[2] *The London Scale of Prices*, 1836, p. 25. The letter of protest is in the British Museum. MSS. Add. 27799, f. 95.

[3] *Report of the Journeymen Members of the Arbitration Committee, or Conference of Employers and Employed*, 1847.

[DOCUMENT LV]

Globe Tavern, March 11, 1816.

At a Meeting of the Committee of Master Printers held this Day,

Mr. Woodfall in the Chair,

It having been stated that doubts had arisen in the minds of several Masters as to what should be considered "Reprinted Works"—

Resolved,

That they be informed that, under the above Resolutions, all "Reprinted Works" were meant to be comprehended, whether printed sheet for sheet or otherwise; it being understood that, in cases where the copy is rendered peculiarly troublesome by intricate manuscript insertions, a reasonable allowance may be made for the same to the Compositor.

The Union Society, formed in 1801, was possibly the first body of London compositors *formally* organized for the protection of the interests of the journeymen and the defence of established customs. The reverse suffered by the compositors in 1816 may partially be attributed to the dissolution of the Union Society, which foundered shortly after the successful termination of the long fight over the Scale in the years 1809 and 1810. The events of 1816 were responsible for the formation, in the same year, of the London Trade Society of Compositors. The book of rules of the Society, printed in 1826, gives the date of its foundation as 17 July 1816. In 1826, thirty-eight regulations were in force, governing the election of members, officials, etc. The following are a selection from them:

[DOCUMENT LVI]

1. This Association shall be entitled The London Trade Society of Compositors; and be held at *The Three Herrings, Bell Yard, near Temple Bar*, as long as may be convenient.

2. The object of this Association shall be—*The Relief of its Members when out of Employment.*

3. Every Compositor of a fair character, who has served an apprenticeship of seven years, shall be eligible to become a Member.

9. Each Member shall subscribe threepence per week to the fund of this Society, and on each Quarterly Night threepence extra, towards defraying the Secretary's salary.

23. Any free Member, when out of employment, where the cause does not originate in his own neglect, and having actually left his situation, shall be allowed ten shillings per week ; but no payment to be made till seven days after the application ; and the like sum per week for nine weeks longer, should he continue unemployed.   No Member can claim the benefit of this Article for more than ten weeks during twelve calendar months.   Any Member being in arrears, and claiming

the benefit of the fund, such deficiencies to be deducted out of the first payment made to him.

34. Any Member proposing a dissolution of this Society shall be expelled.

37. That the sum of £1 be allowed to any Person, belonging to the Society, who may experience the loss of his composing-sticks or galleys by fire at the office in which he was employed at the time of such calamity.

As it is the intention of the Society that its Members should assist each other as far as possible, it is requested that those who know where Compositors are wanted, will immediately communicate the same to the landlord of the Society's House; and it is expected that such of its Members as may be out of employment, particularly free Members, will attend, daily, to ascertain if any situations are on the Society's Book.

The London General Trade Society of Compositors, a rival organization, was founded on 1 May, 1826. In 1832 the two societies combined to send six representatives each to a body to be known as the Union Committee.

"This Committee (which was termed 'The Union Committee of the London Trade Societies of Compositors') had been appointed in agreement with resolutions passed at a General Meeting of the London Trade Societies of Compositors, and consisted of twelve members (six from each society), to whom all important trade questions were to be referred, their decision to be binding upon newspaper as well as book offices. They were empowered to call in the advice of the officers of the respective societies, or of such other persons as they deemed necessary, the expense of their fortnightly meetings, etc., being defrayed out of the funds of each society. They were prevented by rule from assuming any legislative authority, 'being a Committee of final appeal and consultation, and not an executive body.' The Union Committee were not permitted 'to print or deliver summonses, or to make profit in any way whatever, directly or indirectly, of any order or business they may find necessary to have done, thereby keeping themselves above suspicion and setting an example by the rectitude of their motives and transactions'.

"The importance of the task entrusted to the Union Committee will be gathered from the following instruction embodied in the resolutions passed at the meeting which brought the Committee into existence: 'That as soon after their assembling as convenient, the Union Committee shall take into its most serious consideration the Compositors' Scale, in order that some plan may be adopted for more clearly elucidating those parts of it which, on account of their present ambiguity, often create misunderstandings between journeymen and their employers'."[1]

It was due to the work of the Union Committee that the exegesis to the Scale of 1810, published in 1836, as *The London Scale of Prices for Compositors' Work*, but more familiarly known as the "Green Book," from the colour of its cloth binding, was provided for the information of the trade.[2]

The first other important business undertaken by the Union Committee had reference to the variations in the methods of charging for work done on periodical publications, other than monthlies or quarterlies. The anomalies caused by the Newspaper Stamp Acts caused much confusion. Publications containing public news and comments on news, published at intervals of less than twenty-six days, and of a certain minimum superficial area, were liable for a stamp duty of 4d. per copy. The compositors at work on them were wont to charge for their labour according to the News Scale.[3] In the early 1830s, however, there came a flood of new publications, of varying formats, often publishing information which could be construed as "news," and yet paying no stamp duty.[4] It was the task of the Union Committee to examine the physical formats, methods of composing, and matter contained in these publications, in order that a uniform scale of charges for their composition could be arranged. Its *Report of The Proceedings respecting Periodical Publications* was published in 1832 and is here reprinted.

[DOCUMENT LVII]

General Report of the Proceedings respecting Periodical Publications

The Union Committee of Compositors, appointed by the Trade Societies to investigate cases of dispute referred to them by those bodies, having repeatedly been called upon to decide certain questions respecting the nature of Periodical Publications, which involved the interests of the whole Trade, and anxious to secure the rights of the Compositor, which appeared to be menaced by certain practices of recent origin, at length determined to obtain the opinion of the Trade (through

---

[1] *Jubilee of the London Society of Compositors. A Brief Record of Events prior to and since its re-establishment in* 1848 (London, 1898), p. 25.

[2] The commentary on the Scale of 1810 is reprinted in the previous chapter.

[3] See p. 398.

[4] Information on the remarkable impetus in popular journalism in the 1830s can be found in Hunt, F. K., *The Fourth Estate*, 1850; Andrews, A., *The History of British Journalism*, 1859; Grant, J., *The Newspaper Press*, 1871; Bourne, H. R. F., *English Newspapers*, 1887. The Newspaper Stamp Acts are fully discussed in Collet, C. D., *History of the Taxes on Knowledge*, 1899.

the medium of delegates) as to the best mode of checking the existing evils, and securing the rights of the Compositor from infringement.

For this purpose a delegated meeting of the Trade was appointed to be held at the Red Lion, Red Lion Court, Fleet Street, on Tuesday, the 9th of October, 1832, for the purpose of considering the following propositions, which it appeared necessary should be discussed, in order to ensure a clear understanding and adjustment of the various points at issue.

1. Publications, and parts of publications, when pulled in galleys or slips, to be made up at the expense of the employer.

2. All periodical publications containing two bodies (not being notes) and cast up to the respective founts, to be charged the 2s. 6d. allowed by the 7th Article of the Scale.

3. In cases where the employer takes the fat[5] of a publication, such publication to be paid 8½d. per 1000; but when the compositors have the advantage of all the fat belonging to that publication, it is to be considered as common matter, with the extras allowed by Article VII. of the Scale.

4. That weekly publications, whether stamped or unstamped, which contain reports of police or law courts, or foreign or provincial intelligence, reports of accidents, parliamentary reports, or notices of bankrupts, are to be paid according to the existing Scale for Newspapers.

5. That all weekly publications, not containing general news, such as parliamentary reports, reports of law cases, police reports, and reports of daily occurrences, etc., combined, be paid 6d. per 1000, subject to the conditions of Article VII. of the Scale.

6. That any weekly publication which shall contain only reviews of books, notices of dramatic or musical performances, articles on the fine arts, accounts of the meetings and proceedings of literary or scientific societies, and advertisements, be paid according to the Scale established for book-work, with the allowance contained in the second proposition, if consisting of two different-sized letters, and cast up to the respective bodies.

At the hour appointed, the chair was taken by the President of the Union Committee, and it having been ascertained that there were present 138 delegates from book houses, and delegates from the *Herald* and *True Sun* newspapers, the business of the meeting was commenced by the reading of the following :

Report from the Union Committee

Gentlemen—It is unnecessary to describe the object for which we have this night assembled. The circular issued to the Trade apprised you that we were to meet and consider the six propositions which that circular contained; and it is hoped that from the time which has been afforded for the consideration of those propositions, and for the general discussion of the subject, that we shall be enabled to arrive at a decision which shall prove satisfactory to the whole Trade. It is also unnecessary to tell you that the subject we have met to discuss is an important one— it affects every individual in the Trade, and perhaps it is not too much to

---

[5] "FAT. With compositors, short pages, blank pages, and light open matter: with pressmen, light formes, formes that only require one pull at wooden presses; and very small numbers, such as five, ten, fifteen, or twenty copies each, are termed fat." Savage, W., *op. cit.*

13

say, that upon the decision of this question rests the future prosperity of the business.

You are invited, then, to enter calmly and dispassionately on the consideration of the present mode of paying for periodical publications; (not monthly or quarterly, for those are defined, and the charge for them clearly understood); but those which are published weekly, or at shorter periods.

It is necessary that you should now decide how these publications ought to be paid—for the difference of opinion respecting them is great—and the mode of paying for them differs in different houses. One clear and definite standard for the guidance of the workman should be adopted, which will alone remove existing dissatisfaction, and enable all men to receive equal wages.

As many in the Trade may not be acquainted with the number of these journals, it may be necessary to state, that at the present time there are about fifty published every week, and that they afford employment to nearly two hundred persons.

Although these publications are now so numerous, they may all be said to have taken their rise from the establishment of *The Poor Man's Guardian*,[1] which led the way to its more celebrated successor, *The Penny Magazine*.[2] The great success of which latter publication produced the number of rivals and imitators already stated.

During the few months, however, that these publications have existed, they have caused considerable discussion, and, as before stated, much dissatisfaction among certain members of the Trade; some workmen considering that they ought to be paid as newspapers, others that they are jobs,[3] and a third party considering them simply as book-work. You, gentlemen, are summoned for the purpose of deciding to which class of work they strictly belong.

To prove that these publications have been sources of discontent, it is only necessary to state, that, for the last six months, questions respecting them have been continually referred to the Trade Societies, and to the Union Committee; and only six weeks since it was deemed necessary by one Trade Society to appoint a Committee of Inquiry, in order to ascertain the manner in which such publications were paid for, and the mode in which they were conducted.

The following extract from the report of that Committee will show the result of their labours :—

Gentlemen,—" The Committee of Inquiry appointed by this Society to take into their consideration the present mode of working upon the various penny publications, have the unpleasant duty to lay before you the result of their labours, by stating that such a general departure from the usages of the Trade in general, has taken place upon several of the

---

[1] An unstamped publication first issued by Henry Hetherington on 9 July, 1831. "A weekly newspaper for the people. Established contrary to Law, to try the power of 'Might' against 'Right.' Price, 1d."

[2] No. 1, 31 March, 1832. Published by The Society for the Diffusion of Useful Knowledge, a Liberal organization. Its success was immediate, a weekly sale of 200,000 being attained by the end of the year; an unprecedented figure

[3] *i.e.*, of no greater extent than one sheet. See Scale, Art. 20.

publications, and even Annuals, as is truly alarming to us as a Society, and to the profession at large."

With this communication the labours of that Committee terminated—not because they considered the question settled, but because they thought the matter would be more speedily brought to an issue by the Union Committee, who had been engaged in the investigation of this subject for some weeks previous to the appointment of the Committee of Inquiry.

And here it is necessary to state, that though the question respecting periodical publications is complex and difficult, the Union Committee would have met the question, and, aided by the Trade Societies, would have endeavoured to define how the various publications ought to be paid; but they felt that it was a question in which every man was interested, whether in or out of a Society; and though they could not but regret the unwise policy of those who refrain from joining the excellent and useful Trade Societies, they conceived that every man ought, on this occasion, to have an opportunity to declare his sentiments, and by pronouncing a general decision on the subject, ensure the concurrence and unanimous support of the whole Trade.

With respect to the labours of the Union Committee on this subject, it is necessary to state, that they not only employed themselves in investigating the nature and mode of the various publications, but endeavoured to lay down a certain line which might apply to them all. For this purpose they considered them in three distinct points of view : and have investigated them with respect to their form, their manner, and their matter.

First, In investigating them with respect to their form (by which term is meant their shape and size—that is, folio, quarto, or octavo), it was found that no perfectly definite standard could be laid down, since they assume all shapes; and some of them, as *Chambers' Journal* and the *Thief* (as originally published), exceed the size of all known descriptions of book-work, for previous to the appearance of those publications, no journals (unstamped) were in existence, containing four, five, and six columns in a folio page, which were not, by the trade, the public, and the legislature, considered as newspapers.

The fact that both these publications have been compelled to alter their irregular size, in order that their purchasers may have them in a book-like form, is in itself a proof, that, by the publishers and the public, they were not considered books, but as journals imitative of newspapers, but not, like them, compelled to circulate under the imposition of a stamp.

Secondly, With respect to the manner, by which is meant the way in which some of the publications are set up—*i.e.* the Compositor receives short takings of copy, occasionally makes even lines, and corrects in slips or galleys. This is termed the *manner* of doing these publications, which, it is to be observed, is similar to the practice pursued on weekly newspapers.

This *manner*, however, of doing work, is not confined to weekly newspapers. Monthly and quarterly reviews are occasionally set up from small takings, and pulled and corrected in slips and galleys—and sometimes, for the convenience of authors, a volume is done in a similar way; and therefore custom appears to have given a kind of sanction to this mode of doing periodical work, which only the voice of the Trade can alter; but certainly it has been found that the irregular practices in this respect are such as to render it difficult to assume the *manner* of doing the work as the proper criterion by which to decide what price it ought to be paid; for, in some cases, the takings of copy are of a respectable length, and the Compositor never makes even lines.

With regard to the manner, too, in which this work is at present done, it must be observed that certain masters have taken advantage of the opportunity to make a great encroachment on the privileges of the journeyman, by calling in question the right of the workman to have the whole of the advantages which occur in his matter, whether blocks, heads, or short pages.[1] This is a dangerous innovation, and would tend materially to diminish the value of our labour. The principle, once admitted, must lead to alarming results. In deciding upon these publications, therefore, you must not forget this most important branch of the subject, but adopt such measures as will put an end to the present evil practices in this respect, and effectually prevent their future recurrence.

So much with respect to the *form* and *manner*—and we now come to the third division of the subject—and that is, the *matter* of these publications. By the term *matter* is meant the description of articles which the publication may contain; that is, whether political, literary, scientific, or religious. And here the first question which presents itself is—How far we shall be right in assuming the nature of the matter to be the rule by which the charge is to be regulated?—What difference can it make to a Compositor what the nature of the matter may be, whether it be political or scientific?—How shall we be able to define that hitherto indefinable term "news"?—We admit that the task is difficult, but not impossible.

Will the meeting allow us to suppose a case that will in all probability arise, when the stamp shall be removed, or an equal stamp put upon all publications—Let us suppose that a publication should appear, which should consist of police, politics, literature, and science—How is such a journal to be defined?—Is it to be a newspaper or a literary journal?—This is the question which it becomes necessary to determine, and which, it is hoped, this Meeting *will* determine satisfactorily to all parties—and in such a way as to obviate hereafter all doubt and difficulty on the subject.

Having thus shown the difficulties which attend the adjustment of this question, and noticed the probable objections that may be started against assuming the form, the manner, or the matter of the publications, as the rule by which they shall be charged, it may perhaps be here sug-

---

[1] *i.e.*, fat. The compositor would charge the number of lines filled by the block although not required to set them. The practice obtains to-day when advertisements are set on piece and the advertiser supplies the blocks. The deciding factor is—who provides the blocks? Illustrations in the text are usually supplied by the proprietor of the journal. It being unfair to require him to pay twice for filling the space, such blocks are not chargeable by the compositor.

gested to the Meeting, that a most desirable object would be attained, could they define what distinction ought to be made between literary papers and what are generally considered newspapers—for, after all, it is by experience proved that a literary paper, paid as bookwork, may cost more for its composition, with extras, than it would come to, if paid as a newspaper, at $8\frac{1}{2}d$. per thousand. So that, in these cases, to require the higher charge per thousand would be an injury to the Compositor.

The Committee will now briefly advert to the six propositions contained in the circular—premising, however, that they are rather offered to elicit opinion, than to be inconsiderately adopted. Let them be considered, and re-considered, altered, and amended, as much as may be deemed necessary—or, if advisable, let them be wholly rejected—but the Committee entreat that you will not decide on these or any other propositions, without duly considering what effect they may produce on the business, when brought into operation.

The first proposition is offered to meet the irregularities and misapprehensions which prevail respecting the right of charging for making up, when the matter has been pulled in slips or galleys.

The second is calculated to remove all doubts respecting the charge for mixing the bodies in periodical publications.

The third proposition is to remedy the evil practices on these publications, and to ensure to the Compositor the advantages belonging to his work.

The fourth and fifth are opposite propositions, to define what ought to constitute a newspaper, without reference to the government stamp.

The sixth is an attempt to define what are called literary journals, in the hope of preventing all future misapprehensions respecting publications of this description.

In summing up this Report, which is only intended as a prelude to discussion, without any attempt to bias the opinion of the meeting, who, it is presumed, from experience and consideration, are fully capable of entering into the merits of the question, it only remains to add, that the members of the Union Committee, and the officers of the Trade Societies, have hitherto declined to pronounce a general decision which would influence the whole of these publications, until the sentiments of the Trade on the subject had been ascertained.

Finally—It is necessary that, in every step we take in this matter, we should proceed with circumspection, and not decide too hastily on a subject so important in its consequences. Let us not forget the object of this meeting—which is, not to obtain an increase of prices—but to define what the scale and custom allows for weekly periodicals—and by rendering this clear, enable all men easily to obtain it. Above all, let us not rashly endeavour to obtain a higher price than the circumstances demand—lest we should discourage that spirit which appears to have been excited in favour of literary speculations. High prices are not to be desired, when they tend to diminish labour—and we must not close our eyes to this fact, lest, in seeking to gain more, we should, like the dog in the fable, lose that which we have.

The advantages that will result to the trade from the present meeting are likely to be numerous; but above all, it will settle the minds of men respecting an important branch of our trade, and enable them hereafter to decide without doubt or difficulty how publications are to be charged.

In future, it is hoped, they will have an authority for the correctness of those charges which will not be disputed; since, whatever may be the decision of this meeting, and the consequences resulting therefrom— that decision will not be the act of a self-constituted or partially-appointed body—but the act of the trade itself, and, as such, must be obeyed by every member of the trade.

Such a decision—and such a decision only—can ensure the concurrence and support of all those who are interested in the subject; and it is hoped, that when the matter has been fully and fairly discussed, and a decision recorded—that all parties, whatever their opinion may be, will abide by the decision of the majority; and not, by unwise opposition, endeavour to unsettle that which this meeting, in the name of the trade, shall decide.

––––––––

At the conclusion of the reading of this Report, the number of delegates had so much increased, that many were unable to obtain an entrance into the room. An adjournment, therefore, became necessary; and the question of adjournment having been put by the Chairman, was agreed to.

––––––––

On the 16th of October, the delegates assembled at the Hope Tavern, Blackmoor Street, Clare Market, and the chair having been taken by the President of the Union Committee, and the Report again read to the meeting, the consideration of the six propositions was entered upon.

The first proposition was then read by the Chairman.

In discussing this proposition, it was stated by numerous delegates, that no practice contrary to that declared in the proposition had ever come within their knowledge; that the right of the Compositor to be paid for making-up his matter into pages, when that matter had been previously put by him into a shape for pulling, had invariably been admitted in the best and largest houses; and that any departure from a practice so universally recognized, would be a departure from an equitable and long-established regulation, and a great injury to the Compositor.

The proposition being then put by the Chairman, was unanimously agreed to by the meeting.

In considering the second proposition, it was stated, that this article was submitted that the meeting should remove all doubts respecting the seventh article of the Scale; and some of the oldest publications were named as having been paid, during many years, according to the principle laid down in the proposition. No variation had ever been recognized by the Trade, or been required by the employers; and therefore the charge of 2s. 6d. per sheet, for mixing the bodies, which had been so long admitted upon all publications of a larger description, ought unquestionably to be allowed for those of a minor kind, and more recent origin, which were frequently attended with greater trouble and inconvenience to the workman. As, however, it was conceived that the word "and" might serve to hang a doubt upon, the proposition was slightly amended by the meeting; and being put by the Chairman, as altered, was unanimously adopted by the meeting.

The third proposition was then read to the meeting, but after some discussion it became necessary, from the lateness of the hour, that a further adjournment should take place, which was agreed to.

The third meeting was held at the Hope Tavern, on the 23rd of October, and the consideration of the third proposition resumed.

The delegates, in considering this proposition, expressed their surprise that it should ever have been considered right for the workman to enter into a composition with the employer, in regard to the advantages belonging to his work. They denied the power of the meeting to make any set price for those advantages, and affirmed that the Compositor would, in numerous cases, be injured, and could not, under any circumstances, be benefited by the plan proposed. They were instructed, they said, by their constituents, to declare that they could not consent to the third proposition, which they proposed should be altogether *expunged;* and reprobated, in strong terms, the entering into any composition or compact with the employer respecting the long-established right of the Compositor to *all* the advantages of his work. The third proposition, therefore, on being put by the Chairman, was *unanimously negatived* by the meeting, and consequently expunged from the list.*

* The Union Committee take this opportunity to remark that they perfectly agree with the meeting on this subject; but, knowing the unfair practices prevailing, it was necessary that they should bring the subject before the meeting in a tangible shape, in order that the honest reprobation of the delegates might put to shame the evil-doers, and prevent the establishment of a practice at once ruinous and disgraceful.

The fourth, fifth, and sixth propositions were then considered; and the desirableness of drawing a line between the Newspaper and Literary Magazine generally acknowledged. These three propositions were therefore blended together, and that which is numbered three, in the subjoined list of resolutions, was adopted by the meeting.

The desirableness of checking and preventing the practice of employing "establishment clickers"[1] was then considered by the meeting; and with a view of preventing a practice so unfair and injurious, the fifth resolution was unanimously adopted.

[1] "CLICKER. The compositor who, in a companionship, receives the copy from the overseer or other person, gives it out to compose, receives the matter back when composed, keeps an account of what each person does, sets the head and direction lines, and the notes if any, makes up the pages, lays them down on the imposing stone, and makes out the account, apportioning to each his proper share; his own share of the bill being always equal to the highest: this refers to working on lines. In other companionships he receives the copy from the overseer, distributes it to his companions, and receives instructions how the work is to be done." Savage, W., *op. cit.* The first use of the term *clicker* that I have noticed occurs in Stower, C., *Printer's Grammar* (London, 1808), p. 466. The companionship system is examined in the present work on p. 55 *et. seq.*

The thanks of the meeting were then voted to the Union Committee, and to the President, and a resolution passed requiring every member of the trade to subscribe 4*d*. towards defraying the expenses incurred on this subject.

Resolutions agreed to by the Delegates assembled to consider the state of Periodical Publications.

1. Publications, and parts of publications, when pulled in galleys or slips, to be made up at the expense of the employer.[1]

2. That all publications containing two bodies (not being notes) be cast up to the respective founts, and charged the 2*s*. 6*d*. allowed by the seventh article of the Compositors' Scale.

3. All publications which appear weekly, or at shorter periods, whether stamped or unstamped, which contain general news, such as parliamentary reports, reports of police or law courts, foreign or provincial intelligence, reports of daily occurrences, or notices of bankrupts to be paid according to the existing Scale for Newspapers; but all those which contain only reviews of books, notices of dramatic or musical performances, articles on the fine arts, accounts of the meetings and proceedings of religious, literary, or scientific societies, and advertisements, to be paid the same as monthly or quarterly publications.

4. That no companionship allow its work to be made up by an individual on the establishment, or in any other way effect a compromise with the employer, contrary to the usage of the Trade.[2]

No further meeting of the trade took place until December, 1833. Upon this occasion the Union Committee presented a lengthy *Report*, from which extracts are here printed. Among others, the following subjects were discussed: Irregular terms of payment for compositors engaged on composition as opposed to corrections, make-up, imposition, etc.; precedents for fixing the weekly establishment wage at 33s.; the projected formation of a masters'

[1] "This regulation is to guard the compositor from having two makings-up and two impositions; if he be ordered to make up his matter in slips, or have it pulled in galleys, he is not to make it up into pages, without being paid for the time it takes to make-up and impose.

"It is contrary to the spirit of this regulation for any compositor to accept a price for pulling his galleys, and then make his matter up at his own expense." *The London Scale of Prices*, 1836, p. 61.

[2] "This stipulation was to remedy the practice of establishment men making up the matter of compositors on the piece; thus securing the principal advantage to the employers, who paid for the matter, occasionally, only a halfpenny or a penny extra per thousand. It does not prevent, however, a companionship appointing one of their number to make up their matter, on such terms as they may agree among themselves.

"When a publication is pulled in galleys, and afterwards made up at the expense of the employer, the compositors, in casting up their matter, reckon the head and white lines belonging to the pages." *Ibid.*, p. 63.

association; a plan for amalgamating the London Trade Society of Compositors, the London General Trade Society of Compositors and the News Society into one body.

[DOCUMENT LVIII]

Report of the Proceedings of the Delegated Meeting of Compositors, held at the Hope Tavern, Blackmoor Street, on the 12th December, 1833.

The President of the Union Committee in the Chair.

The circular by which the meeting was convened, having been read, the Chairman directed the Register of the Union Committee to call over the names of the offices to which a copy of the circular had been sent.

The lists containing the names of the journeymen employed in the various book-offices, with those of the delegates at the present meeting, were at the same time given in; from which returns it appeared that there were present 185 delegates from book-offices employing 1200 journeymen; and delegates from the *Herald, Morning Chronicle, Age, New Dispatch, News, Spectator,* and *Old England* Newspaper offices.

The following letter from the *Courier* companionship having been delivered to the Chairman, was read to the meeting :

Courier Office, 12th Dec.

The Courier companionship beg to inform the Secretaries of the Trade Societies that they must decline sending delegates to the meeting of this evening, in consequence of the vagueness of the Notice which they have received, and the irregular manner in which it reached them; conceiving, as they do, that the Notice should have been communicated to the Secretary of the News Committee, and through him to the different chapels.

The Courier companionship beg, however, to state, that—should the object of the meeting be one which will tend to the general benefit of the business—they will be very ready to co-operate in its accomplishment.

The Courier companionship deem it necessary to make this communication, to prevent any supposition of intentional neglect.

The Chairman then requested the attention of the meeting to the following

Report from the Union Committee

Gentlemen,

The Union Committee, in detailing the causes which have induced them to convene the present meeting, premise their statement by remarking that they have, since the trade was called together in October 1832, had several causes for convening an Assembly of Delegates; but, fearful that the continued meetings of the trade would excite attention, and be the means of calling into action persons whose interests are in some respects opposed to those of the Compositors of London, they have deferred the meeting until the present period, when honesty, justice, and the preservation of a good understanding amongst Compositors, demand that it should be deferred no longer.

As the practical result of the four resolutions agreed to at the delegated meetings held last year, it may be briefly stated, that they have succeeded in establishing the right of the Compositor to such advantages as occur in his work. Since that time, with only one exception, the cuts have been unreservedly given up to the Compositors, or else the work has been wholly done on the establishment. In the latter case, it may at first sight seem that we have gained nothing—but, upon reflection, it will appear that we have gained every thing—for the object of that meeting was to prevent the *value* of the cuts being taken by those who had no right to them;—and this has been effected—for in publications now done on the establishment, we believe the price paid for them is as great, if not greater, than if they were done upon the piece, and the whole of the cuts shared among the Compositors.

．　　　．　　　．　　　．

The second branch of this Report, as has been already stated, relates to certain improper practices in the business which require immediate correction. Let it, however, be particularly borne in mind that it is not the object of those who convened this meeting to attempt any innovation upon the Scale, or to seek any advance of prices—we do not meet to establish new customs, but to destroy innovations. We meet for the purpose of ascertaining what is the custom of the business upon certain points, and by establishing one uniform practice, render it impossible for either masters or men to plead ignorance as a reason for departing from that custom in future.

The first irregularity to which the Committee desire to direct your attention is one which has been frequently complained of—has often been noticed in the Reports of the Trade Societies, and which is now too much on the increase to be any longer neglected. We mean the practice of paying men 6*d*. per hour while engaged in composition. This system, if universally adopted, would be exceedingly injurious—for its effect would be to render the maximum or highest rate of our earnings 6*d*. per hour. We should almost always have less, but never more; for what master would have a work done upon the piece, which would turn in to the compositors 9*d*. or 10*d*. per hour, when he could have the same done at 6*d*. per hour, and secure the overproduce of 3*d*. or 4*d*. to himself, which overproduce would in a week amount to 15*s*., and thus reduce the wages of those who occasionally receive £2 : 5*s*. down to the low sum of 30*s*. We need not dwell upon this subject, since the numerous evils to which the system would lead, must be apparent to all minds; but we beg the meeting will observe, that they must no longer delay to apply a remedy to this evil, since many journeymen, who have fallen into the practice, do not scruple to defend it, although it is against custom and reason, and in direct opposition to the Scale, which does not allow the master to act in this manner, nor does it justify the compositor in working at this rate, except when he is employed in correcting. The Committee, therefore, suggest the following proposition to the meeting, premising that it is not intended to interfere with those who are under regular weekly engagements, but is levelled at the employment of compositors, for a few days or hours, on good works, at 6*d*. per hour.

"Resolved—That, wherever practicable, all work must be done on the piece; and that the payment of compositors at the rate of 6*d*. per hour, when engaged in composition, is contrary to the custom of the business, and in opposition to the Scale."

.   .   .   .

As some guide to the meeting in legislating on the subject of establishment prices, the Committee have thought proper to inquire "how the present rate of establishment wages became fixed at 33*s*." and they have ascertained, That, previously to the reduction of the reprints in 1816, the lowest recognised price for establishment men was 36*s*.; but at that period a reduction of 3*s*. per week was also effected in the establishment wages, which reduction was considered to be somewhere about the loss that would be sustained by individuals working on the piece upon reprints. Without investigating the means by which the masters and men arrived at this conclusion, it is sufficient to state the plain fact that in 1816, the wages of the establishment were reduced from 36*s*. to 33*s*. and that, from that period until the present hour, no sum lower than 33*s*. has been recognised as fair by the trade. This simple history of the reduction of the establishment prices may not be new to some—but we are well assured, from their conduct, that it is new to a great many; and it is laid before the meeting in order that in future men may know the grounds upon which they can stand when demanding 33*s*. per week, and at the same time to prevent persons from taking less than the sum which appears to have been agreed to at the last alteration of the Scale.

.   .   .   .

The above remarks terminate what may be considered the second branch of this Report. But the Committee must further trespass upon the attention of the meeting for a short time; for although the subjects already brought before the notice of the meeting are highly important, there is yet one remaining of infinitely greater importance, and upon which the just regulation and prosperity of the business must in future mainly depend—and that is, to invite the delegates to the consideration of some plan for establishing a Union of the Compositors of London; by which the better defence of their interests, and the general improvement of the business may be secured.

The Committee have every reason to believe that such a step cannot any longer with safety be delayed. Only a few months back, it is well known, an association of employers and overseers was attempted to be formed, which, we are well assured, had not for its object the increase of the wages of labour; and, in a recent dispute in a large house, the men were informed it would not be long before the masters would be enabled to settle all such matters by themselves. But, whether there be a union of employers or not, it is essential that there should be a union of men; for two purposes, first, the prevention of mal-practices, and, secondly, the maintenance of such prices, as afford a fair remuneration for our labour.[1]

[1] The first Association of Master Printers was inactive after 1816. The second organized body of employers was not formed until 1836. See p. 235.

For nearly twenty years, Trade Societies have been established, and yet not more than one third of the trade have ever contributed to their support—but the Committee, whilst they give these Institutions every praise, and confess that, if they had *not* been in existence, the wages of our labour would, long ere this, have been considerably reduced, are at the same time compelled to acknowledge that they cannot reach every individual, nor does their influence extend into every office; and therefore the good they effect is confined to a comparatively small circle, whilst the active members of those societies are frequently marked out, and, we fear,—nay, we know,—are often deprived of employment, by vindictive employers. But it is not, it cannot be expected, that year after year a comparatively small portion of the trade should sacrifice their time and money, and be pointed at by the masters as disaffected and discontented, while the majority of the trade remain aloof, and participate only in the profit produced by the labour of the few—No, as *all* reap the advantage, it is fit that all should share the burthen.

With this view, the Union Committee beg to submit the following proposition to this meeting—namely,

"That a portion of the delegates of the present meeting be appointed to confer with the Union Committee and the officers of the Trade Societies, in order that a plan may be arranged for uniting the existing societies, and enrolling the whole trade, in one society, under one head."

The Committee earnestly entreat that this proposition may be taken into serious consideration, and whilst they invite the trade to co-operate with the societies, they beg distinctly to assure the members of those societies, that the Union Committee pledge themselves to hold sacred the property which those societies have accumulated. In the steps proposed to be taken, the interests and property of those societies will be protected —whilst upon their superstructure and principles a society would be formed of unequalled durability and usefulness—and by the weekly contribution of almost the smallest coin current in our country, a *fund* equal to every emergency would be easily created, from which men might be *immediately* remunerated, when compelled to quit their situations. By the arrangements proposed under this plan, no man could in future plead ignorance of the customs and laws of the trade—for, if the whole trade were united in one society, and the business managed by a council of delegates, and delegated meetings—if there were then but one journeyman in a house, that individual would be constrained occasionally to attend, and take a part in the proceedings of the trade. Thus no malpractices could be hidden, nor would innovations any longer creep in by slow degrees, until it becomes difficult to ascertain what is really the custom of the trade upon certain points; but from the communion that would be established between every member of the trade, the interests of individuals would be protected, and the general rights of the business at all times clearly established, and easily maintained.

Gentlemen,—This proposition, which is described in the circular as a plan for better protecting the rights of the journeyman, having been the last brought before you in this Report, will naturally be the last that will be taken into consideration. And, lest it may be conceived that the proposition has been suggested by the Trade Societies from improper motives, we beg most explicitly to state that the proposition has originated solely with the Union Committee. The Committee feel no little pleasure, however, in being able to state their belief that the societies are prepared to co-operate with the trade upon this subject, and that they would joyfully hail that day, which shall see the Compositors of London united under one head, governed by one code of laws, and firmly pledged to stand by each other in the defence of their common interests. The present proposition, however, would not have been brought before this meeting, had not the Union Committee been convinced that it is absolutely called for by existing circumstances. The experience of three years has disclosed to the Committee many facts not generally known to the trade. But we need not go over so wide a field—but merely glance at the events of the last six months, and we shall see that something must be done— for many employers, now finding it is in vain to attempt a reduction upon the scale per 1000, catch at every little opportunity of diminishing the advantages of the Compositor.

.   .   .   .

In the consideration of this proposition it was remarked by one of the delegates that it did not contain any allusion or invitation to the News-body—how, then, he asked, was it proposed to treat them? Were they to be considered as a separate and distinct body, or were they to be included in the projected union?—It was true that in this, as well as upon other occasions, they had come forward with an offer of their money—but this was not what the bookmen required—they wanted their hearts, hands, and heads, to advise and act with them, and he for one would not be satisfied until he had secured this—for bookmen they *were*, and (if they lived long enough) they would be bookmen again— and he saw no reason why their temporary elevation, and introduction to a *sanctum sanctorum* which he had never been privileged to enter, should estrange them from that branch of the trade in which they had served their apprenticeship, and which had always upheld the rights and prices of the news business.

In reply to this, one of the newspaper delegates expressed his surprise that the news department should be termed a *sanctum sanctorum*, when it was well known, it was open to all. The news department were at all times ready to assist the bookmen, but it could not be expected that they should unnecessarily incur the loss of time which their attendance at delegated meetings would entail. Indeed, they felt they had not on this occasion been treated with proper respect by the Union Committee— the circular should have been sent to the secretary of the News Committee and then it is probable the result would have been different.

In answer to this, it was urged by a member of the Union Committee, that the course pursued on this occasion was precisely the same as had been pursued at the delegated meetings of the trade for several years past, and no objection to that course had hitherto been raised; and, with regard to the charge of disrespect, it was wholly without foundation. The Union Committee never intended to offer any disrespect to the members of the News department—but might justly retort the charge upon that body, whose treatment of the Union Committee had been unworthy of them; for, although the Union Committee had twice written to the Secretary, upon matters connected with the interests of the trade, they had never deigned to send an answer; and what security had the Union Committee that any communication *now* made, would meet with a different return?—In conclusion he remarked, that, as a part and parcel of the trade, the Union Committee were bound to protect the rights of the News department; and if *they* were prepared to come forward and aid in the general union, he and his colleagues would be happy to have their assistance; but if they declined this offer, they must abide the result of those measures which would be adopted by the delegates chosen at the present meeting.

The Chairman, after a few observations confirmatory of the statement respecting the conduct of the members of the news-department, checked this discussion, and hoped that the news-body would view their interests in a proper light, and join in the present undertaking; for he was sure that they would find the Committee would meet at any place or hour that might suit their convenience.

The General Trade Committee of Compositors, appointed by the Union Committee on 12 December, 1833, drafted twenty-two articles of association for the projected amalgamation of compositors' unions. These were circulated to the trade, together with an Address from the General Trade Committee on 22 February, 1834.

[DOCUMENT LIX]

To Compositors

Red Lion Court, Fleet Street, Feb. 22, 1834.

The General Trade Committee (appointed at the delegated meeting on the 12th December last, "to arrange a plan for uniting the existing societies, and enrolling the whole trade, in one society, under one head") having agreed to twenty-two articles as the basis of a union of compositors of London, hereby announce that a general meeting of the trade will be held at the London Mechanics' Institution, Southampton Buildings, Chancery Lane, on Tuesday, the 4th day of March, 1834, to receive a report of the proceedings of the General Trade Committee, and to consider of the propriety of adopting the plan of union set forth in the third and fourth pages of this circular.

(Signed) W. CREASY | *Secretaries to the*
W. BAYNE | *Trade Societies.*
R. THOMPSON, *Reg. U.C.*

The chair will be taken at eight o'clock, precisely; and the committee entreat that every compositor will attend this highly important meeting—let those who desire a union, testify it by their presence.

Address of the General Trade Committee

The general committee of compositors having received from the union committee, on the 24th of December last, the "Outlines of a plan for forming a union of the trade," and having since that period been engaged in maturely considering and amending those outlines, consider it advisable to offer an explanation of the objects which they have kept in view, during their deliberations; and, at the outset, observe, that, in all their discussions the first and paramount consideration has been—UNION; because they are convinced that only by union can the present prices and privileges of the trade be secured.

With this view, they consider the compositors employed in London as forming but one body, having but one interest; and, consequently, should be regulated by one code of laws, and should have only one tribunal to which their disputes may be referred, and to which all may apply for advice and assistance.

To accomplish this desirable object, they propose that a body of men shall be selected from the whole trade, and chosen for their knowledge and capacity to form a council, who are to be armed with powers to defend the collective and individual interests of every journeyman. This council, however, is not to be a secret and irresponsible body—but its actions and invidious distinctions of a member of "this body," and its expenses are to be subject to the strictest scrutiny, and its proceedings are every month to be made known to the trade.

To give increased efficiency to the measures of this body, an extensive system of communication will be established with the various societies in the country, so that the measures of the different provincial societies may at all times be forwarded, by the co-operation of the compositors of the metropolis; and that the latter, in their turn, may not have (as hitherto) their views frustrated by the introduction of strangers, unaware of the causes of their disputes, and who are frequently lured into engagements by the plausible misrepresentations of unworthy employers.

It will be perceived also, that, while the committee have been desirous of promoting the welfare of the journeyman, they have been anxious to protect the interests of the respectable master. The committee have not forgotten that the interests of the masters and men are so closely connected, that to attempt to deprive an employer of the just reward of his capital, labour, and talent, would be to divert his property into other channels, and thus inflict a death blow on ourselves :—we have not any thing to fear from the honest and respectable—it is only the avaricious master who is the workman's deadly foe :—and, aware that the object of men should be—not to seek high wages, but simply to secure for themselves such a voice in the regulation of the wages of labour, as would enable them to obtain a remuneration sufficient to maintain themselves and their families—they have, by the tenth article, enabled the masters and men at all times to meet upon equal ground, and arrange such a price for a work, as the one party is willing to give, and the other to take.

But the principal aim has been to make every individual in the trade contribute his share of the expenses incurred in maintaining the rights of the business; and, should the proposed plan be adopted, no longer will a portion of the trade be taxed to the payment of sums varying from 6s. to 14s. per year, for the protection of the rights of others; but every journeyman will be constrained to pay equally, and will in return derive equal advice, protection, and support, should he, in the maintenance of the customs of the trade, be compelled to give up a situation. Henceforth, he will claim as a right, that which he is now content to receive as a boon, and the disagreeable member of "that society," will be abolished—and all will be members of a union, extensive, useful, and (while directed with prudence and honesty) indestructible.

Those, however, who would judge correctly of the proposed plan, must not view it as a new and untried measure—but must consider it as being simply an extension of the principles and views which have governed the existing trade societies; and, while the most beneficial results may naturally be expected to arise from its adoption, it will readily be perceived, by the candid and impartial, that no existing body will sustain loss or injury; indeed, the only alteration contemplated is, to transfer the authority they possess, as courts of appeal and decision, into the hands of a more powerful body; and, instead of subjecting the trade to the expense of maintaining four tribunals, as at present, there will henceforth be but one—the approach to which will be open and easy to all, and whose decisions will be prompt and effective.

In the proposed plan, it will be perceived that every arrangement has been made to prevent a profligate expenditure of the funds—the expenses of the committee are to be limited, and the accounts are to be four times in each year publicly audited, while all who stand in need of assistance will be furnished with a prompt and just supply. No vexatious delays can be made against the demands of the claimant—but he will receive the help he requires at the time when it is truly serviceable— the hour of need; and thus, while he will have a prompt reward for doing that which is right, he will henceforth have no excuse for committing evil—for the oppressed will no longer be compelled to submit to injury, or become dependant on the mercy of the trade, but can flee on the instant to the fund they have contributed to raise, and obtain a remuneration adequate to the losses they have sustained.

The committee do not offer the plan as perfect—indeed, there are many minor arrangements which must necessarily be left in the hands of the first-appointed trade council—but, as a system intended to concentrate the energies of the trade, correct the existing evils, and confer equal rights and equal burthens on all—they believe it not to be capable of material improvement; and they therefore present it to the trade as a whole, entreating them not to enter into the dissection and alteration of insignificant points, which would be more readily and satisfactorily adjusted in the council room—but to view it as an enlarged and improved system for maintaining the rights of the trade. They exhort them to weigh it thoroughly—and if, after mature investigation, they are convinced that it is practicable, useful, and necessary—let them come forward to the approaching general assembly of their fellow-workmen, prepared to give their cordial support to a plan which the committee sincerely believe is now become necessary to the security of the most valuable rights of the business.

[*Then was printed the "Proposed Plan for the General Union of London Compositors, as prepared by the General Trade Committee, and agreed to at Special Meetings of the London Trade Societies," containing twenty-one articles and not twenty-two as stated by its compilers in the announcement preceding the above Address. The various clauses deal with matters concerning the internal organization of the proposed General Union.*]

———————

The General Trade Committee presented its *Report* to the London compositors on 4 March and 11 March, 1834. It was explained that the "Proposed Plan of Union" had been submitted to the London Trade Society, the London General Trade Society and the News Society. Satisfactory replies were received from the first two bodies, but the News Society withheld their unconditional co-operation. They required "full jurisdiction to the News Society in matters affecting their own body alone, and not affecting the trade at large. . . ." Although the General Trade Committee suggested a compromise, no answer was received and they "were led to believe that the News Compositors are disposed to maintain their right to the exclusive regulation of their own affairs." It was emphasized, however, that the News Society could not properly have interests separate from those of the bookmen.

Once again there were conflicting interpretations of the Scale of 1810 to be examined. The Committee published rudimentary statistics showing the influx of apprentices during the past twenty years, and claimed that the amount of work given out in London was not in proportion to the increase in the supply of labour. While the number of periodicals had increased, the "heavy standard works" were fewer in number. "They have been stereotyped, and all are gone from the Compositors' hand. . . ." Union was to be the remedy for these and other evils. Wages and prices would then be levelled, also, to the advantage of the masters, whose numbers had increased nearly twofold during the past twenty years, while their profits and condition had deteriorated.

[DOCUMENT LX]

Report of the General Trade Committee to the Compositors of London, assembled in the Theatre of the London Mechanics' Institution, March 4 and 11, 1834.

The President of the Union Committee in the Chair.

Gentlemen,

The individuals who now address you through the medium of this Report, constitute the General Trade Committee which was appointed on the 18th December last, by the delegated meeting, "for the purpose of arranging a plan for uniting the existing Societies, and enrolling the whole Trade, in one Society, under one head."

In presenting to the trade the Report of their Proceedings, the Committee observe, that they fear it will be found to be of a greater length than is usual in documents of this description; but the importance of the object in which they have been employed, will, it is hoped, induce the trade to pardon the length of a Report, which, in their opinion, could not have been shortened, consistently with clearness, nor without injuring the great cause which has been entrusted to their hands.

.   .   .   .   .

The Committee commence the detail of their proceedings in regard to the especial object for which they were appointed, by informing the meeting that they received the outlines of a plan of Union on the 24th December, from the Union Committee; and they would willingly have assembled twice in each week, to discuss those propositions and bring them speedily into operation; but the press of business on the Union Committee, rendered it impossible for them to meet more frequently than once in each week. Their meetings were protracted during five weeks, for the purpose of considering every clause maturely; and, at the end of that period, having completed their deliberations, it was considered necessary that those members of the trade who had formed themselves into Societies should be invited to accede to the plan of Union which the Committee had framed. For this purpose, the Committee unanimously agreed to the following resolution:—

"That a copy of the proposed plan of Union be forwarded to the London Trade Society, the London General Trade Society, and the News Committee, requesting their concurrence and co-operation in the said plan, as a basis for a General Union of the Trade, and soliciting an answer thereto, on or before the 14th day of February next."

On the receipt of this Resolution, the officers of the Trade Societies convened *special* meetings of the members for the discussion of the proposed Plan, and the Committee have received the following Resolutions, which were agreed to at those meetings.

The first to which the Committee call the attention of the meeting, is from the London Trade Society, and is as follows :—

"Resolved—That the London Trade Society of Compositors having been formed for the support of the trade, finding that persons will not voluntarily subscribe to any Society, the members are willing to try the proposed plan of Union. They hail with pleasure the contemplated measures now in progress to unite the trade at large, and are willing to assist with their utmost exertions to carry into full effect so desirable an undertaking."

The following is the decision of the London General Trade Society :—

"That this Society cordially agree to a General Union of the trade, upon the plan proposed by the General Committee, and pledge themselves, individually and collectively, to exert all their influence to promote such an important object."

Upon these Resolutions it is not necessary to offer any comment—

they are highly satisfactory, and contain all that could be expected, or desired—and the Committee congratulate the trade at large upon the stability which the Union will derive from the accession of these two bodies consisting of more than six hundred individuals. The Committee especially rejoice in it—because it must convince the trade that the members of these Societies do not cherish the bigoted and degrading feelings of prejudice and party, but that they are willing to make another sacrifice (in addition to the many they have already made) in order to advance the general interests of the profession.

But there is another portion of the trade to which the attention of the meeting must briefly be directed; and this portion consists of such Compositors as are employed on daily papers. To those who are unacquainted with the manner in which persons employed on daily papers settle their disputes, it may be as well here to state, that at the close of the year 1819, or the beginning of 1820, the Compositors employed on Newspapers appointed a committee of six persons to draw up a statement of the mode of working on daily Newspapers.[1]

These individuals made their report on the 29th July, 1820, and from that period till the present time one individual is delegated from each daily Newspaper-office to form a Committee to decide any matters affecting Compositors on daily papers.

It will be remembered by those who attended the delegated meeting, that a wish was expressed that the News Compositors might be included in the proposed Union. In conformity with this wish, a copy of the proposed plan, and a Resolution requesting their concurrence and cooperation was transmitted to the News Committee.

This proposition was considered at a double-delegated meeting, *i.e.*, a meeting consisting of two Compositors from each of the daily papers, and they agreed to the following Resolution.

"Resolved—That if the members of the Union will so far modify their rules as to allow a full jurisdiction to the News Society in matters affecting their own body alone, and not interfering with the trade at large, they (the News Society) will, at the earliest opportunity, consider their proposal with every view to meet the interests of the trade at large."

This resolution induced the Committee to review the parts of the proposed plan affecting daily Newspapers, and, desirous of affording further accommodation, they introduced the following article, and transmitted a copy of the same to the secretary of the News Committee.

"That on the last Saturday in each month the trade council shall assemble for the purpose of considering all questions affecting newspapers; on which occasions a delegate shall attend from each of the daily Newspaper offices, and form a part of the council for that evening; and that, for the purpose of aiding in the registration of the decisions on these evenings, a person employed on one of the daily papers shall be appointed to the office of assistant-register, with a salary of £   per annum."

[1] This *Report* is printed in full on p. 404, *et. seq.*

To this proposition no direct answer has been received, but the Committee are led to believe that the News Compositors are disposed to maintain their right to the exclusive regulation of their own affairs. It therefore becomes necessary for the Committee to declare their opinion that the News Compositors have no right to a separate jurisdiction. And the first argument which they use to support this opinion is—that newsmen have no *separate interest*, for their prices depend upon what is paid in book offices. When they legislate separately, they do not legislate for newsmen alone, but for bookmen also—for their body is maintained in its number by persons from bookhouses; and as every newsman in London holds his situation by the tenure of a fortnight's warning, and thirty or a greater number of bookmen may become newsmen in a few days, they have no right to legislate for those thirty bookmen, whose wages would depend upon their decision, without the bookmen having a voice in such decision. And when sitting as a separate body they could, at any time, agree to a modification or reduction of their prices, which it is clear would be an injury to the whole body of bookmen, by whom their ranks are supplied.

2dly. The Committee contend they have no right to a separate jurisdiction—because the nature of their work does not justify a separation, any more than any other department of work in the printing business. What is there in the nature of newswork that requires that they should be considered a separate branch?—Bookmen, after a day or two, become equal to all the duties that devolve on a News Compositor, and perfectly understand the system; and printers have been known to offer bookmen the situation of a full hand, when they have been employed only one or two nights. Besides, the questions and disputes of newsmen, like those of the bookmen, must be decided by reason and by precedent; and if their claim to a separate jurisdiction be admitted, it would be equally consistent that Sunday paper men, persons employed on parliamentary work, and persons in jobbing offices, should each be considered separate and distinct branches of the trade.

3dly. That their prices do not depend upon a Union amongst themselves, but upon the aid and co-operation of the bookmen. To prove this, we cite three important facts : 1st. That they never obtained a rise until *after* the bookmen had gained it. 2dly. That when they ejected the apprentices from daily papers, their Resolutions on the subject were sent round the book trade for the sanction, concurrence, or disapproval of the bookmen, without whose assistance they could not have ejected them; and 3dly. That without the aid of the bookmen they never would or could have obtained the final adjustment of their prices; for, in order to carry this, it was necessary for the members of the book trade to come to a resolution that no bookman should apply for a situation on a Newspaper during the dispute. This resolution gained the wished-for object; not the union of the newsmen alone, but the Union of the news and bookmen. It therefore, under the above circumstances, appears idle to contend that a body, which thus depends for its prices upon the aid of others, possesses, or ought for an instant to possess, any separate and exclusive jurisdiction.

It is not necessary to say more at present upon this subject;* for the Committee are convinced that, upon due consideration, the News Compositors must feel that no greater concessions could be made to them than those already offered—and as the Committee have been informed that the news-body are prepared to advocate their cause in this place to-night, they are willing to leave the determination of this affair wholly in the hands of the meeting.

* It having been tauntingly observed, that this Report contains no instances of unfair practices in news offices, and inferred from this silence that the News Committee had always protected the rights of the business, it is necessary to state that a flat contradiction would have been given to the assertions of the news-delegates at the meeting, by the members of the General Trade Committee, had not the latter imposed silence on each other, in order that they might not engross the time and attention of the meeting. So far, however, from the Committee being in ignorance of existing unfair practices in news offices, they were in possession of facts which, if detailed, would have proved to the meeting the existence of many glaring evils and have clearly demonstrated the folly of the present system. And with respect to the conduct of the News Committee, they sincerely believe that the profits of labour have decreased under their management, and must continue to do so, until, by a Union with the bookmen, News Compositors are enabled to maintain not only their Scale, but their *localities* from being violated by the tyranny or caprice of their printers.

As this is the first occasion upon which the trade at large has been assembled upon the all-important subject of Union, it has been deemed advisable to obtain from the Union Committee a statement of the circumstances which led them to endeavour to form a General Union of the Compositors of London; and the following has been stated to the General Committee as the grounds which led to the attempt.

"The Report to the delegated meeting detailed a few and but a few of the grievances of the trade;—but it was not recent and existing oppressions, numerous and galling as they are, that first inspired the Union Committee with the wish to unite the Compositors of London in the protection of the wages of labour : but the necessity for a Union became evident to them, in consequence of a course of investigation in which they were engaged; and which at once convinced them that all their attempts to remove the numerous evils which their investigations brought to light, would be futile, nay, would be injurious, until a Union of the trade could be formed, to give efficacy to their efforts, and permanency to their labours.

"Among the instructions which the Trade Societies gave to the Union Committee, when they called them into being, was one which directed them, 'To take into their most serious consideration the Compositors' Scale, in order that some plan might be adopted for more clearly elucidating those parts of it, which, on account of their ambiguity, often create misunderstanding between journeymen and their employers.'

"In pursuance of this instruction, the Union Committee on the third night of meeting commenced their investigation upon this important subject. And the first question that demanded their attention arose even in the very first line of the Scale—for having read the words "all works in the English language common matter, *with space lines*" they hesitated—for they knew that what was deemed a space line in one house, was not considered a space line in another; and they therefore could proceed no farther until they ascertained how far custom had defined what kind of space line authorized the deduction of one farthing per thousand. They found that the Compositors' Scale did not authorize a deduction to be made for leads used in pearl matter, although such matter should have a lead equal in thickness to the half or the whole of its own body; and they did hope that they should find that employers would not consider thin leads, when used in large type, as constituting leaded matter. They were, however, deceived; and the result of their long-continued inquiries was—that there was no recognized and universally acknowledged rule by which the trade could judge as to what thickness the lead ought to be, in order to constitute it leaded matter. Every office appeared to have its own mode—one paid the matter as solid when the lead was thinner than six to a pica; another when less than eight; another when thinner than ten; and some insisted upon the reduction being made, even though the leads were thinner than the thinnest paper—Who, then, was to reconcile this difference ?—The Union Committee saw that the desire to make the reduction even upon the thinnest lead (although those leads were in pieces) was fast gaining ground; and they feared that the original intention of the framers of the Scale (which appeared to them to warrant a reduction only upon leads thinner than six to a pica) would be lost sight of—but they knew, also, that any decision which the Union Committee might give, would only bind the members of those bodies which called them into action; and that all attempts to define a precise standard, would be futile and dangerous, while the trade at large withheld their sanction, and marred their efforts by their apathy and cold indifference.

"The Union Committee, however, continued their inquiries—and, proceeding with the first article of the Scale, found that it contained no charge for diamond type[1]. They therefore commenced the inquiry, what ought it to be paid per thousand? In endeavouring to obtain an answer to this question, they ascertained that although there are but a few houses in London which possess founts of this description—there was still no uniformity of charge—but that there was, in fact, a difference of one penny per thousand, in the mode of charging at the different places.

"The third object of inquiry that would naturally arise out of the first article of the Scale was—What constituted such a reprinted work, as authorized the masters in enforcing their own law on this subject? And, widely different as the Union Committee had found the practice upon other points, the variety of modes upon this, exceeded every other. It would be disadvantageous to the trade to particularize the different systems adopted by employers with respect to Reprints, and tacitly complied with by the men—and the Committee content themselves with noticing, that while some houses have varied their charges, and consented to receive an *ad valorem* charge for the alterations of copy and the introduction of MS. additions, one house has even gone so far as to adopt an intermediate price per thousand between MS. and reprints—for which, it is believed, they can plead no precedent, nor, certainly, any authority from the Scale. But, the farther the inquiries of the Committee

---

[1] See p. 173, footnote 3.

extended upon this subject, the more they became assured that no efforts of theirs to define what constituted reprinted works, and carry that definition into universal adoption, could be successful, without a Union of the Compositors of London—and such a Union, too, as would enable them to say to all men—'This is the law, see that you obey it.'

"It was the knowledge of these irregularities, and an acquaintance with the daily-increasing aggressions that were made upon the rights of the business, united with the belief that the existing institutions were unable to apply an effectual remedy to these evils, that incited the Union Committee to endeavour to form a Union of the trade:—they found that though they could discover the wound, they did not possess the power to heal—they felt, too, that though men quitted their situations in compliance with their decisions, they were destitute of the means of affording them any assistance—and they entertained the belief that there was yet remaining among the Compositors of London too much honour, too great a love of justice, and too much commiseration for those who felt the iron hand of oppression, to permit them to remain longer passive, could a plan be devised by which the whole trade could be united in the defence of their common interests.

"But there is another reason why men should seize the present moment for Union. An attempt has recently been made to introduce bastard founts of such a peculiar description, as will cause a reduction of one-twelfth part of our earnings; and it is necessary that the whole trade should now—on the instant—not only speak but act with promptitude and determination, in order that this alarming evil may be nipped in the bud."[1]

To this brief statement of the Union Committee, which testifies the necessity that exists for a Union, and proves that the trade at present endures numerous evils, the General Committee give implicit credence, and would only observe that the question respecting reprinted works is one which demands the most serious attention of the whole trade.—That it is a reduction which ought never to have been made:—and when it is remembered that that reduction was the result of our weakness and disunion, and that it was only partially approved of by the masters themselves, may we not hope that one of the first results of the proposed Union you are this night invited to form, shall be an equitable adjustment of this important question, and such a satisfactory explanation of what constitutes reprinted works, as shall put an end to this, at present, endless source of dispute and dissatisfaction.

What has been said will be sufficient to prove that numerous evils do exist; but the Committee would earnestly entreat you to inquire—whether we may not expect that greater and more galling ills are coming fast upon us?—Should the Corn Laws, which so materially affect the price of all labour, be repealed, how would the Compositors of London be prepared to meet the various changes that might be projected?—Would they consent to *any* terms, and submit to receive the law from the mouths of a few? If they would not, then they must admit that it would be wise not to wait until these evils come upon us, but zealously to

[1] *cf.* Annual Report of L.U.C., for 1835, where the question of bastard founts was further discussed, p. 233.

muster our forces *now*—to prepare our plans of operation *now*—and be ready, when the crisis arrives, to defend our interests, and procure such an adjustment of our prices as will place us not in a worse but in a somewhat better situation than we are at present.

It would lead the Committee too far into the labyrinths of the science denominated political economy, were they to attempt to shew you the effects produced upon society by the high prices of labour; or to convince you that it has been a part of the crafty policy of statesmen, to gull the mechanics of England by granting to them *apparently* high wages, at the same time that they trebled their exactions ;—while it will not need any argument to convince you, that high prices are of no advantage to the labourer, if the articles he consumes rise in price at the same time. In all our disputes, however, we do not find that Compositors complain of the insufficiency of the Scale prices; but they *do* complain of the modes which certain masters adopt to evade the generally recognized charges; they complain also of the different prices paid by masters for the same kind of work; and they bitterly lament that frequent want of employment, which reduced the average wages of the Compositors of London to about 27s. each per week.

With respect to the evasion of certain customs, it will be well to inquire to what extent does it exist, and how is it to be remedied ?—With regard to the extent of its existence, we may safely say that it reaches from one end of the metropolis to another—for what is law and custom in one house, is neither law nor custom in another, although both houses be in the same street, nay even next door to each other. And it will no doubt startle some in this assembly to hear that a work is now in the course of printing, in which the difference of price, between that actually paid for it in the house where it is doing, and what it would be paid for in other houses in this city, is no less than 5s. per sheet; and, as the work is of great length, the total loss to the Compositors will not be less than from eighty to ninety pounds. And this, be it observed, not from any willingness in the men to work under price, but because there is a variation in the mode of paying this kind of work, and consequently no *positive* law; and because they fear, from the want of Union amongst us, that if they were to quit their situations, they would be filled by others, who would do the work at the price which they refused to take. Nor is this a solitary case—for there is another extensive work now in progress, in which the price paid for it is below its estimated value— and the Compositors upon this will sustain a loss of more than £70.

These instances will prove that we *do* sustain great injury from our want of power to enforce the proper charge; and we now turn to another ground of complaint—*viz*, that scarcity of employment which reduces the average earnings of the Compositors of London to about 27s. each per week.

In all trades like ours, where the acquirement of the rudiments is easy, and where, after a year or two's practice, the labour of boys approaches in value, in some degree, to that of men—there will, if men are not united, be always a supply of young hands; because thereby the profits of the master are increased, or he is enabled to underwork those who employ men. And, perhaps, from the cupidity of masters, and the want of Union amongst Compositors, it is not too much to say, that in no regular trade have so many apprentices been introduced, as in the printing business during the last twenty-one years.

For if we estimate the number of journeymen in 1813 to have been	1000
We may calculate that there has been an introduction since, of no less a number than	1350
	2350
And if we reckon the deaths at two in every hundred, and the seceders at one in six, which will cause a reduction of . .	600
We shall have a remainder of	1750

which is somewhere about the present number of Compositors in London. Now, this increase is enormous, especially when we consider that there is not a corresponding increase of employment; for it is untrue to say that there is twice as much printing done now, as was done 21 years ago. We grant that the number of periodicals has increased—but where are the heavy standard works, which used to afford constant employment to some of the largest houses in the trade ? They have been stereotyped, and are all gone from the Compositor's hand, while the capital which was employed by masters in the production and re-production of those works, is laid out by them in the purchase of machinery, and the fabrication of stereotype plates; so that the whole earnings of the present 1750 Compositors do not much exceed the earnings of 1000 Compositors twenty-one years since.[1] Now, what is the result of this influx of hands ? Many bad effects might be detailed, but brevity demands that we should notice only one; and that one is, that, long before a Compositor quits labour, labour quits him—In other words, no sooner do the grey hairs of age appear upon a Compositor's forehead, than he is considered an incumbrance upon the establishment, often in the very house where the primest years of his life have been passed—and he is compelled to wander through the trade, year after year, occasionally getting a few days' work; and even then he is only tolerated, because a younger and a brisker hand cannot be procured.

But, perhaps it will be asked, how is this to be remedied ? We answer, by Union—by endeavoring so to prevent the unjust introduction of fresh hands, as that, after we have served seven years' apprenticeship, we may secure to ourselves partial employment as long as we are able to labour. If a man, from the mere fact of having been born upon a particular spot of our island, is entitled to certain privileges, and possesses vested rights, which even monarchs must hold sacred, has not the humble mechanic, after enduring seven years of bodily and mental slavery to his craft—we say, has not *he* a vested right in that trade, to the acquirement of which he has devoted seven of the best years of his existence ? Several

---

[1] The Edinburgh firm of Chambers were in the habit of sending stereotype plates by sea to London, where further editions of their publications were then printed. [*Chambers's Information for the People*, No. 35, 1835.]

instances might be cited of trades who do protect these rights, but we shall mention only one—*viz. Lawyers.* These gentlemen, whose knowledge of what is right and lawful cannot be disputed, and who are pretty good judges of what is good for themselves, have carefully provided against the introduction of too many hands into their *craft.* They regulate the supply to the demand—in other words, they limit the introduction of fresh hands.—And why should not we do the same ? are *our* interests less worthy of our care ? are the means by which *we* live, less worthy of our protection ? Certainly not; and, since it is no doubt right for the legal profession to employ measures for the defence of *their* subsistence—it is surely equitable and necessary that we should defend *ours* by similar means.

Having thus given to the meeting a slight sketch of the present condition of the trade, the Committee will briefly notice the advantages likely to be derived by the Compositors of London from adopting the plan of Union proposed.

The first advantage which a Trade Union would afford is, that it would enable us to regulate (what we alone have a right to regulate) the value of our labour. As a proof that attempts are making to deprive you of this power, the Committee call your attention to the following document, which is prepared by an employer for Compositors to sign.

"I hereby engage with Messrs.   to receive such prices for my work, and abide by such usages and customs as are established in their office, work, or employment. In case of any dispute, I further agree to abide by the opinion and decision of Messrs. A. B. C. D. and E. (*five hired servants of the master*) or any two of them."

The second advantage of Union would be, that we should be enabled to check that influx of hands which renders employment scarce, and induces men to submit to degradation and robbery, rather than give up a situation where there is any probability of their continuing.

The third advantage is, that should any man be injured, he would be shielded, not by a *part* of the trade, but by the *whole* body, and there would always be sufficient means in hand to recompence his weekly loss by a weekly allowance—and men who have made a sacrifice to maintain the rights of others, would not be constrained to wait weeks, nay months, before they received any remuneration.

And the last, but not the *least* advantage to be derived from Union is—that we should be enabled to maintain a standard and uniform price for work; and thus, while we should advance our own interests, we should effectually protect the interests of the honest and respectable employer. To shew that masters would not be injured by the Union we propose, we quote the following passage from a leading journal—"Labour to masters is only a kind of ingredient in their manufacture—a kind of raw material in the finished commodity from which they derive their profits; and provided labour is the *same price* for them all, it does not matter whether the price be high or low."

This is the point which we wish to establish, and to which we call your especial attention—*viz.* That masters derive no advantage from low prices, and that if they are constrained to pay *equal* prices, it is better for them to pay high than low wages—since their profits are proportioned to the wages of the journeyman. And, we ask, what is the result of the system of reduction they have adopted ?—Have the masters derived advantage ? We answer, No. And as a proof of this, direct you to enquire into their present state, and you will find that the profits and condition of the masters have deteriorated as well as ours—and that they are worse off now than employers were twenty years ago. Their number is nearly twice as great as it was, owing to the lowness of the wages of journey-work, which induces many to becomes masters, who, could they have procured the means of living as journeymen, would have been contented to remain so. It is therefore the interest of employers—nay more, it is their duty to assist in advancing the welfare of those from whom their profits are derived. Their capital might lie in useless heaps, if not pro-fitably employed in production by the labour of our hands—and, surely, if from our labour employers derive luxuries, ease, and affluence, it is not too much to ask that we, in return, should possess a sufficient supply of the common necessaries of life.

The Committee will trespass upon your attention for only a few moments longer, and they will then leave this great question in your hands.

Gentlemen,—The art of printing was practised in England for nearly 200 years, before any set scale of prices was introduced; and it is now fifty years since the Scale for regulating our wages received a definite and printed form. During the first half of that period—*viz.* from 1785 to 1810, there was a gradual increase—but from 1810 to the present day, there has been a constant decrease. Every opportunity has been taken so to construe that Scale as to render the wages of labour less—and every alteration that has been made in the customs of the trade has been to our disadvantage. It is time, then, that we should pause in our downward progress, ere it be too late; and, if we cannot recover our loss, let us make a determined stand where we are, and manfully resist every fresh encroach-ment—we cannot, however, succeed in this attempt, unless we are all united in the effort.

The Committee, therefore, put this most important question to the trade—Shall disunion continue to prevail—shall disorder and encroach-ment reign for ever, or will you now at once firmly declare for Union ? —We know that there does lurk in some breasts a spirit of opposi-tion—but every great and good measure has always had its opponents —and we entreat our opponents to consider what benefit will flow to themselves and others, from a display of their opposition here ?—Will it not encourage our common enemies ?—Will it not lead to fresh exactions from our wages, if it is found that, while almost every other trade is concentrating its energies, and uniting for the protection of their interests, the Compositors of London are so self-important, headstrong, and ungovernable, as to be incapable of adopting any measure which requires a cordiality of feeling and a sacrifice of prejudice ? We do not expect an unanimous vote upon this great measure—but we look for firm consistency and determination in those who approve it—and, knowing the strength of those who are for Union, we say, to our friends, unite calmness with consistency, and resolution with temperance—and the most com-plete, the most triumphant success will crown your efforts.

The Committee do not invite you to any new project, for numerous trade Unions have already been established; but unfortunately, almost all trade Unions hitherto formed, have relied for success upon extorted oaths and physical force; and therefore, though we come late into the field, there is yet much glory to be won. Let the Compositors of London shew the artisans of England a brighter and a better example—and casting away the aid to be derived from cunning and brutal strength, let us, when we contend with our opponents, employ only the irresistible weapons of truth and reason. Upon these and these only would the Committee rely for success, and none other will they employ to procure your approbation of their plan. Did we wish to rouse your indignation, and create a momentary excitement in favour of a Union, we might soon read a long list of insults, frauds, and injuries sustained by those who form a part of this meeting—but we will not owe the success of this great measure to any such aids. We will not appeal to your passions, but your reason—we have endeavoured, by facts, to shew you that stern imperious necessity demands this Union; and when the awful question of Union or No Union comes before you, we trust that the uplifted hands of this vast assembly will testify the zeal that exists to serve each other; and that henceforth error, dissatisfaction, and doubt shall disappear, and unanimity, friendly confidence, and prosperity prevail.

Gentlemen, The Committee declare that the crisis of your fate is at hand—you have now another opportunity of securing your future independence, and of establishing a system of regulations whose good effects, it is hoped, will be felt by ages yet unborn——Should you decide for Union, the events of this night will awaken into existence a power whose influence cannot fail to be beneficial to you, whilst directed with prudence and honesty. It will enable you, after having devoted seven years to the acquisition of your trade, so to regulate it as in some degree to prevent your becoming despised and destitute, while you have health and strength to labour;—it will give you the means of defending yourselves from the encroachments and exactions of those to whom you have too long been exposed;—and, finally, it will enable you to take your stand upon higher ground than the trade has ever yet occupied, and, instead of having your wages wholly regulated by others, you will be enabled to assist in their regulation, and make such terms as will secure to you a portion of the comforts as well as the necessaries of life.

Let the Compositors of London, then, decide this night for Union, and forty united Societies in the country are prepared to take you by the hand, and call you brothers—nearly one thousand individuals are willing to aid your cause, and second all your efforts—but if, fearful, timorous, and lukewarm, you longer hesitate, then farewell to every hope of independence. But the Committee do not imagine that you will be thus indifferent—they do not believe that a body which ought and does contain within it men of high intellect and sound practical wisdom, will shut its eyes to the advantages to be derived from Union. They therefore now close their labours, and leave the question wholly in your hands— trusting that you will be temperate in your actions, liberal in your sentiments, and firm and unchangeable in your resolutions. Do not suffer any argument, however specious, or any cry, however loud, to divert you from the pursuit of the noble design you have in view—Let those who are for Union keep their minds fixed upon that great object alone—Be not allured into clamour or intemperance—be just—be resolute—and the cause of Union must triumph !

———————

Eighteen Articles were then separately considered by the Meeting, and adopted as *The Rules and Regulations for a General Union of the Compositors of London.* Of these the first three only need be reprinted. A total of 1584 Compositors signed the original document.

1. That for the better protection of the rights of the Journeymen, the Compositors of London and its Vicinity shall be formed into one Society, to be called THE LONDON UNION OF COMPOSITORS.

2. That the said Union shall have for its object the protection and regulation of the wages of labour, agreeably to the Scale and acknowledged practice of the Trade.

3. That every Compositor of fair character, while working in London, or in the Vicinity of the Metropolis where London Prices are paid, who can prove his right, by privilege or indenture, to work as a journeyman, shall belong to the Union, and shall pay Four-pence per month, to form a fund, which shall be applied entirely to Trade Purposes. Every Member shall be furnished with a printed Ticket, containing his Name, and his No. in the Union.

CHAPTER VIII

THE LONDON UNION OF COMPOSITORS AND THE NATIONAL TYPOGRAPHICAL ASSOCIATION 1834-1848

The London Union of Compositors was established in March, 1834. The following passages are extracted from the proceedings of the first Quarterly Delegate Meeting, held 1 July, 1834:

[DOCUMENT LXI]

Of the various societies recently established for the protection of labour, not one has received such immediate and general support as has been given to the London Union of Compositors; for on the first night fixed for the enrolment of our members, nearly 1,300 persons joined the Union. The second night produced an addition of about 200, and the numbers have been slowly increasing up to the present period, when the actual number is 1,580.

.   .   .   .   .

Much uneasiness having long been prevalent respecting the practice of taking away Wrappers[1] from the Compositors, and causing them when advantageous to be altered on the Establishment, the subject having been repeatedly brought under the consideration of the Council; and after receiving the most unexceptional testimony from men of experience in the business, respecting the ancient practice of the Trade, and finding also that it is now the practice of some of the most respectable houses to give such Wrappers to the Compositors, and allow them to charge them afresh, when only a single figure has been altered in them, the following Resolution, with a view to setting the matter at rest, was agreed to by the Trade Council.

"That all wrappers belong to the companions on works or publications to which the wrappers are attached. That one page only ought to be charged when the wrapper consists of only one page. That in wrappers, stereotype plates are to be charged as pages of the work; but when in moveable type are entitled to be charged their original value."

The standing formes of wrappers, or paper covers, of periodical publications were regarded by men on piece work as "fat." The wrappers were not invariably reset for each successive issue, although the date of publication, number of volume or part would have to be altered. Although the compositor might make no more

---

[1] i.e., the covers of periodicals.

than a trifling alteration, he would charge the wrapper as if he had been obliged to compose it afresh in its entirety.

The question of wrappers still further engaged the attention of the compositors during the period following the first delegate meeting of 1 July, 1834. The five resolutions printed below were agreed to on 24 November, 1834, and communicated to the masters two days later. The compositors' letter also acquainted the employers with the main objects of the London Union of Compositors, and solicited their co-operation in the promotion of the Union's objects.

[DOCUMENT LXII]

Resolutions agreed to at a General Meeting of the Compositors of London, held at the London Mechanics' Institution, November 24, 1834 [to which have been added the comments contained in The London Scale of Prices, *1836, p. 63].*

Resolved,

I. That all wrappers belonging to reports, pamphlets, quarterly, monthly, or other periodicals, similar to the *Quarterly* and *Westminster Reviews*, the *New Monthly* and *Metropolitan Magazines*, *Limbird's Mirror*, the *Penny* and *Saturday Magazines*, &c. belong to the companions on the works or publications to which the wrappers are attached.

Compositors are not by this regulation entitled to *two* wrappers to one work. If a work is published in weekly numbers with a wrapper, and also in monthly parts with a wrapper, the compositors are entitled to the weekly wrapper, but have no claim to the monthly wrapper. Also, should there be an annual wrapper, in addition to the regular monthly wrapper, the compositors are not entitled to it.

The term "Report" is meant to include the quarterly, half yearly, or annual Reports of charitable or benefit societies.

Should the wrappers to any of the above description of works be stereotyped, it does not destroy the claim of the compositor to them, as pages of the work.

II. That when a wrapper consists but of one page, only one page to be charged.

Wrappers of single pages are never charged *less* than a page of the work they belong to; but if they are of larger dimensions or in smaller type than the pages of the work, they are cast up according to their merits, and take the extras of the work.

Wrappers to tables, music, or mathematics, are only charged as plain matter.

III. That when stereotype plates are used in wrappers, they are to be charged at the price paid for the pages of the work to which the wrappers are attached.

IV. That when standing pages which do not require any alteration are used in wrappers, they are to be charged as pages of the work; but when any alteration takes place by the introduction of advertisements, etc., they are to be paid according to their original value.

Standing pages in advertising sheets to publications come under this regulation. Where a stereotype block of an extra width or in smaller type constitutes a part of a wrapper page, it is reckoned of the same width and type as the movable portion of the page of which it forms a part.

V. That the wrappers to all numbers and parts of standard or other regular works, not complete in each publication, such as Fisher's *Josephus*, the *British* and *Penny Cyclopedias*, &c. are not hereafter to be considered as belonging to the compositor.

Sermons and Tracts published in numbers, and having distinct sets of folios and titles, are not the continuous or regular works included in this regulation, and the compositors are entitled to the wrapper to such number of Tracts and Sermons, and other things of a like nature, when complete in each number.

[DOCUMENT LXIII]

To Master Printers

Red Lion Court, Fleet Street, Nov. 26, 1834.

Sir,

The difficulty which you have occasionally experienced in giving in an estimate for the printing of a work, and the surprise you must have felt, after making a calculation at the lowest rate of profit and expenditure, to find that work taken by another printer at a much lower rate than that at which you had offered to print it, must have led you to suspect that there was an inequality in the mode of paying for labour, and that others possessed advantages from which you were precluded.

This circumstance, which could only be conjectured by you, has been long known and felt by the labouring part of the profession, who, moving frequently from one office to another, perceived and felt that there was a variation in the mode of payment, which, if suffered to continue, would prove fatal to all engaged in the printing business—that masters would be deprived of their capital, and that overseers, readers, and compositors, would be unable to procure such a remuneration for their labour as would provide subsistence for their families. For the purpose of averting this rapidly-approaching evil, forty individuals of known respectability, and employed in the largest offices of the metropolis, were appointed to devise a remedy. These individuals, conscious that the price of labour regulated the charges of the master, and knowing also that unjust charges were often made upon liberal employers, projected, and finally succeeded in establishing, in March last, a society for the accomplishment of the following objects :

1st, To establish a uniformity of charges for labour in the printing business.

2dly, To give to employers an opportunity of settling disputed prices by arbitration, and to shield them from unjust and unauthorized charges.

3dly, To protect the established scale and the customs of the trade from innovation.

The Society thus established has been named The London Union of Compositors, it has been in existence eight months, and is continually increasing in numbers and strength.

The object, therefore, of this communication is to convey to you direct information of the existence of this Society, and respectfully to invite you to co-operate in the promotion of its objects. There is no desire to extort unreasonable prices from our employers, towards most of whom the trade feel respect and gratitude; nor is there any dispositon to obtain higher prices than the custom of the trade recognizes; and they trust that, while they continue true to the professions and principles above stated, they shall be honoured with your countenance and approbation.

The accompanying resolutions, which were passed at a General Meeting of the Compositors of London, for the purpose of securing a uniformity in the mode of charging wrappers, will, it is presumed, convince you of what is above stated; and in submitting them to you, it is hoped that you will feel no repugnance to having them adopted in your house, as there is no doubt of their being ultimately beneficial both to employers and the employed.

We have the honour to be,
Yours respectfully,

R. THOMPSON, *Reg.*
W. BAYNE, *Sec.*

The first Annual Meeting of the London Union of Compositors was held on 2 February, 1835, when the Trade Council presented their account of the year's activities. The dispute over wrappers had been settled, but unsatisfactory relations between the L.U.C. and the News Society still persisted.[1] Extracts from the Council's report follow:

[DOCUMENT LXIV]

The question of the wrappers has been so recently before the Trade as to render it unnecessary here to dwell upon the dispute—further than to state that from every quarter to which the Trade Council have had access, the decisions of the General Meeting have been approved of by the masters, and agreed to, in most cases, without a murmur. Two masters did exhibit a momentary opposition—one of them contending that as we had given up *some*, the journeymen should give up *all*—and the other, that he would not allow himself, to use the prevailing terms of the day, to be influenced by "*the pressure from without.*" But we are happy to say they at length both yielded, and the resolutions of the trade were in every respect complied with.

It has been said, that in these decisions the masters have not been consulted, and that they ought to have taken a part in the settlement of these questions. But whose fault is this? Have the Trade Council ever exhibited any backwardness to meet employers or their agents on any point where a doubt of the Compositors' right existed? Have we not invariably invited employers to canvass our decisions, and prove their invalidity, if they could? And are they not at liberty to send forward their agents to maintain their cause in any individual dispute? But do

[1] See p. 401.

15

we not know, nay, does not every man know, who is at all acquainted with the history of the trade for the last twenty years, that there are but a very few employers who can meet each other with unblushing countenances—for it were useless to attempt to conceal the fact that masters are more at enmity with each other than with us; and that, in truth, our wages do not so much depend on the master-printers of London, as on the opulent booksellers, who have contrived to throw the apple of discord among our employers, and have made them underwork each other to such an extent, as has excited a degree of hostility among them, which the lapse of many years and the adoption of a different system alone can remove. And may it not be expected that one of the earliest and most beneficial effects of our Union will be, to emancipate the master-printers from a state of slavery so galling and disgraceful ?

Those, however, who use the argument that our employers ought to have been consulted, do not see the extent to which that argument may be applied—for if it be admitted at all, it will ultimately lead us into the acknowledgment that masters have a right to regulate the price and will convince every one that if in its infancy it could endure such attacks uninjured—it will, in its maturity, defy all opposition.

Those, therefore, who desire to ascertain the future prospects of the Union, may reckon with safety upon such an increase of wealth as will enable us to adopt measures that will divest the Trade of the irksome task of relieving the various casualties which occur amongst us.

Already are measures in preparation to relieve the trade from subscriptions to tramps; and it is hoped that it will not be long before the Union will be enabled to grant a sum of money at the death of its members, which shall prevent the necessity of soliciting subscriptions from the trade to defray the funeral expenses of the necessitous—thus our association may, in time, be made of essential service in diminishing human calamity. The Trade Council also cannot refrain from expressing a hope that that society which exists in London for the relief of persons out of employment will yet consider the expediency of becoming a branch of our association, and thus derive strength from and give aid to the principles of the Union.[1]

.   .   .   .

In addition to the above money subscribed for our own use, the trade have voluntarily come forward to assist the Operative Builders in the struggle against their employers, and the sum of 55*l.* 10*s.* after deducting incidental expences, was paid to them at a time when they stood much in need of every assistance that could be rendered.

This contribution to the Builders, and the establishment of a printing-office under the title of the Grand Lodge of United Operative Letterpress Printers, by some friends of the exchange-labour system, have led to an impression in some minds that the London Union of Compositors has become a part and portion of the Consolidated Trades' Union. The Trade Council, therefore, take the present opportunity of stating that the London Union of Compositors still remains a perfectly independent

---

[1] This may refer to some trade Benefit Society run by a group of compositors. No details are available.

association—they are totally unconnected with the office in question—and have no interest in the cause of other societies, except that which a hatred of oppression ought ever to create. And should any now present hereafter hear our association blended with that of the General Trades' Union, they may boldly assert that no such connexion does exist, or ever can exist, until the principles of our Union are wholly changed.

It is necessary to acquaint the meeting that there are certain members of the book-trade, perhaps about 50, but it is difficult to ascertain the precise number, as, like other noisome creatures, they dwell in holes and corners, shunning alike the association of their fellow-workmen in public and private. We say, there are about 50 persons, perhaps a hundred (for we do not want to misrepresent their number) who yet withhold their subscriptions; or who, flitting from house to house, pay occasionally for a month, and then refrain until they again go to work in a house where a regular chapel exists, and where they are once more constrained to pay. Others there are who profess to object to the Union upon principle—they dislike the name—defy its power—and consider they have a right to follow their opinion, and do just as they please upon this subject.

———

The following *Report* issued by the Trade Council of the London Union of Compositors was printed together with their *Report on the Mode of working on "The Times" Newspaper, with Regulations for Casual Employment and Establishment Hours,*[1] both being read at Special General Meetings, held on 15 and 22 September, 1835. It concerns the latter subjects.

It was stated that while there was less work available than twenty-five years before, there were more hands to deal with it. Thus compositors could be persuaded to work "on the establishment" for a fixed weekly wage, which would in all probability bring them less at the end of the week than if they had been fully occupied on piece-work. Some employers were in the habit of engaging men by the hour, paying them 6d. for every hour worked.[2] The Trade Committee sought to bring such practices to an end, since there was a tendency for work advantageous to the compositor to be paid for at establishment rates, while lean matter would be paid according to a piece scale. The Committee also sought to regulate the hours of work for men on the establishment, since these varied from office to office.

[1] Conditions at *The Times* office are discussed in Document CV, p. 416.
[2] *Cf. Report of Delegated Meeting of Compositors, 12 December, 1833,* from which a resolution condemning the practice is printed on p. 203 of the present work.

REPORT

Gentlemen,

The continued influx of hands into our Trade, without a corresponding increase of employment, has introduced a state of things which our predecessors never could have contemplated, or one would imagine they would have attempted the only practicable remedy, and limited the right of the master to introduce apprentices, which might more easily have been done, when printing-offices and master-printers were less numerous than they are at the present day. Those who can remember the state of the Trade for a few years previous and subsequent to 1810, and can call to mind the fact of each Compositor having three or four stock works in hand, and the booksellers and authors' loud complaints at the tardy progress of their works, may well be struck with surprise, when they behold the state to which our Trade is reduced.—All employment has become uncertain—no situation is permanent—and, instead of having three or four volumes in stock, a dozen and sometimes a score compositors are huddled on to a work which in former times would have been an employment only for one.—Such *was* our Trade.—But while we cannot refrain from looking to such things with regret—the only course that remains to us is to consider them as matters of history, and as times which but for our misconduct, disunion, and selfishness, might still have prevailed. It is our duty, however, to endeavour to avoid the increase of our present evils by unwarrantable neglect of those means which may promote our improvement, and as the Trade have suffered from the introduction of a mode of working every day becoming more prevalent, and consequently every day more injurious, it has been determined to call the attention of the Trade to the subject, in the hope that some effectual steps will be taken to prevent its increase.

On the first occasion of the slackness of business before alluded to, and the desirableness of permanent employment becoming manifest, that mode of working called "the establishment," which had been on the decline ever since the formation of our first regular scale in 1785, again became prevalent; and many persons in the Trade, for the purpose of securing to themselves a certain sum per week, consented to give up all chance of having any advantageous work to remunerate them for the loss they might sustain from time to time by partial slackness. This arrangement was a woful—a dreadful one for the Trade—it was an act of inconsiderate selfishness which the Trade has long regretted, and still must continue to regret;—but we lament to add that this false step only proved the prelude to another—and has been the means of introducing a mode of working by the day and by the hour, as well as by the single week, instead of adhering to the only legitimate mode of remunerating a compositor's labour, viz. by the piece.

Ever since the establishment of the Union, it has been known that a system of casual employment has been in existence, and that men have been taken into various small houses, at 6d. per hour. Indeed, it will not be too much to say that this practice has existed for years, although it has never received the sanction of the Trade. The system, however, has been brought by the Members of the Union under the notice of the Trade Council, and it has become their duty to submit the matter to the Trade for their decision.

By recent investigations into the practice of certain Jobbing Houses, it seems that there are a few offices in the suburbs of London, perhaps more than the Trade Council have been made acquainted with, who have been in the habit of employing men on composition, at 6d. per hour. The employers do not offer to these individuals any regular engagement—they are taken into an office to do whatever is required—and 6d. per hour is the charge made for each hour's attendance. As soon as the job or jobs are completed, no warning is given, the amount earned is paid, and the men discharged.

To secure to persons thus employed a day's work—(for instances *have* occurred where only a few hours have been paid,) it is suggested in the following proposition that such persons may be engaged for one day, two days, or three days, but no period less than a day, at six shillings per day.

That no compositor shall be allowed by the Trade to accept a casual engagement on time for less than a day; and that, for that day's engagement, he shall not receive under 6s.

In behalf of this arrangement, it can only be urged that were masters allowed thus to take men into their houses, when their business required it, it would perhaps restrain them from taking apprentices, while it would at the same time afford employment to a certain class of our Trade whose habits or health render them unequal to the labour and anxiety of permanent or regular employment.

But perhaps it will be necessary, should the proposition be adopted, that, as a preservative principle, the Trade should determine that in every case where casual assistance is required, masters should invariably pay for such assistance upon this principle, viz. 6s. per day, or without a provision of this kind all solid jobs and other *disadvantageous* casual employment would be paid upon the piece, while all tables, broadsides, and other advantageous matter, would be paid on the proposed establishment.

This arrangement would not only be equitable but desirable in some respects—as it would obviate the loss of time which now occurs in short jobs upon the piece, where a man is often called upon to expend more time in waiting for his proofs and clearing away[1] than he has been engaged in composition. The Meeting, however, will weigh the propositions when they are put in their proper order for discussion, and will consider that the permanent interests of the Trade should be taken into account in deciding this highly important question.

The adoption of this proposition, allowing compositors to accept of casual engagements at six shillings per day, is one of considerable importance; and in order that it may be viewed in its proper light, and fully

[1] "CLEARING AWAY. When a work is completed, clearing away is the distributing of headlines, chapters, lines of small capitals, and other useful sorts, taking the lines of quadrats away, and tying up the remainder of the matter in moderate sized pieces with old page cord, so as to be ready to be papered up; and tying the furniture, reglets and leads up, and delivering them to the proper person, who takes charge of them." Savage, W., *op. cit.*

discussed, the following proposition is submitted for the consideration of the Trade.

That no compositor shall be allowed by the Trade to accept a casual engagement on time for less than a week, and that for such week's engagement he shall not receive under 36s.

Should this proposition be adopted, it will not admit of any casual engagements under a week, and will render it unlikely for employers to take on an assistant, unless they are assured that they have a week's certain employment to give him.

But it must be remembered that the arrangements now proposed to be made do not extend only to persons taken into an office for temporary assistance; but to those who are already employed in a house; and whom the employer desires to place on the establishment for the purpose of completing a certain job. The question, therefore, is, will you allow such persons, to suspend their regular and ordinary mode of working on the piece to go on the establishment in order to aid in completing a piece of work. And, if so, upon what terms is he to go—for two or three days at 6s. per day, or for a week at 36s. per week?

It has, however, with the active Members of the Trade long been considered questionable whether the admission of composition at per hour is not extremely injurious to the business, and that in all cases where assistance is required, either from persons in an office, or from strangers casually engaged, the interest of both masters and men would not be best promoted by the payment of such work upon the piece, according to the regular mode of casting up. It is evident that as matters at present stand, masters can put all disadvantageous matter on the piece, and all advantageous work on the Establishment; and the point for the consideration of the Trade is whether by forbidding all casual engagement per hour, per day, or per week, and by constraining employers to give a *regular* engagement (i.e. with a fortnight's notice) to all persons whom they take on the *establishment*, we should not be forcing advantageous work into the hands of those who are on the piece—and, in some degree, return to that state of things when persons on the establishment to set up all advantageous work that came into an office were unknown.

At all events circumstances require that the Trade should decide these points; and also that the hours that a person on the establishment ought to work should be defined; for it appears that there is no law to guide the business in this respect. There is no rule for the hours which persons on the establishment ought to work. And accordingly we find that admirable discrepancy which seems peculiarly to distinguish our business —in one office they work from 7 to 8—another from 8 to 8—and a third from $\frac{1}{2}$ past 8 to 8—in the latter place, however, it should be also noticed that the compositors have hitherto received no regular sums, but 30s., 32s. and 36s. per week, according to the estimate which the employer put on their abilities. The subjoined proposition is therefore submitted for adoption :—

That the regular and recognised hours for persons on the establishment are from 8 o'clock in the morning to 8 o'clock in the evening, deducting one hour and a half for refreshment; and when compositors on the establishment are required to work longer hours they must be paid extra.

The Trade Council, however, in concluding this brief Report, consider it their duty to direct the attention of the Meeting more especially to the practice of paying for composition at per hour, instead of per thousand. It has often been lamented as an evil that Masters should place persons on the Establishment for a few hours, for the purpose of doing any work which they may consider advantageous or to avoid the payment of any doubtful or disputed charge. Instances have been known where employers have consented to pay 8*d*. per hour, for composition—but it has been when the compositor would probably earn them 1*s*. or 1*s*. 3*d*. per hour for it; and it therefore becomes necessary to check the injustice by a strict adherence to the principles countenanced by the scale, and with this view the Meeting are required to consider the expediency of adopting the following proposition.

That the payment of compositors by the hour, when engaged in composition, is contrary to the custom of the business, and in opposition to the scale, and that from henceforth no mode of doing work be recognized by the Trade but by the piece, or a regular engagement on the Establishment.

This proposition lays the axe to the root of the evil alluded to, and renders illegal all casual engagements either by the hour, day or week, and reverts at once to the original system, which requires the notice of a fortnight previous to the termination of an establishment engage-ment. We admit that in some cases the compositor would lose—we allow that there are works which do not produce 6*d*. per hour.—But how few they are compared with those which produce a much greater sum. An instance of the excellent working of this proposition has been given in a circumstance which recently occurred. An individual was called from the Society House,[1] and required by the master to go on at per hour—he declined, unless paid piecework; a second was sent for, he also declined; a third was sent for, and finding it impossible to obtain men at per hour, the master agreed to put this last individual on the piece, when he earned upwards of £2 in 3 days, instead of 16*s*. 6*d*., which is all he would have been entitled to, if he had consented to undertake the work on the establishment.

This proposition, therefore, is one which particularly requires the attention and calm investigation of the Meeting.—The only result to be feared from its adoption, is perhaps the introduction of a few apprentices, but as we are not assured that, under any circumstances, the same would not be introduced if the master were certain of regular employment for him, but little evil would result to the Trade upon that score; at all events, the adoption of the proposition would lay down a certain and not easily to be misapprehended law which the present practices of the Trade imperatively demand.

The Trade Council were for several nights employed in taking evidence upon this subject, which it is not necessary to detail to this meeting. It was deemed sufficient to lay before you the preceding propositions to meet the case, and the personal experience of the Members of the Trade will afford the best illustration of their necessity.

[1] The public house where a list of vacancies was kept for the benefit of the unemployed.

The Trade Council are by no means friendly to establishment engagements under any circumstances, because they are convinced that they are and must invariably be the means of injuring all who are employed on the piece in the same office; but while they feel the system must at present be tolerated, they consider it their duty to call upon the Trade to limit the practice as much as possible.

It is the duty of the Trade Council to state that the decision of this Meeting on this subject will have an important influence on the future practice and welfare of the Trade. They, therefore, trust that the propositions will be fairly discussed, and they cannot neglect this opportunity of stating their hope that no unbecoming marks of derision—which are disgraceful only to those who employ them, and not to the object derided —will be bestowed on any person who from a sense of duty may address the meeting. The hint is almost unnecessary, for we are all well aware that, as the sweetest nut oft lies beneath the roughest shell, so also is much sound sense and practical knowledge often conveyed in a rambling and desultory speech. If, therefore, you have any respect for yourselves, for the Chairman, and for the interests of the Union, which can never be promoted by cabal and clamour, we invoke you not to judge hastily, but by patient attention and mature deliberation endeavour to arrive at such conclusions as shall advance your best interests, and impart stability to our yet infant Union, whose very existence now and at all times must depend on the moderation, the firmness and the unanimity of its Members.

The preceding Report having been unanimously adopted by a Special General Meeting of the Members of the Union, held at the Theatre of the Mechanics' Institution, on the 22nd September, 1835, Mr. John Nichols, Treasurer, in the Chair, the various propositions contained therein were discussed *seriatim*, and the following *Resolutions regulating Establishment Hours and Casual Employment at per day were agreed to, and these Resolutions are to be henceforth strictly observed by every Member of the Union.*

I. That the payment of Compositors by the hour when engaged in composition on bookwork is in opposition to the Scale; and that from henceforth no mode of doing bookwork be recognised by the Trade, but by the piece, or a regular engagement on the establishment.

II. That compositors, when engaged in the composition of jobs, such as handbills, posters, cards, circulars, &c. may accept a casual engagement for not less than a day on the establishment; but that all other descriptions of work must be paid according to the preceding proposition.

III. That the regular and recognised hours for persons on the establishment are twelve hours per day, including the time for refreshment; and when compositors on the establishment are required to work longer hours they are to be paid extra for such working.

Compositors' Trade Council Room,
    Nov. 16, 1835.

N.B. The Trade Council are at present engaged in ascertaining the number and nature of Bastard Founts in use in the business. Any Member of the Trade possessing any information on the subject, is requested to forward the same to the Register. Anonymous *communications will not be noticed.*

The second Annual Report of the L.U.C., for the year 1835, was presented to the meeting assembled in the Theatre of the London Mechanics' Institution on 19 January, 1836. A diversity of subjects was discussed. Those dealing with Apprentices, the News Society and the Parliamentary Scale are noted in other chapters of the present work. A passage respecting Bastard Founts is here reproduced :

[DOCUMENT LXVI]

In directing the attention of the Meeting to the question respecting Bastard Founts, the Trade Council consider it their duty to premise that the Propositions which are required to be considered, are submitted for the express purpose of being added to a complete copy of the Scale of 1810, which has been supplied with copious notes for the purpose of rendering the charges of the Trade upon all points hitherto disputed, permanent and certain. The introduction of Bastard Founts is of so ancient a date that we have been unable to trace when or why they were first introduced. The Trade, however, at all times too prone to submit to innovation, seems to have sanctioned the use of Bastard Founts only one remove without a murmur; for we are able to speak with confidence that they have been in use for thirty years, without any charge being made for them above ordinary type.

Although, therefore, subject to a loss and inconvenience, upon founts only one remove, for so long a period, the neglect of our predecessors affords no sanction for the endurance of a greater evil; and it is the duty of the Trade, while they have the power, to prevent the yet further reduction of the remuneration of labour by framing such regulations respecting Bastard Founts of more than *one* remove, as may tend to check their introduction, or at all events, if not to prevent their introduction, at least to prevent the employment of them from becoming injurious to our interests.

By a fount of one remove, of course the Trade will understand a small-faced letter cast upon a larger body—that is, upon a body the next in size to it—a brevier face on a bourgeois body, or a small pica face upon a pica body. By a fount of two removes we mean a brevier face upon a long primer body, or a small pica face upon an english body. By a fount of *three* removes—(and here we are glad to say that, though a fount of three removes is mentioned, there is no such fount at present in existence; but, as there is no ground for suspecting that successful innovation would not introduce it, it is our duty to provide against the evil). By a fount, then, of three removes we mean a pearl face on a brevier body, or a long primer on an english body. The mere contemplation of the latter anomaly ought to make us diligent and determined in the correction or prevention of the evil which the introduction of such a fount would inflict.

It appears that the introduction of the founts of two removes arose from the printing of works in which such characters as Arabic, Sanscrit, &c. were employed with common roman characters; and the Arabic, &c. requiring a larger surface, were compelled to be cast of a size larger

than the ordinary english type used with them. To prevent, therefore
the justification by leads, &c. of the roman body to the Arabic, the
English alphabet was cast with a large beard; and by this means was
introduced a description of type which when applied to ordinary book
work effects a reduction of nearly 4s. in every pound sterling; and
reduces the remuneration for a week's labour 7s.; that is, to £1. 9s.
instead of £1. 16s.

The investigations of the Council have led to the discovery that there
are only four offices in which founts of two removes exist; in one office
the principle laid down in the circular is admitted; and the Trade will
therefore have to consider the propriety of adhering to the custom there
established, and thus check an evil which is reported to have been in
existence for thirteen years. With regard, also, to another of the offices
in which these founts are more generally prevalent than in the rest, a
proposition has been made by the employer which requires the impartial
and mature consideration of the Trade.

On 2 February, 1836, the following resolution was therefore
adopted:

That Bastard Founts two or more removes from the regular standard
shall be cast up as leaded matter, deducting 1/4d. per 1,000 for leads.
Thus, a Small Pica on an English body shall be considered only a
Small Pica leaded, taking the depth of the face of the letter as the criterion
of ascertaining to what fount any such description of type shall belong.

The following propositions were contained in the agenda for the
eleventh quarterly meeting of the L.U.C., held on 28 December
1836. Four other propositions dealt with at the same time were
concerned with the conditions of entry into the Union.

[DOCUMENT LXVII]

Prop. 4. That Compositors in country towns desirous of uniting
themselves to the London Union of Compositors, may constitute an
Association in their respective towns, nominating a Secretary to correspond with the Register of the London Union; that such Association
shall have the power of settling minor disputes with employers; but no
alteration of the number of hours of labour, or change of prices shall be
made, nor shall any house or prices be deemed unfair, without the
sanction of the Trade Council of the London Union, and shall be
entitled to all the privileges and protection afforded to the Members of
the London Union, upon payment of 6d. per lunar month. The Subscriptions to be transmitted monthly to the Register of the London
Union, carriage paid.

Prop. 5. That it being an undeniable principle that the employed has
an equal right with the employer to fix or adjust the price of labour,
the London Union of Compositors are called upon to use the utmost

vigilance in watching the proceedings of a Society newly established under the name of "An Association of Master Printers."

Prop. 6. That in accordance with the above principle, this meeting earnestly requests the Compositors of London not to submit any disputed question to the above Association of employers; nor to comply with any decision that may be given by them, unless in conformity with the decisions of the Trade Council.

During the summer of 1836 the Newspaper Stamp Tax was reduced from 4d. to 1d. Nevertheless, as the compilers of the *Annual Report for* 1836 of the L.U.C. remarked, ". . . but the last, the worst penny remains to clog the wheels of improvement."

The formation of an Association of Master Printers, announced a year previously as a coming event, was now accomplished. At a meeting held at Stationers' Hall on 8 December, 1836, the employers heard the *Report* of a Provisional Committee and passed seventeen resolutions defining the scope of their activities. A portion of the minutes was reprinted in the L.U.C. Report for 1836, which remains our sole contemporary source of information.

[DOCUMENT LXVIII]

With regard, therefore, to the effect produced in the metropolis by the new law, we feel bound to state that it is trivial and almost unworthy of regard, and would scarcely have been felt if a general dearth of business had prevailed. We are glad, however, to learn that in country towns the result is quite different, and the Secretary of the Northern Union, who was written to for information on the subject, states "the effect of the alteration in the stamp duty has been, as we anticipated, the commencement of a great number of papers, and of course the employment of many more hands in every part of the country. There are at least 35 additional hands in Liverpool alone; and the persons who were formerly obliged to tramp in search of employment are nearly all in work."

. . . . .

We have now to direct your attention to an important event in the proceedings of the past year—*viz.* the formation of an Association of Masters.

The Council know not whether they should call upon the Trade to lament or to rejoice at this circumstance, since they are not aware whether the intentions of the Association be good or evil as regards the interest of those who work for them; but the Council are well assured that if, regardless of our interests, they use the power they possess to depreciate the rate of wages, or augment the present abundance of hands by an unwarrantable increase of apprentices, the evil they intend for *us*, will fall with tenfold vengeance on their own heads; and, in a very brief space of time, their present low rate of profits will be rendered considerably lower by the uprising of many scores of small masters, who, content

with lower gains, will wrest the work from the hands of the presen
opulent and respectable employers. Let the Association, therefore, ponde
well the undeniable fact—that, in proportion to the low rate of wages, i
the number of small masters increased. They need not look far fo
abundant proof of this; as in this city alone, perhaps a hundred instance
might be found of men who have commenced business as masters, solel
from their inability to maintain themselves and their families by thei
labours as journeymen.

Again, let the Masters compare the present state of the business an
the rate of their profits with what they were in 1816, ere the notabl
reduction of reprints took place, and they will discover a woful alteratio
in their condition and ours. And to whom is this change attributable
Assuredly, not to us. We have not willingly yielded to a reduction of th
wages of labour, nor have we sought to swamp the Trade by an influ
of apprentices; but the Masters have done both. In the last 21 years
upon a moderate calculation, they have trained up from 1200 to 150
apprentices; and by the introduction of bastard founts, thin type,[1] an
other injurious speculations and defrauding manœuvres, have cut off a
least one-sixth of the former profits of labour. Now, we would ask the
to consider, Who has benefited by this reduction? Whose happines
comfort, or wealth has been augmented by their efforts? They ma
search the Trade in vain for one who will answer—"I have;" but
they inquire in a certain place northward of the famed St. Paul's, the
may perhaps find some who will admit that *they* have profited from th
reductions made in the price of our labour.

Finding, then, that their past efforts have done no good to themselve
or to us, we would fain indulge the hope that employers will be con
vinced of their true interests, and in future co-operate with us in main
taining a uniform and regular standard for defining the wages of labou
They are as much interested in this as we are; their profits are regulate
by ours; and they should make common cause with us against those wh
would seek to obtain their work done in such a way, and at such a pric
as would rob the respectable master of his fair profits, and the journeyma
of his just hire. We are satisfied that it requires only a good understandin
of the respective rights of the two parties, to effect, in a short space o
time, a wondrous revolution in the affairs of the printing business, an
introduce a state of things highly advantageous to both masters and me

To effect this, however, *we* must stand on high ground. We must t
independent—assuming neither a threatening nor a rebellious aspect—
but conducting ourselves in such a way as to exhibit strength, and cor
fidence, and rectitude. We have no desire to seek an advance of price
High as the rate of provisions has recently been, and difficult as it i
from the very nature of our business, to ensure even one full week's wor
we are content that things should remain as they are. What we want—
and what, indeed, the Union was established to obtain—is a just definitio
and uniformity of price to be paid for our labour; so that, after workin
for a week, we may not expend the next three days in deciding how v
are to be paid; or leave it in the power of an employer to dispute th
week's bill on the Saturday night, and send a journeyman home pennile

---

[1] *i.e.*, condensed founts.

to his family, unless he chooses to take that price which his employer dictates.

We shall, however, now submit to you the circular containing the regulations of the Association of Masters, and as by its general circulation through the trade it has become a public document, we shall take the liberty of offering a few remarks upon it.

ASSOCIATION OF MASTER PRINTERS

Extract from the Report of the Provisional Committee to the General Meeting held at Stationers' Hall, on Thursday, the 8th December, 1836, for the Re-establishment of the Association of Master Printers.

The Provisional Committee, in framing the Rules for the constitution of the Association, have had the advantage of the experience and knowledge of two members of the old Committee of Master Printers; and they have endeavoured, allowing for the altered circumstances of the times, to frame those rules upon the model of the old Society, the principles of which are developed in the following recommendations of the Committee:—

1. That all master printers should be admitted as members, without any form of nomination or election, upon payment in advance of a certain subscription.

2. That the affairs of the Association should be conducted by a Chairman, General Committee, and Secretary; and that these should be honorary offices.

3. That, in the formation of the General Committee, the number should be such, that all branches of the Trade may be represented therein; and in the selection of its members care should be taken that those names only should be proposed that are most likely, from their influence and knowledge of business, to insure respect for their decisions among the members of the association as well as among the journeymen. And the Provisional Committee are from their experience induced to believe, that the number of those among the journeymen who have long desired the re-establishment of such a tribunal for the adjustment of disputes between them and their employers is so great, that a ready acquiescence on their part will attend the decisions of the General Committee.

4. That the Association should afford their assistance to check the dishonest practice too prevalent with some journeymen, of quitting their employers without notice, or in debt. This the Provisional Committee consider no less due to the honest journeyman than to the general interests of the Trade.

———

The following is a Copy of the Resolutions founded on the Recommendations of the Provisional Committee.

At a Meeting of Master Printers held at Stationers' Hall, on Thursday, the 8th *of December,* 1836.   George Woodfall, Esq., *in the Chair.*

Resolved—1. That the old Association of Master Printers be now re-established, under the designation of "The Association of Master Printers," for the purpose of protecting the general interests of the Trade.

2. That all master printers be admitted members of this association, on payment in advance of an annual subscription of 10s. 6d., where the number of presses used by him does not exceed two; of £1 1s. where the number does not exceed four; of £2 2s. where the number does not exceed eight; and of £3 3s. where the number exceeds eight: a machine being considered as equal to three presses.

3. That the affairs of this association be conducted by a chairman, committee, and secretary; and that these be honorary offices.

4. That Mr. George Woodfall be requested to accept the office of chairman, and Mr. Walter M'Dowall that of secretary.

5. That a committee of twelve, exclusive of the chairman and secretary, be now elected, to conduct the affairs of the association, to whom all matters in dispute between master and journeyman may be submitted for decision.

6. That the committee meet on the first Thursday in every month, and on such other days as they may see fit; and that not less than six form a quorum.

7. That it is the opinion of this meeting, that the scale of 1810, as amended in 1816, should form the basis of the decisions of the committee.

8. That the points in dispute to be submitted to the committee for their decision, be delivered in writing to the secretary on or before the Monday preceding the meeting of the committee.

9. That the secretary communicate to the referror the place and hour at which the committee will meet, in order that the referror and one or two of the journeymen belonging to the companionship with respect to which the dispute arises, may attend the meeting of the committee, to support their respective views.

10. That the secretary communicate to the referror the decision of the committee within two days after the matter shall be decided.

11. That the members of the association communicate in writing to the secretary, the names of any persons who may have left their employ without having given and completed the warning required by the usage of the Trade, or who may have left the books uncleared.

12. That the members of the association pledge themselves not to employ, for the space of three months from the date of the secretary's notice apprizing them of the fact, any person who has left his employ without having given and completed the warning required by the usage of the Trade, or who has left the books uncleared.

13. That the names of those who may infringe any of the rules of the association, be reported to the committee for the information of the members.

14. That there be an annual meeting of this association on the first Friday in December, to audit the accounts, and for general purposes.

15. That the committee be empowered to fill up any vacancies that may occur in their body, subject to the approval of the next general meeting of the association.

16. That the thanks of this meeting be given to the provisional committee for the zealous and efficient discharge of the duties confided to them.

17. That the thanks of this meeting be also given to the chairman for his able conduct in the chair.

The Committee elected in pursuance of the 4th and 5th Resolutions are

Mr. Woodfall, Chairman.

Mr. Spottiswoode,	Mr. Clay,
Mr. L. G. Hansard,	Mr. Gilbert,
Mr. J. B. Nichols,	Mr. Balne,
Mr. Clowes,	Mr. M'Intosh,
Mr. Taylor,	Mr. Baldwin,
Mr. Tyler,	Mr. J. L. Cox.

Mr. M'Dowall, Hon. Sec.

The Provisional Committee who framed the above Resolutions have deceived those who appointed them. They have stated that a great number of journeymen are willing to submit their disputes to a tribunal which is composed wholly of masters. Where is their proof of this assertion? Is it to be found in the fact that though the Masters' Committee have been established two months, not a single case has been laid before them by the journeymen? or is the corroboration of their statement to be found in the yet more remarkable circumstance, that one of the selected amongst the Masters, after threatening to refer a disputed work to "The Association," declined so to do, and paid according to our Scale? We regret, therefore, that the Masters should have been deceived by so gross a mis-statement, and we are convinced there is no man who desires to act consistently with the interests of the Trade who would submit any dispute to a tribunal constituted like that of the "Masters' Association."

We hasten on to notice another point in the Masters' Regulations; namely, "that the Scale of 1810 as amended in 1816 should form the basis of the decisions of the Committee." Why, this is exactly the course that has been invariably pursued by the Union—we have adopted the Scale of 1810 as *altered* (for we cannot consider *a reduction* an *amendment*) in 1816, as the basis of every decision that has been given; and we challenge them to exhibit any decision given by the Union contrary to that Scale; but, in thus referring to a document of nearly 40 years' standing, the Masters forget that it is imperfect; that, except in regard to the price per 1000, and one or two other points, it does not apply to the present state of the business—and how do they propose to meet the cases for which that Scale makes no provision? why, doubtless, by laws of their own; by framing rules upon subjects of which their knowledge is only theoretical; for, upon looking over the list of the present committee, it will be found that there is not one *practical* man amongst them —not one operative—not one who by actual experience knows the portion of time required to execute any unusual or difficult work for which the Scale does not provide.* How, then, are they likely to give the due reward for labour, when their knowledge is not derived from the proper source, *viz.*, a capability of executing the work which they are called upon to value? As a proof of this, we may remark that one gentleman amongst them maintains that it is as advantageous to a compositor to set an 8vo. page in two columns as it is to set it in one measure.

* In the above remark there is no desire to stigmatize or depreciate the members of the committee. Some of them have been long known to the Trade as generous and honourable men; all that we have to urge against them, as a committee, is, that they are not, nor for some time past have been WORKMEN, and that their knowledge of the value of labour is not practical but theoretical.

Another rule of the Association is that no Master shall employ a compositor who has left a situation, without giving and completing the "warning" required by the usage of the Trade. We presume by the indefinite expression "*the warning*," that these gentlemen mean a fortnight's notice. And we are somewhat glad to see this public acknowledgment of the custom by the Masters, more especially as one of those most active in forming the Association was bold enough to swear, in a court of justice, that no such custom existed, and that persons came into his office one day, and went out of it the next, without molestation; but, while we admit the right of a master to a fortnight's notice, we deny Mr. Spottiswoode's interpretation of the law, who kept men in his office until the period of their notice had expired, and yet refused to give them fair employment. No, the law of the Trade is, that the compositor should give a fortnight's notice in order that an employer may not suffer inconvenience from his leaving, and in order to afford time for the correcting and finishing of his work; but we deny the right of the master to retain any man in his office to whom he is unable to give employment; and if the Association should in its wisdom deem fit to post any man who should leave under such circumstances, it will be our duty to appeal to the laws of the land for protection against such an injustice.

We have not time to dwell longer upon the principles of the Masters' Association except to notice that it contains the names of some who, from the disregard which they have shown to the interests of the trade, by the introduction of apprentices, can have little claim to the regard or respect of the journeymen. If we are to view this Association as formed for the purpose of opposing our Union—and we know that it was this feeling which called it into existence—have not these gentlemen constantly in their employ a sufficient number of apprentices to execute any disputed work, without thus irritating us by opposing an institution which we deem essential to our welfare. What respect do they suppose will be paid to the decisions of the Association of Masters, where 11 out of the 14 gentlemen of the committee have no less than 179 apprentices in their employment!

If they would win our respect, let them show some sympathy for our sufferings. Let them show some regard for our moral condition and happiness; and not, by an unprincipled introduction of apprentices, compel us to open violence, and to the adoption of measures injurious to the youths whom they trepan into a profession which cannot afford them employment, and which will only yield to them such a miserable pittance as will render life rather a burden than an enjoyment.

Finally, then, before dismissing this Association from our minds—we earnestly solicit the trade not to refer any work to the tribunal their employers have constructed. It is founded upon a wrong principle, and we cannot expect justice from its hands. If you expect to receive a just value for your labour, and to obtain wages sufficient for your maintenance, you must not appeal to those whose exertions have hitherto been employed in sapping the rights of the trade and reducing the wages of labour. If the employers are really desirous to promote the interests of the business and establish a good understanding with the journeymen, let them institute a tribunal where capital and labour shall be equally represented —where an equal number of masters and journeymen shall constitute a committee of reference—but till then we must refuse all reference to them.

With the exception of the controversy on the question of wrappers and standing matter, which engaged the attention of the trade in 1838, there is nothing contained in the Annual Reports of the L.U.C. issued between the years 1837 and 1842 needing examination in this chapter. The Extracts which follow are taken from the L.U.C. Annual Report for 1838.

A dispute had broken out in Bentley's office. The committee of the employers' Association met on 10 December, 1838, for the purpose of "considering the case of the refusal of the compositors in Mr. Bentley's office to work upon his Magazine; and with a view to conformity of practice in our several offices."

[DOCUMENT LXIX]

The Committee of Master Printers being informed that claims have been made by compositors in some offices for all wrappers and advertising sheets to be set up by such compositors only as were employed on the periodicals to which they are attached, it was unanimously resolved

That such claim on the part of the compositors is an innovation on the antient and accustomed usages of the Trade, and wholly incompatible with that control which a Master has a right to exercise over the mode of conducting his own business; and that such claim will in future be resisted by every Member of this Committee.[1]

It having been stated by Mr. Bentley, that the compositors in his office had refused to proceed with his Magazine in consequence of his acting on the general understanding of the Committee, that the compositors were not entitled to the Standing Advertisements in Periodicals, it was resolved

That compositors are not entitled to such *Standing Advertisements*, or to any *Standing Matter*, such claim being also contrary to the antient and established practice of the Trade.

A deputation of compositors conferred with the master printers, and in January, 1839, the following regulations were adopted by mutual consent. The L.U.C. Report reprinted all correspondence and papers exchanged between the Union and the Employers. The Resolutions printed below formed part of a circular issued by the Master Printers' Association on 14 February, 1839.

1. That the Companionship on a Magazine or Review be entitled to the first or title-page of a Wrapper on a Magazine or Review; but not to the remaining pages of such Wrapper, nor to the Advertising Sheets which may accompany the Magazine or Review.

2. That Standing Advertisements or Stereo-blocks, if forming a complete page, or, when collected together, making one or more complete pages, in a Wrapper or Advertising Sheet of a Magazine or Review, shall not be chargeable; the compositor to charge only for his time in making them up. The remainder of the matter in such Wrapper or Advertising Sheet, including Standing Advertisements or Stereo-blocks not forming a complete page, to be charged by the Compositor, and cast up according to the 8th and 20th Rules of the Scale as they may respectively apply. But the charge of 2s. 6d., as given by Rule 7, is not to be superadded.

3. With regard to Standing Matter, the Committee adhere to their Resolution of December 10, 1838.

[1] The Masters resisted the claim in 1834, but gave way. See p. 225.

16

Thus the men relinquished their right to three out of the four pages of a Wrapper. They made the concession in view of "the great alteration that has gradually been taking place in the nature as well as the quantity of matter in the wrappers and advertising sheets or pages of the various periodicals of the day. . . ."

———————

While conditions in the provinces were not mentioned in the first *Annual Report* of the London Union of Compositors, on the occasion of their second annual meeting, held 19 January, 1836, when the Report for 1835 was read, the following information was given :

It is gratifying to add to the previous statements of the London Union, that our brethren in the country are also in a highly prosperous condition. The Northern Union, by whose aid we hold correspondence and are in connection with sixty provincial societies, increases in wealth and influence.

The Northern Union, founded in 1830, consisted largely of local associations active in the larger towns of the midlands and north country.

The L.U.C. Annual Report for 1836 contains this passage :

The delegation to Manchester in the summer of the past year promises to be productive of events highly satisfactory. Encouraged by the strength and unanimity which the meeting of delegates displayed, the compositors of Ireland and Scotland have established a Union in each country for the protection of their interests. Famed as those countries have hitherto been for the rearing of apprentices, it is highly gratifying and encouraging to us to see them now step forward and assist us to the utmost extent of their ability. Since our last Annual Meeting societies have been re-organized or established at Brighton, at Bristol, at Cambridge, at Oxford, and even at the Isle of Man, for the purpose of advancing the interests of the profession; and while we feel the most lively joy in contemplating the glorious results which must arise from a Union so extensive, when its energies and resources are brought into full activity, we trust that our brethren in London will not suffer themselves to be surpassed in zeal and firmness by their brethren in the provinces, but that they will upon all future occasions assist and second their efforts.

No further details on provincial matters were given until the L.U.C. Annual Report for 1839 was published.

[DOCUMENT LXX]

Our fellow-labourers in England, Ireland, and Scotland, we are glad to report, are not inactive in promoting the general good. During the past year societies have been formed at Bristol, Northampton, and

Ipswich. In the West of England, which has long been in a most deranged and disgraceful state, a "Western Union," upon the same principles as those of the Northern Union, has been established, and apprentice-restricting societies now exist in Bath and Bristol. Let us, then, have a Union in the east and the south. Those parts are not wholly destitute of societies—and some check may be afforded to the great evils of which those places are now more especially the cause.

In the use of the words "apprentice-restricting" may be found the key to our understanding of trade organization outside London. Existing sources of information on provincial matters contain little on the subject of Scales of prices or methods of working, but a great deal concerning the surplus of apprentices in a trade which could not provide enough work for its journeymen.[1] The evil known as "tramping," whereby journeymen wandered the country-side in search of an odd day's work, and subsisting on the charity of their fellow craftsmen, arose directly from this state of affairs.

The "Union in the east and the south", which had been suggested in the L.U.C. Annual Report for 1839, did not come about until the beginning of 1845, when the L.U.C. joined the newly formed National Typographical Association.

The Society had been in difficulties for some time. After 1836, when there were about 1,900 subscribers, membership began to diminish. The closing of Spottiswoode's, considered an "Unfair House," was an important factor, since the firm was one of the largest in the trade.[2] In 1838 there was a good deal of unemployment and men were unable to pay their subscriptions. The Special Committee appointed to reorganize the affairs of the Union in 1840 met with little success, since its decisions were negatived by the Council, and dissensions still further weakened its position. By 1843 expenses began to exceed subscriptions, and the complete collapse of the L.U.C. seemed inevitable.

In the meantime the proposal of the provincial societies for the amalgamation of all the printing trade unions in the United

---

[1] The following should be consulted: *The Compositors' Chronicle*, 1840-43, continued as *The Printer*, 1843-45; *The Typographical Gazette*, 1846-47; *The Typographical Protection Circular*, 1849-53; *The Typographical Circular*, 1854-58. These periodicals, all published in London, were addressed particularly to the workmen engaged in the London and provincial printing trades. Unfortunately much of the matter sent in for publication by the secretaries of the provincial unions is extremely dull and tells us little that is useful. A valuable summary of events between 1845-60 is contained in Crompton, J. W., *Report on Printers' Strikes and Trade Unions since January*, 1845, in *Trades' Societies and Strikes*, published for the Nat. Assoc. for the Promotion of Social Science, (London, 1860), pp. 77-92.

[2] See p. 368.

Kingdom was meeting with some success. It was not due in any way to the initiative of the L.U.C., but to the desire of the country associations for the restriction of apprentices and control and relief of "tramps," or unemployed journeymen compositors walking from town to town in search of work. Thus was formed the National Typographical Association. In some despair at the state of their own Society, the leaders of the L.U.C. recommended affiliation to the N.T.A., and in January 1845 the London Union of Compositors was wound up. The organization became known as the London Society of Compositors, being a branch of the South-Eastern District of the N.T.A.

Delegates from all parts of the country had held a meeting at Derby in July, 1844. They then drew up a provisional set of Rules "for the Government of the National Typographical Association." These were considered at a General Meeting of the London trade on 10 September, 1844. The Trade Council conceived that the following could be regarded as the main objects of the Association.[1]

[DOCUMENT LXXI]

1. The diminution of strikes, by vesting the power of closing offices in the whole trade, instead of leaving it, as at present, in the hands of a few individuals.

2. An equitable remuneration to those who make sacrifices for the interests of the trade.

3. The abolition of the present system of tramping and casual relief, by providing a permanent allowance for the unemployed.

4. The concentration of the energies and resources of the trade in all cases of dispute.

5. An equalization of subscription, and bestowal of equal benefits.

The affairs of the Association were managed by a Central Board or Committee, consisting of five District Boards collectively—in which resided the executive power, a majority of whose votes decided every question—and the Committees of each Local Society or Branch belonging to the Union.

The five Districts were:

Northern—Scotland, having Eight Branches or Local Societies at principal towns, with		800	members.
Western—Ireland, Eleven Branches	,,	569	,,
Midland—Twenty-two Branches	,,	714	,,
South-Western—Twelve Branches	,,	237	,,
South-Eastern—Seven Branches	,,	2,000	,,
Total	.	4,320	members.

[1] *Report on the National Typographical Association read at a General Meeting of the Compositors of London*, 10 September, 1844.

The Trade in Manchester did not join the Association, and remained united amongst themselves in a Society which had previously been in association with the Northern Union. Most of the Societies which had formed part of the Northern Union joined the National Association, the Northern Union ceasing to exist.

The National Typographical Association achieved a striking initial success. Trade was brisk during 1845, and the London Society of Compositors ended the year with a balance in hand of more than £1,300. But the Second Annual Report of the L.S.C., covering the whole of 1846, presents a less favourable picture :

[DOCUMENT LXXII]

The two years which the Society has now seen, have been as dissimilar in effect upon the trade as two opposites can well be supposed. . . . In the second year, so great was the change, that from activity the trade was reduced to a dearth that finds no parallel in latter years, and likened only to that known in 1825 and 1826. For all, the past year has been a very trying one. It has obliged the executive to increase the rate of payment at a time when the members were least prepared to pay the same; and it has compelled a large body of men to be dependent upon the Society for the means to obtain bare food and shelter.

Double subscriptions had been demanded in the autumn of 1846, and a document dated 24 December, 1846, informed the London compositors that the same sacrifice would be demanded of them until the close of March, 1847. The condition of affairs was even worse in Edinburgh where, in December, 1846, thirty-eight employers combined to break up the local Association by engaging only non-society men. This was the beginning of the end of the N.T.A.

On 14 July, 1847, a circular containing the following message was sent to the various London chapels :

[DOCUMENT LXXIII]

We are directed by the Committee, in consequence of the great and increasing demands made upon them by unemployed and strike members, to request that if the Chapel hold any money collected on behalf of the Society, the same may be forthwith paid, otherwise the Committee will not be able to meet their engagements on Saturday next.

Half a year later this sad chapter in the history of the London printing trade was brought to a close.

[DOCUMENT LXXIV]

At the Third Annual General Meeting of the London Society of Compositors' Branch of the National Typographical Association, held at the Mechanics' Institution, Southampton Buildings, Holborn, on Tuesday Evening, February 1, 1848, the following Resolutions were unanimously agreed to :

That in consequence of the numerous secessions which have taken place, both in town and country, from the ranks of the National Typographical Association, as also the continued indifference exhibited on its behalf, this Branch deems it necessary, for the maintenance of Union, to cease connection with the afore-named Association, forming in its place a local society apart from, but in friendly connection with, all other typographical societies in the three kingdoms.

That this Meeting hereby establishes a Local Trade Society, to be called The London Society of Compositors, for the purpose of protecting and regulating the wages of labour, agreeably to the provisions contained in the London Scale of Prices (as agreed to by a Conference of Masters and Compositors in 1847); as also the Scales of Prices regulating News and Parliamentary Work; together with such customs and usages as belong to the profession, not directly mentioned in the Scales above alluded to.

The Rules of the Society were passed at a Special General Meeting on 29 February, 1848. Rule 3 specified :

[DOCUMENT LXXV]

That every compositor of fair character, now working as a journeyman in or within fifteen miles of London, or who receives London prices, or who may hereafter prove his right to work as a journeyman either by privilege, seven years' indenture, or clear card of membership of the country society he has just quitted, shall be admissiable as a member; and whilst so, shall pay weekly, or at most every fourth week, a sum proportionate to his earnings; *i.e.* for 15s. or less than 20s. 2d.; for 20s. and less than 30s., 3d.; and for 30s. or more, 4d. per week.

Thus was founded the London Society of Compositors as constituted to-day. Since 1848 it has preserved complete independence from the provincial unions.

ticularly of late years, been afflicted, the price of provisions, and expence of all the necessaries of life, has risen at least one third, nay, it is believed, that a fairer proportion would be one half; and for this fact, an enumeration of particulars, or reference to evidence is quite unnecessary; it is known to every man."[1] It was suggested that in many trades the wages had been increased, but that "During the period now alluded to, the wages of the journeymen compositors have not been altered. No augmentation whatever has taken place, except in the year 1792, when, owing to a particular pressure of work, a very inconsiderable and temporary rise in the price of book-printing was voluntarily given."

The compositors then reminded the employers of the wage increases that had been allowed to their brethren in London, "in consequence of the continual variations in the price of provisions and the rate of living." In Scotland, it was pointed out, no demands had been made. "During those late years of scarcity, which will not soon be forgotten, the memorialists suffered the hardships endured by other workmen; and in order to subsist themselves and their families, were forced to sell or pledge their furniture, and incur debts, which many of them have not been able yet to discharge." Men employed in other trades had not scrupled to cause trouble, but the compositors had endured their hardships with fortitude. "The memorialists were sensible that the state of the printing business in Scotland at that time afforded them no reasonable prospect of an augmentation of wages."

This depressed state of the manufacture however is now at an end. The trade of printing has again become flourishing in Scotland; and that fund, which, if it had existed in the years of scarcity, would have authorised a much larger demand of augmentation than the memorialists have now brought forward, indisputably exists in the hands of the masters. It is a fact capable of the most distinct and easy proof, that there are more books composed and sent forth from this city than from almost all the other cities of the island taken together, with the single exception of London; but even London booksellers have come of late years to employ Scotch printers to print for their market. The Edinburgh work is daily improving in elegance and correctness; it is done at a cheaper rate: and although formerly, when goods were conveyed to London only by a land-journey, in the waggon, or by merchant ships, which stopped perhaps for weeks to complete their cargoes, a traffic in this article was impracticable, nowadays the distance formed no great obstacle; for the smacks lately established afford a very quick, easy, regular, and cheap conveyance; they sail daily; make their voyage in the course of

---

[1] *Cf.* Memorials of London compositors at various dates before 1810, in which were made claims based on similar grounds.

three or four days; are insured for a mere trifle; and the freight is scarcely worth naming.

The judicial bench expressed a desire for exact information on the subject of the compositors' wages in the past. The employers produced their wage-books for the preceding twenty-five years, from which some interesting but complicated statistics were compiled. The simplified table here printed shows the average weekly wages at three different periods.

Average Wage per week	1773	1791	1802
Session work *	15/1$\frac{3}{4}$*d.*	19/11$\frac{2}{3}$*d.*	18/2$\frac{11}{12}$*d.*
Book work	12/7$\frac{1}{12}$*d.*	17/11$\frac{2}{3}$*d.*	17/8$\frac{5}{12}$*d.*, including King's Printers 16/11*d.*, without King's Printers

* The equivalent of London parliamentary or legal printing.

During the whole period the price of 3$\frac{1}{2}$*d.* per 1,000 had remained unchanged. These figures, therefore, simply demonstrate that increased earnings depended entirely upon a sufficient supply of work being available.

The Court decided in favour of the men, their findings being contained in the "*Interlocutor* pronounced by the Lords of Council and Session, in the Process of the Journeymen Compositor Printers in Edinburgh, against the Master Printers there, for a rise of Wages, so as to conform to the preceding Scale."

The Scale mentioned in the *Interlocutor* contained nine articles, which were to remain in force "until altered or augmented by proper authority, or of consent of the parties interested." The Edinburgh composition price was raised to 4$\frac{1}{2}$*d.*, which was $\frac{3}{4}$*d.* per 1,000 less than that paid in London. But whereas the London rate was advanced to 5$\frac{3}{4}$*d.* for leaded and 6*d.* for solid matter in 1810, these prices remaining in force until 1866, the Edinburgh 1805 Scale was not increased until 1862, when an extra $\frac{1}{2}$*d.* per 1,000 was allowed.[1] It may be supposed, therefore, that the Edinburgh masters were not put to any great disadvantage by the *Interlocutor*.

It would appear that the Edinburgh pressmen also received an advance in prices at about the same time. A pressmen's Scale

[1] *Scottish Typographical Circular* (Edinburgh, Jan. 1862).

". . . Agreed upon by the Master Printers of Edinburgh, April 26, 1805," contained the following: "Final Note: N.B.—In agreeing to pay the above Prices to their Pressmen, the Masters must express their firm expectation that the work will be executed in that neat manner, which alone can secure to Edinburgh its due proportion of employment in the English market, without which, it is obvious that the Journeymen will in the end suffer equally with their masters."[1]

MANCHESTER, 1810

Among the Place MSS. at the British Museum there is a copy of a circular addressed to the Master Printers of Manchester by their employees.[2] This document is dated 27 June, 1810, and contains a request for an increase in prices.

We feel it necessary to inform you, that a material advance has taken place, for some time, in London, Dublin, Liverpool, Bristol, and other leading towns throughout the United Kingdom; and if the Journeymen Printers of Manchester are amongst the last in being applicants, it surely is another proof of their forbearance and moderation; nor, indeed, would they at any time wish to urge it, but that there is no instance on record of the Master Printers giving to the Journeymen a rise unsolicited.

No details of existing prices were given. The following were the compositors' demands:

	£	s.	d.
Men employed on the Establishment .	1	15	0 *per week*
Extra Work to be paid			7 *per hour*
Compositors on Piece-work to be paid .			6 *per 1,000*
Jobs of one sheet, or under . . .			7 *do.*
Pressmen on Piece-work to be paid . .			6½ *per hour*
Do. on Messrs. Russell and Allen's grand folio Bible			6 *do.*
All Jobs an advance of one halfpenny per hour.			

It is doubtful whether these advances in prices were granted by the employers, since the Manchester prices would thus have been increased to about the London level. Neither at that time, nor since, has Manchester been an important printing centre.

[1] *Report of Select Committee on King's Printers' Patents*, 1832, p. 260.
[2] MSS. Add. 27799. *f.* 92 *r.* The Manchester Typographical Society was founded in 1797. See Dickson, J. J., *Manchester Typographical Society and Branch of T.A. Centenary*, 1797-1897 (Manchester, 1897).

GLASGOW, 1815

Scale of Compositors' Prices, Agreed to by the Master Printers of Glasgow, May 1, 1815.

This Scale contained sixteen articles. Common matter was cast up at $4\frac{1}{2}d.$, the same as in Edinburgh.

LEEDS, 1826 [1]

The twenty-nine articles of the Leeds Scale, agreed upon 15 March, 1826, are based upon those of the London Scale of 1810. Common matter was cast up at $5d.$ per 1,000. Prices were also stated for Posting Bills, all sizes from double demy at 7s. 6d. to foolscap octavo at 9d. being quoted. Circulars, in quarto or octavo, were charged according to whether they were set in ordinary roman type or in French script, a small extra charge being made for the latter, because the types were not cast on rectangular bodies, but at an angle, thus facilitating the joining of each character. Invoice heads, post or foolscap, 9d. If the date line and £ s. d. columns were added, an extra 3d. was charged.

DUBLIN, 1835

Thirty articles based on the London Scale of 1810. Common matter cast up at $5d.$ per 1,000.

BELFAST, 1835

Thirteen articles. Common matter cast up at $4\frac{1}{2}d.$ per 1,000.

SCOTLAND, 1841

The particulars contained in the abstract of provincial Scales printed on p. 253 are taken from the *Rules and Regulations of the General Typographical Association of Scotland . . . Adopted August 5, 1841.*

---

[1] The following information is taken from the *Centenary Souvenir* of the Leeds Typographical Society, 1910. The Society was founded in 1810. In 1823 the proprietors of the *Leeds Mercury* installed a printing machine, operated by two men turning a handle. 1825: Establishment wages were 26s. per week of sixty hours. 1836: Affiliation with the Northern Union. 1858: 28s. per week of fifty-nine hours. 1872: 32s. per week of fifty-nine hours.

	London 1785	Dublin 1800	London 1805	Edinburgh 1805	London 1810	Glasgow 1815	Leeds 1826	Dublin *c.* 1836	Belfast *c.* 1836	Scotland 1841
	English-Brevier	English-Brevier	English-Brevier	Down to Brevier	English-Brevier	Pica-Brevier	English-Minion	English-Brevier	English-Brevier	Outside Edinburgh and Glasgow.
Common Matter, per 1,000	4½*d.*	4½*d.* [London, Dec. 24, 1800. Price raised from 4½*d.* to 5¼*d.*]	5¼*d.*	4½*d.*	leaded 5¾*d.* solid 6*d.*	4½*d.*	5*d.* news 6*d.* (to allow for short takings)	5*d.*	4½*d.*	4½*d.* Newspapers and pamphlets, 5½*d.*
Establishment wages	21*s.*-27*s.*	—	33*s.*	—	36*s.*	—	26*s.*	—	21*s.*	Rate for Edinburgh and Glasgow, 25*s.* outside, 20*s.*
Foreign languages: roman type	5*d.*	1*s.* per sheet extra.	English-Long Primer 5¾*d.*	5*d.*	leaded 6¼*d.* solid 6½*d.*	5*d.*	5½*d.*	5½*d.*	—	—
Dictionaries	5½*d.*	5*d.*	5¾*d.*	5*d.*	leaded 6¼*d.* solid 6½*d.*	5*d.*	5½*d.*	5½*d.*	—	—
Jobs, generally one sheet or under	—	Increase of one-quarter on book scale	6½*d.*	5½*d.*	7*d.*	5½*d.*	5*d.*	Increase of one-sixth on book scale	5½*d.*	Outside Edinburgh and Glasgow, 5½*d.*
Corrections, per hour.	4½*d.*[?][1]	6*d.*	6*d.*	—	6*d.*	6*d.*	6*d.*	6*d.*	6*d.*	—
Location of document.	St. Bride broadside.	St. Bride broadside.	St. Bride, Savage's *Dictionary of Printing*, p. 749.	*London Scale of Prices*, 1836, p. 84.	St. Bride, Savage, Hansard, *London Scale of Prices.*	Bound in with *Compositors' Chronicle*, 1840, at St. Bride.	*London Scale of Prices*, p. 79.	*London Scale of Prices*, p. 87.	*London Scale of Prices*, p. 91.	Bound in with *Compositors' Chronicle*, 1840, at St. Bride.

[1] See *London Scale of Prices*, 1836, p. 14, footnote.

CHAPTER X

THE LONDON SOCIETY
OF COMPOSITORS (1845-1889)

1. 1845-1856

One of the first documents issued by the London Society of Compositors after the dissolution of the London Union was the *Report of the Commission of Inquiry appointed to investigate the Mode of Payment, &c., practised in those offices in London that have been regarded, for some time past, by Compositors, as Unfair.*[1] The following houses were examined: Spottiswoode's, Johnson's, Fairbrother's (the latter two specialising in theatrical printing), Truscott's and *The Times*. The state of affairs at Spottiswoode's, a parliamentary house, is explained in Chapter XIV, and conditions at *The Times* are examined in Chapter XVI. Only the complaints regarding Johnson's office are reprinted here. The document also contained a discussion on "what size sheet of paper can fairly be considered *one* sheet," which is also reprinted. The *Report* is dated 16 December, 1845.

[DOCUMENT LXXVI]

Mr. Johnson's, St. Martin's Lane, late of Nassau Street.

At this office a somewhat strange system is carried on, different from the understanding of the trade respecting Play-bill Offices, which was put in force some time since by Mr. Johnson. Bookwork as well as play-bills are done here, and the hands upon each are all paid 33s. per week. There are, however, two rooms, and for clearness, they will consider, first.

The Play-Bill Room.—Three hands, winter and summer, playhouses closed or open, are kept at 33s., and another at 36s. per week, and go to work in the morning at half-past ten. This is the understood hour to commence work, but this is altered by circumstances. Supposing them to commence at half-past ten o'clock in the morning, they compose until half-past ten o'clock at night. If they have to work later, which is invariably the case during the months when the majority of the playhouses are open, they take the time out of the next day. Thus, if they left off at one o'clock in the morning, they would not resume work until two the next day, that is with the hour for their dinner. From half-past

---

[1] The only copy of this *Report* known to the author is in the possession of the L.S.C. Two pages of introductory matter are missing.

en o'clock they are kept waiting for the proofs from the managers; consequently, their time for leaving the office is uncertain; yet, if they are not detained above an hour or so, they are expected to begin work in the morning at half-past ten. Instead of staying, as on other nights, late on Saturday, they go *every Sunday*, for a few hours, or so long as the proofs may take them to correct. They go upon this principle: *whatever quantity of work may come in to do, however late it may keep them, or whatever the number of hours they may be called upon to do it; yet it must be done, and for* 33s., no extras being paid to them either for night work, overtime, or Sunday work. The witnesses stated that during one part of the year, and for about three months, they have very little to do, and are seldom called upon to compose other work. But at present they were working a great many hours, consequent upon a heavy play-bill season. These play-bills keep four hands the year together in the office, and one of them reads the bills, for which Mr. Johnson, when he first went, said he would put him upon the full establishment, or 36s. No bills are written.

The Book Room.—Here, the book hands work from nine in the morning until nine at night, and are on the establishment at 33s. They are seldom called upon to work later, but when they are, they are not paid for it. They might, instead of working 63 hours in a week, work 70; if they did, they would only be paid 33s. They do not write any bills, and there are seven of them in the room, all on the same terms. There is not a single apprentice in the whole house.

The differences in the office of Mr. Johnson may be said to be—

1. That he will not pay night-work;
2. That he will not pay overtime; and
3. That he will not pay Sunday work.

With Mr. Johnson, as with Mr. Spottiswoode, they desired to have an interview; but as before, their efforts were frustrated; and the foregoing are facts that are too glaring to pass by your notice unheeded.*

* This Report was read on the evening of Dec. 3; and on the following morning, a letter was received from Mr. Johnson, a copy of which is appended :—

'Mr. Johnson's compliments to Mr. Edwards, and regrets extremely in not replying to his letter sent some time since, which had by accident got mislaid, and the circumstance forgotten until this moment. Mr. Johnson will feel great pleasure in seeing Mr. Edwards, with other gentlemen, any evening, from eight to nine o'clock.

'*Dec.* 3, 1845.'

On the 5th, Mr. Johnson was waited on, and received a deputation of three persons with much courtesy. He entered into a statement of the peculiarities consequent upon theatrical printing; and observed, that he had been in business a great many years, during which he had struggled hard to bring about something like a system in this kind of work, and he does but little other, but had failed. The whims of managers know no bounds: alterations were made at the last moment, and for which he dare not charge a shilling extra. If it were not for his machinery, he could not do as he does, so ruinously low is he cut down in his prices. If he attempted to charge the managers with but the extra for night and Sunday work, he should lose the printing; and where would it go? Why, to some back-parlour, to be done by 'a man, woman and boy.' As a practical printer, he assured the deputation, that he knew well that the charges named were paid by employers, and he would not dissent from paying them himself, if that his work were anything like bookwork. But it was quite an exception; it must be done at all hours; and when it was in the house, he called upon his men to get it out as soon as possible. When done, the hands left the office for a few hours, or until such time as the work was expected in again. He certainly must confess, that he paid but thirty-three shillings per week, though the hands may have been in some weeks more than ordinarily employed: but, as a set-off to this, he kept his men the year round, and in some months of it they have little or nothing to do. He paid all he could afford to pay; and he trusted, that whatever opinion the trade may have of his mode of payment, it would not be pronounced an *unfair* mode, but as *differing* with the majority. If it were at all possible to effect the desired change, he would readily do it; but it was impossible; and as long as the impossibility continued, so long must he be obliged to refuse payment for night-work, Sunday-work, or over-time. Under the head 'theatrical work,' Mr. Johnson includes the plays and operas printed, or any kind of printing at all connected with theatres.

The Report was concluded with a note on the work of the Committee which had been appointed to decide "what size of paper can fairly be considered one sheet." This matter was also considered two years later by the Joint Committee of Masters and men appointed to consider the Scale of 1810.

Upon the size of the sheet depended the number of pages which could be printed at one operation, and hence the complexity or otherwise, of the imposition. At the beginning of the century when the old-fashioned handpress was still in use, the limitations of the apparatus prevented sheets much larger than royal (20 × 25 inches) being printed. Even then, two pulls were often necessary, since the forme was larger than the platen. Then, when printing machines were introduced, with their cylindrical impression, perfected double demy sheets ($22\frac{1}{2}$ × 35 inches), printed on both sides of the paper, could be worked. This would involve the imposition of thirty-two octavo pages. As machines were improved, so was their sheet capacity enlarged. The 1847 Conference reported that "During the last few years, pages which were wont to be called folio have been designated 4[to], and quarto 8[vo], etc. which is no other than increasing the size and number of pages in the sheet at the expense of the compositors' extras." The latter were specified in Article 9 of the Scale of 1810.[1] Hence the desire of the compositors to settle what should be the maximum size of one sheet, so far as the interpretation of the Scale was concerned.

[1] See p. 177.

Having disposed, so far, of the particulars connected with these unfair houses, there remains but one thing more to notice, viz., "To declare what size sheet of paper can fairly be considered *one* sheet."

There are so many publications being done, at the present day, and upon large sheets of paper, that it behoved the Commission to consider which of them would be affected by a decision adverse to the price now being paid for them; and they said if it be possible to determine upon a certain size, that whilst it will not affect the majority of them, at the same time will not occasion the trade any loss in consequence, it would be both commendable and satisfactory. Before, then, they were desirous of meeting the employers, they thought it an advisable step to lay before this Meeting, and subsequently the trade, their views upon it; and if they be satisfied with them, the Committee of the Masters' Association would only have to be written to, asking them to consent to the standard laid down, or objecting to it, would they condescend to arbitrate the matter.

The names given to sheets of paper are no guide, because instead of calling a sheet of paper double-foolscap or double-crown, it might as well be called imperial or any other name, and being a sheet of paper stands as much right to be called so, as a sheet of royal. Looking at it in this point of view, they have reduced a sheet of paper to a certain number of inches, not superficially, but to be one sheet, it must not exceed, either in width or length, the dimensions stated; exceeding them, to be declared as two sheets. This is their resolution :—

"That all works printed on a sheet of paper, not exceeding, in breadth or length, $27\frac{1}{2}$ by $20\frac{1}{2}$ inches, shall be considered as *one* sheet.[1] Should the size of the paper exceed these dimensions in any way—that is, be in the length, longer, or in the width, wider, or *vice versâ*—then such sized paper shall be considered as two or more sheets, as the case may be. This regulation not to affect Parliamentary Work, Appeal Cases, or Bills in Parliament."

The dimensions here named are those taken from a fair sheet of super-royal, and will take in all double-foolscaps; and it is upon this size that so many of the publications are done, and which are only being paid as one sheet.

The following particulars of the relative size of several publications now being done, are taken from the numbers issued for Saturday, November 15 and 22; and are here adduced as examples of to what extent the vague term of one sheet may be carried, if that a limit be not placed upon the size of the paper that these leviathan pages are printed on; as also to show that some of them will not be affected by the proposed scale of $27\frac{1}{2}$ inches by $20\frac{1}{2}$ inches.

The *Medical Gazette*, printed on one sheet of paper, in extent three sheets of demy. This would have to be charged as three sheets of octavo—publications, the same as it is now being paid.

Lloyd's Weekly Volume, consisting of sixty-four pages, worked upon a sheet of paper measuring 29 by 23 inches. The Committee would call this two sheets of 16mo., because it exceeds the dimensions laid down both in width and length.

[1] Altered to 520 square inches in 1847.

17

Lloyd's Weekly Miscellany, consisting of sixteen pages, worked upon a sheet of double-crown, measuring 30 by 20 inches. Here, two sheets of quarto would have to be declared.

Lloyd's Entertaining Journal, sixteen pages. This sheet will not be affected, for it is but a royal, and measures 25 by 20 inches. This would be called a sheet of 8vo.

Sharpe's London Magazine. A sheet of super-royal, measuring 27 by 20 inches. This would be called one sheet.

Cousins' Entertaining Magazine. A sheet of thirty-two pages, measuring $27\frac{1}{2}$ by $17\frac{1}{2}$ inches. This would be called one sheet of 16mo.

The Penny Satirist, printed by Mr. Cousins, on a sheet of double-crown, folio-way. This sheet measures 30 by $19\frac{1}{4}$ inches. Here is an instance of the stated dimensions being exceeded in length only. The extras upon this publication would have to be doubled.

The Family Herald, of sixteen pages, worked upon two sheets of demy, measuring $34\frac{1}{4}$ by $22\frac{1}{2}$ inches. Two sheets of 4to. would have to be declared for this publication.

The London Journal, printed at Mr. Wilkinson's, Brydges-street, Drury-lane. A publication worked upon two sheets of a demy paper, larger in one way than that upon which the *Family Herald* is done, measuring 35 by 22 inches. This would have to be looked upon as two sheets of quarto.

Joe Miller, and the *Sportsman's Magazine*, are worked upon a sheet-and-a-half demy. In length they measure $34\frac{1}{2}$ by only $17\frac{1}{2}$ inches. All extras upon these publications would have to be doubled.

Chambers's Edinburgh Journal is printed on a super-royal sheet, and will not, therefore, be affected by the scale, supposing it to be set up in London.

There are many other publications being done, most of which are believed to be less than the stated dimensions. The preceding ones named will be sufficient to convince you of the necessity for laying down some plan whereby such works as the *London Journal* and the *Family Herald* may not be imposed upon the trade as one sheet, when, in reality, they take up the space of two. The difference made upon many of them would be obvious, if they were publications; the 2s. 6d. per sheet being doubled. Lloyd's works have scarcely a single extra; the alteration therefore, would but little affect them. The *Family Herald* and others must be made conformable to the rule; and but few fears may be entertained that acquiescence will follow a decision, in itself so reasonable and just. The Commission cannot but think that their view of the case will be regarded as honourable by the employers; and believing so, they earnestly hope that it will be, by this Meeting, allowed, that the labours of the Commission have been replete with interest, and if not attended with any immediate success, certainly full of consequence to the trade. The inquiry has extended over a period of eleven weeks, and, but few hours of business time have been sacrificed to it. With these facts before you, they bring their Report to a conclusion, trusting that the trade will derive the benefit from it that was alone desired;—to satisfy men; and give to the Society a document that can be acted on; be a guide to the subsequent deliberations of its Committee, and a warning to the members to avoid the unfair offices it treats of.

The first Annual Report of the London Society of Compositors was published on 4 February, 1846, and is remarkable since it is the earliest trade document to take notice of two important innovations, namely the use of the paper process for stereotype matrices, as opposed to plaster of Paris, and the introduction of composing machinery.

Although Moses Poole, a London patent agent, filed a specification for the manufacture of paper moulds, or "flong," for stereotyping, on behalf of an unknown client in 1839 (Patent No. 8,159), there is no record that the system was worked in England before being introduced and patented by J. M. Kronheim, in 1844 (Patent No. 10,275). In a letter written by him as late as 1883, and preserved in the St. Bride collection, he gives the following information :—

In 1843 being in Brussels I had the opportunity of visiting the establishment of Messrs. Demat, Publishers, Printers, Type and Stereo founders. I there saw a Plate ready for Press, I at once recognized that it was not done by the Plaster process and on enquiry I obtained sufficient information as to the material used instead of the plaster.

Although the process then used (I know not for how long) at Messrs. Demat was very faulty, I thought the discovery important enough to introduce the same in England, with the view of improving the same—I did so successfully after many unsuccessful attempts. In 1844 I took out a Patent and sold it to a firm possessing a stereo casting establishment— the said firm being in many difficulties became bankrupt. The process being no more my property I had neither interest or right to look after its continuance, nor prevent others from practising it.

One Jean Baptiste Genoux, of Lyons, obtained a patent for a paper matrix process in 1829 (French Patent No. 3,965). He sold licences to work his system to at least half-a-dozen printers in France and Germany, and it is probable that Messrs. Demat, of Brussels, were among the licensees.

It was not until the early 1850s that the paper process found its most effective use in this country, when the brothers Dellagana first used it for the manufacture of type-high plates of the individual columns of *The Times* newspaper, and later for complete pages cast at one operation, and of the normal thickness. Until the Dellaganas perfected the paper matrix process, stereotyping was not in use for newspaper production, since plaster of Paris moulds were too easily damaged to be suitable.

The composing machine in question was probably one of the few models of the Young-Delcambre apparatus to be sold in this country. Patented in 1840, it was first described in the *Compositors'*

Chronicle for 6 September, 1841. In the issue of 1 January, 1842, it was noted that the "much-dreaded machine" had been put to work on the composition of *The Phalanx*. Almost twelve months later, the *Family Herald* made its bow on 17 December, 1842, also set by the Young-Delcambre machine. The monthly issues of the *Compositors' Chronicle* throughout the years 1841-1844, contain a number of splenetic articles on the subject of composing machinery. This is an isolated reference to the subject as far as the earlier documents of the trade are concerned. The Young-Delcambre machine did not remain in use for more than a year or two. Another generation of compositors was to be born before composing machinery found an effective use in this country.

The paragraphs which follow are taken from the L.S.C. Annual Report for 1845 :

[DOCUMENT LXXVII]

The Compositors of London have been blind, so far as remedying the evil, to many encroachments that have been imperceptibly thrust upon them; none need a fairer exposition than that respecting the size of the different founts of type, that are daily being cast by the founders, and which are so properly denominated as condensed. If there has been a standard for the depth of type, there cannot be said to be one now. Take, as an instance, the founts of nonpareil and brevier from Scotland, or the founts of pica and long primer lately cast by the London founders; these, with others, are not only diminished in the thickness of the letter, but also in the depth. Yet they are all charged upon the ratio of a certain supposed standard, which regulated the compositor's charge in 1810. Now the effect of all these modern improvements in this wonderful and condensing age, is to reduce the wages of the journeyman. Yet you never hear of compensation for these losses; but you do hear of attempts of reduction, still further, of those wages that but barely procure for the compositor sufficient means to sustain a respectable position in society.

The new system of stereotyping, under the patent of one Kronheim, in which the casting of the types by stucco is superseded, we have determined as entitled to be charged at the same rate as if cast by the ordinary method, with *high* spaces, viz., 1s. 4d. per thousand extra. These are our reasons : 1. That but little trouble is occasioned to the compositor by the stucco, when cast with high spaces; 2. That the charge for stereo is made because of the loss accruing to the compositor, by the imposition, the many formes he has to lock up, and the loss of time he sustains, from the work being stereotyped. Except that the stucco is not used under the new system, which we take to be but of little consequence, with high spaces, the other contingencies mentioned are found to exist still; the trouble of imposition, in fact, is increased, at least two-fold, by the large bevels that encircle the pages; so also is the weight of the formes and the loss of time found to exist in connection with the patent mode. The trade will understand from the foregoing that 1s. 4d. per thousand extra is charged upon all works stereotyped under Kronheim's system.

In a chamber remotely situated in a printing office contiguous to Fleet-street, a nonpareil composing machine was supposed to be at work, setting up the most profitable part of a publication that is paid by the employer as newspaper for obvious reasons; the compositors in the office being called upon to set up the larger type, and make up the matter composed by the machine. This was the general impression, but it proved to be a false one; the machine being but a curtain to hide the practices being carried on behind it. Two men and three boys were employed in this room. The boys distributed the letter for a *halfpenny* per thousand, which enabled these men to have full cases of nonpareil type to compose from in the ordinary way, the machine being but seldom used. One of these men enacts the part of the master; engages the second man and the boys, and agrees to set up nonpareil matter at a price less, by one-third, than the scale allows. The boys are not apprentices, nor are their fathers printers, consequently they have no claim to the business whatever. We were determined to state, at once, the right of the members of this Society to make up the matter composed by the machine, or said to be so; and passed a resolution to that effect. By this resolution we wished to establish the understanding that this Society will not identify itself with the products of machinery, nor allow one of its members to be engaged upon them. The compositors in the office are not called upon now to make up the matter, or in fact have anything to do with, this said machine, and one of the two men spoken of has quitted the office; yet we have not wholly succeeded in preventing the continuance of the evils connected with the machine—such, for instance, as the employment of these boys, or the progress of the individual who calls himself the master of it. These boys continue to distribute, and a portion of the publication is still composed as before : we wait but for a few weeks to receive the sanction of the Executive upon the subject of apprentices, to enable us to require the withdrawal of these boys from the establishment, and endeavour to get this machine-master subject to the rules of the chapel of the office where he works. But it is not the machine, nor the man who is supposed to work it, that the Society cares for, as doing an injury to the trade, but it is the system of inducting boys in the art of the business, taken as they are from a street or from a type-foundry, and learned to distribute and partially compose;— in a few months we shall see them engaged upon some of the weekly papers, or working in an office unknown to the generality of men : but we are determined not to admit, as members of this Society, any person but who can clearly establish his right to the trade, either by indenture or patrimony.

The Scale of 1810 was in force for thirty-seven years before the men discussed the document as a whole with their employers. During April, 1847, a meeting of compositors was held "To consider the propriety of requesting the Master Printers' Association to agree to the formation of an Arbitration Committee, composed of masters and men, to whom every charge *not* decided in the Scale of 1810 shall be submitted for final settlement." At the Conference resulting from this resolution the compositors were represented by eight of their body, who met an equal number nominated by the masters, among whom may be mentioned Messrs. Clay, Clowes, and Harrison.

At the conclusion of the meetings the compositors published their *Report of the Journeymen Members of the Conference of Master Printers and Compositors held in the year* 1847. The preliminary section of this document, containing a summary of events since 1785, is not reprinted in this work. A series of glosses on the articles of the Scale of 1810 are reprinted as footnotes to the Scale in Chapter 6 of this book. That part of the 1847 Report dealing with Reprints and Addenda to the Scale of 1810 follows here :

[DOCUMENT LXXVIII]

Having thus gone through the Scale, we come to what is called a rider to the Scale, which at the will of twenty masters took off one-eighth of the price per 1000 allowed in 1810 upon Article I., which Article is said to have been mutually agreed to by masters and men in 1805, and therefore, in justice, ought only to have been altered with the approval of the men. It relates to reprint; and is an ever-memorable instance of the condition of the trade, in and out of society. We approached this 1816 modification with much concern; indeed we repudiated its authority to be ranked as part of the Scale, from the fact of its being a rule of the masters' own creation. Having at some length pointed out the losses the trade experienced from this excessive reduction, and the extraordinary definitions given to the word "reprints" by several masters, we sought for an advance of $\frac{1}{4}d$. per thousand upon plain reprints, and an understanding of the term itself. The masters seemed prepared for this attempt, and met our proposition by a counter one : viz., "That in consequence of the great facility of communication now existing between all parts of the kingdom, and the low rate of wages paid in many places, it is not advisable for either masters or men to add any inducement to the removal of reprints from London, by advancing the price per 1000." The employers added, "They would feel a pleasure in granting the advance sought, but such was the effect of provincial competition, that to increase the price of reprints would be to lose them entirely to London." Cases were given even under the present mode of payment. One gentleman said, a work of fourteen or fifteen volumes was lost to the London business, and had gone to Oxford, because the London masters could not do the work so low as it was agreed to be taken for. Other gentlemen observed, that they had lost works in a like manner; and one employer stated that he had estimated for some volumes that had gone to Bungay,[1] in Suffolk, though his compositors were walking about for want of employment. The employers generally said that we would be best consulting the interest of the trade if we did not further persist in this matter, as it would only tend to increase apprentices, and lead to other improper measures being resorted to to get this kind of work out of the respectable offices where journeymen were employed. Met by such experience as the foregoing, we set about obtaining something like a distinct understanding in regard to what was and what was not a reprint. After considerable difficulty the conference succeeded in settling what may be called four kinds of reprints. There may be said to be, 1. Reprints composed from print copy, unaltered by the author or corrector, and not derived from various sources; for such works $\frac{3}{4}d$. per 1000 will have to be deducted. 2. Reprints having manuscript alterations; for such $\frac{1}{2}d$. per 1000 will have to be deducted. 3. Reprints consisting of half manuscript and half reprint; these will be paid as manuscript. And 4. Reprints having manuscript insertions numerously interspersed throughout the work, although amounting, when reckoned together, to but one-fourth, or even less, of the work; these will also be paid as manuscript. We conclude our notice of this much-disputed question by saying, that our right to an advance upon plain reprint was admitted but its effect was so much questioned as to render it dangerous to grant it.

The next heading in the new Scale, under the title of "Addenda," is Appeal Cases. It may be naturally supposed that if the masters anticipated our attack upon reprints, we certainly ought not to be alarmed if we heard from them of reduction upon Appeal Cases. We doubt not that the majority of the trade expect to hear that this reduction has been agreed to by us; and perhaps not alone upon the price per thousand, but also the usual, but disputed charge, for side notes. Now this payment of 8d. per 1000 for Appeal Cases has ever been objected to by certain employers. In many offices establishment hands and boys have engrossed this work; and even when piece hands have done it in these offices, the money has been indirectly paid. The masters frankly said they never would admit the charge, because no authority nor labour could be shown for the demand made. They also said, in answer to a statement made by us, that those who had Appeal Cases done could afford to pay the extra 1d. per 1000; that there was as much competition going on and estimates given for this work as any other. Well, we had two important charges to struggle for in settling the price of Appeal Cases; and looking at the position of the trade, and always wishing to destroy any incentive for boys being taken, we held it advisable to yield a little to secure the remainder. And we think that when the alteration is calmly considered, and Rule XXII. of the Scale read, which gives a higher price for an increased measure, the trade will be satisfied with our arrangement. First, as to the price per 1000. By limiting the dimensions of this work, we still preserve the old price of

---

[1] Doubtless to the country establishment of Mr. Child, a fellow member of the employers' committee. The firm was later taken over by Clay's.

8*d*. per 1000; that is, where the compositor has to set up Appeal Cases exceeding 40 ems pica wide, 8*d*. per 1000 will be charged; 40 ems and under, 7*d*. per 1000. The noted M'Dowall case was 42 ems pica wide; so that, after all, 8*d*. per 1000 would be paid for it if again done. This being settled, the masters said piece-hands would in future have this work to do. Then we come to side notes. At the time of the strike,[1] the masters said these side notes should be charged according to the Book Scale, which would give about 1*s*. or 1*s*. 6*d*. per sheet. However, no such price was mooted to us, and we have the satisfaction of saying that side notes to Appeal Cases will be paid, if a broad, 3*s*.; double narrow, 5*s*.; double broad, 6*s*. per sheet, or 4 pages folio.

Column Work.—A distinction has been made between column work and tabular and table work; and column-matter, as distinguished from table and tabular, is matter made up continuously in two or more columns, not dependent upon each other for their arrangement; that is, matter running from the first column into the second, and so on, such as ordinary two-column matter. In 4to and 8vo, 1*s*. per sheet for two columns will be charged. Need we say that, at present, no more would be charged for 12mo and 16mo ? But, in future, 12mo will be paid 1*s*. 6*d*.; 16mo and smaller sizes, 2*s*. per sheet. The employers laid before us specimens of column-work which admitted of no charge for columns in measures above 17 ems in width of the type used. This was so different to our views, that we at once said such a proposition could not be entertained; for in nonpareil, if the measure were nine ems pica wide, no charge for columns was proposed to be made. By practically showing the difficulties belonging to column-work, we succeeded not only in obtaining the advance mentioned upon 12mo and 16mo, but also the prices clearly stated in the Scale to be paid for column-matter.

The next is Tabular and Table-work. Table and Tabular-work is matter set up in three or more columns depending upon each other, and reading across the page.

Wrappers will be paid as settled in 1839, an addition being made to the resolutions then passed, affecting advertisements in the body of weekly publications, such as the *London Journal*, &c. These will be paid in the same way as occurring in advertisement sheets; when a whole page is standing, it is the property of the master; when less than a page, the property of the men.

Under the head "Miscellaneous," will be found many important methods of charging what may be called additions to works, and matter beyond the ordinary character. Prefatory matter, which includes Prefaces, Contents, Preliminary Dissertations, Biographical Memoirs, &c., making a sheet, or under, set up in larger type than, or the same size as, the body of the text, to be paid as pages of the work; if in smaller type, to be cast up according to their bodies, the extras of the work being added to the cast-up. But when either of the above-named exceeds a sheet, then it must be regarded as appendix matter.

"All works to be cast up as sent to press." This sentence gave rise to considerable discussion; the employers wishing works to be cast up as first sent out. This we opposed firmly; for no limit could be placed upon

---

[1] Probably a strike confined to one or two offices.

the extent the compositor would be thus injured. All woodcuts inserted in proofs, chapters made pages, and so on, would be lost to the compositor. After several sittings, we heard that our objections had prevailed; but to suit cases that may demand a casting up, in consequence of great delay, or even the work not going to press, another sentence has been added, so that the rule will read, "All works to be cast up as sent to press, except by mutual agreement between employer and employed."

Slip-matter, which has become so frequent nowadays, was wished to be cast-up at an advanced price of ½*d*. per 1000, as sent out in slips.[1] This was even less than the 2*s*. 6*d*. given upon publications. The proposition was declined acceptance. Considering, however, the difference to the compositor of first making up his matter, and from sending it out in slips, in justice to the employers we agreed to the following modifications :—Works in two or three columns, sent out in single columns, to abandon the column charge, providing each column exceeds 12 ems pica wide; the extras given by Article IX upon long primer and smaller type, for 16mo, 18mo, &c., to be relinquished; and matter sent out without head-lines, the value of the head-lines to be deducted. Thus, as the compositor has not to make up columns above 12 ems pica wide, or make up his pages in a 16mo or 18mo form at his own expense, or to set the head-lines to his matter when first sent out, it seemed proper to admit of these trifling reductions. In deducting for head-lines, the compositor should cast up his work in the usual way, *i.e.* inclusive of the head-line; and then ascertaining, say in 8vo, the exact value of sixteen solid lines, deduct it from the actual cast-up of the sheet. Example : price per sheet, by letters, 19*s*. 10*d*.; deduct value of sixteen head-lines, 6*d*.; price per sheet, 19*s*. 4*d*., which is 19*s*. 6*d*. Before dismissing the modifications connected with slip-matter, the compositor should particularly observe, that if he be on a work in columns 12 ems pica or less wide; or the work be set in small pica or larger type; or the work be made up in pages with a folio or any head-line, yet sent out in a slip form; the reduction mentioned will not have to be made, as the regulation only applies to "works sent out in slips *not* made up into perfect pages."

The rule respecting woodcuts was made in order that the piece-hands might get the composition of these advantageous works. It will be noticed it is the woodcuts, not the matter, which is to be mutually settled; and this only where they exceed one-fourth of the work; thus insuring the piece-hand a charge of one-fourth for wood-cuts; and if the trouble requires a higher charge, the sum to be arranged between the master and the men.

The scale, with the additions, definitions, and explanations settled by the Committee of Conference, comes into operation on the 1st of December, 1847, and will be applicable to all descriptions of work mentioned therein, commenced on or after that date.

---

[1] *i.e.*, proofs in galley, not made up into pages.

The Conference of 1847 was followed by a period of calm. Although the newsmen were involved in at least one serious dispute, little occurred to disturb the peace in the general trade. The employers' organization "fell into abeyance."[1] The London Society of Compositors, on the other hand, was busily engaged in consolidating its position after the *débâcle* of 1847, caused by the collapse of the National Typographical Association, and was much strengthened by the amalgamation of the two News Societies in 1853. The masters considered it expedient to re-establish their Association and were persuaded to appoint delegates to a permanent joint Arbitration Committee, the rules of which came into force in January, 1856. Three journeymen and three employers sat under the chairmanship of a barrister, the latter having a casting vote. It was hoped that the Committee would "serve for the amicable settlement of all Disputes which may hereafter arise relative to the Prices to be charged and paid for Work, without incurring the expense, trouble and irritation, consequent upon an appeal to a Court of Law."[2]

Two minor questions were settled without difficulty, but the first important difference submitted to arbitration was finally settled only at the cost of litigation. Once again the question of payment for wrappers was the cause of the contention. The following passage is extracted from *Association of Master Printers: Report of the Committee*, 10 August, 1858.

[DOCUMENT LXXVIII A]

The interpretation put by the Compositors on the terms in which the agreement of 1839 was expressed, by which the companionship on a Magazine or Review gave up their claim to the Wrapper and Advertiser thereof, and to all complete pages of standing advertisements, though partially submitted to in most of the London printing offices in slight and unimportant cases, was felt by the Masters as an infraction of the spirit of that agreement, and it was accordingly generally evaded, that class of work being done by the establishment hands or by the apprentices whenever the different amount of cost was at all important. This anomaly was therefore generally exhibited—that whilst in many offices the Wrapper and Advertiser of *one* or *two* Magazines were done according to the Compositors' interpretation of the agreement, others, and those the most important in a pecuniary sense, were kept from the piece hands

---

[1] Evidence of George Levey in *Tenth Report of the Commissioners appointed to inquire into the Organisation and Rules of Trades Unions and other Associations*. 1868, p. 83.

[2] Association of Master Printers: Report of the Committee, 7 Feb., 1856.

altogether, often to the great inconvenience of business arrangements, and often with the effect of keeping many "piece" hands idle while the "establishment" hands were working late and early. It was also felt by the Masters that, whilst there was some plausability for the claim of the companionship on a Magazine to the standing advertisements, while their right to the Wrapper or Advertiser was admitted or conceded, as a compensation for the insufficient employment at one period, and the excessive efforts necessary at another, which characterize periodical work, all idea of compensation was absurd as soon as the great extension of magazine advertising had necessitated the abandonment of such claim on the part of the companionship, and the Advertisers were composed by men totally unconnected with the Magazines to which they belonged, and who could have no moral ground of claim beyond payment for their actual work.

As time passed on, and the repeal of the advertisement duty [1853] extended advertising both greatly in quantity, and from 8vo pages of bourgeois and brevier to 4to pages of nonpareil and pearl, at the same time greatly increasing the quantity of Standing Advertisements, the injustice and absurdity of the Compositors' claim in this matter became more and more apparent and more and more intolerable; until at length, in September, 1856, it was thought advisable by Mr. J. A. D. Cox, the Honorary Secretary of the Association, to bring the question before the Arbitration Committee which had been constituted a few months before, on a case which had occurred in his office. The Masters' interpretation of the clause in question was, that the Compositors were entitled by that clause to be paid for that portion only of Standing Advertisements which remained after *the quantity sufficient to make complete pages had been measured off*, altogether irrespectively of the position of such Standing Advertisements in the re-making up, whether all together, or with new advertisements interspersed amongst them—the time occupied in re-making-up such Standing Advertisements being also paid for. . . .

The employers then cited an instance of the problem that confronted them :

. . . the meaning put upon the clause by the Compositors was both unreasonable and unjust, and involved the anomaly, that in a case of sixteen pages of 4to advertisements in pearl, at 20*s.* each, of which fifteen were standing, it would entirely depend on all the new matter being concentrated into one page, or scattered over all the sixteen pages, whether the Compositors should be paid *thirty shillings*, or *sixteen pounds*, for *exactly the same amount of work.*

Establishment hands, the permanent staff of a printing office, were generally kept as few as possible in number, since it was necessary to pay them even if there were not enough work to keep them fully occupied. They could not be dismissed without a fortnight's notice. In return for steady employment and a guaranteed wage they gave up all claims for extra remuneration for difficult or fat work. The piece hands, the majority in any office, were more at the mercy of circumstances. They earned much or little, according to the supply and the nature of the work available.

The Wrapper dispute of 1856 was caused by the desire of the employers to have wrappers and standing formes handled by the piece workers at what amounted to an establishment rate. Since work in periodical houses was not regular, it was not economic to retain establishment hands in such large numbers that, at the busiest times, the whole of the production could be done by them. By the regulation of the L.S.C., it was not possible to put piece hands on the establishment for any period less than fourteen days.

When the matter was brought before the Arbitration Committee, the barrister gave his casting vote in favour of the masters. Some of them immediately gave wrappers and standing advertisements to their piece hands, being under the impression that no more than a charge for making-up would be made. The L.S.C., however, refused to acknowledge the Committee's decision, instructing its members to charge the full rate. The masters declined to pay, and one of them was sued in the Court of Exchequer for a trifling sum. Eventually the Court decided in favour of the men, the defendant, Mr. George Levey, being liable for costs amounting to £846. These were paid by subscription among his colleagues. The case was of the utmost importance, since the piece hands' right to benefits deriving from standing formes has never since been seriously challenged.

II.   THE ADVANCE OF 1866

On 6 December, 1865, a Special Committee was appointed at a General Meeting of the London Society of Compositors, "to draw up and present a Memorial to the Master Printers of London and its Vicinity for an advance in prices." The rates settled in 1810 were still in force, as well as the reduction on reprints imposed by the employers in 1816. The men had asked for an advance of one farthing per thousand on periodical composition in 1839, which had been refused them, but otherwise no effort had been made to alter the main provisions of the Scale of 1810.

Although there were more men engaged in the London trade than in 1810, the amount of work available for their occupation had increased enormously. Piece hands in regular employment would be able to earn the equivalent of the existing establishment rate of 33ˢ. by setting 66,000 ens solid in 63 hours. Such a task would have been strenuous but not exceptional. There were, however, many different varieties of composition for which the Scale allowed an increased rate, and with which the Conference of 1847 was mainly concerned. The average skilled compositor made his living through his ability to execute at a fair speed all these classes of work for which extra payment was made.

Changing economic and social conditions, however, encouraged the compositors to petition for an advance. In the Memorial presented to the Master Printers on 16 January, 1866, there was contained a reasoned justification for their claims.

[DOCUMENT LXXIX]

To the Master Printers of London and its Vicinity

Gentlemen,

We, the Compositors of London, beg most respectfully to solicit your attention to, and consideration of, the following propositions :—

1.—That a rise of $\frac{1}{2}d$. per 1000 on all descriptions of work (exclusive of Newspapers), and of $\frac{3}{4}d$. per 1000 on Reprints, be paid. [The following to be the definition of Reprints:—Works reprinted, free from alterations or interlineations, save a remodelling of punctuation or orthography, which shall be done, if at all, before giving out of copy to compositor.]

2.—That the minimum rate for Establishment Hands shall be 36s. per week of not more than 58 hours.[1]

3.—That Overtime be paid for at the rate of 3d. extra per hour after 8 o'clock in the evening, till 8 o'clock in the morning; but that no charge be made of less than 1s. extra between the hours of 10 p.m. and 6 a.m.

4.—That Sunday-work be paid for at the rate of 6d. per hour extra, but that in no case shall the compositor receive less than 2s. 6d. extra.

5.—That no deduction be made for Pieced Leads in measures of less than 26 *ems* wide.

6.—That $\frac{1}{4}d$. per 1000 extra be paid on all Founts for every *en* below 12 *ems* of their own bodies in thickness.

7.—That Corrections be paid for at the rate of $7\frac{1}{2}d$. per hour.

Gentlemen,—Your Memorialists, in placing these various propositions before you, do so in the full confidence that you will recognise in the circumstances of the times the necessity and the justice of considering the position which the Journeyman Printer now holds, looking to the vast changes which have been of late years effected in the direction of the printing trade by the removal of fiscal and other burdens.[2]

With respect to the proposition to advance the price of general work one halfpenny and Reprints three farthings per 1000, your Memorialists trust that the increased expense of living consequent upon the general prosperity of the people, will be a sufficient justification for the rise

---

[1] The existing hours of work were sixty-three.

[2] *i.e.*, the repeal of the Advertisement Tax (1853), Newspaper Stamp (1855) and Paper Tax (1860).

they are seeking upon the prices at present paid; for, in the matter of rent alone—always so important an item in London—the working man is now called upon to pay from 15 to 20 per cent. more than he did a few years back; nor is this all, as he is compelled, by the large displacement of population arising from the requirements of our railroad system and other improvements, to seek lodgings far away from his work, thus increasing considerably the cost of the family living; and this, taken in connexion with the high prices prevailing in some articles of paramount necessity, and which are likely to increase rather than decline, render it imperatively necessary that, where the purchasing power of a fixed standard of wages is so materially depressed, some advance in that standard should be sought for and established.

The raising of the minimum rate of payment for Establishment Hands to 36s. per week is a necessary consequence of the preceding proposition, and your Memorialists do not deem it necessary therefore to enlarge upon that point; but with respect to limiting the hours of labour to 58 per week, they venture to call to your attention the fact, that while there is hardly a trade which exercises so great a strain upon the system, both mentally and physically, as that of an operative printer, there is at the same time scarcely one in which the workman is compelled to work so incessantly and under such disadvantageous circumstances; for proof of which we need only turn to the terrible fact shown in the labours of a recent Royal Commission, that the death-rate of printers is 47 per cent. higher than that of the whole community, and that 70 per cent. of the deaths occurring are ascribable to some form of chest disease.[1] So startling a statement as this surely calls for a remedy; and although we are aware that there are some employers who have already put in practice the very salutary measure now sought, yet we respectfully ask that it be a principle with all, believing that none would lose, even in a pecuniary point of view, by thus reducing the hours of labour; for it must be evident to all who reflect upon the subject that an overworked man will not produce so much as one whose vigour and strength are not impaired by such excessive toil.

With regard to the question of Overtime, your Memorialists respectfully ask you to reflect upon what the present system involves—that a man can actually be called upon to be at his employment 16 hours daily, without the slightest additional remuneration for such increased toil, being paid only at the same rate for his over-hours as for his regular ones—a position which no other body of working men in the kingdom occupy. Under these circumstances we cannot but hope that the proposition we now lay before you to regulate this crying evil will meet with your approval and assent.

In respect to the payment of Sunday-work, your Memorialists trust that, looking to the character of the day, the sanctity of which is thus invaded, it is not too much to expect that if the exigencies of the public require a working man to sacrifice his only day of rest to their service the public must be content to pay for it; and we hope, gentlemen, for

---

[1] For a vivid description of conditions in a typical London printing office at the time, see [Smith, Charles Manby], *The Working Man's Way in the World* (London, 1854).

your assistance in this rather in the direction of really securing Sunday as a day of rest than from any desire to reap a profit from its use; for we believe that both the physical and moral well-being of our class would be best consulted by reducing to as low a point as is consistent with the absolute necessities of society the labour required on that day.

With respect to Piecing Leads, your Memorialists place this before you, gentlemen, because they feel that it is one of those evils which have gradually crept into the trade, and for which they think, now that they are seeking an amelioration of their condition, they have a claim for a remedy, inasmuch as when the distinction was drawn between leaded and solid matter, it could never have been contemplated that a Compositor would have to lift and adjust two, and in many cases three pieces, to fill his space line; thus causing a loss of time which destroys the balance sought to be established in the charges for the two descriptions of work.

There is, however, another evil which has for some years been developing itself, that of Thin Founts—an evil of no ordinary magnitude, because in numerous cases the Compositor, according to the present mode of casting-up, is called upon to set a much larger number of letters than he is paid for;—as a proof of which (and the instances have not diminished), of 656 founts examined and tested in 1846, no less than 478 were found to be below what we think may fairly be considered the standard thickness of a fount, namely, 13 *ems* to its own 26 lower-case letters, their measurement ranging from $12\frac{1}{2}$ to 11 *ems*, the exact number of each being 114 founts $12\frac{1}{2}$ *ems*, 245 at 12 *ems*, 87 at $11\frac{1}{2}$ *ems*, and 32 at 11 *ems*, while of the remaining 178 founts 70 were 13 *ems* each, and the remainder ranged from $13\frac{1}{2}$ to 15 *ems*. Thus, it will be observed that over two-thirds of the founts examined were under 13 *ems*, and of that proportion more than one-half were 12 *ems*. It would appear, therefore, to your Memorialists, that, considering these facts, a standard of 12 *ems* for the 26 lower-case letters should be established, below which a rise of $\frac{1}{4}d.$ per 1000 for the loss of every *en* in thickness should be paid.[1]

Then, with regard to the question of Corrections, your Memorialists would respectfully suggest that it is not in accordance with justice to call upon a man to do such a description of work for a price less than the rate which is paid to an establishment hand; as such work is commonly of that character as more than any other in the business to try and exhaust the physical powers of those engaged in it.

Having thus, gentlemen, touched as briefly as possible on the various points which your Memorialists desire to bring under your notice, they would now take leave to point out some more general reasons why they think themselves entitled to your favourable consideration.

If we look back upon the style and method of doing work, when our present scale was settled over fifty years ago, and compare it with that which now prevails, there can, we think, be no doubt that the latter system is in every respect less profitable to the Compositor than the former, arising from the tendency to crowd as much as possible into a

---

[1] Thin, or condensed founts, are also discussed in Document LXXVII, p. 260.

volume, the hurried way in which work is performed, the loss occasioned by frequent stoppages, the Clicker System, and, above all, the introduction and extension of Establishment Hands (so profitable to the employer), who necessarily take away from the piece hands a large amount of that work which formerly acted as a compensating balance against the less remunerative labour he was engaged in—which elements, had they existed at the time of the settlement of 1810, must, we think, have had considerable weight with the parties to it, and have secured a more liberal remuneration in some respects than that now afforded by it.

Another reason we think we may adduce in support of our claim upon your attention is the wonderful impetus which has been given to the printing business by the repeal of the Taxes on Knowledge, resulting in an expansion of Trade that must largely have increased the profits of capital, and which we think should in some degree have improved the position of those whose labour capital employs, and through whose toil the public is benefiting so largely.

There are yet two other reasons which we would ask to submit to your consideration in support of the prayer of this Memorial : firstly, the very general advance which has taken place in the wages of almost all classes of working men during the last thirty years, amounting on the average to 20 per cent.; and, secondly, the fact that in most of the larger towns of England and Scotland (such as Manchester, Liverpool, Birmingham, Edinburgh, Glasgow, and Aberdeen, &c.), advances in the wages of our own trade have been already cheerfully and liberally accorded by the Employers, and the hours of labour have been shortened below the point we now submit to you for your approval.

In conclusion, gentlemen, your Memorialists, in thus respectfully laying their claims before you, beg to state that they are actuated by no desire to disturb existing contracts, or in any way to act otherwise than in a spirit of fair dealing, believing that it is of the first moment that a mutual feeling of respect and confidence should exist between the employer and the employed; and we therefore leave this Memorial in your hands in the perfect belief that it will meet with a full, careful, and impartial consideration from you, and that you will not deem it either desirable or right that in the Metropolis, the great centre of the nation's intellect and wealth, the followers of that art to which the world owes so much should occupy an inferior position to that of other classes of their fellow-working men.

Trusting to be favoured with an early reply to this Memorial, we have the honour to be, gentlemen, on behalf of the Memorialists,

Your most obedient Servants,

C. T. HENLEY, *Chairman.*
H. SELF, *Secretary.*

The *Report* of the L.S.C. Special Committee, published in March, 1866, contains the following account of the meeting between the compositors' deputation and the masters' committee, held on 12 March :

[DOCUMENT LXXX]

Mr. W. Clowes in the chair.

Members of Committee

Messrs. Adlard, Barrett, Burt, Geo. Clowes, Edwards, Thos. Harrison, Kinder, Levey, J. G. Nichols, Pardon, Rivington, and C. W. H. Wyman.

The following seven gentlemen being also present by invitation : viz. Messrs. W. Bradbury, W. Clowes, Griffith, H. Hansard, Harrild, G. A. Spottiswoode, and Wilkins.

On entering the room the deputation from your Committee were again received with every mark of courtesy, and having been requested to take seats, the following resolutions were read by the secretary to the association, and a copy at once placed in the hands of your secretary.

ASSOCIATION OF MASTER PRINTERS OF LONDON

Freemasons' Tavern, March 12, 1866.

For the Deputation of Compositors who presented to the Committee of the Association of Master Printers, on the 16th January, 1866, a Memorial for an Advance of Wages.

At a General Meeting of the Master Printers of London and its vicinity, held at the Freemasons' Tavern on the 6th March, 1866, for the purpose of taking into consideration the Memorial of the Compositors (Mr. Wm. Clowes in the chair), it was
Resolved unanimously—

1. That the Master Printers here present have individually the strongest possible evidence that large and increasing quantities of work are going into the provinces, to Scotland, and to the Continent, owing entirely to the question of price.

2. That after a careful examination of the Edinburgh and Glasgow and Leeds scales, and of the establishment wages paid to Compositors in English provincial printing-offices, this Meeting is unanimously of opinion that a compliance with the request of the London Compositors for a general rise of wages will very much increase the tendency of London Publishers to employ provincial printing-offices—a result which would be as disadvantageous to the Compositors themselves as to the Master-Printers.

3. That while on the one hand it would be most inexpedient to raise the London scale at a time when London Master Printers are hardly able to hold their ground against Country Printers, on the other hand the Master Printers of London are ready to meet the Compositors in conference to consider any question arising out of a change in the method of doing business, or otherwise.

W. CLOWES, *Chairman.*

This was followed by Mr. Rivington reading a report of a sub-committee which had been appointed to examine into the Memorial, and lay the results of that examination before the general Committee, two-thirds of that document being taken up in analysing the differences between our own scale and the prices paid in Edinburgh, Glasgow, and the English provinces.

After this paper had been read, a lengthened discussion ensued between the deputation from your Committee and the masters present, which had no other result than a general expression of feeling on their part that they regretted not being able to comply with the claims set forth in the Memorial, but the close competition to which they were subjected prevented their doing so. A respectful request was then made to be furnished with a copy of the report which had been read, embodying as it did, the reasons for the masters rejecting the prayer of the Memorial, and the deputation having been requested to leave the room to enable the Committee to consult upon the propriety of acceding to the application, were, after a few minutes absence, recalled, and informed that the required document would be forwarded at the end of the week, and at the same time they were distinctly told that the resolutions placed in their hands were simply a negative to the first and seventh propositions in the Memorial, the rest being left open for conference.

On the Saturday following this interview, the report was accordingly forwarded, and in dealing with the reasons contained therein your Committee feel that it is unnecessary to read the whole of the document in question to you, for the reason already stated, that the greater portion of it is taken up with a comparison between the Scotch and London scales, and they feel that it will be sufficient for the purpose of this report to take such portions as more immediately bear upon the points raised in the Memorial. With regard to the first proposition, the report proceeds thus :—

Your Sub-Committee have carefully examined the Scales of Prices for Compositors' work in force at *Edinburgh* and *Glasgow* comparing them with the *London* Scale, both present and proposed, and now proceed to lay before you the results of their investigation.

Proposition 1.

The price per 1000 for ordinary bookwork at *Edinburgh* and *Glasgow* in founts ranging from English to Minion inclusive, is 5d., in Nonpareil 5½d., in Pearl 6d.[1] No distinction is made as in London between manuscript and reprint, or between leaded and solid matter, notwithstanding their variations in trouble and difficulty all works of plain matter are placed on one level.

The following table will show the comparative prices in *Edinburgh*, *Glasgow*, and *London*, of a sheet of demy 8vo. manuscript and solid on a page in 23 *ems* Pica wide, and 48 Small Pica lines long, including head and white lines in six founts, from Small Pica to Nonpareil without extras.

							London.						
Edinburgh and Glasgow.							Present.				Proposed.		
	1000			£	s.	d.		£	s.	d.		£	s.	d.
Small Pica ..	41	At 5d.		0	17	0	At 6d.	1	0	6	At 6½d.	1	2	0
Long Primer..	48	„ 5d.		1	0	0	„ 6d.	1	4	0	„ 6½d.	1	6	0
Bourgeois	62	„ 5d.		1	6	0	„ 6d.	1	11	0	„ 6½d.	1	13	6
Brevier	74	„ 5d.		1	11	0	„ 6d.	1	17	0	„ 6½d.	2	0	0
Minion	91	„ 5d.		1	18	0	„ 6¼d.	2	7	6	„ 6¾d.	2	11	0
Nonpareil	124	„ 5½d.		2	17	0	„ 7d.	3	12	6	„ 7½d.	3	17	6

[1] The Edinburgh 1805 price of 4½d. per 1000, common matter had been increased to 5d. in 1862. Later in 1866, a few weeks before the London employers granted an advance, the Edinburgh price was increased to 5½d., the Establishment wage being raised from 25s. to 27s. 6d. per week of 57 hours. (*Scottish Typographical Circular*, Oct., 1866). See also p. 248.

The excess of prices proposed by the *London* Compositors over those of the *Scotch* Scales on the castings in the foregoing table is as follows:

	£	s.	d.			£	s.	d.
Small Pica	0	5	0	Brevier		0	9	0
Long Primer ..	0	6	0	Minion		0	13	0
Bourgeois	0	7	6	Nonpareil		1	0	6

The following table will show the comparative prices of the same sheet, if it consists of mere reprint solid:

	1000			£	s.	d.			£	s.	d.			£	s.	d.
					Edinburgh and Glasgow.			*Present.* (London.)				*Proposed.* (London.)			
Small Pica....	41	At	5d.	0	17	0	At	5¼d.	0	18	0	At	6d.	1	0	6
Long Primer..	48	„	5d.	1	0	0	„	5¼d.	1	1	0	„	6d.	1	4	0
Bourgeois	62	„	5d.	1	6	0	„	5¼d.	1	7	0	„	6d.	1	11	0
Brevier	74	„	5d.	1	11	0	„	5¼d.	1	12	6	„	6d.	1	17	0
Minion	91	„	5d.	1	18	0	„	5½d.	2	1	6	„	6¼d.	2	7	6
Nonpareil 124		„	5½d.	2	17	0	„	6¼d.	3	4	6	„	7d.	3	12	6

Excess of proposed *London* over *Scotch* price:

	£	s.	d.			£	s.	d.
Small Pica	0	3	6	Brevier		0	6	0
Long Primer ..	0	4	0	Minion		0	9	6
Bourgeois	0	5	0	Nonpareil		0	15	6

Now, in dealing with the question of the difference of prices in the cases just cited, the Masters' Committee totally ignore the fact that for fifty years prior to 1862 they had been paying, in the case of Edinburgh, just the precise difference for MS. works of a solid character which they point out would exist between our proposed price and the present Edinburgh scale, while they are entirely silent as to the point that, under that scale, no deduction is made for leads, and the same remarks apply with greater force to Glasgow, where the rise of ½d. per 1000 was not established till the latter end of last year while one of the same amount had taken place in Edinburgh 5½ years prior to that period, and where the masters might have said with quite as much truth as the employers of London do now, "Look at Glasgow, if we grant you this rise all our work will go there," yet the rise was conceded, and it does not appear that the trade of Edinburgh suffered in the period elapsing between their advance and a similar one in Glasgow.

With respect to reprints the case is somewhat different, inasmuch as we are seeking a rise in that description of work to the extent of ¼d. per 1000 beyond that which has, within the last four years, been established in the two great Scotch cities, the relative increase being in a sheet of small pica 1s., long primer 1s., bourgeois 1s. 6d., brevier 1s. 6d., minion 2s., and nonpareil 2s.; but it may be said that the London employers are at present reaping the full benefit of the advance in Scotland; indeed, the difference between a Scotch reprint solid and one of a like character here, is only 1s. per sheet higher from small pica to bourgeois, and 1s. 6d. on brevier, while with respect to a leaded reprint, they pay in

Scotland at present as much as is paid in London. The Report having
dealt with every kind of work common to the Scotch and London
scales, and also that of Leeds, by way of comparison, then proceeds:

With regard to England generally, it is stated that bookwork and jobbing
are almost universally executed on the establishment. It appears from a tabu-
lated list which has been furnished to the sub-committee, that the establishment
wages paid in fifty-six towns vary from 20s. paid in Plymouth to 31s. in
Liverpool, the general average being about 25s. per week of from fifty-four to
sixty hours. The examination instituted by your sub-Committee shows, as
the general result, that the prices of composition in *Edinburgh* and *Glasgow*,
and *the provincial towns of England*, are very considerably lower than those
paid under the present scale in *London*.

With regard to *reprints*, the facility of their execution at a distance renders
them more liable than any other species of work to be removed from London
to Scotch or English provincial offices. Such removal must always form a
serious loss to both masters and journeymen in the slack seasons of the year.
In addition to an advance in the prices per 1000, it is proposed to abandon the
distinction between different kinds of reprints which were agreed to at the
conference of 1847 after long and careful consideration. The inevitable result
of the adoption of the proposed definition would be at once to convert a large
class of reprints into MS. works and greatly to increase the difficulty of meeting
competition in this department with Scotch and English provincial offices.

With regard to the comparison of the establishment rates paid in the
56 towns alluded to, that comparison is not complete unless the average
amount received is put against the average hours worked, which is 58;
hence it follows that if you add 5 hours on, which would be paid as overtime, to bring the number of hours worked up to the London standard of
63, the country master would then have to pay 27s. 6d. as against 33s.; and
with respect to the facility for doing reprints to any extent at a distance
from London, that is a very doubtful point, for there is an element in
the question which your Committee believe to be of great importance in
considering this matter, and that is, the difficulty of securing the necessary
amount of labour in isolated country towns to execute the work with
despatch; for the tendency in the present day is to do almost all descriptions of work in the shortest possible time, a thing which can only be
done in great centres of labour, where a master pressed by orders has a
ready means of obtaining that which he requires; and, besides, we
maintain that the masters of London have been competing successfully
with a state of things very much worse in the provinces than that which is
now presented, or that would be likely to arise from the adoption of the
first point in our Memorial. Then with respect to the proposed definition
of a reprint destroying the distinction between different kinds of reprints
which was agreed to at the Conference of 1847, our object is to obtain a
clear definition of what should constitute a reprint proper, for under the
very elastic phrase of "verbal alterations," the most extraordinary
claims have been set up, and masters, in some instances, have sought to
pay as simple reprints works infinitely more troublesome to the compositor than many bad MSS., thus placing him in a position, coupled
with the low price paid for this description of work, of being unable to
earn a bare subsistence on it.

On proposition 2 the Report remarks :—

Proposition 2.

The present rate of establishment wages in *London* is not less than 33*s.* per week for 10½ hours of full work per day. Considering the great diversity between individual journeymen in skill and quickness, and industry, it appears unreasonable to pay to all without distinction so high a *minimum* rate as 36*s.*, especially when it is remembered that in London compositors claim to consider no engagement on the establishment as lasting for less than a fortnight.

With respect to the argument contained in this paragraph your Committee venture to think that the skill, quickness, and industry of the workman are not paid for at the present minimum rate, although all these qualities are demanded of men even upon the low establishment; and with regard to the statement that the London compositors claim to consider no engagement on the establishment as lasting for less than a fortnight, this is a mistake, for a master taking on a new hand is not bound to keep him a fortnight unless he suits; but if he continues beyond that time he is entitled to a fortnight's notice, a position quite as beneficial to the master as the man; but it is correct that if a man is working in a house on the piece he cannot be put upon the establishment for less than a fortnight; but surely a master so situated has it in his power, and does put the most capable of his piece hands on the establishment : under such circumstances the proof therefore that a master would suffer any great loss by admitting the claim contained in proposition 2 seems to us to fail.

On proposition 3 the Report goes on to say :—

Proposition 3.

The scale defines Overtime as commencing at 10 p.m. and ceasing at 6 a.m. It is now asked that it shall commence at 8 p.m. and cease at 8 a.m.

As the ordinary time of closing in *London* offices is 8 p.m., it seems desirable that an interval should be allowed to separate the two periods, otherwise a strong temptation to delay the completion of the regular business of the day would be afforded to the Compositor who would derive a pecuniary profit from what may often be the result of his own want of exertion or of the lateness of his arrival at the office in the morning.

Now the assumption contained in the paragraph just read is one that we venture to think will not bear examination; for it assumes a very low tone of morality among the compositors of London, as well as very great short-sightedness; for we are not aware that the habitually negligent workman would long maintain his position in any house; and were it true that some individuals could be found so wanting in what is due to common honesty and to the welfare of their families, it would afford no sufficient justification for keeping the great bulk of the operative printers of the metropolis in so disadvantageous a position. At any rate, no such fear as that put forth in this Report seems to actuate the masters of the provinces, or of Scotland and Ireland, where it is the universal custom to pay an enhanced price for labour done after the regular working hours; and it may be noted as remarkable that in Dublin a compositor is paid threepence per hour extra from 8 to 10, and from that time till 6 in the morning sixpence per hour extra.

On proposition 4 the Sub-Committee say that they have no remark to offer on it. May we hope from this that that at least is a point gained ?

Then with respect to proposition 5 it is said :—

Proposition 5.

With regard to pieced leads, it is to be observed that the proposed regulation embraces all works in demy 8vo. and under. The supply of pieced leads is often as advantageous to the Compositor in preventing his standing still while waiting until leads of the full measure can be procured, as it is to the master in the expeditious execution of the work in hand.

With regard to pieced leads being advantageous where they are systematically used, your Committee must demur, as we do not see—looking to the readiness with which leads of all sizes can be obtained—that any appreciable delay need occur; while in the adjusting of such leads we believe that a far greater impediment to the expedition of the work is apparent, as well as loss to the compositor.

Proposition 6.

This proposition, if adopted, would lead to very great inconvenience, and does not seem to be called for by any disadvantages *generally* experienced in London offices.

That in such a reform as that which we propose with regard to the thin founts, certain inconvenience might at first occur may be admitted, but we cannot accept the statement that it would be very great, the more so as in Glasgow, and in the provinces the natural standard of 13 ems to the 26 lower case letters is adopted, which involves a more complex system of casting up than that which we propose. Nor can we admit the affirmation that the disadvantages resulting from the use of these thin founts is not very general, for we believe the experience of most of you will suffice to disprove that assertion, and there can be no doubt justice might fairly demand 13 ems for all founts below that point, and therefore in making the concession we do of an em, we cannot be charged with mooting the question in an exacting spirit, for we presume it will not be disputed that a thin fount involves a reduction in the price per 1000.

In regard to proposition 7 the masters say :—

Proposition 7.

An increased charge for corrections would give a high price as a minimum to Compositors of all classes, however slow or incompetent. It is believed that in practice good compositors obtain now at least 7d. per hour.

It may be that in some instances good compositors do obtain 7d. per hour for corrections, but how do they get their claims allowed ? Why, the conscience of the employer tells him, that the work the men have done is worth it, and he pays in face of a scale that says corrections shall be paid at 6d. per hour, and all we desire is that the scale should agree with the practice and not leave it in the power of particular employers to exact the letter of such a clause against a man who is worth more; and with reference to this it may be also observed that in the provinces there is no parallel for paying a man less **per hour** for correction than an ordinary establishment hand gets, but on the contrary, he is paid at a higher rate for such work and that apparently without any very great evils arising from the different capacities of various men.

In conclusion the Masters observe :—

In conclusion, your Sub-Committee would offer a few general observations. The terms of the present scale were settled in the early part of the present century, in consequence of the high price of living occasioned by the great continental war and have never since been reduced, although cheaper times have intervened. The reduction in the rate for reprints was agreed to in 1816 as a measure of self-defence against the competition of country offices. The compositors obtained many concessions at the conference of masters and journeymen in 1847. May not the present difference between the prices for compositors' work in London and in other cities and towns be reasonably regarded as an ample equivalent for any greater expense incurred by the London workman in consequence of his residence in the metropolis ?

It is perhaps needless to suggest that in coming to a decision upon the Memorial, the greatly increased facilities of communication with distant parts of the country, both by land and water, as well as by the book-post and telegraph, coupled with the adoption of free trade principles as regards foreign parts form most important elements of consideration. While such facilities exist it can scarcely be expected that publishers will hesitate to transfer a still larger portion of their work even than at present, rather than incur the increased cost which must be the result of compliance with the requisitions of the compositors.

In reply to this your Committee would observe that, although it is true wages were raised in 1810 in consequence of the high prices of provisions prevailing at that period, yet the different style of working then adopted gave men many advantages of which they have since been deprived and which enabled them to make good earnings at the rates then settled; and if some articles of consumption are cheaper resulting from the removal of certain excise and custom duties, the increased rate men have to pay for rent outweighs by far any relief afforded by such matters, and this coupled with the high prices of prime articles of consumption arising from no temporary cause but produced by the enormously increased and increasing wealth of the nation justifies the claims we make for an advance, and we maintain that that free trade to which the Master Printers point, and the remission of all those duties which specially pressed upon them, have given an expansion to the Trade which has largely increased their profits, but which have not hitherto touched us; and whatever may be the difference between the London prices as they stand and those of the country, it is for you to ask yourselves whether 30s. will go as far now as that sum did 20 years ago, and if it does not is it not a proof that while the master is getting richer you are getting poorer ?

Having thus, gentlemen, placed before you the reasons given by the employers for rejecting the main propositions in your Memorial, your Committee feel that those reasons are not sufficient to justify you in abandoning one single claim set forth in that document, but at the same time they do not think it would be advisable at the present moment to reject the proposition of the masters to confer on those points not negatived in the resolutions adopted, because we feel that in a movement of this kind it is desirable, if possible, to bring about a settlement without being forced into a course of action that might result in leaving behind a feeling of annoyance or ill-will. Besides, it must be acknowledged that in questions of this nature it is a work of time to bring men's minds to a full conviction of the justice or necessity for such a movement; and it is possible that even in our own ranks there may be found men who have not yet fully recognized the propriety of the claims put forth, or the danger they are in of falling behind the age; and if that be so, it can hardly be matter of surprise that the employers should be slow to recognize their necessity. The Memorial is, however, in your hands, and we invite you to ponder over it, and if upon examination you believe its provisions to be just, then give it all the aid you can. Amongst your companions and with your employers urge the rightfulness of the claims put forth, and by so doing you will bring such a mass of opinion to bear upon the propositions submitted as must result in their entire acceptance. In the meantime your Committee would recommend that the Conference proposed by the employers be adopted; but with the reservation that the Committee entrusted with the duty of conferring shall not accept any modifications of the five points open for discussion without first referring such modifications to a Special General Meeting. And, in coming to this resolution, your Committee do so because they believe that there is hardly one of those points which in itself would not justify a strong effort for its adoption. And at the same time they would have it clearly understood that the two other points which have been for the present rejected shall not be abandoned, but that the question with respect to them shall be kept open for future action—and that at no distant date.

In conclusion, gentlemen, your Committee felt that in a movement such as that which has been initiated, you would not desire to maintain an isolated position with respect to those who have not yet joined the ranks of the London Society of Compositors, and they therefore thought it expedient to throw this Meeting open to all who chose to attend; and we would strongly and earnestly urge those who have hitherto stood aloof from us to make this cause their own, and by throwing their weight into the scale secure for it a more general acceptance, and thus assist in obtaining for themselves and for future generations a better position than that which they at present occupy. Union and earnestness of purpose can accomplish much, while disunion leaves you a prey to the undue exactions of capital, and cripples every effort that may be made to resist its encroachments. Your Committee, therefore, confidently hope that the compositors of London will not lag in the rear of that great army of industry which of late years has awakened to a knowledge of its power, and which if rightly directed and governed by temperance and justice will secure for its members a fair and honest share in that wealth towards the production of which they contribute so largely.

The compositors' memorial had been presented in January, 1866, but no settlement was reached between employers and employed until the following November.

AGREEMENT WITH THE COMPOSITORS

At a Meeting held November the 21st, 1866, of the Committees of Master Printers and Compositors of London and its vicinity, appointed respectively, viz., of Masters at the General Meeting of Master Printers held at the Freemasons' Tavern on the 8th of October, 1866, and of Compositors at the General Meeting of Compositors held at Exeter Hall on the 8th of November, 1866, and empowered to settle finally all matters relating to the subjects comprised in the Memorial of the London Compositors presented in January, 1866, it was mutually agreed :—

1. That a rise of one halfpenny per thousand be paid on all descriptions of work, whether manuscript or reprint, excepting newspapers.[1]

2. That the definitions of Reprints in the Scale of 1847 be adhered to, but that remodelling of punctuation or orthography shall be done before giving out copy to the Compositors, or be paid for.

3. That the Establishment Wages be 36s. per week of 60 hours, the apportionment of the 60 hours to be mutually agreed upon between the Employers and the Journeymen in each office.[2]

N.B.—The increase on Establishment Wages to 36s., and the reduction of hours to Sixty, to take effect on the first Monday in December, notwithstanding existing contracts.

4. That Overtime be paid for at the rate of 3d. extra per hour after 9 o'clock in the evening till 6 o'clock in the morning, provided that when the Compositor, having worked during the night, is required to continue working after 6 a.m., he is to be paid 3d. per hour extra until 8 a.m. No charge to be made of less than 1s. extra between the hours of 10 p.m. and 6 a.m.

Schedule of Prices for Overtime

			s.	d.					s.	d.
From	9 till 10	..	0	3	From	9 till 4	..	..	2	0
,,	9 ,, 11	..	1	0	,,	9 ,, 5	..	..	2	3
,,	9 ,, 12	..	1	0	,,	9 ,, 6	..	..	2	6
,,	9 ,, 1	..	1	3	,,	9 ,, 7	..	..	2	9
,,	9 ,, 2	..	1	6	,,	9 ,, 8	..	..	3	0
,,	9 ,, 3	..	1	9						

Provided also—That no Compositor be required to work more than 10½ hours per day without being paid 3d. per hour as Overtime.

5. That Sunday work be paid for at the rate of 6d. extra per hour; but that in no case shall the Compositor receive less than 2s. 6d. extra.

---

[1] Scale of 1810: English-Brevier, 5¾d. leaded, 6d. solid.

[2] 1847: Establishment wages 33s. per week for 10¾ hours full work per day. 1835 : 12 hours per day including time for refreshment.

6. That no deduction be made for Pieced Leads in measures of less than 26 ems wide.[1]

7. That one farthing per thousand extra be paid on all Roman founts for every en below 12 ems of their own body in thickness.

8. That Corrections be paid for at the rate of 7½d. per hour.

And that the foregoing Modifications of Prices be adopted, except as regards all works already in progress, or contracted or estimated for, or the current volumes of periodical publications, from and after the first Monday in December next.

All works already estimated or contracted for, if not put in hand before the first day of January, 1867, to take the advanced price.

(*Signed*)

On behalf of the Masters	*On behalf of the Compositors*
Robert Kingston Burt, *Chairman*	Charles Thos. Henley,
	Chairman
Wm. Clowes	Samuel Harvey
George Levey	William Hinds
Wm. Rivington	H. Self

At the Annual General Meeting of the Association of Master Printers, 12 October, 1870, it was unanimously resolved :

That, having regard to the existing relations with our Workmen, the continuance of this Association is unnecessary, and that it be accordingly dissolved.

That Mr. Harrison, the Chairman, Mr. Griffith, the Deputy Chairman, and Mr. Pardon, the Treasurer, of the Association for the past year, be requested to settle the affairs of the Association; and that Mr. Pardon be requested to take charge of all books, papers, or other property belonging thereto.

"It has sometimes been supposed, when this resolution has been quoted apart from the context, that its meaning was to the effect that the Association was disbanded because its relations with the men were so harmonious. But the exact opposite is the truth, strange as the conclusion may appear, and its explanation seems to be that as the Association was formed mainly with the object of amicably settling points at issue between masters and men, and as this had become impossible in the embittered state of affairs, it was no use continuing it.

"As a consequence there was no regular Association in existence to deal with such subsequent memorials of the compositors as that

---

[1] *i.e.*, instead of ¼d. per 1000 reduction being made for leaded matter, the composition was to be charged as solid. In assembling small pieces of spacing material the compositor lost much time and all the advantages inherent in composing a work that was leaded.

of 1872, when, although a meeting of Master Printers was summoned, it was eventually decided to leave the matter to the individual action of each employer.

"This resolution was reached at a meeting held at the Freemasons' Tavern, on the 14 March, 1872, and presided over by Mr. T. D. Galpin. The result was the success of the nine hours movement and an advance in rates."[1]

III.   1872.   THE NINE HOURS MOVEMENT

On 19 January, 1872, the London Society of Compositors presented the following Memorial to the employers. Their principal demand was that the hours of work should be reduced from 60 to 54 per week, and that an advance of $\frac{1}{2}d.$ per 1,000 ens should be allowed in compensation to the piece hands. The Nine Hours Movement was at that time supported by the majority of the Trade Unions.

[DOCUMENT LXXXII]

NINE HOURS MOVEMENT

To the Master Printers of London and its Vicinity

Gentlemen,

In January, 1866, the Members of the London Society of Compositors appealed to you on the question of the hours of labour, and the rate at which that labour should be paid, and, after considerable delay, they were enabled to come to an agreement on the points then raised, although it was one not altogether satisfactory to themselves. Since the period alluded to, the labour question has entered upon a phase of a more definite kind than that which then seemed to exist, when, although shorter time was one of the points insisted on, no very clear or general standard appears to have been arrived at. Now, however, in all directions and in all sorts of trades, the limitation of the week's work to 54 hours, or nine per day, has become an accepted creed with the great mass of skilled workmen, both of the Metropolis and of the Provinces. Nor have the large employers of labour been found altogether averse to this change, although, necessarily, some differences upon the point have been evinced; but, supported as it is, by public opinion, the justice of the limitation sought to be established will, we venture to predict, soon meet with general acceptance. Encouraged by these symptoms, your Memorialists, therefore, can hardly suppose that you, Gentlemen, are unprepared to have the question submitted to you : for there are few occupations which strain more severely both the physical and mental powers of men than those of the operative printer, whose position, therefore, pre-eminently claims relief in the direction of shortening the hours of labour. Before,

---

[1] [Austen Leigh, R. A.] Notes in the *Programme and Handbook of the Twenty-Sixth Annual Meeting of the British Federation of Master Printers*, 1926.

however, pressing the matter upon your attention, steps were taken, both by balloting our Members and by a subsequent meeting of 350 Delegates, representing all the chief offices in London, to ascertain the views and the desires of those we represent. Consequent upon the action thus taken, the Committee of the London Society of Compositors have received directions respectfully to place before you the following propositions for your consideration, and which, we trust, will meet with your assent.:—

1. That the Master Printers of London be memorialised for a reduction of the hours of labour to 54 per week.

2. That overtime shall commence after 7 p.m. from Monday to Friday, and after 2 p.m. on Saturday, each day standing on its own merits.

3. That an advance of ½d. per 1,000 on all descriptions of composition (newspapers excepted) be conceded.

4. That the above alterations shall come into operation on all works put in hand on and after the first day of March, 1872.

In submitting these propositions to you, your Memorialists do not feel it necessary to go at length into the arguments which justify the claim for shortening the day's labour, as they have been, of late, so constantly urged in the public press that it would be an insult to you to suppose you unacquainted with them; but, with respect to the period at which it is desired that the day's labour should close, we wish to press upon your consideration the following facts:—

It is, unhappily, too true, as the experience of past years proves to us, that the influence of close and unhealthy offices operates fearfully upon our death-rate, as is shown in the amount disbursed by our Society in funeral payments, over fifty per cent. of our Members dying from diseases of the air passages, which is almost entirely referable to the vitiated atmosphere we are compelled, in too many instances, to breathe, and which, we need hardly say, is intensified by having to work late at night. Independent of which, were this reason not patent, the increased and increasing cost of rent in central London compels us to make our homes at a considerable distance from our various places of employment, and hence a further necessity exists for restricting the hours of labour within such limits as will enable us to spend some little time with our families, and to obtain that relaxation which is so essential in sustaining bodily health.

In regard to the position of those who work upon the piece, and on whose behalf the claim of ½d. per 1000 extra is made, we deem it right to point out to you that that appears as a necessary corollary to lessening the hours of labour, otherwise a compositor so situated would, from a monetary point of view, be a loser by the reduction in time; and, further, it is conceived that he has a claim for an advance for another reason, and that is, that the establishment system deprives him to a great extent of that share of profit which he has a right to expect from a scale constituted on a basis such as that upon which ours rests—for the establishment system has exercised an increasing pressure year by year on his condition, until it becomes a matter of the utmost difficulty for the piece compositor in many houses, even with the closest application, to earn the means of decent subsistence. We would also urge, in support of the plea for an advance in piece prices, that the employers of Edinburgh and Glasgow have recently granted the advance which we are now seeking; and, therefore, should you accede to the prayer of our Memorial, the London Master Printers would occupy as good a position with respect to those towns as hitherto, and in some respects a better one, inasmuch as the Glasgow employers have conceded an advance of ¾d. per 1000 on solid manuscript, while, in the former town, the week has also been reduced to one of 54 hours; and not only has this advance in piece prices, and a reduction of the hours of labour to 54 begun to take effect in Scotland, but in the provincial towns of England also, for already Newcastle, Sheffield, Manchester, Chester, Bath, and Bristol, have obtained advances in their prices, and with one exception a reduction of the hours to 54, and in every direction other towns have commenced to follow the example set them, so that we may confidently affirm that London employers would not be placed at a disadvantage with the Provinces in the event of their favourably entertaining the application we now make to them.

If we turn our eyes from Home to Foreign Competition, we believe that you, Gentlemen, have still less to fear (if there was any cause for apprehension in such a direction before), for not only were prices raised in Paris in 1868, but it must strike even the most unreflective that the condition of affairs in France at the present time, resulting from the disastrous war in which she has recently been engaged, has fearfully affected her industry, and with a considerable diminution of workmen the cost of production must necessarily be enhanced, while the imposition of new and onerous fiscal burdens, and heavier ones in prospect, must tend to leave her out of consideration as a competitor in any degree with English employers for some time to come. In Germany also the workmen have diminished, and the purchasing power of money decreased—a state of things which has led to a general advance in wages, and a reduction of the hours of labour to the present London standard, notwithstanding which the agitation continues, and the aspect of affairs is by no means reassuring; it is therefore quite certain that the employers of this country need apprehend no disturbing influences from that quarter.

Owing to the non-existence of any Association representing the Master Printers of London, we are compelled to apply to you, in the first instance, personally; but if you think it preferable that a Committee should be appointed to act on your behalf in the settlement of the question, we shall be quite ready to fall in with such a view, and hold ourselves prepared to meet your representatives on an early day.

In conclusion, Gentlemen, we earnestly pray you to consider this Memorial in a spirit of fairness and candour; and if you do so, we feel satisfied that you will not reject the signs of the times, or permit the Compositors of this great city to occupy an inferior position to that of their fellow-workmen in the Provinces or in other Trades.

Trusting to receive a favourable and speedy reply to this Memorial, we have the honour to be, Gentlemen, on behalf of the Memorialists.

Your most obedient Servants,

RICHARD LEE, *Chairman.*
HENRY SELF, *Secretary.*

January 19th, 1872.

In reply to the compositors' Memorial the masters, who had appointed a Committee to negotiate with the men, submitted two alternative propositions, suggesting concessions in the matter of the hours of labour, but offering no advance in prices. This compromise was immediately refused by the L.S.C., which reiterated its original demands, with the addition of a clause requiring that corrections should be paid at 8d. instead of 7½d. per hour. At the same time it was stated that "unless the above terms are conceded by Saturday, March 16, Compositors shall tender their employers a fortnight's notice on that day, but that no overtime shall be worked during the running of the said notice."

It was not necessary for so drastic a threat to be put into force, for the majority of firms complied with the compositors' demands without further discussion. Since no properly-constituted Master Printers' Association existed, no fresh agreement was signed between the conflicting parties.

The Masters' Committee, appointed at a General Meeting, held 12 February, 1872, published a Report from which extracts are here reprinted:

[DOCUMENT LXXXIII]

Report of the Committee appointed at a General Meeting of Master Printers of London, held at The Freemasons' Tavern, on Monday, 12th February, 1872.[1]

Your Committee have to report that, in discharge of the duty confided to them at the last General Meeting of the Masters Printers of London, in accordance with the following Resolution, they placed themselves in communication with the London Society of Compositors on the subject of their Memorial.

"That this Meeting, having regard to the fact that an advance of wages and a reduction of the hours of labour were recently made to those employed in the printing trade; to the low prices now received by the London master printers, and the great competition with which they have to contend, owing to the transfer of a large amount of work to country printers who pay much lower wages; and also to the fact that the last advance of one halfpenny per 1000 is not now being paid by some of the oldest and largest houses in London, deem it inexpedient, alike in the interests of the employed as well as of the employers, to grant the advance of one halfpenny per 1000 asked for by the Compositors in their Memorial, but is willing to consider the possibility of some reduction in the hours of labour."

[1] The *Report* was read at a General Meeting of Master Printers held on 14 March, 1872.

On the 22nd February a conference was held with the Compositors, their deputation consisting of Mr. Lee (Chairman), Mr. Self (Secretary), and twelve Compositors—all the members of your Committee* being present.

* The Committee, as nominated by the General Meeting, consisted of—

Messrs. Adlard,
   ,, Burt,
   ,, W. C. K. Clowes,
   ,, L. Collingridge,
   ,, Edwards (Savill and Edwards),
   ,, Galpin,
   ,, Griffith,

Messrs. Judd,
   ,, Kemshead,
   ,, Pardon,
   ,, Rider,
   ,, Robson,
   ,, Unwin, and
   ,, Wyman.

At the commencement of the interview, in reply to a question from the Chairman, the Compositors stated that they had no power to conclude any agreement with the employers; and being invited to state any further arguments they desired to bring forward in support of their Memorial beyond those they had advanced therein, they replied they had none to offer. After these and a few other preliminaries, the Chairman of your Committee read to the Deputation a brief statement, in which the Committee expressed regret that they did not see their way to grant the prayer of the Compositors' Memorial in its entirety, and adduced reasons for their inability to do so.

It was moreover pointed out that the Master Printers of London employing Society hands have not only to compete with the Continent, Scotland, and the Provinces, but actually with several of the largest firms here in London, who are paying a lower rate of wages than the Scale of 1866, and that they were already told by their employers, "It is no use your coming to us for work; your men belong to the Society, and you, therefore, pay more for labour than other printers. Why do you do so?" We stated to the Deputation, that in consequence we were forced to send in our estimates based on the old Scale, in order to secure the work we had to compete for; and we urged, that while the London Society of Compositors were unable to bring the non-Society men into their Union, yet they came to us who have adhered to the Agreement of 1866, and asked for a further rise in wages, which would take still more work from us, and give it to those who have made themselves independent of their Society. We told them that, although desirous to work with their body, there was a point beyond which we could not go, in justice to ourselves, and that they, in their Memorial, had gone beyond that point.

With respect to the diminution in the hours of work, we stated that after giving this portion of their Memorial our careful consideration, and having regard to the foregoing Resolution passed at the General Meeting of the Employers constituting this Committee (which was read to the Deputation), we were prepared to recommend the Master Printers of London to accept either or both of the following proposals, at the option of each Office.

The eight propositions submitted by the employers were rejected by the L.S.C., and the following communication was sent in reply.

[DOCUMENT LXXXIV]

London Society of Compositors,
3, Raquet Court, Fleet Street,
March, 7, 1872.

Sir,

I beg to inform you that an aggregate Meeting of the Members of our Society was held at Exeter Hall last night, when the reply of the Committee of Master Printers to the Compositors' "Memorial" was laid before them, resulting in an animated discussion thereon, which terminated in the adoption of a revised series of propositions and a further resolution as to the period when the Compositors request that they may be carried into effect. I enclose copies for the use of your Committee, in the hope that you will take immediate steps to place them before the gentlemen comprising it.

The parts marked in italics point out the alterations effected by the Meeting.

I am, Sir,
Your most obedient Servant,

B. Pardon, Esq.   H. SELF, *Sec.*

LONDON SOCIETY OF COMPOSITORS

NINE HOURS MOVEMENT

At an aggregate Meeting of the Members of the London Society of Compositors, held in Exeter Hall on Wednesday Evening, March 6, 1872, to take into consideration the reply of the Committee of Master Printers to the "Memorial" of the Compositors, the following revised Propositions were unanimously adopted :—

1. That the hours of labour shall consist of 54 per week.[1]

2. That overtime shall commence after 7 p.m. from Monday to Friday, and after 2 p.m. on Saturday, each day standing on its own merits.

3. That an advance of ½d. per 1,000 on all descriptions of composition (Newspapers and *Parliamentary Work* excepted) be adopted.[2]

4. [*That corrections be paid at the rate of 8d. per hour*].[3]

5. That the above alterations shall come into operation on all works put in hand on and after the First day of March, 1872.

It was also unanimously resolved :—

That unless the above terms are conceded by Saturday, March 16, Compositors shall tender their employers a fortnight's notice on that day, but that no overtime shall be worked during the running of the said notice.

March 7, 1872.

[1] Reduced from 60 hours per week.
[2] Advance of 1866 gave 6¼d. leaded, 6½d. solid.
[3] Price for corrections in 1866 was 7½d. per hour.

There were no further negotiations. The employers' committee concluded its *Report* with a resolution condemning the alleged intransigence of the L.S.C.

A communication regarding the *Report* published by the Masters' Committee was sent to the employers shortly after the dispute had received its arbitrary settlement. The men defended themselves against the charges of discourtesy levelled against them and justified their actions.

[DOCUMENT LXXXV]

In conclusion, Gentlemen, we were as desirous as yourselves that no feeling of bitterness should have been imported into the matters placed before you, and if we have been compelled to assume an attitude that has unfortunately placed us in antagonism, we must respectfully decline to admit that we are in any way answerable for the result, which we hold is entirely attributable to the delay which took place between the issue of our Memorial and the period when your Committee first proposed to meet us, and to the utter insufficiency of the offers then made; for we think that had they looked fairly at their position, and recognised that our movement was not an isolated one, but formed a part of the national progress, they would have dealt with us in a spirit totally different from that which seemed to pervade their counsels, and thus have averted a struggle which we neither courted nor desired; and further, it is evident from the notices constantly flowing in to us of firms who have conceded our Memorial, that your Committee failed to appreciate the true sentiments of those they represented. However, we trust that means may yet be found to settle any questions of detail which may arise by the collective action of the Employers and the Employed, and thus put an end to the continuance of irritating topics, which will be alike inimical to the interests of both parties.

IV. A LETTER FROM WILLIAM BLADES

The efforts put forth by the London Society of Compositors in the 1880s to induce public bodies to confine their work to employers recognized by the Society as "fair" must also be noted. That so prominent and experienced a Master Printer as William Blades was prepared to lend his support, indicates the accretion of power and prestige enjoyed by the Society at that date, the fruits of a century or more of endeavour. The following letter, addressed by William Blades to the members of the London School Board, is taken from the Report of the 167th Quarterly Delegate Meeting of the L.S.C.

19

[DOCUMENT LXXXVI]

TO THE MEMBERS OF THE LONDON SCHOOL BOARD

PRINTING CONTRACTS

23, Abchurch Lane, London,
October, 1889.

Gentlemen,—I beg with all respect, as a Master Printer of old standing, to lay before you a few remarks bearing upon the question of what are called "fair" and "unfair" houses in the Printing Trade, and upon the effect of the Trade Union among Printers.

I am strongly of opinion that the Trade Union, with all its imperfections, is a necessary institution, good for the employers, good for the workmen, and good for the general welfare. It should always be remembered that the present scale of prices is not one-sided, imposed by the workmen upon their unwilling employers; but a compact settled by mutual agreement, and varied, as occasion required, from the year 1810 to 1874.

1810.—In this year a representative body of employers, and a similar body empowered by the men, met, and after long discussion, came to a perfect agreement.

1816.—Alterations were made, again by a Committee of Master Printers, to which the consent of the men was given.

1847.—Other changes were made in the Scale, which were agreed to by eight Compositors representing the Union, and the following eight Master Printers who signed "On behalf of the Employers" :—

William Rivington	Richard Clay
John A. W. Cox	George Clowes
Alex. Macintosh	J. Iliffe Wilson
T. R. Harrison	Chas. Whittingham

1866.—A Committee of four Employers and four Compositors agreed to certain Addenda which bound both sides. The Masters who signed "On behalf of the Employers" were :—

R. K. Burt	George Levey
Wm. Clowes	Wm. Rivington

1872.—In this year an Agreement was made by which the Union is now governed; it originated in the desire of the Compositors to define the length of a day's work, the payment of overtime, and other important matters. Here, although no agreement was signed, the new arrangement was accepted by the whole London trade, with the exception of half-a-dozen firms.

1874.—Further alterations were made this year by mutual agreement, the Signatories "On behalf of the Employers" being :—

R. K. Burt	J. Judd
Horace Cox	C. W. H. Wyman

E. J. Francis

I have mentioned these successive changes to prove that from 1810, up to now, there has been a continuity of agreement between employers and workmen. Such mutual agreements have had a most beneficial effect upon the peacefulness of the trade, and I think it would be a great calamity were they now ignored, in favour of a free fight between Labour and Capital. Indeed, no better plan for the welfare of the trade could be devised than the appointment now of a truly representative Committee of Employers, to arrange with a Committee of the Union, a scale, which could be accepted and adhered to by all parties.

I would like to add that while unable to endorse all that has been said about "sweating," I have no hesitation in repeating that the Union is advantageous to both sides. It does not, as some people accuse it of doing, "reduce the good and the bad workman to one dead level." It does its best to prevent the employer obtaining work at a lower scale than he or his representatives have agreed to pay, but it only fixes a *minimum*, below which no man ought to work, and above which many Compositors are now paid. I refer to men on weekly wages, irrespective of what they really earn; and here, although 36s. is the lowest wage, the cases are numerous in which the same roof covers men receiving, as abler journeymen, 38s., 40s., or 42s.

The benefit of a Trade Union to the employers is, to me, patent. In these days of severe competition, when a long schedule of work is given out to be tendered for, it is of vital importance for an employer to know that his competitors must pay for the workmen's labour the same price as he does. Not unfrequently it happens that anxiety to get work induces an employer to put in a tender which he finds, too late, will not pay. His great aim then is to pare down cost, and wages is naturally the first thing which tempts him. In such a case the workman, unsupported by his Union, would be at the mercy of the employer, and reduction would slowly succeed reduction, until "sweating" would really be reached. The employer who wished his men to be paid fairly would be compelled to follow suit or see his trade collapse. Then would ensue a series of strikes, and the formation of fresh Trade Unions—there would be friction everywhere, and renewed war between Capital and Labour, a certain result of what is called Freedom of Contract. This word "freedom" is perhaps the most ill-used word in our language. Obedience to a generally-received scale is not curtailing the employer's freedom of contract with his men. On the contrary, it is the absence of such laws that would surely intensify unnatural competition, and lead to tyranny on the one hand and hate on the other.

But do the so-called "unfair" houses pay their men "sweating" wages ? To no great extent, at present, because the Union rate of wages working all around them keeps up the wage of the Non-Unionist workman to the same, or nearly the same, level as the Unionist. To force down wages much below the Union standard would certainly drive the Non-Unionist into the Union ranks; but should the Union ever be thrown over, through the opposition or apathy of the majority of Employers, the system of "sweating" would soon be reached. All employments prove the truth of the axiom : "Where Unionism is weak, wages are low."

As to the effect of the Union on its members, I have no doubt that its moral influence is good. No man found guilty of crime is allowed to remain a member, and therefore cannot be employed in any Printing Office where Union rules are in force. The inner rules of the Union, by which members must abide, tend to promote foresight, brotherhood, self-respect, and a feeling of corporate responsibility, thus fostering in the mind a true sense of manhood. Unrestrained competition, whether Capital against Capital, or Labour against Labour, leads to social cannibalism, so that the less scrupulous a man is, the better chance there is of rising upon the body of his brother. To avoid this a scale of wages accepted and adhered to by both Employers and Employed seems the real remedy.

As an old Master Printer, whose business lies outside such Contracts as are now under debate, and whose position will be unaffected by a decision either way, I have ventured to address you, feeling strongly that your action in this question will have an important effect upon the future of both Employers and Workmen.

WILLIAM BLADES
(*Firm:* Blades, East and Blades).

CHAPTER XI

PRESSMEN AND PRESSWORK

In 1816, when the employers imposed a reduction upon the compositors, the pressmen were also obliged to accept a lower rate. (See p. 189.) The author has found no documents dealing with the affairs of the pressmen between 1816 and 1866, an interval of half a century. During that time the number of compositors and the strength of their trade organisation increased enormously. It may be surmised, however, that the number and influence of the pressmen did not grow in the same manner. This was probably due to the introduction of the printing machine. The hand press, and the technique of its operation was outmoded. However, until the invention of the treadle-operated platen machine in the 1860s, the press was still used for short runs, jobbing, proofs, and bookwork (limited editions) of the finest quality.

In 1866, when the compositors petitioned for an advance in wages (see p. 269), the pressmen and machine minders immediately followed suit. No details of their memorials and the subsequent negotiations have been found. The texts of their new agreements were published at the same time as those of the compositors. Before dealing with these new accords, it is necessary to make a short examination of mechanical and technical developments in the press and machine-room during the previous years of the century.

The iron press perfected by Lord Stanhope *circa* 1800 was not patented and a number of "machinists" undertook the manufacture and sale of more or less close copies.[1] It was not long before the new press entirely superseded the wooden presses, which were as ancient as the craft itself, in the principal London offices.[2]

"The improvements that Lord Stanhope introduced were an increased power, by means of a compound lever attached

---

[1] An illustrated account of these presses is in Hansard, T. C., *op. cit.*, chapter on "Improved Manual Presses," pp. 637-688.
[2] A most useful essay on the construction of the wooden press can be found in: Wroth, L., *The Colonial Printer* (Second Edition, Portland, Maine, 1938), pp. 69-86.

to the screw. This increased power was the means of producing larger presses, which enabled the printers to print larger sheets of paper than before with one pull, even to the extent of a double royal; and these new presses, being made of iron, produced better workmanship than wooden ones, with less trouble, the wooden platen being subject to being indented, which occasioned the impression to be irregular. This difficulty required much time and trouble to equalize it, particularly in fine work."[1]

An even more important innovation was Koenig's steam-driven printing machine, the prototype of the flat-bed cylinder presses in universal use for book and general printing to-day. Its first effective use in commerce was for printing *The Times*, two models being bought for this purpose in 1814.[2] The machine was capable of an output of at least 1,000 impressions per hour, four times greater than that of the hand-press. The general adoption of this type of machine was comparatively slow. Few other than the proprietors of the London daily newspapers cared to spend the thousand-odd pounds required for their purchase. In 1820 there were only eight machines among six printers, and of these two were not in use.[3] The mechanization of the machine-room did not begin until fifteen years later, when William Clowes assembled the largest plant then known for printing the *Penny Magazine* and other cheap literature. By 1850 most periodicals were printed "by steam." Small cylinder machines for jobbing work were introduced at about the same time, and the treadle platen some ten years later.[4]

The introduction of the iron press had a profound influence on printing technique and, as it will later be shown, on wages and conditions of work for the pressmen. It is therefore necessary to discuss briefly the methods of operating both the old and the new models.

The wooden press was not an instrument of precision. If a sheet of paper were placed on an inked forme and an impression made, the latter would not be even. Some letters might not show, while others would be over-inked, resulting in uneven colour.

[1] Savage, W., *op. cit.*, art. Press.
[2] See *The History of "The Times"* (London, 1935), vol. I, pp. 109-119.
[3] See Goebel, Th., *Frédéric Koenig et l'invention de la presse Mécanique.* Traduit par P. Schmidt (Paris, 1885), p. 209.
[4] The best account of the machine-room equipment of the London trade during the nineteenth century may be found in Wilson, F. J., and Grey, D., *A Practical Treatise upon Modern Printing Machinery* (London, 1888). See also the present writer's *Newspaper Printing in the Nineteenth Century* (London, 1943).

The difficulty was dealt with in the following manner : soft blanket material was placed between paper and platen, and a heavy, crushing impression made. The tough hand-made paper ordinarily in use was damped in order to avoid injury to the types and so that the ink might better adhere to it. The printed sheets were more or less heavily indented in the process and later had to be pressed smooth in the warehouse.

The introduction of the iron press during the first decade of the nineteenth century coincided with the spread of the then fashionable disease known as "Bibliomania."[1] Those afflicted by it were assiduous in collecting old and rare books and sponsoring the production of new and sumptuous works. Whereas the new iron press was an utilitarian acquisition to any printer, for the reasons stated above by Savage, it was especially useful to the select band of printers employed on the best class of bookwork : Messrs. Bulmer, Bensley, M'Creery, Nichols, Whittingham, Rickaby and others.

Writing as late as 1841, William Savage thought that "Fine printing . . . . is the art of obtaining impressions from an engraving on wood, of the surface and the surface only, so as to produce the effect which the artist intended, in the highest state of perfection."[2] It must be emphasized that at first the new white-line engravings, made popular by Bewick and his followers, presented considerable difficulty to the pressman.[3] Unless the greatest care was taken in their inking and impression the results were deplorable. This was specially the case when the old presses were used. The introduction of the iron press made possible the evolution of a new technique, which is the real foundation of letterpress printing as we understand it to-day. It is probable, therefore, that exact methods of presswork were not primarily evolved for the perfection of letterpress, but for obtaining the best possible results from white-line wood engravings, with their delicate incisions and variations in tone.

The new technique at press was in all respects the reverse of the old : a hard packing replaced the blankets and a "kiss" impression took the place of one that was heavy and crushing. The paper was printed dry instead of damp. Even impression was

---

[1] For an account of the cult, reference should be made to the works of Thomas Frognall Dibdin, chronicler and high-priest of the movement, also to Jackson, Holbrook, *The Anatomy of Bibliomania* (London, 1930).

[2] *Dictionary of Printing*, art. Engravings on Wood.

[3] The matter is discussed at some length in Chatto, W. A., and Jackson, J., *A Treatise on Wood Engraving*. Second edition by H. G. Bohn. (London, 1861.)

obtained by a process known as "make-ready." This involved, then as now, building up a series of thin paper overlays on the tympan sheet in places where the impression was faint, and in cutting away parts where the impression was too heavy. The process was simple enough with text matter, but required some ingenuity in the case of engravings with a considerable variation of colour.

Soft packing, heavy impression and damp paper were used in machine printing until the end of the century, when the introduction of accurately designed presses, such as Robert Miehle's two-revolution machine, made it possible to duplicate the best hand-press work by adopting hand-press technique.[1]

. . . . . .

It will be noticed that in 1866 no alteration was made in the pressmen's Piece Scale. Two years later, W. H. Blatchley gave evidence before the "Commissioners appointed to inquire into the Organisation and Rules of Trades Unions and other Associations."[2] He stated that their original Scale was now something of a dead letter. It had formerly been drafted for charging rough work, but now that make-ready was expected on a great many jobs, it was impossible to charge the old rates. A contract price was therefore made between master and man. Should special care be needed, 8*d*. or 9*d*. per hour would be asked instead of the usual 7*d*. The old Scale was still used, but only for posters, small runs of pamphlets and cheap jobbing work.

[DOCUMENT LXXXVII]

AGREEMENT WITH THE PRESSMEN [3]

Resolutions agreed upon November 27, 1866 :—

1. That the Establishment Wages be 36*s*. per week of 60 hours, the apportionment of the 60 hours to be mutually agreed upon between the Employers and Journeymen in each office.

---

[1] The first attempts were made in the U.S.A. About 1875, T. L. de Vinne experimented with some success in printing the "cut" formes of the *Century Magazine* on dry paper ". . . producing a more brilliant effect from fine engravings than had been thought possible." *American Dictionary of Printing* (1894), art. De Vinne.

[2] Tenth Report, p. 101.

[3] The Agreement with the Machine Minders was substantially the same. J. Shreeve, Secretary of the Printing Machine Managers' Trade Society, also gave evidence to the 1868 Commission. He stated that his Society was then twenty-nine years old. It was, therefore, founded in 1839. In 1838, according to Charles Knight, there were from 300 to 400 machine men in London who were paid 32*s*. to 42*s*. per week. *The Guide to Trade*, p. 53.

2. That Overtime be paid for at the rate of 3*d*. extra per hour after 9 o'clock in the evening till 6 o'clock in the morning, provided that when the Pressman having worked during the night, is required to continue working after 6 a.m., he is to be paid 3*d*. per hour extra till 8 a.m. No charge to be made of less than 1*s*. extra between the hours of 10 p.m. and 6 a.m.

Schedule of Prices for Overtime :—

			s.	*d.*							*s.*	*d.*
From 9 till 10	..	..	0	3	From 9 till 4	..	..	..	2	0
,, 9 ,, 11	..	..	1	0	,, 9 ,, 5	..	..	..	2	3
,, 9 ,, 12	..	..	1	0	,, 9 ,, 6	..	..	..	2	6
,, 9 ,, 1	..	..	1	3	,, 9 ,, 7	..	..	..	2	9
,, 9 ,, 2	..	..	1	6	,, 9 ,, 8	..	..	..	3	0
,, 9 ,, 3	..	..	1	9						

Provided also—That no Pressman be required to work more than 10½ hours per day without being paid 3*d*. per hour as Overtime.

3. That Sunday work be paid for at the rate of 6*d*. extra per hour; but that in no case shall the Pressman receive less than 2*s*. 6*d*. extra.

4. That Pressmen employed on Time for any portion of a day be paid at the rate of 7½*d*. per hour, and that after the first hour time shall be reckoned in half-hours.

5. That, in lieu of an advance upon agreed piece work, which, from the frequent abandonment of the Scale, would be beset with difficulties, the deductions for proof-pulling and wetting be discontinued.

6. That these Resolutions take effect on and after the third day of December next.

(*Signed*)

On behalf of the Masters.	*On behalf of the Pressmen.*
Robert Kingston Burt, *Chairman*	E. Eatley, *Chairman*
Wm. Clowes.	A. S. Froom.
George Levey.	J. Staines.
Wm. Rivington.	J. Dickinson.
	J. P. Killingback.

CHAPTER XII

THE APPRENTICE QUESTION
(1835-1896)

Discontents caused by the excessive number of apprentices were as prevalent in the 1830s as during the first decade of the century. According to the Annual Report of the L.U.C. for 1835, there were then 500 apprentices as against 1,750 journeymen in Union offices. The same Report also published two resolutions passed at a Meeting held on 2 February, 1836. It is improbable, however, that these regulations were strictly obeyed.

That no journeyman compositor shall be allowed to bring up more than one boy or apprentice to the business, or more than one in a year.

That no journeyman shall be allowed to bring up more than one son to the business, without being bound to an employer.

The Annual Report for 1839 gave the number of men and boys in ninety-five London offices as 1,343 and 534 respectively. There were at that date approximately 300 printing houses in the metropolis.[1]

It is probable that the compiler of the 1839 Report based his list on one of the guides issued for the benefit of the trade. I have inserted the addresses and the side headings showing the geographical situation of the various firms as given by Cowie, and also indicated, where known, the type of work done. An asterisk after the name of a firm indicates that the concern still exists (1945) under the same name.

[DOCUMENT LXXXVIII]

	Blackfriars, etc.			MEN	BOYS	
1.	Baldwin ..	..	..	47	12	Union Street. (*The Standard* newspaper. Books.)
2.	Davidson..	..	..	12	6	Tudor Street. (Books.)

[1] Cowie, G., *Printer's Pocket Book and Manual*, third edition (London, c. 1836-7), lists 280 names and addresses. The seventh edition, published c. 1842, lists 309 firms.

	Fleet Street, etc.			MEN	BOYS	
3.	Neal	..	.. ..	2	—	7, Fleet Lane.
4.	Hill	..	.. ..	1	5	Black Horse Court.
5.	Wood	..	..	3	12	18, Poppin's Court.
6.	Cunningham		..	15	12	Crown Court.
7.	Bentley	..	..	18	9	Bangor House, Shoe Lane. (Books.)
8.	Whitehead		..	8	5	——
9.	Hughes	..	..	3	1	King's Head Court, Shoe Lane.
10.	Mills & Co.	..	..	2	6	Crane Court. (Successors to Bensley.)
11.	Tyler	..	.. ..	30	15	Bolt Court.
12.	Leighton	..	..	8	3	11, Johnson's Court.
13.	Evans & Co.	..	..	2	1	——
14.	Nuttall & Co.	..	..	5	5	
15.	M'Dowall		..	32	11	4, Gough Square.
16.	Macintosh		..	20	7	Great New Street.
17.	Hartnell	..	..	8	4	Red Lion Passage. (Stationery Office contracts.)
18.	Taylor, R.★	..	..	21	14	Red Lion Court. (Periodicals.)
19.	Palmer & Co. (Clayton)	..		16	4	Crane Court.
20.	Last	..	.. ..	6	1	——
21.	Riley	..	.. ..	1	1	10, Gough Square.
22.	Bradbury & Co. (Evans)★			43	19	Lombard St., Whitefriars. (Later printers of *Punch*.)
23.	Rayner & Co. (Hodges)	..		12	6	109, Fetter Lane.
24.	Shaw & Co.★	..	..	18	4	137, Fetter Lane. (Local Government work.)
25.	Wilcoxson		.. ..	6	1	Rolls Bdgs., Fetter Lane.
26.	Roworth★		.. ..	17	5	Bell Yard. (Books and general.)
27.	Stevens	..	.. ..	17	5	Bell Yard.

	Temple Bar to Westminster.					
28.	Watts	..	.. ..	9	8	12, Crown Court, Pickett Street. (Law and Oriental Printing.)
29.	Kelly	..	.. ..	13	5	Old Boswell Court. (Directories.)
30.	Rogerson	..	..	13	10	24, Norfolk Street.
31.	White	..	.. ..	—	1	——
32.	Berger	..	.. ..	2	2	1, Bell Yard, Strand.
33.	Hetherington		..	2	1	126, Strand. (Radical periodicals.)
34.	Limbird	..	..	1	2	143, Strand. (Radical periodicals.)
35.	Ibotson & Co. (Palmer)	..		21	6	Savoy Street.

Temple Bar to West-
minster—contd.   MEN BOYS

			MEN	BOYS	
36.	Whiting ..	.. ..	17	8	Beaufort Buildings, Strand, (Colour printing.)
37.	Norman ..	.. ..	20	4	29, Maiden Lane.
38.	Clowes★ ..	..	21	16	14, Charing Cross. (Books and government contracts.)
39.	Nichols ..	.. ..	24	6	King Street, Westminster. (House of Commons' *Votes, Gents.' Mag.*)

Long Acre to Piccadilly.

40.	Gadsden ..	.. ..	3	1	100, St. Martin's Lane.
41.	Harrison★	.. ..	40	14	St. Martin's Lane. (War and Foreign Offices.)
42.	Richards ..	..	18	8	100, St. Martin's Lane.
43.	Levey (Franklyn) & Co. ..		16	4	60, St. Martin's Lane.
44.	Saville ..	.. ..	15	9	107, St. Martin's Lane. (Books.)
45.	Moyes ..	.. ..	27	10	Castle Street, Leicester Sq. (Now Strangeways Press.)
46.	M'Gowan	.. ..	3	3	16, Great Windmill Street. (Periodicals and newspapers.)
47.	Crozier ..	.. ..	1	3	37, Silver Street.

Tottenham Court Road.

48.	Bradley ..	.. ..	2	—	78, Great Titchfield Street.

Oxford Street.

49.	Reynell ..	.. ..	26	11	18, Little Pulteney Street. (Periodicals.)
50.	Gardiner & Co. ..	..	3	—	Princes St., Cavendish Sq.

Holborn.

51.	Hansard (Old House) ..		53	5	Tichborne Court. (House of Commons' printing.)
52.	Hansard (New House) ..		41	1	Parker Street, Drury Lane. (House of Commons' printing.)
53.	Cox, W. H.	.. ..	7	7	Parker Street, Drury Lane.
54.	Cox & Sons	.. ..	37	10	75, Great Queen Street. (Now Wyman's.)
55.	Cousins ..	.. ..	5	5	18, Duke Street.
56.	Spetigue ..	..	2	7	67, Chancery Lane.
57.	Whittingham	..	9	7	21, Took's Court. (Now *Chiswick Press*. Books.)
58.	Holmes ..	.. ..	7	7	4, Took's Court.
59.	Green ..	.. ..	6	3	—
60.	Hodson ..	.. ..	9	2	15, Cross St., Hatton Gdn.

Clerkenwell.	MEN	BOYS	
61. Roche	2	5	23, Gloucester Street.
62. Gilbert & Co. (Rivington)	68	18	St. John's Square. (Theological and Oriental.)

Bartholomew Close.			
63. Rider	10	6	14, Little Britain. (Theological.)
64. Adlard★	4	6	22, Bartholomew Close. (Founded *c.* 1767.)
65. Compton & Co. (Ritchie)	4	3	23, Middle St., Cloth Fair.

Skinner Street.			
66. Woodfall	24	4	Angel Court, Skinner Street. (Books.)
67. Kinder	14	2	Green Arbour Court, Old Bailey.
68. Stewart & Co. (Murray) ..	18	5	Angel Court, Skinner Street.
69. Knight	6	1	——

Paternoster Row.			
70. Hansard	22	6	Paternoster Row. (Hansard's *Debates*.)
71. Pitman	5	3	Warwick Square.
72. Thoms	10	5	Warwick Square.
73. Stevens	7	3	Warwick Lane.

Cheapside to Aldgate.			
74. Clay★	26	14	8, Bread Street Hill. (Books.)
75. Lewis	2	1	21, Finch Lane, Cornhill.
76. Unwin★	5	4	Bucklersbury.
77. Smith	5	5	Corner of Mincing Lane.
78. Darling	6	3	31, Leadenhall Street. (Later Stat. Off. contractors.)

Lombard Street to Whitechapel.			
79. Rickerby	4	7	3, Abchurch Lane.
80. Blades & Co. (East)★ ..	3	1	11, Abchurch Lane. (Now Cheque and Security printers.)
81. Marchant	9	4	Ingram Ct., Fenchurch St.
82. John(s ?)ton	12	6	13, Mark Lane.
83. Maurice	6	4	4, Howford Buildings, Fenchurch Street.

Upper Thames Street, etc.			
84. Renshaw	4	—	Budge Row.

Gracechurch Street to
*   Shoreditch.*   MEN BOYS

		MEN	BOYS	
85.	Balne	11	—	38, Gracechurch Street. (Colour printing.)
86.	Dean & Co. (Munday) ..	6	6	Threadneedle Street.
87.	Varty	7	3	Camomile St., Bishopsgate.

Eastcheap.

88.	Skipper	5	5	St. Dunstans Hill.

St. Martin's-le-Grand to
*   Islington.*

89.	Doudney..	7	6	Corner of Long Lane.
90.	Clarke	15	2	1, Dudley Court, Silver St.
91.	Norris	7	4	138, Aldersgate Street.
92.	Fisher	8	4	Angel Street.

Barbican to Hoxton.

93.	Haddon*	15	12	Castle Street, Tabernacle Walk. (Now printers' suppliers.)
94.	Wertheimer	13	5	Finsbury Crescent. (Now Williams, Lea.)

Surrey Side and Borough.

95.	Clowes*	125	24	Duke Street, Stamford St. (Books, periodicals, Stat Off. contracts.)
		1,343	534	

From the numbers in the returns we shall therefore not err in assuming, that if the proportion in those offices which have made no returns be the same as in those that have, the number of apprentices in book offices and weekly newspapers must be nearly 700.

In the year 1836, the attention of the trade was called to this subject, and in 1837 a specific proposition for limiting the number of apprentices was brought before a general meeting. At that time the number of apprentices was considered to be about 500. In the short space of three years that number has increased to 700.

In April, 1841, the following resolution was passed at a general meeting of the L.U.C. It is extracted from the Annual Report for the Years 1840–41.

[DOCUMENT LXXXIX]

That this meeting views the late increase of apprentices with feelings of alarm, and that it pledges itself to assist the respectable master-printers of the metropolis in restricting them to the following proportion—viz. One apprentice to every four journeymen employed throughout the year, and for which purpose it is hereby resolved that no journeyman shall bring up more than one son to the business until the number shall be reduced within the above bounds, and that no journeyman shall bring up or assist therein any apprentice in any establishment where such proportion is not observed.

A Memorial was sent to the employers on 4 May, 1841, with a request that the above proportion of apprentices to journeymen should not be exceeded. It is stated that there were 700 apprentices at case in London, and that the number of journeymen in book-offices amounted to about 2,000; and if the newspaper compositors were included that not less than 3,000 men were employed in the composing department of the printing business. According to the annual reports of the L.U.C. for the years 1840 and 1841 combined, the men met with some success in their endeavours to limit the number of boys engaged in the London trade.

From the condensed mode of printing, and the practice of stereo-typing all successful works, full employment for 3,000 persons is not afforded; and a considerable number of compositors therefore cannot obtain any employment for several weeks in the year, while the earnings of a vast proportion of those who hold situations in the book offices vary from 15s. to 20s., and from 20s. to 25s. per week, upon an average throughout the year.

The status of Turnovers was examined in an appendix to the first Annual Report of the London Society of Compositors, read at a general meeting held 4 February, 1846. The following extract is from the Committee's Address on the subject of Apprentices and Turnovers :—

[DOCUMENT XC]

A turnover, at the present day, is a person who seems to possess an undisputed right to traverse the trade in search of the most profitable employment, or to locate himself in an office that will best suit his quali-fication and purpose. For these privileges he is content to make a reduction in his week's wages, shielding himself under the assumed guard of being an apprentice, or one who is serving his seven years to the trade. We are disposed to deny to such a person the right to do anything of the kind, believing that there should be but three grades, viz. the master, the journeyman, and the apprentice. If he pretends to be the latter, he cannot possess the liberty of going from house to house, as he does now, in search of work; and the power to refuse doing any kind of composition but that which is the most lucrative. No, the duty of an apprentice is known to be bona fide; he is the servant of his master, and cannot leave him without his sanction, and his indentures being transferred to another employer.

(The Executive have resolved, "That persons known in the business as *turnovers* shall no longer be recognised—they must be turned over to an employer by a legal or written witnessed agreement; and unless this agreement or indenture be produced, at the completion of their servitude, they shall not be eligible to become members of this Society.")

An essay entitled "The Disease and the Remedy," by Edward Edwards, the first Secretary of the re-established London Society of Compositors, appeared in 1850.[1] His thesis was that the distressed state of the printing trade was "mainly attributable to excessive boy labour."

[DOCUMENT XCI]

Observe, however, what the introduction of so many boys has led to. It has given birth to practices decidedly detrimental to the employment of capital. The *farming* system owes its existence to the large number of boys and turnovers partially initiated in the business, who work for half wages, and, upon newspaper composition, set up a goodly number of types. This plan is the annihilator of masters' profits. Newspapers and periodicals which, but for it, would be done in respectable offices, are now printed by individuals possessing all the advantages and none of the responsibilities of mastership. Some of the followers of this mode of working apprentice lads in the usual way. A change takes place, consequent upon some person underbidding the present holder. The boys are then turned on the trade, as the newcomer has some of his own, by agreement, to employ, or he obtains lads who will work for less money. Yet what are such men ? Not master printers, but working conductors; who contract to perform a given amount of work for less money than, as journeymen, they would be paid for the same. Who can question the wrong that has thus been done to the employers? Yet the whole plan would tumble to pieces, like a house of cards, if its chief support—boy labour—were withdrawn.

And, again, who has failed to remark the lamentable incapacity of journeymen to discharge the duties of a compositor ? Good practical workmen are, year by year, decreasing in numbers. Taste in display how few men possess serviceable ideas of? Rule-work is but imperfectly understood; and intricate or difficult composition frightens many. This is not to be wondered at. We should rather be surprised to see even so much ability prevalent. What knowledge of his business can that man have who has served seven years' apprenticeship on the *Times* newspaper ? All he knows of his business is the composition of advertisements and such like matter. The same question may be asked respecting the acquirements of those persons who have been bound to newspaper proprietors. Boys, in large numbers, throughout the empire, during their servitude, are never called upon, or taught how, to make up a 12mo. page, impose a sheet of 18mo, or set a title or dedication page ! Incapacity of workmen (organic defect excepted) is entirely owing to imperfect tuition; and we hold it to be totally imprac-

---

[1] It was first published in *The Typographical Protection Circular* (February, 1850) and subsequently reprinted in pamphlet form.

ticable for a boy working exclusively on a newspaper, to master the "art and mystery of a compositor." The system of *clicking*, either by placing lads in companionships with journeymen, or causing them to work together with a maker-up at their head, is another reason why so many indifferent workmen are to be found. The real art of the trade is centred in one particular person, the clicker; and the remainder of the companionship are but one remove from the position of those described as working on newspapers.

As Secretary of the L.S.C., Edwards had access to well-authenticated information, and the statistics showing the rates of payment and number of men and apprentices in seventy-nine provincial towns, printed below, are of considerable value.

It will be noted that the wage rates for Oxford and Cambridge were high in comparison with those of other towns of similar size. This is accounted for by the presence of the University printing offices, where skilled, and therefore highly paid, compositors were required for the execution of works in foreign and exotic languages. Good prices were also paid at Hertford, a small country town, where Stephen Austin's establishment made a speciality of Oriental printing.

Table showing the rate of wages per week, number of journeymen and apprentices, and unfair offices in seventy-nine towns of the United Kingdom :—

NAME OF TOWN	RATE OF WAGES	No. OF JOURNEY-MEN	No. OF APPREN-TICES	No. OF UNFAIR HOUSES
	Shillings			
Aylesbury	24	9	9	0
Banbury	24	9	5	0
Bath	25	64	49	0
Bedford	21—24	12	20	0
Berwick-on-Tweed	18—20	10	15	0
Bradford	24—26	18	26	0
Brecon	23	5	4	0
Brighton	29	30	50	2
Bristol	24—25	120	100	0
Bolton	27	12	22	3
Blackburn	24	7	12	2
Canterbury	20—24	10	18	4
Chichester	21—30	3	2	0
Cardiff	21—24	16	11	0
Chester	27	31	17	0
Cheltenham	24	24	33	0
Cambridge	27—40	67	35	1

20

Name of Town	Rate of Wages	No. of Journey-men	No. of Appren-tices	No. of Unfair Houses
	Shillings			
Durham	21	23	24	1
Darlington	18—24	11	11	0
Doncaster	22—24	20	14	0
Dover..	21	7	14	0
Exeter	18—19	30	50	0
Hereford	21—24	17	12	0
Halifax	24	24	18	0
Hertford	28	10	7	0
Huddersfield	24	10	16	2
Isle of Man	12—20	10	58	0
Kendal	24	12	14	0
London	33—48	3000	1500	6
Liverpool and Birkenhead ..	30	280	100	20
Leeds	26	118	50	1
Lancaster	24	10	10	6
Leigh	24	2	2	0
Leicester	24	30	30	0
Lewes	29	18	20	2
Maidstone	24—25	13	17	0
Manchester	30	300	80	5
Macclesfield	18—24	11	7	0
Nottingham	27	55	60	3
Newport (Mon.)	21—24	12	10	0
Northampton	24	11	22	0
Oxford	30—33	58	46	0
Preston	27	36	28	5
Portsmouth and Portsea ..	21—28	20	20	0
Rochdale	24	6	8	0
Scarborough	21	11	6	0
Sheffield	28	62	32	3
Southampton	20—25	21	22	0
South Shields	21—24	15	8	0
Stafford	24	11	7	0
Shrewsbury	24	22	23	0
Stamford	27	22	13	0
Ulverstone	21	6	14	0
Warwick and Leamington ..	21—25	29	12	4
Wakefield	24	14	24	1
Worcester	24	31	19	2
Warrington	24	4	7	1
Woking	27	8	6	0
Wolverhampton	24	25	22	0
Wigan	27	11	7	0
Yeovil	21	4	15	0
York	24—26	40	30	0
		4,937	2,943	74

SCOTLAND

NAME OF TOWN	RATE OF WAGES	NO. OF JOURNEY-MEN	NO. OF APPREN-TICES	NO. OF UNFAIR HOUSES
	Shillings			
Dundee	20—21	40	35	0
Edinburgh	25	598	329	0
Glasgow	25	280	150	0
Kilmarnock	20	6	6	0
Perth	20	21	18	0
Stirling	20	9	12	0
		954	550	0

IRELAND

NAME OF TOWN	RATE OF WAGES	NO. OF JOURNEY-MEN	NO. OF APPREN-TICES	NO. OF UNFAIR HOUSES
Belfast	25	63	100	0
Cork	20—26	58	32	5
Dublin	30—32/6	380	270	11
Galway	15	9	5	1
Kilkenny	20—21	10	8	0
Londonderry..	18—21	12	24	0
Omagh and Armagh ..	15	12	22	0
Sligo	12—15	4	14	0
		548	475	17

RECAPITULATION

NAME OF TOWN	RATE OF WAGES	NO. OF JOURNEY-MEN	NO. OF APPREN-TICES	NO. OF UNFAIR HOUSES
London	33—48	3000	1500	6
England and Wales	18—30	1937	1443	64
Scotland	20—25	954	550	0
Ireland	12—32/6	548	475	17
		6,439	3,968	87

This table is presumptive evidence—considering the number of towns unnoticed, and their known appreciation of boy-labour—that the following

Statement of the numbers of the trade (case in London, press and case elsewhere) approximates to correctness :—

London*	..	..	..	3,000	1,500
Provinces of England and Wales				2,500	2,000
Scotland	..	..	..	1,500	1,200
Ireland ..	..	..	..	1,500	1,300
				8,500	6,000	14,500**

* In London there are, besides the numbers stated, 850 men and 450 boys, who work exclusively at the press.[1]

** There are printed in London, 50 weekly, 294 monthly, and 55 quarterly publications. The majority of the weeklies, and about 100 of the monthlies, are chiefly composed by boys; but the quarterlies are mostly done by the journeymen. In the United Kingdom there are 14 daily papers, 18 tri-weekly papers, 41 bi-weekly ones, and 403 weekly journals; total 476. Of these, 84 are printed in London; 238 in the provinces of England and Wales; 70 in Scotland; and 84 in Ireland.

On the London daily press 460 men are employed.

In 1867 a Sub-Committee was appointed by the L.S.C. to examine and report on a number of questions, including the "Turnover System."[2] Ninety-nine offices supplied information, and it was established that in them there were employed 2,344 journeymen as against 547 apprentices and 103 turnovers. The proportion of apprentices and turnovers to journeymen was, therefore, 2—7½.

[1] "The 'aristocratical few' of this part of the business have for some years separated themselves into sections—comfortable little *coteries*—nicknamed Gifts, and to the institution of these miserable monopolies all the disturbances known are assignable. Six of these bureaucracies are now in actual confederation. Four of them number about 60 men each; another has 45; and the sixth 25; so that, in all, there may be said to be 310 'Gift men,' leaving full 490 others unconnected with these lordly formations. In this way London is geographically subdivided, each district having its 'Gift,' and of course its own particular connections, there being a slate kept at each 'Gift' house, on which those out of work belonging to the Society insert their names. The qualification of a 'Gift man' is, *that he shall not be, at time of joining, 45 years of age;* and to this is added an understanding or agreement, *that he shall not acquaint any but his own Gift men where employment is to be obtained.* By such agency, about 300 men arrogantly attempt to monopolize all the press-work of the metropolis, shutting out from their select circles all men of middle age, and withholding from their fellow workmen that knowledge by which the labour of the trade may be generally diffused and properly executed." (*The Typographical Protection Circular*, November, 1849.)

[2] *Report of the Sub-Committee to the Trade Committee on the Prices paid for the Composition of Books of Reference; the Standard adopted by Founders to gauge the relative Thicknesses of the different letters in a Fount; and the Turnover System.* (n.d.)

[DOCUMENT XCII]

With regard to the mode of paying Turnovers, there seems to be little variation, the general report being that they receive half their earnings on news, and two-thirds on book-work, while in some few instances they are placed on the establishment, receiving from 13s. to £1 a week.

And with respect to the answers received as to the practice adopted in dealing with Turnovers, the general tenor is that the Turnovers come and go as they like, while in two or three instances it is stated that the firm holds their indentures, or has them re-bound; but this is very exceptional, and the same laxity appears to have been generally adopted by the Chapels in regard to Turnovers, they seldom interfere in the matter.

It was established that out of 92 replies to the query as to the method generally pursued by the firm in training apprentices, so as to qualify them as efficient workmen on the expiry of apprenticeship, 46 stated that no set instruction was given, in 12 instances partial instruction was given at the outset, and in 34 offices a fair amount of teaching was provided. A letter was sent to the employers with the request that they should "adopt such a system as will secure to their apprentices a larger amount of instruction in the various branches of the business than is at present apparent." No reply was received.

The subject was re-examined ten years later, when a report was issued, of which the first portion only is here reprinted. In the part that is omitted was discussed the motion of limiting the period of apprenticeship to five years. This suggestion was not adopted then or subsequently.

[DOCUMENT XCIII]

Report of the Special Committee on the Apprenticeship Question, appointed at the 117th Quarterly Delegate Meeting, held on the 28th of February, 1877.

Gentlemen,

Although the Committee on the above question was appointed in February last, there have been only 15 meetings since its nomination; various causes combining to prevent more frequent sittings, in addition to it having been imperatively necessary to obtain the fullest possible information upon a matter involving such vital interests. It is worthy of remembrance that attempts have been made to deal with the same question on four previous occasions during the last forty years, viz., in 1837, 1840, 1847, and 1867.

After a lapse of ten years, then, when there prevails a growing demand for technical education, and when it has been emphatically proclaimed that there shall be at least an universal education, the present is perhaps an opportune period for once more considering the question of apprentice labour. If, therefore, the subject be approached in a spirit of impartiality, and an attempt be made to deal with it by the light of that advancement which the last decade has reflected, the result may prove of no inconsiderable advantage, notwithstanding the difficulties to be overcome and the inefficiency of the efforts hitherto attempted.

The following is a summary of the returns made on five occasions of the subject being inquired into :—

Year	Houses	Journeymen	Apprentices	Turnovers	Proportion
					A. J.
1837	94	1,110	425	..	2—5
1840	95	1,343	534	..	2—5
1847	124	1,901	495	140	2—6
1867	99	2,344	547	103	2—7½
1877	180	3,601	961	112	2—6⅔

By the above returns of the proportion of boys to journeymen in the two periods of 1867 and 1877 the average appears to be slightly in favour of the former period; but as in 1877 returns were obtained from houses which would perhaps not have given them had not special and exceptional means been adopted, it may be assumed that the actual average of journeymen to boys at the present is quite equal to any former period.

As a preliminary measure in the present inquiry a circular, containing ten queries, was issued; but the returns not being so complete as desired, a personal application was made to those from whom no replies had been received, resulting in the fullest returns that have ever been made upon any question submitted.

The following comprise the ten queries referred to, and a summary of the answers :—

QUESTIONS

1. The number of journeymen employed ?

2. The number of apprentices, and how paid ?

3. The number of turnovers, if any, and their mode of payment ?

ANSWERS

Returns were made from 180 houses, employing 3,601 journeymen (exclusive of the daily papers), 961 apprentices, and 112 turnovers.

Nine hundred and sixty-one. An establishment payment adopted in the great majority of cases, at all events for a considerable portion of the term; the returns showing that in 122 houses an establishment payment was in existence while piece rates were adopted in only 37.

One hundred and twelve. In some few cases turnovers taken in a legitimate manner, and treated as regards payment, as house apprentices; but in the greater number of instances treated

QUESTIONS

ANSWERS

merely in the light of cheap journeymen, and set to work on remunerative matter (chiefly newspaper) at reduced prices, the firms getting the advantage of the reduction and giving nothing in return. The number of houses are—piece payment, 22; establishment, 11; but where the establishment rate is adopted, the number of apprentices is small, while in those cases where large numbers are employed, they are invariably paid on the piece.

4. The practice adopted by the firm with regard to turnovers?

In 21 cases rebound or possession of indentures demanded by the firm, and terms of service indorsed on them; but in 21 other cases (more particularly where any large number are employed) taken on much in the same way as journeymen, with power on their own part or that of their employer to determine the engagement at a moment's notice or, at all events, in a week, and without showing any right to work at the trade at all.

5. The practice adopted by the Chapel with regard to turnovers, more particularly with reference to Rule X?[1]

Rule almost invariably ignored; in a few cases an effort appears to have been made to carry it out, but in the great majority no notice at all taken of the existence of such a safeguard. In only 7 Chapels is any attention paid to the rule, while in 28 it is entirely neglected.

6. The method generally pursued by the firm in training apprentices, so as to qualify them as efficient workmen on the expiry of apprenticeship?

In the larger number left to pick up what they can how they can; in several intrusted to the general supervision and occasional teaching of the overseer; in some few large houses formed into an apprentice companionship under the management of an establishment clicker; and in 12 cases only placed under efficient tuition (either companionship or individual), and the teaching paid for by bonus or a proportion of earnings.

7. Has there been any improvement or deterioration in the general capacity of boys placed in the business during the past four years?

Answers rather vague, but a pretty general impression that the class of boys brought into the business is not so good as formerly. Where a decided reply is given the consensus of opinion points to deterioration.

---

[1] L.S.C. Rules. The text of the rule is substantially the same as that of the resolution passed on 4 February, 1846. See p. 304 *supra.*

QUESTIONS

ANSWERS

8. Does a system exist in the office in which you are employed of placing boys at case before being bound and, if so, for how long a period ?

Great laxity exists in many cases. An almost universal custom of some probation, but in about 30 cases prolonged to an unreasonable extent—9 or 12 months, or even longer. In other firms apprentices (nominal) working for years before indenture executed, which is not done in at least one large firm until completion of term.

9. Are there any apprentices serving according to the provisions contained in the note to Rule V., viz. "A compositor's eldest son can serve without indenture, but must prove that he has served seven years to the business" ?

Custom dying out and almost extinct. Only 25 apprentices working under these conditions, viz.:—

15 houses with 1 apprentice each.
3   ,,   ,, 2 apprentices ,,
1   ,,   ,, 4   ,,   ,,

10. State the relative number of journeymen, apprentices, and turnovers employed in March, 1872, and at the present time ?

Returns not sufficiently complete or certain to give them any value; but evidence that there had not been any organized or extended attempt to import an undue proportion of apprentice labour during the last five years. At the same time two or three large firms have certainly considerably increased the number of their apprentices during that time.

*Analysis of the Comparative Number of Journeymen and Apprentices**

	Houses	Journeymen	Apprentices
Where apprentices equal or exceed journeymen	19	136	172
Where the proportion of journeymen to apprentices does not exceed 2 to 1	34	502	304
Where the proportion of journeymen to apprentices does not exceed 3 to 1	34	563	216
Where the proportion of journeymen to apprentices exceeds 3 to 1 ..	76	2,276	381

* For the purposes of this statement apprentices and turnovers are treated together, the relative proportions being 961 apprentices and 112 turnovers.

In 17 houses 124 journeymen are employed without any apprentices. The daily newspaper offices, employing journeymen only, are not included in this statement.

In a group of 7 houses in the first classification there were 61 journeymen to 90 apprentices—one house returning 5 journeymen to 15 apprentices.

In a group of 18 houses in the fourth classification there were 1002 journeymen to 122 apprentices—two of these houses giving a proportion of 220 journeymen to 19 apprentices.

In dealing with the foregoing questions, No. 1 presents various phases : 3,601 journeymen (exclusive of 542 newspaper hands, together showing 4,143 journeymen) as compared with 1,073 apprentices and turnovers, presenting an average of nearly 3⅓ journeymen to one boy, thus comparing favourably with those branches of the trade in the metropolis which have made the limitation of apprentices one of their fundamental principles; the Machine Managers and Pressmen's Societies stipulating for one apprentice where only one journeyman is employed, two apprentices to four journeymen, and an additional apprentice to every three additional journeymen who have been employed for six months consecutively, or a fraction under three journeymen to one apprentice. Unfortunately, however, the question presents other and altogether opposite phases, as shown in the analysis at the end of the ten questions, namely—on the one hand 19 houses employing together only 136 journeymen, but 172 boys; on the other, 76 houses employing together 2,276 journeymen, but only 381 boys. To cope with this vast disparity in the proportionate numbers has been one of the chief difficulties of your Committee, and will form the subject of special comment, conjoined with the apprentice period of servitude, in another portion of this report.

Regarding the remaining queries and the answers thereto, they are but adjuncts to the main question. It may be gathered from them, however, that apprentices are principally paid at an establishment rate of wage; that the method pursued by firms in training them is far from satisfactory, as they are mostly left more to chance than to any other influence, which, combined with the fact that boys of an inferior status are put to the trade, renders a deterioration of their general capacity an obvious consequence.

Turnovers, however, are treated very differently, in some few instances only being dealt with legitimately, the vast majority being utilized as cheap journeymen (mainly on newspapers), an entirely one-sided arrangement on the part of the firms employing them, who make as much as possible out of their labour, but teach them nothing in return; and as they are retained at the option of their employers, turnovers are frequently incapacitated from showing any right to work at the trade at all. But with respect to this particular element of the question the returns show that great remissness has prevailed with Chapels, as, notwithstanding the existence of a rule appertaining to the class of persons referred to, the application of Rule X (stipulating that all turnovers shall be rebound to an employer) has virtually become obsolete. Your Committee therefore recommend that a probationary period of one month prior to being rebound be a stipulation in regard to all turnovers entering a house, and that the condition be strenuously enforced in every instance.

That the evils attendant on the treatment of apprentices and turnovers are sufficiently potent will be readily admitted, but it must also be conceded that many of those evils have been long accruing, and consequently cannot readily be effaced. Nevertheless it is of the highest consequence that remedial measures should be adopted in order to avoid a still further extension of the complaint which would unquestionably affect the interests of the whole body; for if, when arriving at manhood, a compositor discovers that he is wanting in the chief attributes of his craft, that few employ him beyond the urgency of the moment, and that he is more frequently out of work than otherwise, it is but a natural result that he at length accepts any terms obtainable by him.

With a view therefore of attaining greater efficiency amongst journeymen, it is recommended that a circular to master printers be issued by the executive of the Society, urging employers to an equitable fulfilment of their part of the contract with apprentices, pointing out the custom which existed years ago of placing boys under the tuition of competent workmen, and recommending a return thereto; advocating also the desirability of teaching apprentices more ample details of their trade, not only for the boys' sake, but as a means of their becoming of greater utility to employers themselves. And in the event of failing to obtain any concessions, then, in justice to fair employers, to apprentices, and to the journeymen of the future, it is recommended that every effort be made to obtain parliamentary and other powers to enforce such conditions as shall provide for the effectual training of those who are now treated by many as mere factors for gain, utterly regardless of every other consideration. Acting in conjunction with other recommendations to follow, the foregoing will, it is thought, effect proportionate results.

Respecting evils of a more general character, which, it may be acknowledged, have developed mainly from laxity on the part of our own Members, two may be here cited :—(1.) The existence of a system of placing boys at case for lengthened periods prior to being indentured. (2.) A practice prevailing amongst Members of the Society of accepting engagements in other offices than those in which they are regularly employed, assisting not unfrequently in making-up matter which has been composed entirely by boys. In reference to the first mentioned, it is recommended that a probationary period of not more than one month be allowed, and that this condition be strictly enforced. With regard to the last mentioned, that Chapels be instructed to exercise every available influence to prevent Members from accepting engagements under such circumstances, and report to the Executive any Member so contravening the spirit of the rules. It is also recommended to abolish entirely the provisions contained in the note to Rule V., viz. :—"That a compositor's eldest son can serve without indenture, but must prove that he has served seven years to the business." In addition to the custom having become almost extinct, it is advisable to expunge the provision altogether, as by its retention an additional apprentice may be introduced into a house where there is already a fair proportion, and which there is no desire on the part of the firm to increase.

In the course of the inquiry it has been rendered quite manifest that the situations of members are frequently jeopardized by personal efforts to prevent infractions of the rules of the nature here referred to, and in order to minimize such responsibilities, it is recommended that quarterly returns be made from each office, on forms to be provided, of the number of journeymen, apprentices, and turnovers employed therein, together with any special circumstance contrary to the spirit of the rules which may be deemed worthy of notification. By submitting a summary of such returns to the Delegates quarterly, evils may be dealt with at their inception.

In 1896, when the first definitive composing machine Scale was negotiated between masters and men, it was enacted in the first article of the Book Scale that "Apprentices in the last two years of their time can be employed in due proportion to the number of journeymen operators—*i.e.*, one apprentice to three journeymen operators."[1]

Thus for the first time in the history of the London trade there was a convention limiting the apprentices in proportion to the number of journeymen employed. Their restriction in the hand composing room followed as a matter of course.

[1] See p. 506.

CHAPTER XIII

THE SCALE OF 1891

Early in 1890, and for the first time since 1872, the London Society of Compositors decided to memorialize the masters for an advance in prices. The following letter accompanied a voting paper, the answers of the Society's members to nine propositions being required. It was suggested that present conditions in the printing trade justified an attempt to better their lot. The men were reminded of the growth of the establishment system to the detriment of the piece hands, of the many innovations for which the Scale provided no ruling, and of the advantages enjoyed by their brethren in the provinces, where the hours of work were somewhat shorter than those in London.

[DOCUMENT XCIV]

LONDON SOCIETY OF COMPOSITORS

Advance of Wages Movement

Gentlemen,—

At the 168th Quarterly Delegate Meeting, held at the Memorial Hall, Farringdon Street, on Wednesday Evening, February 5th, 1890, it was unanimously resolved, on the recommendation of your Committee, to take a plebiscite of the Members on the propriety of approaching the Employers with the view to an Advance of Wages.

We need scarcely remind you, that the present conditions under which our Members work, were fixed 18 years ago, and that with the exception of the advances obtained in 1866 and 1872, no alteration has been made in the Book Scale since 1847.

That we have not kept pace with the times must be admitted by both Employers and Workmen, many anomalies having crept into the trade as the result of the altered state of things arising from the requirements of modern times. The rapid growth of the 'stab system has rendered the condition of the piece hand in many instances almost unbearable, and without seriously increasing the cost of production, we trust means may be devised whereby the piece hand and the 'stab hand may be placed more on an equality than at present.

In some provincial towns, and also in some parts of Scotland, the working hours have for years been only 51 per week, and while keeping in view the Eight Hour Day, which we hope may at no distant date be secured by

ll trades, we see no reason why an effort should not be made to dispose of
ome of our surplus labour by reducing the working week.

This reduction will however be but of little value unless at the same
ime the Members set their faces against Systematic Overtime, and firmly
ut respectfully decline to kill themselves in order to live. This question
f Overtime we believe to be all important, and in order as far as possible
o reduce it to a minimum, we trust you will empower us to make an effort
o increase the price paid, as we feel convinced such a course is the only
ractical method to be adopted.

While dealing with Overtime in Book and Jobbing Offices, we are con-
inced that the time has arrived when Compositors employed on Weekly
Newspapers should also be paid at the same rate, and we have little doubt
herefore that the Members will desire to so far modify the arrangement
nade with the Weekly Newspaper Proprietors in 1874,[1] as to abolish the
listinction between the Book and News hand in this matter, especially as
oth are frequently employed in the same office.

It is of course impossible to forecast the views and wishes of the Machine
Managers and Pressmen, the former being already far better paid as a rule
han Compositors, owing to the fact that they have no Piece Scale to con-
end with; but it must be patent to all that an alliance for a purpose of
his kind would be mutually advantageous, and would go a long way
o secure an improvement of the condition of all three branches of the
rade.

In asking for power to temporarily increase your subscriptions, we are
ollowing the precedents adopted on former occasions, and although it
loes not follow that we shall call upon you to pay an increased rate, the
ower to do so necessarily places us in a far better position than we shall
therwise be, as it is a practical proof of your earnestness. In addition to
his, it shows the Employers that so far as you are able you are determined
y every legitimate means to enforce if need be any just demand you may
nake, and altogether gives a tone to the movement which cannot be
btained in any other way. In the event of you determining to proceed
vith the matter we have no doubt as to the result of your vote on this
oint, for you have at all times most liberally responded to any similar
all.

In order, as far as possible to ascertain the views and wishes of the mem-
ers generally, we earnestly invite them not only to reply to the proposi-
ions submitted for their consideration, but also to favour us with the
easons which have led them to record their votes either *pro* or *con* as the
ase may be. We shall also be glad if Members will favour us with their
iews, not only on these propositions, but also upon such other phases of
he question as may be germane to the subject matter of this proposed
Advance of Wages Movement, more especially with respect to the mode
f working in their own offices and the best method to be adopted in their
pinion to improve it, together with the result of such experience as they
nay have obtained elsewhere, either in the Metropolis, the Provinces, or
n fact any other country in which they may have been employed.

In entering upon a movement of this character it is obviously impossible

[1] See Document CXII, p. 444.

to foresee what may happen, and it is therefore necessary that you should
place, as we have no doubt you will, the most implicit confidence in your
Executive, as any captious criticism at a time like this would only weaken
our influence and thus prevent us from obtaining that recognition at the
hands of the Employers, which nothing but a bold and united front can
secure. At the same time we shall endeavour to proceed with tact and
discretion, and to assume that such propositions as may ultimately be submitted for the consideration of the Employers will be received by them in
the same spirit in which they are offered, viz., a desire to leave the Printing
Trade of the Metropolis, if possible, in a better condition than we
found it.

In the past all advances in prices, all agreements between masters
and men, had taken the form of amendments and addenda to the
Scale of 1810, and that document was always taken as the basis of
discussion. During the course of eighty-one years the Scale had
become a labyrinth, unsatisfactory to employers and employees
alike. In 1890 the L.S.C. proposed a complete revision of the Scale
for which was to be substituted a document which "while retaining
many of the provisions of the present Scale, would also, as far as
possible, codify the rules and customs of the trade generally, and
contain at the same time such further amendments as in our
opinion are necessary."

The compositors' Memorial and draft for the new Scale were not
presented to the Master Printers until 24 November, 1890, ten
months being required for the compilation of the latter document.

[DOCUMENT XCV]

To the Employers in the Printing Trade of the Metropolis

Gentlemen,—

A wide-spread feeling having existed among the compositors employed
in the various printing offices of the Metropolis that the time had arrived
when an effort should be made to better their condition, a series of questions was submitted to a ballot of the members of the London Society of
Compositors in February last, with the result that the Executive were
authorised to memorialise the Employers for an Advance of Wages and
Revision of the Scales of Prices. After lengthened and very careful consideration by a Committee specially appointed for the purpose, a draft of
the proposed Revised Scale was, in due course, submitted to the Executive
who, having also given it their serious attention, now submit it to the
Employers, with full confidence that it will be favourably received.

When it is borne in mind that the existing Scale for Bookwork was
framed so far back as 1810, no apology can be necessary for an attempt
being made by the compositors to bring this 80-year old document up to
date, in the interest both of employers and workmen. It is true that modi-

fications and alterations were made in the years 1816, 1847, 1866 and 1872, but these changes tended very greatly to complicate matters and to render a proper interpretation of the Scale exceedingly difficult. As, therefore, any further change would necessarily accentuate this state of things, we have deemed it advisable to prepare for your consideration a document which, while retaining many of the provisions of the present Scale, would also, as far as possible, codify the rules and customs of the trade generally, and contain at the same time such further amendments as in our opinion are necessary.

Speaking generally, our desire has been so to amend the Scale as to place all compositors, practically, on an equality, no matter upon what class of work they may be engaged, whether as piece or 'stab hands—allowance, of course, being made for the varying capabilities of those employed. With this object in view, we do not propose an increase in the price per thousand on all descriptions of work, as was done in 1866 and 1872, believing that it is not so much the price per thousand compositors complain of, as the prices paid for certain descriptions of work, for which the Scale either does not provide at all, or for which an inadequate payment is made. Should you endorse our view, we believe that much, if not all, of the long-existing discontent would be removed, and that such amended Scale would fairly meet the present requirements of the trade.

Among other matters with regard to which alterations are proposed, will be found :—

Reprints.	Grammars.	Narrow Measures.
Bastard Founts.	Spelling Books.	Clearing Away.
Leads.	Side Notes.	Mixture.
Foreign.	Catalogues.	Parliamentary Work.
Dictionaries.	Column Work.	Chancery Cases.
Gazetteers.	Corrections.	&c., &c., &c.

Turning from the piece to the 'stab hand, we are convinced that, taking all things into consideration, he is justly entitled to an increase of 4s. upon his present rate of wages—the minimum in future to be 40s. per week. Bearing in mind also, that it is now a quarter of a century since any alteration was made in the establishment wage, and that so far back as 1810 the sum of 36s. per week was paid in many cases, it cannot possibly be said that the London compositor has been extravagant in his demands—on the contrary, it is quite clear that he has not kept pace with the times, for while other trades have improved their position, he has looked on and contented himself with subscribing towards their support. It is true that in 1872 the working hours were reduced from 60 to 54 per week, but, advantageous as that undoubtedly was, it must not be forgotten that the Nine Hours Movement was one in which the trades of the country generally shared, and it would therefore have been impossible to deprive us of the advantages accruing from a national movement of that character. In order to show that the rate of wages paid to compositors in the Metropolis is, generally speaking, lower than in most trades, we append the following table, which, while scarcely so complete as we had hoped to make it, will, we believe, go a considerable way to prove our case.

Minimum Rates of Wages and Hours worked by various Metropolitan Trades :—

TRADES.	Wages per hour.		Number of Hours per week.	Extra Rates per hour, Overtime.	General Remarks.
	Day Work.	Piece Work.			
BARGE BUILDERS ..	9d.	—	54	1½d.	
BOILER MAKERS AND IRON SHIP BUILDERS ..	New work 10d.	Platers.			
,, ,, ,,	Repairs 10½d.				
,, ,, ,,	New 8½d.	Riveters.	54	Double.	
,, ,, ,,	Repairs 9½d.				
,, ,, ,,	New 7½d.	Holders-up.			
,, ,, ,,	Repairs 8d.				
BOOKBINDERS	7d.	—	54	Time and an eighth after 57 hours.	Finishers, 36/- to 50/-
BRICKLAYERS	9d.	—	52½ 44½	1d. first hour; 2d. until 8 p.m.; after, time-and-a-half.	
CABINET MAKERS ..	9d.	—	54	Time-and-a-quarter.	Piece workers' wages vary from 35/- to 50/- per week.
CARPENTERS AND JOINERS	9d.	—	52½ 47	1d. first hour; 2d. till 8 p.m.; 8 till 10, 1/1½d.; after, double till 6 a.m.	
COACH MAKERS ..	Wheeler 8d. Smith 9d.	—	55½	—	Piece workers' wages vary from 50/- to 60/- per week.
COOPERS	—	—	54	6d. extra, limited to one hour per week.	
CURRIERS	8d.	—	54	No overtime.	
DECORATORS AND PAINTERS	8½d.	—	52½ 48½	1st hour, 1d.; 2d. till 8 p.m.; after, time-and-a-half; Saturday, time-and-a-quarter till 5 p.m.; after, time-and-a-half.	
ENGINEERS	8½d.	1/-	54	Time-and-a-quarter, first two hours; time-and-a-half afterwards.	
FARRIERS	—	—	—	Same rate.	Firemen, 38/- per week; Doorkeeper, 33/- per week.
GLASS MAKERS	1/-	—	48	10 per cent.	
HATTERS	—	1/-	65	No overtime allowed.	Working hours 55, from 1891.
IRON FOUNDERS ..	8½d.	—	54	Time-and-a-quarter, first two hours; time-and-a-half afterwards.	

Trades.	Wages per hour.		Number of Hours per week.	Extra Rates per hour, Overtime.	General Remarks.
	Day Work.	Piece Work.			
Lithographic Artists	9d.	—	47½	Various rates.	
Lithographic Printers	10d.	—	54	Time-and-a-half.	
Plasterers	9d.	—	52½ 47	1d. first hour; 2d. second hour; after 8 time-and-a-half; after 12 double.	
Plumbers	10d.	—	47 44½		
Shipwrights	Old work 11d. New 9d.	—	54		
Slaters	9d.	—	56½ 51½		
Stereotypers	8d.	—	54	No fixed scale.	
Stone Carvers ..	1/-	—	47		
Stone Masons ..	9d.	—	51 47		
Upholsterers	9d.	1/-	54 46	Time-and-a-half.	
Zinc Workers.. ..	8d.	—	54	After 8 p.m. or 1 p.m. on Saturdays, time-and-a-half; from 12 midnight till 6 a.m., double.	

With regard to overtime, there is probably no trade that suffers more from the evils arising therefrom—especially systematic overtime—than our own, and while we are not prepared to say that generally speaking the evil is greater to-day than formerly, still we are convinced that very much of this overtime could and should be avoided. Much of the blame no doubt rests with the public, who, as the result of existing competition, are in some cases promised proofs of their work in a ridiculously short space of time, when a little pressure would induce them to supply the copy earlier; while in other cases they insist upon work being done at overtime rates, when such work could be produced in the ordinary way without the least disadvantage. To obviate this, or at least to reduce it to a minimum, is no doubt a difficult problem, but nevertheless it is one well worthy the serious consideration of both employers and workmen, and, as we believe, the only way to accomplish it is to increase the cost of production, we submit an amendment of the overtime rule.

In the first place, we request that all overtime be paid for at the rate of 4d. per hour extra instead of 3d., which although a very moderate increase, will, in many cases, mitigate the evil.

Next, we propose that after 10 p.m., from Monday to Friday inclusive, and after 2 p.m. on Saturday, 6d. per hour extra shall be charged—a return to some extent to the system in vogue prior to 1872. By this means we are convinced that the amount of overtime now worked will be considerably curtailed. The object of an extra charge for overtime being to make the price as far as possible prohibitive, we believe we shall in this way prevent compositors being called upon to work night after night, as at certain seasons of the year they do at present, to the detriment of their health and personal comfort, and with little or no advantage to the employer. In addition to this, as many compositors are compelled to reside at considerable distances from their employment, ten o'clock at night is certainly as late as they ought to be expected to work, if they are to do justice to their employers and themselves on the following day; and we believe, therefore, that this alteration will prove advantageous to all concerned.

In the case of compositors called upon to work during their meal-times, we submit that the custom of allowing an hour's overtime to be charged should be made universal, in order to put a stop, as far as possible, to a great and growing evil; for although the meal-time may be subsequently taken, the inconvenience, and in some cases loss, occasioned cannot be remedied, to say nothing of the compositors' health being impaired by the irregularity. In the case of females and young persons, the Factory Acts effectually prevent anything of this sort occurring, and we believe the liability to pay 4*d*. extra will have a similar effect in the case of journeymen compositors.

The oft-disputed question as to how much or how little time shall be given by the employer for refreshment when working late should, in our opinion, be met by the insertion of a clause on the subject, it being customary in all cases to allow at least half an hour after each three hours of overtime have been actually worked—an allowance obviously as much in the interest of the employer as of the journeyman.

Sunday work, which we are glad to know is now seldom resorted to, should be paid for proportionately, and we therefore propose that in future compositors should receive 8*d*. per hour extra from 12 o'clock on Saturday night to 8 o'clock on Monday morning—the minimum charge to be 4*s*. instead of 2*s*. 6*d*.; Christmas Day to be paid at the same rate.

With regard to the Weekly News Scale we do not submit for your consideration an increase in the price per thousand, our desire being so to amend this Scale also as to render it clear and easily to be understood in future.

The many changes that have taken place in recent years both in the character of these publications themselves, and their mode of production, render an alteration of the News Scale a necessity, and while the amendments made in 1874 were, so far as they went, undoubtedly advantageous, the interpretations placed upon them from time to time have been of a very conflicting nature. In order, therefore, to remedy this state of things we propose to put—

1. A broad interpretation upon the word newspaper.
2. Compositors called in for casual assistance in a similar position to book hands.
3. 'Stab hands, piece hands and apprentices on an equality, when the line is on.
4. Compositors pulling and seeking for galleys in a better position.
5. A broader interpretation on the term bastard fount.
6. Compositors employed on foreign languages in a better position.

In addition, we also propose for your consideration—and this, in our opinion, is a most important matter—an assimilation of the Book and News Scales in so far as the minimum establishment rate is concerned, and also the charges for overtime. This will necessitate an abolition of the present system of piece hands working six hours of overtime before being entitled to an extra charge—a system which has led to more unpleasantness, probably, than any other that was ever introduced, owing to the mixed nature of the work produced in London printing offices—for, as matters stand, if a compositor is called upon to work late under the Book Scale he is entitled to 3*d.* per hour extra, while if the same compositor is called upon to work late under the Weekly News Scale he must first work six hours of overtime before being entitled to 3*d.* per hour extra, although working for the same employer and in the same office. As we have abundant evidence that the amount of overtime worked on weekly newspapers has been considerably curtailed since 1874, when the principle of payment was first established, we see no reason why such overtime should not be still further reduced.

Having thus given a general idea of the nature of our application, we will briefly touch upon one or two additional reasons why, in our opinion, an advance of wages is due to the compositors in your employ.

1. In the first place, there can be no doubt that the general condition of the country is, and has been for some time past, very flourishing, and that while our employers have, to a greater or lesser extent, shared in that prosperity, the journeyman compositor's position has remained stationary.

2. That while considerable improvement has in recent years been made in the sanitary condition of many of the Metropolitan printing offices, the fact remains that upwards of 50 per cent. of the members of the London Society of Compositors die annually at a comparatively early age from diseases of the air passages and lungs, thus proving beyond doubt that the nature of our avocation is one that renders us peculiarly liable to disease and premature death.

3. That the growth of the 'stab system has led to compositors, in many cases, being kept at continued high pressure, through everything being "wanted in a hurry," with the result that although our trade is, as compared with many others, a moderately light one, the strain in such cases, both mentally and physically, is so great as to prove exceedingly exhaustive.

4. That the cost of living, especially for rent, rates, taxes and travelling, continues to increase, and that the distance most compositors are compelled to reside from their work reduces their home comforts and opportunities for improvement or relaxation to a minimum.

5. That, notwithstanding the lower wages paid in other portions of the United Kingdom, compositors, all things considered, occupy a better social position in the provinces than in London, the purchasing power of their money being greater owing to the fact that they are able to reside near to their employment and to go home to their meals.

In view of the comparisons frequently drawn between the London compositor and his provincial fellow-craftsman the following list of towns, in which, among others, advances of wages or reductions of hours, or both, have been obtained since 1872 will doubtless be of interest :—

Aberdeen.	Burnley.	Durham.	Inverness.	Newcastle.	Southport.
Airdrie.	Cardiff.	Edinburgh.	Ipswich.	Newry.	Stafford.
Arbroath.	Carlisle.	Falkirk.	Kelso.	Northampton.	Stirling.
Ardrossan.	Carlow.	Forfar.	Kendal.	Nottingham.	Stockton.
Ashton.	Castlebar.	Galashiels.	Kilmarnock.	Oban.	Stranraer.
Ayr.	Cheltenham.	Galway.	Kirkcaldy.	Oldham.	Sunderland.
Banbury.	Chester.	Glasgow.	Lancaster.	Oswestry.	Walsall.
Banff.	Chesterfield.	Greenock.	Leamington.	Paisley.	Warrington.
Barnsley.	Coventry.	Guildford.	Leeds.	Perth.	Warwick.
Barrow.	Darlington.	Halifax.	Leicester.	Potteries.	West Bromwich.
Bath.	Derby.	Hamilton.	Limerick.	Preston.	Whitehaven.
Belfast.	Doncaster.	Hartlepool.	Liverpool.	Rochdale.	Wigan.
Birmingham.	Drogheda.	Hawick.	Manchester.	Rugby.	Wolverhampton.
Blackburn.	Dumbarton.	Hereford.	Macclesfield.	Scarborough.	Worcester.
Bolton.	Dumfries.	Hertford.	Middlesboro'.	Sheffield.	Wrexham.
Bradford.	Dundee.	Huddersfield.	Montrose.	Shrewsbury.	York.
Bristol.	Dunfermline.	Hull.			

While having no desire to disturb existing contracts entered into prior to it having become generally known that we were about to approach our Employers with the view to an Advance of Wages (except in cases where advances upon the present rates can be obtained), we trust that arrangements will be made whereby the Revised Scale may come into operation on the first day of January, 1891. With this object in view, therefore, we shall hold ourselves free to meet our Employers, either individually or through the medium of a representative Committee as may be most agreeable, in order that the whole question may be considered in a friendly spirit and an understanding arrived at of a mutually satisfactory and permanent nature, which shall be binding upon the trade generally.

I have the honour to remain, Gentlemen,

On behalf of the Committee,

Yours faithfully,

C. J. DRUMMOND, *Secretary.*

London Society of Compositors,
3, Raquet Court, Fleet Street, E.C.,
November 24th, 1890.

The Printing and Allied Trades Association, founded by the employers on 29 October, 1890, appointed a committee to examine the draft Scale submitted by the compositors.[1] In a letter to the L.S.C. the secretary of the Association mentioned the sympathetic interest of his colleagues who had, in their turn, compiled a draft Scale. "In drawing up this Amended Scale, the aim of my Committee has been to work in friendly co-operation with your Society, as they hold that the interests of employers and journeymen are identical." The preliminary paragraphs of the letter are not reprinted.

[1] The first executive included the following names : W. C. Knight Clowes, P. H. Waterlow, W. P. Griffith, C. Harrison, W. Hazell, G. Unwin, G. F. McCorquodale.

[DOCUMENT XCVI]

In respect to your proposal of an establishment wage of 40*s.* per week, my Committee and employers generally have decided that such an advance in the minimum wages would be injurious to the trade, and to a very large number of your older members; and they, therefore, recommend an increase to 38*s.*, which will confer a substantial benefit on journeymen generally, and will afford opportunity for increasing the amounts now paid in advance of the minimum to the more skilled hands in many offices.

On the question of overtime my Committee concur with you in principle, and would be much gratified if they could totally abolish it. But it is well known that there are kinds of work on which overtime is absolutely unavoidable, and to raise the price to the extent you have suggested, would not secure your object, which is to make it prohibitive. The more the charge for overtime is increased, the greater will be the opportunity, where overtime work is a necessity, as in the case of weekly papers, prices current, warrant notes and similar productions, for small offices now employing unskilled labour, to take over printing at present in the hands of Society houses, and this will inevitably lead to more offices being closed to your members. While not adopting your rates in full, my Committee have granted a very substantial advance on the present Scale for prolonged night work and for Sunday work; and they think the prices proposed will compare favourably with those paid in other trades, and tend considerably to reduce the excessive overtime which is so much deplored.

My Committee wish me to refer to some observations in your Memorial which are open to comment. You remark that the trade of the country is very flourishing, and that you consider the employer to have shared in the general prosperity, while the journeyman's position has remained stationary. They think your attention should be drawn to the fact that, while the printing trade has enormously increased of late years, thereby supporting more employers and more journeymen, the employers' profits have notably decreased. Competition has never been keener than at the present time : prices have never been so low.

It is further stated in your Memorial that, as far back as 1810, 36*s.* a week was paid in many cases to establishment hands. If a comparison be desired with the minimum wage of the present day, you must also take the minimum of the earlier date. Whatever the minimum may have been in 1810, 37 years later it was 33*s.*, and it was not until 1866 that 36*s.* was the recognized establishment wage. Even supposing that the minimum wage of 1810 can be ascertained, there would still be no comparison, as the hours comprised in a week were then very much longer. The fact that the Scale of 1810 provides that corrections should be paid at the rate of sixpence per hour, affords pretty strong evidence that the present minimum wage for time work is at least one-third higher than it was at that date.

Your observation that the cost of living continues to increase cannot be endorsed. On the contrary, it was shown by Mr. Chamberlain, in his speech on Provident Societies on the 5th inst., that the cost of living has been much reduced during the last 50 years, some of the principal articles of food being from 25 to 75 per cent. and clothing quite 50 per cent. cheaper.

With regard to competition, you are of course aware that for a long time Scotland and the Provinces have competed for the London book trade, and carried off the greater portion of it. Public attention has been drawn to the anticipated appearance of a fresh competitor in America, when the new Copyright Bill becomes law. But you may not be aware that a London publisher has, during the last few months, opened another source of competition by getting a reprint produced in Holland at 15 to 20 per cent. below the lowest English rates. It must be borne in mind that many of the large London houses have established branch offices in the country to avoid paying the high prices of the London Scale, where not only book work but also some jobbing is already done, and more will inevitably follow if such a rise as you propose is adopted.

My Committee wish to draw your particular attention to the fact that many firms hold contracts having several years to run, on which a serious loss would be incurred if estimated upon the increased Scale which you have suggested, and it is felt that it is not the desire of your Society to inflict such loss.

Taking into consideration all the facts, my Committee have every confidence that your Society will accept the proposals herewith submitted, as being calculated to promote the best interests of both employers and journeymen.

Some employers have strongly urged on my Committee the necessity of journeymen having a certificate of efficiency granted to them by your Society, after passing a proper examination. The examiners should be a combined Board of Employers and Journeymen, and the examinations be conducted in the same manner as those of the City of London Technical Institute. This principle has already been recognized as fair, equitable and essential to the public interest in another skilled trade in London.

It must be distinctly understood that the Revised Scale only applies to those of your Society who are employed in London, and that the question of Daily Papers has not been considered by the Committee.

Finally, my Committee direct me to inform you that they have selected the seven gentlemen whose names are given below to confer with an equal number of your Executive as already agreed; and they will be pleased to arrange the date of meeting as early as you may desire.

W. C. KNIGHT CLOWES, Esq. (*William Clowes & Son, Limited*),
    Chairman of the Association.
P. H. WATERLOW, Esq. (*Waterlow & Sons, Limited*), Vice-Chairman.
H. BURT, Esq. (*Hansard Publishing Union, Limited*).
T. CATLING, Esq. (*Edward Lloyd, Limited*).
C. R. HARRISON, Esq. (*Harrison & Sons*).
G. F. MCCORQUODALE, Esq. (*McCorquodale & Co., Limited*).
J. F. WILSON, Esq. (*Cassell & Company, Limited*).

          I am, Dear Sir, yours faithfully,

              H. VANE STOW, *Secretary.*

The following is extracted from the *Digest of Revised Scale*, which was published for the information of their constituents by the compositors' committee on 13 February, 1891, five days before an agreement was ratified with the masters. Here will be found the principal features of the Scale of 1891 :—

[DOCUMENT XCVII]

An advance ranging from $\frac{1}{4}d.$ to $1\frac{1}{4}d.$ upon certain classes of book work.
A further advance of $\frac{1}{2}d.$ per 1000 on all descriptions of solid book work.
Sundry increases in the prices per sheet.
Abolition of the liability to clear away (equivalent in some houses to a further increase in the price per 1000).
The right of piece companionships to appoint their own clickers.
An advance of $1d.$ per 1000 on the worst description of Parliamentary work.
A re-modelling of the Weekly News Scale in the interest of the piece hands.
An advance in the rates for Overtime—Book and News—the minimum price being $1s.$ per hour.
Abolition of six hours at present worked by news compositors without extra.
An advance in the charges for Sunday work.
An advance of $2s.$ per week on the establishment rates—Book and News.

These substantial advantages having been gained, it now remains for the members to say whether they are prepared to accept them as a fair and equitable re-adjustment of their mode of working, or whether they are prepared to risk the loss of all that has been obtained for the purpose of endeavouring to still further increase the remuneration of the establishment hands. Failure to accomplish this would doubtless place our members in a worse position than they have ever been, and might possibly wreck our Society; while in any event we should be unable to procure the signatures of the Employers to the London Scale, which in itself would be a misfortune it is impossible to over-estimate. Whatever success we, as a Society, have hitherto met with is due in no small degree to the fact that we occupy the somewhat unique position of working under a Scale of Prices, for both piece and 'stab, that has been mutually agreed to by representative employers and workmen, and it is difficult to foresee what condition the London trade would be in but for the existence of this all-important document.

On this occasion we are bound to record the fact that the Employers have met us all through in a fair spirit, and are, we believe, as desirous as we are to improve the condition of the trade. At no period in our history has the relationship between the Employers and ourselves been so good as at the present time, for we have no reason to believe that any of them will decline to accept the decision of the Conference; and when we look back to the friction that existed in 1866 and 1872, and to the houses that were lost to the Union, some of which have never been recovered, we should fail in our duty were we not to earnestly beg of you to seriously reflect upon the present aspect of affairs; for not only are we unlikely to lose any houses on this occasion, if the conclusions arrived at by the Conference are ratified, but we have reasonable hopes of winning over in the near future some of the houses now outside the Union.

The London Society of Compositors issued a pamphlet showing, in four parallel columns, their own draft Scale, the one made by the employers' committee, the original Scale of 1810 with its amendments, and the Scale of 1891 as agreed upon by all parties. The two latter versions are here reprinted. The prices per 1,000 in the old Scale take into account the advances of 1866 and 1872, totalling an increase of 1*d.* per 1,000 over those of 1810. To each paragraph or sub-paragraph of the original Scale has been added the date of its introduction in the Scale, which is not necessarily that of any preliminary agreement between masters and men. For instance, the rule relating to wrappers printed under Art. 7 of the old Scale was made in 1838, but did not form part of a complete Scale until 1847.

The Scale of 1891, then, took into account every agreement reached over a period of eighty-one years. The twenty-five articles of the 1810 Scale and the addenda of 1847, 1866 and 1872 were replaced by a document containing fifty-eight articles applicable to contemporary conditions and requirements.

[DOCUMENT XCVIII]

Note.—Original London Scale prices are corrected to those of 1872.

ORIGINAL LONDON SCALE	SCALE OF 1891

Art. 1. All Works in the English language, common matter, *with space lines*, including English and Brevier, to be cast up at 6¾*d.* per 1000; if in Minion, 7*d.*; in Nonpareil, 7¾*d.*;— *Without space lines*, including English and Brevier, 7*d.* per 1000; in Minion, 7¼*d.*; in Nonpareil, 8*d.*; in Pearl, *with or without space lines*, 9*d.*; Head and Directions or Signature lines included. A thick space to be considered an en in the width, and an en to be reckoned an em in the length of the page; and where the number of letters amounts to 500—1000 to be charged; if under 500, not to be reckoned; and if the calculation at per 1000 shall not amount to an odd threepence, the odd pence to be suppressed in the price of the work; but where it amounts to or exceeds threepence, there shall be sixpence charged. Em and en quadrats, or

1. All works in the English language, common matter, including English and Brevier, to be cast up at 7½*d.* per 1000; Minion, 7¾*d.*; Nonpareil, 8½*d.*; Ruby 9*d.*; Pearl, 9½*d.*; Diamond, 11½*d.*; head and white lines included. A thick space to be considered an en in the width, and an en to be reckoned an em in the length of the page. 1000 to be charged where the number of letters amount to 500; under 500 not to be reckoned. If the calculation per 1000 shall not amount to an odd threepence, the odd pence to be suppressed in the price of the work; but where it amounts to or exceeds threepence, sixpence to be charged.

ORIGINAL LONDON SCALE	SCALE OF 1891

whatever is used at the beginning or end of lines, to be reckoned as an em in the width. (1810.)

Ruby, *with space lines*, to be cast up at $8\frac{1}{4}d$. per 1000; *without space lines*, $8\frac{1}{2}d$. per 1000.

Diamond, *with space lines*, to be cast up at $10\frac{3}{4}d$. per 1000; *without space lines*, at $11d$. per 1000.

The extra price per 1000 for Minion and all founts below Minion to be paid upon all descriptions of work. (1847.)

All reprinted works to be paid Three Farthings per 1000 less than the Scale of 1810. All Manuscript or Original Works shall continue to be paid for as at present. (1816.)

Reprints, with numerous MS. insertions interspersed throughout; or so materially altered as to consist of half MS. and half reprint; or derived from various sources not being the compilation of the works of one author, to be considered Manuscript or Original Works.

[An entire chapter or portion in MS. not to be considered as part of the one-half above mentioned, but to be paid as MS.]

Reprints having less MS. alterations than above stated, to be paid one-halfpenny per 1000 less than the scale of 1810.

[Verbal corrections, simple alterations of style, or typographical alterations, not to be considered MS. alterations.]

The text of an author reprinted with a MS. Commentary at the foot of the page, to be paid one-halfpenny per 1000 less than the scale of 1810. (1847.)

That the definitions of Reprints in the Scale of 1847 be adhered to, but that the remodelling of punctuation or orthography shall be done before giving out copy to the compositor, or be paid for. (1866.)

Reprints in every respect exact reproductions of the originals to be cast up at $\frac{3}{4}d$. per 1000 less. Reprints not in every respect exact reproductions of the originals, which may be set in a different sized type and to a different measure, containing verbal corrections, simple alterations of style, and typographical alterations, to be cast up at $\frac{1}{2}d$. per 1000 less. Reprints with MS. insertions not exceeding one-eighth of the volume to be cast up at $\frac{1}{4}d$. per 1000 less; and such reprints may be derived from various sources although by one author.

Original London Scale	Scale of 1891
That $\frac{1}{4}d$. per 1000 extra be paid on all Roman founts for every *en* below 12 *ems* of their own body in thickness. (1866.)	Thin founts to be cast up at $\frac{1}{4}d$. per 1000 extra for every en below 12 ems of their own body in thickness.
Bastard founts of one remove to be cast up to the depth and width of the two founts to which they belong. (1847.)	Bastard founts of one remove to be cast up to the depth and width of the two founts to which they belong; of two removes to be cast up to the smaller body, both in depth and width.
All matter stereotyped by the present method, namely, by using plaster of Paris, to be cast up, if with high spaces, at $\frac{1}{4}d$. per 1000 additional; if with low spaces, at $\frac{1}{2}d$. per 1000 additional. Should any other method be adopted obviating the inconvenience experienced by the compositor, no extra charge per 1000 to be made; but, if imposed in small chases, 1s. per sheet to be allowed. (1847.)	Matter stereotyped by the plaster process to be cast up, if with high spaces, at $\frac{1}{4}d$. per 1000 extra; if with low spaces, at $\frac{1}{2}d$. per 1000; but should any other method be adopted entirely obviating the inconvenience occasioned, no extra charge per 1000 to be made.
The usual deduction for leaded matter to be made for 8 to Pica leads when used with Long Primer or smaller type; for 10 to Pica leads with Brevier or smaller type; and for 12 to Pica leads when used with Nonpareil or smaller type; Pearl not excepted. If leads of intermediate size be used, 9 to Pica to be reckoned as 10 to Pica, and 11 to Pica as 12 to Pica. No deduction to be made for any thinner lead than 12 to Pica with any sized type. (1847.)	The price per 1000 throughout to apply to solid matter; $\frac{3}{4}d$. per 1000 to be deducted in all cases when 6-to-pica leads or upwards are used; when 8-to-pica are used for brevier or smaller bodies; and when 10-to-pica are used for pearl or smaller bodies; but no deduction to be made for leads thinner than 10-to-pica, or for pieced leads. Distinct portions of a work or publication which are uniformly leaded or solid to be so charged.
That no deduction be made for Pieced Leads in measures of less than 26 ems wide. (1866.)	By the term "common matter" is understood the usual description of bookwork, but where any departure whatever is made, by the introduction of peculiar matter, extraneous sorts, contractions, &c., the compositor to be entitled to an extra charge, in accordance with the time occupied.
2. Works printed in Great Primer to be cast up as English; and all works in larger type than Great Primer, as half English and half Great Primer. (1810.)	2. Works printed in Great Primer to be cast up as English; in larger type than Great Primer, as half English and half Great Primer.

ORIGINAL LONDON SCALE	SCALE OF 1891
3. All works in Foreign languages, though common type, *with space lines*, including English and Brevier, to be cast up at 7¼*d.* per 1000; if in Minion, 7¾*d.*; Nonpareil, 8½*d.*; *without space lines*, including English and Brevier, 7½*d.*; Minion, 8*d.*; Nonpareil, 8¾*d.*; and Pearl, *with or without space lines*, 9¾*d.* (1810.)	3. Works in Foreign and the Welsh language, Roman type, including English and Brevier, to be cast up at 8½*d.* per 1000; Minion, 9*d.*; Nonpareil, 9¾*d.*; Pearl, 10¾*d.*
If Dictionary matter, to take ½*d.* advance per 1000. (1847.)	
14. Greek, *with space lines,* and without accents, to be paid 9½*d.* per 1000; if with separate accents, 11*d.*; *without space lines,* and without accents, 9¾*d.*; with accents, 11¼*d.*; the asper not to be considered an accent. (If Dictionary matter to take one halfpenny advance.) (1810.)	4. Greek without accents, Russian, Saxon, German and similar languages in their own characters, to be cast up at 10¼*d.* per 1000; with accents (whether cast on the body or not), 11¾*d.*
Works in the Saxon language, set up in common type with the two Saxon characters for *th*, to be cast up ½*d.* per 1000 additional. (1847.)	Dictionaries, and works in the Saxon language, in Roman type, with the two Saxon characters for *th*, to be cast up at an advance of ½*d.* per 1000.
Works in the Saxon or German languages set up in the Saxon or German character, to be paid 1*d.* per 1000 extra. (1847.)	
15. Hebrew, Arabic, Syriac, &c., to be paid double. Hebrew with points to be cast up as half body and half points doubled. (1810.)	5. Hebrew, Arabic, Syriac and similar languages, to be paid double the price of common matter; if with points to be cast up as half body and half points doubled.
Foreign. — Works done in the Russian character should be charged at the same price as Greek without accents.	
All accented Greek words, whether the accents be cast on the body or separate, should be charged according to Art. 14 of the Scale.	
Works in the Oriental languages, with points similar to those used in Hebrew, should be charged in the same manner as Hebrew with points, according to Art. 15 of the Scale.	

ORIGINAL LONDON SCALE	SCALE OF 1891

Works with Hebrew interspersed in a different body to the text should be charged 1s. per sheet for mixture of bodies, in addition to the extra value of the Hebrew as measured off and cast up.

[The above four paragraphs appear in the *Trade Memoranda* printed in Edition of the Scale published in 1879.][1]

13. Greek, Hebrew, Saxon, &c., or any of the dead characters, if one word and not exceeding three lines in any one sheet, to be paid for that sheet 1s. extra; all above to be paid according to their value. (1810.)

Greek, &c. exceeding three lines in any one sheet, to be paid 1s. per sheet, in addition to its value as cast up; the 3 lines specified for the 1s. charge being deducted. (1847.)

4. English Dictionaries of every size, *with space lines*, including English and Brevier, to be paid 7¼d. per 1000; *without space lines*, 7½d.

Dictionaries of two or more languages, of every size, *with space lines*, including English and Brevier, to be paid 7½d. per 1000; *without space lines*, 7¾d.;—If smaller type than Brevier, to take the proportionate advance specified in Article 1.

(In this article are not included Gazetteers, Geographical Diction-

---

Works interspersed with Hebrew, or similar languages, in a different body to the text, to be paid 1s. per sheet extra for mixture of bodies.

6. Greek, Hebrew, Saxon, and similar languages, if one word or not less than three separate letters, and not exceeding three lines in any one sheet, to be paid for that sheet 1s. extra; above three lines to be paid according to their value as cast up, with the addition of 1s. for placing on each sheet in which they occur.

7. English Dictionaries of every size, and works of a similar description, including English and Brevier, to be cast up at 8½d. per 1000 when expressing only the meaning of words; 9d. per 1000 when marked for pronunciation or accents.

8. Gazetteers, Encyclopedias, Geographical Dictionaries, Dictionaries of Arts and Sciences, and works of a similar description, including English and Brevier, to be cast up at 8d. per 1000.

9. Dictionaries in two or more languages, of every size, including

---

[1] The *Trade Memoranda* consisted of amendments, definitions and additions to the Scale claimed by the men, and not necessarily agreed to by the Masters, since they formed no part of the officially recognized Scale. These *Memoranda* were often published by the L.S.C. together with the official Scale. In the present case, the quotations were taken from the *Memoranda* printed in the editions of 1879 and 1889.

ORIGINAL LONDON SCALE	SCALE OF 1891

aries, Dictionaries of Arts and Sciences, and works of a similar description, except those attended with extra trouble beyond usual descriptive matter.) (1810.)

English and Brevier, to be cast up at 9½*d.* per 1000.

5. English Grammars, Spelling Books, and works of those descriptions, in Brevier or larger type, *with space lines*, to be paid 7*d.* per 1000; *without space lines*, 7¼*d.*

If in two languages, or foreign language, *with space lines*, 7¼*d.* per 1000; *without space lines*, 7½*d.* (1810.)

10. Grammars, Spelling Books, and works of a similar description, including English and Brevier, to be cast up at 8½*d.* per 1000; if in a foreign or two languages, 9*d.* per 1000.

Grammars wholly in a foreign language to be paid ¼*d.* per 1000 extra beyond the price of works in foreign languages, as settled by Art. 3. (1847.)

9. Works done in Sixteens, Eighteens, Twenty-fours, or Thirty-twos, on Small Pica and upwards, to be paid 1*s.* 6*d.* per sheet extra. If on Long Primer or smaller type, 1*s.* per sheet extra. Forty-eights to be paid 2*s.* per sheet extra, and Sixty-fours 2*s.* 6*d.* per sheet extra. (1810.)

11. Works in Sixteens, Eighteens, Twenty-fours, or Thirty-twos, in Small Pica and upwards, to be paid 1*s.* 6*d.* per sheet extra; if in Long Primer, or smaller type, 1*s.* Forty-eights to be paid 2*s.* per sheet extra, and Sixty-fours 2*s.* 6*d.*

If imposed in small chases, 1*s.* per sheet to be allowed.

Works imposed in small chases, or with stereo furniture, to be charged 1*s.* per sheet extra on the above charges.

10. Works requiring an alteration or alterations of margin, to be paid for each alteration 1*s.* per sheet to the pressmen, if altered by them, and 6*d.* to the compositor, as a compensation for making up the furniture; if altered by the compositor, then he is to be paid 1*s.* for the alteration, and the pressmen 6d. for the delay.—This article to be determined on solely at the option of the employer. (1810.)

ORIGINAL LONDON SCALE	SCALE OF 1891

6. Small-sized Folios, Quartos, Octavos, and works done in Great Primer or larger type (English language) which do not come to 7s. when cast up at the usual rate, to be paid as follows :—English and larger type, not less than 7s.; Pica 8s. 6d.; English 12mo. to be paid not less than 10s. 6d.; and Pica not less than 11s. 6d. per sheet. (1810.)

The words "including every item of charge" to be understood after the words "when cast up at the usual rate." (1847.)

In casting up, no sheet to be considered single which exceeds 520 superficial inches of printed matter, including borders and rules and the inner margins; all of larger dimensions to be cast up as two single sheets of half the number of pages of which the whole sheet consists, viz., 4to. as folio, 8vo. as 4to., &c., as the case may be. This rule not to include Parliamentary work. (1847. Art. 9.)

Works, although printed in half-sheets, to be cast up in sheets. (1847.)

8. Pamphlets of five sheets and under, and parts of works done in different houses, amounting to not more than five sheets, to be paid 1s. per sheet extra; but as it frequently occurs that works exceeding a pamphlet are often nearly made up without a return of letter, all such works shall be considered as pamphlets, and paid for as such. (1810.)

In works of more than five sheets, where two-thirds are made up without a return of letter and leads, either of its own or of a similar work, 1s. per sheet extra to be paid upon the whole work. If, however, the work be published in separate volumes, and

Small-sized folios, quartos, octavos and works in Great Primer or larger type (English language) which do not come to 7s. when cast up at the usual rate, including every item of charge, to be paid as follows :—English and larger type, not less than 7s.; Pica, 8s. 6d.; English 12mo., not less than 10s. 6d.; Pica, 11s. 6d.

In casting up, no sheet to be considered single which exceeds 520 superficial inches of printed matter, including borders, rules, and inner margins; all of larger dimensions to be cast up as two single sheets of half the number of pages of which the whole sheet consists, i.e., 4to. as two sheets of folio, 8vo. as two sheets of 4to. Works, although printed in half-sheets, to be cast up in sheets.

12. Pamphlets of five sheets and under to be paid 1s. per sheet extra. Parts of works done at different houses to be cast up according to the respective merits of the different parts; if consisting of a sheet, or less, to be cast up according to Art. 19; if amounting to not more than five sheets, to be paid 1s. per sheet extra.

In a work of more than five sheets, where one-half is made up without a return of letter and leads, either of its own or of a similar work, 1s. per sheet extra to be paid upon the whole work; but in all instances it is to be distinctly understood, that the letter

ORIGINAL LONDON SCALE	SCALE OF 1891

the letter of the first volume be used for the second, or of the second for the third, no charge for making up letter to be made beyond the first volume.

Parts of works done at different houses to be cast up according to the respective merits of the different parts; and if consisting of a sheet, or less, to be cast up according to Art. 20. (1847.)

25. Different volumes of the same work to be paid for distinctly according to their value. (1810.)

11. Bottom notes consisting of twenty lines (or two notes though not amounting to twenty lines) and not exceeding four pages in every ten sheets, in quarto or octavo;—one page (or two notes, though not amounting to one page) and not exceeding six pages, in twelves;—two pages (or two notes, though not amounting to two pages) and not exceeding eight, in eighteens or above, to be paid 1s. per sheet; but under the above proportion, no charge to be made. Bottom notes consisting of ten lines (or two notes, though not amounting to ten lines), in a pamphlet of five sheets or under, and not exceeding two pages, to be paid 1s. per sheet extra. Quotations, mottoes, contents to chapters, &c., in smaller type than the body, to be considered as notes. [Where the notes shall be in Nonpareil or Pearl, in twelves the number of pages to be restricted to four; in eighteens to five pages.]— *This Article is intended only to fix what constitutes the charge of 1s. per sheet for bottom notes: all works requiring a higher charge than 1s. for bottom notes are to be paid for according to their value.* (1810.)

and leads must be the same kind of letter, the same sized leads; if not, the charge for making up letter will still stand good. If, however, the work be published in separate volumes, and the letter of the first volume be used for the second, or of the second for the third, no charge for making up letter to be made beyond the first volume.

Different volumes of the same work to be paid for distinctly according to their value.

13. Bottom notes to be measured off and cast up to their own body, with an addition of 1s. for placing in folio, quarto, and octavo; 1s. 6d. in 12mo.; 2s. in 16mo., 18mo. and above, for each sheet in which they occur.

Quotations, mottoes, contents to chapters, &c., in the same fount as the notes to be reckoned as notes.

In order to constitute the charge of 1*s*. per sheet for notes, there must be, on the average, in every ten sheets in 4to. or 8vo. one note of 20 lines, or two notes though not amounting to 20 lines; in 12mo. one page, or two notes, though not amounting to one page; in 18mo. and above, two pages or two notes, though not amounting to two pages.

Thus, in 4to. and 8vo. work, there must be—

In 10 sheets, 1 note of 20 lines .. or 2 notes not amounting to 20 lines,

15	,,	2 notes amounting to 40 lines	..	or 3	ditto
20	,,	ditto	.. ..	or 4	ditto
25	,,	3 notes amounting to 60 lines	..	or 5	ditto
30	,,	ditto	..	or 6	ditto

and so on in proportion.

Notes exceeding the maximum quantity specified in this article, to be paid 1*s*. 6*d*. per sheet. If the quantity of notes entitle to a further advance, the whole to be measured off and cast up as a distinct body, 1*s*. per sheet being paid for placing.

Example:—In a work of Sixteen Sheets—

	£	s.	d.
Pica, 12 sheets, at 14*s*. per sheet	8	8	0
Long Primer, 4 sheets at 21*s*. 6*d*. per sheet	4	6	0
Placing	0	16	0
	£13	10	0

In measuring off notes, quotations, &c., the actual quantity of small type to be reckoned; and when it exceeds one line, one line extra to be allowed for the white, but when there is only one line of small type, one line only to be reckoned; *i.e.* for each separate quantity of note, quotation, &c., exceeding one line, one line extra to be reckoned for the space which separates it from the text. Where no space appears, no line to be reckoned.

In measuring off notes, quotations, &c., the actual quantity of small type to be reckoned, and when it exceeds one line, one line extra to be allowed for the white, but when there is only one line of small type, one line to be reckoned; *i.e.* for each separate quantity of note, quotation, &c., exceeding one line, one line extra to be reckoned for the space which separates it from the text, but where no space appears, no line to be reckoned.

ORIGINAL LONDON SCALE	SCALE OF 1891

If two or more notes occur in one line, each reference to be considered a note in counting, but not a separate line in measuring off.

In calculating the charge of 1s. per sheet for notes, the note type to be considered as two sizes less than the text type. Notes set up in a type three or more removes from that used for the text to be reckoned according to the relative proportions of two removes.

"23. NOTES.—*Notes in the same Type as the Text.*—The compositors are entitled to charge 1s. per sheet for placing.

"*Notes occurring only in the Preliminary Matter to a Pamphlet* entitle the compositors to charge 1s. per sheet throughout such pamphlet." [*Trade Memoranda.*]

Works having notes upon notes, quotations, etc., set up in a smaller type than the notes, to be paid 1s. per sheet extra on every sheet where such notes, &c., occur. If, however, this extra charge be not equivalent to the value of the matter set in any one sheet, such matter to be measured off and paid for upon the same principle as bottom notes.

Type between the sizes of the text and the notes to be paid for as follows :—The quantity to be measured off, and the difference of value between it and the text type charged, with the addition of 1s. per sheet for placing in every sheet in which it occurs; if occurring in three-fourths of the work, 1s. per sheet for placing to be paid throughout. (1847.)

Double Column Bottom Notes (1s. per sheet if in 16mo., 6d. if in 8vo.)—although there may be no other double column matter in the volume—entitle the compositor to the above charges. [*Trade Memoranda* in Ed. of Scale published 1879.]

Types between the sizes of the text and the notes, or smaller, to be measured off and paid 1s. per sheet extra for placing in those sheets in which they occur, for every sized type used.

Double column notes, interspersed through a volume, to be charged, in addition to the price for notes, 1s. per sheet extra in 8vo.; 1s. 6d. in 12mo.; 2s. in 16mo.

22

ORIGINAL LONDON SCALE	SCALE OF 1891

When, in consequence of notes being struck out in authors' proofs, the *pro rata* charge per sheet is destroyed, the compositor shall only charge for notes upon the sheets where they originally appeared.

12. Side notes to folios and quartos not exceeding a broad quotation, if only chapter or date, and not exceeding three explanatory lines on an average in each page, to be paid 1s. per sheet; in octavo, if only chapter or date, and not exceeding three explanatory lines on an average in each page, 1s. 6d. per sheet. Cut-in notes in smaller type than the body, to be paid for in a similar manner. (1810.)

14. Side notes, not exceeding a broad quotation or five lines on an average in each page, to be paid, for each sheet in which they occur, 1s. in folio; 1s. 6d. in quarto; 2s. in octavo; 2s. 6d. in 12mo; 3s. in 16mo., 18mo. and above. Double-narrows 1s. 6d. in folio, 2s. 6d. in quarto. Cut-in notes to be paid as side notes, with the addition of 2d. for each justification.

Side notes in 12mo. to be paid 2s. per sheet; in 16mo., 18mo., and above, 2s. 6d. per sheet.

Side notes set up in Nonpareil, though not exceeding the quantity specified in this Article, and not cast up to their value, to be paid 6d. per sheet additional; if in Pearl, 1s. per sheet additional.

Side notes in nonpareil, though not exceeding the quantity specified, and not cast up to their value, to be paid 6d. per sheet additional; if in pearl, 1s. per sheet additional.

Where side notes exceed the maximum quantity specified, viz., chapter or date, and three explanatory lines on an average in each page, the actual number of lines set up to be counted and paid at treble their price as common matter, as an equivalent for composing and making up. In casting up the actual width only of the text and side notes to be taken respectively.

Where side notes exceed the maximum quantity specified, viz., five lines on an average in each page, the actual number of lines set up to be counted and paid treble the price of common matter, as an equivalent for composing and making up. In casting up, the actual width only of the text and side notes to be taken respectively.

Side notes and Cut-in notes, occurring in distinct portions of works, or in less than one-fourth part of a work, not to form a *pro rata* charge per sheet, but to be paid on those sheets only in which they appear.

ORIGINAL LONDON SCALE	SCALE OF 1891

Double side notes, or notes upon each side of the page, to be paid double the price specified for notes on one side of the page; but if occurring occasionally, to be paid on those sheets only in which they appear.

Figures in the margin down the side of a page not to be considered as side notes, but to be charged extra according to the trouble occasioned.

Under-runners not to be cast up with the side notes, but to be paid by agreement between the employer and journeymen. (1847.)

Side and bottom notes to many, particularly historical and law works, if attended with more than ordinary trouble, to be settled between the employer and journeymen. (1810.)

18. Booksellers' catalogues (in whatever language) to be cast up at 8*d*. per 1000; not including the numbering. (1810.)

This Article applies to Booksellers' Catalogues only.
"Not including the numbering" means, that, when the compositor has to supply or correct the numbers used in a booksellers' catalogue, an extra charge shall be made equivalent to the loss of time occasioned.
Notes or remarks in smaller type inserted in a booksellers' catalogue, to be paid as bottom notes.

The words "in whatever language" mean those in which common type is used. (1847.)

Auctioneers' Catalogues and Particulars to be cast up at 7*d*. per 1000, leaded or solid, and irrespectively of extent. Small type introduced, or any other extra, to be paid as in bookwork. (1847.)

Double side notes, or notes upon each side of the page, to be paid double the price specified for notes on one side of the page, for each sheet in which they occur.

Figures in the margin down the side of a page not to be considered side notes, but to be charged extra according to the trouble occasioned.

Under-runners not to be cast up with the side notes, but to be paid by agreement between the employer and journeyman.

Side notes, attended with more than ordinary trouble, to be paid by agreement between the employer and journeyman.

15. Library Catalogues, in whatever language (Roman type), to be cast up at 8*d*. per 1000; Booksellers' Catalogues at 9*d*. per 1000; not including the numbering. Small type, or any other extra, to be paid as in bookwork.

16. Auctioneers' Catalogues and Particulars (other than Catalogues of Books provided for by Art. 15) to be cast up at 7½*d*. per 1000 solid, 7*d*. leaded. Small type, or any other extra, to be paid as in bookwork.

ORIGINAL LONDON SCALE	SCALE OF 1891
The "Conditions" page, if standing, to be paid as a page of the catalogue; but if composed, according to the type in which it is set up. (1847.)	The "Conditions" page, if standing, to be paid as a page of the catalogue; if composed, according to the type in which it is set.
7. Reviews, Magazines, and works of a similar description, consisting of various sized letter, if cast up to the different bodies, to be paid 2*s.* 6*d.* per sheet extra. (1810.)	17. Reviews, Magazines, and works of a similar description, consisting of more than one fount and cast up to the respective bodies, to be paid 2*s.* 6*d.* per sheet extra.
No deduction to be made for printed copy partially introduced in Reviews, Magazines, &c.; nor for leads occasionally used in them, unless with sizes of type leaded throughout according to the plan of the work. (1847.)	No deduction to be made for leads occasionally used, unless with sizes of type leaded throughout according to the plan of the publication.
	Contents and other prefixed matter to a volume of a publication belong to the companionship who has done the parts, but such matter may by mutual arrangement be given to another piece companionship in an emergency.
The companionship on a Magazine or Review to be entitled to the first or title-page of the Wrapper of such Magazine or Review; but not to the remaining pages of such wrapper, nor to the Advertising Sheets which may accompany the Magazine or Review. (*Addenda*, 1847.)	18. Wrappers may by mutual agreement between the employer and journeyman be set up either by piece or establishment hands; if by the latter, such wrappers belong to the house.
Standing Advertisements or Stereo. Blocks, if forming a complete page, or, when collected together, making one or more complete pages in a Wrapper or Advertising Sheet, of a Magazine or Review, not to be chargeable; the compositor to charge only for his time in making them up. The remainder of the matter in such Wrapper or Advertising Sheet, including Standing Advertisements or Stereo. Blocks not forming a complete page, to be charged by the compositor, and cast up according to the 8th or 20th Articles of the Scale as they may respectively apply; but the charge of 2*s.* 6*d.*, as given by Article 7, is not to be superadded. (1838.)	Standing advertisements, wood cuts, or stereo. blocks, in a wrapper or advertising sheet, not to be chargeable, except for the time occupied in making up.

ORIGINAL LONDON SCALE	SCALE OF 1891

Advertisements and Wood-cuts connected with Advertisements, occurring in Periodical Publications, to be charged in a similar manner. (*Addenda*, 1847.)

20. Jobs of one sheet or under (except Auctioneers' Catalogues and Particulars) to be cast up at 8*d*. per 1000; if done in smaller type than Brevier, to take the proportionate advance specified in Article 1.—If in foreign language of one sheet or under (except Auctioneers' Catalogues), to be cast up at 9*d*. per 1000; if done in smaller type than Brevier, to take the proportionate advance specified in Article 1. (1810.)

19. Jobs of one sheet or under to be cast up at 8½*d*. per 1000; in foreign language, 10*d*. Jobs in smaller type than brevier to take the proportionate advance specified in Art. 1.

Two pages only, irrespective of imposition, to be paid as two pages; if with an indorse or any other kind of matter constituting a third, then as three pages.

Jobs of the character of book-work to be cast up in sheets, with the usual extras, and the portion of the sheet which is actually set up or imposed to be charged. (1847.)

Jobs of the character of book-work to be cast up in sheets, with the usual extras, and the portion of the sheet which is actually set up or imposed to be charged.

Tracts of one sheet or under, printed for Religious or other Societies, or forming part of an uniform series, not to be considered jobs, but to be cast up according to Article 1, with the addition of 2*s*. 6*d*. per sheet. (1847.)

Tracts or papers of one sheet or under, forming part of an uniform series, not to be considered jobs, but to be cast up according to Art. 1, with the addition of 1*s*. per sheet for folio, 1*s*. 6*d*. for 4to., and 2*s*. 6*d*. for 8vo. and smaller sizes, provided the compositors obtain a return of letter, &c., in each case.

21. Where two pages only are imposed, either opposite to or at the back of each other, they shall be paid for as two pages; but if with an indorse, or any other kind of matter constituting a third, then to be paid as a sheet if in folio, a half-sheet if in quarto, and so on. (1810.)

In works printed on every alternate page only, the blank at the back of each page not to be charged. 1847.)

20. Where works are printed on alternate pages, the compositor to be entitled to charge for the time occupied in making up the blanks.

22. Broadsides, such as Leases, Deeds, and Charter-Parties, above the dimensions of crown, whether table or common matter, to be paid the double of common matter; on crown and under, to be paid one and one-half common matter. The indorse to be paid one-fourth of the inside page as common matter. (1810).

This Article to apply to undisplayed Broadsides of one measure; if set up in 2, 3, or 4 columns, to be paid one-fourth the price of common matter extra.

Displayed Broadsides to be paid as follows :—
If containing more than 16 lines—

		s.	d.
Foolscap or Crown		5	0
Demy		7	0
Royal		8	6
Double Crown	..	10	0

If containing 13 and not more than 16 lines, three-fourths of the prices specified; if 12 lines and under, one-half. (1847.)

Tabular and Table work is matter set up in 2 or more columns depending upon each other and reading across the page. To be paid as follows :—

3 columns without headings, one-fourth extra.

3 columns with headings, or 4 columns without, one-half extra.

4 columns with headings, and 5 or more with or without, double the price of common matter.

Headings in smaller type than the body, but not exceeding two removes from it, if not more than three lines in depth, to be paid 1s. per sheet extra; if more than 3 lines, or if in smaller type than two removes, to be

21. Undisplayed broadsides in one measure, such as leases, deeds, and charter-parties, above the dimensions of crown, whether table or common matter, to be paid double the price of common matter; on crown and under, one and one-half common matter; if set in 2, 3, or 4 columns, one and one-fourth common matter ; 5 columns, one and one-half; 6 columns double. The indorse to be paid one-fourth of the inside page as common matter. Displayed broadsides, if containing more than 16 lines, to be paid as follows :—

		s.	d.
Foolscap or Crown		5	0
Demy		7	0
Royal		8	6
Double Crown	..	10	0

If containing 13 and not more than 16 lines, three-fourths of the prices specified; if 12 lines and under, one-half.

Broadside descriptions of plates to be paid one and one-fourth common matter, and each turnover page to be paid as a full page.

22. Tabular and table work is matter set up in three or more columns depending upon each other and reading across the page. To be paid as follows :—

3 columns without headings, one-fourth extra.

3 columns with headings, 4 columns without, one-half extra.

4 columns with headings, and 5 or more with or without, double the price of common matter.

Headings in smaller type than the body, but not exceeding two removes, if not more than three lines in depth, to be paid 1s. extra; if more than three lines, or if in smaller type than two removes, to be cast up according

ORIGINAL LONDON SCALE	SCALE OF 1891

cast up according to the relative values of the two bodies; the greatest number of appearing lines being considered the depth. (*Addenda*, 1847.)

The following to be considered a definition of the word heading :—

Parish.	Name of Voter.	Residence.
Chelsea ..	John Smith..	Belgrave Place.

Or thus, when set in smaller type, and forming three or more lines :—

Name of Voter.	Trade or Profession.	Place of Residence.
John Smith	Wheelwright	Chelsea.

Blank Tables to be cast up double the price of the text type of the work. No extra charge to be made for headings in smaller type, unless such headings constitute one-half of the table.

The extra price for table, tabular, and column matter to be paid upon its actual dimensions only, with the following exceptions :—Title headings to table and tabular matter to be reckoned as part of such matter; but if they exceed 5 ems of the body of the table, &c., in depth, 5 ems only to be charged as table, the remainder as common matter.

Bottom Notes to tables to be paid on the same plan as Title Headings; not to constitute a *pro rata* charge per sheet.

The extra price for table, tabular, and column matter, when paid by an addition to the price per 1000, to be cast up according to Art. 1 : thus a Greek table to be paid as once Greek and once English matter. (*Addenda*, 1847.)

---

to the relative values of the two bodies; the greatest number of appearing lines being considered the depth.

The following to be considered a definition of the word heading :—

Parish.	Name of Voter.	Residence.
Chelsea ..	John Smith..	Belgrave Place.

Or thus, when set in smaller type, and forming three or more lines :—

Name of Voter.	Trade or Profession.	Place of Residence.
John Smith	Wheelwright	Chelsea.

Blank tables to be cast up double the price of the text type of the work. No extra charge to be made for headings in smaller type, unless such headings constitute one-third of the table.

The extra price for table, tabular, and column matter to be paid on the actual dimensions only, with the following exceptions:—Title headings to table and tabular matter to be reckoned as part of such matter; but when exceeding 5 ems of the body of the table, &c., in depth, 5 ems only to be charged as table, the remainder as common matter.

Bottom notes to tables to be paid on the same plan as title headings; not to constitute a *pro rata* charge per sheet, provided they do not exceed 5 ems of the body of the table.

Table, tabular, and column matter, when paid by an addition to the price per 1000, to be cast up according to Art. 1 : thus a Greek table is cast up as once Greek and once English.

Tables belonging to a work to take the extras of that work.

Column matter, as distinguished from Table and Tabular, is matter made up continuously in two or more columns, not dependent upon each other for their arrangement. To be paid as follows :—

2-column matter—in sizes less than folio :—

In quarto and 8vo.   1s. 0d. per sheet
    12mo.   ..   ..   1s. 6d.   ,,
    16mo. and smal-
        ler sizes   ..   2s. 0d.   ,,

3-columns :—

In pages 21 ems Pica or less wide, one-fourth more than common matter.

In pages of greater width, 2s. per sheet extra.

4-columns :—

In folio and 4to., 4s. per sheet.

In 8vo. and smaller sizes, in pages 22 ems Pica and less wide, one half more than common matter; in pages of greater width, one-fourth more than common matter. (*Addenda,* 1847.)

5-columns—in folio and 4to., one-half more than common matter; in 8vo. and smaller sizes, double the price of common matter. (*Addenda,* 1847.)

Column matter not exceeding 5 ems Pica in width to be paid one-half more than common matter; not exceeding 4 ems Pica, double the price of common matter.

Parallel matter, dialogues, vocabularies, comparative statements, and matter of a similar description, although arranged in columns depending upon each other, to be considered as column matter; if attended with extra trouble, to be arranged between the employer and journeymen.

23. Column matter, as distinguished from table and tabular, is matter made up continuously in two or more columns, not depending upon each other, and reading down the page. To be paid as follows :—

2-columns :—

In folio and 4to. ..   1s. 0d. per sheet
    8vo.   ..   ..   2s. 0d.   ,,
    12mo.   ..   ..   3s. 0d.   ,,
    16mo. and smal-
        ler sizes   ..   4s. 0d.   ,,

3-columns :—

In folio and 4to., 2s. per sheet.

In 8vo. and smaller sizes, one-fourth more than common matter.

4-columns :—

In folio and 4to., 4s. per sheet.

In 8vo. and smaller sizes, one-half more than common matter.

5-columns :—

In folio and 4to., one-half more than common matter.

In 8vo. and smaller sizes, double the price of common matter.

6-columns :—

In all cases double the price of common matter.

Column matter not exceeding 5 ems pica in width to be paid one-half more than common matter; not exceeding 4 ems pica, double the price of common matter.

Parallel matter, dialogues, vocabularies, comparative statements, and matter of a similar description, although arranged in columns depending upon each other, to be considered as column matter; if attended with extra trouble, to be paid by agreement between the employer and journeyman.

ORIGINAL LONDON SCALE	SCALE OF 1891

Two-column matter interspersed throughout the text of a work, to be paid in 4to., 8vo., and 12mo., 6d. per sheet extra; in 16mo, and smaller sizes, 1s. per sheet extra; if constituting more than half the work, to be paid as if the whole sheet were column matter. (*Addenda*, 1847.)

Two-column matter interspersed through a volume, to be charged 1s. per sheet extra in 8vo., 1s. 6d. in 12mo., 2s. in 16mo., on the sheets in which such matter occurs.

Three columns, depending upon each other, when made up forming six across the page; and six columns, depending upon each other, across two pages, to be charged double.

The above charges to be made upon every description of work, and to include the insertion of column rules when required. (*Addenda*, 1847.)

The foregoing charges to be made upon every description of work, and to include the insertion of column rules when required.

Algebraical and other mathematical works, consisting of mathematical fractional workings numerously interspersed throughout, to be paid double the price of common matter. When, however, such workings are not numerous, they shall only be cast up as double, the remainder of the work being cast up as common matter, with such extra for fractions, &c., as shall be mutually agreed upon between the employer and journeyman. (*Addenda*, 1847.)

24. Algebraical and mathematical works, consisting of mathematical fractional workings numerously interspersed throughout to be paid double the price of common matter.

Where lines or small portions of algebraical or mathematical workings occur in different parts of a work, such lines or portions are not to be measured and cast up, but to be paid for in proportion to the labour or time employed in executing them.

Chemical and medical works to be cast up as common matter, with such extras for split fractions, superiors, inferiors, signs, &c., as shall be mutually agreed upon between the employer and journeyman for the time occupied.

Pedigrees to be paid double the price of common matter; and the heads and notes upon the same principle as the heads and notes of tables. (*Addenda*, 1847.)

25. Pedigress to be paid double the price of common matter; and the heads and notes upon the same principle as the heads and notes of tables.

Pedigrees worked separately to take the extras of the work.

ORIGINAL LONDON SCALE	SCALE OF 1891

Interlinear matter, on the plan of the Hamiltonian system, to be cast up as one and one-half the price of common matter; the actual number of lines of small type only being reckoned.

In grammars, &c., where words and figures, not being a literal translation, are arranged between the lines, one-fourth more than common matter to be paid. (*Addenda*, 1847.)

Works sent out in slips not made up into perfect pages, to be made up at the expense of the employer; if in two or three columns, provided that each column exceeds 12 ems pica in width, no charge for column matter to be made in the casting up. If set up in long primer or smaller type, the charges for 16mo., 18mo., &c., under Art. 9, to be relinquished; if sent out without head-lines, the value of the head-lines to be deducted from the casting-up. (*Addenda*, 1847.)

Matter driven out by insertions to be charged by the compositor, but the value to be deducted from the

---

26. Interlinear matter, on the plan of the Hamiltonian system, to be paid as one-half the large and one-half the small type, and to be cast up as one and one-half the price of common matter.

In grammars, &c., where figures and words are arranged between the lines (not being a literal translation), one-fourth more than common matter to be paid.

27. Works set up in slips may be paid for in either of the following ways :—

a. To be cast up and charged at 8*d.* per 1000 leaded or solid, with all such extras as may actually occur in the slips, the compositor to be relieved from all further responsibility. Matter set to less than 16 ems of its own body in width (not being table, tabular, or column matter), to be charged one-fourth extra; less than 10 ems of its own body, one-third extra. Slips so charged to become the property of the employer, who shall not be liable to any further claim, anything otherwise stated in the scale notwithstanding; the copy to be given out and proofs pulled by the house.

b. Works sent out in slips, not in perfect pages, to be corrected and made up at the expense of the employer, and charged as sent to press; but if in two or three columns, provided that each column exceeds 12 ems pica in width, no charge for column matter to be made; if set in long primer or smaller type, the charges for 16mo., 18mo., &c., under Art. 11, to be relinquished; if sent out without headlines, the value of the headlines to be deducted.

Matter driven out by insertions to be charged by the compositor as the work goes to press, but the value to be

ORIGINAL LONDON SCALE	SCALE OF 1891

time taken in driving out such matter; when driven out by leads, the over-matter to be charged by the compositor, deducting the time taken in inserting the leads; when driven out by the insertion of wood-cuts, the matter to be charged, but the time taken in justifying such wood-cuts to be deducted. (*Addenda*, 1847.)

17. Index matter, though but one measure, to be paid 2*s.* per sheet extra. (1810.)

Prefatory matter, preliminary dissertations, biographical memoirs, &c., not exceeding a sheet, if set up in type not less than the body of the text, to be paid as pages of the work; if set up in smaller type, to be cast up with the addition of the extras of the work; but if either exceed a sheet, to be cast up as appendices. Half-titles, titles, dedications, &c., in all cases to be paid as pages of the work. Appendices, portions of works, &c., set up in a different type from the text, and made up in separate pages, to be cast up upon their own merits; and if not exceeding five sheets, or if made up without a return of letter, to take one shilling per sheet extra, according to Art. 8. Indices, being provided for by Art. 17, are not included in this rule. (*Addenda*, 1847.)

STANDING MATTER.—Standing Preliminary Matter to a Work should be charged according to the decision of the Arbitration Committee in 1856, viz. :—

"That the compositors are entitled to the Preliminary Matter as pages of

deducted from the time taken in setting insertions and driving out such matter; when driven out by leads, the over-matter to be charged by the compositor, the time occupied in inserting leads to be deducted; when driven out by the insertion of wood-cuts, the matter to be charged, but the time taken in justifying such wood-cuts to be deducted.

28. Indices, though but one measure, to be paid 2*s.* per sheet extra.

29. Appendices, portions of works, &c., set up in a different type from the text, and made up in separate pages to be cast up on their own merits; and if not exceeding five sheets, or if made up without a return of letter, to take 1*s.* per sheet extra, according to Art. 12. Prefatory matter, preliminary dissertations, biographical memoirs, &c., not exceeding a sheet, if set up in type not less than the body of the text, to be paid as pages of the work; if set up in smaller type, to be cast up with the addition of the extras of the work; but if either exceed a sheet, to be cast up as appendices. Half-titles, titles, dedications, etc., in all cases to be paid as pages of the work. Indices, being provided for by Art. 28, are not included in this rule. Compositors engaged on a volume to be entitled to the preliminary, appendix, index, &c., but such matter may by mutual arrangement be given to another piece companionship in an emergency.

30. Matter having been once used becomes the property of the employer at whatever time lifted, the compositor to be entitled to charge for correcting, making up, &c.

the Work; but should the alterations in the small type have exceeded the value of a like number of pages of the Work, then such small-type matter shall be charged as if recomposed." This has been decided to mean, that if the corrections on any page exceed the value of a page of the work, such page (or pages) should be cast up according to their respective values— the remainder to be charged as pages of the work.

When a work has considerable quantities of standing matter interspersed throughout, all complete sections of a sheet of standing matter belong to the house; those sections consisting partly of newly-composed and partly of standing matter belong to the compositors.

"*Standing Matter from a Magazine introduced into a Work by the same Author.*—The compositors are entitled to charge the work as it goes to press, including the matter from the magazine."

"A standing price current, with corrections, introduced into a monthly magazine, but not forming a distinct portion of the same, should be charged as composition."

"*Standing pages*—such as a balance sheet, &c.—the compositors are entitled to charge at the price of pages of the body of the work." [*Trade Memoranda in* Ed. of Scale published 1879.]

MIXING BODIES.—Works (not reviews or periodical publications) in which more than one type is used in various parts of the text, are charged 1*s*. per sheet for every body above one. Thus, a work in pica and long primer is charged 1*s*. per sheet; and one in pica, small pica, bourgeois, and nonpareil is charged 3*s*. per sheet extra. Notes not to be reckoned a body. [*Trade Memoranda* in Ed. of Scale published 1879.]

31. Works, other than reviews or periodicals, in which more than one type is used in various parts of the text, to be charged 1*s*. for every fount above one for the sheets in which the mixture occurs.

'ORIGINAL LONDON SCALE	SCALE OF 1891
Works with rules or borders round the pages to be cast up according to the actual dimensions of the type, an extra price being paid for the rules or borders according to the trouble occasioned. (*Addenda*, 1847.)	32. Works with rules or borders round the pages to be cast up to the actual dimensions of the type, an extra price being paid for the trouble occasioned.
Blank pages to be filled up at the option of the author, the compositor charging for his previous trouble in making up the blank. (*Addenda*, 1847.)	33. Blank pages to be filled up at the option of the author, the compositor to be entitled to charge for making up the blanks.
	34. Specimen pages in all cases to be paid as jobs.[1]
Cancels in all cases to be charged as pages of the work. (*Addenda*, 1847.)	35. Cancels to be paid as pages of the work, with all extras.
When wood-cuts constitute more than one-fourth of the work, the mode of charging such wood-cuts shall be settled between the employer and journeyman. (*Addenda*, 1847.)	36. No deduction to be made for woodcuts, when constituting one-eighth of a volume or less; when exceeding that quantity, the mode of charging to be arranged between the employer and journeyman. Run-in wood-cuts to be paid not less than 2*d*. each extra.
AUTHOR'S PROOFS.—A piece companionship is entitled to author's proofs of all works they have composed and sent to press. [*Trade Memoranda* in Ed. of Scale published 1889.]	37. Compositors to be entitled to the author's proofs of all works they have composed, except when paid for in slip, in accordance with Art. 27, clause (*a*); but such proofs may by mutual arrangement be given to another companionship in an emergency.
23. All Corrections to be paid 6*d*. per hour. (1810.)	38. Corrections and time-work to be paid at the rate of 8½*d*. per hour.
4. "That corrections be paid at the rate of 8*d*. per hour." (1872.)	

[1] "So far as the London Scale is concerned, this is a new paragraph although a very old custom; but as we have found it dealt with in other scales we have incorporated it here." (*Report of Sub-Committee appointed to revise the London Scale of Prices*, L.S.C., 1890, p. 11.)

ORIGINAL LONDON SCALE	SCALE OF 1891
All works to be cast up as sent to press, except by mutual agreement between the employer and journeyman. (*Addenda*, 1847.)	39. All works to be cast up as sent to press, except when paid for in slip in accordance with Art. 27, clause *a*.
	40. Turned letters, when ordered to be used, to be altered at the expense of the employer.
	41. Clarendon,[1] or other fancy type, to be paid not less than 1s. per sheet for each fount in such sheets in which it is used.
	42. Hair-spaced headlines to be charged 1s. per sheet extra in 8vo., 1s. 6d. in 12mo., and 2s. in 16mo.; headlines requiring justification to be paid at the same rates. Hair-spaced words introduced into the body of a work to be paid according to the time occupied. Brass rules after headlines, or used continuously throughout the sheet, if cut by the compositor, to be paid 1s. per sheet extra.
	43. Braces and justifications, letters or words of a smaller or larger size than the depth of the line in which they occur, requiring justification, inferior or superior letters or figures made up of two pieces, and split fractions, to be paid according to the time occupied, but not less than 6d. per sheet for those sheets in which they occur.
	44. Initial or ornamental letters to be paid, if justified, in solid matter, 1d.; in leaded matter, 2d. Cut-in initials to be paid not less than 1d. extra on the above charges.

[1] Clarendon is not, properly speaking, a "fancy type," but a bold face with bracketed slab serifs and even colour. According to Gray, N., *Nineteenth Century Ornamented Types and Title Pages* (London, 1938), p. 51, it was introduced by Besley in 1845. The extra charge was to remunerate the compositor for his trouble in setting from and distributing into an additional pair of cases.

ORIGINAL LONDON SCALE	SCALE OF 1891

45. In all works where the last word of a line is taken into the line above or below, the compositor to charge at the rate of one full line for every four words, or portion thereof, taken above or below.

46. Matter overrun to be paid one-half of the measure to which it is overrun, with all the extras; this charge to include making up and imposition.

47. Matter set to less than 16 ems of its own body in width (not being table, tabular, or column matter), to be charged one-fourth extra; less than 10 ems of its own body, one-third extra.

16. Music to be paid double the body of the sonnet type. (1810.)

Music to be paid by agreement between the employer and journeymen, the foregoing Article being wholly inapplicable to instrumental music. (1847.)

48. Music to be paid by agreement between the employer and journeyman.

49. Suitable distribution for each work to be provided, but if matter interspersed with clarendon, italic, figures, etc., be given out, an arrangement to be made between the employer and journeyman whereby the latter may be compensated for the extra time occupied.

50. Compositors not to be called on to clear away any description of work at their own expense.

By mutual arrangement between the employer and journeyman and with the approval of the Chapel, compositors 55 years of age and upwards may accept employment at the minimum rate of 30s. per week, provided they are regularly engaged in clearing away and not called upon under any circumstances to assist at case or to take up any description of composition, etc. The ordinary extra

ORIGINAL LONDON SCALE	SCALE OF 1891

rates for overtime to be paid to compositors so engaged.

51. By mutual arrangement between the employer and journeyman, piece companionships to have the right of appointing and controlling their own clickers, who must not be establishment hands.

The members in offices shall not be called off the piece to be put on the establishment for any description of composition, unless engaged for at least a fortnight, according to the terms in Rule XLI; nor shall any member contract, by way of farming, to do any description of bookwork or jobbing, or accept an engagement on any such work so contracted for. (No. 43 of L.S.C. Rules, 1889.)

52. Compositors not to be called off the piece on to the establishment for any description of composition, unless engaged for at least a fortnight, except with the consent of the Chapel, when they may assist in a case of emergency.

53. Compositors not to contract, by way of farming, to do any description of bookwork or jobbing, or to accept an engagement on any such work so contracted for.

That members called in to assist in the composition of bookwork or jobbing, may take a casual engagement for not less than a day on the establishment, but not of a greater length than a fortnight; at the expiration of which time they must either be paid on the piece, or, if not then discharged, be entitled to a fortnight's notice. (No. 41 of L.S.C. Rules, 1889.)

54. Compositors called in to assist in the composition of bookwork or jobbing may take a casual engagement for not less than a day on the establishment, but not of greater length than a fortnight without being entitled to a fortnight's notice, except when specifically engaged for a particular job and retained for that job only, in which case the engagement can be terminated on its completion, without notice.

Compositors on the establishment to receive not less than 33s. per week, for 10½ hours of full work per day. An extra allowance to be made for working beyond the time specified. (*Addenda*, 1847.)

3. That the establishment wages be 36s. per week of sixty hours, the apportionment of the sixty hours to be mutually agreed upon between the employers and the journeymen in each office. (1866.)

1. That the hours of labour shall consist of 54 per week. (1872.)

55. Compositors on the establishment to receive not less than 38s. per week of 54 hours, the apportionment of hours to be mutually agreed upon between the employer and journeymen in each office, and to govern all the compositors employed.

ORIGINAL LONDON SCALE	SCALE OF 1891

ORIGINAL LONDON SCALE

Compositors to receive and give a fortnight's notice previously to their engagement being terminated. (*Addenda*, 1847.)

19. Night work to commence and be paid for, from ten o'clock till twelve, 1*s.*; all after to be paid 3*d.* per hour extra till 6.—Morning work, commencing at four o'clock, to be paid 1*s.* extra. (1810.)

2. That overtime shall commence after 7 p.m. from Monday to Friday, and after 2 p.m. on Saturday; each day standing on its own merits. (1872.)

Sunday work, if not exceeding six hours, to be paid for 1*s.*; if for a longer time 2*d.* an hour. (1810.)

5. That Sunday work be paid for at the rate of 6*d.* per hour extra, but that in no case shall a compositor receive less than 2*s.* 6*d.* extra. (1866.)

24. The imprint to be considered as two lines in the square of the page. (1810.)

SCALE OF 1891

56. Compositors, whether piece or establishment hands, if retained beyond a fortnight, to receive and give a fortnight's notice prior to their engagements being terminated.

57. Overtime to be paid at the rate of 3½*d.* per hour extra for the first three hours; after that time, but in any case after 10 o'clock from Monday to Friday inclusive, at 4*d.* per hour till 12 o'clock, after that at 5*d.* per hour. On Saturday, for the first three hours, 4*d.* an hour, and after that time 5*d.* The charge for overtime to be governed by the ordinary working hours of each office, and to commence in any case before 8 a.m., after 8 p.m., and after 2 p.m. on Saturday, each day standing on its own merits. Compositors called upon to work the whole of the dinner-hour to receive 4*d.* extra. Compositors regularly employed in a night companionship for a fortnight at least to charge 3½*d.* per hour extra, including meal-times. Compositors called upon to work overtime for more than three consecutive hours to be entitled to half-an-hour for refreshment after each three hours of overtime have been worked. Fractions of hours to be paid as complete hours. Lost time to be deducted at the ordinary rate, but a compositor coming in more than half-an-hour late may be called upon to work the first hour of overtime the same day without charging extra, each day standing on its own merits.

58. Sunday work to be paid at the rate of 8*d.* per hour extra from 12 o'clock on Saturday night to 8 o'clock on Monday morning, when such work is continuous; compositors in no case to receive less than 3*s.* 4*d.* extra. The same rule to apply to Christmas Day. Compositors called in at 12 o'clock on Sunday night to be paid at the same rate; if at 6 o'clock on Monday or any other morning, except Sunday, at 4*d.* per hour extra.

In spite of the immense amount of trouble taken, upon the initiative of the L.S.C., to evolve the piece-work Scale of 1891, it was soon to become a dead letter. An ever-increasing amount of work was done by the establishment hands at fixed weekly wages. The employers were not willing to pay the extras demanded for such items as tabular setting and other types of setting which were now more profitable to the piece-hands. Their answer was to give all such work to the establishment men, and to allow the piece-work compositors only the straightforward solid composition, which had to be accomplished with considerable celerity (to the benefit of the employers) if the men were to earn a reasonable wage. Again, if there was a shortage of work, the establishment compositor was kept busy at the expense of the piece-hand who stood idle and therefore unable to earn. If men on piece-work objected to conditions in their office, they were free to give a fortnight's notice, but were liable to find the same conditions elsewhere. Alternatively, an employer could always tender the same notice to a piece-hand if, in his opinion, the man's earnings were too considerable. Then, if he felt so disposed, he offered to re-engage the man as an establishment hand, and in such cases the compositor had little option but to accept.

Work which was required in a hurry was still done on the piece, especially Parliamentary and Periodical printing. However, shortly after 1900, the Linotype composing machine, first used in London for daily newspaper composition in 1893, was being installed in general offices as well, and more and more composition was mechanically set, the make-up and imposition being attended to by the establishment hands. This was the death-knell of the traditional hand-compositor's trade and of the piece-work system. Although piece Scales were soon evolved for machine operators in the general offices, such men were almost universally paid at establishment rates slightly higher than those of the hand compositors.

The composing machines (as opposed to the already obsolete type-setting machines) were extremely productive in the hands of a well-trained operator, since an output of anything between 6,000 and 8,000 ens per hour was feasible, and with no distribution cost, since unwanted used matter was melted down. The first composing machine Scales were favourable to the operators, but it was not long before employers in the general trade decided to pay establishment as opposed to piece rates.

Thus by 1910 composing-room practice and methods of

charging had become completely altered. And whereas the compositor of 1810 worked under much the same conditions as his predecessors in 1710, by the turn of the nineteenth century a revolution had taken place in both the organization, economy and technique of the composing department.

CHAPTER XIV

GOVERNMENT AND LEGAL PRINTING

I. VARIETIES OF PARLIAMENTARY PRINTING

In describing the organization of government printing at the beginning of the nineteenth century, a distinction must be made between the work ordered by the two Houses of Parliament in connection with the conduct and record of their business, and the printing handled by the Stationery Office acting for the various public departments. Whereas the work under the control of the Stationery Office was put out on tender to the general trade, parliamentary printing was the specialized activity of a limited number of offices.

The printing done by order of the two Houses of Parliament between 1660 and 1837 is divisible into the printed records of their proceedings and the printed versions of papers which came into their possession. The printed records of the votes and proceedings of the House of Commons consisted, in 1800, of the *Votes* and *Journals*; those of the House of Lords, of *Journals*. The printed versions of papers which came into the possession of Parliament were the reports and returns of various committees and government offices, *i.e.*, Blue Books and White Papers. There were also the texts of Bills put before Parliament, of the Acts as passed into law, and the Appeal Cases and other legal documents of the House of Lords.[1]

During the eighteenth century printing for Parliament became concentrated in the hands of a few firms. As may be expected, the King's Printer was represented among them. The first King's Printer's Patent, granted by Queen Elizabeth to Christopher and Robert Barker in 1589, gave the patentees the right to print,

---

[1] These terms are merely descriptive of a physical difference in parliamentary papers. A Blue Book, so called from the colour of its cover, is a paper the number of sheets of which made sewing, glueing and covering necessary. That the colour of the cover was originally blue is quite fortuitous. A White Paper is a piece of printing whose sheets, being few in number, do not require anything more than simple stitching.

The writer must here state his indebtedness to H. Hale Bellot's paper on *Parliamentary Printing*, 1660-1837, in *Bull. Inst. Historical Research*, November, 1933. This study contains much valuable information on the origins of the various kinds of printing done for both Houses.

inter alia, "omnium et singulorum statutorum, librorum, libel-
lorum, actuum parliamenti, proclamationum, injunctionum, ac
bibliorum, et novorum testamentorum." In 1769, when the
patent was transferred to Eyre, Strahan and Reeves, the King's
Printers were still entitled to print "all and singular Statutes,
Books, small Books, Acts of Parliament, Proclamations and
Injunctions, and Bibles and New Testaments."[1]

According to a statement made by Andrew Spottiswoode to
the Select Committee on King's Printers' Patents in 1831, the
printing of the House of Lords "was transferred to the firm with
which his name is connected [*i.e.*, Eyre and Strahan], upon an
estimate of charges being sent in, about sixty years ago." The first
thirty-one volumes of the *Journals* of the House of Lords were
printed by William Bowyer, the last volume of the series being
completed in 1777, the year of his death.[2] The order to print
the *Journal* was not given again until 1793.[3] It is probable that
the contract then passed to the King's Printers. Although their
imprint cannot be found on this work until after 1850, it is on
record that they had the printing of it in 1800.[4]

The first general order to print the votes of the House of
Commons was made in 1680. It was repeated in 1681 and extended
to read "and Proceedings." The text of the *Votes* was derived
from the entries made by the clerks at the table during the sitting
of the House, but included, besides the record of all the acts of
the House, all public petitions. From 1680 onwards the *Votes*
were placed on sale to the public, but from 1772, as J. B. Nichols
reported to a Select Committee in 1822, the sale gradually
diminished, occasioned by the proceedings being reported in the
newspapers.

Until 1729 the *Votes* were printed by a number of different
firms, including the King's Printers. In the latter year, however,
the contract was given to William Bowyer. "Through the friend-
ship of the Right Honourable Arthur Onslow, he was appointed
Printer of the Votes of the House of Commons in 1729; and
continued in that employ under three successive Speakers, for
almost fifty years."[5] Bowyer was followed by John Nichols

---

[1] For the texts of the Patents of 1589 and 1769, as well as a summary list
of the King's Printers, see Hansard, T.C., *op. cit.*, pp. 175-187.

[2] Nichols, J., *Anecdotes of William Bowyer* (London, 1782), p. 476.

[3] Hale Bellot, *op. cit.*, p. 91.

[4] Report from *Select Committee on King's Printers' Patents* (1832), Appendix
(C), p. 304.

[5] Nichols, J., *op. cit.*, p. 61. Hansard, T. C., *Typographia*, p. 328.

(1745–1826), in turn his apprentice, partner, successor and biographer. The firm of Nichols printed the *Votes* until 1940, when it closed its doors. The *Votes* are now printed by the Stationery Office.

The *Journal* of the House of Commons is a fair and enlarged record, in narrative form, of the proceedings, compiled from the minutes and other papers in possession of the clerks, namely *Votes and Proceedings*, papers printed by order of the House, petitions and other manuscript and printed papers presented to the House.

The printing of the *Journals* and, far more important, the miscellaneous papers of the Commons, was in the hands of a third firm. About the year 1763 John Hughs "obtained through the interest of Lord North, who had been his schoolfellow at Eton, the appointment as printer of the Parliamentary Papers and Journals of the House of Commons; by him thus was laid the foundation of a business brought to a high degree of prosperity."[1] Hughs died in 1771. His son Henry directed the firm until 1799, when it was sold to Luke Hansard who had long been employed in the business.

II. THE STATIONERY OFFICE

The following remarks, relative to the foundation of the Stationery Office in 1786, are taken from the evidence of Samuel Brooke, printer in Paternoster Row, before the Select Committee on Printing and Stationery of 1822 :[2]

The Stationery-office was originally established in consequence of there having been patents where the patentees were not printers or stationers, but employed printers or stationers to do the business, and

---

[1] Hansard's *Parliamentary Debates*, commonly known as "Hansard," was founded by T. C. Hansard, eldest son of Luke, who conducted his own business. Both firms were merged into Horatio Bottomley's ill-starred Hansard Publishing Union in 1889 and 1890 respectively. The Hansard Union collapsed in 1891. The firm of Hansard and Sons, founded by Hughs, was then taken over by Eyre and Spottiswoode. The *Parliamentary Debates* were, in turn, printed by Reuter, Eyre and Spottiswoode, Waterlow, Wyman and Truscott. Since 1920 they have been printed by H.M.S.O. See the genealogical chart compiled by the present writer in *The Monotype Recorder*, Vol. 38, No. 2 (1939).

[2] p. 235. See also his *An Appeal to the Legislature on the Subject of the Office of the King's Printer in England* (London, 1830), and *A Second Appeal*, etc. (1832). Both contain much useful information concerning government printing arrangements at the time. Hansard, Luke James, *Proposition for a National Printing Office* (London, 1848), is also indispensable. The only copy I have seen is in the British Museum.

charging a very large profit upon the work, thereby getting a very great income. I think it is now about thirty years since it was determined by Mr. Pitt, that the Stationery-office should be established to save those great additional sums the public were paying; we were employed by the patentee as tradesmen, at the trade price, as it is commonly described; our employer was Mr. Vincent; we printed for the Customs, and the major part of the Excise; the Customs was afterwards taken from us, and given to Mr. Walter, the printer of *The Times*, by Mr. Pitt; it afterwards went into other hands; we were likewise the printers of *The London Gazette*, under a patent likewise; we were the mere mechanics that carried on the business, at as low a rate as the patentees could get it done; this went forward till the patents were expired, and then we printed the Excise business, under the Stationery-office. . . .

The initial turnover of the Stationery Office was about £17,000. Besides printing, it supplied pens, paper, ink, sealing wax, red tape and all other necessary supplies for the public offices. The first accounts were with the following departments :—

Stamp Office, Distributor's Branch	India Board
	Pay Office
House of Lords	The Lord Chamberlain
House of Commons	Comptroller of Army Accounts
Salt Office	Hawkers and Pedlars
Tax Office	Commissioners of Audit

The Patent granted to Edward Castles in 1717 for the supply of four offices finally expired in 1797, when the following accounts were transferred to the Stationery Office, with an accretion of revenue of £7,000 per annum :—

Secretaries of State	Master of the Great Wardrobe
Customs	Excise

The only remaining Patent had been granted to Jacob Tonson and Son, dated January, 1720, for supply to :—

Post-master General	Secretary at War
Treasurer of the Navy	Stamp Office, Incident Branch
A part of the Excise Office	

This Patent had been originally granted for forty years, and was renewed on two subsequent occasions for like periods, the last being to Messrs. Mount and Page. Upon its expiration in 1800 the offices mentioned above fell to the Stationery Office.[1]

In 1830 the Stationery Office supplied one hundred and twenty-two public offices (including those in Ireland) with printing and

[1] The whole of the above information is taken from *Select Committee on King's Printers' Patents*, 1832, p. 235.

stationery to the value of about £300,000. At that date, with
the exception of certain work printed by the Excise Office with
plant owned by it, all work was put out to tender.

III. SCALE OF COMPOSITORS' PRICES FOR PARLIAMENTARY WORK

It will be noticed that no agreement reached between the
employers and compositors between 1785 and 1810 mentions any
special scale of prices for parliamentary work. It is probable that,
since this class of work was concentrated in the hands of three
firms, any special regulations were of no immediate interest to
the greater part of the body of journeymen. It would appear,
however, that from time immemorial compositors engaged on
certain classes of parliamentary work demanded and received
greater remuneration than that earned by their brethren engaged
on books and jobbing.

In brief, it may be said that all parliamentary work which had
to be completed with expedition was liable to the extra charge.
Thus, for example, the *Votes* (Nichols), Miscellaneous Papers
(Hansard), Appeal Cases, Acts of Parliament, Proclamations
(King's Printer) were all of such a nature that their rapid delivery
was essential for the proper conduct of public business. The
Journals of both Houses being historical records of each Session
were not required with such urgency, and were compiled and
printed in a more leisurely fashion.

When they appeared before the Select Committee of 1822,
Luke Hansard and his son Luke Graves Hansard were asked
"why the difference was made between the rate paid for private
work and the rate paid for government work . . .?"[1] Their
answer was that

The principle upon which the difference was made is from time out
of mind; the ground-work of it is the greater expedition with which the
work is expected to be done. The workmen are always expected
to be in attendance, and to submit to certain general arrangements in
the management of the printing-office, which is not customary in other
description of employment, nor required in other offices. The difference
in wages is likewise upon the principle, that the compositors have to set
up the whole of the presses, and therefore have no advantage from what is
technically called a return of the letter,[2] but which is the case in the usual
process of the printing business; for a few sheets being set up, the men in

---

[1] *Select Committee on King's Printers' Patents*, 1832, pp. 182-6.
[2] *i.e.*, distribution of formes from which an impression has already been
taken.

setting up these first few sheets lose a considerable portion of time in collecting together the necessary materials, which in the return affords them an advantage in doing their work, by enabling them to use the same materials repeatedly for the progressive performance of their work. But in Parliamentary printing, as the whole of the presses are set up,[1] they have not that advantage, and that is the cause of the custom in the trade to pay higher wages for pamphlets than for large books; and upon this difference is grounded the principle of the difference in the rate of wages.

Although the pressmen's prices for pulling Bills before Parliament were published in 1801, those for the composition of parliamentary work were not included in any of the early Scales nor in the Scale of 1810 itself. The draft Scale of Prices, dated 29 January, 1805, prepared by the London compositors for circulation among themselves, contained one clause which did not appear in the final version sent to the employers a few days later. This clause was to regulate the prices to be paid for the composition of Bills in Parliament of a regular and standard size. The prices contained in it may be compared with those published by Caleb Stower in 1808, and in the *London Scale of Prices*, 1836. None of the other trade manuals printed similar details.

	Compositors' Draft Scale January 29, 1805	C. Stower, *Printers' Grammar*, 1808, p. 428	*The London Scale of Prices,* 1836
	25 ems, English wide, 43 deep per sheet	Bills in English, 25 ems wide, 43 deep	Bills, in English, 26 ems wide, 47 deep
ENGLISH			
Without side notes	6s. 6d.	7s. 6d.	6s. 0d.
With side notes	7s. 6d.	—	—
With broad quotation side-notes	—	—	9s. 0d.
With double narrow side notes	—	—	10s. 0d.

[1] The composition was entirely completed before a work was sent to press. The formes could then be put on a number of machines at the same time and the job completed faster than if the press was kept waiting for each individual forme. The amount of material necessary for this method of composition was enormous. According to J. Rickman's evidence before the 1828 Select Committee (p. 47), the Hansards possessed type to the value of £47,000. At that date they employed 200 men.

	Compositors' Draft Scale January 29, 1805	C. Stower, *Printers' Grammar*, 1808, p. 428	*The London Scale of Prices*, 1836
PICA		Bills in pica, 29 ems wide, 42 deep	Bills in pica, 29 ems wide, 53 deep
Without side notes	8s. 6d.	6s. 6d.	7s. 0d.
With side notes	8s. 6d.	8s. 6d.	—
With broad quotation side notes	—	—	10s. 0d.
With double narrow side notes	—	—	11s. 0d.

It may be assumed, however, that these sets of prices did not cover all contingencies. Varying formats, sizes of type, and complicated tabular and column matter would require a more comprehensive Scale. Although the clauses contained in it may have been operative over a long period of years, such a document was not published by the men until 1836. But it is possible to obtain certain information regarding the prices paid to compositors from the reports of the various Select Committees appointed to deal with questions affecting printing and stationery.

In his evidence to the Committee on Public Expenditure (Printing and Stationery) in 1810, Luke Hansard pointed out that, whereas the compositors' price per 1,000 ens for bookwork had been increased from 4d. to 5¼d. since 1785, the price for parliamentary work had remained the same throughout the whole period, *i.e.*, 6d. per 1,000 ens.[1] He and his son, Luke Graves Hansard, appeared before a Select Committee appointed to deal with the same subject in 1822. They then stated that "we now pay 6½d. for wages for parliament work; but there was an advance after 1810, in consequence of the general advance made throughout the trade to the workmen; the price then amounted to 7d.; we have since made a reduction (in 1816) which brought it down to 6½d., and at that rate it has stood ever since."[2]

[1] p. 202. Hansard gave evidence on 9 February, 1810. The employers decided to grant an increase in prices on 12 March. The book scale was then advanced to 5¾d. for leaded and 6d. per 1,000 for solid matter.

[2] In 1816 a reduction of ¾d. per 1,000 for bookwork was forced upon the men by their employers, see p. 189, *supra*. Their evidence appears on p. 190 of the

The firm of Hansard submitted a statement "relative to the Rates of Wages, and Charges for Printing" at the request of the Select Committee of 1822.[1]

RATE OF WAGES PAID TO COMPOSITORS FOR PARLIAMENTARY WORK

Plain matter	6½*d.* per 1,000 letters.
Table matter.	13*d.* ,, ,,

RATE OF WAGES PAID TO PRESSMEN

		If Brevier
From 250	6*d.*	6½*d.*
500 to 750 . . .	5½*d.* per 250	6*d.*
1,000	5*d.* per 250	5½*d.*
For every token of 250 above the first four	4½*d.*	5*d.*

RATE OF CHARGE FOR REAM-WORK

When the rate of Wages paid is	The charge is
4½*d.* per 250, or Token	7*s.* per Ream.
5*d.*	8*s.* ,,
5½*d.*	9*s.* ,,
6*d.*	10*s.* ,,
6½*d.*	11*s.* ,,

Prices for folding, sewing, ordinary stitching, and stitching in Blue Covers were also given.

It was not until immediately after the establishment of the London Union of Compositors that the men decided to draw up and publish a Scale of Prices for parliamentary printing. This followed the action of the Stationery Office in issuing a set of regulations for the guidance of their contractors. According to a statement contained in the L.U.C. circular dated 6 September, 1836, these regulations were published in 1833. No copy of the original version has been found, but "The Conditions under which the Printing Work for the Two Houses of Parliament is executed, showing the Rate paid for Composition and Press-work, for Tabular and Table Matter, Headings, Notes, Corrections and Alterations, and for the various other Services incidental to this Description of Printing" was published as Appendix 13 to the Second Report from the Select Committee on Printed Papers,

---

Report. According to Hansard, T. C., *Typographia*, p. 784, a distinction was made between *public* and *private* parliamentary work. The latter, done at the request of members, was charged at the rate of 7d. per 1,000 ens.

[1] p. 311. Apparently no distinction was made between leaded and unleaded matter.

1835. The regulations are dated from the Stationery Office, 13 March, 1835.

The L.U.C. took immediate exception to this Scale imposed by the Stationery Office, since it contained several regulations not recognized in the Scale of 1810. Most obnoxious of all was that making pica type the standard by which certain classes of composition were to be paid. "This appears, at first sight, to be one of the strangest of human inventions. For let us take the case of a sheet of long primer folio, the last half page of which is blank—and by this system three pages and a half receive a long primer price, and the half page blank is paid as pica, although (it may be) there is not a single pica letter in the whole sheet."[1]

In order to clarify the situation, the L.U.C. appointed a number of delegates to frame a Scale of Parliamentary Prices, since none compiled and approved by the men existed. The men who framed the provisional regulations were selected from firms undertaking that class of work :—[2]

Spottiswoode's	employing	100 men
Hansard's two houses[3] . . .		140
Harrison's		40
Clowes', Stamford Street . .		130
Clowes', Charing Cross . . .		20
Nichols & Sons		20

This Committee drafted a Parliamentary Scale which was discussed at the Annual General Meeting of the L.U.C. on 19 January, 1836. In spite of a protest, dated 23 January, from the chapels of Messrs. Hansard's two establishments, where separate agreements had been made, the fourteen clauses of the Scale were adopted at a Special General Meeting on 12 April, 1836.

---

[1] L.U.C. Annual Report for 1835, p. 14. The point is that there would be potentially fewer pica than long primer ens in the half page, pica being a larger size type than long primer.

[2] *The Compositors' Chronicle*, No. 1, 7 September, 1840, p. 3.

[3] The original firm of Hansard had two offices. The reference does not include T. C. Hansard's establishment. (Hansard's *Debates*.) The "Old House" was in Great Turnstile, between Holborn and Lincoln's Inn Fields, and the "New House" nearby in Parker Street. According to the *Proceedings of the Second Quarterly Meeting of the Delegates of the London Union of Compositors*, 7 October, 1834, Spottiswoode's then had men working in four buildings: Old and New Houses, Law House and Cooperage.

The following *Scale for Parliamentary Work*, adopted by the trade in April, 1836, was printed in *The London Scale of Prices*, *op. cit.*, pp. 66-70. It was also included as an Appendix to the *Report of the Journeymen Members of the Arbitration Committee*, published in 1847.

With the exception of the advance of 1866, the Parliamentary Scale of 1836 remained in force until 1891, when its clauses were revised at the same time as the main Scale. Although prices have since been considerably raised, the terms of the 1891 Parliamentary Scale are still in force, two short paragraphs being added.

[DOCUMENT XCIX]

SCALE FOR PARLIAMENTARY WORK

1. That all work for either House of Parliament, such as Reports, Minutes of Evidence, etc., as well as Reports of Royal Commissions of Inquiry, whether manuscript or reprint, leaded or solid, to be charged at 6½*d*. per 1000,[1] including English and brevier; and always to be cast up according to the type in which it is composed. Tables to be charged 1*s*. 1*d*. per thousand.

2. That all works not intended for either House of Parliament, but executed for the Public Departments, to be paid according to the Scale for Book-work, with all the extras.

3. That Private Parliamentary Bills be charged 7*d*. per thousand, and table-matter in them at 1*s*. 2*d*. per thousand.
This Article does not interfere with those Bills in Parliament which are of the *regular* size, and for which a stated price is paid.

4. That pica or any other type as a standard is in opposition to the practice of the business, and in no case to be admitted; but all Reports, Minutes of Evidence, Accounts, Appendices, &c., are to be cast up according to the type in which they are composed.

5. That pages consisting of two or three columns, with one or more headings, or three or four columns without headings, to be charged as tabular, or one and one-half common matter.

6. That pages consisting of four or more columns, with one or more headings, or five or more columns without headings, to be charged as table, or double the price of common matter.

7. That when short pages occur in a series of tables, to be charged as full pages; but where a table or piece of table occurs in a Report, &c., to be charged only the depth of the table, measuring from the head to the conclusion of the table. The same rule to apply to tabular.

In a *series* of tables all *pieces* of pages left blank are charged as table; in jobs or works consisting of plain matter, where tables or tabular matter are introduced, whatever blank occurs is considered as common matter, unless the table

---

[1] Increased to 7*d*. in 1866, together with the other prices quoted in the first three paragraphs of the Scale. When the book compositors received an advance in 1872, Parliamentary work was specifically excepted.

or tabular matter forms more than three-fourths of a page; in which latter case the page is charged as a full page of table or tabular, as the case may be.

8. That all headings to table or tabular matter, when in smaller type than the body of the table, to be charged extra.

9. Pages consisting of four or five blank columns to be charged tabular; but when the columns are six or more, to be charged table, cast up to the size of the type used in the Reports or Bills in which they occur.

10. When blank forms are used by themselves, detached from any Bill, &c., to be charged as pica table or tabular, according to the number of the columns, as specified in Resolution IX.

11. Plain matter divided into two columns to be charged not less than 1s. per sheet.

12. All read-over pages (as in Dr. and Cr. accounts of two pages), where one page only is tabular or table, the same charge to be made for both pages, and in no case shall read-over pages be charged less than tabular.

13. Side-notes of "broad quotations," and not exceeding five lines per page, in quartos and folios, to be charged 1s. 6d. per sheet; in "double narrows," not exceeding five lines per page, 2s. per sheet, throughout such Report, Appendix, &c., excepting when pages comprising the whole width of the page (including the space for side-notes) shall occur; all above that proportion to be paid *ad valorem*. Where double side notes occur in a page, to be charged double the above sum.

Reports, Minutes of Evidence, and Appendices, are all cast up separately, and take only the extras which strictly belong to them. Thus, if a Report, &c., have side notes, and the Appendix is without side notes, no charge is made on the Appendix for side notes.

14. Where two bottom notes, or one note of twenty lines, occur in a Report, Bill, Appendix, &c., a charge of 1s. per sheet to be made throughout such Report, Bill, Appendix, &c.; all above to be charged according to their value.

N.B.—The foregoing Regulations are applicable solely to Parliamentary Work.

The L.U.C. succeeded in obtaining recognition of the new Scale by six out of the seven offices engaged in that branch of the business. The exception was Spottiswoode's, whose proprietors refused to adopt the regulations, whereupon upwards of sixty men handed in their notices. The members of the L.U.C. then decided to close the office to their members.

[DOCUMENT C]

TO THE COMPOSITORS OF LONDON

Trade Council Room, Red Lion Court,
Sept. 6, 1836.

Gentlemen,

As a considerable number of persons were, from the crowded state of the meeting, unable to obtain admission to the Mechanics' Institution on

Thursday evening last, it is considered necessary to circulate through the Trade a brief statement of the circumstances which have led to the adoption of the following Resolutions.

At the close of the year 1833, the Government, through the medium of the Stationery Office, issued certain Regulations for charging all kinds of work done for the Houses of Parliament. As no Society at that time existed possessing the whole confidence of the Trade, the compositors in certain Parliamentary houses accepted those Regulations, with certain modifications.

At the close of the year 1835, a well-founded rumour prevailed that, as the Regulations of 1833 had only been received by certain houses, and were not at all binding on the general trade, any office was at liberty to make its own regulations for this description of work, and propositions were made to depart even from those regulations and work at a lower rate. The evils likely to arise from this state of the question naturally excited the attention of the London Union of Compositors, and the whole subject was brought under the consideration of the Trade in January, 1836. Repeated discussions took place on the subject—a committee, consisting of *forty-five* individuals, investigated the customs of the Trade, and considered the various points in the Regulations of the Government, several of which were found to be innovations on the long-established rights of the business; and, finally, at a Special General Meeting of the Trade, the plan of the Government was partially modified, and *fourteen* Regulations based on the general practice of Parliamentary houses were adopted for charging Parliamentary Work.

The 16th of May was the time appointed for these Regulations to come into operation; and, within a few days, six out of seven Houses in which Parliamentary Work is done, agreed to pay according to the 14 Regulations. Mr. Spottiswoode's establishment was the seventh, and the only office which refused to adopt those Regulations. His answers to those who have solicited his compliance with the Regulations has been, that "Though the difference in the price is no object, he will not be dictated to; that no alteration will be made in the prices of any of his works; that for every man that leaves he will take an apprentice in his place; that the name of every person quitting the office on the present occasion shall be entered in a book, and the individual shall never again, upon any consideration, be employed in that establishment."

This language and conduct is at once so daring and contemptuous, as to awaken indignation in every free and honest breast; but Mr. Spottiswoode has even dared to do more than this. In the hope of punishing those who, according to his own estimate of their criminality, have done no more, to use his own words, than seek "an increase of price,"—he has posted through the Trade the names of several individuals who left their frames perfectly clear, had made no overcharges, but *who did his work at his own terms*, and gave him *a fortnight's notice* of their intention to leave.

We cannot go into further particulars at present. Suffice it to say, that at a meeting of Thirteen Hundred Compositors, the following Resolutions were *unanimously* agreed to.

Resolved,—That in consequence of the refusal of Mr. Spottiswoode to pay the prices for Parliamentary work agreed to by a General Meeting of the Trade, and as paid in all other Parliamentary houses, as also small type in headings to tables, column matter, and appeal cases, this meeting refuses to recognise the offices of Mr. Spottiswoode until those prices are paid.

Resolved,—That this meeting consider it highly expedient that no member of the Union should remain in the offices of Mr. Spottiswoode after the 17th of September.

Resolved,—That a subscription of 1s. 6d. from every member of the Union be entered into, to be paid in three weeks, or in the course of the month of September.

The Trade Council conceive they know the feeling of the Trade too well to utter a word soliciting immediate and strict compliance with the above Resolutions. The unanimous and unequivocal expression of sentiment at the Meeting was a sufficient testimony that the Trade are awakened to the importance of the present dispute. We ask from Mr. Spottiswoode no more than other masters pay, and require only from him that which the Scale and general custom justifies.

By Order of the Trade Council,

R. THOMPSON, Reg.
W. BAYNE, Sec.

[DOCUMENT CI]

The King's Printing Office (Spottiswoode's) remained a non-union house until 1917. The following document, published in 1854, further summarizes the differences between the firm and the Union.

Report of the Select Committee appointed by the Committee of the London Society of Compositors on the Origin of the Closing of Messrs. Spottiswoode's Houses, together with the subsequent proceedings thereon. 1836-1854.

Without occupying the time of the Meeting with introductory remarks, the Select Committee would draw the attention of the Delegates to the following brief history of the closing of Spottiswoode's Houses, and the subsequent proceedings thereon :

"In the month of December, 1833, a copy of the Treasury Propositions was laid before the chapel of the two houses of Messrs. Hansard. It was found that the proposed adoption of a Pica standard was the most objectionable feature. A deputation was sent from the above chapel to the compositors of the King's House, with the view of having their assistance in resisting the attempted innovation, when, to the surprise of all, it was discovered that the very same principle had been recognised and acted upon there for *upwards of half a century !*"

The above is an extract from a statement of the chapel of the late Mr. Hansard's, read at a meeting of the London Union of Compositors, January 19, 1836; the meeting at which the present Parliamentary Scale was agreed to.

In August, of the same year, a number of men were posted through the trade by Mr. Spottiswoode, "because," to use his own words, "a demand, made by them for an increase of wages, was not complied with."

At a General Meeting, held at the Mechanics' Institute, September 1, in the same year, the following resolution was unanimously adopted :

"That in consequence of the refusal of Mr. Spottiswoode to pay the prices for Parliamentary work, as agreed to by a General Meeting of the trade and as paid in all other Parliamentary houses; also, small type in headings to tables, two-column matter, and Appeal Cases—this Meeting, in justice to themselves, and other employers, resolve : 'That the houses of Mr. Spottiswoode shall not be considered fair till those prices are paid.' "

This short statement is sufficient to show the original cause of the closing of Messrs. Spottiswoode's houses. Your Committee will now proceed to show what subsequent proceedings have been adopted, with the view of clearing away the differences between the firm and the trade.

On the 19th of August, 1845, at a meeting of the members of the South-Eastern District Board, and of the Committee of the London Society of Compositors, the following resolution was agreed to :

"That a Commission of Inquiry be opened, as to the prices paid in those printing-offices in London, considered by compositors to be unfair."

The following is their Report on Spottiswoode's :

"It would be, perhaps, a work of supererogation were they to detail to you the proceedings that occurred in the year 1836—the time when the Parliamentary scale was made, which scale Mr. Spottiswoode refused to acknowledge. Suffice it to say, they find, in a measure, that the evils then in being continue to this day; only, they have discovered additional ones which have crept in, no doubt, with time; and which will serve to swell the already known causes which justify the closing of the office.

"There are two offices which these differences concern; in themselves they are regarded as distinct, and go under two names : the Queen's House, and the New House—both, however, belong to Mr. Spottiswoode. Under this head, then, they first treat of—

"*The Queen's House.*—In this part the Parliamentary work is carried on, which principally consists of Lords' and Commons' Bills, Public Acts, and local Acts.* A bill is called a *Lords' Bill*, if it be one that has been introduced into Parliament by the members of the Government. The Reform Bill—when first printed—was called a Lords' Bill. A *Commons' Bill* is one that is printed from manuscript copy, for the use of the members of the Upper House, introduced by a company or private individual. When these bills have been passed by the house, as also all other bills agreed to by it, and to which the Royal assent has been given, if it be, say, such a one as the Reform Bill, it is unleaded,

---

"* Commons' Bills are paid 10s. per sheet, without reference to casting up.

		s.	d.
Lords' Bills—57 by 58—13,000, at 6½d. . .		7	0
Broad side-notes		2	6
Back figures		0	6
		10	0
Public Acts—56 by 58—13,000, at 6½d. . .		7	0
Broad side-notes		3	0
		10	0
Local Acts—56 by 58—13,000, at 6d. . .		6	6
Broad side-notes		2	0
		8	6

and made into and becomes a Public Act, and is paid as Parliamentary work, because it concerns the civil, criminal, and municipal laws of the country. A Local Act is a Commons' Bill, such as the 'London and Birmingham Railway Act,' and all such schemes, which having been granted, and the regal signature given, is reprinted by Mr. Spottiswoode from the print copy, and as it concerns but a portion of the community, or the interests of a company, is called a *Local* Act. All the bills are paid a stated price; so also are the Public Acts; but the Locals being printed from a Commons' Bill, not a point allowed to be altered, and going line for line and page for page, are, by Mr. Spottiswoode called only book-work, because they are printed at his order, and under the patent he holds, which binds him to keep in print, a certain number of copies for sale to that portion of the public concerned in such local matter. Having explained the meaning of these acts and bills, the next thing to show will be the price paid for them.

"They are paid upon the 'lumping' system, or 10s. per sheet. They contain 13,000 letters, which if rated at 7d. would be equal to 7s. 6d., leaving 2s. 6d. for side-notes, light or heavy. This is the price for private work. Some are cast up at 6½d. and are paid 10s. for, giving them 3s. for notes, etc. Locals are cast up at 6d., equal to 6s. 6d., and are paid 2s. only for notes, or 8s. 6d. per sheet. This difference is, because, as has been before observed, they are reprint. With the exception of the Locals, which the London Union have decided to be Parliamentary work, the price per 1,000 for the public Acts and Bills, and, in fact, the price per sheet for them, may be said to be by no means encroached upon. The lumping system itself is not recognized by the trade; nor is the deduction for reprint upon the Locals allowed. Passing by these, the following are real objections :

"Suppose an appendix to a bill to be in long primer, and it makes several sheets, any blanks occurring therein are not paid as long primer, but as pica; simply because that was the fount the bill itself was set in. It would seem that they set up pica as the standard body for everything done in this part of the building, and from it they charge their extras. Thus, if they had seven sheets of an appendix in long primer, they would charge the seven sheets as pica, and so much extra for the long primer, occasioning two castings-up where one would do.

"Again, if they have any tables, the headings to which might be set up in minion or nonpareil, they are not allowed to charge the value of the small type in the headings, but reckon them according to the body of the table; thus setting nonpareil headings at the same price as long primer, unless they be very heavy. There are about forty-five men and twenty apprentices employed in this part of the firm.

"In the *New House* the worst evils exist. *Two column matter* is never paid for; such a charge is wholly disregarded; though the compositors are paid, sometimes, for what is called extra trouble; thereby proving the justice of the charge, and yet directly refusing it. Here, also, payment for *headings to tables in small type* is refused; and here *Art. 20, or the job rule of the scale*, is positively set at nought. Mr. Spottiswoode says, 'That if he have a pamphlet of one sheet or less, such is not a job, but applicable to the rule which gives 1s. per sheet for pamphlets of five sheets or under.' Now the scale distinctly says, '*Jobs of one sheet or under*,' etc.; therefore Mr. Spottiswoode's argument cannot be said to be tenable; and yet he will not pay it, though the men say they have refused to work upon them, and the boys, generally, get these things to do: and when the men have been desired to go upon them, they are told they may charge it at 7d., but they must not view it as a precedent. In this part of the building the *appeal cases* are mostly done, which are paid a certain price per sheet, with or without notes. Their dimensions are 83 by 79, or 26,000, which rated at 7d., is equal to 15s., leaving them 4s. for notes (and these only a broad; if in double-narrow, they charge 6d. per page extra), they being paid 19s. per sheet. When the appeal cases are less in width or length than is here stated, a deduction of 1s. per sheet is made by the compositors. There are about eighty-six men and thirty-five apprentices in this part. Add to this the number in the Queen's House, and we shall find 121 men and fifty-five apprentices, or but eleven short of half the number of men employed, and the houses are very full now.

"Looking at the several innovations here noticed, the following may be said to be the differences existing in the offices of Mr. Spottiswoode :

1. That Pica is, in all parliamentary work, considered as a standard type, to which all others must be subservient. Whereas, such a plan is declared in the Scale to be improper.

2. That Blanks, in this kind of work, are paid, not according to the type the Appendix to a bill is set in, but as Pica; which is not the practice of the trade.

3. That the extra for small type in Headings to Tables, either in Parliamentary or book-work, is not paid for; which is an innovation of the Scale.

4. That two-column matter is not recognised, and never paid; which is contrary to the practice of the trade.

5. That Appeal Cases are paid only 7*d.* per 1,000, instead of 8*d.*, as they should be.

6. That the system of Lumping, adopted in all Parliamentary Work and Appeal Cases, is a system not observed by the trade, as being founded upon a sense of injustice, alike to the public, the employer, and the employed.

7. That the Job Rule of the Master's Scale is, by Mr. Spotiswoode, violated. Instead of paying a sheet-work at 7*d.*, he will only pay it at 6*d.*, in defiance of the said rule.

IV. PARLIAMENTARY SCALE OF 1891

With the exception of the advance of 1866,[1] the Parliamentary Scale of 1836 remained in force until 1891, when the text was revised. Although prices have since been considerably raised, the terms of the 1891 Scale are still in force, two short paragraphs being added.

[1] $\frac{1}{2}d.$ per 1,000 ens on all classes of work.

CHAPTER XV

THE NEWS COMPOSITORS' REPORT
OF 1820

The Report "of a Committee appointed to draw up a statement of the regular Mode of Working on Newspapers . . ." (1820) is at once the most comprehensive and important of all the earlier documents concerning that branch of the trade. The *Report* contains transcriptions or excerpts from all known documents relating to the subject, and reprints several of which no separate copies can now be found.

Among the many subjects discussed were : the physical formats of the late eighteenth and early nineteenth century sheets, innovations in typographical arrangement and display as applied to newspapers, and the negotiations preceding the advances in wages of 1786, 1793, 1801, 1809 and 1810. Apprenticeship questions, conditions of work on evening papers, and remuneration for the various classes of workmen were also considered and an Abstract of the News Scale appended.

Some preliminary account of the organization of newspaper composing rooms is necessary. In 1785, when the book compositors' memorial, with their propositions for the first Scale of Prices, was presented to the Employers, an increase in wages for the newspaper compositors was requested in the fourth paragraph (see p. 73). There was then no trade division between book and news hands. "Most of the papers were small folios . . . they were nearly all connected with or done in book-houses." But the conditions under which daily newspapers were composed were rapidly changing. Circulations were rising, due to increased public interest in foreign affairs (particularly the French Revolution) and domestic politics. There were also more newspapers and more energetic competition between their proprietors. This affected the composing department. The later a newspaper could be sent to press, the better the chance of including late despatches or parliamentary reports. On the other hand, lateness in the composing room had its effect in the pressroom, and hence in the hour at which the newspaper was on sale to the public. Thus the organization of newspaper composition became increasingly involved, the newspaper compositor's trade more specialized in its technique, and, in time, separate from that of the book or jobbing hand. This was probably already the case by 1793, when the first printed document, *solely* from the newsmen and signed by 145 of their number, was submitted to the proprietors.

The 1820 Report will show that, with the changing conditions, there were classes of labour employed on newspapers which did not exist in general offices, and that the compositors' methods of working and charging for their labour differed greatly from the practices of their brethren in the book and jobbing houses.

There were three classes of newspaper compositor, namely, the *Full Hands*, the *Supernumeraries* and the *Assistants*.

The *Full Hands* on daily newspapers were compositors engaged to attend the office for the maximum number of hours allowed in the agreement between the proprietors and the men. At any time between 1793 and 1820 this would appear to be twelve, including time for refreshment. It is probable that a further couple of hours were required for distributing the types used for the previous day's issue, but distribution was not chargeable by the compositors.

The *Supernumeraries*, a class of labour introduced about 1770, had no fixed hours of work and were guaranteed nothing more than a galley per day, whether on morning or evening newspapers, although by 1820 they invariably received sufficient copy to enable them to earn as much per week as the full hands. They were entitled to give and receive a fortnight's notice.

There was also a third class, known as *Assistants*, introduced in the 1790s. They were called in as and when required, not receiving copy until the Supernumeraries were supplied. They were paid by galley according to the Scale. They were not entitled to a fortnight's notice.

The complete attendance of Full Hands, Supernumeraries and Assistants was not necessary at the commencement of the day or night's work. Sufficient copy would not be available for their employment. Therefore only the Full Hands were required when the office was opened. After they had distributed their letter, they were given the advertisements and such copy as happened to be ready. The Supernumeraries on morning papers were not needed until from two to six hours later. On the evening papers, where the Full Hands mostly began at 5 a.m., the Supernumeraries came at 9 a.m. The Supernumeraries and Assistants, therefore, were not required to attend until such time as there was a fair press of copy. A large number of men could then be employed on short takings, and the inner forme completed with rapidity in order that the paper might be sent to press. This system also permitted the editorial staff to keep the columns open for the reception of late news until the last possible moment.

Full hands were guaranteed a weekly minimum at all times, and for this sum they contracted to perform a stipulated amount of work, based on a long primer galley of 5,000 ens, with smaller size reckoned in proportion. In 1810, for example, the weekly guarantee was 48s., or 8s. per night. The nightly labour was divided into two halves, the "first work," consisting of a galley and one third, to be completed within seven hours, and a "finish" of five hours, in which composition was required to be done at a speed of at least one-fifth of a galley per hour. Thus for $2\frac{1}{3}$ galleys, the compositor would receive 8s. 11d.

The Supernumeraries, who commenced work later than the Full Hands, were engaged for a minimum of one galley, to be composed in four hours. It will be noticed that, at this later stage in the production of a newspaper, the required speed of setting was accelerated. It will be noticed, too, that the Supernumerary's guaranteed weekly wage, on the basis of a galley per night, was a little under half that of the Full Hand, who produced $2\frac{1}{3}$ galleys. In effect, however, the Supernumeraries generally received at least two galleys per night to compose.

The Assistants received no guarantee, but were entitled to a galley per night, copy to be furnished at the rate of a quarter of a galley (1,250 ens) per hour.

The table printed below, showing the changes in newspaper composition prices over a period of forty years, will assist the reader to grasp the essentials of the system.

MORNING NEWSPAPERS

Year	Full-hands	Super-num.	Assistants	Per Galley	Per 1,000	Over Hours
1770	27/-	13/-	—	2/2	5d.	6d.
1786	31/-	15/-	—	2/6	—	—
1793	36/-	17/-	—	2/10	—	—
1801	40/-	19/-	$9\frac{1}{2}d$. p.h.	3/2	—	—
1809	42/-	20/-	10d. p.h.	3/4	—	—
1810	48/-	23/-	$11\frac{1}{2}d$. p.h.	3/10	9d.	—

The following extracts from the *Report, Rules and Regulations* of the Society of London Daily Newspaper Compositors, published in 1848, supplement the information contained in *The London Scale of Prices*, 1836 (reprinted at p. 398 *et seq.*), and throw further light on the organisation of newspaper printing.

[DOCUMENT CII]

MORNING PAPERS

FULL HANDS

The system of doing work by "Full Hands," originally including the majority of the Companionship, is fast taking its place among the things that were. The regulations for their guidance appear, however, to be strictly acted upon, and the Committee have, therefore, to propose no more than verbal alterations in the last paragraphs under this head.

The duty of Full Hands upon these journals is what is termed a First-work, and a Finish of five hours. The First-work, which consists of one galley and one-third,[1] must be completed in seven hours from the time specified for beginning, including refreshments, and the correction of one galley; any time which may be gained in the completion of this quantity, by the ability of the Compositor, within the above period, to be at his own disposal; but in such case, should the press of matter cause the Printer to require any assistance from those individuals during such interval, then such of the persons as may be engaged charge all work so done by the value per line, or, in other words, at $11\frac{1}{2}$d. per quarter galley; always bearing in mind that no less than that quantity is allowed to be charged; that is to say, if there be not time to complete the quarter-galley that night, the remainder of it to be done on the next night's First-work, and that no corrections of such extra work be made or allowed for.

The Finish, which includes composition, correction of proofs and revises, and putting the Paper to Press, must be completed in five hours

---

[1] *i.e.*, one galley and the after-lines. "With regard to after-lines upon the first work on morning papers, we find that the custom existed as far back as the year 1770, but no reason for the practice can be assigned, though it is understood to have been adopted to lighten or leave nothing to compose for the finish, and thus enable the compositors to go early to their beds; an advantage which, from the complete alteration in the nature of Morning Papers, it is totally impossible they now can enjoy.

"By a finish of five hours on Morning, and six hours on Evening Papers, it was not meant that the compositors should produce five or six quarters of a galley, as that would produce considerably more than they were paid for; but from the best information that can now be obtained of the nature of newspapers at the time this mode of work was introduced, it appears that the *first work and after-lines* of the full-hands and the *galley* of the supernumeraries were sufficient to produce the Paper, and that the "finish" was merely waiting to see whether any news of importance should arrive (during which time they might put in letter for the next day), and assisting to put the Paper to press."
The London Scale of Prices, 1836, p. 57.

from the hour appointed for such work to commence. The duties of the Full Hand whilst engaged in composition during this portion of the work is reckoned at the rate of one-fifth of a galley per hour. Should the period of time taken in putting the Paper to Press exceed the five hours from the hour originally stipulated, then such overtime may be disposed of as follows, according to agreement between the employer and the employed : On Papers where the time of going to Press one morning regulates the hour of commencing the following day's work, the number of hours so over may be taken from the First-work of the following day, by deducting so many quarters of galleys; for example, where the Finish terminates at Five, but the Paper does not go to Press before Six, then one quarter may be deducted from the First-work of the following day, the Full-hands commencing the day's work at Six accordingly; but should the Printer require them to commence at the regular hour, then the hour before mentioned to be charged $11\frac{1}{2}$d. for, extra and above their previous day's work. On some Journals a different plan is adopted, and all time over the five hours' Finish is paid for as extra, and no deviation made in the time of beginning or the quantity composed for the following day's work. The day's work being completed when the Paper goes to Press, should the Printer detain the Full Hands, or any portion of them, beyond that time, the same to be paid at the rate of $11\frac{1}{2}$d. per hour; any time over even hours on the regular day's work to be paid for according to agreement between the Printer and the Full Hands.

SUPERNUMERARIES

Supernumeraries are now in a very different position to that which they occupied a few years since. They now form the bulk of every companionship, and, instead of being engaged for a galley, galley and a half, and so forth, are, as a matter of course, engaged for one galley, and as many more as may be required. The following, therefore, may be taken as the recognised Rule with regard to Supernumeraries :—

Supernumeraries are engaged to do one galley, and no engagement to be for less than that quantity; the galley being considered four hours' work, including corrections, from the time of taking copy. Supernumeraries to correct as nearly the amount of their composition as possible. Should the Printer require their attendance beyond the time above stated, and be unable to furnish copy according to the above specification, in such case $11\frac{1}{2}$d. per hour is charged for that attendance.

ASSISTANTS

Though the employment of what are called "Assistants" is now a matter of very rare occurrence on a Morning Paper, yet, as such is occasionally necessary, the following regulation is proposed :—

Assistants are not under any special engagement, that is, not entitled to the recognised fortnight's warning; but are entitled to a galley, and must be furnished at the rate of a quarter per hour from the time of taking copy.

EVENING PAPERS

The Rules for the guidance of Full Hands and Supernumeraries on Evening Papers being similar to those with respect to Morning Papers, the Committee have to propose only a few verbal alterations as follows :—

The Full Hands upon Evening Papers are employed ten hours per day, and the work is divided into two proportions, viz., one galley as a First-work, and a Finish of six hours. The time for taking copy for the First-work is regulated by the hour for commencing the Finish, being four hours previous to that time. Any time which the Full Hands may have between the completion of the First-work and the time of commencing the Finish is at their own disposal. Should the Printer find occasion for their services during this interval, then such assistance to be charged for according to galley quantity, in quarters or half-galleys, as the case may be, namely, one quarter, 10½d.; two quarters or half a galley, 1s. 9½d.; three quarters, 2s. 8½d.; galley, 3s. 7d. No charge less than one quarter; that is to say, if there be no time to complete the quarter-galley that morning, the remainder of it to be done on the next day's First-work. One galley to be corrected for the First-work, or a sixteenth of a galley composed as an equivalent, if agreed upon between the Printer and the Full Hands.

The duty of the Full Hands upon the Finish, like that of the Morning Papers, consists of composition, correcting proofs and revises, and putting the paper to press. The quantity calculated for each Full Hand whilst engaged in composition was, in former years, at the rate of one galley within the six hours prescribed; but in the progress of time, circumstances have occurred occasioning different arrangements to be made, and, by some Printers, as much as a quarter per hour has been enforced; but if, through compulsion, that quantity should be exacted, still it must be understood that in no case shall it be exceeded. Any time which may be over the six hours to be paid or accounted for according to agreement between the Printer and Full Hands, the same as on Morning Papers.

The Supernumeraries are guided by the same rules as laid down for those on the Morning Papers, claiming a galley, or charging the same, at the expiration of four hours from the time of taking copy. The day's work finishing when the Paper goes to Press, any work required afterwards to be paid for extra, and nothing less than one quarter charged.

Assistants are more frequently employed on Evening than on Morning Papers, and it has been the practice to ensure them half a galley only, the inconvenience being much less than on Morning Papers. The following rule is therefore submitted :—

Assistants are not under any special engagement, and have no claim upon a particular quantity of work beyond half a galley, being liable to be called on at a late period of the day; therefore they cannot claim more of the employer than at the rate of a quarter per hour from the time of taking copy.

[DOCUMENT CIII]

Report of a Committee appointed to draw up a Statement of the regular Mode of Working on Newspapers, for the Information of the Trade ; to examine Documents, and to report the same—Read July 29, 1820.[1]

The object which your Committee were directed to accomplish (that of giving a fair scale of work, mode, time, and price, on *all Newspapers*, wherever published) has been entered into with zeal on their parts, and they trust will be found to your satisfaction. They have examined the bases of all official agreements, and all acknowledged and understood rules; and have particularly adhered to their instructions, by keeping in view, "that it was to guide the ignorant, to prevent the evil intentions of the unprincipled, and, if possible, to form a closer bond of union among yourselves."

Laws are rendered more sacred, more valid, by age; and in performance of the task assigned them, the Committee commenced their labours by tracing the Regulations for News Work back to a certain period, in order to support them in their declaration, that they had been introduced on fair principles, that they had been cordially agreed to by the Masters, had been acted upon by the employed for so great a length of time, and that any innovation made on those regulations by an Employer, or *set of men* acting for themselves, without the concurrence of the general body of News Compositors, should be opposed, and those concerned in such an attempt treated as enemies to their fellow-workmen, and marked as acting inimically to the interests of their profession.

It was necessary for your Committee, for the maintenance of the superstructure, to examine its foundation; with this view they have, from oral testimony, been enabled to collect the size and price of various Newspapers from 1770. They consisted of 16 small columns, some 18, some 19, and others 20 ems Long Primer wide. The galley was 130 or 132 lines, and 50 *after-lines*, Long Primer; Brevier galley 96, *after-lines* 38. (The only exception was the old *Daily Advertiser,* which contained 12 columns, of 25 ems Long Primer wide, the galley in proportion). The prices were, full hands 27s.; Supernumeraries 13s.; galley 2s. 2d.; 5d. per thousand, and *over-hours* 6d. *Supernumeraries* (a term which explains itself) were not known ten years prior to this date. Most of the papers were small folios; and as they were nearly all connected with, or done in Book-houses,[2] the eldest apprentice, upon a press of matter, was usually called in to assist. Upon the subdivision of the labour into galleys, and the size of the papers extending, a man was employed if any deficiency arose in the quantity required. Advertisements increased; the use of small type was extended, and the *Supernumerary* became a fixture.

Prior to 1776, controversial essays, domestic news, and extracts from

---

[1] The only copy known to the writer is in the possession of the London Society of Compositors. Excerpts from it are given at some length under *Newspapers* in Savage, W. *op. cit.*

[2] *The Times*, for instance, founded by John Walter I in 1785, was printed at the establishment opened by him for printing books by the logographic system. John Bell, owner of a number of newspapers, was also a book printer.

the official communications in the *London Gazette*, appear to have filled the small columns of the Journals, but the American war commencing this year, they assumed a new consequence, by first venturing to give daily Reports of the Debates in Parliament.

In 1777 there were seven Morning Papers, eight of three times, one twice a week, and two weekly. The first *Sunday Paper* came out in 1778; in a few weeks it was followed by a second; and a third was brought out in the succeeding year. The Weekly Journals paid 24s. In 1780 a new Daily Journal arose, with a different appearance from the others, which seems to have induced a further alteration.[1] The prices remained the same, but the employment of more hands was rendered necessary. The hour of beginning varied, some commencing business at eleven, others at two, and some so late as three o'clock.

In 1784, the first year after the peace, another Journal started for public favour, in which Minion was introduced.[2] The old method of display was discarded, a new taste appeared in the arrangement of the matter in the inner form, and the former advertisement style was completely exploded. Rivalry commenced, and the other Newspapers soon made a correspondent change. Your Committee have thus reached the period when they meet with the first printed document relating to the composing part of the printing business.[3] It is a request, in the form of a Circular, by the *body* of Compositors, for an advance of *one halfpenny* (Book-work being then paid 4d. per 1,000), dated April 6, 1785, and consisting of eight propositions; which were not finally determined upon by the Employers till the 25th of November following. The proposition and answer relating to Newswork were as follows:

"Prop. 4. That the Compositors employed on Daily Newspapers, now paid at the rate of 27s. per week, be in future paid £1 11s. 6d. per week, and over hours paid as at present.—*Answer:* This cannot be a matter of general regulation, as the trouble of every paper differs from that of another."

Your Committee have no other document of this date: it will be observed that the prices were low, and that the over-hours were paid for, but it was considered impossible to make the request "a matter of general regulation," as every Journal differed in its trouble from another. The Bookmen, however, received an advance of one-eighth, or 2s. 6d. in the pound, and the establishment in Book-houses varied from £1 1s. to £1 7s.

1786—The advance on Book-work commenced on the 1st of January, and in the month of March following the Newsmen, on Daily Papers

---

[1] The first Sunday paper was the *British Gazette and Sunday Monitor* founded actually in 1780. The only daily paper founded in 1780 was the *Morning Herald*. The information concerning the total number of journals published in various years and the dates of their respective foundations is often inaccurate. Reference should be made to: Morison, S., *The English Newspaper* (Cambridge, 1932), and the relevant portions of Mr. Graham Pollard's contributions on English Newspapers, 1660-1800, in the *Cambridge Bibliography of English Literature*.

[2] The reference is probably to John Walter's *Daily Universal Register*, first published 1 January, 1785. Its title was changed to *The Times* in 1788.

[3] Document I, p. 72.

only, received a rise of 4s. 6d. which made the price for full hands £1 11s. 6d. and for Supernumeraries 15s.; the galley 2s. 6d. A few Journals only of the other class rose to 27s. At this time there were eight Morning Papers, eight of three times a week, two Weekly, and three Sunday Journals. In 1788 the first *Daily* Evening Paper made its appearance, and the men received the same price as the Morning Papers; a second came out in 1791, and was paid in like manner.

1793—For a number of years the Compositors employed on Book-work had been labouring under an intolerable grievance, and although they did not demand a rise per thousand, requested, as a new regulation, that the head and direction lines of pages, and the en and em quadrats at the sides, should be paid for. Their Circular was dated the 14th January, and on the 11th March following, the Masters agreed to the proposition of paying the head and direction lines, but not the ens and ems.

The News department appears to have been in full employment at this period. By a strong competition for public favour (which commenced, as already observed, prior to the termination of the American war—and from the year 1785 to 1793), the Journals underwent a most material alteration. It was a remarkable epoch, including the most eventful seven years of the last century. The disarrangements, both civil and political, concomitant to a return to peace after a long war—the wars in India—the troubles in Germany, in Flanders, Brabant, Holland—the French Revolution—and the commencement of a war with France—all occurring within the dates just mentioned, caused a strong political feeling in the public mind; of course, information from all quarters was eagerly sought, and as readily given by the Editors of the Daily Journals, among whom, as with their readers, party spirit rose to its utmost height, and no expense was spared to gratify it.

In this period nineteen *new* Journals put forth their claims for public support—the majority, however, were "born but to die!"—two of the older Papers also expired; but their places were occupied by *seven* juniors. The number now amounted to eleven Morning and two Evening Papers; seven of three times a week, one Weekly, and five Sunday Papers. An alteration in the method of display, and a new mode in the arrangement of the matter, became now very general. One Journal went beyond the rest, by its introduction of French rules, the small capitals for particular paragraphs, and discarding nearly all the double letters, and the *long s*.[2] Your Committee are also enabled to state, by comparing the modes of work prior to 1785, with the necessary alterations at the

---

[1] The first *daily* evening paper was *The Star and Evening Advertiser* (No. 1 appeared on 3 May, 1788).

[2] French rules were introduced by *The Morning Post* in 1772. The abandonment of the long s in a newspaper is first seen in *The English Chronicle* in 1786. This sheet was partly owned by John Bell, who was also the first to dispense with the long s for bookwork. The journal which "went beyond the rest" was undoubtedly *The World*, another of Bell's creations, which made its debut on 1 January, 1787. *See* Morison, S., *The English Newspaper*, op. cit., p. 175 *et seq*. where a full account of the typographical development of these journals is given, also the same author's *John Bell* (London, 1930).

period they have now mentioned, that a complete revolution was also effected in the *nature* of Newswork. It became necessary, therefore, that the price should keep pace with the labour, and an advance was solicited. The first printed document, *solely* from Newsmen, is dated April 4, 1793, signed by 145 Newsmen, and their request was supported by the signatures of 281 Bookmen.[1] It contains four propositions :—the first for an advance of 4s. 6d. per week on *Morning* and *Evening* Papers; the second related to the *hours* of working and the charge for *over-hours*, which then was but 6d. per hour; the third, to Papers published *three times a week*; and the fourth to Supernumeraries, but it did not state their price. All these propositions were modified ten years afterwards.

The address which accompanied these propositions, and the requests made in it, being so applicable to the present mode of work, your Committee are satisfied with defending every iota required by their predecessors. Although twenty-seven years have elapsed since they were submitted to the Employers, yet, if required at the present moment, the same argument might be used in their support. In fact, they must be considered the foundation-stones of the edifice. Your Committee will introduce the document.

Sir, London, April 4, 1793.

The Compositors employed on Newspapers, impressed with the opinion of your candour in hearing and redressing any real grievances they may complain of, presume to submit to your consideration the following statement :

Previous to the year 1786, the Weekly Salary of *Daily* Newspaper Compositors was £1 7s. a sum which, considering the regularity and moderation of the hours of attendance, was thought fully adequate to their trouble. Owing, however, to a competition for Public favour among the various Newspapers, by giving a long detail of Parliamentary Debates, entering at large into the politics of Europe, and the irregularity and uncertainty of the arrival of Mails, the hours of attendance were necessarily increased, which, together with the enhanced price of Provisions, made an advance of Salary necessary, and which was at that time cheerfully acquiesced in by the Proprietors of *Daily* Newspapers, as perfectly reasonable; but no advance was then given to *Evening Papers*.

The Compositors on both *Daily* and *Evening Papers*, upon a comparative view of the trouble and attendance requisite at that period and at the present time, and the still increased price of the necessaries of life, humbly propose and request an addition to their Salary, which they trust the Gentlemen Proprietors of Newspapers will not think unreasonable, when the following circumstances are taken into consideration :

That at the rate of twelve hours' Composition, and at least two hours' Distribution, the present Salary of Compositors employed on *Daily Papers* amounts to no more than Fourpence Halfpenny an hour, which considering the irregular hours of attendance, working by night, and on Sundays, and of being constantly at command, the Compositors humbly think, and trust, the Gentlemen Proprietors of Newspapers will agree with them in opinion is by no means adequate to their labour.

That as Compositors on *Evening Papers* obtained no advance in the year 1786, and that as their labour has been gradually increasing ever since that time, it is hoped their joining in the present application will not be thought unreasonable.

[1] No copy of this document is known.

It is humbly proposed, for the above reasons, that an increase should take place upon the Salaries of Compositors on Newspapers, in the following proportion, viz.

I. That an advance of 4s. 6d. per week take place on the present Salary of every Compositor fully employed on *Daily Papers*.

II. That if owing to the length of Proceedings in Parliament, or other late Matter, the Compositors employed on Daily Papers should be detained above twelve hours on Saturday, to be reckoned from the time of beginning to compose on Friday, they be paid Sixpence per hour extra for the same, or an equal proportion of time allowed on Sunday, in the same manner·as is usual on other Days of the Week.

III. That 3s. be added to the present Weekly Salary of Compositors fully employed on *Evening Papers, published three times a Week*.

IV. That the Salary of Supernumeraries employed on either of the above be increased in proportion.

These, Sir, are the Propositions submitted to you, to be laid before the Gentlemen Proprietors, not doubting but that the reasonableness of the Compositors' demands will be evident to you, and that it will meet with your approbation and concurrence, especially when it is considered that the advance they require is so nearly proportionate to that lately obtained on Book-work.

It will be necessary to state that the terms Evening Papers used in this document, allude only to the desire expressed in the third proposition. The words *Daily Newspapers*, repeated in the second and fourth paragraphs of the Address, and in the first Propositions, sufficiently show that no distinction was intended to be made between *Daily Morning* and *Daily Evening Papers*. But this request of the Newsmen did not seem to be answered with cordiality by the Masters, for your Committee have a copy of the Report of the News Committee, dated April 20, 1793, which, after mentioning the names of 15 Delegates present, at two in the afternoon, previous to the general meeting to be held at seven in the evening, states :

That, pursuant to a printed circular setter, signed 'J O H N B E L L,' the Committee adjourn to Anderton's Coffee-house, to hold a Conference, as requested, on some Propositions laid before the Printers and Proprietors of Newspapers, by the Journeymen employed by them.—Adjourned accordingly.

Six o'clock, P.M.

The Delegates having returned to the Hole-in-the-Wall, report to the General Meeting,

That they met with the Representatives from the following Newspapers, viz. *Ledger, Herald, World, Morning Chronicle, Oracle, True Briton, Sun, Star, Times,* and *Diary.*

That these Gentlemen did not chuse to hold any conference on the Subject to which your Delegates were invited.

That the professional Printers present, though personally requested, declined entering upon the Subject, the Discussion of which your Delegates were required to attend.[1]

That the above-mentioned *John Bell*, instead of attending to the Business to which they were expressly called, endeavoured to persuade them to accede to the following Resolutions, as particularly *advantageous* to the Employers and *Employed*, viz.

[1] The "professional printers" were the individuals responsible for the production as distinct from the editorial side.

NEWSPAPER PROPRIETORS' RESOLUTIONS

April 20, 1793.

At an Adjourned Meeting of the Proprietors and Representatives of the Daily Newspapers, held this day at Anderton's Coffee-house, to consider the Propositions of the Daily Newspaper Compositors,

Present,—The Representatives of the *Ledger, Herald, World, Morning Chronicle, Oracle, True Briton.*

Considering the Requisitions and Pretensions of the Newspaper Compositors in the most extensive and liberal Points of View, so far as they are connected with the fair Interests of their Employers, it was resolved, to recommend the Prices and Regulations in future for Newspaper work to be fixed on the following Plan :

That each regular Compositor be paid One Pound Fourteen Shillings *per* Week.

That the Hours of regular Attendance for composing, be from Three o'Clock in the Afternoon until the Paper goes to Press.

That whenever the Time of going to Press shall exceed Three o'Clock in the Morning, the Times of Attendance on the same Day shall be in the following Manner, *viz.*

When the Paper goes to Press at——

3	to begin at	3		8	to begin at	5
4	....	3		9	....	6
5	....	3		10	....	7
6	....	4		11	....	8
7	....	4		12	....	9

That the Supernumerary Compositors shall be allowed One Shilling *per* Week over and above their present Pay, supposing that such Supernumerary shall compose *one Column* per *Day*, and so in Proportion.

That your Delegates felt the Indignity offered to them, but bore it with the Patience which the Justice of the cause in which they were engaged only could warrant.

That your Delegates, with a becoming Dignity rejected the Resolutions of the said *John Bell.*

That your Delegates, from the Consideration of the Labour required, find their first propositions unanswered, unopposed, and therefore just.

Ten o'Clock, P.M.

The General Meeting unanimously approve of the Conduct of the Delegation and further resolve,

That the Original Propositions standing uncontroverted, the same be strictly adhered to.

The Resolution in the last paragraph of this Report was most rigidly adhered to ; and your Committee cannot but lament, that the first attempt of your brethren to introduce *Laws and Regulations* for the reciprocal benefit of the employer and employed, was met by such propositions on the part of one Proprietor, that, in order to carry their point, they were obliged to enter into a Resolution that a general notice of quitting their situations, according to the custom of the trade, should be given. Before the expiration of the fortnight, however, an accommodation was proposed by the Employers individually, but upon the principle that a material difference existed, both in labour and comfort, between an Evening and a Morning Paper, the Newsmen agreed to a distinction being made in the price. Morning Papers received the sum required of 4s. 6d., but Evening Papers only 2s. 6d. The wages of the former were £1 16s.; Supernumeraries 17s.; the galley 2s. 10d.: the Evening Papers were 34s.; Supernumeraries 16s.; the galley 2s. 8d. Within this period the term *Assistants* was first recognized. Your Committee are not enabled to state whether any satisfactory agreement was entered into with respect to the second Proposition of the Journeymen relating to the commencing work on Sundays. It would appear that they only requested that day's indulgence, for they already possessed it on the others. Some of the Journals at this time paid but 6d. per hour, while others, more liberal, paid on those of the Morning $7\frac{1}{2}$d. and on the Evening 7d. for over-hours or Assistants.

In the month of October, 1793, the same year of the rise, your Committee find that the Journeymen had occasion, from the accumulation of labour on Daily Newspapers, to object to the employment of Apprentices, as a strong desire was evinced, at this period, of returning to the system, by employing *run-aways*, or *turn-overs*, as they were denominated. The Employers conceiving they had been *forced* to accede to the rise in the month of April preceding, appeared determined to take advantage of the men, by paying themselves for their defeat by the difference of price between Apprentices and Journeymen. Suspicion had been long awake that some innovation was intended, and the scheme soon developed itself; the Newsmen assembled, and entered into certain Resolutions, which, with a statement of their case, were sent round the Trade for the concurrence or disapproval of the Bookmen. They were readily adopted by the latter, and your Committee present an extract from the Journeymen's Address, and their Resolutions.

October 1, 1793.

Can any reasonable Advocate be found for the Introduction of Apprentices on Newspapers? We do not believe there can.—A Companionship on a Newspaper, distinct and different in its Nature from Book-work, requires equal Attention, equal Exertion, and equal Interest. And can this be expected (we ask) from an Apprentice? Companionships find it their mutual Interest to be watchful over each other, and see that each does an equal Share; which, if not done, is easily remedied among themselves. But who is it that will say this can be done with an Apprentice? A Journeyman must be attentive, or, from the Representations of his Companions, he loses his situation. But how is this to take place in regard to Apprentices? If Complaints are made to the Printer, how can he rectify them? It is evident to us that he cannot. Your time of employment is not to be forced on an Apprentice; he can refuse to work either by Night or on Sunday, and be justified in his refusal; and Magistrates *must* sanction him. Indeed, experience has proved, that it is generally impossible to keep an Apprentice to the Business on a Newspaper with regularity; they have no interest to bind them; they have no obligation to compel them. Need there be a further Argument used in support of our opinion? We trust not. Under these circumstances then there is only one thing remaining for us to recommend—to unite in a firm Phalanx, and to be *unanimous*.

[COMPOSITORS'] RESOLUTIONS

I. That Newspaper printing, being necessarily conducted by Companionships, requires in each Companion corresponding abilities, corresponding modes of reasoning, and corresponding interests.

II. That an Apprentice, not being at liberty to act for himself, cannot be supposed to possess an equal and independent mode of reasoning, and therefore has not a corresponding interest.

III. That the introduction of an Apprentice upon a Newspaper will occasion a clashing of interests, which may, in the end, prove highly detrimental, not only to the Companionship, but to the Property on which they are engaged, and likewise to the whole body of Compositors, by enlarging the field for the employment of Apprentices.

IV. That therefore the Compositors on Newspapers are firmly and decidedly of opinion, that an Apprentice is by no means an adequate Companion.

V. And therefore they will resist, to the utmost of their power, any attempt (if any such attempt should happen) to obtrude an Apprentice upon them.

The system, however, commenced in the month of October, upon one Journal, which lasted about five years—and upon another which continued nearly eleven years; but in the end you were successful; and men were again engaged upon these Journals on a fair principle. The fate of some who had worked with the boys should have served as a warning—they were neglected, despised, and ultimately driven from the profession.[1] Your Committee cannot refrain from congratulating the Journeymen of that period on their unanimity and perseverance; and at this moment, upon a due consideration of the present state of our business, rejoice in their patriotism, and return thanks to every individual now in being concerned in the opposition given to the attempt.

1801—Your Committee have thus led you to the conclusion of the second period of seven years, through the whole of which the country was engaged in a war with nearly all the European quarter of the globe, and, as has been stated for 1793, your labour increased with the demand for news by the public, and by the struggles of the Journals for pre-eminence, which, added to the alarming price of provisions and all other family requisites, made it again necessary to solicit an advance of wages. In the month of November, 1800, the Bookmen requested a rise, and certain regulations applicable to their department. It was granted to the amount of 1-6th, and took place on the 1st of January, 1801. Shortly after, almost gratuitously, the News department received an advance of 1-9th (or 4s.) on Morning, and 1-11th (or 3s.) on Evening Papers. The former were now £2; Supernumeraries 19s.; per galley 3s. 2d.; Assistants 9½d. per hour; the Evening, £1 17s.; Supernumeraries 17s.; per galley 2s. 10d.; Assistants 8½d. per hour.

Thus terminated the third rise from 1785. In this period several disputes occurred; but your Committee will only repeat those relating to the general interest. From the extensive sale of some of the Evening Papers, the work was obliged to be performed in a manner that, from its evil tendency, required some modification; the hours for composition were not so well defined as hereafter they appear to have been, and the following Resolution, as applicable to Evening Papers, was agreed to among the Newsmen; "That all composition cease when the day's

---

[1] The newspaper referred to was the *Morning Chronicle*.

publication goes to press—all work afterwards to be paid for as extra, or deducted from the first work of the next publication." This did not apply to the second or third editions of the day's paper; that being completed, those *additions* could have no claim on the following publication. The quantity and quality of the matter were also better defined within this period. Brevier was the smallest type till 1784, when Minion was introduced; and the adequate number of lines, by their proportion to Long Primer and width of column, were regulated by the Companionships and their *Printers*. This continued till 1793, when the different proportions were *generally* understood, and a printed graduated Scale for Long Primer, Brevier, and Minion, according to width, was found in each News-house. This appears to have been requisite, as your Committee learn, that from 1789, it was the custom on some Journals to widen their columns during the sitting of Parliament, one or two ems, and reducing them in the recess. At this date a misunderstanding still existed relative to the hour of beginning on Sundays. Certain regulations were adopted respecting the twelve hours' work (including refreshment time, galley and *"lines,"* and correcting), and the time of commencing on that day.—Your Committee must observe, that the Compositors employed on Morning Papers at this period were not uniform in their hours of beginnings on Sundays, and disputes frequently occurred on that point. This might have arisen from the different *temper* and *politics* of the Journals on which they were engaged; some entering at length on the Friday night's Debates in Parliament, Foreign News, etc., while others were content with giving the Public a moderate portion of both. Competition, however, soon made the labour on the Journals equal, and, in 1803, the hour of commencing on the Sunday, regulated by the Saturday's finish, became general.

Your Committee also state that they have endeavoured to trace the origin of what are termed the *"after-lines"*[1] of the first work; tradition has vaguely assisted them in their research. They learn that they were general in 1777, but differing in amount. The term is not mentioned in the Propositions of 1793, but is acknowledged in the Regulations before mentioned; your Committee are therefore led to conclude that they arose with the subdivision of labour on the smaller Papers, prior to 1770, and suppose that custom, arising from local convenience, sanctioned their adoption by your predecessors.

1809—In pursuing their plan, your Committee observe nothing of material consequence occurring in the News department till the year 1809, when the still-increasing price of provisions rendered it necessary for the Compositors to solicit a rise of prices, and on the 19th of May the Newsmen issued a Circular, addressed "To the Proprietors of Newspapers," requesting an advance of 1-5th on their wages—*i.e.*, 8s. per week on Mornings, and 6s. per week on Evening Papers.[2]

---

[1] The expression *after-lines* is discussed on p. 375.

[2] The compositors' letter of 19 May, and the Report of the employers' committee of 30 June, 1809, printed together in one document, are preserved at the Cambridge University Press. The extracts given in the 1820 *Report* contain all the essential information with the exception of the commodity price lists printed opposite.

In the two former Circulars, certain propositions were submitted, to be accepted, modified, or rejected; but the present one was accompanied by the first and regular *Scale for News Work*, and signed by 198 Newsmen. Your Committee will introduce an extract from the introductory paragraphs, and the Scale itself, which complete the edifice you had long laboured to rear.

After stating the necessity the Newsmen were under of soliciting the assistance of the Employers to enable them, by their industry, to make their existence comfortable, they point out the moderation of their request, by giving a comparative statement of the prices for family necessaries, between 1793 and 1809, by which it appeared, that in sixteen years they were nearly doubled.[1] They further add, that :

It has been observed by the Duke of Portland, in his letter to the Lord Lieutenant of Oxford, that *"there is no reason why the labour of the Handi-craftsman, the Mechanic, and the artizan, should not keep pace with the advance on the articles of the Farmer, Grazier,"* etc.[2] Upon this principle, the justice of which is too evident to need the smallest comment, might we not calculate, as Morning Papers, in 1793, were paid 36s. and Evening Papers 34s. that we should now receive nearly £3 12s. on the Morning Papers, instead of £2; and nearly £3 8s. instead of £1 17s. on the Evening ?

There is another consideration to which we must beg to call your attention; at the time of the last advance a ratio of one-sixth was obtained on all works in Book-houses, which proportion was not received by those employed on News-papers; four shillings only being granted on Morning Papers, which before that time were 36s. and three shillings on Evening Papers, which previously were 34s. being only one-ninth on the former, and scarcely an eleventh on the latter These circumstances, together with the great increase of labour on Papers of late years, arising from the introduction of *so large a portion of small letter*, are considerations which, we hope, will not be passed over without that deliberation they deserve.

From an impartial view of the comparative statements and the proposed advance, it will be seen that we have kept perfectly within the limits prescribed by justice. We have pursued this line of conduct from a solicitude to avoid the introduction of any thing which might prevent your ready compliance with our request.

[COMPOSITORS'] PROPOSED SCALE

Daily Morning Papers to be paid	..	..	..	£2	8	0	
Per Galley on ditto	..	..	..	..	..	0	3	9½
Daily Evening Papers	..	..	..	..	..	2	3	0
Per Galley on ditto	..	..	..	..	..	0	3	7

----

[1]

Article	1793	1809	*Article*	1793	1809
	d.	s. d.		s. d.	s. d.
Bread, per quartern ..	9	1 2¾	Candles	8	1 1
Meat, per pound ..	4½	10	Small beer, per gallon	4	8
Butter	8	1 4	Milk, per gallon ..	9	1 4
Cheese ..	5	1 0	Coals, per bushel ..	1 3	1 10
Soap	8	1 0½		5 10½	10 4½

[2] See Dodsley's *Annual Register for* 1800. Appendix, p. 141.

That Ten Hours Composition be the specific time for Daily Evening Papers.

That Assistance be paid at per Hour in proportion to the sum per Galley, considering the Galley as Four Hours' Composition.

Papers Three Times a Week, and Weekly Papers, to take an advance in proportion to that on Evening Papers.

That the above advance do take place from Saturday the 3rd of June, 1809.

This request was verbally and negatively answered in the different News Houses, and the 3rd. of June passed over as if no solicitation for a rise of prices had been made. The Journeymen felt the necessity of perseverance, and the following Circular was sent to the Employers, dated June 13, signed by the same number of men :

Gentlemen—We cannot help expressing our surprise at the manner in which our request has been passed over; nearly a month has elapsed, and no answer has been communicated. Had we in our Scale gone further than the urgency of the times renders necessary, or had we neglected to show that respect which your situations in life require, we might have anticipated such indifference; but feeling our conduct not liable to such objection, we are entirely at a loss to assign any motive for the want of attention to our present circumstances; and we feel ourselves under the necessity of requesting an answer by Saturday next; a non-compliance with which will be considered as a refusal of our propositions.

This second Circular received no answer, and on the 29th of June, the regular notice of quitting was given to the different Printers; but before the fortnight had elapsed, each Journeyman received a copy of a Report of a Committee of Masters, dated June 30, accompanied by a string of Resolutions, but not meeting the request of the men.

Your Committee regret that the document is too voluminous for insertion, but they will make a few extracts in furtherance of their present object. It commences with stating that "A General Meeting of the Proprietors of London Morning and Evening Papers, was held this day (June 30, 1809), Mr. Stuart in the Chair, to take into consideration the Report of the Committee appointed to enquire into, and report their opinion upon the *Circular Letter* of the Compositors, respecting certain alleged grievances, and *demanding* an advance of Wages; present five Daily Morning, and five Daily Evening Papers," and that the said Report was read.—To answer the above-mentioned "Circular Letter," eleven paragraphs are given, and a comparative Table of the Prices of Necessaries, from 1793 to 1809, in contradiction to that given in by the Journeymen.

The *first* paragraph condemns the strong spirit evinced by the men in demanding so large a rise as 20 per cent. on their labour; and protests against the "Scale proposed," as containing *"Rules and Restrictions* new to the Trade, and embarrassing to the Proprietors, while no reciprocal benefit or advantage is held out."

The *second* attempts to controvert the assertion of the Newsmen, that they "experienced difficulties in procuring the necessaries of life," by declaring it "a matter of surprise and regret, that anything so unfounded should be advanced on so serious an occasion by a body of men, generally speaking, so intelligent and respectable," and after comparing your prices and situation with your brethren on Bookwork and other mechanics, conclude with stating, that :

"Their claims to high wages do not rest on the difficulties in obtaining the necessaries of life, but on the disagreeable hours of labour. They make more money than falls to the lot of 39-40ths of the men in Britain, and they can procure not only all the necessaries of life, but even *more of its comforts* than 99 out of every 100 men in Europe. It is lamentable to see men so insensible to the *blessings* of their situation !"

Your Committee cannot congratulate you on the *comforts* or *blessings* of your situation; they leave to your own feelings the fallacy of assertions so hacknied, and proceed to the *third* paragraph, which calls the quotations from the "Duke of Portland's Letter," a "misrepresentation and a pretended extract," and concludes with finding a meaning, not intended by his Grace of Portland—"that the arbitrary fixing of wages was a most alarming evil."

The *fourth* respects the statement of the prices of necessaries, and will not admit the propriety of introducing the year 1793 in comparison with 1809, because the Compositors "then received all they asked, and a *new compact* was formed with them on their own terms." A difference appears in the Compositor's statement and that of your Employers, for the year 1793, of 2½d.

The *fifth* acknowledges the calculation for 1809 to be correct— 10s. 4½d., and as the prices for 1800 were 8s. 9½d., there only remained a difference of 1s. 6½d. to 1809; a loss they conceived you might well bear, "without incurring the penalties of starvation."[1]

Your Committee feel it necessary to quote the *sixth* at length—it needs no comment.

The reference the Compositors make to the increased labour on Newspapers, in consequence of the introduction of *small letter*, is unjust, is absurd, and we cannot understand how they could allow so unfounded a complaint to escape them. The proprietors have always paid, and paid smartly too, for this introduction. The Compositors have limited hours of employment, limited quantities of work, and they *compose only one number of letters*, whether small or large, *agreeably to the universal rule of the business*.

The *seventh* mentions Apprentices, which your Committee will not repeat, considering that question set at rest.

The *eighth* recommends that "the false assertions, groundless complaints, and extravagant pretensions of the Compositors should be met by a firm and determined resistance," and for fear that you should be intoxicated by success to demand "double wages," state, that they "have therefore considered a plan of establishing a society of Compositors under an Act of Parliament, connecting with it a benefit society, which, they are confident will enable the trade to go on, and which they may hereafter submit to you"; but without stating who were to be the *honoured* Members of such society.

The *ninth* paragraph, after expressing the indignance of the Masters at the extravagant demands of the Men, recommends that the wages should be put upon a footing with Book-work in 1800; acknowledging

---

[1] According to the employers' calculations, the chief rise since 1800 was in soap, candles, etc., "occasioned by the interruption in the Baltic trade."

that the rise on the latter was 1-6th while that on News-work was but 1-9th on Morning, and 1-11th on Evening Papers, and propose that 2s. per week should be added to the Morning Papers, but that only 1s. should be given to the Evening Papers, "the difference in the labour and hours of work, being much more than 4s. per week."

The *tenth* recommends that no alteration in the hours of composition on Evening Papers be permitted.

The *eleventh* expresses the anxiety of the Committee to give the Compositors a detailed answer, in order that the latter might clearly understand and appreciate their own interests; and the whole concludes with the following :

[EMPLOYERS'] RESOLUTIONS

Resolved—That the Report of the Committee now read be agreed to.

Resolved—That the Newspaper Compositors have not made out a case entitling them to a rise of Wages; but that as they complain their rise in 1800 was not equal to the rise in Book Houses, a Regulation do now take place, putting them both on a footing.

Resolved—That as the labour on Morning is considerably heavier than on Evening Papers, the latter are not entitled to the same indulgence on this occasion the former.

Resolved—That from Saturday the 15th of July, 1809, the Wages of Compositors on Daily Morning Papers shall be Two Guineas per week, and on daily Evening Papers, Thirty-Eight-Shillings; and that the Galley on the former shall be Three Shillings and Four-pence, on the latter Three Shillings and Twopence.

Resolved—That the Circular Letter of the Journeymen Compositors together with the Report of the Committee of Masters and these Resolutions, signed by the Chairman, be printed in the form of a letter, and that some one Proprietor of each Newspaper shall personally deliver to each Compositor while at work in his house, a Copy of the said printed Letter.

(Signed)   D. STUART, *Chairman.*

Turk's Head Coffee House, Strand.
June 30, 1809.

After some discussion, the Newsmen agreed to accept the offer made by the Proprietors in the Resolution above stated; but as the sums given were declared to be on the principle only of putting you on an *equality* with the Bookmen, in their advance in 1801, it was determined to continue united to support the original Propositions when an opportunity offered. This regulation gave the Morning Papers £2 2s.; Supernumeraries £1; per galley 3s. 4d.; 10d. per hour; and Evening Papers £1 18s.; Supernumeraries 19s.; per galley 3s. 2d.; 9d. per hour.

At this period the Book Compositors were soliciting a rise of 1-7th on their prices. The Newsmen were not long behind their brethren in claiming the same advance on their labour, and the long Report of the Masters, before mentioned, was answered, paragraph by paragraph, in a manner which must have convinced them, that if they would not allow the talent, they must acknowledge that all the justice in the dispute lay on your side. This answer is dated January 18, 1810. Your Committee cannot, in consequence of its length, insert it here, but, to suit their present purpose, will extract the answers to the *second* and *fifth* paragraphs.

The profession of a man should always be equal to the support of himself and family in a decent way. They should be supplied with not merely what will preserve animation, but what custom has rendered necessary for our comfort; and every man of family must feel the truth of the assertion—that at the present time he experiences difficulty in procuring such necessaries. With respect to the difference between the wages of Book and News Compositors, it will be observed, that the expenses of a News Compositor are necessarily more than that of a Book Compositor, arising from the unseasonable hours of labour.—We believe the latter part of their paragraph will be found very deficient of truth; for there are but few mechanics with the same constant and regular exertion, but would equal, and exceed by far our incomes.

As the two dates given by the Journeymen for the prices of provisions were to be contradicted, they introduced *three* tables, and made a calculation by the rule of Subtraction. But the men were not to be deceived by this *new* system of Arithmetic, and combated it by the *old* mode, as follows :

It would seem as if the sum of 1s. 6¾d. was considered as the loss we sustained in the course of a week; but it is the proportion it bears to 8s. 9½d. and we find that it makes a difference in our weekly incomes of 7s. 1d., a sum which must be felt particularly by those having families.

The assertions made in the other paragraphs were most ably controverted, and your cause made doubly sure by the truths which accompanied its defence. The Employers never made a reply to it, because it was unanswerable : and your Committee cannot refrain from expressing their gratitude to all concerned in its production.

1810—To proceed. The Book Masters acquiesced in the request of their Compositors for an advance, which was to take place on the 1st of May, and the Newsmen taking advantage of the acknowledgment made in the *ninth* paragraph before mentioned, demanded the rise of 1-7th to place them on an equality with their brethren in the Book department. Their request was not noticed. They still persevered, and to assist their cause the Bookmen came to a Resolution, that no man should apply for a situation on a Newspaper during the dispute.—Highly to their credit, and honourable to their character, not one application was made.

The Newsmen still continued their exertions, and, on the 14th of May, the following proposition in MS. was presented to each Companionship.

The Proprietors of the Daily Newspapers, having taken the request of their Compositors for an advance of wages into consideration, and on referring to the whole series of rises from 1783[5], when Book-work was 4d. per thousand, and Morning Papers were £1 7s. per week, find that £2 0s. 6d. on Morning Papers would be equal to 6d. per thousand, the present advanced price on Book-work.

But the Proprietors, unwilling wholly to disappoint the expectations of their Compositors, consent to give them an advance of 4s. on Morning Papers, and 3s. on Evening Papers, per week, making the Wages on Morning Papers, £2 6s. per Man per week, and on Daily Evening Papers £2 1s.; to take place from Monday, May 21, 1810.

This was answered by the following Resolutions :

At a General Meeting of the Compositors employed on Newspapers, held May 19, 1810, the following declarative Resolutions were agreed to *unanimously* :

Res. I. That in tracing our advances of Wages from the year 1783[5] up to 1800, there not being extant any clear and certain records, and a perfect collection of documents containing all the circumstances, many important facts and transactions may be forgotten and lost.

Res. II. That from the above consideration, it is evident, that to refer further back than 1800, in order to determine what ought to be the advance of Wages on Newspapers is unfair and improper; and it is contrary to right, according to the declared opinions of the Newspaper Proprietors themselves as expressed (in a Report of their Committee, dated June 30, 1809, and generally circulated) in the following words of their own : "The Compositors have no right to refer further back than the year 1800, as they then received all they asked, and a *new compact* was made with them on their own terms."

Res. III. That the Newspaper Proprietors ought to give their Compositors an advance of Wages fully equal to the advance on Book-work since 1800, conformably to the principle admitted by themselves in the above-mentioned document : where, after stating the allegation of the Newspaper Compositors that their advance in 1800 was not equal to the advance on Book-work, and admitting the fact, they allow it to be (using their own words) a "reasonable ground of complaint in your Compositors' Circular."

Res. IV. That, in the Scale of 1805, a considerable advance was granted to the Compositors on Book-work, in respect to Sunday-work, Night-work, and Morning-work, which required a correspondent advance on Newspapers, to which it is particularly applicable.

Res. V. That, even if we had not the above indisputable grounds, we have in justice sufficient grounds in the exigencies of the times, as, according to the News Proprietors' own statement of the comparative prices of the necessaries of life between 1800 and 1809, there was a rise of 1s. 6¾d. on 8s. 9½d. which makes a difference in our weekly incomes (taking the medium of Morning and Evening Papers) of upwards of 7s.

Res. VI. That the Compositors on Book-work have received less from their Employers than their exigencies required, and only what circumstances allowed. Those unfavourable circumstances were alleged to arise principally from the war, and, consequently, far from being applicable to the Newspaper branch of the Business, which derives its prosperity from the war. Therefore, there could be no reason why Compositors employed on Newspapers should not have an advance fully adequate to their exigencies.

A fortnight's notice to quit was then given upon the Daily Papers, and on the day of its expiration the News Compositors were given to understand from the individual Printers, that the demand was acquiesced in, and your Scale, as it now stands, was acknowledged—Morning Papers £2 8s. ; Supernumeraries £1 3s. ; galley 3s. 10d. ; 9d. per thousand ; and Assistants 11½d. per hour.—Evening Papers £2 3s. 6d. ; Supernumeraries £1 1s. 6d. ; galley 3s. 7d. ; 8½d. per thousand ; and Assistants 10½d. per hour.

Thus terminated your last struggle. It will be found that in the space of twenty-four years, your prices and modes of work have equally changed with the appearance of the Journals. From the former rise to the present nothing appears worthy notice, excepting the alteration of measure during the sitting of Parliament ; but from the great pressure of matter, and an alteration in the size of the paper used, most of the Journals retained the same measure during the recess.

Your Committee feel that some apology may be necessary for giving so minute a detail of what perhaps has occurred within your own memory but the task imposed upon them embracing so wide a field, must plead their excuse; and having introduced the latter document to your notice, considering it the precursor of an understood and established "Scale of Prices," they trust its utility will compensate for the trespass.

Having now advanced to the period (May, 1810) when your endeavours, after twelve months' struggle, were crowned with success, your Committee, trusting to your own feelings, must beg to pause on the events of that time. Would they not be guilty of an act of injustice; would they not betray a want of feeling, did they not call to your recollection the sufferers in that contest ? In various disputes in your profession, advantage has been taken of the most prominent characters; dismissal from their situations has been the awarded punishment—they are cheered and assisted by their fellows, and the sacrifice is but lightly felt—yet, in this instance (although solicited and dealt with according to the immemorial custom of the trade), in opposition to the concurrence in your request by eleven other Newspaper Proprietors, one Employer alone refused, and by a paltry subterfuge and mean advantage, was the means of incarcerating eleven of your brethren in a manner worthy alone the character of a feudal tyrant triumphing over his vassals. Torn from their families, separated from their associates, months rolled over them in the gloom of a prison. Their brethren were alive to their sufferings; they felt, they commiserated; and what comfort they could afford was cheerfully given, and as gratefully received. This unfortunate circumstance is still in your memories; cherish it; and when sinking in the vale of years, may the sufferers be enlivened by the smiles of their younger brethren, and ever be remembered when departed from us !—One, unhappily, fell a victim to his punishment; and when the name of Malcolm Craig shall be repeated, the glow of sympathy shall rouse us to despise his persecutor, and encourage us in maintaining the cause for which he suffered !

The vacancies on this persecuting Journal[1] were filled partly by boys and partly by *men*; in a few years this system failed; it was again thrown open, but in its usual encroaching spirit it was shortly after closed upon an entire *new* principle, and *"as it was in the beginning,"* etc.

In the year 1811, a dispute occurred on an Evening Paper, respecting the introduction of Apprentices, which lasted but six weeks.

About the year 1813, Morning Papers of 20 columns became almost general. Papers of the present size have not rendered the use of small

[1] The newspaper referred to was *The Times*. The issue for 9 November, 1810, gives an account of the trial. A score of men, encouraged by the companionship of *The Day*, handed in their notices. The prosecution suggested that sabotage was intended, that the men proposed to "Bishop the balls," *i.e.*, soak the pressmen's inking balls in water, and render them unfit for further use. Street, the publisher of *The Times*, reckoned a pressman's average weekly wage at £3 15s. od., the average working hours being 15 or 16 one day and 10 or 11 the next. When the companionship left, Mr. Flint, a notorious taker of apprentices (see p. 119), supplied *The Times* with a number of boys.

type less necessary than when they consisted but of sixteen columns; and the remarks made in the extracts from the documents before your Committee, of the years 1793—1810, are equally applicable, as the same causes exist.

In the commencement of the year 1816, the Trade was thrown into confusion by the introduction of Nonpareil, a type not recognized in former agreements respecting the price for Newspapers.[1] The companionship were required to compose it at Minion price and quantity; they refused, and in consequence left their situations; but others, in direct opposition to the interests of the profession, submitted to the demand. Ignorance could not be pleaded by them; for your Committee are well aware, that few men can be found incapable of casting up the galley on a newspaper, or be unacquainted with the difference in price of Nonpareil and other types used in Book-houses. The bad example set by these men, with the desire of gain, may have induced others to follow their steps; but they cannot, unless you lose your unanimity, sap the foundation of your rights. It is therefore incumbent on your Committee to protest against any men taking upon themselves the right of deviating from your regulations, or of settling either the price or quantity of the galley of smaller type than Minion, without a general understanding with their brethren of the profession. It has caused both trouble and expense, and been the means of removing good men to gratify the meanness or greediness of those, who have in the end been necessitated to throw themselves upon the mercy of their fellow-workmen, for permission to gain a subsistence among those they had, by their previous conduct, deprived of bread. Your Committee beg to state, that adding to the difference in price given on Nonpareil or Pearl in Book-work to the price per thousand in News-work, will be found the equitable charge for those sizes; that is, 1d. per thousand extra on Nonpareil, and 2d. on Pearl. Thus the fair charge for Nonpareil on Morning Papers would be 10d. per thousand, Evening Papers $9\frac{1}{2}$d.—Pearl 11d. per thousand on Morning, and $10\frac{1}{2}$d. on Evening Papers—or a *reduction, in proportion to value, on the galley quantity*.

In the latter end of the same year a misunderstanding arose in consequence of a Morning and Evening Paper being done in the same place. It might have been considered a local dispute; but as certain Resolutions were passed at a delegated Meeting held on the 3rd of January, 1817, your Committee cannot refrain from noticing it.

At a Delegated Meeting of News Compositors, held at the Coach and Horses, Water Lane, Fleet Street, Jan. 3, 1817, the following Resolutions were passed unanimously :

Resolved, I. That it is the opinion of this Meeting, that there are but three classes of Workmen on Morning Papers that can be acknowledged by the Profession, viz. *Full hands*, £2 8s. per week; *Supernumeraries* at £1 3s. per week; and *Assistants* at $11\frac{1}{2}$d. per hour.

Resolved, II. That we consider the Situation of *Finishers* on a Morning Paper, (where no person is employed to do the preceding part of the work), as an innovation that would tend to disorganize the system hitherto acted upon.

---

[1] An innovation made by *The Times*.

Resolved, III. That under this consideration we recommend to our fellow-workmen to refuse any such situation should it be offered them.

Resolved Unanimously.—*That with respect to the——(having no precedent to act upon) and there not being a regular Companionship, we recommend to the persons employed thereon to regulate the trifling difference between them and their employer as amicably as possible, keeping in view that the interests of the profession are not invaded thereby.*

This matter was amicably adjusted; but your Committee regret to state, that at the commencement of the following year, a dispute arose on another Journal, by a demand being made for eleven hours' work (time and quantity)—or two measured galleys and a finish, sometimes extending to three hours. This mode was declared inadmissible by the trade; it was resisted, and you again triumphed by the sacrifice of situation only of those that refused their acquiescence.

Nothing appears worthy of notice after the above date till the month of May in the present year, and while your interests impose upon your Committee, the necessity of laying before you the circumstances that then arose, they will trespass upon your patience only so long as the subject demands.—After the introduction of Nonpareil on the Journal mentioned in the year 1816, the Trade were ignorant of the *men* and their *modes of work;* you had no interest in the enquiry, for they never could be respected who had deserted your standard, nor pitied when labouring under difficulties they had brought upon themselves.[1] From an accidental occurrence, not necessary here to repeat, a request was made, that a statement of the situation of that Journal might be laid before you. Policy dictated the propriety of receiving it; if those employed acted up to the spirit of your laws, you would have nothing to condemn; but if, on the contrary, they had violated your system, you would have the opportunity of declaring against it, and of preventing the evil example from spreading further. Custom, it is said, will in time become law; so would your silence have permitted the unprincipled to gratify themselves by the sacrifice of your rights and interests, and to undermine your whole system before you were aware of the danger.

By this statement it was discovered there were two *modes* of work on that Journal, both in direct opposition to the rules and prices agreed upon in 1810. From the pressure of advertisements, two companionships were formed, one for the outer, and another for the inner form; those engaged on the former were offered, and accepted an Evening Paper price per galley for Nonpareil, Minion quantity; while those on the latter were employed according to the custom of the trade. It is unnecessary to comment on the introduction of *two companionships* on a Daily Paper, much less to point out the absurdity of consenting to receive an Evening Paper price on a Morning Journal, upon the plea of its being performed by daylight; by the same parity of reasoning, you might demand a Morning Paper price for an Evening Journal, because, for a great part of the year, a portion of the work is done by candlelight. But an alteration on the inner-form system was shortly proposed, which was that rejected by yourselves in the year 1818—*viz. two galleys*, and

---

[1] These and the following remarks refer to *The Times*.

remaining till the paper went to press. This was refused by the employed, and seven out of twelve deserted this "flag of blackest hue."

This circumstance, from the consequences that might probably follow, led to the appointment of a Committee to draw up, and circulate, for the information of the trade, a statement of the regular mode of working on Newspapers—"to guide the ignorant, to guard the unwary." To assist them in their labours, and to maintain that harmony which should ever subsist between two branches in one profession, your Committee requested, at a delegated Meeting of Bookmen, the appointment of a gentleman from their body to assist them in the task assigned, which was most cheerfully met and cordially assented to.

After the appointment of your Committee, another circumstance arose which necessarily occupied a portion of their time. The Proprietor of an obscure Evening Journal, out of which a Sunday Paper is formed, made a demand on the employed to complete the Weekly Journal, not merely with a *reduction* of wages, but absolutely for *nothing !*—as a kind of make-weight for the salary they received upon the other. This not being found in any article of your scale, was, of course, refused by the companionship, and the loss of situation followed: their places have been filled by some *distinguished* characters, now out of the pale, but whose *memories* will be cherished.

Your Committee will, by recapitulating the events related under each date, bring the various Regulations into one point of view, which, attached to your Scale of 1810, will, it is trusted, fully accomplish the purpose for which your Committee received their appointment. In 1786 a rise of 1-6th (or 4s. 6d.) was obtained on Newspapers, but no Regulations were generally adopted; each Paper having its own mode, its internal management was regulated by existing circumstances; but in the year 1793, the nature of News-work, in a progress of seven years, was completely changed, and the price of necessaries increasing with the labour imposed, rendered it incumbent on your predecessors not only to solicit an advance of wages, but that the time and quantity should also be defined. This request was made by the Newsmen, and though sanctioned by the signatures of their brethren in the Book department, your Committee consider it as the first division of the Compositors into two branches of one profession. Their wishes were granted so far as related to a rise of 1-7th (or 4s. 6d.) on Morning Papers; but nothing relating to the hours of work or time of commencing on Sundays was determined upon. It was acknowledged that the Supernumeraries should receive a proportionate advance, but your Committee cannot pass over the distinction then made between Morning and Evening Papers without expressing their regret at the circumstance. The latter only received a rise of 1-13th, or 2s. 6d.

In the same year the Resolutions were passed against the employment of Apprentices on Papers. Some years prior to this date they were to be found on many of the Journals, and particularly on those called *Weekly*, arising from the connection of both classes with Book-houses; but, from the circumstances already mentioned (1793), when Daily Papers required separate establishments, and were conducted by non-professional men, your brethren took the opportunity of objecting to their re-admission on the latter class. The Resolutions of that day now stand as Laws; you struggled—you conquered; and your Committee can only add that five attempts against them failed of success.

A rise was gained in 1800 of 4s. on Morning and 3s. on Evening Papers, making a still greater difference between the two classes of Journals. It was given and accepted without any reference to further regulations in the spirit of the propositions before quoted.

The nature of the work and increase of labour on the Evening Journals, from 1793 to 1800, required the adoption of the Resolution mentioned under the latter date :—"That all Composition cease when the day's publication goes to press—all work afterwards to be paid for as extra, or deducted from the first work of the next day's publication." This regulation (with one exception) was generally accepted; the Printer had the choice of paying or deducting. A Scale of quantity, and a regulation for the twelve hours' work, was also adopted.

In the year 1809 it became necessary to solicit another rise. Twenty-four years had passed away; the system of News-work had ripened into perfection, and it merely required registering for the mutual convenience of the parties interested. With the request for an advance a Scale was introduced, which specifically defined the sum to be paid for labour. You accepted the offer of the Employers, which was a rise of 2s. on Morning, and 1s. on Evening Papers; but nothing was answered respecting the Scale, the sole object of your wishes. The following year you succeeded; and your Committee merely notice a fractional difference in the sums proposed and those now paid. The galley on a Morning Paper is stated at 3s. $9\frac{1}{2}$d., now 3s. 10d.; and the Evening Journals at £2 3s., instead of £2 3s. 6d. per week. With this difference the Scale stands complete; and for its support, with a clear definition, have the labours of your Committee been wholly directed.

"To guide the ignorant, to frustrate the machinations of the unprincipled, and, if possible, to form a closer bond of union among yourselves," has been their pleasing task. By a reference to the first Resolution of the Newsmen of May 19, 1810, it will be observed, that they lament the want of a perfect collection of documents, by which they might correctly trace the advances of wages from 1785 to 1800— indeed they assert that no records were extant. Your Committee congratulate themselves upon being more fortunate, and have extracted from, or inserted at length, every document relating to Regulations or Prices since 1785, which they trust will not be considered uninteresting, and, handed down as records, may yet be useful. To prove the strength of your foundation, the Committee have embraced a period of fifty years, in which is included fifteen years prior to the date of the first document, and subsequently, through a space of thirty-five years, to the present time. In pursuing their duty, your Committee have not deviated from their path to obtrude upon your notice at this day all the misunderstandings which have arisen among the Journeymen, nor have they paused to revive the memory of local disputes with the employers; they have sought not "to rake the ashes of the dead"—they have endeavoured to avoid any reflection that might cause a blush in the living.

The labours of your Committee will close with an Abstract of the Scale, and the Laws and necessary Regulations attached, which they trust will satisfactorily answer the purpose of their collection. You require nothing of the employers—they demand nothing from you; and shall it be said that your privileges must be forfeited by your own negligence; be scattered into air by the unprincipled; or sacrificed to the interest of a designing few ?—Forbid it, spirit ! while the recollection of the struggles of our predecessors lives amongst us ! Your Committee conclude with soliciting your indulgence for any deficiency on their parts; but as your interest has been their sole object, your approbation their reward, they confidently trust the purity of their motives will be a sufficient apology for their unintentional errors.

P. CHALK	W. YOCKNEY
H. WARREN	T. PATERSON
E. M. DAVIS	J. B. SPENCE.

ABSTRACT OF THE SCALE[1]

	Per Week	Per Galley	Per Hour
1. Morning Papers	£2 8s. 0d.	3s. 10d.	11½d.
Evening Papers	£2 3s. 6d.	3s. 7d.	10½d.

The charge of tenpence halfpenny per hour refers solely to employment upon time; every odd quarter of a galley, on quantity, must carry the charge of 11d.; as the charge of 10½d. would bring down the galley to 3s. 6d.; which is contrary to the scale.

2. Assistants on other Journals are paid the same as Evening Papers; the Sunday Papers, having their galleys of various lengths, are paid at the rate of 8½d. per thousand, or 10d. per hour.

The only meaning that can be gathered from the first part of this article is, that papers which are published twice or three times a week are paid the same as Evening Papers. With respect to the second part, the price per thousand for a Sunday or weekly paper is the same, but time-work is paid only 10d. per hour.

3. Long Primer and Minion galleys, cast as nigh 5,000 letters as possible (at present varying from that number to 5,200 partly arising from a variation in the founder's standards), are, per thousand, on

	Morning	Evening
Long Primer and Minion	9d.	8½d.
Nonpareil	10d.	9½d.
Pearl	11d.	10½d.

Or a reduction, in proportion to value, on the galley quantity.

This article has been greatly misunderstood; it has been supposed to contain a licence for the news compositor to set up 5,200 letters for a galley, but it does

[1] The explanatory notes on the various clauses are taken from *The London Scale of Prices*, 1836, p. 55. In 1851 the Glasgow Typographical Society referred to the London News Scale as "excellent rules, by which the destructive effects of constant night-work on man's constitution are mitigated as much as human ingenuity can devise." *Typographical Protection Circular* (London, February, 1851), p. 118.

not *say* any such thing; it simply states the fact, that at the period when the Scale was framed, some galleys contained more than 5,000 letters. As the price per thousand is clearly established, the compositor should set up neither more nor less than just such a number of lines as will amount to 3s. 10d. on a Morning Paper, or 3s. 7d. on an Evening Paper.

4. The galley on Morning Papers consists of 120 lines Long Primer, and 40 *after-lines*—Minion 88, and 30 *after-lines*—on Papers 22 ems Long Primer wide; other widths in proportion; and a *finish* of five hours. Another *mode* is, one galley and a *finish* of six hours. Twelve hours on and twelve off (including refreshment time) was the original agreement.

"The galley on Morning Papers consists of 120 lines long primer, and 40 after-lines;" which amounts to just this, that it consists of a galley and a quarter and ten lines (long primer); that the workmen shall compose 7,040 letters for 3s. 10d., instead of receiving his just reward, 5s. 3½d.; and that the full hand on his first work is paid at the rate of 6½d. per thousand, though the Scale gives him 9d.

There is also a mis-statement in respect to the length of the galley; for it will be found that on casting up a galley of the length and width given, it would contain 5,280 letters, thus exceeding the legal quantity by 280 letters, and being at direct variance with the first part of the Scale, which directs "that long primer and minion galleys are to be cast as nigh 5,000 letters as possible." The *first* direction is that which is really meant to be adopted, and which the remaining regulations of the Scale alone sanctions.

With regard to after-lines upon the first work on Morning Papers, we find that the custom existed as far back as the year 1770, but no reason for the practice can be assigned, though it is understood to have been adopted to lighten or to leave nothing to compose for the finish, and thus enable the compositors to go early to their beds; an advantage which, from the complete alteration in the nature of Morning Papers, it is totally impossible they now can enjoy.

By a finish of five hours on Morning, and six hours on Evening Papers, it was not meant that the compositors should produce five or six quarters of a galley, as that would produce considerably more than they were paid for; but from the best information that can now be obtained of the nature of Newspapers at the time this mode of work was introduced, it appears that the *first work and after-lines* of the full-hands and the *galley* of the supernumeraries were sufficient to produce the Paper, and that the "finish" was merely waiting to see whether any news of importance should arrive (during which time they might put in letter for the next day), and assisting to put the Paper to press.

5. The *time* of beginning to be the same uniformly as agreed upon by the Printer and Companionship—*i.e.*, either a two, three, or four o'clock Paper—and at whatever hour the Journal goes to press one morning regulates the hour of commencing work for the next day's publication, provided it should be over the hour originally agreed upon—if under, the time is in the Compositors' favour. The hour of commencing work on Sunday is regulated by the time of finishing on Saturday morning.

This article it is impossible to understand; but the general practice appears to be, when the paper goes to press two or three hours after the specified time, to take off one, and sometimes two, quarters from the first work of the next day; but generally commencing at the time originally agreed upon on a Sunday, making each week's work complete in itself.

6. Ten hours' Composition is the specified time for Evening Papers.—All Composition to cease when the day's Publication goes to Press; any work required afterwards to be paid for extra, or deducted from the first work of the next publication.—This does not apply to *Second Editions*; they being connected solely with the antecedent Paper, must be paid for extra.

Matter set up for a morning paper is invariably paid morning paper price, although such matter is set up in London, and the paper is published in the provinces.

7. Newspapers in a foreign language take, of course, the same advance as is allowed on Book-work.

8. A system termed *Finishing* having been formerly introduced, it is necessary to state, that no mode of working can be considered fair (except as before stated) otherwise than by the galley or hour.

No Apprentices to be employed on Daily Papers.

Apprentices are not permitted to work on *daily* papers, whether stamped or unstamped.

Compositors on weekly papers, when employed on time, charge one hour for every portion of an hour.

Compositors called in to assist on weekly papers are entitled to charge not less than two hours if employed on time, or less than half a galley if paid by lines; and persons regularly employed in a house where a weekly paper is done, if required to leave their ordinary work to assist on the paper, are entitled to not less than a quarter of a galley or an hour for each time of being called on.

The method of charging column work upon Newspapers is as follows : half measure is charged one-third more, third measure is charged one-half, and four column measure is charged double.

One-fourth is allowed for distribution on weekly papers, where more than one galley has been composed; but if less than a galley, no deduction is made.

Although a Committee had been appointed to draw up the *Report* printed above, there was no properly constituted trade union for the news compositors. Within a few months of the publication of the *Report*, its compilers proposed the organization of the one hundred and ninety-three men who subscribed to it, as members of a trade society. Thus was founded the *News Society*, some four years after the inception of the London Trade Society of Compositors.

CHAPTER XVI

NEWS COMPOSITORS'
METHODS OF WORKING
1833 - 1840

There is a complete lack of documentation concerning the affairs of the newspaper compositors and the progress of their Society from 1820 until the year 1833, when the Union Committee advised the amalgamation of all the printing trade organizations. The discussions on the subject of the News Society's refusal to co-operate are printed elsewhere in this work.[1]

When the first Annual Meeting of the London Union of Compositors was held on 2 February, 1835, it was stated that the unsatisfactory state of affairs with regard to the News Society still persisted. The following are the relevant paragraphs from the report of the meeting.[2]

It will be remembered, that, at the meeting of the trade to establish the Union, an objection was made, by the compositors employed on daily papers, to the endeavour to establish one executive head for the transaction of the business of the trade; and that it was their desire that they might constitute a separate class, having the jurisdiction of all matters affecting newspapers left in their own hands. The general meeting refused to accede to their wishes, and declared, that from the time of the establishment of the Union, there should not exist any tribunal, whose decisions should guide the compositors of London, except the Trade Council. The majority of the compositors on newspapers have refused to comply with this resolution, and have continued to support a separate Society, and constrained members of the Union to contribute indirectly to its support. They have even done more than this—they have, in one case, questioned the right of a member of the Union to work at the business, unless he enters the Society for the relief of persons out of employ.

This opposition, however, to the interests of the Union, has not been answered by the display of a similar spirit on the part of the Trade Council. They have abstained from any violence, or aught that might irritate, in the hope that conviction of the necessity of Union would induce the news compositors to join themselves to their brethren in the

---

[1] *Report of the Delegated Meeting of Compositors*, 12 December, 1833, p. 201. and *Report of the General Trade Committee*, 4 and 11 March, 1834, p. 209.

[2] Other subjects discussed at the meeting will be found in Document LXIV, p. 225.

book department, and aid them in the vindication of their rights. For this purpose (it having been intimated to the officers of the Union by members of the news trade that the fear of the number of the Council alone deterred the newsmen from joining the Union), the Trade Council considered whether they had the power of limiting their number on the monthly news-nights, but found that they were forbidden by the laws of the General Meeting to take this step. Determined, however, to remove this apparent obstacle, they resolved to recommend such a measure to the present General Meeting; and in order that they might with certainty report to this meeting that such a proposition, if carried, would remove all existing obstacles, they addressed a circular to the father of the chapels in the respective news offices, requesting him to ascertain how many members approved of an arrangement that would limit the number of the Council on news nights to the same number as the delegates from daily papers. To this communication no answer has been received from those chapels where the majority are anti-unionists, but the following letter has been received from Mr. Steel, who it seems, yet holds the office of Secretary to those who are opposed to the present principles of the Union.

Red Lion, Red Lion Court, Jan. 3, 1835.

Sir—At a double delegated meeting of newspaper compositors, held for the purpose of taking into consideration a circular issued by the London Union of Compositors, the following resolution was unanimously agreed to, and ordered to be forwarded to you the earliest opportunity.

"That no answer be given by any chapel to the circular sent by the Union; and that no notice for the future be taken of any communication unless through the medium of the Secretary."

I remain, Sir, yours, etc.,

R. STEEL, *Sec. News Society.*

The Trade Council conceived that they could not, consistently with the resolutions of the General Meeting in March last, treat with the agent of any organized body opposed to the spirit and letter of the Union, and therefore no answer to this letter was sent. They, however, intended no slight or disregard to the writer of that letter—but are willing, in the face of the whole trade, to bear testimony to his straightforward and manly conduct and candour upon all occasions, and sincerely to declare their regret at seeing his talents still employed in an unworthy and dangerous cause—dangerous to both parties, and profitable to neither. It remains, however, for this meeting to take up the subject in the course of the evening—but the Council cannot dismiss it now without expressing their earnest desire that it may be treated with calmness and a due allowance for the opinions of others. If we are by reasoning to convince our opponents of their folly, we must argue with them coolly; and if we are driven to the necessity of employing measures to subdue them, we shall be more likely to succeed by cool and well-timed movements than by rash and ill-digested attacks.

The conduct of the affairs of the newspaper compositors was not vested solely in the News Society. The London Union of

Compositors, which had failed to recruit the News Society into its ranks, also concerned itself with this section of the trade, since many members of the L.U.C. were employed on newspapers, without necessarily subscribing to the News Society.

A question of vital importance to the newsmen was discussed at the first Quarterly Delegate Meeting [1] of the L.U.C., held 1 July, 1834, when it was resolved :

> That, as it appears to the Trade Council that a practice exists upon the daily papers of casting up their galleys at amounts fluctuating from 5,000 to 5,200 letters; and as such a custom is manifestly unjust, inasmuch as it not only compels the proprietors of newspapers to pay unequally for the work done for them, but also forces the journeymen to do more labour in one house than another, for the same remuneration; it is resolved, That the Officers of the Trade Council be instructed to require of the companions on the different daily papers the castings-up of their respective galleys, with a view to a general assimilation of the mode of work in that department of the trade, and the establishment of one uniform principle between the employer and the employed.

In the course of the following year much information was collected and published as the *Report of the Committee of the Trade Council appointed to enquire into the present mode of working on "The Times" and other newspapers*. According to the L.U.C. Annual Report for 1836, the inquiry into conditions at Printing House Square "was undertaken at the request of the compositors on *The Times*. They challenged investigation, and that challenge was met by a diligent inquiry."

The companionship of *The Times* had "challenged investigation" of the methods of working at Printing House Square, an office which had been closed to union labour since 1816, when the proprietors refused to pay extra for nonpareil type. During the twenty years that followed, under the management of John Walter II and the editorship of Thomas Barnes, the paper achieved for itself a position unrivalled in the Press of this or any other country.

"The dominating political position of *The Times* during the 1830's is partly explained by its superiority in circulation, its printing facilities, its matchless reporting by express. . . . Meanwhile advertisements poured into the office in such numbers that supplements (themselves an enormous advertisement of the paper) became first frequent and finally regular. These supplements,

---

[1] Other subjects discussed at the meeting will be found in Document LXI, p. 222.

more than anything else in *The Times*, convinced the world of its unique position, which after 1832, was almost that of an estate of the realm."[1]

"The first additional four-page sheet, printed for delivery with a four-page paper, was occasioned on 13 June, 1806, by *The Times* report of the impeachment of Henry Dundas, Lord Melville. This issue consisted of three four-page sheets, the extra four-pages being headed respectively 'First Supplement' and 'Second Supplement.' Similar extra sheets were published in the same year, but afterwards there was no repetition of the enterprise known to the trade as the 'double paper' until 1817. The first gratis supplement came out in 1822 (22 July); it was composed entirely of advertisements, then an exceptional expedient. The six-column format, 16½ by 22½ inches, first appeared on 12 July, 1825. From 1825 onwards, 'double,' *i.e.*, eight-page papers became increasingly frequent. By 1831 such issues of *The Times* came out more than once a week, and by January, 1836, they averaged four a week. The *Morning Post* and the *Morning Herald* seldom produced supplements, but they printed on as large a sheet as *The Times*."[2]

Thus can be explained the division of *The Times'* compositors into two companionships, the first attending during the day to compose the supplement or advertisement forme, and the second occupied at night on news formes. The complaint of the London Union was not that there were two companionships, but that the day shift, at work on matter to be used in a morning paper, were not remunerated according to the morning paper scale of prices.

[DOCUMENT CIV]

Report from The Trade Council of the London Union of Compositors, preparatory to a Special General Meeting to be held on Tuesday, the 15th September, with a Copy of the Proposition to be submitted to that Meeting [1835].

The Trade Council having been called upon to consider the mode of working on *The Times* newspaper, have felt it to be their duty to summon a General Meeting of the Trade to decide upon the fairness or unfairness of the system prevailing thereon; and in order that the Trade at large may become acquainted with the results of a long investigation into the system of newswork, have considered it advisable to print the subjoined Report from a Section of the Council especially appointed to consider this description of work, and to compare the general mode of

---

[1] *The History of "The Times"* (London, 1935), vol. I, p. 247.
[2] *Ibid.*, p. 324.

working in news offices, with the peculiar system adopted on *The Times* newspaper. By a careful perusal of this document it is conceived the Members of the Trade will be enabled to comprehend the nature of the question at issue, and at the appointed General Meeting be in a state to enter fairly upon the discussion of the Propositions at page twenty-one of this Report.

Report of the Committee of the Trade Council appointed to inquire into the present mode of working on "The Times" and other Newspapers.

Gentlemen,

The committee intrusted to inquire into the present state of *The Times* newspaper, immediately after their appointment proceeded to adopt such measures as seemed to them best calculated to carry your intentions into effect.

Your committee more particularly directed their attention in the course of this inquiry, to the investigation of the three following points :

1st. The mode of executing the work, and the price paid for labour, as compared with other daily papers.

2nd. The acknowledged irregularity of introducing apprentices.

3rd. The state of the nonpareil galley, whether as fair as other papers, or whether totally inadmissible.

In order to arrive at the most correct information on these points, your committee requested the attendance of a full-hand from *The Times*, and summoned the chapels of the different daily morning and evening papers to send down a person fully instructed to give evidence as to the mode of doing work on their respective papers.

In compliance with the request of your committee *The Times* companionship, after having had a meeting to consider the letter which your Registrar had sent to an individual working on that paper, requesting his attendance to give evidence, and which he considered it his duty to submit to his companions, who consented to his attending, and put him in the full possession of every circumstance connected with the mode of doing work on their paper, and also expressed their anxiety to afford every information that it was in their power to render.

But your committee are sorry to report that they have not met with the same willingness and desire to afford information from the news-body at large, as they had a right to expect from them, in the prosecution of an inquiry in which their interests, as well as those of the trade at large, are so deeply involved; and have thus been the means of preventing your committee from laying before you such a complete body of evidence, as to the mode of doing work on the other daily papers, as they were desirous of doing, in order to enable you to form a just and sound judgement on this important question—a question which has so long disturbed the trade, and for the settlement of which they have so long been anxiously looking. You will no doubt feel surprised to learn that your committee were enabled to obtain evidence from only six morning and evening papers, namely :—*The Morning Chronicle*, *The Morning Herald*, *The Ledger*, *The True Sun*, *The Standard*, and *The Courier*; and that out of this number *three* only sent delegates. Finding that they could not obtain the required information in a direct manner from the chapels of the different papers, your committee sought to obtain it from individuals engaged on those papers, but were successful in only three instances, namely :—*The Morning Chronicle*, *Morning Herald*, and *Standard*.

In pursuing their investigation of the mode of doing work on *The Times*, as compared with other papers, your committee divided their inquiry into the following heads :

1. The hours of work.
2. The price per galley on the morning papers.
3. The price per galley on the evening papers.
4. The quality of the letter.
5. The number of lines per galley.
6. What paid for extra time.
7. The number of men and apprentices.
8. The average amount of earnings.

The following is the mode of doing work on *The Times*, and the other papers, as given in evidence before your committee.

THE TIMES

The Times is divided into two companionships, and is paid *two* prices for : the *inner*, or *news* form, and the *outer*, or *advertisement* form. The *advertisement* part is done during the day, the companions commencing at six o'clock in the morning and leaving off at eight o'clock in the evening.

The companions on the morning (or news) part of the paper all commence at six o'clock in the evening, and finish at five o'clock on the following morning, being eleven hours in all. It is called a four o'clock paper. The compositors are required to set two galleys in the eleven hours. All done above the two galleys in the eleven hours is paid extra for. The extras commence at 4 o'clock. If there is a press of copy, the printer avails himself of the eleven hours, and the extras do not commence until five o'clock. Extras after the eleven hours are paid for at the rate of $11\frac{1}{2}$d. per hour until the paper goes to press. The price paid per galley is 3s. 10d., the nonpareil galley included. The number of lines in a

Bourgeois galley is	..	..	110
Minion	..	..	..	90
Nonpareil	..	..	..	70

The number of letters in a

Bourgeois galley is	..	..	5060
Minion	..	..	..	5040
Nonpareil	..	..	..	5040

The nonpareil is a *bastard* fount, being a Scotch letter, which is not so deep as the English nonpareil, and the compositor sets above four hundred letters more than he is entitled to do, as will be seen from the following calculation :

Bastard fount	..	..	5040 letters
Regular nonpareil	..	..	4600
			440

The supernumeraries are paid by the piece, and the assistants 1s. per hour. They agree with the printer what will remunerate them individually for usual standing still during the night, after the expiration of the four hours, such as waiting for expresses, etc. No individual charges, but taken in the gross, unless any person is specially standing. This applies only to supernumeraries and assistants, full hands taking the price at 11½d. per hour after the eleven hours have expired.

The number of men employed on this part of the paper is :

Full-hands	..	..	..	10
Supernumeraries		..	..	10
Assistants	..	..	..	13
		Total	..	33

and their average earnings during the last twelve months have amounted to :

			£	s.	d.
Full-hands	..	..	£3	5	0
Supernumeraries	..	..	2	15	0
Assistants	..	..	2	10	0

The advertisement form.—The companions on the *advertisement*, or *outer* form commence at six o'clock in the morning and leave off at 8 o'clock in the evening. Sometimes they are required to work till ten o'clock, but not later. They are paid by the lines, and there is no specific time to do any quantity of work in. The price of the galley (nonpareil) is 3s. 6d., being *one penny under evening paper price, fair galley, and four pence under the morning galley.* When called on to assist on the morning part of the paper, they commence at 9 o'clock, and are paid 11½d. per hour. The apprentices are not required to assist on the news part of the paper.

The number of persons in the advertisement companionship is :

Men	..	..	..	17
Apprentices	..	..	..	7
				24

making a total of 57 compositors engaged on the whole of the paper.

THE MORNING CHRONICLE

The full hands on the *Morning Chronicle* commence at five o'clock, p.m. Four o'clock is the proper time. The *finish* commences at eleven o'clock, and ends at four o'clock. After four o'clock the compositors are paid 11½d. per hour. They are required to produce one galley and one third (called *after lines*) for the first work, which must be done by eleven o'clock. All done above the one galley and one third is paid for extra. The first work is six hours, the finish five hours; extras after that time 11½d. per hour. The *nick*—if the half of a quarter, a quarter of an hour is charged, and so on in proportion.

Supernumeraries.—There is no specified time for the supernumeraries to commence. They are engaged to do one galley, and are paid for it whether they have it or not, generally they do two galleys. They have made an arrangement among themselves not to remain in the office ten minutes after being told by the printer that there is no more copy for them. Four hours is the specified time for doing a galley in; if anyone should take five hours it is his own loss. Expected to do quarter per hour for the finish, which is as much as ought to be done; some do more, some less. They are paid 4s. for the finish, which is five hours work, and cannot earn more during that time. When called on to assist in correcting they charge per quarter of an hour in the same proportion as at the nick on the conclusion of the night's work.

The number of lines in a

Long Primer galley is	..		..	124
Brevier..	..	..	..	100
Nonpareil	..	..	..	72

The number of letters in a

Long Primer galley is		..	..	5002
Brevier..	..	..	..	5000
Nonpareil	..	..	..	4608

The number of hands engaged is 30, whose average earnings amount to £3.

THE MORNING HERALD

The full hands on the *Morning Herald* commence at two o'clock p.m. It is called a two o'clock paper, on the minute system, the Printer sometimes deducting from the following days' work. The *finish* commences at nine o'clock and ends at two o'clock. They are required to do one galley and about one-third as afterlines, for the first work, which must be done by nine o'clock. There are no extras on the first work, which consists of advertisements. The first work is seven hours, finish five hours, after that time 11½d. per hour is paid.

Supernumeraries and Assistants.—The Supernumeraries are insured one galley per night. Assistants are not engaged for any particular quantity, they all taking the first choice of copy, according to seniority, and then go on till all the copy is out. Supernumeraries or Assistants have no connection whatever with the full hands. They have no specified time for commencing, but are expected to be ready by eight o'clock. None are allowed to remain in the office after the Printer has told them that there is no more copy, excepting those included in the pulls, above five minutes, they having the advantage of any copy that might come up. If they are engaged in correcting for the property, they charge a quarter per hour. If desired to wait for an express, put on time. Rarely ever stand still, advertisements and other copy being given out not being wanted for the current Paper. There is no charge made less than one hour. They correct in turn, but have no particular quantity to correct, except in the nonpareil, which, if it exceeds five rules, or equivalent to it. is divided.—No distribution allowed after taking copy.

The number of lines in a

Long Primer galley is	..		106
Minion	..	..	..	88
Nonpareil	..	..	..	64

The number of letters in a

Long Primer galley is	..	4664
Minion	..	..	..	5104
Nonpareil	..	..	..	4672

The number of persons employed is

Full hands	..	..	..	6
Supernumeraries	..	..	5
Assistants	..	..	..	27
		Total	..	38

whose average earnings amount to

In Session

Full hands	..	..	£3	18	0
Supernums. and Assistants		2	10	0

Out of Session

Full hands	..	..	£3	3	0
Supernums. and Assistants		1	16	0

THE LEDGER

The *full hands* on the *Ledger* commence at six o'clock, p.m. The *finish* commences at twelve o'clock and ends at five o'clock, being a five hours' finish, after which 11½d. per hour is charged. They are required to do one galley and one third (being after lines) for the first work. All done above that is paid extra for. Time after five a.m. is charged upon the minute system.

Supernumeraries.—The Supernumeraries have no specified time for commencing, but in general begin at about half-past seven or eight o'clock. They are engaged to do one galley per night, which they must get out in the four hours. Corrections are paid at per hour. None are allowed to remain in the office after being told by the printer that there is no more copy.

There is a minion fount used on the paper, which the printer allows to be cast up as a *minion nonpareil*, on account of its extreme thinness, thereby making a difference of *nine* lines in the galley in favour of the compositor.

The number of lines in a

Bourgeois galley is	..	..	115
Minion	..	..	..	88
Nonpareil	..	..	..	77

The number of letters in a

Bourgeois galley is	..	..	5060
Minion	..	..	4576
Nonpareil	..	..	4620

The number of men employed is

Full hands	..	..	5
Supernumeraries	..	..	18
	Total	..	23

whose average earnings amount to about £2 14s. 0d.

THE COURIER

Full hands. The full hands on the *Courier* are presumed to commence at five o'clock a.m. and the galley to be got out by nine o'clock. Formerly they commenced at half-past four, the galley to be got out by half-past eight, and the finish by half-past two o'clock; but there was a change made by the present proprietors. The finish is now completed by three o'clock. There are no afterlines on the first work, and the full hands are expected to set a galley and correct one by nine o'clock; but if the galley is not corrected by nine o'clock, no allowance or deduction is required. Extra work above the first galley is paid for in the usual way— nothing less than a quarter of a galley is charged. The full hands' time is completed at three o'clock. If the paper goes to press at twenty-nine minutes after three, no overtime is allowed; if it goes to press any time over half-past three an hour is charged. There are no half-hour charges on the *Courier*, and the amount of each days' work is kept complete. In the finish of six hours, composing a galley is considered fair work, and no demand of more has ever been made. Full hands on *second* or *subsequent editions* are paid by the hour. At eight o'clock the full hands and a specified number of assistants are required to attend; an edition is done, when nothing less than an hour is charged. Even when not employed at all, one hour is paid.

Supernumeraries.—The copy for the supernumeraries is generally ready at nine o'clock for them to commence; sometimes it is as late as half-past nine. All begin at the same time. They are engaged to do one galley, which is required to be out by one o'clock. If not supplied with sufficient copy during the four hours the galley is charged. When they are employed after one o'clock, the supernumeraries are on their lines until the copy is all out. If there is more copy than a galley to be had, it is given to them, and they charge what it makes above the galley. If there is not a sufficient supply of copy, and they are kept standing, which occurs but very seldom, they are expected to remain until one o'clock. If the supernumeraries assist the full hands in correcting for five or six minutes, they charge a few lines, according to the number of lines that might be composed within the time they are so employed; but if they are employed for half an hour, they charge one hour. There are no assistants employed on the paper.

The number of lines in a

Bourgeois galley is	..	..	104
Minion	..	..	89
Nonpareil	..	..	68

The number of letters in a

Bourgeois galley is	..	..	4992
Minion	..	..	5162
Nonpareil	..	..	4604

The number of men employed is

Full hands	..	..	6
Supernumeraries	..	..	16
		Total ..	22

whose average earnings amount to

Full hands	..	.. £2	10	0
Supernumeraries ..	..	2	0	0

THE TRUE SUN

Full hands.—The full hands on the *True Sun* commence at five o'clock a.m., and are expected to get the galley out by nine o'clock. The finish begins at nine and ends at three o'clock, being six hours. Extras paid on the first work, and not less than a quarter of a galley is charged. After three o'clock every minute is charged; they are cast up at the end of the week at the rate of a quarter per hour. The full hands can be called upon to do a quarter per hour on the finish of six hours, for which they are paid 3s. 7d. being the price of a galley, and which is half a galley more than what they are paid for; but this is seldom enforced.

Supernumeraries.—The Supernumeraries commence at half-past nine o'clock; all begin at the same time; they charge from that time whether they have copy or not, sometimes they take copy at half-past seven. They are engaged to do a galley, which is required to be done in four hours, from the time of taking copy. After they have got the galley out they go on the lines till the copy is finished. Sometimes the printer calls them on to assist the full hands in correcting. When correcting they charge minutes the same as the full hands, which are reduced into lines, at the rate of a quarter of a galley per hour.

Second Editions are paid for at the rate of a quarter per hour. After the first hour go on the minute system. All subsequent editions commence afresh on the same system, charging not less than a quarter.

Assistants.—The assistants are paid in the same way as the supernumeraries, but are not entitled to commence at the same time with them.

The number of lines in a

Long Primer galley is	..		132
Bourgeois	..	..	115
Minion	..	..	97
Nonpareil	..	..	76

The number of letters in a

Long Primer galley is	..	5016
Bourgeois	..	..	..	5060
Minion	..	..	..	5044
Nonpareil	..	..	..	4636

The number of men employed is

Full hands	..	..	..	3
Supernumeraries	..	..	21
Assistants	..	..	..	2
		Total	..	26

whose average earnings amount to about

Full hands	..	..	£2 12 0
Supernumeraries ..	..	2 2 0

THE STANDARD

Full hands. The full hands on the *Standard* commence at five o'clock
a.m., and are required to get the galley out by nine o'clock. The finish
begins at nine, and ends at three o'clock, making six hours, during
which time they are expected to produce a quarter per hour. There are
no extras on the first work. After three o'clock, 10½d. per hour is charged.
The *nick*, half an hour is paid. It appears doubtful whether any extras
can be charged before half-past 3 o'clock.

Supernumeraries.—None.

Assistants.—The assistants, who are all elderly men, come at six
o'clock, but have no specified time for commencing, and sometimes
do not get any copy before half-past nine or ten o'clock. They do not
declare out of the galley at any particular time, nor do they make any
charge for standing still. They are not called on to assist in correcting,
nor are they expected to wait for second editions, which are done by
bookmen in the house, and who are likewise employed on the paper
whenever there is a press of copy. If the full hands are not there by six
o'clock, the assistants are expected to occupy their frames, but this is
only an arrangement amongst the companionship.

Second Editions commence at half-past five o'clock, and are charged
by the line if exceeding a quarter of a galley, but an hour is charged for
any quantity under that.

The number of lines in a

Bourgeois galley is	..	..	112
Brevier..	..	..	..	106
Minion	..	..	..	94
Nonpareil	..	..	..	64

The number of letters in a

Bourgeois galley is	..	..	5040
Brevier..	..	..	..	5194
Minion	..	..	..	5170
Nonpareil	..	..	..	4544

The number of men employed is

Full hands	13
Assistants	4
	——
Total ..	17

whose average earnings amount to about

Full hands £2	4	4½
Assistants 1	10	0

———

It will be seen from the foregoing evidence, which was all that your committee were able to obtain, that the principal points of difference in the mode of doing work on *The Times*, and the other daily papers are three in number.

1. The existence of *two* companionships (a day and a night companionship) on the same paper, which is paid *two* different prices for.

2. The nonpareil galley, which is 440 letters above the 4600, and paid one penny under the evening paper price, and fourpence under the morning paper.

3. The employment of apprentices.

With respect to the mode of doing work which is adopted on the *inner*, or *news*, form of *The Times*, there does not appear to be anything objectionable with the exception of the nonpareil galley, the irregularities existing on that paper being principally on the *outer*, or *advertisement* form.

With respect to the mode of doing work on the other daily papers, your committee cannot help observing that several irregularities have also crept in amongst them, and they wish particularly to draw your attention to the system of doing what is called the *finish* and the setting a number of lines over and above the galley, which are called *after-lines*. Your Committee have endeavoured to trace the origin of this latter practice, but have not been able to arrive at any certain information on the subject. It appears that they were general in 1776, since which time they have been regularly acknowledged by the trade.

The evils resulting from this system will be best seen from the following statement.

The full hands on morning papers are required to compose one galley and a third for their first work, the value of which is 5s. 1¼d., leaving 2s. 10¾d., for the finish, which is five hours work. On the *Morning Chronicle* the full hands are expected to produce a quarter of a galley per hour while on the finish. In such case the value of the lines on the finish will amount to 4s. 9½d., which added to 5s. 1¼d., the value of the first work, will produce 9s. 10¾d., for which they receive only 8s. namely :

First work

1 Galley	3	10
After lines, ⅓ of a galley ..	1	3¼
	——	
	5	1¼

Finish

1 Galley	..	..	..	3 10
¼ of a galley	..	..	..	11½

    4   9½

First Work	..	..	..	5 1¼
	Total	..		9 10¾

      6 days

Making per week	..	£2 19 4½
For which they are paid	..	2 8 0

Thus producing a clear
profit of £0   11   4½

per week to the establishment more than what they are paid for.

The Times nonpareil galley, cast up to its own body, consists of 5040 letters, and is paid 3s. 6d. for, equal to 8¼d. per 1000, which is one penny under evening paper price and fourpence under morning paper.

The *Morning Herald* nonpareil galley consists of 4672 letters, to which must be added (for the full hands) a third of a galley for after-lines, thus making 6229 letters, which is paid 3s. 10d. for, and is equal to 7¼d. per 1000 (which thus reduces it to one penny less than *The Times*) leaving 10d. an hour for a finish of five hours to make up the established wages. It must also be borne in mind that the full hands are required to have a sufficient quantity of letter in their case to do the finish before they commence it. If we therefore deduct a fourth for distribution, it will necessarily reduce the price per hour on the first work to 7½d.

The *Standard* brevier galley consists of 5194 letters, and is paid 3s. 7d. for, which is equal to 8d. per 1000, leaving 3s. 8d. for a finish of six hours to make up the sum of £2 3s. 6d. per week, the regular wages of a full hand. If we add the distribution, it will make it seven hours and a half, for which 3s. 8d. is paid, consequently the full hands barely receive 6d. per hour for the finish. To take this in another point of view :—The full hands are required to produce one galley for the first work, and a quarter of a galley per hour on the finish. The first work, Brevier lines, is 5194 letters and the finish 7791 letters, making altogether 12,985 letters, for which they are paid 7s. 3d. which is equal to 6¾d. per 1000.

The above calculations, as will be perceived, are made from two of the worst cases which came before your committee, in order to show to what lengths the evil of the after-lines and finish are capable of being carried.

On *The Times* there is no such thing as after lines or a finish. There are ten full hands employed on the news part, who are paid £2 8s. 0d. per week for the composition of the two galleys per night, in the eleven hours, and although they may not be able to produce it in consequence of an insufficiency of copy, still they are ensured the £2 8s. 0d., and if they produce more than the specified quantity (2 galleys) they are paid extra for it at the rate of 3s. 10d. per galley. When the eleven hours have expired and the paper has not then gone to press, they are paid 11½d. per hour until it does. Should any nonpareil advertisements be set up by the compositors on the news department, they are paid 3s. 10d. per galley. It will thus plainly appear that when the compositor has set his two galleys, all that he may do after is paid for extra; thus, if there is plenty of copy and he sets up three galleys before the expiration of the eleven hours, he is paid one galley extra, and all the time that he may stop after the eleven hours he is paid 11½d. per hour for; he having merely to complete his two galleys per night during the week for his £2 8s. od.

There are 17 journeymen and 7 apprentices employed on the advertisements during the day, from 6 o'clock in the morning till 8 at night, but it sometimes happens that the journeymen are required to stop at night to assist in the inner form, and in such case they are paid 11½d. per hour. The boys are never called upon to assist on it, or to work during the night. They are principally the sons of men employed in the office.

On the *Ledger* there is a minion in use, which on account of its extreme thinness, the printer allows to be cast up as a minion-nonpareil, thus reducing the galley by *nine* lines.

There is a bastard nonpareil in use on the *Standard*, 64 lines to the galley, and there is also another irregularity existing on that paper, namely, the practice of the assistants coming at six o'clock in the morning and sometimes waiting until half-past nine or even ten o'clock before they have any copy given them, thus waiting for three or four hours without making any charge for standing still.

Your Committee having thus brought under your notice all the material points of the evidence which was given before them, now beg leave to close their Report, leaving it in your hands to make such deductions from it as may best suit the difficulties and justice of the case, and the great and important principles which are involved in its final adjustment. They have refrained from expressing any opinion on the merits of the question, conceiving it to be their duty merely to investigate and to lay before you the evidence which they might be enabled to obtain, which evidence is, they regret to say, owing to the obstacles and prejudices which they had to contend with, from those whose interest it will more particularly affect, not so copious or so complete as they could have wished.

[*Then followed six propositions which were to be put to the Meeting on 15 September, 1835. These are printed after the* Report *of that meeting on p. 424*].

The following figures, extracted from the Report, show the numerical superiority of the supernumeraries and assistants over the full hands.

	Full hands	Sups.	Assts.
The Times			
(night news ship) ..	10	10	13
Morning Herald ..	6	5	27
Ledger	5	18	—
Courier	6	16	—
True Sun	3	21	2
Standard	13	4	—
	43	74	42

At the meeting held on 15 September, 1835, a further Report on "the mode of working on *The Times* newspaper" was read. The companionship of *The Times* sent a communication with five arguments in defence of the customs of their office. These were also read to the assembly. In conclusion, six resolutions respecting the situation were agreed upon by the London Union of Compositors.

[DOCUMENT CV]

Report of The Trade Council of the London Union of Compositors, on the mode of working on The Times *newspaper . . . adopted at Special General Meetings held on the 15th and 22nd of September, 1835, in the Theatre of "The London Mechanics' Institution."*

Amid the many important matters which from time to time have engaged the attention of the Trade at our General Meetings, there has been none so important as that which has caused our assembling together this evening. Those upon former occasions have been only of partial interest—but the present is one which involves the interest of the whole Trade. It is therefore necessary that the utmost attention should be paid to the details which it has been considered necessary to lay before you, in order that our conclusions may be founded upon justice, and that the events of this evening may tend to the stability of the Union, and the advantage of every individual member of the Trade.

The period when the first dispute between the proprietors and the compositors on *The Times* newspaper occurred, is now so far back, being upwards of 25 years since, that the particulars and all remembrance of the event would have passed away, had not the occasional return to the book trade of some individual who had worked on that paper, and thus subjected himself to the reproach of the business, brought the facts to our recollection.

The compositors of the present day (those who work in London, at least) are told that *The Times* office is considered unfair, and they know that those who have worked on that paper are the subjects of reproach and persecution, but why it is closed, and why the men are persecuted, is not known, perhaps, to more than two hundred persons in the whole trade. We have so long been accustomed to hear, at almost every turn, that the men on *The Times* are "liberally paid for their labour," that hundreds doubt the justice of closing an establishment which employs more persons than any other daily journal, and which to many has been represented as a kind of Valley of Diamonds, in which it is only necessary to enter in order to secure an ample supply of present necessities, and a handsome competency for old age.

It therefore became the duty of the Trade Council to examine into these rumours, to investigate these representations—and convey to the Trade a just knowledge of the present state of this oft-agitated question; for as one of the first principles of the London Union of Compositors is, justice to the employer and the employed—and as it was evident from the isolated condition of *The Times* office that this golden rule had been violated—that either the men were suffering injustice from their employers, or that the employer was kept out of the pale of the Trade, by an unforgiving spirit, it became necessary for the character and honour of the London Union that the question no longer should remain uninvestigated.

It is necessary, however, to state that as there are several persons now working on sufferance in the Trade, who cannot by the present laws be admitted into the Union, it has become necessary that a General Meeting should decide whether these individuals have so transgressed as that they can never hereafter be considered fair and honourable workmen, or whether their exclusion is not uncalled for and unmerited, the establishment of the Union having cancelled all previous offences.

There is one other reason, too, why an investigation into the mode of working on *The Times* should not be delayed, and that is the belief that the Union sanctions the practices on that paper. This erroneous idea must therefore be removed or confirmed, and the proceedings of this night will doubtless speak the sentiments of the Members of the Union on this subject in a language that cannot in future be misunderstood.

A tedious history of the disputes of *The Times* office is not necessary for our purpose. But we must observe, that at the last rise obtained by the News Trade, now a quarter of a century ago, circumstances arose at *The Times* office, which led to the imprisonment of the workmen employed thereon, and during the term of that imprisonment one of the compositors expired. This unfortunate case the Trade has been repeatedly called upon to cherish; and to perpetuate the memory of the event from son to sire and from sire to son—but as the grave has closed upon most of the sufferers, and the rest of the actors in this melancholy drama must soon follow them, the event should, in the remembrance of the Trade, henceforth seem but as a dream, whose impressions are so faint and so uncertain, as cannot influence a well-directed mind.

In 1810, then, *The Times* office was closed, and men and boys[1] were employed upon the paper for a few years, when at length the house was again opened, and declared fair—but in 1816, nonpareil was for the first time introduced on the paper without an allowance for the smallness of its size, agreeable to the first article of the Book Scale. The proprietors insisted that the Nonpareil galley should contain the same number of letters as the minion galley, and the house was again closed; and has never since been re-opened. Several internal disputes have caused men at various times to leave; but it is nineteen years since this house was under the influence of the Trade—and in considering this question it must not be forgotten that the prevailing irregularities which we have now to lament have been introduced during that period.

Pursuing, therefore, the course which has always characterized the London Union, viz., to judge of things as they are, not as they have been—and labour to remove those evils which generally have been found to have arisen from our hitherto disunited state, and from the want of any appointed head which was entitled to general respect and obedience, we proceed to direct the attention of the Trade to the *present* condition of *The Times* office.

[1] The boys were supplied by Mr. Flint, whose office was in Little Green Arbour Court, Old Bailey. He employed only youths. See also p. 119.

The printed Report of the Trade Council has already shown to the Trade the mode of work in that office and in a few others. And we find that the only important particulars in which *The Times* differs from other offices are the three following :

1. The payment of less than evening paper price for work done on a Morning Paper.[1]
2. The existence of a Nonpareil galley which is paid considerably less than its value.
3. The employment of apprentices.

It is not necessary, we apprehend, here to enter into the question why apprentices should not be admitted on Daily Papers—it is sufficient for us that for forty years they have by common consent and agreement been forbidden to work on Daily Newspapers, and the crowded state of the Trade forbids that that door for the introduction of apprentices, so long shut, should at present be opened. We say, therefore, that this Meeting, before it sets aside a regulation which has existed for so long a period, ought to weigh well the consequences which would arise to the Trade from their decision on this point.

In considering the question of apprentices, however, we must not forget that feelings of humanity as well as a sense of moral propriety forbid that youth should turn night into day, and immolate their strength, their health, and their morality at the shrine of interest. Indeed, we apprehend, it would be difficult to find parents who would thus sacrifice their children by introducing them to a nauseous nocturnal employment; and if lads are to be admitted into Newspaper Offices to work there only in the day time, and do the desirable and profitable part of the labour, would it be right for the Trade to submit to have this kind of work thus divided with boys, who might be sufficiently numerous on a paper to do all the required work during the day, leaving it to half a dozen men to complete the remainder of a Morning Paper during the night ?

The second infraction of the Scale is the division of labour—or the payment of a less price for that which is done in the day, to that which is done in the night. We are aware that this question is one of paramount interest, and request your attention to a few remarks respecting it. We will assume, for instance, that the work *should* be thus paid, we will *presume* the absence of any positive law—though, at the same time be it observed that there is a clear, distinct, and positive law on the subject—and what is the conclusion ? It is this—that if 8½d. per thousand be paid for that part of a Morning Paper which is done during the day, an additional charge for night work must be paid on that set up during the night, for the ½d. per 1000 now paid extra for it, above Evening Paper price, is not the just remuneration for Morning Paper work, if the WHOLE of that work is to be done during the hours of night. The advocates of the division of labour must bear in mind that the present price of 9d. per 1000 for Morning Paper, was made with the understanding that a portion of that work should be done in the day; and the recognition of a division of labour must therefore involve a total alteration of the present mode of

---

[1] *i.e.*, to compositors employed during the daytime.

charging; for it is clear that that which is done in the night is not equitably paid for, unless a portion of the Morning Paper be set up during the day, *i.e.*, before eight at night. Upon investigating the scale, we shall find that the Morning Paper prices are calculated upon the supposition that the compositor should do about half his work in the day and half in the night. That is, he should compose a galley in the day, and a galley in the night; the amount of two galleys being all that he is justly entitled to compose; and in the case of a two o'clock paper—which, at the framing of the scale, was perhaps the average hour of beginning work—it must be evident to all that half of the work *would* be done in the day and half in the night.[1] To recognize, therefore, the division of labour, would be to abrogate a positive law, as well as render necessary a new system and a new scale of prices for charging Morning Paper work. Had there been a proportionate increase on the night-work part of the paper, when the day-work system was introduced, there would have been some show of equity in the arrangement. But when it is borne in mind that from the late hour of beginning, viz. six o'clock, but a small portion of the paper can be composed in the day-time; it is evidently a total departure from that scale which was framed with the understanding that the Morning Paper work should be half day and half night work.

We now turn to the third irregularity—and the Trade Council deem it right to observe that they notice these irregularities, not for the purpose of prejudicing or swaying the minds of the Meeting, but in order that the facts of the case may be clearly before you. The third irregularity is, what is called the Nonpareil galley, which, it will be remembered, was the cause of closing the house. The history of the news department of our Trade acquaints us, that the compositors having admitted Minion into Newspapers without any additional charge—that is, composing it as Brevier—5000 letters, or thereabouts, for the galley—when Nonpareil was introduced, that type also was expected to be composed as minion— that is, no advance on account of the diminution of size. We know it has been said that if a news compositor sets up a certain number of words, and they form a certain number of lines, and stand within a depth of four inches long; if he compose the same number of words in a shallower type, and make the same number of lines, and they stand within a depth of *three* inches, he does not pick up a *greater* quantity of types. Granted— but does not law and justice require that the compositor should be remunerated according to the depth of his letter ?—Are we not paid more per 1000 for Nonpareil than for Brevier; and why ? Simply because its diminution in size renders its composition more difficult ? And, with respect to the breadth of the letter, it should be remembered that it has never been adopted as a principle to regulate our charges—if it is broad,

---

[1] The preliminary report showed that the *Morning Herald* was a two o'clock paper, while work on the *Chronicle*, *Ledger* and *Times* began at five or six. The introduction of the steam-driven printing machine, with an output five or six times greater than the 250 impressions per hour of the hand press, would permit a later time for going to press. *The Times* possessed more efficient machines than any other newspaper, and was thus in a position to go to press late. For an account of this aspect of newspaper printing see the present writer's *Newspaper Printing in the Nineteenth Century* (London, 1943).

it is advantageous, if narrow, it is, on the contrary, disadvantageous; and, heaven knows, the number of disadvantageous founts now vastly preponderate. The Pica of former days has in breadth become a Small Pica—the Long Primer a Brevier—the Brevier a Nonpareil, and the Nonpareil, in some cases, not broader than Pearl—the argument, therefore, that a compositor on a newspaper has nothing to do with the depth of the type is not tenable; if it were, he ought to compose Pearl and Diamond at the same price as Long Primer.

In discussing and adjusting the present question, however, it is advisable that we leave out of consideration all former founts employed on the paper. We are to speak of *The Times as it is*, not as it *has been*. And what is the present state of the Nonpareil galley ? When cast up to its own ems, which is the only legitimate mode of casting up, we find that in its width, which is 16 ems Pica, and which of a true Nonpareil, would only admit 32 ems, that the one used on *The Times* admits four ems more, making 36 ems wide or 72 ens, which width, when multiplied by 64, the proper length of the galley, would give 4608 letters—which at 10d. per 1000, entitles the galley to be charged 3s. 10d. But the compositors are required to set 70 lines of Nonpareil, which is, consequently, *six* lines above the quantity which constitutes a regular galley.

There is also one other point connected with this galley, which the investigations of the Trade Council have disclosed, and which their duty to the Trade will not permit them to pass unnoticed—viz. That this fount, though described and recognized as a Nonpareil, is in fact, a Ruby; that is, a letter whose body is precisely half-way between a Nonpareil and a Pearl. On measuring it with the standard which guides our founts, we find that 161 lines of this fount are one foot in depth; and as a standard Nonpareil is only 143—we have, consequently, eighteen lines over the proper depth; now, as it only requires $17\frac{1}{2}$ to constitute the proper body for a legitimate Ruby, or a fount half-way between Pearl and Nonpareil, we are by these facts driven to the conclusion that it is a legitimate Ruby, and should in conformity with the principles of the Scale be cast up at $10\frac{1}{2}$d. per 1000, the intermediate price between Nonpareil and Pearl.

Having noticed the prevailing irregularities, we must advert briefly to the propositions which are set forth for the consideration of the Meeting, premising, at the same time, that they are not to be considered as sanctioned, or advocated by the Trade Council—they are not to be viewed as expressing their sentiments; but are employed as mere leaders to discussion, and to elicit the sentiments of the Trade, by inducing them to propose others of an opposite nature, or to suggest amendments upon those.

From what has been already urged, the advantages which the Proprietors derive from this mode, must, it is presumed, be apparent; but the following calculation which occupied a considerable portion of time in forming, and which has been executed by a Member of the Council, will throw some light on the first proposition. It was found that in a week's papers of *The Times*, consisting of two supplements, there were no less than 25490 lines of advertisements, or 364 galleys, which at 3s. 6d. per galley would come to £63 14s. Now, the same quantity of work, done in any other office by the assistants and supernumeraries, would cost £76 5s. or a difference weekly of £12 10s. But, to make allowance for errors, we will take it at £10—and this brings us to the conclusion that the saving by *The Times* system is at least £500 yearly. As a counterpiece or set-off to this gain it is but just that we should state that the arrangements and payments for the night-work or news part of the paper are most liberal—and the compositors employed on it enjoy important advantages which are not enjoyed by the compositors on any other Morning Paper. The amount of work required from them amounts to only £2 6s., while they are paid £2 8s.;[1] and all standing tables, as the revenue quarterly forms, and other advantageous matter, as funds, markets, etc., are given out to them, and charged as new matter. Indeed, they have no disadvantage or unfairness on the news department to complain of, except when engaged in the composition of Nonpareil, which, as before stated, is six lines above its legitimate quantity.

The printed Report and what has already been read render all observations on the remaining propositions unnecessary—except those which relate to the necessity for the present meeting and its probable results. And, in the first place the necessity for the present meeting will be evident from the fact that matters in *The Times* office are not in a state of improvement—that success in the first innovation on the recognized scale has led to many others, and will probably lead to more—the first innovation by the introduction of a minion nonpareil has led to the introduction of a nonpareil pearl or ruby; and the admission of day-work upon a part of the paper, has led to an additional encroachment even in that department—for, instead of its being wholly set up in the day-time, according to the original agreement, the compositors are now required to work during the hours of the night, and occasionally till two or three o'clock in the morning, at the price stipulated for day-work, namely, 3s. 6d. per galley of 5040 letters. But it may be asked, why do men submit to this ? Why will they permit this injustice ? The answer is obvious—they have no resource; they must submit, or fly to a persecuting Trade, and starve—they have, in entering that house, exposed themselves to condemnation, and they cannot quit it with safety. Many of them, we are led to believe, from the want of an investigation like the present, have erred in ignorance, and would be glad once more to be associated with their fellow-workmen and by future exertions endeavour to benefit that Trade they have contributed to injure—and it therefore becomes a question, which the concluding proposition will bring before the Meeting, whether it is just and expedient that those who have left and those who may leave until the decisions of this meeting are recognized, should be admitted as Members of the Union—remember that the grounds of their exclusion have not been investigated by the Trade, but only by a portion of it. Let the London Union therefore pronounce its decision on the subject—let us forgive what is past, and define what is right for the future.

We are persuaded that many in the present meeting have never contemplated how dreadful would be the effect upon the Trade, if the system

---

[1] The compositors on the inner forme were only obliged to set two galleys at 3s. 10d. the galley per night. See p. 398.

of *The Times* were generally adopted. We have shown that its gain to the Proprietors is about £500 yearly. Now, if the principle were adopted upon the other eleven papers, and the loss to the Compositors were only one-third of what it is on *The Times*, it would cause an additional loss to the Trade in one year of about £1600. Let the Trade, therefore, weigh well these facts, and deliberate on the consequences which may result from a single vote upon this most important question.

As a summary to this Report, and in order that the points in dispute may be fresh in the memory when we enter upon discussion—we would in the first place desire the Meeting to observe that there exists a positive law for the regulation of the price of Morning Paper work—a solemn compact between employers and employed, of twenty-five years' standing, which has never been altered or abrogated since it was agreed to by the separate parties—the journeymen and their masters. By that compact, the galley of a Morning Paper, no matter at what time composed (but we are sure that when the bargain was made it was half composed in day-time), was agreed to be paid 3s. 10d. The question on this point is, will you, can you, recognize the charge of 3s. 6d. per galley ?

Secondly, in 1793, the whole Trade, bookmen and newsmen, joined in expelling apprentices from newspaper offices, and are you now prepared to recognize their admission ? Is the trade in such a state that it can permit an increase of its hands through a channel which for 40 years has been closed against them.

Thirdly, the number of letters in a nonpareil galley. It is shown that the galley at present required on *The Times*, considered as nonpareil, contains 5040 letters, but from the nature of the type it should not be above 4400. Were it a true nonpareil it would be 440 letters above the proper quantity; but as it is an intermediate and smaller type it is nearly 200 more than this; the question, therefore, is, will you recognize a galley which has no parallel in any other office in the news department ?

But it has been urged, and it is a point which the meeting must duly weigh, that as from the evidence it is clear that the compositors on *The Times* receive what is considered a remunerating price for their labour, those on the day part averaging fifty shillings per week, what ground is there for contending that such working is unfair ? We admit that they earn £2 10s. per week, and we admit also that that sum is above what evening paper supernumeraries obtain—but let us not forget the number of hours *The Times*' men have to work; and let us also bear in mind that for the work which they perform for £2 10s. an evening paper man would receive about £2 16s. But the question of "adequate" remuneration is put out of view by the fact that there is A SCALE for the regulation of the remunerating price for this description of labour. While such a document exists, it is wrong for either bookmen or newsmen to take any other price, because they please to denominate it a remunerating price. An agreement having once been made between masters and men, the price agreed upon ought to be paid, until the parties who framed that law agree to its abrogation.

The Trade Council do not consider it consistent with their duty to the trade to stand forward as the advocates of any innovation upon established law. Any step inconsistent with those which they have taken in this affair, would be in violation of the second rule of the Union, which declares "that the said Union shall have for its object the protection and regulation of the wages of labour, agreeably to the Scale and acknowledged practice of the Trade."

They, therefore, cannot stand forward as the advocates of the practices of *The Times*, which are evidently in opposition to the recognized law for the regulation of the News Trade. But they at the same time feel that as the following statement has been placed in their hands, it is but performing a simple act of justice to the individuals interested, to put the meeting in possession of the following arguments in extenuation of the existing system adopted on *The Times* newspaper, and the palliation which has been urged by those employed thereon.

First, That the compositors employed on *The Times* are, upon the whole, remunerated for their labour, and the office of that Journal has never been closed or even condemned by the general voice of the Trade, but merely by a small body, the Newsmen, who are at this moment at variance with and unacknowledged by the Union.

Secondly, The apprentices, which form one of the grounds of complaint, cannot be received as a just one, as they are not nor ever were a principle of the House, and not at all connected with the closing it, but were forced upon it in its own defence, by a species of dictation which no men (whether masters or journeymen) have a right to use towards others, and which the present Union will not attempt to defend. Had it been a principle of the firm in question to carry on its Journal by apprentices, time enough has elapsed since its quarrel with the journeymen, to have reared three companionships; one for the night, one for the day, and one as a *corps de reserve*—this has not been done. There have been but few apprentices taken, compared with the long lapse of time since the period referred to, and the small number now in the Establishment are employed in the day department and on the same principle as the book houses. The night work (that is the genuine morning newspaper work) is performed entirely by journeymen procured from the Trade at large.

Thirdly, The division of the work into day and night ought not to be condemned as unfair, without the most careful investigation and grave deliberation; for it should not be forgotten that persons employed on the day establishment, have not to make those sacrifices of comfort which are incidental to an Evening paper, and much less those which are inseparable from a Morning one.

Fourthly, The Trade having formed itself into one body, called the Union, its Members are bound in fairness to commence with their own formation; the laws of the London Compositors ought to be in reference to the *present* and the *future*, for they cannot with justice be acted upon retrospectively. The Union has no right to visit with punishment any offence committed previous to its own existence, *unless that offence is persevered in, after it has been clearly pointed out by some definite resolution of the Trade.*

Fifthly, Time and circumstances having produced a complete revolution in the system of all newspapers, scarcely two Journals are now conducted on the same principle in the printing department, and not more than one or two on the original plan. *The Times* companionship then is entitled to the same plea as that of other papers for any irregularity (or presumed irregularity) that may exist, namely, time and circumstances, especially as every sacrifice of repose and comfort on the premises of that Journal is amply paid for.

Finally, In the investigations which have preceded this Meeting, and in the Report now submitted, it has been the object of the Trade Council to furnish the Trade with all the facts connected with the present condition of *The Times* newspaper, in order that ignorance of its state and practices should not be pleaded in extenuation by those who hereafter may work upon that Journal; and in order to guide the Trade in their decisions upon the subject; believing that a knowledge of the evil will go far to effect a cure—and trusting that the Trade will believe that the efforts of the Trade Council in this particular result from a sense of duty and a love of justice.

They have not assumed the office of counsellors to direct the Trade what steps ought to be taken—but they leave the affair wholly in the hands of the meeting, entreating them not to look back vindictively upon what had passed, but to hear all calmly, to deliberate dispassionately —and resolve firmly; and while they are honoured with the support of the Trade, they may rely that no efforts will be spared to give effect to the resolutions of this Meeting, whatever those resolutions may chance to be.

The following Resolutions were then considered by the Meeting, and adopted.

Resolutions respecting the mode of working on the "Times" Newspaper, agreed to on the 15th September, 1835.

1. That the division of labour on the *Times* newspaper into day and night work is contrary to the long-established practice of the business and cannot be recognised by the London Union of Compositors.

2. That the bookmen having, in 1793, joined with the newsmen in ejecting apprentices from newspapers, the present employment of them on the *Times* newspaper cannot be recognised by the London Union of Compositors.

3. That the nonpareil galley on the *Times* newspaper containing more letters than a nonpareil galley ought to contain, cannot be recognised by the London Union of Compositors.

4. That if the irregularities of different prices for night and day work, the improper quantity of the nonpareil galley be corrected, and no more apprentices be introduced, the Establishment shall henceforth be considered fair.

5. That in the event of the above alterations not being made on the *Times* newspaper, such compositors as quit that Establishment on the announcement of such refusal of the proprietors, shall be received into the London Union as fair Members.

6. That individuals who previous to this Meeting have quitted the *Times* newspaper, shall receive their Union Cards upon such terms as the Council may deem fit; but individuals working on that paper after this examination and attempt at adjustment shall be deemed unworthy members of the Trade, and forfeit all claim to the consideration and protection of the compositors of London.

The Meeting then adjourned till the 22nd instant.

Adjourned Meeting, Sept. 22

Before entering upon the special business of this evening, the Trade Council invite the Meeting to take the first step towards carrying the Resolutions of the previous Meeting into effect. That first step they propose should be in the shape of a Memorial from the Trade, conveying to the Printer of *The Times* the proposition of that Meeting, and soliciting his compliance with the proposed regulations. In the Memorial which has been prepared for the adoption of the Meeting, care has been taken to render it as free from offence as possible, to avoid all that might appear like dictation, and to offer the terms of reconciliation in as unassuming a form as possible. The proposed Memorial is as follows :—

Memorial of the Compositors of London to the Printer of "The Times" Newspaper, agreed to at a Special General Meeting of the Trade, assembled in the Theatre of the London Mechanics' Institution on the 22nd day of Sept. 1835,

Sheweth,

That your Memorialists, with a view to the removal of the ill-will and differences which have existed between the workmen employed on the *Times* newspaper and the Trade, have considered it their duty to investigate the causes of this long existing dissension, and finding them to be of such a nature as may without material detriment to your interests be removed, respectfully request your consent to the three following propositions—

> First—That the present variation of price between day and night-work may be discontinued—and the recognised charge for Morning Paper work be paid to the Compositors for the whole.
>
> Second—That no other apprentices than those at present belonging to the *Times* establishment, may be employed upon the Paper.
>
> Third—That what is denominated the nonpareil galley may be cast up according to its own body, in conformity to the practice of the Trade.

In soliciting compliance with these Propositions your Memorialists consider it unnecessary to dwell on the advantages that will arise to both parties from their adoption; but they would venture to observe that as they solicit no higher price than is paid to Compositors on other daily Journals—as they require nothing but what their long-established Scale of Prices warrants—and as your compliance would effectually remove all existing dissensions between the Trade and your Workmen, and secure to you the thanks of the Compositors of London, you will be induced on these considerations to comply with their earnest request.

Signed on behalf of the Meeting,

JOHN NICHOLS, *Chairman.*

It is of course impossible to ensure compliance with our request—but surely none will say that the request ought not to be made. And what more desirable form of making it ? What way more likely to ensure success than a memorial of this description, coming from a meeting of such extent and respectability as the present. It is, therefore, particularly desirable that the form should be unanimously adopted, that our opponents (if we have any) may not say there is a division in our camp. Let the present step be unanimously agreed to, and it may go far towards effecting that adjustment so long desired, and so earnestly sought for.

In spite of the representations of the L.U.C., the methods of work at *The Times* were not altered, and the compositors at Printing House Square continued to remain outside the Union until 1908, when Lord Northcliffe gained control. Contemporary trade union influence was never strong enough to bring them within the fold. On the other hand, rates of pay at *The Times* were always satisfactory and continuity of employment assured to steady workers. I imagine that *The Times'* chapel remained "non-union" by tradition rather than for any other reason.

———

In spite of the aloofness of the News Society, the news department of the London Union of Compositors began to develop. The Annual Report for 1838 informs us that "In respect of the news department, the Trade Council have only to state that in consequence of certain arrangements made in July last, about 40 additional members were added to the Union; thus giving us a majority in the News Trade."

The next document is noteworthy since it is the first in which printing machinery is mentioned, although cylinder machines, as opposed to hand presses, had been in use for newspaper printing since 1814. The year in which the document was printed is not stated, but the resolution was probably passed in 1839. J. Darkin, the Assistant Registrar whose signature the circular bears, was appointed to his office early in that year (*Annual Report of the London Union of Compositors for* 1839); and the last issue of *The Weekly True Sun* was on 29 December, 1839.

[DOCUMENT CVI]

TO THE COMPOSITORS OF LONDON

At a Double Delegated Meeting of the News Council of the London Union of Compositors held on Saturday, December 21, to receive from a Deputation from the *Weekly True Sun* office, a statement of the nature of the dispute between the Printer and the Compositors employed on that Journal, the following Resolution was unanimously agreed to, and ordered to be circulated through the Trade.

"Resolved—That to call upon journeymen (who are employed on their lines) to carry the forms of a newspaper to or from the machine without payment for the same, is contrary to every rule and practice of the business."[1]

Persons engaged on Weekly Newspapers are requested to bear in mind that a meeting of delegates is held on the first Saturday in each month, at eight o'clock, to whom all matters connected with the Journals on which they are employed, may be referred.

By Order of the News Council,

J. DARKIN, *Assist. Reg.*

[1] Savage, W., *op. cit.*, under *Newspapers*: "The full hands have each three pairs of cases—Nonpareil, Minion and Bourgeois; and as the most advantageous matter is generally set up in the smaller type, they claim the benefit of it as an equivalent for the labour of putting the formes to the machine. . . . The full hands take it in turn to correct the revises, lock up the formes, and take them to the machines to be worked off."

CHAPTER XVII

DISPUTES ON LONDON NEWSPAPERS
1845-1852

During the decade following the investigation into the conditions at *The Times* in 1835, the Annual Reports of the L.U.C. contain little or no information about their news compositors' department. It is evident, however, that relations with the rival newsmen of the Society of London Daily Newspaper Compositors were no more friendly than in the past. The following is extracted from the first Quarterly Report, dated 16 April, 1845, of the London Society of Compositors, as the L.U.C. became known after the foundation of the National Typographical Association.[1]

[DOCUMENT CVII]

Out of this 140 [members of the News Department] there are 120 employed upon daily newspapers, which argues much against the usefulness of the society that is still estranged from us, we mean "The Society of London Daily Newspaper Compositors," consisting, we suppose of about 120 men."

The latter organization never became a branch of the National Typographical Association. Although invited to join, it preserved its independence.

The terms of the Agreement "between the Printer and the Persons employed on the Establishment" of the *Morning Post*, dated 11 December, 1846, caused considerable unrest in the London news trade. According to a circular issued by the L.S.C. on 22 December, 1846, the *Morning Post* office had been closed to its members on their refusing to accept it.

[DOCUMENT CVIII]

A few weeks since, a Mr. Crosbie was introduced on the *Morning Post* as the general director of affairs. This person, the Companionship were informed, had been discharged from *The Times* for selling situations on that paper; and naturally regarding their own frames to be unsafe— having fully satisfied themselves of the truth of the allegations laid to

---

[1] The formation of the National Typographical Association is discussed in chapter VIII.

his charge—submitted a candid and comprehensive statement to the proprietor, who refused to interfere.

The Companionship received a fortnight's notice from Mr. Crosbie, with an intimation that if they chose to retain their situations, they were open to them. Acting under the advice of the trade, a communication was made to Mr. Crosbie, by the Companionship, agreeing to remain—the answer to which was the document hereafter mentioned, which they were all required to sign.

.   .   .   .   .

Mr. Crosbie stated to the Companionship, "*that he was engaged to* R E D U C E the expenditure," and he has since remarked, that in order to do so he should carry out the principle adopted on *The Times* as far as possible (including the employment of apprentices). As the first step to enable him to effect his object he produced the following form of agreement, which he required the Companionship to sign, and which they were told *they must do, or resign their situations.*

[DOCUMENT CIX]

MORNING POST

Agreement between the Printer and the Persons employed on the Establishment

Morning Post Office, Wellington Street, Strand, 11th December, 1846.

The proprietors of the *Morning Post*, being desirous that there should be a clear and distinct understanding between themselves and the several persons who are or may be employed on their establishment of the rules and regulations henceforth to be enforced therein, have authorized the undersigned, Mr. Arthur Aurelius Crosbie, as the printer on their establishment, to require that the following rules be observed, and accordingly the several other persons who respectively have hereunto subscribed their names, do severally agree with Mr. Arthur Aurelius Crosbie to be bound by and observe the rules following; that is to say :—

That no meeting of the compositors shall henceforth take place in the office of the *Morning Post* for the purposes of what is known by the name of a "chapel."

That the printer shall employ, as occasion shall require, any person whom he may from time to time think fit, on the work or in the business of the establishment, without regard to the connection or the non-connection of such persons with any union or association whatsoever.

That every compositor employed or to be employed upon the news-paper, previously to leaving his employ in the establishment, shall be required to give a fortnight's notice in writing of his intention to quit, and to give the same in writing unto the printer at the office of the establishment on any day, not being Sunday, between the hours of twelve and three.

That in every case of fraud, disobedience of, or inattention to orders, insubordination, or insulting behaviour, the printer may discharge any compositor or other person employed or to be employed in the printing department of the establishment forthwith; but in any other instance he shall not discharge any such person, except on a fortnight's notice.

That all work to be done in the office of the establishment shall be paid for according to the acknowledged scale of prices without any alteration whatsoever, except in the case of readers and other persons who may receive weekly salaries, the amount of which salaries shall, from time to time, be determined on by the printer; but the same shall be subject to alteration as circumstances may require, notice of such intended alteration being in every case given by the printer to the person whose salary it may be intended to alter.

These rules will take place upon and after the 18th day of December instant; and any person who may be unwilling to conform thereto, and will not sign the same as here written, shall not be retained or allowed to work on the establishment.

The management of the *Morning Post* were unable to enforce the agreement, and the whole of the companionship was reinstated on 1 January, 1847.[1]

Four years later, in January, 1851, the proprietors of the *Morning Post* made yet another attempt to reduce their production costs at the expense of the Society hands employed by them. The owners of the *Sun*, a paper supporting the Liberals, followed their example. On 28 October, 1852, the L.S.C. published the following observations, for circulation among the general public, in the form of an oblong quarto handbill.

[DOCUMENT C X]

EMPLOYERS' STRIKE

London, Thursday, October 28th, 1852

A Coalition having been entered into between the proprietors of two Metropolitan newspapers, of distinctly opposite principles, to reduce the recognized price of compositors' labour (as mutually agreed upon between the employers and their workmen) the whole of the men employed upon the *Evening Sun* having been dismissed at the shortest notice which the law allows; the compositors on the *Morning Post* having been similarly treated a short time previously.

Under these circumstances, it becomes a question for the working classes whether the *Sun* newspaper is any longer worthy of their support.

No documents relating to the dispute at the *Morning Post* office have been found, but the state of affairs received the fullest

[1] *Typographical Gazette*, January, 1847.

examination in the pages of the *Typographical Protection Circular*, a monthly periodical addressed to the London compositors.[1] The relevant passages are here summarized.

A certain Robert Dickson, overseer on the Glasgow *North British Daily Mail*, was appointed to a similar position at the *Morning Post*. His first act was to discharge the whole of the companionship, which he replaced with thirty-two men specially brought down from Glasgow. The conditions of their employment were contrary to the London News Scale. They were each to be paid £2 8s. per week of sixty hours, working ten hours per night. The London wage of £2 8s. per week for full hands was in return for a stipulated amount of work. The system of employing full hands was by then "an all but exploded one, there being but eight men employed in that manner, out of the whole number engaged on Morning newspaper work in London."[2] Under the present system, no man need limit himself to 48s. worth of work as long as there was sufficient copy, and provided he was paid the regulation price.

The men from the north, however, were to perform an *unlimited* amount of work for their money. Their status would be that of 'stab hands. Ten hours work, according to the Scale, at 11½d. per hour was worth 9s. 5d., or £2 17s. 6d. per week, and even on those terms production would be limited to a quarter of a galley per hour, the maximum allowed on time work.[3]

On 1 October, 1852, the companionship of the *Sun*, and the Printer of the paper, thirty-three men in all, were given a fortnight's notice, and immediately replaced by additional hands imported from Scotland.[4]

The chief novelty of this new move of these ruthless invaders consists in the strong delusion offered both to the trade and to all who aspire to

---

[1] No. 1. January, 1849 (price 2d.)—No. 59. November, 1853, are in the St. Bride collection. It was founded by J. Catchpool who also published *The Typographic Gazette*. No. 1. April, 1846—No. 16, May, 1847. The later numbers of the *Typographical Protection Circular* were edited, printed and published by Luke James Hansard, at the office of the Universal Working Class Association. Hansard, who was a grandson of Luke Hansard, was House of Commons Printer until 1848.

[2] *The Typographical Protection Circular*, February, 1851, p. 117.

[3] *Ibid.*, October, 1851, p. 155. The Scots claimed that they only performed eight hours per day composition. "We receive 1s. per hour on time, mon; but that does not include *deestri-boo-tion* or *stonding steel*, mon."

[4] *Ibid.*, November, 1852, p. 212. "We append the names of some of the persons employed on the *Sun :* M'Lean, M'Bride, M'Naught, M'Quail . . M'Donald . . . M'Laren, M'Nott . . . !"

enlist under their banner. The recognized wages of the trade are pretended to be paid, viz., £2 3s. 6d. per week. But to be entitled to this sum, each man is bound to give ten hours composition, or 2,040 lines per week. The value of these lines, at the Scale price, is £3 18s. 7d. or £1 15s. 1d. *more* than is even promised to be paid. Now comes the delusion of the scheme. Not only are ten hours' presence in the office exacted, but each man must show that he has set the said number of 2,040 lines, failing which deduction commences in the same *pro rata* principle. Thus if, from inability, from want of copy, etc., any hand shall produce only half the number of lines (which is but little short of that which can be furnished to any one man on an evening paper), then the man only receives £1 1s. 9d., notwithstanding he may have placed at the call of his hirer sixty hours of his time. So that, in fact, and as will be found to be the case practically, the deluded men are giving ten hours' labour for 3s. 7½d., believing that they would receive 7s. 3d. as the result of their day's occupation.[1]

A defence Committee appointed by the L.S.C. immediately approached the independent London Daily Newspaper Society with the object of securing combined action, and a joint committee was formed on 6 November, 1852.

Deputations were sent to the various trade organizations, inviting financial assistance; also to the principal licensed victuallers and coffee-houses, who, by refusing to take in the particular paper, rendered the Defence most valuable assistance. . . . Addresses were distributed broadcast throughout the country, and posted in public houses and coffee shops in the metropolis, and at one time members of the "rat" companionship were engaged to go round and collect the bills, stating that they were authorized to do so by the Defence Committee, as the employers had given way.[2] Although a heavy expenditure had to be met, the members eventually had the satisfaction of attaining the desired result, the employer being badly beaten in his attempts to introduce a system of working at variance with the established customs of the trade.[3]

[1] *The Typographical Protection Circular*, November, 1852, p. 211.

[2] Half a dozen window bills and broadsides relating to the dispute at the *Sun* are preserved in the St. Bride collection.

The Members of the Metropolitan Society of Operative Bricklayers to their Fellow Workmen (December 16, 1852).

To the Working Men of England (Issued by the Defence Committee from the Falcon Tavern, Gough Square, December 22, 1852).

To the Members of the Bookbinders' Trade Society (Issued by their Committee from 5 Pemberton Row, Gough Square, n.d.).

To all the Carpenters and Joiners of London and the Suburbs (Issued by the Friendly Society of Carpenters and Joiners, held at the George IV, Leicester Street, Regent Street, n.d.).

To the Carpenters and Joiners of the Metropolis (Issued by the "Friends of Freedom" Society of Carpenters and Joiners, n.d.).

[3] *A Brief Record of Events* (Jubilee publication of the L.S.C.) (London, 1898), p. 72.

The dispute with the proprietor of the *Sun* was explained, albeit none to clearly, in the "Second Address" printed below. No copy of the first manifesto has been found.

[DOCUMENT CXI]

*Second Address of the Compositors of London
to the Trades of the United Kingdom*

London, November 23, 1852.

Fellow workmen,

We take the first opportunity of thanking you for the efforts you have made in our behalf. Your exertions have already had much effect. That the shoe already pinches tightly is evidenced by the production of a long array of words, in the name of "The compositors of the *Sun* newspaper," as an "answer" to our first address, but which, in reality, answers nothing. When we say that the so-styled "answer" is nominally the production of the compositors on the *Sun*, we speak advisedly; for every line of it points out to the initiated that it is the concoction either of the man who has entered on this crusade against us, or has been produced to his order, by one of the practised writers, over whom, as manager or the *Sun*, he has control. Indeed, if other testimony were required to show that the alleged source from which it emanates is as great a fraud as the contents of the document itself, the place from which it is issued would be sufficient to settle any doubts that might arise. Again, the men were not attacked; and, consequently, were not called on to reply. We have hitherto withheld our strictures on their conduct, inasmuch as we regard them simply as tools—dangerous instruments in the hands of unscrupulous men, but popular evils that nothing but public opinion can modify or eradicate.

Before refuting the specious statements in the "answer," it may be remarked that the contest is not between the old hands and the new, but between the entire fair trade of the kingdom and the introduction of a system opposed to a custom of forty or fifty years' standing, and inimical to the interests of the whole body.

First, then, they profess to lay before the public the rule of the society (which was framed by a committee of employers and employed) as regards the established wages per week, and the hours of labour, as follows :—"Morning papers, £2 8s.; evening papers, £2 3s. 6d. Ten hours' composition is the specified time for evening papers." There they stop, as they cannot proceed without being self-condemned; they have carefully omitted, among other matters which would tell against them, the following :—"A system termed finishing having been formerly introduced, it is necessary to state that no mode of working can be considered fair otherwise than by the galley or hour." "The rule of the society of daily newspapers," as they term it, has also the following explanation, which they fail to give, for the simple reason that it is the very opposite of the system under which they are engaged :—

The full hands upon evening papers are employed ten hours per day, and the work is divided into two proportions, viz., one galley as a first-work, and a

28

finish of six hours. The time for taking copy for the first-work is regulated by the hour for commencing the finish, being four hours previous to that time. Any time which the full hands may have between the completion of the first-work and the time of commencing the finish, is at their own disposal. Should the printer find occasion for their services during this interval, then such assistance to be charged for according to galley quantity, in quarters or half-galleys, as the case may be, namely, one quarter, $10\frac{1}{2}$d.; two quarters or half a galley, 1s. $9\frac{1}{2}$d.; three quarters, 2s. $8\frac{1}{2}$d.; galley, 3s. 7d. No charge less than one quarter.

Why, if they had truth on their side, did they omit these particulars? The answer is obvious.

Secondly. As there is an evident intention to mislead the public as to the necessity for introducing a new system, it is stated "that nearly a fourth of the number of the late workmen received from 15s. to 20s. per week more than the others." To this we give a flat contradiction. Moreover, to step in and supplant the whole of the hands is a singular method of assisting those with whom they affect to sympathize for having had but a small share of the work under the old system—the imperative condition of the introduction of the new system being that every compositor, reader, and reading boy must be discharged!

Thirdly. It is stated, "there is a rule, as we have informed you, in the union printed documents, recognizing £2 3s. 6d., as the legitimate sum per week, which sum we duly receive." We reply, that the old hands did not average 36s. per week; consequently, as they have thirty-one hands now engaged on the paper (one less than before), if they pay them £2 3s. 6d. per week, we are at a loss to discover the saving, and therefore repeat, that if such promises were made they were not intended to be kept, especially as the proprietor stated, when he gave the late overseer notice to quit, that his reason for so doing was, "that a similar step, taken by the *Morning Post*, had been productive of a considerable saving to the proprietors," and he was going to adopt the same principle. A proprietor of a large establishment would never revolutionize his arrangements and risk his property for the mere sake of change; and certainly no one will deny him the credit of being sincere when he stated that the course he had entered upon was for the purpose of reducing expenses. Should any further proof be required, the following letter, addressed to a daily paper office, may be deemed conclusive :—

———, November 5th, 1852.

Sir,

I beg to call your attention to the new system of working daily papers, whereby a considerable saving is effected. I mean the system carried out upon the *Sun* and *Post*. Being a party employed upon one of these papers, and understanding the working of the system, I undertake to procure a staff of workmen competent to produce the——in good condition, and in good time, effecting a great saving to the property. By granting an interview, I will explain the above system.

I am, Sir, your obedient servant, ———.

To ———

Fellow workmen, weigh well the avowed object of the proprietor, and the statement that the men are getting £2 3s. 6d. per week, and judge for yourselves.

"The compositors of the *Sun*" are next made to say, "It is not improbable that the inference may perhaps be deduced by some that we hold our present situations in consequence of our hostility to the principle of union. With a view to erase such impressions, we distinctly state that the question whether we did or did not belong to any union, has never been asked either prior or subsequent to our engagement." This is true. They were not engaged in the ordinary way, but were brought together by the person who put himself at their head, and their services were tendered as a body to the proprietor of the *Sun*, at a tempting price, much in the same way that the tender is made in the above letter. To show the value of the statement, as to the question of belonging to the union entering into the proprietor's mind, he asked, at the time of giving the notice to quit, whether all the men employed on the *Sun*, at that time belonged to the union ? and, receiving an affirmative, he further asked whether the men employed in the book offices in the neighbourhood belonged to the society ? Meeting with a similar reply, he remarked that "the trade were all alike"; and it was evident that union men would not suit the scheme upon which he was about to enter.

Fourthly. In justification of the new method of working, we find the following :—"In accepting an established weekly wage, we are only carrying out the principle of the union, in regard to daily evening papers." How does this statement harmonize with the foregoing document, which expressly declares it is a "new system";—nay, that it requires "explanation" ?

It is stated, further, that the system on which the *Sun* is now produced is "recognized in regard to weekly papers and book establishments"; and here the writer of the "answer" either betrays his ignorance of the legitimate system of working, or, stoops to a wilful falsehood. The merest tyro in the trade knows that there is no analogy between the daily newspaper department and the rest of the business—that while the introduction of apprentices in the other branches is in accordance with trade usages, in the daily newspaper department they are, for substantial reasons, by mutual agreement, not employed—and also that though any man in the "receipt of established wages" is very properly "expected to be attentive to the hours of labour, and to be industrious while at work," as regards one portion of the trade, it is a matter of notoriety that a man engaged on "established wages" on a daily paper, has a stated amount of work to perform per hour, technically called "a quarter," as is shown in the extract given above from the rules of the newspaper trade, which state clearly that "any time which the full hands may have between the completion of their first work" (a "galley") "and the time of commencing the finish, is at their own disposal. Should the printer find occasion for their services during this interval, such assistance to be charged for" extra. Independently of all this, the advantages to the compositor from the second or third editions are altogether abandoned under the new system. This, again, is a violation of the London scale for daily news work.

We come now to the moral part of the subject. The writer here charitably expresses a hope that the "design" was entered into " in moments of warmth of temper." It will be sufficient to remark, that, however individuals may act from sudden impulse, large bodies of men, seldom, if ever, act in concert unless some great principle is at stake. It is not we who have "entered upon a design." We have but taken up arms in self-defence; and the "charitable" writer of the "answer" must have been weak-minded indeed, if he supposed that a mere passing "warmth of temper" would have been evoked by the thrusting out, without the shadow of a cause, of upwards of thirty men from situations which they had held for years with credit to themselves and profit to their employer, or if he thought that the interests of some thousands of an intelligent profession were to be considered as nought by the proprietor of a news paper. He (the proprietor) has used his power—legally, we admit, but not morally—for the sake of adding a trifle to his gains. Shall we then be denied the right to resist an aggression on our trade—which, if successful, will debar us from providing the decencies of life and education for our children, and reduce us to the lowest condition in the social scale ?

There is an evident intention in the last paragraph, to lead the reader to infer that the present hands, in addition to being the pioneers of "equality" as regards the newspaper compositors of London, mean to practise something more than "mere lip expressions of sympathy" towards the unemployed members of the trade. But their antecedents will lead no one to give them credit for such good intentions; for they are a class of men who have never supported the charitable institutions of the profession. And it may here be remarked, that many of those at present engaged on the *Sun* were not forced by want of employment to supplant others, at a reduced rate, for several of them, less than two years ago, threw up good and fair situations at Glasgow, to assist in introducing the "new system" on the *Morning Post*, and have now branched off from that paper to introduce their system on the *Sun*. Thus the spirit of these men is rendered apparent; and, that they may be condemned by their own words, we will introduce a letter from a compositor on the *Post*, in reply to a request for assistance from a friend of his who was attempting to infringe the trade rules at Liverpool :—[1]

Morning Post Office, London, 2nd October, 1852.

Dear Andrew,

I received yours of the 29th, and I do assure you I was not aware you had pitched your camp in Liverpool. Believe me, Andrew, I am very sorry, but I fear I cannot lend you a helping hand at the present moment. I will tell you my reason for stating so. Alexander M'Lean, one of our men, has undertaken to work the *Sun* newspaper on the same principle as that of the *Morning Post*, and he has been recommended to it by Mr. Robert Dickson, and is engaging all the superfluous hands he can get hold of here. The wages are to be two pounds three shillings and sixpence a week. You will at once have an idea, Andrew, of the chance I have in securing a few hands for you, however willing I may be, and you such a distance from London. The pressmen have almost always been the cause of differences between the masters and the men, and it is a pity you could not crush them alone; but if the comps. have joined them, they must take the lean along with the fat, and they have only themselves to thank for it. If I can do you any good, I assure you, Andrew, I will not leave a stone unturned to do so. The Messrs. Dickson are getting on swimmingly. So is

[1] The text of this letter, with further comments, was also published in *The Typographical Protection Circular*, November, 1852.

the whole concern. Do not be afraid to oppose these fellows; you are sure to beat them. I am glad that there is another of ours who has courage enough to oppose the English. They have always thought that a Scotchman had no right to come to their country, far less to dictate to them. Now we will show them the other side of the picture. Write almost every day, and let me know how you are getting on. I hope you will beat them.

Yours sincerely,

P. WILSON.

In reference to the postscript of the "answer," it may be stated that the usual course was adopted, and that their conduct received the "general"—in fact, the unanimous—condemnation of the members of the union in public meeting assembled.

And now, fellow workmen, we trust the speciousness of the document headed "Hear both sides" is made clear to you. We ask you not only to listen, but to judge; and we shall be content to leave the matter in your hands. We trust we can safely anticipate your verdict; and we earnestly exhort you to continue the moral and legal course which you have so far, and with so much success, entered upon in this matter, and we have no doubt of the issue. Our cause is yours.

We remain, fellow workmen, on behalf of the trade,

Yours faithfully,

THE DEFENCE COMMITTEE

CHAPTER XVIII

NEWS COMPOSITORS'
METHODS OF WORKING
1868-1894

Although unsatisfactory relations had persisted for twenty years, the two London news societies co-operated in the dispute with the management of the *Sun* newspaper, and the year 1853 "witnessed the long-delayed but much-desired amalgamations of the two societies, the Annual Report for 1854 announcing that in the previous March the Old Daily News Society had joined the London Society of Compositors. . . . The membership of the Society was thus increased to over 2,600 paying members. . . ."[1]

The News Scale was not altered in 1866, when the general trade received a number of concessions from the employers. Before the Memorial was sent to the Association of Master Printers, the News Department was invited to participate. Their refusal was contained in the following resolution :—

> That whilst this Committee express their sympathy with the efforts now being made to obtain an advance in the book scale, and their earnest desire that it may prove successful, they are of the opinion that it would not be desirable to make any claims for an advance in the News Department, which perhaps, might rather embarrass than forward the movement in the Book Department.

In 1868, following the publication of a report issued by a Special Committee appointed by the L.S.C. News Department "to revise the Trade Rules, examine into the System of Working in each Office, and frame a Report upon the Evidence that may come before them," new and amended rules and regulations for news work were issued. These, together with the addenda of 1874, are printed parallel with the revised News Scale of 1891 on pp. 449 *et seq.* of this work.

Six years later, in 1874, the state of affairs in both daily and weekly newspaper offices was examined by a committee appointed

---

[1] *A Brief Record of Events, op. cit., p. 72.*

"to consider the best means for improving the condition of news-paper compositors." Their report was divided into two parts, dealing with compositors in daily and weekly newspaper offices respectively.

It was recommended that the following demands should be addressed to the proprietors of daily newspapers :—

1. An advance of ½d. per 1,000 on all founts.
2. That 3d. extra per hour be paid for Sunday work from the time of lifting copy till the cut.[1]
3. That on morning papers a quarter [of a galley] per hour should be guaranteed from the time of lifting copy till the cut, and the cut must be a general and not an individual one; but work done in the first four hours, shall be independent of that subsequently performed.[2]

The first only of these propositions was included in the Memorial subsequently sent to the employers on 13 June, 1874.

The daily newspaper proprietors did not accede to the men's request for an advance. No document containing the reasons for their refusal has been found.

The second section of the report, dealing with weekly newspaper conditions, is here reprinted in full :—

[DOCUMENT CXII]

Report of the Weekly Newspaper Sub-Committee to the Daily Newspaper Committee

Gentlemen,

At the commencement of our proceedings we issued a circular asking for information as to the mode of working on the various weekly news-papers. This having been sent to seventy offices thirty-seven replies were received thereto, and as a basis for a clearer comprehension of the details to follow, they may be thus briefly summarized: The thirty-seven offices referred to in the returns contained 552 journeymen and 239 boys, the latter comprising 152 apprentices and 87 turnovers; the number of journeymen as compared with boys being about 2⅛ journeymen to one boy; but as about 60 "grass" hands are not included in the comparison, the proportion of journeymen is somewhat above that given. The number of "'stab" hands engaged on those weekly papers from which returns have been received is 164, leaving 388 line hands. 89 "'stab" hands are

---

[1] "CUT" is a contraction of the phrase "cut the line," meaning the end of the day's work. The start of the day (or period after idle time or "slating") is known by the expression "the line is on."

[2] The morning newspaper compositor was frequently urged to work at his utmost speed during the first part of the night and in the latter part was com-pelled to remain in the office with very little work provided for him. The adoption of this proposition would have provided for a more even flow of work,

receiving but 36s. per week; the remaining 75 from 36s. to 55s. The number of journeymen as compared with boys in any given office is, in the maximum case, 24 journeymen to 2 boys; in the minimum, 5 journeymen to 23 boys.

Respecting the special grievances, the undermentioned cases may be taken as illustrative of those calling for remedial measures, and the kind to which we have specially directed our attention.

1. Much loss of time occasioned by the system of giving out copy in an unfair manner, the "fat" being selected from the solid portions, the former given to the 'stab and boys, the latter to line hands, and, as a consequence, involving innumerable pullings and loss of time.

2. A custom of putting piece hands on "time" to compose advertisements.

3. Newspaper and publication matter both being charged at 3s. 7d. per galley, notwithstanding that the latter may be of so "fat" a description that were it charged upon its own merits it would realize, it is assumed, much above that which is paid under the existing conditions.

4. A system of holding the compositor whose turn it is to pull a galley responsible for the whole of the copy, although the person who has composed a portion of it may have neglected to put his copy into the place provided for the purpose; also of compositors having to seek for a galley and pull the same after inserting a few lines which may be added thereto, irrespectively of the galley having been previously pulled by a time hand, or, as may happen, by a 'stab hand. Of 'stab hands having invariably the first portion of "takes," thus depriving the line hands of a fair share of the heads belonging thereto; and of "takings" being cut up into minute portions, and given out irregularly and partially, the "fat" to the 'stab, the solid to the piece. Of 'stab hands being expected to produce, and not unfrequently producing, a much larger amount than they receive; and, although there is obviously no actual stipulation to that effect, it is an inferential condition from the fact of 'stab hands writing "time" on occasions when unable to produce what would be considered by the employer sufficient in lines.

5. Unlimited composition by 'stab hands frequently earning half as much again as they receive; all the "fat," or almost all, being extracted from the line hands. Extraction of pieces of advantageous matter from the middle of articles, which are given to boys or 'stab hands. Line hands being kept an unlimited amount of time "slating" without any compensation. Compositors employed on time work during the day being put on the papers at night, and expected to write bills for such work. Regular book 'stab hands going on piece work on the papers at night. Excessively late hours. News hands being employed upon book work during the day, and book hands being employed on papers after 7 p.m. in order to save overtime charges. Line hands being put on time at 10d. per hour when the line is on, thereby putting the best workmen (those put on time) at a disadvantage with inferior workmen. Excessive late work on 'stab; insufficient for overtime; and having to write bills, making up full, and much above full time of the actual hours paid for; and to such an extent is this latter condition enforced, that a 'stab hand has been known to write "on account" to make up for the deficiency in his bill.

6. Another case where it appears 'stab hands are expected to write a bill which must exceed in amount 10s. above that actually received by them, and where also line hands are continually kept standing whilst the 'stab and boys are provided with copy.[1]

7. Over-hours after 7 p.m. An undue proportion of boys to journeymen.

It is felt that the grievances comprised in the foregoing illustrations are such as undoubtedly call for redress, as by their existence compositors engaged upon weekly papers are placed in a much worse position with respect to the conditions under which they work than those who are engaged upon book or jobbing work; for while the latter have for some years past enjoyed the advantage of having some compensation for being obliged to continue at work after the regular leaving-off time, the former have no corresponding advantage, and are in no better position, in most respects, than they were before measures were taken to raise the status of the members generally.

After examining the whole of the returns made, and it having become obvious therefrom that the grievances referred to are almost universal, the Sub-Committee have come to the unanimous conclusion that very strenuous means should be adopted to repress entirely those which are serious and palpable infractions of the Scale Rules, and that unremitting efforts should be made to obtain for Weekly News hands advantages corresponding to those which other members of the trade already enjoy. With this view they have framed the following proposed Rules, which are recommended for the reasons appended to each of them :—

1. "That on the completion of the ordinary working day of 9 hours, or 9½ hours for the first five days and 6½ hours on the Saturday (as may be mutually agreed upon), a compositor shall be entitled to charge 3d. extra for each additional hour (or part of an hour) that he is required to remain in the office; and that in any case, irrespective of the number of hours that he may have been in the office, he shall be entitled to charge 3d. extra for each additional hour he may be required to remain after 9 o'clock p.m."

---

[1] "This system of working, known as 'piece-'stab,' was for a long time a cause of much dissatisfaction. Up to the early years of the twentieth century it was prevalent in weekly newspaper and periodical offices. The composing staff in these houses was roughly of three kinds, piece-hands, 'stab-hands and apprentices, all writing weekly bills as if on piece. The 'stab hands, on the minimum wage, were kept busy on the more advantageous matter (*e.g.*, wider measures, small type) and were expected to write several shillings over the amount they received. If they frequently failed to reach the required standard of earnings, they were placed under notice and offered a piece job. On the other hand, if a smart piece-hand, albeit kept on disadvantageous copy (*e.g.*, narrower measures, large type), consistently earned more than the 'stab minimum, he was offered a 'stab job. The apprentices also worked on a piece-work system. Their copy was, in the main, all 'fat' (*e.g.*, standing headings to articles, table-work, small type), which was frequently picked out for them. On their earnings as shown by their weekly piece bill the apprentices received a 'bonus'—in one office a fifth of all they earned over 30s. Notwithstanding many efforts to end this system, 'piece-'stab' remained till the composing machine brought about a revolution in composing-room organisation."   (Contributed by Mr. Harold E. Waite.)

This being made an established rule will, it is considered, act beneficially in a three-fold manner. First, it will be the means of putting those engaged upon weekly papers on a par with the members of the general trade, in respect to being paid some compensation for having to continue at work after an average day is completed. Secondly, that it will tend greatly to decrease the excessive hours which those on weekly papers are frequently called upon to endure—the adoption of similar means by those engaged in the general trade having already demonstrated the effectiveness of the remedy. And, thirdly, that by thus decreasing the number of hours, the extensively complained-of grievance, both by regularly engaged line hands and "grass," viz. that of "slating,"[1] will be considerably lessened, and thereby render unnecessary the seeking of an advance per thousand; for it has been elicited from a large number of those interested, that it is not so much the price per galley that militates against those engaged upon weekly papers as it is the inordinate, and what is believed to be to a considerable extent unnecessary, time which they are kept standing idle. The next proposed rule is—

"That a compositor shall not be expected to gather copy and be held responsible for the same; that in no case shall he be expected to pull a galley containing less than 5,000 letters fresh matter; nor shall he be expected to seek for a galley containing other matter for the purpose of inserting a few lines therein without being entitled to charge three lines for the trouble occasioned thereby."

So serious is the loss sustained by the existence of the circumstances which induced the foregoing, that your Sub-Committee feel constrained to recommend the adoption of the same on the grounds that the grievances to be inferred therefrom are entirely an innovation of recent times, arising out of conditions that did not exist when the original rules appertaining thereto were framed, and consequently now calling for special arrangements respecting them. As regards 'stab hands, it is proposed—

"That in no case shall a 'stab hand be called upon or expected to write a bill; and when engaged on the line he shall lift copy fairly and in regular numbers with the piece hands."

A stipulation of this kind is urgently needed to interdict the largely increasing evil of 'stab hands being expected to produce an amount far exceeding what they are paid for; and as they are mainly assisted thereto by the unfair assortment of copy, the latter portion of the proposed rule would both remedy the evil referred to and prove of advantage to line hands. And further, with regard to 'stab hands, it is proposed—

"That £2 per week of 54 hours be the minimum 'stab wages; 10*d*. per hour overtime, with 3*d*. extra for each additional hour that a compositor is required to remain in the office after the completion of the ordinary working day, or in any case after 9 o'clock p.m."

---

[1] SLATING. "The paper being produced entirely on the piece system, the compositor, having taken copy, strains every nerve to secure as many takings as he can whilst there is work to give out; for the time frequently arrives all too soon when the stone is clear, and the men as they come out, write their names upon the slate, pending the arrival of more copy." Gould, Joseph, *The Letter-Press Printer* (London, 1876), p. 119.

The foregoing is recommended as being but a fair request on the part of those engaged on the 'stab, as may be implied from the fact of 75 out of 164 receiving, at the present time, wages ranging from 36*s.* to 55*s.*, as also from the additional fact, that even prior to the advance of the general 'stab from 33*s.* to 36*s.*, now some years since, it was almost universally the custom to pay the latter sum on weekly papers; besides which, it is thought that by making the minimum £2, it will tend, in some degree, to rectify the evil of 'stab and piece being engaged on one work—an evil existing in no other trade having an organized society.

Respecting Sunday work, the following is recommended :—"That special Sunday work be paid for at the rate of 6*d.* per hour extra, from 12 o'clock on Saturday night to 12 o'clock on Sunday night; but that in no case shall a compositor receive less than 2*s.* 6*d.* extra." And although there does not appear to be much Sunday work on weekly papers, yet it is so evidently a fair concession to be made to those so engaged, that it is deemed essential to recommend the adoption of the proposition.

With respect to assistants on weekly papers, and "pulling out" on extra editions, the two following propositions are recommended :— (1) "That when a compositor is called in to assist, he shall be entitled to charge not less than four hours, if employed on time, or less than a galley if paid by lines." (2) "That when a compositor is required to 'pull out' (that is, to compose more than a quarter per hour), he shall be entitled to charge the lines so composed. That is, if he is detained three hours for an extra edition, and then ordered to 'pull out' for another hour, during which time he may compose half a galley, he shall be entitled to charge a galley and a quarter, instead of only the four hours actually engaged." The first of these propositions will, it is considered, be but a fair stipulation as regards those who may be called in for the purpose of getting out an edition, and having nothing to do beyond that; and the second proposition will be merely adopting the same principle with respect to "pulling out" on weekly papers as is already applied on morning and evening papers, and which, it is maintained, the former are justly entitled to.

A special grievance relating to undistributable matter having been brought to the notice of your Sub-Committee, and the heavy loss occasioned thereby being evident, the following proposition is made, with a view to meet similar cases:—"That all type involving additional labour in distribution resulting from the use of strong ley, turpentine, or other spirits in the process of cleansing, shall be paid ½*d.* per thousand extra."[1]

In reference to the apprentice grievance, while it is admitted to be an evil, and one which, if practicable, should be dealt with, we have to report to you that the question was thoroughly gone into by the Trade Committee so recently as 1867, when, by returns, it was rendered apparent that, proportionately with the increase of journeymen, the number of apprentices was at that time decreasing; and inasmuch as it

---

[1] Mr. Waite tells me that old ale was frequently used to prevent spaces rising, especially with new founders' type. Type treated in this way by the machine-minder was extremely difficult to separate when being distributed.

was not deemed advisable to take any active measures then, neither is it thought prudent to do so now, as such a step would lessen the prospects of gaining the more substantial advantages which we are seeking.

Thus, gentlemen, we submit to you the chief results of our labours, and, as the conclusion of our report, we most earnestly desire that you will be able to reconcile the adoption thereof with the views entertained by yourselves respecting the claims of newspaper compositors to some amelioration in their condition. But of one thing we feel confident, that whether our labours result in the accomplishment of our desires or not, much good will evolve from the impetus that has been given to those engaged in our special branch of the trade, to interest themselves actively in extinguishing those evils which have been brought to light by our instrumentality.

A Memorial was presented to the proprietors on 5 June, 1874. In the course of the subsequent negotiations the compositors' propositions were slightly amended, the final agreement taking the following form :—

[DOCUMENT CXIII]

LONDON SOCIETY OF COMPOSITORS

WEEKLY NEWSPAPER COMPOSITORS' MEMORIAL

Notice

At a meeting of Master Printers, held at the Freemasons' Tavern, on Tuesday, the 15th day of December, 1874, the following Resolution was passed with respect to the above Memorial :—

That this Meeting, on behalf of the London Master Printers engaged in the Printing of Newspapers, and employing Union hands, hereby accepts and agrees to the Modified Propositions submitted as the result of a Conference between a joint Committee of Employers and Journeymen, on the subject of the Weekly Newspaper Compositors' Memorial, and requests their Committee, Messrs. Burt, Cox, Francis, Judd, and Wyman, to take the necessary steps to give effect to this resolution. The Modified Propositions to come into operation as and from Monday, January 4th, 1875.

In accordance with the above, the Trade Committee hereby inform Fathers of Chapels and the Members generally, that the subjoined Modified Propositions having been accepted by the Delegates, at the Special Delegate Meeting of November 25th, 1874, on behalf of the London Society of Compositors, will come into operation on and after Monday, January 4th, 1875.

WEEKLY NEWSPAPER COMPOSITORS' MEMORIAL

Amended Propositions as accepted by Employers and Journeymen

1. That no compositor on the piece shall be called upon to work more than six hours of overtime during the week without charging 3d. per hour extra. The week to consist of 54 hours, and the overtime to commence when 60 hours

are completed, such hours to be governed by the ordinary working hours of the house, and may all be worked in one night or divided as may suit the convenience of the employer; provided that in no case shall a piece compositor be called upon to work after 12 p.m. without receiving the extra for overtime.

2. Without mutual arrangements exist thereon, that no compositor be called upon to pull a galley containing less than a quarter of a galley of fresh matter. Nor shall a compositor be expected to seek for a galley wherein to insert less than one-eighth of a galley of fresh matter without being entitled to charge 1*d.* for the trouble occasioned thereby.

3. 'Stab hands when engaged on the line shall lift copy fairly and in regular numbers with the piece hands. Apprentices who have served four years of their time to lift copy with the men. The foregoing not to apply either to advertisements or articles given out in their entirety to 'stab hands or apprentices. The minimum 'stab wages to remain at 36s. per week of 54 hours, the overtime thereon to be paid at not less than 11*d.* per hour.

4. Time-work to be paid at the rate of 10*d.* per hour, subject to the extra for overtime when the 60 hours have been worked.

5. That when a compositor is called in* to assist, he shall be entitled to charge not less than four hours, if employed on time, or less than a galley if paid by lines. That when a compositor "engaged on extra editions" is required to "pull out," that is, to compose more than a quarter per hour, he shall be entitled to charge the lines so composed. That is, if he is detained three hours for an extra edition, and then ordered to "pull out" for another hour, during which time he may compose half a galley, he shall be entitled to charge a galley and a quarter, instead of only the four hours actually engaged.

6. That special Sunday work† be paid for at the rate of 6*d.* per hour extra from 12 o'clock on Saturday night to 12 o'clock on Sunday night, but that in no case shall a compositor receive less than 2s. 6*d.* extra.

* By "a compositor called in" is understood *not already employed in the house.*

† By special Sunday work is meant work performed after the ordinary and regular edition or editions of any weekly paper have been sent to press and worked off: the proposition not being intended to affect those journals the getting out of which regularly enters into Sunday morning.

By order of the Committee,

H. SELF, *Secretary.*

3, Raquet Court,
   Dec. 22, 1874.

On 18 December, 1889, the News Department of the L.S.C. addressed a Memorial to the proprietors of the London morning and evening newspapers. They requested payment for slating and for Sunday work and an agreement on the length of the working day. Although no fresh agreements resulted in 1889, the compositors received satisfaction of most of their demands in 1891.

[DOCUMENT CXIV]

To the Proprietors of the London Morning and Evening Newspapers

Gentlemen,

In the early part of the present year steps were taken to convene a Conference composed of compositors employed in the different Morning and Evening Newspaper Offices, to take into consideration various disadvantages under which they labour—more particularly that of "slating," or enforced idleness—with the view of endeavouring to provide such remedies as, while proving satisfactory to the compositors, should, by their moderation, commend themselves to the acceptance of the employers. After several sittings (the first taking place on May 25th) a series of resolutions was drawn up, and embodied in a Report submitted to a Special General Meeting, held at the Memorial Hall, Farringdon Street, on October 19th. The Members unanimously approved and adopted this Report (a copy of which is forwarded herewith) and directed that a Memorial should be forwarded to the employers, accompanied by a request that they or their representatives would meet the journeymen in Conference, at which the various resolutions could be amicably discussed, and a mutual understanding arrived at.

The first and most important subject which we desire to submit to your earnest consideration is that of "slating," which has for many years past been a source of great discontent. While frankly admitting that a certain amount of "slating" time on newspaper work is unavoidable, we feel convinced that employers have but a slight knowledge of the extent to which this system is carried in the majority of offices, or of the serious manner in which it affects the labour of the compositors therein employed. Speaking generally, about one-fourth of the time the "line" is on is spent compulsorily upon the slate, for which the compositor receives no remuneration whatever, thus reducing the value of the work done either in the earlier or later portion of the day or night—work performed under very high pressure, and, particularly in the case of night work, not altogether under the healthiest conditions. As the News Scale stands at present, a compositor is guaranteed a quarter-galley per hour so long as the "line" is on. Should he be fortunate enough to do eight hours' work in five hours—that is to say, should he do a sufficient quantity of work in five hours to amount in value to the sum guaranteed him according to Scale at the expiration of eight hours from the commencement of work— he can be compelled to remain idle in the office for three hours longer without receiving any recompense whatever. Naturally, this enforced idleness is a source of great irritation, as, instead of men deriving the full benefit of their extra exertions during one portion of the night, it resolves itself into a means by which they can be retained a much longer time in the office than is absolutely necessary, at no expense to the employer.

With respect to evening paper hands it is generally admitted that the conditions under which evening newspapers are produced at the present time are entirely different to those which prevailed when the Scale of Prices was mutually agreed upon, such altered conditions entailing upon the compositor the necessity of remaining in the office an excessive number of hours, without the satisfaction of receiving a proportionate increase in his remuneration. In order to keep pace with the requirements of the public, and owing to the pressure of competition, those responsible for the production of evening newspapers have found it necessary to publish very early and occasional late editions. As a result of this, the men are sometimes called down at seven o'clock in the morning, or as early as six, and retained until nine o'clock, or even later, at night. It being impossible to keep them employed during the whole of this time, a system of "cuts" has been very largely taken advantage of, and it is a common occurrence for men to be "cut" two or three times during the day, the time varying in duration from two to three hours. In addition to this, they are subject to a certain amount of "slating." Of course, under these circumstances, the day's work practically extends over a period of thirteen or fourteen hours; and, so strong is the feeling against a continuance of this system, that it has been considered advisable to endeavour to define an ordinary working day for evening paper hands, and a time both before and after which extra remuneration can be claimed.

In laying before you resolutions on this subject, and asking your careful consideration of the same, we are encouraged in so doing by the fact that one of the leading evening journals recently referred to the greatly altered conditions under which evening papers were produced, generously acknowledging that such conditions were unfavourable to the compositor, and expressing willingness to favourably entertain and consider whatever recommendations might result from the deliberations of the Conference then sitting.

During our deliberations, the conviction was forced upon us that, as a certain amount of "slating" is unavoidable, it would not only be reasonable, but absolutely necessary, to allow the "house" some latitude on each day or night's work—this necessity being recognised on some provincial journals where "slating" is paid for. We trust, therefore, that the allowance of one hour—or half-an-hour when the "line" is on for less than six hours—will be considered a fair and equitable arrangement.

In approaching you with the request that you will seriously consider the points submitted, we desire to assure you that we are not giving expression to any feeling of discontent from a wage-earning point of view, but merely seeking to diminish the friction that arises in the majority of newspaper offices in consequence of the undue advantage taken of the quarter-per-hour guarantee, which we are convinced, from a long experience, is not only unnecessary, but baneful and demoralising in its tendency.

Under these circumstances, we submit the following resolutions for your favourable consideration :—

"Slating," or "Standing" time to be paid for at the rate of a quarter per hour; but if the standing time does not exceed one hour on the completion of the day or night's work, no charge to be made, the first hour being given to the Property, provided the "line" be on six hours; if less than that time, half-an-hour only to be given.

Rule 6, Section iv. (Evening Papers).—Regular hands are guided by the same rules as laid down for those on morning papers, claiming a galley, or charging the same [at the completion of the first edition].

That no "cut" between editions shall be of greater length than a quarter of an hour.

That the ordinary working day be nine hours (to include all cuts, except between any two editions that may be mutually agreed upon for meal times, which must not exceed one hour), on the completion of which a compositor shall be entitled to charge 3*d.* extra for each additional hour (or part of an hour) that he is required to remain in the office; and that in any case 3*d.* extra per hour be charged before 7 a.m. or after 8 p.m.

That Sunday work be paid for at the rate of 6*d*. per hour extra from 12 o'clock on Saturday night till 12 o'clock on Sunday night; but that in no case shall a compositor charge less than 2*s*. 6*d*. extra.

That 3*d*. per hour, or part of an hour, shall be paid as overtime for all extra editions upon morning papers.

The following proposed Rule respecting special Sunday work is intended to apply to the case of men called down early in order to publish a second edition of Saturday's paper:—

That all special Sunday work shall be paid for at the rate of 6*d*. per hour extra, but in no case shall a compositor charge less than 2*s*. 6*d*.

We gladly avail ourselves of this opportunity to return, on behalf of the members of the News Department of the London Society of Compositors, their very cordial thanks for the benefits of late years received at the hands of several of the Proprietors—in particular, by the granting of an annual holiday, subscribing to office sick funds, and improving our composing rooms by introducing the electric light and better ventilation; and we sincerely trust that the harmonious relations hitherto existing between the employers and employed may not only be fully maintained, but materially strengthened in the future.

Having thus laid before you the views of the compositors employed on the daily papers, we would respectfully request a reply, signifying your acquiescence or otherwise in the above resolutions, not later than January 1st, 1890; and in the event of your accepting our invitation to confer we shall be pleased if you will kindly arrange to meet us at Anderton's Hotel, Fleet Street, E.C., on Tuesday, January 7th, at Three o'clock p.m., for the purpose of discussing the various matters contained in the Memorial, with the view of their coming into operation, if agreed to, on February 1st, 1890.

We beg to remain, Gentlemen,

Yours faithfully,

C. W. BOWERMAN, *Secretary* (*News Department*).
C. J. DRUMMOND, *General Secretary*.

3, Raquet Court, Fleet Street, E.C.
December 18th, 1889.

In 1891 the bookmen's Scale of 1810 was completely revised, and a general advance in prices was arranged. Upon this occasion the *Rules and Regulations for News Work*, published by the L.S.C. in 1868, with the addenda of 1874, were also made the subject of a detailed inquiry. While the prices per galley and per thousand ens were not altered, a number of important additional clauses were inserted into the re-drafted Scale. These related to cuts, the definition of the working day on evening papers, together with overtime charges for both morning and evening journals. Since the wages of the establishment hands in the general trade had been increased by 2s. to 38s., those of the same class of workman employed on weekly periodicals were raised a like amount. The *Rules and Regulations for News Work* of 1868, together with the additional clauses agreed upon in 1874, are here reprinted parallel with the News Scale as revised in 1891. It will be noted that the concessions granted in the latter year largely correspond to those requested in the Memorial of 1889 printed above.

[DOCUMENT CXV]

NEWS SCALE OF 1868	NEWS SCALE OF 1891
1. All newspapers or publications partaking of the character of a newspaper, composed in London, to be charged according to the following scale of prices :—[1]	1. All newspapers, or publications partaking of the character of newspapers, composed in London, to be charged according to the following scale of prices :—

News Scale of 1868

Description of Paper		Morning	Evening	Weekly and wider periods
Per Hour.	d.	11½	11 {10½}	10
Per Galley.	s. d.	3 10	3 7	3 7 / 3 0 3
Salaries of Establishment Hands.	£ s.	—	—	16 0 / 1 16 0
Diamond.	d.	13	12½	12½
Pearl.	d.	11	10½	10½
Ruby.	d.	10½	10	10
Nonpareil.	d.	10	9½	9½
Emerald.	d.	9½	9	9
Minion Nonpareil.	d.	9½	9	9
Minion and larger sizes.	d.	9	8½	8½

(Per 1000 en quads* of own body.†)

News Scale of 1891

Description of Paper		Morning	Evening	Weekly and wider periods
Per Hour.	d.	11½	11 {10½}	10
Per Galley.	s. d.	3 10	3 7	3 7 / 3 0 3
Salaries of Establishment Hands.	£ s.	—	—	18 0 / 1 18 0
Diamond.	d.	13	12½	12½
Pearl.	d.	11	10½	10½
Ruby.	d.	10½	10	10
Nonpareil.	d.	10	9½	9½
Emerald.	d.	9½	9	9
Minion Nonpareil.	d.	9½	9	9
Minion and larger sizes.	d.	9	8½	8½

(Per 1000 en quads* of own body.†)

* A thick space to be reckoned an en in the width. As the price per thousand is clearly established, the compositor should set up neither more

* A thick space to be reckoned an en in the width. As the price per thousand is clearly established, the compositor should set up neither more

[1] The prices for minion, nonpareil and pearl and the galley prices, morning and evening papers, are the same as printed in the 1820 Report.

29

nor less than just such a number of lines to the galley as will amount to 3s. 10d. on morning, or 3s. 7d. on evening and weekly papers.

† Depth of Type :—

Lines to a foot.		Lines to a foot.	
English ..	64	Minion ..	122
Pica ..	71½	Emerald ..	128
Small Pica	83	Nonpareil .	143
Long Primer	90	Ruby ..	166
Bourgeois .	102	Pearl ..	180
Brevier ..	110	Diamond..	204

In founts below minion, when the type comes under the above standard, an advance of price is granted, if it is equal to or exceeds half of the difference between the larger fount and the next smaller one, but under that proportion no extra charge is made. Thus, when a bastard nonpareil contains half as many more ems to the foot as the difference between nonpareil and ruby, a farthing extra is charged, but if under that proportion no charge is made. In every instance, of course, the founts are cast up to their own ems. One farthing extra to be paid on all founts for every en below 12 ems of their own body in thickness.

nor less than just such a number of lines to the galley as will amount to 3s. 10d. on morning, or 3s. 7d. on evening and weekly papers.

† Depth of Type :—

Lines to a foot.		Lines to a foot.	
English ..	64	Minion ..	122
Pica ..	71½	Emerald ..	128
Small Pica	83	Nonpareil .	143
Long Primer	90	Ruby ..	166
Bourgeois .	102	Pearl ..	180
Brevier ..	110	Diamond..	204

In founts below minion, when the type comes under the above standard, an advance of price is granted, if it is equal to or exceeds half the difference between the larger fount and the next smaller one, but under that proportion no extra charge is made. Thus, when a bastard nonpareil contains half as many more ems to the foot as the difference between nonpareil and ruby, a farthing extra is charged, but if under that proportion no charge is made. In every instance the founts are cast up to their own ems. One farthing extra to be paid on all founts for every en below 12 ems of their own body in thickness.

II.—DAILY PAPERS*

Engagements on daily papers are of two kinds, viz. :—

1. Regular hands, secured one galley per day, and as much in addition as the requirements of the paper will admit of their obtaining.

2. Assistants, secured one galley on morning, and half-a-galley on evening papers, each time of working.

Engagements on daily papers are of two kinds, viz.: —

1. Regular hands, secured one galley per day, and as much in addition as the requirements of the paper will admit of.

2. Assistants, secured one galley on morning, and half-a-galley on evening papers, each time of working.

* Full Hands.—The employment of full hands formerly existed on daily papers, but the system, being found to be entirely unsuited to their present requirements, has gone into disuse.

NEWS SCALE OF 1868	NEWS SCALE OF 1891

III.—MORNING PAPERS

1. Regular Hands are engaged (by the fortnight) to do at least one galley per night, and as much more as the requirements of the paper will admit of; the galley reckoned as four hours' work, including corrections. To correct as nearly as possible the amount of their composition. Should the printer be unable to furnish copy according to the above specification, at the rate of one-quarter per hour is to be charged from the time of taking copy until the finish.

2. Assistants.—Assistants are not under any regular engagement, but are entitled to a galley, and must be furnished at the rate of a quarter per hour from the time of taking copy.

3. Assistants employed by the property at a galley per night are entitled to a fortnight's notice.

4. Time Work to be paid at not less than 11½d. per hour.

5. Corrections.—All matter composed after the paper has gone to press, when making less than a galley, shall be corrected by the property.

---

3. Regular hands are engaged (by the fortnight) to do at least one galley per night, and as much more as the requirements of the paper will admit of; the galley reckoned as four hours' work, including corrections. To correct as nearly as possible the amount of their composition. Should the printer be unable to furnish copy according to the above specification, at the rate of one-quarter per hour is to be charged from the time of taking copy until the finish.

4. Assistants are not under any regular engagement, but are entitled to a galley, and must be furnished at the rate of a quarter per hour from the time of taking copy. Assistants employed by the property at a galley per night are entitled to a fortnight's notice.

5. Time work to be paid at not less than 11½d. per hour.

6. Matter composed after the paper has gone to press, when making less than a galley, to be corrected by less property.

7. Threepence per hour, or part of an hour, to be paid as overtime for all extra editions upon morning papers.

8. Special Sunday work to be paid for at the rate of 6d. per hour extra, but a compositor in no case to charge less than 2s. 6d. extra.

IV.—EVENING PAPERS

6. Regular Hands are guided by the same rules as laid down for those on the morning papers, claiming a galley, or charging the same, at the expiration of four hours from the time of taking copy.

---

9. Regular hands to be guided by the same rules as laid down for those on morning papers, claiming a galley, or charging the same, at the completion of the first ordinary edition.

NEWS SCALE OF 1868	NEWS SCALE OF 1891

10. No "cut" between editions to be of greater length than half-an-hour, except the dinner hour.

11. The working day to be nine hours, exclusive of all "cuts," which shall not exceed one hour and a half, on the completion of which the compositor to be entitled to charge 3*d.* extra for each additional hour, or part of an hour, that he is required to remain in the office, but in any case 3*d.* extra per hour to be charged before 7 a.m. or after 8 p.m.

12. Sunday work to be charged at the rate of 6*d.* per hour extra from 12 o'clock on Saturday night to 12 o'clock on Sunday night; but a compositor in no case to charge less than 2*s.* 6*d.* extra.

7. Time Work.—Every odd quarter, or hour, to carry the charge of 11*d.* Thus the first quarter, or hour, would be 11*d.*, the second 10½*d.*, the third 11*d.*, and the fourth 10½*d.*, making the four quarters, or hours, 3*s.* 7*d.*

13. Every odd quarter, or hour of time work, to carry the charge of 11*d.* Thus the first quarter, or hour, would be 11*d.*, the second 10½*d.*, the third 11*d.*, and the fourth 10½*d.*; making the four quarters, or hours, 3*s.* 7*d.*

8. Compositors (not forming a portion of the regular companionship) called in, or ordered to attend, after copy has been taken, to assist on the first edition of an evening paper, are entitled to not less than half a galley.

14. Compositors (not forming a portion of the regular companionship) called in, or ordered to attend, after copy has been taken, to assist on the first edition of an evening paper, are entitled to not less than half a galley.

V.—RULES APPLICABLE TO BOTH MORNING AND EVENING PAPERS

9. Time Work.—Not less than one hour to be charged on time; but the fractional parts of an hour beyond that period to be charged at their value in lines.

15. Not less than one hour to be charged on time; but the fractional parts of an hour beyond that period to be charged at their value in lines.

10. Extra Editions are done on time or lines, at the option of the printer. If on time, only the rate of a quarter per hour is produced; if on lines, and there be not a sufficient supply of copy, the rate of a quarter per hour is charged. No charge less

16. Extra editions are done on time or lines, at the option of the printer. If on time, only the rate of a quarter per hour is produced; if on lines, and there be not a sufficient supply of copy, the rate of a quarter per hour is charged. No charge less

NEWS SCALE OF 1868

than a quarter. Each edition is a separate charge, unless several editions are going on continuously, in which case time or lines is to be charged from the commencement till the finish of these editions. On morning papers an extra quarter allowed to persons called in to assist, if the quantity composed be less than a galley.

[On extra editions, when the compositor is required to "pull out" (that is, to compose more than a quarter per hour), the general practice is to charge the lines so composed. Thus, compositors detained for three hours for an extra edition, and then ordered to "pull out" for another hour, during which time they might compose half a galley, would charge a galley and a quarter, instead of only the four hours they were engaged.]

11. All composition or corrections in hand when the paper goes to press must either be suspended or charged as a second edition—that is, charging not less than a quarter of a galley.

12. On daily papers, matter composed before the usual time of commencing work, such as leading articles for editors, advertisements as copy for other papers, &c., to be charged distinct from the day's work. If less than a quarter, a quarter to be charged; if more, the number of lines.

13. Assistants, if ordered to attend at the ordinary time of taking copy, are entitled to the charge of a galley; but if holding a *bonâ fide* employment by the property, and taken from other work when their services are required, are entitled to not less than a quarter for each time of being called on.

14. Apprentices.—No apprentices to be employed on daily papers, morning or evening.

NEWS SCALE OF 1891

than a quarter. Each edition is a separate charge, unless several editions are going on continuously, in which case time or lines is charged from the commencement till the finish of these editions. On morning papers an extra quarter is allowed to persons called in to assist, if the quantity composed be less than a galley.

[On extra editions, when the compositor is required to "pull out" (that is, to compose more than a quarter per hour), the general practice is to charge the lines so composed. Thus, compositors detained for three hours for an extra edition, and then ordered to "pull out" for another hour, during which time they might compose half a galley, would charge a galley and a quarter, instead of only the four hours they are engaged.]

17. All composition or corrections in hand when the paper goes to press must either be suspended or charged as a second edition—that is, charging not less than a quarter of a galley.

18. On daily papers, matter composed before the usual time of commencing work, such as leading articles for editors, advertisements as copy for other papers, &c., to be charged distinct from the day's work. If less than a quarter, a quarter to be charged; if more, the number of lines.

19. Assistants, if ordered to attend at the ordinary time of taking copy, to be entitled to the charge of a galley; but if holding a *bonâ fide* employment by the property, and taken from other work when their services are required, to be entitled to not less than a quarter for each time of being called on.

20. No apprentices to be employed on daily papers, morning or evening.

NEWS SCALE OF 1868	NEWS SCALE OF 1891

51. Declaring on Time.—The system of declaring on time on daily newspapers is at variance with the Scale, and is therefore abolished.

21. Declaring on time on daily papers is contrary to Scale.

VI.—TRI-WEEKLY AND BI-WEEKLY PAPERS

15. Tri-weekly and bi-weekly papers to be considered weekly; but in all cases of newspapers published oftener than three times a week, the mode of producing which is similar to that of a morning paper, the same shall be paid for in accordance with the morning paper scale.

22. Tri-weekly and bi-weekly papers to be considered weekly; but in all cases of papers published oftener than three times a week, the mode of producing which is similar to that of daily papers, the same to be paid for in accordance with the daily paper scale.

VII.—WEEKLY PAPERS

24. Publications containing only reviews of books, notices of dramatic or musical performances, articles on the fine arts, accounts of the meetings and proceedings of religious, literary, or scientific societies, and advertisements, to be paid the same as monthly or quarterly publications. Should the mode, however, of getting up these publications materially differ from the common mode of doing book-work, and the compositors have frequently to make even lines, with takings of a few lines each, and other disadvantages connected with a newspaper, then they take the newspaper charge.

23. Publications containing news of any description, and produced by the ordinary method of weekly news-papers, to be paid accordingly. Commercial prices current, shipping lists, and similar publications not necessarily to be considered newspapers.

Extra editions are done on time or lines, at the option of the printer. If on time, only the rate of a quarter per hour is produced; if on lines, and there be not a sufficient supply of copy, the rate of a quarter per hour is charged. No charge less than a quarter. Each edition is a separate charge.[1]

24. Extra editions to be done on time or lines, at the option of the printer. If on time, only the rate of a quarter per hour to be produced; if on lines, and there be an insufficient supply of copy, the rate of a quarter per hour to be charged. No charge to be less than a quarter, and each edition to be a separate charge.

5. That when a compositor is called in[2] to assist, he shall be en-

25. Compositors, not already employed in a house, called in to assist

[1] In the *Rules and Regulations* of 1868 this paragraph formed the second part of clause 16.

[2] By "a compositor called in," is understood *not already employed in the house.*

titled to charge not less than four hours if employed on time, or less than a galley if paid by lines. That when a compositor "engaged on extra editions" is required to "pull out," that is to compose more than a quarter per hour, he shall be entitled to charge the lines so composed. That is, if he is detained three hours for an extra edition, and then ordered to "pull out" for another hour, during which time he may compose half a galley, he shall be entitled to charge a galley and a quarter, instead of only the four hours actually engaged. (1874.)

Persons regularly employed in a house where a weekly paper is done, if required to leave their ordinary work to assist on the paper, are entitled to not less than a quarter of a galley, or an hour, for each time of being called on.[1]

19. Assistants employed in the house not to be called on to correct their matter unless they compose a galley.

20. No deduction to be made for letter when the composition is under a galley. When the composition exceeds a galley, the letter shall be either deducted for or returned, at the option of the compositor.

21. Compositors not to be called off piece-work to compose on time.

3. 'Stab hands, when engaged on the line, shall lift copy fairly and in regular numbers with the piece hands. Apprentices who have served four years of their time to lift copy with the men. The foregoing not to apply either to advertisements or articles given out in their entirety to 'stab hands or apprentices. (1874.)

are entitled to charge not less than eight hours if employed on time, or less than a galley if paid by lines, claiming a galley, or charging the same, at the expiration of four hours from the time of taking copy. Compositors regularly employed in a house where a weekly paper is done, if required to leave their ordinary work to assist on the paper, are entitled to not less than a quarter of a galley, or an hour, for each time of being called on, but not to correct their matter unless they compose a galley.

26. No deduction to be made for letter when the composition is under a galley, but when it exceeds a galley, the letter to be either deducted for or returned, at the option of the compositor.

27. Compositors not to be called off the piece to compose on time.

28. 'Stab hands and apprentices, when engaged on the line, to lift copy fairly and in regular order, and pull, slate, and cut with the piece hands. This rule not necessarily to apply to advertisements, nor to articles given out in their entirety to apprentices who have served less than three years of their time; but no particular article or portion thereof shall be

---

[1] In the *Rules and Regulations* of 1868 this paragraph formed part of clause 18.

|

given to apprentices while the line is on because of the profitable nature of such article.

4. Time-work to be paid at the rate of 10*d*. per hour, subject to the extra for overtime when the 60 hours have been worked. (1874).

29. Time-work to be paid at the rate of not less than 10*d*. per hour, subject to the extra for overtime.

The minimum 'stab wages to remain at 36*s*. per week of 54 hours, the overtime thereon to be paid at not less than 11*d*. per hour.

30. Compositors on the establishment to receive not less than 38*s*. per week of 54 hours, the apportionment of hours to be mutually agreed upon between the employer and journeymen in each office, and to govern all the compositors employed.

16. The engagement for establishment hands on weekly papers to be 10 hours' work per day. The time of commencing, from six to eight o'clock in the morning, to be the same each day; such time to be fixed at the option of the employer; and all employment prior to or after the specified time to be paid at 10*d*. per hour.

1. That no compositor on the piece shall be called upon to work more than six hours of overtime during the week without charging 3*d*. per hour extra. The week to consist of 54 hours, and the overtime to commence when 60 hours are completed, such hours to be governed by the ordinary working hours of the house, and may all be worked in one night or divided, as may suit the convenience of the employer; provided that in no case shall a piece compositor be called upon to work after 12 p.m. without receiving the extra for overtime. (1874.)

31. Overtime to be paid at the rate of 3½*d*. per hour extra for the first three hours; after that time, but in any case after 10 o'clock from Monday to Friday inclusive, at 4*d*. per hour till 12 o'clock, after that at 5*d*. per hour. On Saturday, for the first three hours, 4*d*. per hour, and after that time 5*d*. The charge for overtime to be governed by the ordinary working hours of each office, and to commence in any case before 8 a.m., after 8 p.m., and after 2 p.m. on Saturday (except in the case of weekly newspapers the getting out of which regularly enter into Sunday morning and produced in offices where no other description of work is done, when the charge of 5*d*. per hour extra shall commence not later than 8 p.m. on Saturday for grass hands, and not later than 12 o'clock (midnight) for establishment

hands, provided that in the case of the latter a regular weekly holiday in lieu of Saturday is mutually agreed to between the employer and journeyman), each day standing on its own merits. Compositors called upon to work the whole of the dinner-hour to receive 4d. extra. Compositors called upon to work overtime for more than three consecutive hours to be entitled to half-an-hour for refreshment after each three hours of overtime have been worked. Fractions of hours to be paid as complete hours. Lost time to be deducted at the ordinary rate, but a regular hand coming in more than half-an-hour late may be called upon to work the first hour of overtime the same day without charging extra, each day standing on its own merits.

6. That special Sunday work* be paid for at the rate of 6d. per hour extra from 12 o'clock on Saturday night to 12 o'clock on Sunday night, but that in no case shall a compositor receive less than 2s. 6d. extra. (1874.)

32. Special Sunday work, performed after the ordinary and regular edition or editions of a paper have been sent to press, to be paid at the rate of 8d. per hour extra from 12 o'clock on Saturday night to 8 o'clock on Monday morning, when such work is continuous; compositors in no case to receive less than 3s. 4d. extra. The same rule to apply for special work to Christmas Day. Compositors called in at 12 o'clock on Sunday night to be paid at the same rate; if at 6 o'clock on Monday or any other morning, except Sunday, at 4d. per hour extra.

33. Compositors, whether piece or establishment hands, if retained beyond a fortnight, to receive and give a fortnight's notice prior to their engagements being terminated.

* By "special Sunday work" is meant work performed after the ordinary and regular edition or editions of any weekly paper have been sent to press and worked off; the proposition not being intended to affect those journals the getting out of which regularly enters into Sunday morning.

NEWS SCALE OF 1868	NEWS SCALE OF 1891

VIII.—DAILY AND WEEKLY PAPERS (INCLUDING SUNDAY PAPERS)

25. Number of Slips to be Pulled.—Not more than three slips to be pulled of each galley, including the revise. If more than three are required, lines to be charged equivalent to the trouble, but not less than three lines to be charged.

34. Not more than three slips to be pulled of each galley, including the revise. If more than three are required, lines to be charged equivalent to the trouble, but not less than three lines to be charged.

2. Without mutual arrangements exist thereon, that no compositor be called upon to pull a galley containing less than a quarter of a galley of fresh matter. Nor shall a compositor be expected to seek for a galley wherein to insert less than one-eighth of a galley of fresh matter, without being entitled to charge 1d. for the trouble occasioned thereby. (1874.)

35. No compositor to be called upon to pull less than half a galley of fresh matter; nor shall a compositor be expected to seek for a galley wherein to insert fresh matter, without being entitled to charge three lines for the trouble occasioned.

26. Leaded Matter.—All leads other than those used in making up are to be charged by the compositor.

36. All leads other than those used in making up to be charged by the compositor.

27. Bastard Founts. — Bastard founts of one remove to be cast up to the depth and width of the two founts to which they belong; of two removes to be cast up to the smaller body, both in depth and width.

37. Bastard founts of one remove to be cast up to the depth and width of the two founts to which they belong; of two removes to be cast up to the smaller body, both in depth and width.

28. Matter having been once used becomes the property of the employer.

38. Matter having been once used becomes the property of the employer, at whatever time lifted.

29. All matter with head or first-lines larger than the body to be charged according to the depth of the body of the taking; but all rules to be charged as distinct lines, except advertisement rules, which in all cases are to be placed with the first line, and, thus combined, counted as two lines only.

39. Matter with head or first-lines larger than the body to be charged according to the depth of the body of the taking; but all rules to be charged as distinct lines, except advertisement rules, which in all cases are to be counted with the first line, as two lines only.

30. General heads of articles, and the rules after, whether standing or not (such as latest news, law intelligence, police intelligence, &c.), rules in the middle of articles (unless placed

40. General heads of articles, and the rules after, whether standing or not; rules in the middle or at the end of articles; and blocks inserted by the compositor, to be charged.

NEWS SCALE OF 1868	NEWS SCALE OF 1891

by the printer for the convenience of making up), half-doubles, or other rules, at the end of articles, let-in blocks and wood-cuts inserted by the compositor, are to be charged by the compositor.

31. Standing advertisements, brass or other clump heads, and the date line attached thereto (such as the scroll heads preceding leaders, fashionable and table talk, &c.), wood-cuts, leads, and rules in the middle of articles inserted for convenience of making up, being placed on the galley or in the form by the printer or his time hands, are the property of the employer.

41. Brass or other clump heads to sections, wood-cuts, &c., placed on the galley or in the form by the printer or his time hands, are the property of the employer.

32. Greek, &c., left blank, or paid for according to the value of the time occupied in composition, but not less than one shilling to be charged.

42. Greek, &c., to be left blank, or paid for according to value, not less than one shilling to be charged.

33. Newspapers in a foreign language take the same advance as allowed on book-work. Portions of newspapers in foreign languages to take the charge of one-sixth extra.

43. Newspapers in a foreign language to take the same advance as bookwork. Portions of newspapers in foreign languages to take the charge of one-fourth extra.

34. Supplements.— Supplements to newspapers to be charged according to the scale for the paper to which they are attached.

44. Supplements to be charged according to the scale for the paper to which they are attached.

38. Alterations from Copy in first proofs, if done by the compositor correcting such proof, to be charged according to the time occupied in making such alterations, not less than three lines being charged.
[This applies solely to alterations made by the reader, and not to authors' corrections, the latter being charged according to Rule 9, Sec. V. for daily papers.]

45. Alterations from copy in first proofs, if done by the compositor correcting such proofs, to be charged according to the time occupied, not less than three lines to be charged.

39. Copy making less than three lines not to be considered a take; if less, three lines to be charged.

46. Not less than three lines to be considered a taking; if less, three lines to be charged.

40. Clearing Away.—No compositor to be called on to clear away newspaper work.

47. Compositors not to be called on to clear away newspaper work.

44. Matter consisting of subscribers' names, with sums of money run out to the end of line; names of horses, with age, stone, lb. run out; measurements of land, and all composition of the same description, takes no extra charge; but when there are two columns of such figures brought into the same width, one-third extra to be charged; three columns, one-half extra; four or more columns, double. Other matter which requires casting off for the purpose of ascertaining proper widths for the purpose of ranging, whether such matter consists of words or figures, each width or ranging to be considered a column. In matter other than the exceptions given above, each arrangement to be considered a column, with or without rules.

48. Matter consisting of subscribers' names, with sums of money run out to the end of line; names of horses, with age, stone, lb. run out; measurements of land, and all composition of the same description, to take no extra charge; but when there are two columns of such figures brought into the same width, one-third extra to be charged; three columns, one-half extra; four or more columns, double. Other matter which requires casting off for the purpose of ascertaining proper widths for the purpose of ranging, whether such matter consists of words or figures, each width or ranging to be considered a column. In matter other than the exceptions given above, each arrangement to be considered a column, with or without rules.

TABLE, TABULAR AND COLUMN MATTER

41. Two Columns.—Two justifications or arrangements to constitute half-measure—one-third extra.

49. Two Columns.—Two justifications or arrangements to constitute half-measure—one-third extra.

42. Three Columns.—Three justifications or arrangements to take the charge of one-half extra.

50. Three Columns.—Three justifications or arrangements to be charged one-half extra.

43. Four Columns.—Four or more justifications or arrangements to be charged double.

51. Four Columns.—Four or more justifications or arrangements to be charged double.

45. Matter set to less than 16 ems of its own body in width (not being table, tabular, or column matter, as defined in Rules 41 to 44 inclusive) to be charged one-fourth extra; less than 10 ems of its own body, one-third extra.

52. Matter set to less than 16 ems of its own body, and not being table, tabular, or column matter, to be charged one-fourth extra; less than 10 ems of its own body, one-third extra.

46. The top and bottom rules of tables are charged as distinct lines; but cross rules in the body of a table are only reckoned in the depth.

53. The top and bottom rules of a table to be charged as distinct lines, double; but cross rules in the body of a table to be reckoned in the depth.

NEWS SCALE OF 1868	NEWS SCALE OF 1891
47. The signature, date-line, and rule, after a table, if making three lines, to be charged as common matter.	54. The signature, date-line, and rule, after a table, if making three lines, to be charged as common matter.
48. Heads.—Title-headings, to table or tabular matter, not exceeding five lines, take the charge of the matter to which they are attached; above five lines, no extra to be charged.	55. Title-headings to table or tabular matter, not exceeding five lines, to take the charge of the matter to which they are attached; above five lines, no extra to be charged.
49. Lines between table or tabular matter, not being headings to such matter, take no extra charge.	56. Common matter occurring between table or tabular, not being headings, to take no extra charge.

35. Reprints.—When duplicate copies of newspapers are composed, no reduction shall be made for the reprint copy.

36. Matter composed in London for a paper printed in the country to be paid according to the London Scale, whether daily or weekly.

37. Stereotype. — Newspapers stereotyped with plaster of Paris, or any other matter giving equal additional trouble, to take an advance of one halfpenny per thousand.

22. Periodicals partaking of the nature of a newspaper, although published regularly at a period exceeding a week, are to be considered as newspapers, and paid agreeably to the scale for weekly papers.

23. Definition of a Newspaper.— Publications which appear weekly, or at wider periods, containing general news—either parliamentary reports, reports of police or law courts, foreign or provincial intelligence, reports of daily occurrences, or notices of bankrupts or insolvents—to be paid according to the scale for newspapers.

** In the event of any question arising whereon either the Book or News Scale is silent or not clearly defined, such question shall be governed by the custom of the trade (if any) or decided by mutual agreement; it being understood that for work of an exceptional character the compositor is entitled to charge such special rates as will adequately remunerate him for the time occupied on the work.

The London Scale of 1891 was put into force in February of that year. Within a few weeks the News Department appointed a committee with the task of "inquiring into, and reporting upon, the systems prevailing in the various daily-paper offices, with the view to ascertaining whether—and if so, to what extent—irregularities existed either of scale or custom. . . ." Their findings were published in October, 1891. The two principal subjects of inquiry concerned the manner of paying for the composition of the contents bill and the status of "grass" hands, neither of which have been discussed in any previous document.

The contents bill, it appeared, was either composed by a line hand, who was put on time for the purpose, or by a 'stab hand. In some cases, when the bill was set by a line hand, more than the bare time rate was paid. On the *Daily News*, for instance, time and a half was allowed. Alternatively, line hands so engaged were guaranteed a galley, or 3s. 10d., morning paper rate. Generally, when piece workers composed the contents bill, the practice was to pay rather more than the minimum galley guarantee, since the average compositor could earn more than 3s. 10d. in four hours, the standard time for the composition of a galley.

A "grass" hand was defined by C. T. Jacobi as "a compositor temporarily engaged—a practice common in newspaper offices."[1] The term is not used by William Savage, but writing of contemporary practices on *The Times* he refers to the "*outsiders* who fill the frames of absentees in cases of sickness, or from other causes: they are not considered as belonging to the establishment, inasmuch as they hold no situation, and are consequently dependent upon the workmen."

Compositors in regular employment who desired to take occasional leave of absence "sold out," a "grass" hand taking over their frame. The committee were concerned at the conditions under which these substitutes were employed. In the most unsatisfactory cases the "grass" did not receive the guarantee of a galley, was liable to be "cut" earlier than the companionship, and be obliged to collect his earnings through the man he represented. The committee recommended that "grasses" be abolished altogether, failing which a guarantee of a galley should be insisted upon.

[1] Jacobi, C. T., *The Printers' Vocabulary* (London, 1888).

[DOCUMENT CXVI]

Report of the Committee on the System of Working adopted in each Office.

Gentlemen,

When, in May last, we were entrusted with the task of inquiring into, and reporting upon, the systems of working prevailing in the various daily-paper offices, with the view of ascertaining whether—and if so, to what extent—irregularities existed either of scale or custom, we had every reason to hope that the task would prove comparatively light. Although no such inquiry had taken place since 1868, we felt that the Slate Conference of last year resulted in good work being done in the direction of bringing about a greater uniformity of working. For instance, at the initial meeting of the delegates to that Conference, it became apparent that a difference of practice existed with regard to the charge for the first edition of an evening paper, some companionships not claiming the galley upon such edition going to press, but making a continuous charge up to the time of being "cut," which was usually after the second edition. As a result, the Rule bearing upon the subject was more clearly defined by the insertion of the words, "at the completion of the first edition," and as amended by the delegates (subject to the insertion of the word "ordinary"), met with the approval of the Conference. Several other instances might be given, were it necessary, of anomalies brought to light and remedied (not so much by Rule as by Chapel action) through the interchange of views which took place upon that occasion; sufficient to say that at its conclusion a better understanding existed between the members regarding matters upon which previously there had been a wide divergence of opinion, thus anticipating, in a degree, the inquiry upon which we have been engaged. Naturally enough, when it was borne in mind that every Chapel had for years been directly represented on the Board, considerable surprise was felt at the irregularities which were proved to exist, and that a closer system of working should not have prevailed as a result of what may be termed the monthly delegate meetings. The necessity for further investigation having been clearly demonstrated, we trust that the result of our labours, as contained in the recommendations about to be laid before you, will tend to greater uniformity of working.

Our first meeting was held on the 6th of May, and as we were without specific instructions concerning the intended direction and scope of the inquiry, except on one point—the mode of producing the contents' bill— we could only be guided, in the words of the Report read to the members at the May quarterly meeting, "by the belief that the desire of the delegates was simply to bring about, as far as practicable, a more uniform system of working without undue or unnecessary interference with the systems pursued at present—excepting, of course, where existing systems or customs involve an infringement of Scale." After discussing the matter at some length, it was agreed that we should proceed on lines similar to those of the 1868 inquiry, by requesting Fathers of Chapels to furnish a detailed description of their mode of working; should such statement not be forthcoming, the necessary information to be obtained by summoning a deputation. A circular to this effect was issued, and we desire to take this opportunity of acknowledging the excellent and prompt manner in which, in the majority of cases, such reports were drawn up. To fully examine and discuss these documents thirteen meetings were held, and in only six instances was it found necessary to supplement the information therein contained by means of a deputation. The results of our investigations may be described as follows:—

ST. JAMES'S GAZETTE.—There being one or two points in this report upon which further information was desired, a deputation was summoned. It appeared that two 'stab hands, whose hours of working were the same, with a slight difference in the rate of pay, worked for about one hour per day after the paper went to press. Exception had been taken to this, but as the hour was included in the number fixed by the terms of their engagement, we could see no objection to the practice so long as the minimum was enforced. The same men worked three hours overtime on one evening during the week (with half-an-hour for refreshment, this being deducted), and one hour's overtime the following morning, for which they received 4*s.* 7*d.*, or about ½*d.* per hour less for overtime work than their average "per" for the ordinary week's work. With respect to the refreshment half-hour (which had never been claimed) we are of opinion that it should not be deducted, and that all overtime charges must commence from the finish of the ordinary working day; and, whilst admitting the anomaly of overtime work being paid for at a lesser rate—however slight—than the ordinary work, we fail to see how, under the circumstances, we can advise that a claim should be made, or the matter treated in any sense as an infringement of Scale.

On extra editions a system prevails of retaining the men for about half-an-hour after the edition goes to press before an intimation is given of the number required for the succeeding editions. This practice we consider manifestly unfair; and if men are systematically retained for lengthened periods between the editions they should be entitled to charge time up to the moment of receiving the final "cut."

Another matter had reference to the contents' bill, which was occasionally produced by a "line" hand, who was put on "time" for the purpose. The question had been submitted to the Committee, and it was considered advisable to inquire into the general manner of doing such work.

PALL MALL GAZETTE.—The statement furnished from this companionship was considered very satisfactory, the only point giving rise to comment being that the Chapel permitted the "line" hands to distribute their type during the dinner hour. This practice we regard as objectionable, but it was not considered necessary to deal with it by special resolution. The contents' bill is produced by a permanent time-hand.

EVENING NEWS AND POST.—In this case, also, a generally satisfactory report was forthcoming, with the exception of the manner of employing "grass" hands. It appeared to be the custom for the "grass" to belong to the companionship, except in the event of a frame being vacant through sickness, when the Printer would claim a "grass" hand for such frame; otherwise they were under the entire control of the companionship. Consequently they received no guarantee from the Printer. This practice is one which cannot be too strongly condemned, as it must inevitably place the member in a disadvantageous position; and we earnestly recommend that in future Chapels shall not be allowed to employ "grass" hands, but that it shall be a *bonâ fide* engagement, subject, of course, to the usual guarantee. Contents' bill done by 'stab hand.

STAR.—Statement considered in every respect satisfactory. No "grass" hands except during the holidays, when they are exactly on the same footing as the men whose frames they fill. A 'stab hand is specially engaged to do the contents' bill.

EVENING STANDARD.—The communication forwarded from the Chapel being somewhat brief, it was considered advisable to obtain further information by means of a deputation. Several matters were inquired into, notably the manner of doing the contents' bill, the system of pulling and correcting, how tables were given out, with the extra charges thereon, cricket scores, etc., also whether any special work was done by arrangement. The replies disclosed a particularly satisfactory method of working. The scale was interpreted in a liberal spirit, the only matter calling for comment being that a small standing table, in which there were five columns, was given out to the 'ship, and charged as ordinary matter. This arrangement was understood to be in accordance with a decision of the Committee some years previously; but we are certainly of opinion that such an arrangement would not be sanctioned at the present time, and consider that such matter, if given out, should be charged on its merits. The contents' bill is done by a piece hand, at a sufficient rate.

ECHO.—Here, again, it may be said that the report laid before us was fairly satisfactory, the revised rules of working resulting from the recent Slate Conference, together with the Committee's decisions, being strictly carried out, and the entire work of the office performed in accordance with the rules and customs of the trade. No mention, however, was made as to the manner in which the contents' bill was produced, but, acting upon your instructions, we ascertained that a man was specially engaged to do the work in question, working about forty-eight hours per week, and receiving a stated wage—as nearly as possible bare time. The most disagreeable feature of the matter was that this person did not belong to the Society, but communications were opened up on the subject which, we are pleased to report, had the desired effect.

SHIPPING GAZETTE.—The information supplied in reply to our request was of so meagre a character that it became necessary to supplement the same by summoning a deputation. From the evidence thus taken it appeared that a contents' bill was unknown. The work was of a peculiar but advantageous character, quite distinct from the ordinary methods of evening-paper production. No "grass" were employed, frames vacant through illness being left blank. Only one edition was published, the paper going to press about 3.30. A weekly paper was published every Friday morning, and produced at weekly-paper price. If, however, work was given out for the weekly concurrently with the evening-paper matter, it would be charged according to the daily-paper scale; and, further, no matter set for the weekly appeared in the evening paper.

MORNING POST.—From this companionship a clear and satisfactory statement was furnished, the only matter giving rise to discussion being the system of employing the "grass" hands. They were practically engaged by the Printer, but guaranteed nothing, and handed over to the 'ship to fill the frames of full-hands desiring to "sell out." On certain nights of the week a portion—occasionally the whole—of the "grass" were claimed by the Printer. They were entitled to the "fat" that might fall to the frame in which they were engaged, and were allowed by the companionship to take their names off the list on any night, except general holidays. The contents' bill was done on 'stab, at an adequate remuneration.

MORNING ADVERTISER.—Nothing calling for special comment was shown to exist in the working of this office, both the letter and spirit of the rules being strictly carried out. The "grass" were in precisely the same position as the full-frame hands, so far as the lifting of copy, "cut," etc., were concerned. The contents' bill was done by two "line" hands, who received a galley each.

DAILY NEWS.—The matters upon which information was desired were fully dealt with in the reply received from the companionship. In this case, also, the only question requiring comment was that of the "grass" hands, who were engaged solely by the Printer, guaranteed but very rarely "cut" at the galley, and, with the exception of not holding advertisement cases, in every sense on an equality with the frame hands. Men are taken off the line to do the contents' bill, receiving time and a half.

DAILY CHRONICLE.—No irregularities were shown to exist in the system of working prevailing in this office. On the contrary, so far as the scale was concerned, it was interpreted in a liberal spirit; and, with regard to custom, a sweeping departure had been made by the entire abolition of the "grass" system, all being made frame hands, and thus placed on an equality, enjoying the same privileges. The selling-out slate is controlled by the Printer, who nightly announces the number of hands he can allow away. We cannot but think that this innovation will commend itself to the members, more especially in those offices where at present the "grass" system is conspicuous for its complication, and consequent confusion. So far as we can ascertain, the new arrangement has worked very satisfactorily, and certainly deserves to be given a trial, if for no other reason than its extreme simplicity. With respect to the contents' bill, two line hands were put on time for the purpose, being paid a trifle over a quarter per hour.

MORNING STANDARD.—Although in the reply received the ground of our inquiry was tolerably well covered, it was considered advisable to examine, by deputation, into the system of working. Every information was afforded, and may be briefly stated, as follows :—

Most of the tables and bond advertisements were given to one man, with assistance, if required, from the first in the lift. This system, although acquiesced in by the companionship, we consider unsatisfactory, and recommend that all copy should go out from the stone in the ordinary manner.

Certain standing tables were given out to the piece hands to correct, who were paid double time, and lifted copy again upon the completion of such time work. The custom undoubtedly is for a man once on time to remain on time; and we have, therefore, no alternative but to condemn the practice.

Standing traffic returns were also given out to the line hand to be corrected, and charged as common matter, any fresh lines that might have to be set being charged double. As in the case already commented upon, we consider that such matter should be charged on its merits.

With respect to the "grass" hands, they held all cases, but did not lift ruby copy unless ordered to do so. With this exception, and occasionally lifting before the 'ship (for which a satisfactory reason was given), they were virtually in the same position as the frame hands, always working, and continuing on to the finish of the night.

The contents' bill was done by two line hands, who received a galley each; if an extra bill was done, time and a third was paid.

DAILY TELEGRAPH.—The only matter calling for special comment in this case was the fact that time work is paid for at the bare quarter per hour. In nearly every other office an increased payment is made, and we strongly recommend the companionship to endeavour to obtain better remuneration for the work. In other matters, as in this, the scale is rigidly adhered to. The "grass" hands are in exactly the same position as the frame hands, taking their share of "fat" work, enjoying the holiday, etc., and only occasionally getting a galley "cut." The contents' bill is done by a 'stab hand (regularly engaged on the work) with the assistance of a semi-'stab hand, the latter receiving bare time.

DAILY GRAPHIC.—There was nothing noticeable in the method of conducting work at this establishment, the report being considered entirely satisfactory. "Grass" hands were engaged by the house, receiving the usual guarantee, but seldom, if ever, "cut" at the galley. A "line" hand is called on to do the contents' bill, at the rate of one shilling per hour, but never receiving less than a galley.

DAILY ORACLE.—In this case, also, there was little to criticize, the method of working bearing favourable comparison with that of much older companionships. The "grass" hands, however, were employed by the 'ship for the purposes of "selling out" and filling sick-frames, receiving no guarantee; and, as in the case already reported upon, we recommend that this system be discontinued. Contents' bill produced by 'stab hand.

PUBLIC LEDGER.—A fairly satisfactory report was returned from this companionship, one matter only requiring notice—the manner of producing displayed advertisements. In consequence of the 'ship not possessing the necessary material, these advertisements, which only came in occasionally, had to be done on 'stab in another part of the house; but they had never been claimed, nor, so far as we could ascertain, had any attempt been made to obtain the requisite type. Under these circumstances, we recommend the companionship to make a move in the latter direction; and, until successful, to claim the difference between the time occupied by the 'stab and the value of such composition. No contents' bill.

SPORTSMAN.—The first matter calling for consideration in this report was that of the "grass" hands, who were engaged by the Father—in reality, in the employ of the companionship, and guaranteed nothing from the house. Up to recently they had to get their money through the men they represented, but were now allowed to write their own bills. The Printer had been asked to employ them in the same manner as on other papers, but hesitated on account of the want of room. The system was entirely satisfactory to the Chapel, who forwarded a request that in this respect matters might be allowed to remain as they were, fearing that, should the practice be abolished, four men would be thrown out of casual employment, and the members deprived of taking a holiday whenever they felt so disposed. As in the former cases, we had no alternative but to condemn the system.

The next debatable point had reference to the employment every Sunday night of two semi-time hands after the paper went to press, who were retained for about three hours, in case late news arrived, and received one hour's time each and as much as they could compose on the line. Naturally enough, the copy supplied to them was for the following day's paper; so that, in reality, the 'ship, not the house, were paying for their overtime work. This practice we consider to be wrong, and unhesitatingly condemn it.

The only other point arose out of the manner of producing the contents' bill, which was done by contract, a line hand being put on time for the purpose, the remuneration being satisfactory.

A further matter, not referred to in the report, was inquired into—namely, the manner of dropping insertions in and additions to articles, and it was ascertained that the compositor had to drop such takings in their respective places, the galley being found and the matter opened up by a 'stab hand.

SPORTING LIFE.—A very full report was forthcoming from this companionship, the matters giving rise to discussion being the following : The "grass" hands are termed first (four), second (three), and outside (one). During the holidays the four "first grass" work every night, the rest being guaranteed Tuesdays and Fridays only. Throughout the remainder of the year two only of the "first grass" are guaranteed four nights per week; should the Printer require the services of the other two on those nights, he communicates with the Father, and they are ordered in and expected to occupy their frames, and would be held responsible did they not attend. All the "grass" enjoy the same privileges as the full hands when at work, the grades taking preference for "selling-out" purposes; should no member of the 'ship "sell-out," they are not paid at all. By this system they are precluded from taking other employment.

The system of correcting was then inquired into, and it appeared that frequently the matter was made up by the house, and the compositor had to correct his proof in the column. If divided on two galleys, he would only be expected to correct one portion. We are of opinion that the proofs of all uncorrected matter removed from the galley should be taken over by the house.

A further question arose out of the system of dropping insertions and additions to articles. If a member had to take a galley from the rack, and open out the matter to drop his taking, he would charge three lines; but should the galley be on the random no charge was made, although being responsible for opening out the matter. Although this is a matter which was dealt with by the Committee some years since, we are decidedly of opinion that additions and insertions should be dropped in by the house; or, if done by the piece hands, a charge should be made.

The contents' bill is done on time, at a special rate.

FINANCIAL NEWS.—A satisfactory reply in every respect was received from this companionship, the "grass" hands being engaged by the house, guaranteed a galley per night, lifting with and sharing in the privileges of the frame hands, and only "cut" at the galley when a small paper is published. The contents' bill is done by the 'stab.

FINANCIAL TIMES.—The information supplied by letter being somewhat slight, a deputation was summoned, the evidence thus taken proving that the system was, with two or three exceptions, fairly satisfactory. The unsatisfactory features were :—First. The "grass" hands, two of whom were engaged by the companionship for selling-out purposes, and, as in the previous instances, not guaranteed the galley per night. Formerly, about a dozen "grass" hands were employed, who had recently, at the instigation of the 'ship, been made frame hands—the system being thus practically abolished; and it was at their suggestion that the two men were engaged for the purpose stated. We can only repeat our previously-expressed condemnation of this system, and our opinion that the hands in question should be guaranteed a galley per night.

With respect to holidays (which formerly were paid for, with the exception of holy days), the house was now opened for men to compose the galley, which they did, under a Chapel fine for non-attendance. In connection with this matter, 'stab hands used to be paid their full night's money, but since the opening of the house on holiday occasions they only receive one galley. This is undoubtedly a breach of contract, and we recommend the members in future to claim the full amount.

In this case, also, the contents' bill was done by the 'stab.

FINANCIER.—The report furnished from this companionship was of a most voluminous character, and raised so many debatable issues that it was considered necessary to have before us representatives from the Chapel, and accordingly a deputation attended.

The first matter dealt with had reference to the employment of a turn-over, who had been there six months, and, although a doubt was felt as to his having been properly indentured, we were reassured upon this point by the statements of the deputation. This lad was engaged on a weekly and a fortnightly paper, composing ordinary advertisements (which he completed), and bond advertisements, the fag end of which was frequently given out to the 'ship; and he was kept going while the 'ship slated. He received a stated wage, and a bonus upon whatever he earned over a certain amount. Exception was taken to his employment, on the ground that he was engaged in a morning-paper office, although, at the same time, he was not allowed to lift copy for the daily paper; and a protest had been made against column-figure matter being given to him and the solid portion to the 'ship. Some few years back the Committee had agreed to the retention of an apprentice, provided he was not allowed to work on the daily paper. This understanding has, apparently, been thoroughly observed; but it is extremely doubtful if it was intended to allow others to be introduced. Believing that it was not so intended, and taking all the circumstances into consideration, we are of opinion that after the present lad has served his time, no further apprentices should be allowed.

The question of "grass" hands was then dealt with. They numbered eleven; two of them being guaranteed five nights per week, but invariably working six; the claim of the others to the galley guarantee and a fortnight's notice not being recognized. Recently, however, this matter had been the subject of dispute, and we are in a position to state that their claim has been fully admitted and that the Chapel will, in future, support them in obtaining everything that custom entitles them to receive.

Complaint was also made that no copy-time was announced, so that the men never knew for certain at what hour they were likely to commence their night's work. As a matter of fact, the time for lifting copy did not vary much—perhaps to the extent of half-an-hour; and, although the Printer had been applied to on the subject, he expressed his inability to comply with the wishes of the companionship, on the ground of the difficulty he experienced in obtaining copy. It must be apparent that it is a great convenience and safeguard, not only to a companionship, but to a Printer, to have an announced or fixed time for commencing work, and we desire to recommend that in all cases the following night's copy-time should be given with the "cut."

Several other matters were dealt with, some of which have since been referred to and decided by the Committee; the others, being of a purely local character, need not be referred to here. Two points upon which we were enabled to enlighten the members of the deputation were—first, that the "grass" hands (who had not hitherto been allowed to participate in certain advantageous work) were, by the ruling of the Committee, entitled to share in such work, a promise being given that, for the future, this ruling should be observed; and, secondly, that as an outcome of the Slate Conference, an overtime charge on morning papers could be claimed, a fact of which they appeared to be entirely unaware. It was also pointed out that all work done on a morning paper must be paid for at morning-paper price.

With this office our investigations came to a conclusion. From the replies received in answer to our inquiries, it became apparent that the contents' bill was done in one of two ways—either at the ordinary time-work rate of the office, or at a figure specially agreed upon. After fully considering the question, we would recommend that, as the work is of a special character, it should be paid for by arrangement—at any rate, wherever a member is called off the line for the purpose.

It will be observed that one of the principal subjects of our inquiry has been the method of employing "grass" hands, and it is remarkable that in this respect no two offices are exactly alike. In some the hands are employed by the companionship, for the "selling-out" of full frame hands, and although they would be held responsible in the event of "bridging," and are, indeed, sometimes claimed by the property, no guarantee of a galley is given. Under other systems the "grass" are seldom "cut" at the galley, but are subject to various restrictions, such as not holding certain cases, not lifting certain copy unless specially ordered, lifting earlier or later than the 'ship, etc. Under yet another management, there are three grades of "grass" hands. It must be obvious that this great want of uniformity leads to much unnecessary confusion, if not to breach of trade rules, and in the most favourable circumstances has the practical effect of making a man serve a second apprenticeship.

We, therefore, earnestly recommend that Chapels endeavour to follow the lead set by the *Daily Chronicle* in this matter, by abolishing "grass" hands altogether. We are aware, of course, that in exceptional cases this may be somewhat difficult, but are convinced that generally the alteration will be satisfactory to the companionship, and no inconvenience to the property, since the Printer would always retain control of the "selling-out" slate. Where, however, this is found to be impracticable, the guarantee should be insisted on.

We would, also, strongly urge Chapels to insist upon all work that has been considered by the decision of the Committee, or in accordance with the Scale, to be the property of the 'ship, being given out from the stone, and not to allow of any contract for the production of the same, thus avoiding the establishment of precedents which may be used to the detriment of other companionships.

Although numerous matters have presented themselves requiring careful consideration at our hands, we feel justified in congratulating the members upon the fact that we have been unable to discover any very serious infringement of scale or departures from sound and established custom, and we trust that, wherever it has been found necessary to condemn a particular practice, our recommendations will result in its removal with the least possible amount of friction and the greatest amount of benefit to the members.

We remain, Gentlemen,

On behalf of the Committee,

Yours faithfully,

S. G. M. RICHMOND, *Chairman.*

C. W. BOWERMAN, *Secretary.*

October, 1891.

At a Special General Meeting of the News Department, held 17 December, 1892, a committee was appointed to consider the revision of the News Scale. This body presented its findings in June, 1893. The Report stated that "the chief reason for the appointment of that Committee was to ensure a uniform charge for page advertisements in particular and advertisements generally. . . ."

To mention one point, the full-page advertisement, set in a variety of type sizes, was a recent innovation, for the charging of which the Scale gave no guidance. "A portent had appeared in the advertisement columns of *The Times* during the autumn of 1866: nothing less than the first 'displayed' advertisement. It took an elementary form—namely, the line-by-line repetition of the name of the firm or its product, or both. In 1868 there are numerous instances of columns being given to this form of advertising, set in all cases in the capitals of the news fount."[1]

Advertisements thus arranged in the normal column measure and set in the body fount of the paper caused no particular trouble to the compositor and were charged as column matter. The development, however, of more complicated display, with head-lines set over the breadth of seven columns of text matter in a number of sizes and to varying measures, brought matters to a head. Thus, in 1893, the newspaper compositors demanded the provision of a definite schedule of prices for such work.

The claim of the companionship to produce the whole paper was of importance. The purchase of space in any paper bought with it the right to have the advertisement set at the expense of the vendors of that space. But, with the development of displayed advertising and the planned advertising campaign, where the same advertise-ment was inserted in a number of different journals, it was an advantage to the advertiser or his agent if identical stereotype casts or moulds could be supplied to all publications in which an iden-tical text was to appear. Duplicates of copy and layout, corrections in proof and misprints, were all rendered unnecessary or avoid-able.

Advertisement setting was thus to become the minor specialised activity of a number of general printing offices situated in the neighbourhood of Fleet Street with access to stereotyping plants. Not only were they equipped with display types not to be found in the normal newspaper composing room, but they employed compositors accustomed to setting display matter. The average news hand, constantly employed in picking up small sizes of type with all the speed at his command, was not trained for this class of work. Nor did it pay the newspaper proprietor to install, and place at the disposal of his advertisers, sizes and founts he did not employ in his news columns.

The news compositors' claim to charge for the space occupied by advertisements set and stereotyped outside their own office was based on the long-established custom that the 'ship was engaged to produce the whole of the paper, and that the advertiser was not compelled to have recourse to outside composition.

A Memorial was presented to the proprietors on 28 August, 1893. The propositions contained in it were almost identical with

---

[1] Morison, Stanley, *The English Newspaper*, *op. cit.*, p. 285. The fifth of the examples shown in the appendix to the 1893 Report, and printed in the London Scale to this day, show that the style was still in use at that date. See p. 486.

those contained in the report printed below. Where necessary the latter have been amended to show their final form:—

The News Revision Committee's Report to the Members

Gentlemen,—In accordance with the decision of the Special General Meeting held on December 17th last, the Revision Committee beg to submit the result of their deliberations to the members, who will recollect that although the chief reason for the appointment of that Committee was to ensure a uniform charge for page advertisements in particular and advertisements generally, other questions of equal importance demanded final settlement and recognition by employers— a course which was anything but premature when it is borne in mind that, with the exception of recent regulations as to "cuts" and the definition of a working day on Evening Papers, together with a charge for overtime on all daily papers, the News Scale remains in its original form. The importance and extent of the questions assigned to us may be described by quoting the following extract from the Report adopted by the members at the Special Meeting before referred to, and will, we think, fully account for the apparently protracted inquiry :—

"Upon comparing the composition and methods of the daily papers of to-day with those of the period when the Scale was framed, it will naturally strike most people that it can scarcely be considered up to date. That it has been our guide through the vicissitudes of daily paper printing for so many years testifies to the wisdom of its constructors and to the soundness of its principles; and the framers of the Scale cannot be blamed if they did not provide for the unforeseen. The increase in the number of references to your Committee, and the nature of the questions submitted have led them to think that the time has arrived when certain customs should be legalised by insertion in the Scale, and grievances peculiar to some offices abolished or provided for. They therefore consider that various other matters should also be adjusted at the proposed conference."

ADVERTISEMENTS

While still in agreement with the decision already given on the principal question—viz., that the provisions in the Scale for ordinary measure should equally apply to larger measures—we were impressed with the obvious difficulty of framing a rule to govern all page advertisements; but, with a view to overcome the opposition to this decision on the part of some employers, we have re-examined the question from all points, and as it cannot be admitted that we should forgo the extras when advertisements exceed a certain size, we have endeavoured, after careful consideration, to formulate charges which, it is hoped, will meet with your approval and be acceptable to employers.

All advertisements being the property of the companionship, the compositor should naturally be held responsible for their production, and, notwithstanding the opinion held by some Printers, that only a select few are capable of undertaking the responsibility of such work, which we controvert, it cannot be admitted that the extras which are allowed in the scale for trouble involved in casting off, &c., are therefore to be surrendered to the House. Specimens can be produced to show that even the disputed extra charges have not always compensated for the time occupied; and it is not reasonable to contend that the lucrative nature or extraordinary size of an advertisement should nullify the terms of the Scale.

The following resolution which we now submit for your approval has been conceived in a spirit of equity, and, upon being applied to the specimens accompanying this Report, it will be seen that it is a modification of the instruction of July last; at the same time, it must not be forgotten that the disputed charges have been allowed for several years at other offices :—

All advertisements on first appearance to be the property of the companionship, entire, and when given out to make a certain quantity shall carry the following charges:—Full columns of ordinary measure or measures to be charged as common matter : broken columns to take tabular or table charges, viz.— two columns, one-third extra; three columns, one-half extra; four columns or more, double. When such advertisements are made up by the House all extras to be charged as above, but a proper allowance to be made according to the time occupied. When an advertisement consists of full columns of ordinary measure or measures the same shall be made up by the House; or, if made up by the 'ship, a time charge to be made at a rate per hour not less than that paid to ordinary time hands.

In agreement with the first portion of the foregoing resolution, and considering that a 'ship is engaged to produce the paper—a principle which has been recognized on some papers—we contend that *all* advertisements, however executed, should be charged on the first insertion; therefore the following resolution has been framed to meet a style of advertising which has recently developed in a remarkable manner, and, if not provided for, would be a serious matter for some companionships, considering the number of times advertisements of this class are repeated :—

That all block advertisements should be charged by the companionship according to scale on their first appearance.

The three following resolutions are simply a codification of well-established customs :—

Advertisements set in larger type than that used in the news portion of the paper to be charged in the type in which the major part of the news portion is composed; but where advertisements are set in more than one of the types used in the paper the smallest type in such advertisement to be the type in which it shall be charged. This to apply to all advertisements, whether set up as ordinary articles or otherwise.

All advertisements, tables, or text (or portions of such) in which the corrections or alterations in form amount to one-half, to be considered fresh matter.

Introductory matter not exceeding five lines (inclusive of the head) shall take the same charge as the body of the article to which it belongs, whether the same be given out as a separate taking or in conjunction with a portion of such article.

BOXING, HALF-WHITES, ETC.

To ensure uniformity in the charges for boxing and the trouble involved when half-whites are used in brace matter, we propose to insert the following in the Scale :—

That sixpence extra be charged for each single-rule boxing, irrespective of size.

That one line extra be charged for each pair of half-whites.

That all diagonal, curved, diamond-shaped, and matter of a similar character be charged not less than double.

That where side-heads, first words, or speakers' names in articles or paragraphs are set out of a general case, a charge of one line be made on all takings containing three such headings or words, or less.

RUN-ON NAMES, FIGURES, ETC.

For some time past it has been considered that this kind of composition should carry an extra charge, especially as in some instances the copy is given out unprepared. Frequently the compositor has to repeat the headings after each item in tabular copy, and in other cases names have to be transposed and contracted. We contend that although such matter has now become common in daily papers it ought not to be regarded as common matter. In this view we are supported by the Provincial Trade, and upon their Scale we have based the following proposition :—

That matter consisting of names run-on, names and figures, with fractions and signs (as for example—prize lists, balance-sheets, *Gazette* news, programmes, mining reports, and similar matter) or italics shall, when exceeding three lines, be charged one-third extra.

SHORT TAKINGS

It being our opinion that it is altogether erroneous to suppose that work is expedited by giving out two or three line takings, and believing that, as a rule, it occupies no more time to complete longer takes, we have arrived at the following conclusion as much with the object of putting an end to an irritating and, as we think, unnecessary system, as to compensate the compositor for the trouble and loss of time involved in casting off, giving and taking words, booking, and walking to and from the random, which is now carried to an immoderate degree :—

That one line extra be charged on all takings under seven lines when the compositor has to make even; but no "take" shall be of less value than threepence.

LIFTING PREFERENCE COPY

In order to supply proofs of articles required immediately, it is a common practice in some offices to order the suspension of copy in hand, so that certain copy shall be taken up at once; and on some papers it is not an uncommon occurrence for a compositor to have even three takings in hand. At one office where this system is in vogue a charge of three lines is allowed each time a taking is suspended, the justice of which induces us to propose that the following should be inserted in the Scale :—

That when compositors [on Morning Papers are] called upon to stop the taking in hand and lift preference copy, a charge of three lines should be made.

TIME WORK

Another matter claiming attention is the lack of uniformity in the payment for time work, the spirit of Clause 5 not being generally acknowledged. As a rule, time hands are selected for their ability, but considering the high pressure at which news hands have to work nowadays, whether on composition or in assisting to "get the formes away," we submit that the remuneration is insufficient for such work if advantage is taken of the literal interpretation of this clause. Some Printers recognize the value of the work done by their time hands by allowing more than the minimum rate, and in view of the responsible nature of the work and the disproportion to the amount earned while on composition we think it only just to propose the following :—

That any piece hand required to go upon time shall be paid at the minimum rate of 1s. 6d. per hour [on Morning Papers, and 1s. 3d. on Evening Papers].

All composition done upon time to be charged by the 'ship.

SLATING

Some interesting and instructive information has been forthcoming from different offices as to the amount of standing time, average earnings, &c., of line hands. In spite of the promise made by the representatives of the employers at the Slate Conference four years ago, the same state of things appears to exist in a varying degree in the majority of houses as at that time. But in the opinion at least of the hands engaged, many offices could, with a little trouble, be worked much more smoothly, and with almost an absence of that demoraliser of companionships—the system of "slate and take." A day or night's work on a London paper now consists of short "takings" and "slates" of varying length; or, pulling out for a couple of hours, and then spending a great proportion of each succeeding hour on the slate. To this rule there are, of course, a few exceptions; but the idea is pretty general that, payment for slate once enforced, arrangements would be made for copy to be supplied in a more regular and systematic way. The experience of the *Daily News* Companionship goes far to prove that contention, where piece hands are paid for standing time, less a certain deduction for exigencies of working. As a matter of fact, however, the advantage is found in what may be termed the "closing up" of the night's work rather than in any direct monetary gain, but tending to the comfort of the 'ship, the payment for standing time at the office referred to during the past nine months being practically *nil*. Being of opinion that the question is one of management, we therefore propose :—

That slating be paid for at the rate of a quarter per hour.

That when the "line" is on less than five hours, *all* slating time to be charged; five hours and less than seven, thirty minutes to be allowed to the House; seven hours and more, one hour allowed. This to apply to Morning Papers only.

That no charge be made for slating on the first edition of Evening Papers, provided that the "line" does not exceed four hours; the House to be allowed at the rate of ten minutes' slate per hour on after editions.

GUARANTEE

With regard to the Guarantee Question, although the financial papers do not appear to be suffering from galley "cuts" to the extent they were twelve months ago, it is urged that, so long as the rule stands as at present, we shall always find advantage taken of it. The practice now adopted by many Houses of giving papers varying daily in size has, no doubt, tended to increase the strength of the 'ships, and the cancelling of orders for large-sized papers often places a Printer in a fix, as he cannot keep his large staff going. While standing time is not a financial consideration to the House this need not trouble him—he can cut a small section at a galley and the others drag along; but if payment for slate becomes law there would possibly be a resort to galley "cuts" more frequently, and the line hand's condition would scarcely be improved. An increase of the guarantee might not remedy everything, but it would at least take away the power of cutting a portion of a 'ship for a so-called night's work at the miserable sum of 3s. 1od. It may be argued that raising the guarantee will in some offices cause the discharge of hands—a result which would be a great misfortune; but such action is most unlikely, as the present tendency is rather to keep a large 'ship to produce the bulk of a paper in the shortest possible time. These and other views of the subject having been duly considered, and bearing in mind that one of the rules in Provincial Scales provides "that 36 hours' *composition* per week be guaranteed to piece hands on Morning Papers (not less than five hours to be *worked* on any one night)," we have come to the following conclusion :—

That the guarantee of one galley on Morning Papers be increased to one galley and a half.

NON-PUBLISHING DAYS

Taking into consideration the amount of money spent by our Society in establishing the principle of payment for compulsory holidays, we propose that the following should form part of the Scale, in accordance with well-established custom :—

That one galley be charged on all days on which the House is compulsorily closed.

OVERTIME

As regards the limit of a day's work on Morning Papers, the evidence given in support of the previous questions pointed rather to a lack of work and a decrease in the average earnings than otherwise; and, in view of the proposed increase of the guarantee and the payment for slate, we do not think it advisable to interfere with the hours of working on Morning Papers. That it should be found necessary to formulate a rule to provide for an excess of work appears for the moment superfluous; but the recent production of certain weekly journals by Evening Paper 'ships renders it necessary, on behalf of those who have been compelled to work an unreasonable number of hours, and likewise in the interests of those who would be glad to obtain employment, to propose that the overtime rate should be increased after a certain time, believing that where excessive hours are unavoidable the present rate is inadequate, and, on the other hand, that the higher rate would be the means of bringing about a more equal distribution of work. It is therefore proposed :—

That overtime on Evening Papers be charged, after nine working hours, at the following rates :—3*d.* per hour extra for the first three hours, and 6*d.* per hour for each following hour.

MEAL TIMES

With few exceptions it is now the custom to allow a supper-time on Morning Papers, and experience having removed the doubts not long since entertained that a temporary cessation of work would be impracticable, we confidently anticipate that the following resolution will be agreed to :—

That a regular meal-time of not less than fifteen minutes be taken on all Morning Papers, and if called upon to work during that time, or more than thirty minutes beyond it, 3*d.* extra to be charged.

The tendency to call "copy" on some Evening Papers at an exceptionally early hour has led us to adopt the following resolution, which is in accordance with the custom of all other trades :—

That when the "line" on Evening Papers is put on before 7 a.m., a breakfast time be taken from 8 to 8.30. [In the event of hands being called upon to continue work during that period, 3*d.* extra to be charged.]

UTILISING EVENING PAPER MATTER

Considering the advantage gained by proprietors in lifting matter from one paper to another, it is thought that a slight compensation should be made to those affected by the system; therefore it is proposed :—

That where matter is set up at Weekly or Evening Paper price and afterwards inserted in a Morning Paper, the difference in price per galley be charged by the Morning Paper 'ship.[1]

PRICE PER THOUSAND

Although an advance on the Book Scale was granted both in 1866 and 1872, an endeavour made on behalf of News hands in 1874 to obtain threepence per hour extra for Sunday work and an increase of one halfpenny in the price per thousand proved unsuccessful. While progress has been made in the Book Department and in all other trades, the News hand, whose occupation deprives him of most of the comforts enjoyed by others, still works, with slight modifications, by the original Scale. Bearing in mind that a Morning Paper compositor is unable to enjoy a complete day's recreation during the week unless at his own expense, whereas other workmen have the Saturday half-holiday and the whole of Sunday, we seriously considered the advisability of proposing a substantial charge for Sunday work, but the idea was eventually dismissed in favour of an increase in the price per thousand, which is only logical when it is remembered that, although no increase has been made in the News Scale as originally framed in 1810, a third advance of one halfpenny per thousand was granted for bookwork in 1891. We now propose :—

That the price per thousand on all founts on Morning or Evening Papers above nonpareil be the present price of nonpareil—that is, 10*d.* and 9½*d.* respectively.*

* This proposition was redrafted and took the following form : "That an increase of a halfpenny on the present price per thousand to be paid on all founts on Daily Papers."

[1] This proposition was not included in the Memorial.

The absence of specific provision in the Scale for most of the foregoing matters, which are now common to daily papers, but not uniformly recognized, clearly shows the necessity for re-opening the Daily Paper Scale. As before observed, "the frequent application of the final clause of the Scale to a certain class of work is much to be regretted, as in some instances the charge agreed to might be regarded by the Printer as a concession, and, on the other hand, the compositor would probably consider he was only receiving that which he was justly entitled to, and which should have been indisputably laid down in the Scale." It has even been contended that certain charges could not be allowed because they were not mentioned in the Scale, and with the object of supplying such deficiencies and removing grievances which have almost been regarded as unalterable because of their long standing, we have formulated proposals the necessity and fairness of which will, we trust, ensure their recognition and final adoption by all concerned.

We remain, Gentlemen, yours faithfully,

THE REVISION COMMITTEE

June 28th, 1893.

No agreement was reached until almost a year after the submission of the Memorial. The newspaper proprietors had insisted that, before any discussion could be held, a Scale of Prices for machine composition must be arranged. The compilation of such a document delayed the negotiations by many months.

While no increase in the price per 1,000 ens was granted, the compositors received a number of important concessions, since the composition of advertisements in the office was made extremely profitable to them. In addition, they were now permitted to charge on their first appearance, for the space occupied by advertisements set by outside labour.

[DOCUMENT CXVIII]

London Society of Compositors (News Department). New and Amended Rules agreed to at a Conference between the Representatives of the London Daily Newspaper Proprietors and of the London Society of Compositors, held at Anderton's Hotel on June 7th, 1894.

1. Advertisements, or portions of advertisements, set in the width of the page, or a broken measure of the paper (excepting single or double column advertisements, broken measures in which shall be charged in accordance with Scale, sections 48 to 51),[1] and which advertisements contain type smaller than Long Primer, to be charged one-fourth extra. Matter of the ordinary width to take no extra charge. All display lines

[1] *i.e.*, as table, tabular and column matter.

to be marked in the type in which they are to be set, and such advertisements to be made up by the house and charged as they appear. (See specimens.)

[It is to be understood that in the event of an insufficiency of display type, compositors will be allowed to "turn" for deficient sorts, the same to be rectified by the house.]

2. All complete block advertisements to be charged by the companionship as common matter, in the body type of the paper, on first appearance.

3. All let-in blocks in single columns (viz., blocks with matter running down the side) to be charged one-fourth extra. When matter which has already been charged is given out to fit such blocks, the extra not to apply.

4. Advertisements set in larger type than that used in the news portion of the paper to be charged in the type in which the major part of the news portion is composed; but where advertisements are set in more than one of the types used in the paper, the smallest type in such advertisement to be the type in which it shall be charged. Blocks forming part of such advertisement to take the same charge. This to apply to all advertisements, whether set up as ordinary articles or otherwise.

5. The guarantee of one galley on Morning Papers to be one galley and a half for all piece-hands.[1]

6. One galley to be charged on all days on which the house is compulsorily closed.

7. Any piece-hand required to go upon time shall be paid at the minimum rate of 1s. 3d. per hour on Morning Papers and 1s. 1d. on Evening Papers throughout the day.[2]

8. No composition to be done upon time (corrections excepted), except in case of emergency, when such composition shall be charged by the companionship, less the time occupied by the 'stab.

9. When compositors on Morning Papers are called upon to stop the taking in hand and lift preference copy, a charge of three lines shall be made.

10. A regular meal-time of not less than fifteen minutes to be allowed on all Morning Papers, and if called upon to work more than thirty minutes beyond the supper "cut," threepence extra to be charged.

11. When the "line" on Evening Papers is systematically put on before 7 a.m., a breakfast-time shall be allowed from 8 to 8.30. In the event of hands being called upon to continue work during that period, threepence extra to be charged.

---

[1] *i.e.,* 5s. 9d. per night as opposed to 3s. 10d.
[2] Raised from 11½d. per hour on Morning Papers and 10½d. per hour on Evening Papers.

12. Overtime on Evening Papers to be charged, after nine working hours, at threepence per hour. Half-an-hour's refreshment time to be allowed at the expiration of nine hours and after every subsequent three hours when work has to be continued.

13. All advertisements, tables, or text (or portions of such) in which the corrections or alterations in form amount to one-half (see specimens), to be considered fresh matter. In estimating half corrections in tables, only those columns in which half the figures have to be altered shall be reckoned against the bulk. All Stock Exchange or other tables that appear daily to be excepted. Advertisements in which the additions amount to three-quarters of the whole to be the property of the companionship.

14. Introductory matter not exceeding five lines in depth (inclusive of the head) shall take the same charge as the body of the article to which it belongs, whether the same be given out as a separate taking or in conjunction with a portion of such article.

15. One line extra to be charged for each pair of half-whites.

16. Sixpence extra to be charged for each single-rule boxing, irrespective of size.

17. All diagonal, curved, diamond-shaped, and matter of a similar character, to be charged not less than double.

18. Where side-heads, first words, or speakers' names in articles or paragraphs are set out of a general case, a charge of one line to be made for every three such side-headings or words, or less.

Then were printed eight pages of examples of advertisement settings. The blocks from which the following illustrations are printed have been loaned by kind permission of the London Society of Compositors. They are used to this day in the Scale of Prices issued by the Society.

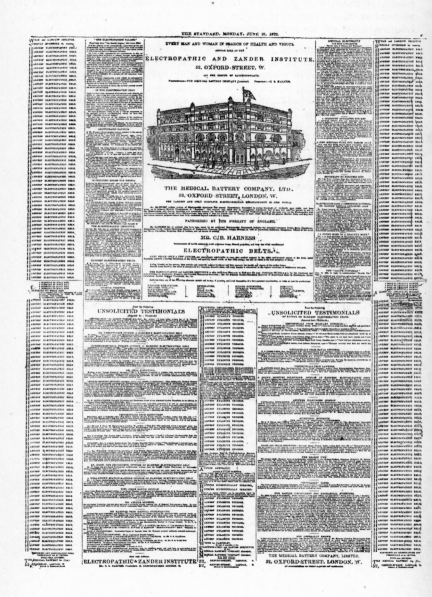

THE FINANCIAL NEWS, WEDNESDAY, MAY 25, 1892.—SIX PAGES.

THE LONDON AND CHICAGO CONTRACT CORPORATION, LIMITED, IN LONDON, AND THE LONDON AND CHICAGO CONTRACT CORPORATION, LIMITED, THE ILLINOIS TRUST AND SAVINGS BANK, THE AMERICAN TRUST AND SAVINGS BANK, AND FOREMAN BROTHERS, BANKERS, IN CHICAGO, WILL RECEIVE SUBSCRIPTIONS FOR THE UNDERMENTIONED CAPITAL

THE SUBSCRIPTION LIST WILL CLOSE ON OR BEFORE MONDAY, MAY 30, 1892

THE
INTERNATIONAL PACKING AND PROVISION COMPANY,
LIMITED.
HAM, BACON, AND PORK CURERS, PACKERS, &c.

Incorporated under the Companies Acts of Great Britain and Ireland, 1862 to 1890.

AMALGAMATION OF THE IMPORTANT PACKING BUSINESSES OF THE INTERNATIONAL PACKING COMPANY, THE T. E WELLS COMPANY, THE ALLERTON PACKING COMPANY, JOHN CUDAHY, J. C. HATELY, HATELY BROTHERS, AND JONES AND STILES.

SHARE CAPITAL   £850,000.

DIVIDED AS FOLLOWS:—

THE FINANCIAL NEWS, WEDNESDAY, NOVEMBER 9, 1892.—SIX PAGES.

GEORGE GREGORY AND COMPANY.

FROM BIRTH AND PROGRESS, WITH SOME ACCOUNT OF THEIR MANAGEMENT, POLICY, AND SURROUNDINGS.

GREGORY'S.—THE PICCADILLY CIRCUS BRANCH OFFICE.

GREGORY'S.—THE PRIVATE ROOM, HEAD OFFICE.

GREGORY'S.—THE OXFORD CIRCUS BRANCH OFFICE.

GREGORY'S.—THE HEAD OFFICE.

GREGORY'S.—THE BRIGHTON BRANCH OFFICE.

GREGORY'S.—THE SAFE, &c., HEAD OFFICE.

GREGORY'S.—THE HASTINGS BRANCH OFFICE.

THE DAILY TELEGRAPH, WEDNESDAY, NOVEMBER 19, 1890.

THE SECOND "BURNAY" PORT SALE

NOVEMBER 23, 24, 25.

ORDER OF SALE.

MESSRS. SOUTHARD AND CO., SWORN BROKERS

MESSRS. HENRY BURNAY AND CO., OF LISBON,

COMMERCIAL SALE ROOMS, MINCING LANE, E.C.

EXTRACT FROM THE "TIMES," MARCH 14, 1876.

A GRAND TRIAL OF SEVENTEEN THOUSAND FOUR HUNDRED PIPES,

THE DAILY TELEGRAPH, THURSDAY, JUNE 16, 1892.

LANCASHIRE, DERBYSHIRE and EAST COAST RAILWAY.

INCORPORATED 1891.

NORTH SEA

The Subscription List will Close at four o'clock To-morrow (Friday), 17th inst., for Town, and twelve o'clock noon on Saturday, 18th inst., for Country.

THE LANCASHIRE, DERBYSHIRE, & EAST COAST RAILWAY COMPANY.

(INCORPORATED BY ACT OF PARLIAMENT, 54 AND 55 VICT.: C. 189.

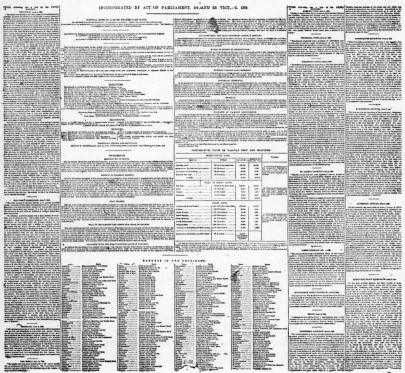

CHAPTER XIX

THE FIRST COMPOSING MACHINE SCALES

The introduction of the Young-Delcambre composing machine was recorded in the Annual Report of the L.S.C. for 1845.[1] Apart from this isolated notice, the problem of mechanical composition does not appear to have been mentioned in any L.S.C. document until at least forty-five years later. Although from 1866 onwards composing machines were to be found at work in the provinces, it was not until 1890 that the question of their use in London became one of vital importance to either employers or employed. The following extract introduces us to a problem of outstanding technical and economic importance, the solution of which revolutionized both the general and newspaper printing trades of this country.

[DOCUMENT CXIX] [2]

No subject of greater importance could well engage the attention of a trade organization than that which has necessitated the convening of the present meeting—namely the attempt to substitute machine for hand labour. During the past fifty years rumour has from time to time been busily engaged in magnifying the capabilities of the various inventions which have been designed ostensibly for the purpose of supplanting the hand compositor; and looking at the number and variety of machines which have during that period been introduced, and the signal failure which has attended the various and costly experiments, it is, perhaps, excusable that members should have allowed themselves to be lulled into a false sense of security against the prospective competition of machinery, and to feel that, come what may, they have nothing to fear from its attacks. Now, however, and for the first time in the history of the Society, the general Trade is confronted with the same problem that other industries have had to solve, a demand having been made for the fixing of a Scale of Prices and Conditions of Working to govern machine work, which shall be applicable to the Trade as a whole. Happily, as far as can be judged at present, machinery can only be partially used, and for certain classes of work, although looking at the marvellous developments of recent years, it is impossible to say what the future may bring forth.

[1] See p. 261.
[2] *Report of the Committee to a Special Delegate Meeting held December 14, 1895, and convened to take into consideration the Provisional Agreement re Scale and Conditions to govern Machine Composition. The result of a Conference between the Employers and the Society's Representatives.* (MS. Report. L.S.C. Collection.)

For some time, however, an unmistakable desire has been evinced by the employers to try machinery, although it is held in many quarters that, when the cost of the machine or the royalty (if on hire), with the various incidental expenses are taken into account, the saving in comparison with hand composition is *nil*. Whether this be so or not, the fact remains that machines are being introduced into different offices, and, once introduced, have a disagreeable habit of remaining. Therefore, by common consent, it will be agreed that the time has arrived when a workable Scale should be fixed, enabling the operator to earn a good wage, while at the same time protecting as far as possible the interests of the case hand.

At this point a brief account of the historical development of composing machinery in this country during the nineteenth century may be useful. The earliest recorded proposal for mechanical composition is contained in the British patent No. 4664 of 1822, granted to Dr. Church, an American.

"The types are arranged in 'files' in a case at the top of the machine, each file being directly over a slit in a horizontal frame. One of a 'number of jacks' protrudes through each of these slits, each jack being connected with a key in a manner somewhat 'similar to the jacks and keys of an harpsichord.' On the depression of any particular key, the upper part of its jack pushes forward the undermost type of the file into a 'race,' to the centre of which it is swept by collectors, so as to come under the beak of a lever by which it is pushed down an aperture answering the purpose of a composing stick."[1]

The system invented by Church was adopted by the majority of the inventors of type-setting machinery in this country during the nineteenth century. There is no evidence to show that Church ever actually built a machine, but twenty years later, in 1840, Messrs. Young and Delcambre patented and constructed the first composing machine to be put to work in London or elsewhere.[2] The Young-Delcambre machine attracted to itself the hostility of the London compositors, who feared for their employment. It was withdrawn from use in London after an intermittent trial extending over a couple of years.[3] Mechanical deficiencies militated against its use as much as the antagonism of the workers.

Of the multitude of machines invented, patented and offered

---

[1] *Abridgments of Specifications relating to Printing* (London, 1859), p. 159. *Cf.* Johnson, J., *Typographia* (London, 1824), vol. II, p. 545; Hansard, T. C., *Typographia* (London, 1825), p. 665.

[2] *Abridgments, op. cit.*, p. 216. Patent No. 8428.

[3] *The Compositors' Chronicle* (London, Sept., 1840—August, 1843) contains much interesting information on the subject.

to a sceptical printing trade between the years 1850-90, four only need be mentioned in these pages, those designed by Messrs. Hattersley, Kastenbein and Thorne respectively, and the Linotype, the invention of Ottmar Mergenthaler.[1] The Hattersley and Kastenbein machines incorporated many of the principles originally suggested by Church. They were loaded with foundry type, which was arranged in magazines and released into the composing stick by a keyboard operator. Justification was effected by hand, either by the operator or a second workman. Distribution required a separate machine or, alternatively, could be accomplished by hand in the normal fashion. The Thorne incorporated in its mechanism an automatic distributor, for which the type required to be specially nicked.

The Linotype machine was constructed upon an entirely different plan. Matrices took the place of movable types in the storage magazines. The keyboard operator assembled a line of matrices which, combined with a casting apparatus, produced a solid "slug" or "line o' type." Justification was automatic, the matrices for each word being spaced with expanding wedge-shaped space bands. The problem of distribution did not arise, since the slugs were put back in the metal pot after printing. The matrices were automatically returned to the magazines, ready for use.

The Hattersley was first in the field. Between 1866, when two models were put to work at the *Eastern Morning News* office in Hull,[2] and 1891 when they made their first appearance in a London newspaper office, that of the *Daily News*, the Hattersley machines found their most extended use in the provinces, particularly in the North of England.[3]

The Kastenbein machine, much the same as the Hattersley in

---

[1] The best technical descriptions of these and other composing machines are to be found in, Legros, L. A., and Grant, J. C., *Typographical Printing-Surfaces: the Technology and Mechanism of their Production* (London, 1916). See also Herrmann, C., *Geschichte der Setzmaschine und ihre Entwicklung* (Vienna, 1900); Thompson, J. S., *History of Composing Machines* (Chicago, 1904); Höhne, O., *Geschichte der Setzmaschinen* (Leipzig, 1925).

[2] *The Printers' Register*, February, 1866. In the April issue there was a note to the effect that there was a machine at Reuter's. See also Hunt, W., *Then and Now; or, Fifty Years of Newspaper Work* (Hull, 1887).

[3] In 1877 the Hattersley machine was in use on the *Southport Daily News, North Cheshire Herald, Midland Gazette* (Sutton-in-Ashfield), also at the office of John Bellows in Gloucester. By 1890 models were also installed at the offices of the *Liverpool Courier, Liverpool Daily Post* and *Newcastle Daily Chronicle*. This list does not claim completeness. Its purpose is to show the class of office operating the machine.

design, was installed at *The Times* in 1872, although some years passed before its use at Printing House Square was other than experimental.[1] With one or two unimportant exceptions the Kastenbein was not used elsewhere in this country.[2] Since the composing room of *The Times* was closed to members of the London Society of Compositors, the rates of payment for operating the machine were outside the jurisdiction of the Society. Until August, 1890, when the *Sportsman* bought the Thorne machine, which was already in use for the *Manchester Guardian* and *Bradford Observer*, *The Times* alone among the London daily newspapers used mechanical composition. This would explain the complete lack of L.S.C. documents dealing with composing machine questions before 1891.

The Linotype machine, first used on the *New York Tribune* in 1886 and in England for the *Newcastle Chronicle* in 1889, was soon to supplant the machines in which the storage and manipulation of movable types were the main features, for it proved itself equally efficient and distinctly more economical. Although the practicability of type-setting machines had been proved, the savings effected by them, compared with hand composition, were not firmly established. The Hattersley machine, in particular, was handicapped by the want of an economically run distributing apparatus, such as the automatic appliance on the Thorne. In the provinces, where composing machines were in use long before being generally adopted in London, cheap boy or girl labour was often employed exclusively for distribution. This practice was impossible in London, since under no circumstances could it be countenanced by the London Society of Compositors. The difficulty of obtaining economic distribution therefore prevented the use of the Hattersley machine in London at a time when the machine was making headway in the provinces. When, in December, 1891, the proprietors of the *Daily News* put in six Hattersleys, and sought to employ female labour on the distributing machines, there was an immediate and successful protest from the L.S.C. It may be remarked that these early composing machines do not appear to have found a use in any of the leading provincial book-printing houses. Their employment was largely confined to the production of local newspapers.

---

[1] See *The Times*, 3 July, 1872.

[2] On the Continent the Kastenbein was used by the Agence Havas in Paris, *L'Echo du Parlement* at Brussels. In the U.S.A. it was installed at the office of the *Christian Union*, New York. (Advertisement in the *Printers' Register*, 1877.)

The Typographical Association had been compelled to consider rates of payment for operating composing machinery as early as 1877, when the *Southport Daily News* was in the process of building up the first large Hattersley plant, a modest start having been made there in 1874. In 1891, when the London Society of Compositors was engaged with the first two disputes over composing machine questions that had arisen in its area, and confined to two offices only, the Typographical Association held a conference on the composing machine situation at Manchester, attended by forty delegates from Bradford, Liverpool, Manchester, Newcastle and Nottingham.[1] It is evident from the report of the proceedings that the increasingly widespread use of mechanical composition was disturbing the normal conditions of the trade. It was established that, wherever machines were installed, there was a tendency for the operators to be kept in copy at the expense of the case hands. It could thus be taken as a rule that a reduction of hands followed the installation of the machine. Equally disturbing was the difficulty in arriving at an equitable method of settling the operators' wages. The various makes of machine differed in productivity, and the Typographical Association felt itself obliged to combat the custom of paying a bonus to operators on the establishment for all composition effected above a certain weekly minimum, since they received sums out of all proportion to those earned by the case hands.

In 1893 the Typographical Association again discussed the composing machine question at the Delegate Meeting held at Sheffield. Upon this occasion the Secretary of the London Society of Compositors, Mr. C. W. Bowerman, informed the assembly of recent developments in London. His remarks will serve to introduce the series of documents relating to the formation of the first London Scales for composing machines in both the book and news sections of the trade.

[DOCUMENT CXX]

In London they had not had much experience of piecework. In fact they had practically none at present; but they had not been able to resist the demand of the employers, where these machines had been introduced, the demand to formulate a piece scale.[2] The first office with which they had negotiations was the *Sportsman*, where the Thorne machines were

---

[1] *Conference on the Working of Composing Machines*. Report published by the Typographical Association (Manchester, 1891).

[2] Piece-work encouraged fast composition and large outputs, making the heavy cost of installing the machines an economic proposition.

tried. They were started on 'stab—a very low 'stab, he was sorry to say—but all were entirely in the dark as to what the machines were capable of doing, and met them rather too fairly. After they had been running twelve months, the proprietors of the *Sportsman* made a claim for the piece system. Their association resisted it, but the proprietors put up their backs, and insinuated that the reason they declined to frame a piece scale was that they were antagonistic to the machines, and would not allow the men to show what they were capable of doing. A piece scale was framed which did not meet with approval; a split took place, and the house was closed to the Society. The next case was the *Daily News*. There they had the most liberal 'stab terms for fifteen or sixteen months. At the end of that time they were met with the same demand for a piece scale. They framed a scale as high as possible, but not so high that the employers could very well reject it. But after the scale had been agreed to between the Executive and the proprietors, the men stepped in and declined to accept it, alleging that the rate was too low. The Executive were, perhaps, not very sorry that they did decline. There was a certain amount of friction caused by this, but at length it was tried. This scale had only been in operation for a very short time, so they were not able to give any very definite opinion on the subject.[1]

To the information given by Bowerman must be added the fact that the proprietors of the *Daily News* made a determined but unsuccessful attempt to introduce girl and boy labour for distribution purposes. The minimum of 38s. per week of 48 hours eventually agreed upon for this class of work was the same as paid to compositors on 'stab in weekly paper offices, who were required to work fifty-four hours, as in the general trade. The sum of 4d. per 1,000 for night work on the Hattersley was slightly higher than the prices prevailing in the provinces, where 3¼d. for Bourgeois and 3d. for smaller sizes was paid.

The document printed below, a handbill circulated upon the occasion of the dispute with the *Sportsman* office, is apparently the first issued by the London Society of Compositors specifically relating to a composing machine question:—

[DOCUMENT CXXI]

To the Workmen of the United Kingdom

Fellow Workers,—

We beg to call your attention to the fact that the Proprietors of the "*Sportsman*" have *Locked Out their Union Compositors*, and have replaced them by Non-Unionists, consequently this paper is now produced exclusively by *Non-Union Labour*.

The ostensible reason assigned for this high-handed proceeding is that

---

[1] *Extracts from Report of the Delegate Meeting of the Typographical Association . . . Sheffield*, 1893. (London, 1893, published by the Linotype Co., Ltd., an early piece of Linotype composition.)

a small strap or two about half an inch wide were said to be cut, although it is well known that the Union compositors had left the office several hours before. If anything of the sort happened, which is doubtful, it was evidently done for the purpose of prejudicing our Union, and enabling the Proprietors to find a pretext for severing their connection with us, which they have been threatening to do for years past.

The real cause of the *Lock-Out* is that *we decline to submit to a reduction of wages* in order that the Thorne type-setting machine may prove a source of profit to the Proprietors of the "*Sportsman*." The London daily papers are produced in accordance with a *scale of prices mutually agreed to* by representative employers and workmen, and while no advance of wages has for years been obtained by the compositors employed on such papers, we are naturally not inclined to submit to a reduction, and deny the right of either party to break an agreement thus entered into.

We shall probably be charged with hostility towards machinery; but we challenge the Proprietors to publish the whole of the correspondence that has taken place between this Society and themselves with respect to the introduction of the Thorne machine. So far from opposing it, we have gone out of our way to meet the wishes of the Proprietors to the fullest possible extent, until we have been compelled to decline the prices offered, as such prices are far below those already paid, which only enable our members, owing to the peculiar nature of the work, to earn a fair living wage, looking to the fact that such work is performed at night. If machinery is to be introduced, we claim a right to benefit by its introduction; but if it can only be made to pay at the expense of those who have served an apprenticeship to a trade, we submit that in such an event no real advantage is to be derived. This and other machines, we may add, are at present being worked by our members in other houses.

We have the best reason for believing that the *Proprietors of the* "*Sportsman*" *fear anything in the nature of a Boycott;* but we venture to appeal to all who have the welfare of the Workers at heart to bear in mind that the *Compositors on the* "*Sportsman*" *have been Locked Out after many years' faithful service* in some cases, and that there are *other Sporting Papers* produced exclusively by Union Labour, which, under the circumstances, deserve to be supported *in preference* to the "*Sportsman*," the Proprietors of which are sparing neither time, trouble, nor expense, to injure the cause of Trade Unionism, in order to still further enrich themselves at the expense of the Workers.

By order of the Committee,

C. J. DRUMMOND, F.S.S., *Secretary.*

London Society of Compositors,
  3, Raquet Court, Fleet Street,
    London, E.C.

February, 1892.

The statistics printed on pp. 498–99 formed part of a confidential memorandum sent by the Executive Committee of the Typographical Association to their Representative Council. Although undated the document may be ascribed to the year 1893-4.

The Linotype machine was already sweeping the field. There were at least 250 models known to be at work in the provinces, as against thirty-three Hattersleys (of which twenty-three were in Liverpool) and fourteen Thornes. Although the returns respecting the number of case hands employed in each office are not complete, it will be seen that, while there were at least 1,445 men employed prior to the introduction of machinery, their number had since dropped by 564, or approximately a third, to 881. The dismay with which the men greeted the introduction of composing machinery is understandable.

In August, 1893, following the publication of the Report [1] of the L.S.C. delegates appointed to revise the News Scale, a Memorial requesting an advance in prices was sent to the employers. The latter declared that they would not enter into negotiations unless the men's representatives were prepared to discuss the formation of a Scale for machine composition.

The composing machine Scale here printed, the first to be drawn up for the London trade, formed part of a document entitled *New and Amended Rules agreed to at a Conference between the Representatives of the London Daily Newspaper Proprietors and of the London Society of Compositors held at Anderton's Hotel on June 7th, 1894.*[2]

Prices for Linotype composition were scheduled for the first time. The *Globe* led the way in adopting this machine, the *Financial Times* following suit shortly afterwards. These installations took place before the end of 1893. By the middle of 1894 Linotypes were used in half-a-dozen offices, including that of the *Daily Telegraph*. It was not long before all the London daily papers were set by this type of machine.

[DOCUMENT CXXII]

COMPOSING MACHINES

1. All skilled operators—*i.e.*, compositors, justifiers, and distributors, as distinct from attendants or labourers—shall be members of the London Society of Compositors, preference being given to members of the companionship into which the machines are introduced. Distribution to be paid at a minimum rate of 38s. per week of 48 hours, day work.

2. A Probationary Period of three months shall be allowed, the operator to receive his average weekly earnings for the previous three months. During this period he shall not undertake piece-work.

---

[1] The Report is printed on p. 473 *et seq.*
[2] The rules affecting hand compositors are printed on p. 479 *et seq.*

Name of Office	Number and Description of Machine	How Worked, Piece or 'Stab	Hours Worked		Rate of Wages: Piece per 1000 ens		Rate of Wages: 'Stab		Average Earnings for Four Weeks		No. of Operators Employed		No. of Apprentices Employed on Machines	No. of Case Hands Employed	
			Day	Night	Day	Night	Day	Night	Day	Night	Day	Night		Prior to Introduction of Machinery	Present Time
					d.	d.	s. d.	s. d.	s. d.	s. d.					
Accrington: *Observer* and *Times*	1 Lino.	'Stab.	..	..	..	..	40 0	..	..	..	1	..	1	3	1
Bath: *Chronicle* ..	2 Linos.	..	..	..	..	..	..	..	..	..	..	..	..	..	..
Belfast: *News Letter* and *Evening Telegraph*	10 Linos.	Piece.	9	8	2½ & 2¾	3	..	..	60 0	60 0	6	6	2	78	54
Blackpool: *Times*	2 Linos.	'Stab.	55	..	..	..	30 7	..	..	..	2	..	..	8	7
Birmingham: *Daily Gazette*	15 Linos.	'Stab.	..	42	..	..	..	50 0	..	..	..	15	1	58	24
Blackburn: *Express*	5 Linos.	'Stab.	48	..	..	..	40 0	..	..	..	5	..	..	26	11
,, *Times*	2 Hatts.	Piece.	48	..	2½	..	..	..	..	..	2	..	..	6	0
Bolton: *Evening News*	10 Linos.	Piece.	49¾	..	2½	..	..	..	65 1	..	10	..	..	41	7
Bradford: *Observer*	10 Thornes.	'Stab.	52½	51	..	..	..	..	..	45 0	2	20	3	56	33
,, *Argus*	2 Linos.	'Stab.	52½	..	..	..	34 0	..	..	..	2	..	..	28	24
Brighton: *Guardian*	1 Lino.	'Stab.	60	..	..	..	..	..	..	..	..	..	1	9	5
Burnley: *Express*	1 Lino.	..	..	..	..	..	..	..	..	..	..	..	1	..	..
Carnarvon: *Herald*	2 Linos.	Piece.	48	42	2½	3	..	..	36 0	36 0	2	2	..	12	4
Cardiff: *Western Mail*	13 Linos.	Piece.	48	45	2½	3	..	..	42 0	55 0	10	12	..	30	6
Chester: *Chronicle*	2 Hatts.	Piece.	48	..	2½	..	..	..	38 0	..	2	..	..	14	11
Halifax (Brighouse): *Echo*	1 Lino.	'Stab.	54	..	..	..	29 3	..	..	..	..	..	..	9	8
Hull: *Morning News*	9 Linos.	'Stab.	48	46	..	..	40 0	46 0	..	..	2	8	2	21	4
,, *News*	7 Linos.	'Stab.	48	..	..	..	40 0	..	..	..	7	..	..	27	11
Kendal: *County News*	1 Lino.	..	..	..	..	..	..	..	..	..	..	..	1	3	2
Liverpool: *Courier*	11 Hatts. (Courier and Express)	Piece.	..	50	..	3¼ to	..	..	..	72 0	..	13	2	..	62*
,, *Express*		Piece.	51	..	3	3¾	..	..	50 0	..	8	..	..	..	..
,, *Daily Post*	12 Hatts.	Piece.	51	50	3	3½	..	..	50 0	63 0	12	12	..	93	40
,, *Mercury*	9 Linos.	Piece.	48	42	3¼	3¾	..	..	..	70 0	..	9	..	84	56
,, *Journal of Commerce*	2 Hatts.	'Stab.	48	..	..	..	60 0	..	..	..	2	..	..	22	19

Paper	Machines	System												
LEICESTER: Mercury and Post	4 Linos.	Piece.	48	42	2¼	2¾				57	6	4	4		38	18
MANCHESTER: Courier	12 Linos.	Piece.		44		3½				66	0		15		75	20
„ Guardian	14 Linos.	'Stab.		44				47/6					14		79	72
„ Sporting Chronicle	6 Linos.	'Stab.	48	42	3		52/6	52/6				3	6	2	28	20
„ Evening Mail	6 Linos.	Piece.	48						60/0			6			25	11
„ Evening News	8 Linos.	'Stab.	52½									4 to 8			46	46
„ Excelsior Works	1 Hatts.	'Stab.	48									5	13	1		1
„ Guardian Jobbing	4 Thornes.	'Stab.	52½												88	88
„ Percy Brothers	3 Linos.	'Stab.										5	13			
NEWCASTLE: Daily Chronicle	26 Linos.	'Stab.	48	45			47/6			47/6			13	1	46	11
„ Evening Chronicle	}	'Stab.	48				52/6						3	1	40	13
„ Journal	Hatts.	'Stab.	48	45			47/6					5	11		49	23
„ Leader	11 Linos.	'Stab.	51	45			47/6					4	11		51	19
NORTHAMPTON: Herald	5 Linos.	'Stab.	50									1			23	7
„ Mercury	5 Linos.	'Stab.				2¼	50/0					3		1	21	7
OSWESTRY: Advertiser	1 Lino.	Piece.	48									3	8	1	10	8
OLDHAM: Chronicle	5 Linos.	'Stab.	48				40/0					4		1	16	1
PLYMOUTH: Mercury	8 Linos.	Piece.	42				40/0		46/0			4		1	47	42
„ Independent	4 Linos.	'Stab.	48				35/0					5		1	12	5
POTTERIES: Staffordshire Post	5 Linos.	'Stab.	48				37/4					2			23	8
ROCHDALE: Star	2 Linos.	'Stab.	48				40/0					2		1	6	2
„ Observer	2 Linos.	'Stab.	48				40/0								20	17
„ Leach's	1 Lino.	'Stab.												1		
ROSSENDALE VALLEY: Times	1 Hatts.						33/0					4			9	0
SCARBORO': Mercury	4 Linos.	'Stab.	48				33/0					3		1	14	1
„ Gazette	1 Lino.						36/0					9	20	2	90	31
„ Post		'Stab.	32¼	40½	3	3			54/8½			9			10	6
SHEFFIELD: Telegraph	20 Linos.	Piece.	48						47/8			2				
SOUTHPORT: Guardian	Hatts.	Piece.	48													
STAFFORD: Advertiser	2 Hatts.						34/0					1			15	13
„ Chronicle		'Stab.	48				55/0								7	3
SWANSEA: Leader	2 Linos.	'Stab.	48				48/0					3				
WARWICK: Advertiser	1 Lino.	'Stab.	48													
WIGAN: Examiner	3 Linos.	'Stab.	57													

*Number previously employed not stated.

3. In all offices where composing machines of any description are introduced the operators and case hands shall commence composition simultaneously. Machine operators can work seven hours per day on Morning Papers, and on Evening Papers forty-two hours per week. Machine operators on Morning Papers to be paid threepence per hour extra after seven hours' work. Compositors and operators in such offices to be guaranteed two galleys per day of seven working hours on Morning Papers and on Evening Papers twelve galleys per week of forty-two hours.

4. Any machine hand required to go upon time shall be paid at the ordinary rate of the office whilst so employed. The same rate of payment to apply to any case hand sent temporarily to a machine. This regulation to apply only in cases of emergency.

5. No man shall be permanently changed from machine to case or *vice versâ* without a fortnight's notice, except for wilful neglect or carelessness.

6. The scale of prices for machine work shall be

LINOTYPE

3¼*d*. per one thousand ens for day work in Evening Paper offices.
3¾*d*. per one thousand ens for work done in Morning Paper offices.
¼*d*. per one thousand extra on all types above brevier.

HATTERSLEY

4*d*. per one thousand ens for Evening Paper work, and
4½*d*. per one thousand ens for Morning Paper work.

GENERAL REGULATIONS AFFECTING COMPOSITION BY MACHINERY

(*a*) Any stoppage for repairs of or over fifteen minutes to be charged at the ordinary time rate of the office; not less than half-an-hour to be charged.

(*b*) Twelve lines to constitute a machine "take" of copy; less than that number to be charged as 12 lines.

(*c*) All standing headings, leads, rules, &c., other than those required in making up to be charged by the operator. Headings not composed by the operator to be given out to the piece hands.

(*d*) Matter above eight lines composed in other than ordinary English (*e.g.*, dialects) to be charged one-half extra; and foreign languages above four lines, double.

(*e*) Matter consisting of names run on, names and figures, with fractions and signs (*e.g.*, prize lists, balance-sheets, "Gazette" news, programmes, &c.), shall, where exceeding eight lines, be charged one-fourth extra; all lines in which small capitals or italics appear to be charged double.

(*f*) The usual piece regulations as to bad copy or MS. to apply to operators; copy not properly sub-edited to rank as bad MS.

(*g*) All corrections to be done by the operator, except machine errors and "house" marks, which shall be charged double.

(*h*) In all cases not covered by the foregoing the provisions of the London Scale shall apply.

The rules with regard to type-composing machines shall remain in force until the end of 1895.

At the end of 1895 the newspaper proprietors exercised their option to demand a revision of the composing machine Scale of 1894. It was remarked in the L.S.C. *Report,* quoted below : .

It can be asserted unhesitatingly and without fear of contradiction, that the Scale then agreed upon was from first to last most favourable to both case and machine hands; and it has on more than one occasion been suggested that the employers representatives were "caught napping" when assisting to frame it. However that may be, circumstances since have clearly shown the impossibility of obtaining a renewal of the terms then agreed upon.

Evidence was submitted by the masters that machine operators were able to earn sums varying from £3 10s. 0d. to £4 5s. 0d., a week, amounts greatly in excess of those received by the case hands, and gained, too, in a shorter time. A long and difficult series of negotiations followed. Besides proposing a general reduction in machine piece rates, the employers were no longer willing to pay learners. When a provisional agreement was at length reached, the rank and file of the Society refused to vote in favour of its acceptance.

The following extracts from the *Report of the Adjourned Special Delegate Meeting held* . . . *Jan.* 11, 1896, some days before the ballot was taken, reflect the attitude of the L.S.C. Committee :

[DOCUMENT CXXIII]

In casting their votes it is earnestly to be hoped that members will realize to the full the responsibility devolving upon them. It must be remembered that this machine question is no longer in its experimental stages, but that, on the contrary, its practicability has been placed beyond all doubt. It is perfectly true that at present its adaptability is limited to certain classes of work, which, however, by comparison, are well paid for; but when it is remembered that throughout the United States, and in nearly every provincial town of importance in the United Kingdom, machinery has been introduced to a more or less general extent, it becomes a duty to recognize that it can no longer be treated as some plaything to be toyed or trifled with, but rather that it is a factor to be reckoned with, and one which the Trade would be well advised to treat with seriousness and firmness.

.   .   .   .   .   .

In voting upon this question, however, the members will do well to bear in mind that an adverse vote will probably place them—so far as public sympathy is concerned—in the undesirable position of attempting to fight machinery. Time after time charges of hostility towards the machines have been levelled against the Executive and the members, and as often refuted; but the experience of other industries has clearly demonstrated that wherever machinery has been introduced in which was embodied the elements tending towards success, time has eventually proved its success, despite the opposition levelled against it. In the case of the composing machines none are perfect, although the strides made towards perfection during the past few years cannot and must not be ignored.

Six months passed before an agreement on the composing machine question was finally reached between masters and men. The composing machine Scale of 1896 was more comprehensive than that of 1894. Whereas the 1894 Scale was confined to daily newspaper offices, prices were now given for work on weekly newspapers and in book houses. In addition, rates were also given applicable to the Empire typesetting machine, an apparatus constructed on the same mechanical principles as the Hattersley or Kastenbein machines.[1] While the Hattersley prices remained unchanged for both morning and evening newspapers, a reduction of $\frac{1}{4}d$. per 1,000 on morning paper work was made for the Linotype machine.

[DOCUMENT CXXIV]

Rates and Rules for working Composing Machines in London, agreed between Representatives of Employers and of the London Society of Compositors, on July 27, 1896.

NEWS SCALE—DAILY PAPERS

1.—All skilled operators, justifiers, and distributors (as distinct from attendants or labourers) shall be compositors and members of the L.S.C.

2.—Members of companionships into which machines are introduced or existing installations increased shall be given facilities to learn them in their own times (matter so composed not to be used), and when learners have reached an output of 4,000 ens in a test hour, or 12,000 ens in a test of four hours, preference shall be given to such qualified learners, and they shall be paid (when put on machines) for six weeks their average earnings of the previous three months.

3.—In all offices where composing machines of any description are introduced, or are in use, composition to be commenced simultaneously; and on morning papers the "cut" to apply to both case and machine hands, any stoppers required to be in the proportion of three case hands to one machine. Disadvantageous portions of articles not to be selected for either case or machine; and copy generally, whether advertisements or news matter, to go out in fair proportion. Case hands and operators to lift from separate heaps of copy, but when one heap is run out copy to be taken from the heap remaining for either case or machine hands. Compositors and operators in such offices to be guaranteed two galleys (7s. 8d.) per day of seven working hours on morning papers; on evening

---

[1] Models were in use at the *St. James's Gazette* office.

papers twelve galleys (£2 3s.) per week of 42 hours. This not to interfere with the existing guarantee of a galley on first edition of evening papers.

Machines may be employed on morning papers in the day time, provided that three case hands are called in to each machine, and that not more than three machines are thus employed. The earnings of such operators to be restricted to £3 per week.

4.—Any machine hand required to go upon time to be paid at the ordinary rate of the office. The same rate of payment to apply to any case hand sent temporarily to a machine, and to any machine hand sent temporarily to case. This regulation to apply only in case of emergency.

5.—No man shall be permanently changed from machine to case, or *vice versâ*, without a fortnight's notice.

6.—The scale of prices for machine work shall be :—

LINOTYPE

$3\frac{1}{4}d.$ per 1,000 ens for day work in evening paper offices.
$3\frac{1}{2}d.$ per 1,000 ens for work done in morning paper offices.
$\frac{1}{4}d.$ per 1,000 ens extra on all types above brevier.
Matter requiring two bars to complete one measure (not being tabular matter) to be charged one-third extra; three or more, one-half extra.

HATTERSLEY

$4d.$ per 1,000 ens for evening paper work, and
$4\frac{1}{2}d.$ per 1,000 ens for morning paper work.
Distribution to be paid for at a minimum rate of 38s. per week of 48 hours day work, or 3d. per 1,000 piece work.

EMPIRE

$4\frac{1}{2}d.$ per 1,000 ens for evening paper work, and
$5d.$ per 1,000 ens for morning paper work.
$\frac{1}{4}d.$ per 1,000 ens extra for measures below 20 ems of its own body.
Distribution to be paid for at a minimum rate of 38s. per week of 48 hours day work.

Machine operators on morning papers to be paid 4d. per hour extra for the first hour after seven hours' work, and 6d. per hour afterwards. On evening papers they shall be paid 4d. per hour extra for all hours between 42 and 48 per week, and 6d. per hour extra afterwards. At any time after nine hours' consecutive work 3d. per hour extra shall be charged, when overtime is not otherwise chargeable.

7.—All stoppages of ten minutes and upwards to be cumulative, with a minimum charge of twenty minutes, and to be charged at the ordinary time rate of the office. Such charges to be countersigned by the mechanic.

8.—Twelve lines of 16 ems pica or less, or its equivalent in wider measures, to constitute a machine "take" of copy; less than that number to be charged as twelve lines (or its equivalent).

9.—All standing headings to be charged by the operator. All leads and rules, other than those required in making-up, to be charged by the operator. When leads are cast on the bar, the operator to charge half the additional depth, the time taken in changing knives not to be counted a stoppage. Headings not composed by the operator to be given out to the piece hands.

10.—Matter of and above four lines composed in other than ordinary English (*e.g.*, dialects) to be charged one-half extra, and foreign languages double for each line.

11.—Matter consisting of names run on and figures—*e.g.*, prize lists, balance sheets, Gazette news, programmes, etc.—shall, where exceeding eight lines, or where containing fractions, signs, or accents, where exceeding two lines, be charged one-fourth extra; one line extra to be charged for each word of small caps, italic, or clarendon, etc. When two-line-letter matrices are dropped in, they shall be charged one line extra for every two two-line letters.

12.—The usual piece regulations as to bad copy or MS. to apply to operators; copy not properly sub-edited to rank as bad MS.

13.—All first-proof and revise corrections (marks left undone in the first proof) to be done by the operator, except machine errors and house marks, which shall be charged double. Charges for machine errors to be countersigned by the mechanic.

14.—If a machine is changed by order to a different type, operators shall not be required to change it again to make corrections, which shall be done by the operator on a vacant machine, or by the house.

15.—Matter which requires more than one justification for the purpose of ranging to be paid for in proportion to the time occupied.

16.—No operator shall be compelled to do engineers' or labourers' work.

WEEKLY PAPERS

1.—All skilled operators, justifiers, and distributors, as distinct from attendants or labourers, shall be compositors and members of the L.S.C. Apprentices in the last two years of their time can be employed in due proportion to the number of journeymen operators—*i.e.*, one apprentice to three journeymen operators.

2.—Members of companionships into which machines are introduced or existing installations increased shall be given facilities to learn them in their own time (matter so composed not to be used), and when learners have reached an output of 4,000 ens in a test hour, or 12,000 ens in a test of four hours, preference shall be given to such qualified learners, and they shall be guaranteed (when put on machines) for six weeks 38s. per week of 48 hours.

3.—In all offices where composing machines of any description are introduced, or are in use, composition to be commenced simultaneously. Disadvantageous portions of articles not to be selected for either case or machine; and copy generally to go out in fair proportion. Case hands and operators to lift from separate heaps of copy, but when one heap is run out copy to be taken from the heap remaining for either case or machine hands. But giving out complete articles not to be considered a breach of this rule. When operators and case hands work together on the same papers they shall be guaranteed a quarter per hour (unless exempted by the chapel) while the line is on.

4.—Any machine hand required to go upon time upon machine work shall be paid 1s. per hour, but any operator required to go upon stone work shall be paid at the ordinary time rate of the office, such work to be confined to papers produced wholly or partially by machinery.

5.—No man shall be permanently changed from machine to case, or vice-versâ, without a fortnight's notice.

6.—The scale of prices for machine work shall be :—

LINOTYPE

$3\frac{1}{8}d$. per 1,000 ens.

$3\frac{1}{4}d$. per 1,000 ens for all types above brevier.

Matter set to less than 20 ems of its own body, or more than 24 ems pica in type below bourgeois, to be charged $\frac{1}{4}d$. per 1,000 ens extra. Matter requiring two bars to complete one measure (not being tabular matter), to be charged one-third extra; three or more, one-half extra.

HATTERSLEY

$4d$. per 1,000 ens.

Distribution to be paid at a minimum rate of 38s. per week of 48 hours.

EMPIRE

$4\frac{1}{4}d$. per 1,000 ens.

$\frac{1}{4}d$. per 1,000 ens extra for measures below 20 ems of its own body.

Distribution to be paid for at a minimum rate of 38s. per week of 48 hours.

Overtime to be paid at the same rate as case hands, taking the day as eight hours.

7.—All stoppages of ten minutes and upwards to be cumulative, with a minimum charge of twenty minutes, and to be charged at the rate of 1s. per hour. Such charges to be countersigned by the mechanic.

8.—Twelve lines of 16 ems pica or less, or its equivalent in wider measures, to constitute a machine "take" of copy; less than that number to be charged as twelve lines (or its equivalent).

9.—All standing headings, leads, rules, etc., other than those required in making up, to be found and placed on the galley and charged by the operator. Where leads are cast on the bar, the operator to charge half the additional depth, the time taken in changing knives not to be counted a stoppage. Headings not composed by the operator to be given out to the piece hands. In no case are complete block-headings or blocks to be charged.

10.—Matter of and above four lines composed in other than ordinary English (*e.g.*, dialects) to be charged one-half extra, and foreign languages double for each line.

11.—Matter consisting of names run on and figures—*e.g.*, prize lists, balance sheets, Gazette news, programmes, etc.—shall, where exceeding eight lines or where containing fractions, signs, or accents, where exceeding two lines, be charged one-fourth extra; one line extra to be charged for each word of small caps, italic, clarendon, etc. When two-line-letter matrices are dropped in they shall be charged one line extra for every two two-line letters. Rules to advertisements and leads to be put in and charged by the operator.

12.—The usual piece regulations as to bad copy or MS. to apply to operators; copy not properly sub-edited to rank as bad MS.

13.—All first-proof and revise corrections (marks left undone in the first proof) to be done by the operator, except machine errors and house marks, which shall be charged double. Charges made for machine errors to be countersigned by the mechanic.

14.—If a machine is changed by order to a different type, the operator shall not be required to change it again to make corrections, which shall be done by the operator on a vacant machine or by the house.

15.—Matter which requires more than one justification for the purpose of ranging to be paid for in proportion to the time occupied.

16.—One-fourth extra, to the full width of the article, to be charged for matter run down blocks.

17.—The minimum rate for establishment hands shall be 45s. for 48 hours.

18.—No operator shall be compelled to do engineers' or labourers' work.

BOOK SCALE

1.—All skilled operators, justifiers, and distributors, as distinct from attendants or labourers, shall be compositors and members of the L.S.C. Apprentices in the last two years of their time can be employed in due proportion to the number of journeymen operators—*i.e.*, one apprentice to three journeymen operators.

2.—Members of companionships into which machines are introduced or existing installations increased shall be given facilities to learn them in their own time (matter so composed not to be used), and when learners have reached an output of 4,000 ens in a test hour, or 12,000 ens in a test of four hours, preference shall be given to such qualified learners, and they shall be guaranteed (when put on machines), for six weeks, 38s. per week of 48 hours.

3.—Any machine hand required to go upon time upon machine work shall be paid 1s. per hour, but any operator required to go upon stone work shall be paid 9½d. per hour.

4.—No man shall be permanently changed from machine to case, or vice-versâ, without a fortnight's notice.

5.—The scale of prices for machine work shall be :—

LINOTYPE

3d. per 1,000 ens.

3⅛d. per 1,000 ens for all types above brevier.

Matter set to less than 20 ems of its own body, or more than 24 ems pica in type below bourgeois, to be charged ¼d. per 1,000 ens extra.

Matter requiring two bars to complete one measure (not being tabular matter) to be charged one-third extra; three or more, half extra.

4*d*. per 1,000 ens.

Distribution to be paid for at a minimum rate of 38*s*. per week of 48 hours.

4¼*d*. per 1,000 ens.

¼*d*. extra per 1,000 ens for measures below 20 ems of its own body.

Distribution to be paid for at a minimum rate of 38*s*. per week of 48 hours.

Overtime to be paid for at the same rate as case hands, taking the day as eight hours.

6.—All stoppages of ten minutes and upwards to be cumulative, with a minimum charge of twenty minutes, and to be charged at the rate of 1*s*. per hour. Such charges to be countersigned by the mechanic.

7.—All leads, rules, etc., other than those required in making-up, to be charged by the operator. Where leads are cast on the bar, the operator to charge half the additional depth; the time taken in changing the knives not to be counted a stoppage.

8.—Matter of and above four lines composed in other than ordinary English (*e.g.*, dialects) to be charged half extra, and foreign languages double for each line.

9.—Matter consisting of names run on and figures—*e.g.*, prize lists, balance sheets, Gazette news, programmes, etc.—shall, where exceeding eight lines, or where containing fractions, signs, or accents, where exceeding two lines, be charged one-fourth extra. One line extra to be charged for each word of small caps, italics, clarendon, etc. When two-line-letter matrices are dropped in, they shall be charged one line extra for every two two-line letters.

10.—The usual piece regulations as to bad copy or MS. to apply to operators; copy not properly sub-edited to rank as bad MS.

11.—All first-proof and revise corrections (marks left undone in the first proof) to be done by the operator, except machine errors and house marks, which shall be charged double. Charges for machine errors to be countersigned by the mechanic.

12.—If a machine is changed by order to a different type, the operator shall not be required to change it again to make corrections, which shall be done on a vacant machine, or by the house.

13.—Disadvantageous portions of articles in magazines and serials not to be selected for either case or machine. This not to apply to volume work.

14.—Matter which requires more than one justification for the purpose of ranging to be paid for in proportion to the time occupied.

15.—One-fourth extra, to the full width of the article, to be charged for matter run down blocks.

16.—The minimum rate for establishment hands shall be 45*s*. for 48 hours.

17.—All matter to be set in slips and made up by the house.

18.—No operator shall be compelled to do engineers' or labourers' work.

1st Resolution.—"That the foregoing List of Rules for composing by hand and machinery agreed upon by representatives of the London Morning, Evening, Daily, and Weekly Newspapers and Printers and the London Society of Compositors be and are hereby adopted, and that from and after the first working week in September, 1896, the said new rules shall be substituted for those hitherto in force."

2nd Resolution.—"Resolved, that in cases of dispute between the London Society of Compositors and any London newspaper proprietors or printers in regard to the interpretation to be placed upon the foregoing rules, the point at issue may, at request of either side of the parties concerned, be referred for arbitration to a Committee consisting of five employers' representatives and five representatives of the London Society of Compositors—the gentlemen forming such Committee of Arbitration to be nominated hereafter by the Employers and Society respectively."

On behalf of the Employers:

> Alf. H. Hance.
> Henry Burt.
> Geo. Eaton Hart.
> S. C. Straker.
> E. H. Mayo Gunn.
>
> H. Vane Stow,
> > *Hon. Secretary.*

On behalf of the L.S.C.:

> C. F. Davis.
> Frank A. Hortop.
> Herbert Geo. Arnold.
> J. Mortished.
> Harry Whitehorn.
> W. C. Archer.
>
> T. Sanders,
> > *News Secretary.*
>
> C. W. Bowerman,
> > *General Secretary.*

Salisbury Hotel, 27th July, 1896.

Although the widespread introduction of composing machinery, and particularly the Linotype, caused the displacement of hand compositors, particularly in the provinces, the effect was only temporary. The constant expansion of the printing trade, both in and out of London, speedily absorbed any surplus of men and many more in addition.

During the first decade of the twentieth century the Monotype composing machine was brought over from the U.S.A. This apparatus worked on principles entirely different from the Linotype system. Since the Monotype machine is complicated in design and operation, suffice to say that while the Linotype product is a solid bar or line of type, the Monotype sets and casts lines of single type, mechanically and accurately justified. As with the Linotype system, there is no distribution, unwanted standing matter being thrown into the melting-pot. Corrections are made by hand compositors working from normal type cases filled with sorts cast by the machine. Linotype corrections require resetting a complete line or lines.

The Linotype was specially suited to and favoured by newspaper printers, for in the rush of newspaper make-up the solid slugs could not be "pied." The Monotype found its principal market in the book printing and general trade. An output of at least 6,000 ens per hour, coupled with the machine's suitability for composing tabular matter and work requiring a mixture of light and bold faces, or a multiplicity of accents and special sorts, made it an attractive proposition to master printers. The hand compositors, with whom old traditions died hard, faced with the revolution caused in their trade and technique, felt at home with the single-type product of the Monotype. This machine, therefore, has become intimately connected with the general printing trade of this country and is responsible for the increasingly high standard of book and commercial printing.

The turn of the century is a convenient point at which to bring this book to a close. By 1900 the introduction of mechanical composition had already begun to revolutionize composing-room practice; and the piece-work system, except on daily newspapers, was giving way to weekly wage payments. The London Scale of Prices continues to be published, but for the past forty years has not had the same importance for the general trade. This study ends, therefore, with the impending disappearance from the scene of the old-fashioned piece hand compositor.

APPENDIX I

THE LONDON SOCIETY OF COMPOSITORS 1900–1943

1900, September. The L.S.C. proposed the following advances : Establishments rates to be increased from 38s. to 40s. Hours of work to be reduced from 54 to 48. Piece rates to be increased by 1d. per 1,000. The employers refused to consider these propositions, and a general strike of the London compositors appeared imminent. It was averted when all parties agreed to settle the dispute by arbitration.

1901, March. G. R. Askwith, later Lord Askwith, acted as Arbitrator and made the following award: Establishment rates advanced from 38s. to 39s. Hours of work reduced from 54 to 52½. Piece rates increased ½d. per 1,000 on bookwork.

1907. The question of the 48-hour week again taken up by the L.S.C., but this time as part of a national movement for its adoption.

1910. Protracted negotiations on the same question were held between the National Printing Trades Federation, representing all Trade Unions in the printing industry, and Federation of Master Printers. The result was a deadlock.

1910, October. The following demands were made by the L.S.C.: 50-hour week to be in force as from 1 January, 1911, with a further reduction to 48 exactly a year later. The Federation of Master Printers refused to accept these proposals and a widespread strike ensued. A few large firms gave way immediately.

1911. Agreement was finally reached with a section of the employers, mainly periodical houses. The working hours were reduced from 52½ to 50 per week.

1914–23. Increases and reductions in London weekly wages consequent upon the rise and fall in the cost of living during and after the First World War. (Hand compositors.) 1914 'stab rate : 39s. 1915–17 several increases brought total weekly wage to 53s. In 1918, 1919 and 1920 there were advances of 19s. 6d., 12s. 6d. and 15s. respectively. In 1920 the 'stab rate was 100s. per week.

In 1921, 1922 and 1923 there were reductions of 5*s*., 4*s*. and 2*s*. The 'stab was finally settled at 89*s*.

1919. Following negotiations between the Printing and Kindred Trades Federation, representing all the Unions, and the British Federation of Master Printers, the 48-hour week was generally adopted throughout the country. The new agreement included payment for statutory holidays and a week's holiday in Summer.

1924. The Periodical Scale made piece-work compulsory for the text of weekly periodicals for all types of composing machines.

1937. Hours of work reduced to 45 per week. No change in 'stab rate.

1941–43. War bonus of 17*s*. 6*d*. per week obtained, bringing 'stab rate for hand compositors to 106*s*. 6*d*. Machine operators on the establishment are paid extra.

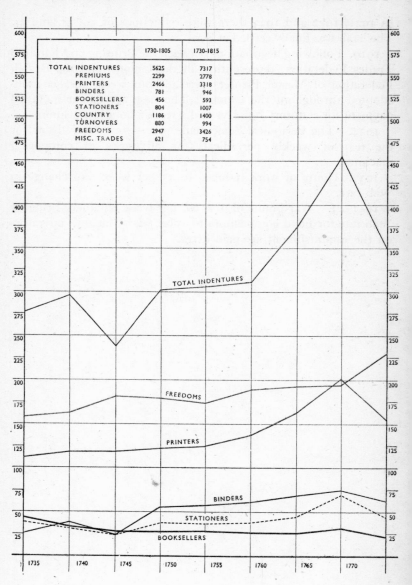

	1730-1805	1730-1815
TOTAL INDENTURES	5625	7317
PREMIUMS	2299	2778
PRINTERS	2466	3318
BINDERS	781	946
BOOKSELLERS	456	593
STATIONERS	804	1007
COUNTRY	1186	1400
TURNOVERS	880	994
FREEDOMS	2947	3426
MISC. TRADES	621	754

TOTAL INDENTURES

FREEDOMS

PRINTERS

BINDERS

STATIONERS

BOOKSELLERS

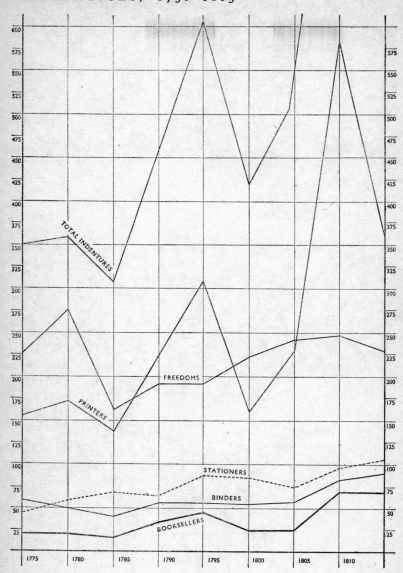

I

GENERAL INDEX

Principal references are shown in heavy figures.

II

NAMES OF FIRMS, MASTER PRINTERS
AND MISCELLANEOUS PERSONS

This book contains three extensive lists of London printing offices :

(i) by Samuel Negus (printed in John Nichols, *Literary Anecdotes*, Vol. I, pp. 288 *et seq.*), giving the names of master printers active in 1724. These are printed, with annotations, on pp. 36–39, and reference should be made to this source for available particulars of men active in the late seventeenth and early eighteenth centuries. Except in certain instances these names have not been repeated in the Index.

(ii) by John Pendred, and published by him in 1785 as *The London and County Booksellers and Stationers Vade Mecum*. (My thanks are due to Mr. Graham Pollard for the use of the proofs of his forthcoming monograph on Pendred, to be published by the Bibliographical Society.) Pendred's list, with annotations, is reprinted on pp. 43–50, and should be used in conjunction with the Index, where subsequent references to the firms named are also given. Names printed in italic will be found in Pendred.

(iii) by the compiler of the Annual Report of the London Union of Compositors for 1839, reprinted on pp. 298–302.

This book does not claim to provide exhaustive biographical material for the study of the London printing trade in the eighteenth and nineteenth centuries, and only in the case of the Negus and Pendred lists has any attempt been made to sort out the ramifications and successions of the firms mentioned therein.

(a) NAMES OF FIRMS

(Names italicised will be found in Pendred's list of firms, printed on pp. 43–50)

(b) MISCELLANEOUS NAMES

III

NEWSPAPERS AND PERIODICALS

527

HOWE   The London compositor